Reconstruction Effects in Relative Clauses

studia grammatica 75

Reconstruction Effects in Relative Clauses

Edited by
Manfred Krifka and Mathias Schenner

DE GRUYTER

ISBN 978-3-05-006274-7
e-ISBN (PDF) 978-3-05-009515-8
e-ISBN (EPUB) 978-3-11-038077-4

Library of Congress Control Number: 2018958373

Bibliographic information published by the Deutsche Nationalbibliothek
The Deutsche Nationalbibliothek lists this publication in the Deutsche Nationalbibliografie; detailed bibliographic data are available on the Internet at http://dnb.dnb.de.

Printing and binding: CPI books GmbH, Leck

www.degruyter.com

Contents

Mathias Schenner

An introduction to reconstruction effects in relative clauses

Reconstruction effects in relative clauses are a class of phenomena where the external head of the relative clause seems to behave as if it occupied a position within the relative clause, as far as some commonly accepted principle of grammar is concerned. An often cited example is (1), where the pronoun *his* in the relative head appears to be bound by the quantified noun phrase *every man* in the relative clause – although the latter does not c-command the former, which is commonly required for binding.

(1) The [$_{NP}$ relative of *his*] [$_{CP}$ which *every man* admires most] is his mother.

Several solutions have been developed in various theoretical frameworks. One interesting aspect about reconstruction effects in relative clauses is that they can be used as a benchmark for competing theories of grammar: Which architecture of the syntax-semantics interface can provide the most satisfying explanation for these phenomena? This volume brings together researchers working in different frameworks but looking at the same set of empirical facts, enabling the reader to develop their own perspective on the perfect tradeoff between syntax and semantics in a theory of grammar.

The following sections provide some background for the discussions in this volume and include pointers to relevant contributions. Section 1 introduces reconstruction effects in general, section 2 adds relative clauses to the picture and surveys the empirical focus of this volume. Sections 3 and 4 sketch and compare the two main lines of analysis, known as syntactic vs. semantic reconstruction, and section 5 concludes.

Mathias Schenner, Leibniz-Centre General Linguistics (ZAS) Berlin

https://doi.org/10.1515/9783050095158-001

1 Reconstruction effects

1.1 Introducing reconstruction effects

One way to view reconstruction effects is as a class of systematic counterexamples to otherwise well motivated grammatical principles. Let's take Principle A of Binding Theory (Büring 2005). A simplistic version is given in (2).

(2) Reflexive pronouns must be locally bound.

For our purposes it is useful to disentangle this principle in two ways. First, we want to avoid the use of a deontic modal and replace (2) by the more explicit conditional statement in (3), following the standard view that binding principles are filters on grammatical structures.

(3) If a sentence contains a reflexive pronoun that is not locally bound, then the sentence is ungrammatical.

Second, we supply a simple version of the notion of binding in terms of coindexing and c-command in (4) and (5). The notion of locality will be left unanalyzed; for our illustrative purposes this qualification could be dropped entirely.

(4) A DP α *binds* a DP β iff
(a) α and β are coindexed, and
(b) α c-commands β.

(5) A constituent α *c-commands* a constituent β iff
(a) α does not dominate β, and
(b) every (branching) node dominating α also dominates β.

Finally, there is one additional principle that we would like to use:

(6) Observational adequacy: A sentence is grammatical iff it is acceptable.

Now we are ready to look at an example sentence that is said to exhibit a reconstruction effect:

(7) Which pictures of *herself*$_1$ did *Alice*$_1$ see?

Here are two observations about this sentence a linguist might make:

(8) The sentence (7) is acceptable.

(9) The sentence (7) contains a reflexive pronoun that is not locally bound.

The first observation is an empirical generalization that utterances of the sentence are acceptable to speakers of English. The second observation in (9) is less empirical in that it depends on several theoretical assumptions of our theory of grammar. Still, based on standard assumptions about constituent structure in the generative tradition and the definition of binding in (4), it should be uncontroversial that the reflexive pronoun *herself* in (7) is not bound. In particular, it is not bound by the coindexed *Alice* because the latter does not c-command the pronoun.

At this point we can easily derive a contradiction from the set of principles and observations introduced above. From (6) and (8) it follows that (7) is grammatical. From (3) and (9) it follows that (7) is ungrammatical.

Of course, this argument is usually not spelled out at this level of detail, because it is intuitively clear that in the light of examples like (7), a grammar that contains a principle like (2) faces an undergeneration problem: There are sentences that are acceptable but ruled out by Principle A. However, this setup allows us to think more systematically about how we can avoid this contradiction. It has been derived from four main premises, so we have at least the following four options:

- Reject (8). We could question the relevant empirical data.
- Reject (6). We could willingly give up observational adequacy and restrict our grammar to a proper subset of the English language that does not contain violations of Principle A.
- Reject (9). We could modify our syntactic assumptions in such a way that reflexive pronouns can somehow be bound by seemingly non-c-commanding antecedents in cases like (7).
- Reject (3). Finally, we could modify the binding principle itself in some way to allow for cases like (7).

While the first two reactions are adequate moves under certain circumstances, we will only consider the last two possible remedies for the contradiction here. First, we could reject (9) by revising our notion of binding in such a way that the reflexive pronoun in examples like (7) comes out as being bound. There are several ways to do this, for example by switching to a weaker command relation or by relaxing the c-command requirement to include traces, like in (10).

(10) A DP α *binds* a DP β iff
(a) α and β are coindexed, and
(b) α c-commands β or a trace of a phrase containing β.

Second, we could replace the formulation of Principle A in (3) by a qualified version that is hardened against the mentioned contradiction. So far, we have tacitly assumed that sentences like (7) are associated with exactly one syntactic structure and that this is the one relevant to Principle A. But in a derivational syntactic theory that assumes multiple stages or levels of syntactic representation, it needs to be clarified what exactly constitutes the input to filters like Principle A. Assuming that the wh-phrase in (7) occupies a derived position and originated in the direct object position of the verb, where it received its thematic role, as in (11), a straightforward revision would be to require that Principle A holds at a stage in the derivation before any wh-movements happen (at NP-structure, see Riemsdijk & Williams 1981) or even before any movements happen at all (at D-structure).

(11) did *Alice*$_1$ see [$_{DP}$ which pictures of *herself*$_1$]

However, this approach has largely been abandoned in the light of examples that suggest that overt wh-movement can create new binding options for reflexive pronouns contained in the wh-phrase (see e.g. Barss 2001: 676 for a summary). From a semantic point of view, there is another problem with this approach, at least if it is assumed that the interpretation function does not take D-structures like (11) as input, but post-movement structures like (7) where the original bindee is no longer in the c-command domain of the original binder. The problem is more prominent in cases like (12), where the reflexive pronoun depends on a quantified noun phrase. This shows that a purely syntactic solution to the problem why Principle A should not rule out sentences like (7) or (12) is not enough, unless it also provides an explanation for why a reflexive pronoun like *herself* can semantically depend on a non-c-commanding quantificational noun phrase like *no girl* in a sentence like (12).

(12) [$_{DP}$ which pictures of *herself*$_1$]$_2$ did [*no girl*]$_1$ see $\_{}_2$

This observation and the fact that neither D-structure nor S-structure are appropriate as inputs for binding principles suggests that yet another level might play a role: Logical Form (LF). But how can we, starting from S-structures like (13), arrive at a syntactic structure that satisfies Principle A?

(13) [$_{DP}$ which pictures of *herself*$_1$]$_2$ did *Alice*$_1$ see $\_{}_2$

Two options come to mind: Move again or move back. First, we could (covertly) move the binder (here: *Alice*) further up the syntactic tree to a position from which it c-commands the phrase containing the bindee (here: *herself*) again. This option turns out to be insufficient: excessive wh-movement cannot solve the problem in general (see e.g. Fox 1999: 160–161 for an argument and also the discussion of example (24) below). Second, we could undo the wh-movement of the phrase containing the bindee. This idea of undoing movements at later stages motivated the term *reconstruction* and goes back to Chomsky (1977). The effect of pushing moved phrases back into their original positions can also be achieved by conceptually perhaps more appealing mechanisms, for example by defining binding in terms of trace-aware command relations, like in (10).

The advent of the Minimalist Program (Chomsky 1995) and its elimination of intermediate representational levels like D-structure and S-structure further backed the idea that principles of Binding Theory are applied at LF. An important innovation was the copy theory of movement that replaced the move-and-undo operations required for reconstruction by copy-and-delete operations. More concretely, while wh-movement in pre-Minimalist generative grammar used to index the moved constituent and create a coindexed trace at the origin, as in (13), it now just introduces an identical copy at the target position, as in (14).

(14) [which pictures of *herself*$_1$] did *Alice*$_1$ see [which pictures of *herself*$_1$]

Logical Forms are subject to economy principles that regulate the deletion of superfluous copies, which results in stripped-down structures like (15) for (14).

(15) [which] did *Alice*$_1$ see [pictures of *herself*$_1$]

While it is intuitively clear that an LF like (15) satisfies Principle A, it is less clear how the semantic component should deal with economized representations of this kind and it turns out that some non-trivial woodworking is required to prepare these tree structures for compositional interpretation (as discussed in Fox 2000 and Heim this volume; also see section 3.1 for some hints).

1.2 Defining reconstruction effects

The previous section introduced reconstruction effects by way of the example in (7), repeated here as (16) with movement decorations, where the reflexive pronoun *herself* behaves as if it were in its pre-movement position as far as Principle A is concerned.

(16) [$_{DP}$ which pictures of *herself*$_1$]$_2$ did *Alice*$_1$ see $\__2$

But can we have a more general characterization of reconstruction effects? Extrapolating from the example just given, it seems that reconstruction effects involve (i) some subexpression that is somehow connected to two different positions in the syntactic structure of the containing expression and (ii) a principle that senses the subexpression in the position in which it is not spelled out, i.e. phonologically visible. Chomsky & Lasnik (1993: 536) describe the notion of reconstruction as follows, where *P* is a property of linguistic expressions:

> *P* holds at LF under *reconstruction*, that is, with the moved phrase treated “as if” it were in the position of its trace

If we abstract from the movement dependency between the two connected positions, we arrive at the more general phenomenon of connectivity effects. Sportiche (2006: 38) gives the following characterization:

> Connectivity effects are cases in which a phrase seems to behave as if it occupied a position different from its 'surface' position, i.e., the position that it seems to be occupying in the spoken string.

It is clear from the discussion in Sportiche (2006) that the "behavior" of a phrase is judged relative to certain principles (or properties). Let's try to turn this into a more explicit definition:

(17) An expression E within a phrase P shows a *connectivity effect* with respect to a principle R iff there are positions p_1 and p_2 within P, such that
(a) E is phonologically realized at p_2,
(b) E is visible to R at p_1, and
(c) $p_1 \neq p_2$.

Schematically, this can be represented as follows:

(18) Phonological: $[_P \ldots [_{p_2}\ E\ ] \ldots [_{p_1} \ldots] \ldots]$
Input to R: $[_P \ldots [_{p_2} \ldots] \ldots [_{p_1}\ E\ ] \ldots]$

This captures the idea that connectivity effects arise when an expression is somehow connected to two different syntactic positions: one where it is spelled out and one where it is visible to some grammatical principle. There are still some aspects to be filled in. For instance, we might want to require that E is invisible to R at p_2, or add a general rule that expressions are never visible at multiple positions at the same time, i.e. to the same principle.

Reconstruction effects are special cases of connectivity effects where the connected positions are related by movement. However, merely adding the clause 'p_1 and p_2 are related by movement' does not suffice, because this would include cases where the non-surface position of E is not one of its past positions, but a future position in its movement chain, as with covert Quantifier Raising. By contrast, the term *reconstruction* is reserved for moving things back into positions that they have previously occupied.

(19) An expression E within a phrase P shows a *reconstruction effect* with respect to a principle R iff there are positions p_1 and p_2 within P, such that
(a) E is phonologically realized at p_2,
(b) E is visible to R at p_1,
(c) $p_1 \neq p_2$, and
(d) there is a movement chain $(p_2, \ldots, p_1)$.

Schematically, this can be represented as follows:

(20) Phonological: $[_P \ldots [_{P_2}\ E_i\ ] \ldots [_{P_1}\ \__i\ ] \ldots]$
Input to *R*: $[_P \ldots [_{P_2} \ldots] \ldots [_{P_1}\ E\ ] \ldots]$

One problematic aspect of this definition is the use of the term *movement chain* in the definiens. Ideally, we would like to characterize reconstruction effects in a theory-neutral way in order to identify the empirical facts to be explained and then compare the predictive success of different theoretical approaches to them. There are two ways to think about this: First, one could speculate that any sufficiently rich theory of grammar will have some mechanism that corresponds to movement dependencies in derivational frameworks. This intertranslatability would ensure a certain degree of theoretical innocence of the notion. Second, reconstruction effects might be an artifact of movement-based syntactic frameworks and might not correspond to a natural class of empirical facts. However, in that case, we can at least resort to the more general concept of connectivity effects that can be defined in a more theory-neutral way (albeit it still relies on some theoretical concepts like tree positions and visibility to principles).

1.3 Classifying reconstruction effects

The definitions given in the previous section suggest some natural parameters for classifying connectivity and reconstruction effects. We will discuss five parameters in the following: principles, optionality, partiality, movement type, target position. More detailed overviews are provided by Barss (2001) and Sportiche (2006).

Principles. One obvious parameter is the principle that triggers the reconstruction effect. In our introductory example (7) it was Principle A from Binding Theory. Reconstruction effects are discussed with respect to all *Binding Theory* principles. If there are world or situation pronouns in syntax, we might also need a Binding Theory for them to prevent overgenerating coindexing patterns, and reconstruction effects have been discussed for these principles as well (Percus 2000, Lechner 2013).

A second principle, related to but distinct from the syntactic Binding Theory filters, is *pronominal binding* between a quantificational noun phrase and a pronoun. We have already encountered this principle in our discussion of example (12). The general configuration is indicated in (21).

(21) [... *bindee*$_1$ ...]$_2$ [... *binder*$_1$ ... [... $\__2$ ...]]

Some instances are (22) from Riemsdijk & Williams (1981: 188) and (23) with examples from German involving topicalization and scrambling that are discussed by Frey (1993), Sternefeld (1997) and Lechner (1998) among others.

(22) [which of *his*$_1$ poems]$_2$ would [*every poet*]$_1$ like to read $\_\_2$?

(23) a. [*Seine*$_1$ Mutter]$_2$ liebt *jeder*$_1$ $\_\_2$
his mother loves everybody
'Everybody loves his mother'

b. dass [*seine*$_1$ Mutter]$_2$ *jeder*$_1$ $\_\_2$ liebt
that his mother everybody loves
'that everybody loves his mother'

A third principle is *relative scope*. Like Binding Theory, this is an extensive topic by itself (see Ruys & Winter 2011 for a survey). The general idea is that syntactic c-command corresponds to semantic scope. If the c-command relations at surface structure do not match the observed scope relations, syntactic approaches employ movement operations to provide appropriate c-command relations at the level of syntactic structure that is visible to the semantic component. For most cases, a rule of Quantifier Raising (QR) is used that covertly moves a quantified DP to a specifier position of a local clause, typically higher up the tree (May 1977). However, there are instances of scope ambiguity that are not naturally accounted for by QR but seem to require reconstruction. A case in point is the example in (24), which allows for an inverse scope reading where the raising verb *expected* has scope over *someone* (which receives a non-specific interpretation this way). No raising of nominal elements will yield this reading, whereas reconstructing the overt subject of the raising verb into its original theta position will.

(24) [*Someone from New York*]$_1$ is *expected* [$\_\_1$ to win the lottery]

Of course, there are other strategies to derive the intended meaning. In fact, May (1977: 18) formulates QR in a way that allows downward movement and makes use of this fact in his analysis of quantified subjects in raising verb constructions (May 1977: 188–196).

A fourth principle concerns *idioms*, syntactically complex expressions whose meaning is not a function of their parts. This characterization implies that idioms need to be interpreted as a whole, i.e. their syntactic parts need to reach the interpretation function as a unit. If an idiom appears to be teared apart at surface structure, some mechanism has to put it together again before handing it to the semantic component. So goes the argument for reconstruction for idiom interpretation. (25) is an example from Sportiche (2006: 47) that illustrates this point.

(25) [How much *care*]$_1$ do you think Mary *took* $\_\_1$ of Bill?

Summing up, we have mentioned four areas that provide principles relevant to reconstruction effects: (1) Binding Theory, (2) pronominal binding, (3) relative scope, and (4) idioms. Except for Binding Theory, all of the mentioned principles are interpretive principles: They require a certain syntactic configuration (e.g. c-command, syntactic binding) to yield a certain semantic effect (e.g. scope, semantic binding). With respect to these principles, reconstruction effects are instances of apparent *syntax-semantics mismatches*, where an expression is spelled out at one position but interpreted at another. Not all of these mismatches are reconstruction or connectivity effects, some show a different footprint and can be handled by other mechanisms like QR. Nor are all reconstruction or connectivity effects syntax-semantics mismatches: Reconstruction for mere filtering principles, like Binding Theory, does not directly relate to interpretation.

Optionality. Another parameter for classifying reconstruction effects is optionality. As we have seen, a reconstruction effect involves a principle R, an expression E and two positions p_1 and p_2 that are related by movement. Reconstruction is *obligatory* if E is only ever visible to R at its origin p_1, never at the movement target p_2. Reconstruction is *optional* if the grammar allows for cases in which E is visible to R at p_1 and also for cases in which E is visible to R at p_2. Finally, reconstruction is *impossible* if E can only be visible to R at p_2, never at p_1. If we use '✓' to indicate that the grammar allows for E to be visible to R in that position and '$*$' to indicate that the grammar does not allow this, we can summarize these three cases as in (26).

(26) a. $[_{\mathrm{P}} \ldots [_{p_2} \ast] \ldots [_{p_1} \checkmark] \ldots]$ obligatory reconstruction
b. $[_{\mathrm{P}} \ldots [_{p_2} \checkmark] \ldots [_{p_1} \checkmark] \ldots]$ optional reconstruction
c. $[_{\mathrm{P}} \ldots [_{p_2} \checkmark] \ldots [_{p_1} \ast] \ldots]$ obligatory non-reconstruction

Optional reconstruction for interpretive principles, like relative scope, enables multiple readings of a sentence. For example, (24) is ambiguous between a surface scope reading that corresponds to the syntactic structure without reconstruction (*someone from NY* c-commands *expected*) and an inverse scope reading that corresponds to the syntactic structure with reconstruction (*someone from NY* is c-commanded by *expected*).

The principles of Binding Theory are considered to differ in optionality. Roughly speaking, reconstruction for Principle A is optional, while reconstruction for Principle C is obligatory (Sportiche 2006: 56). The latter case is illustrated by (27a) which would not be ungrammatical if reconstruction were not obligatory. However, there are similar examples like (27b) that are grammatical. Analyses of this *anti-reconstruction* effect bring in additional factors like differences between arguments and adjuncts (Barss 2001: 689–692).

(27) a. *? [Which argument that *John*$_1$ is a genius]$_2$ did *he*$_1$ believe $\__2$?
b. [Which argument that *John*$_1$ made]$_2$ did *he*$_1$ believe $\__2$?

Reconstruction is not always optional for interpretive principles either. For instance, (28) lacks a reading in which *every building* is in the scope of *10 percent likely*, suggesting that reconstruction is impossible in this case (Sportiche 2006: 57).

(28) [*Every building*]$_1$ is *10 percent likely* [_$_1$ to collapse].

Partiality. So far, we have assumed that an expression E that shows a reconstruction effect is visible as a whole to a principle R in a previously occupied position. But this might not always be the case. A common way to split up E is to distinguish the *movement trigger* (e.g. a wh-word) from the *pied-piped material* that is pulled along. It is often assumed that in wh-movement, the wh-operator itself does not reconstruct, only the pied piped material (see (15) above for an example). The partiality parameter concerns the portion of the expression E that undergoes reconstruction: In *radical* (or *total*) reconstruction, the whole expression E is affected, whereas in *partial* reconstruction only its pied piped parts are.

Movement type. Reconstruction effects can also be classified by the type of movement relation that holds between the two involved positions p_1 and p_2. It is commonly assumed that reconstruction effects can be found with both A-movement and A$'$-movement (see Sportiche 2006: 50–56 for an overview), although reconstruction of A-movement is more controversial because of examples like (28) that don't allow for it.

Target. If an expression undergoes movement multiple times, additional reconstruction possibilities might arise. For instance, if E moves from its original position p_1 to p_2 and then on to p_3, as sketched in (29), reconstruction might in principle target either p_2 or p_1.

(29) $[_{\mathrm{P}} \ldots [_{p_3}\, E_j\,] \ldots [_{p_2}\, [\, \__j\,]_i\,] \ldots [_{p_1}\, \__i\,] \ldots]$

In general, reconstruction effects are not limited to positions that are immediately related by movement but can involve positions that are separated by multiple hops (see e.g. Sportiche 2006: 49). This is consistent with our definition in (19), which only requires that the two relevant positions are part of a single movement chain.

2 Relative clauses

Relative clauses come in many varieties. We will limit ourselves to restrictive headed relative clauses, characterized by Bianchi (2002: 197) as follows:

> A headed relative clause is a syntactically complex modifier involving abstraction over an internal position of the clause (the *relativization site*) and connected to some constituent it modifies (the *relative "head"*).

According to this, headed relative clauses crucially involve two syntactic positions, the relativization site and the relative head. It is the connection between these two positions that forms the basis for all reconstruction effects that have been argued to arise with relative clauses. More concretely, in example (30) the relative head *book* is related to the object position of *wrote* in the relative clause. The position of the relativization site is marked by '_' in the following examples, which should be understood as a purely descriptive device that does not imply the presence of a trace or copy.

(30) the book [which Alice wrote _]

The next two subsections summarize basic assumptions about the syntax and semantics of restrictive headed relative clauses. The third subsection surveys reconstruction effects found with relative clauses.

2.1 Syntax

There are two major issues in the syntax of relative clauses (Bianchi 2002):

- The *Modification Problem*:
  How is the relative clause syntactically related to the modified phrase?
- The *Connectivity Problem*:
  How is the surface head connected to the relativization site?

Modification problem. Starting from (30) as a simple example of a relative clause in a minimal context, we can identify three main components, as shown in (31): a determiner (D), a relative head (NP), and a relative clause, which we assume to be an instance of a complementizer phrase (CP).

(31) $[_{D}$ the] $[_{NP}$ book] $[_{CP}$ which Alice wrote _]

If we assume binary branching, no movement and surface order, then there are only two structural possibilities:

(32) a. [[D NP] CP]
b. [D [NP CP]]

If we add headedness specifications, assuming endocentricity, we get four possibilities for each structural variant in (32), as shown in (33). Headedness is indicated using the projection relation < from Stabler (1997).

(33) aa. $[_< [_<$ D NP] CP] ba. $[_<$ D $[_<$ NP CP]]
ab. $[_< [_>$ D NP] CP] bb. $[_<$ D $[_>$ NP CP]]
ac. $[_> [_<$ D NP] CP] bc. $[_>$ D $[_<$ NP CP]]
ad. $[_> [_>$ D NP] CP] bd. $[_>$ D $[_>$ NP CP]]

Some of these structures are unlikely candidates, in particular (33ac), (33ad) and (33bd) are sentential phrases which fail to capture the nominal properties of constructions like (31). However, most of the remaining structures found their proponents. (33bc) is the NOM-S analysis (e.g. Partee 1975) that later morphed into (33ba) when the idea became popular that the determiner is the head of nominal phrases. The structure in (33ab) corresponds to the NP-S analysis (e.g. Ross 1967), its DP variant in (33aa) is a more modern contender adopted by Sternefeld (this volume). By contrast, (33bb) is the analysis proposed by Kayne (1994), which assumes that the determiner takes a sentential complement, with the head noun sitting in the specifier position of the relative clause.

Connectivity problem. The relative head provides a link between the relative clause (in particular, the relativization site) and its external environment. But how is this link represented in syntax? There are three main lines of competing analyses (see de Vries 2002 or Salzmann 2006 for detailed surveys).

First, the *Head External Analysis* argues that the relative head originates outside the relative clause, there is A′-movement of a relative operator (a pronoun like *which* or a silent *Op*) within the relative clause, and the relative clause is adjoined to the head NP. Assuming a TP layer below the CP layer of the clause, this results in the structure (34) for our example (30).

(34) $[_{DP}$ the *book* $[_{CP}$ [*which*$]_1$ $[_{TP}$ Alice wrote $\_{}_1$]]]

Second, the *Head Raising Analysis* (also known as *Promotion Analysis*) states that the relative head originates inside the relative clause, mediated by a movement of a wh-phrase to the edge of the embedded CP, as indicated in (35). This opens the possibility to reconstruct it in a position inside the relative clause.

(35) $[_{DP}$ the *book*$_2$ $[_{CP}$ [*which* $\_{}_2$ $]_1$ $[_{TP}$ Alice wrote $\_{}_1$]]]

Third, the *Matching Analysis* assumes that corresponding to the external head there is a separate internal head which is phonologically deleted under identity (or recoverability) with the external head. In contrast to the head raising analysis, the internal head and the external head are not part of a common movement chain. This analysis is sketched in (36).

(36) $[_{DP}$ the *book* $[_{CP}$ [*which ~~book~~* $]_1$ $[_{TP}$ Alice wrote $\_{}_1$]]]

These analyses differ in their empirical predictions. In fact, reconstruction effects in relative clauses are the main line of argument for a head raising analysis. The contributions by Salzmann and by Webelhuth, Bargmann and Götze in this volume explore and analyze the available syntactic evidence in detail. In any case, many apparent reconstruction effects do not necessitate a syntactic head raising analysis and several contributions in this volume show how these effects can be derived based on a head external analysis, e.g. for Binding Theory (Krifka) or for pronominal binding (Barker, Jacobson, Sternefeld).

2.2 Semantics

From a semantic point of view, relative clauses are a means to construct complex adjectives from clauses. This idea goes back at least to Quine (1960: 110):

> A relative clause [...] has the form of a sentence except that a relative pronoun stands in it where a singular term would be needed to make a sentence[.] [...] At any rate the peculiar genius of the relative clause is that it creates from a sentence '... *x* ...' a complex adjective summing up what that sentence says about *x*.

Accordingly, we assume that simple relative clauses like (37a) denote properties of individuals, represented in (37b) as a pair of a lambda term and its type, separated by a colon. Here we use expressions of a simply typed lambda calculus to represent meanings, leaving their model-theoretic interpretation implicit. Metalanguage constants are written in bold.

(37) a. $[_{CP}$ which$_1$ Alice wrote $\_{}_1$]
b. λx [**wrote**(x)(**Alice**)] : (e, t)

The basic idea is that the relative clause expresses a proposition that is abstracted over at the argument corresponding to the relativization site. This is combined by intersection, expressed as conjunction in the metalanguage, with the meaning of the head noun, as in (38b) for (38a).

(38) a. $[_{NP}$ book] $[_{CP}$ which$_1$ Alice wrote $\_{}_1$]
b. λx [**book**(x) **and wrote**(x)(**Alice**)] : (e, t)

The meaning of the head noun combined with the relative clause can then form the argument to a determiner, for example as in (39) or (40). Here we are assuming a head external syntactic analysis of relative clauses with a structure based on (33ba).

(39) a. $[_{DP}$ $[_D$ the] $[_{NP}$ $[_{NP}$ book] $[_{CP}$ which$_1$ Alice wrote $\_{}_1$]]]
b. **the**(λx [**book**(x) **and wrote**(x)(**Alice**)]) : e

(40) a. $[_{DP}$ $[_D$ every] $[_{NP}$ $[_{NP}$ book] $[_{CP}$ which$_1$ Alice wrote $\_{}_1$]]]
b. λQ [**every**(λx [**book**(x) **and wrote**(x)(**Alice**)])(Q)] : $((e, t), t)$

There is an intimate connection between relative clauses and questions, both syntactically and semantically. Simple constituent questions like (41a) have been argued to denote properties like (41c), just what we have assumed for relative clauses like (41b).

(41) a. who did Alice meet?
b. who Alice met
c. $\lambda x\,[\mathbf{met}(x)(\mathbf{Alice})] : (e,t)$

This parallel extends to functional readings of questions and relative clauses (Engdahl 1986, Jacobson 1994, Sharvit 1999, Krifka 2001). In its functional reading, the question in (42a) does not ask for an individual such that everybody met that individual, but for a function from individuals to individuals such that everybody met the individual the function returns for them. Formally, this can be represented as a property of individual-valued functions, as shown in (42c). A possible answer is the expression *his mother* that can be interpreted as a function that returns the unique mother for its argument, as indicated in (42d), where **the** maps a two-place predicate of type $(e,(e,t))$ to an individual-valued function of type (e,e). Roughly speaking, $\mathbf{the}(R)$ is the function λx [the unique y such that $R(x)(y)$].

(42) a. Who did everybody$_1$ meet? His$_1$ mother.
b. The relative [$_{CP}$ who everybody$_1$ met _] was his$_1$ mother.
c. $\lambda f\,[\mathbf{everybody}(\lambda x\,[\mathbf{met}(f(x))(x)])] : ((e,e),t)$
d. $\mathbf{the}(\lambda x\,[\lambda y\,[\mathbf{mother\text{-}of}(x)(y)]]) : (e,e)$

One crucial aspect of the formal representation of functional readings is that the relativization site is analyzed as a *layered trace* (von Stechow 1990) that combines two bound variables, f and x. The functional relative clause in (42b) exemplifies a type of relative clauses that is often discussed in the context of reconstruction effects, as we will see shortly.

2.3 Reconstruction effects

We are finally ready to bring the two topics of sections 1 and 2 together and survey empirical phenomena that have been characterized as reconstruction effects in relative clauses. The common structure of these phenomena is that (part of) the relative head E is visible to a principle at the position of the relativization site. This configuration is sketched in (43).

(43) Phonological: [$_{NP}$ ... E ...] [$_{CP}$ ... _ ...]
Input to R: [$_{NP}$ ... ...] [$_{CP}$ ... E ...]

Strictly speaking, the term *reconstruction effect* is only appropriate against the background of a theory of relative clauses that assumes, like the head raising analysis does, that the relative head and the relativization site are linked by a movement chain. Here we use it in a weaker sense as a descriptive term for a class of empirical phenomena that have at least been argued to involve reconstruction, whatever their most satisfying analysis will turn out to be.

There are four main types of principles that play a role in discussions of reconstruction effects in relative clauses: principles of Binding Theory, pronominal binding, relative scope, and idioms. We will discuss them in turn.

First, there are reconstruction effects for principles of *Binding Theory* that involve relative clauses, parallel to the cases we have seen for wh-questions in section 1. Schachter (1973: 32) gives the following examples. In (44a), Principle A can only be satisfied if the reflexive pronoun *himself* is visible at the relativization site rather than in the position of the relative head. Similarly, the ungrammaticality of (44b) is taken to show that the full DP *John* can only be visible to Principle C at the relativization site, where it is c-commanded by a coindexed pronoun, rather than in the position of the relative head, where no violation of Principle C would occur.

(44) a. The $[_{NP}$ portrait of himself$_1]_2$ $[_{CP}$ that John$_1$ painted $\_{}_2]$ is extremely flattering.

b. * The $[_{NP}$ portrait of John$_1]_2$ $[_{CP}$ that he$_1$ painted $\_{}_2]$ is extremely flattering.

Reconstruction for the principles of Binding Theory, which are non-interpretive, as mentioned in section 1.3, might seem to necessitate a syntactic approach to reconstruction. However, Krifka (this volume) develops an alternative analysis of apparent Condition C effects under reconstruction that does not require any syntactic movement.

Second, reconstruction for *pronominal binding* concerns cases where the external relative head contains a pronoun that appears to be bound by an element inside the relative clause. This configuration is known as *binding into the head* (Jacobson 2002a). An example is given in (45), where the quantified DP *every man* inside the relative clause appears to bind the pronoun *his* in the relative head.

(45) The $[_{NP}$ relative of his$_1]$ $[_{CP}$ $[_{DP}$ every man$]_1$ admires _ most] is his$_1$ mother.

One origin of this type of examples is the discussion of functional relative clauses in Geach (1968: 124), who explores the contrast between the sentences in (46).

(46) a. The one woman $[_{CP}$ whom $[_{DP}$ every true Englishman$]_1$ honours _ above all other women] is his$_1$ Queen.

b. The one woman $[_{CP}$ whom $[_{DP}$ every true Englishman$]_1$ honours _ above all other women] is his$_1$ mother.

While these sentences do not involve binding into the head, they do exhibit pronouns that appear to be bound by a quantified DP inside a relative clause that is not c-commanding them. These kinds of *connectivity effects*, discussed in detail by Romero (this volume), are mostly restricted to copular sentences (see Cecchetto 2005), but there are some examples of similar effects in non-identity sentences, like (47) from Sharvit (1999: 449) or (48) from Safir (1999: 613).

(47) The $[_{NP}$ picture of himself$_1]$ $[_{CP}$ which $[_{DP}$ every student$]_1$ hated _] annoyed his$_1$ friends.

(48) The $[_{NP}$ picture of his$_1$ mother$]$ $[_{CP}$ that $[_{DP}$ every soldier$]_1$ kept _ wrapped in a sock] was not much use to him$_1$.

The phenomenon of binding into the head plays a central role in several contributions in this volume, including those by Barker, Heim, Jacobson, and Sternefeld. We will also peek at possible analyses in section 3.

Third, there are several types of examples where an element *E* in the relative head appears to take scope below an element *F* inside the relative clause. This is schematically shown in (49), where *R* is a *relative scope* principle that maps syntactic c-command to semantic scope.

(49) Phonological: $[_{NP}$ ... *E* ...] $[_{CP}$ ... *F* ... _ ...]
Input to *R*: $[_{NP}$ ... ...] $[_{CP}$ ... *F* ... *E* ...]

Some examples are given in (50). The first example in (50a) from Salzmann (2006: 22) involves two nominal elements, where the denotation of *two patients* can depend on the interpretation of the lower DP *every doctor*.

(50) a. the $[_{NP}$ two patients] $[_{CP}$ that $[_{DP}$ every doctor] will examine _ tomorrow]
b. The $[_{NP}$ longest book] $[_{CP}$ that John said $[_{CP}$ that Tolstoy wrote _]] is *War and Peace*.
c. The $[_{NP}$ gifted mathematician] $[_{CP}$ that Bill claims to be _] should be able to solve this equation.
d. The $[_{NP}$ book] $[_{CP}$ John needs to write _] must have more impact than the one he has already written.

In (50b), Bhatt (2002) argued, the adjectival modifier in the relative head can scope above or below *John said*. This has been taken as evidence for a syntactic account of reconstruction that allows to interpret a copy of the relative head in any of the positions generated by successive cyclic movement. A critical discussion of this argument can be found in the contribution by Heycock to this volume.

Grosu & Krifka (2007) discuss another scope-related effect, illustrated in (50c), where the relative head is interpreted below an intensional operator within the relative clause. Moltmann (this volume) develops a semantic analysis of the related class of intensional relative clauses that includes examples like (50d).

A fourth class of reconstruction effects involves *idioms*. As mentioned in section 1.3, the idea here is that, if the chunks of an idiom need to form a syntactic unit when they are handed to the semantic component, examples like (51) from Schachter (1973: 31–32) require syntactic reconstruction.

(51) a. The $[_{NP}$ headway$]_1$ $[_{CP}$ that we made $\_{}_1]$ was satisfactory.

b. The $[_{NP}$ careful track$]_1$ $[_{CP}$ that she's keeping $\_{}_1$ of her expenses$]$ pleases me.

Idioms and their implications for the analysis of relative clauses are discussed in detail by Webelhuth, Bargmann & Götze (this volume).

This completes our short inventory of reconstruction effects in relative clauses. For a more extensive collection, see Salzmann (this volume).

3 Analyzing reconstruction effects

Reconstruction effects involve phrases that are said to behave "as if" they were in a different position. But what does that really mean? How can we analyze reconstruction effects formally in a theory of grammar?

According to Gazdar et al. (1985: 1), a grammar is an "interpreted formal system defining the membership of the collection of linguistic expressions, and assigning a structure and an interpretation to each member". In other words, we want a system that is able to derive correct pairings of form (syntactic structures) and meaning (semantic representations). In particular, we want the system to capture that the relative head may depend (in some sense) on elements within its associated relative clause, i.e. account for apparent reconstruction effects in relative clauses. In this section we will explore different strategies for achieving this.

We can broadly distinguish two basic approaches to the design of the syntax-semantics interface. One approach is to organize syntax and semantics in a *serial architecture* where "syntax feeds semantics". This perspective is taken by mainstream generative grammar implementing the Minimalist Program (Chomsky 1995). The syntactic component operates autonomously – syntactic operations like internal and external merge have no direct semantic effects – and hands in completed structures (LFs) to the semantic component for subsequent interpretation.

The second main approach is to setup a *parallel architecture* where syntax and semantics work hand in hand, in the sense that every syntactic operation is coupled with a semantic operation. At every step in the structure-building process, we are dealing with expressions that have phonological, syntactic and semantic structure. This perspective on grammar architecture, also known as *direct compositionality* (Barker & Jacobson 2007), is embodied in frameworks like categorial grammar or type-logical grammar.

In the following subsections we will sketch how sentences involving reconstruction effects in relative clauses, in particular binding into the head, can be analyzed under these two approaches. The constructions in (52) will serve as the probes.

(52) a. the $[_{NP}$ book] $[_{CP}$ which Alice wrote _]
b. the $[_{NP}$ relative of his] $[_{CP}$ which every man admires _]

Syntactic reconstruction, characteristic for serial grammar architectures, is discussed in section 3.1. Semantic reconstruction, typically found in parallel grammar architectures, but also compatible with serial architectures, is introduced in section 3.2. The approaches will then be compared in section 4, addressing the question whether there are reasons to favor one approach over the other.

3.1 Syntactic reconstruction

Syntactic reconstruction is based on the idea that phrases that behave "as if" they were in a different position really are in that different position at the relevant level of representation. But how does this work in detail? We will look at two versions of a serial grammar architecture, both grounded in mainstream generative syntax. The first one uses a trace-based approach to movement, the second one adopts the copy theory of movement.

3.1.1 LF with traces: Analysis of a simple relative clause

First, we sketch the derivation of the meaning of a simple relative clause against the background of a generative syntax framework in the style of Government and Binding that assumes a level of Logical Form as input to the interpretation function and that assumes that movements leave coindexed traces. The setup of the framework follows Heim & Kratzer (1998).

In order to arrive at appropriate LFs, a syntactic rule of Quantifier Raising (QR) is assumed that moves the relative pronoun from the relativization site within the relative clause to its edge. This rule leaves a trace at the origin and inserts a coindexed binder just below the target position. It can be stated as follows (based on Heim & Kratzer 1998: 185–188 and Büring 2005: 164):

(QR) Replace $[_{CP} \ldots [_{DP}\ \alpha] \ldots]$ by $[_{CP} [_{DP}\ \alpha] [\lambda_i [_{CP} \ldots \__i \ldots]]]$, where i is a positive integer.

Note that binder indices of the form 'λ_i' are part of the syntactic structure, at least at LF, and as such they are elements of our object language.

Under a head external analysis of relative clauses, we arrive at the following LF for a simple example:

(53) $[_{DP}$ the $[_{NP} [_{NP}$ book$] [_{CP}$ which $\lambda_1 [_{TP}$ Alice wrote $\__1]]]]$

It is straightforward to interpret this structure using standard semantic tools. For the sake of explicitness, we use the following set of (slightly adapted) interpretation rules from Heim & Kratzer (1998).

(FA) If α is a branching node and $\{\beta, \gamma\}$ the set of its children, then, for any assignment g, if $[\![\beta]\!]^g$ is a function whose domain contains $[\![\gamma]\!]^g$, then $[\![\alpha]\!]^g = [\![\beta]\!]^g([\![\gamma]\!]^g)$.

(PM) If α is a branching node and $\{\beta, \gamma\}$ the set of its children, then, for any assignment g, if $[\![\beta]\!]^g$ and $[\![\gamma]\!]^g$ are both functions of type (e, t), then $[\![\alpha]\!]^g = \lambda x\, [[\![\beta]\!]^g(x)\ \textbf{and}\ [\![\gamma]\!]^g(x)]$.

(PA) Let α be a branching node with children β and γ, where β dominates only a binder index λ_i. Then, for any variable assignment g, $[\![\alpha]\!]^g = \lambda x\, [[\![\gamma]\!]^{g[i \mapsto x]}]$.

(PR) If α is a pronoun or a trace, g is a variable assignment, and $i \in \mathrm{dom}(g)$, then $[\![\alpha_i]\!]^g = g(i)$.

The type-driven rule of Functional Application (FA) is the default mode of combination. For semantically combining the relative head with the relative clause, the rule of Predicate Modification (PM) can be used. The binder indices introduced by the syntactic rule of QR are interpreted using Predicate Abstraction (PA). Finally, pronouns and traces do not have lexical entries under this setup but are handled by the rule (PR).

If we assume that our lexicon contains the entries in (54), we can apply these rules to the LF in (53) as shown in (55) in order to arrive at its interpretation in (56).

(54)
a. $[\![\text{the}]\!] = \lambda P\, [\textbf{the}(P)] : ((e,t), e)$
b. $[\![\text{book}]\!] = \lambda x\, [\textbf{book}(x)] : (e,t)$
c. $[\![\text{which}]\!] = \lambda P\, [P] : ((e,t),(e,t))$
d. $[\![\text{Alice}]\!] = \textbf{Alice} : e$
e. $[\![\text{wrote}]\!] = \lambda x\, [\lambda y\, [\textbf{wrote}(x)(y)]] : (e,(e,t))$

(55)

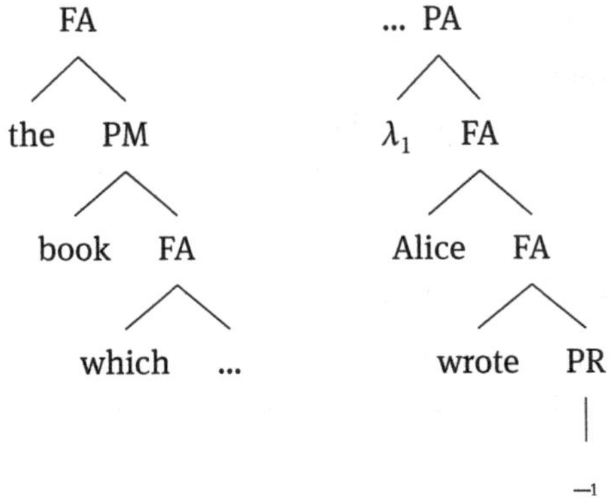

(56) $\textbf{the}(\lambda x\ [\textbf{book}(x)\ \textbf{and wrote}(x)(\textbf{Alice})])$

Under this analysis the relative pronoun *which* does not make any substantial contribution because the conjunctive linking of relative clause and relative head is handled by a separate rule of composition (PM). We have chosen to render the relative pronoun effectively invisible in the semantics by assigning an aptly typed identity function to it in (54c); for the general case one could use the polymorphic version in (57) instead. Alternatively, one could assume that the relative pronoun is invisible or deleted at LF by some rule that eliminates superfluous elements.

(57) $[\![\text{which}]\!] = \lambda\xi\ [\xi] : \forall\alpha\ [(\alpha, \alpha)]$

We will use evaluation trees like (55) with lexical items as leaves and interpretation rules as inner nodes for summarizing the analyses in all approaches below. They are intended to show at a glance which semantic mechanisms are involved in the interpretation of a construction.

3.1.2 LF with copies: Analysis of a simple relative clause

Now we move on to a head-raising analysis of relative clauses based on the copy theory of movement, mainly following the footsteps of Bhatt (2002) and Heim (this volume). If we were assuming, as before, that movement leaves traces, a head-raising analysis of (52a) would result in an LF like (58). However, with the copy theory of movement, we end up with what we might call a Proto-LF like (59).

(58) $[_{DP}$ the $[_{CP}$ $[_{NP}$ book$]$ λ_2 $[_{CP}$ $[_{DP}$ which $\_{}_{-2}$ $]$ λ_1 $[_{TP}$ Alice wrote $\_{}_{-1}$ $]]]]$

(59) $[_{DP}$ the $[_{CP}$ $[_{NP}$ book$]$ $[_{CP}$ $[_{DP}$ which book$]$ $[_{TP}$ Alice wrote which book $]]]]$

It is unclear how to interpret this structure using standard semantic tools. There are two ways to go: First, we could enrich the semantics in such a way that it recognizes copies and knows how to treat them directly as variables, as discussed in Ruys (2011, 2015). Second, we could add an intermediate step at the interface in which we refurbish Proto-LFs in such a way that the result can be consumed by a standard interpretation function. In particular, Fox (2000) develops a mechanism called *Trace Conversion* for this purpose. The specifics of the presentation below more closely follow Heim (this volume), who implements the idea using two type-shifters.

In order to refurbish a Proto-LF, the following three mechanisms are required, which we will label (TCB), (DEL) and (TCT). First, given a structure with two copies of a constituent, (TCB) simultaneously inserts a binder index in the immediate scope of the higher copy and a matching variable as a sister to the lower copy. In effect, this mimics the creation of operator-variable dependencies that is achieved as a result of applying (QR) in trace-based approaches to movement and LF.

(TCB) Given a Proto-LF of the form [... α ... [... [α] ...]] in which the two occurrences of α are copies of each other, transform it as follows, where i is a positive integer: [... α [λ_i [... [... [[α] $\_\_i$] ...]]]],

Second, (DEL) deletes appropriate parts of each copy in accordance with certain economy principles that structures must satisfy at LF, like Copy Economy (CE) and Operator Economy (OE) (see e.g. Barss 2001: 682 for a summary).

(DEL) Delete superfluous material.

(CE) Copy Economy: Eliminate redundancy of copies, down to recoverability.

(OE) Operator Economy: Minimize the content of operator positions.

Third, (TCT) injects two type-shifters at appropriate places in the remains of the lower copy in order to render it locally interpretable.

(TCT) Given a syntactic structure that contains a constituent [[α] $\_\_i$], replace it by [†the [[α] [†ident $\_\_i$]]].

These two type-shifters are defined as follows (adapted from Heim this volume), where the '†' prefix only serves the purpose of distinguishing these elements from other potentially homophonous elements in the object language. We will simply treat these two entries as additional items in our lexicon as shown in (60).

(60) a. $[\![\text{†the}]\!] = \lambda P\,[\mathbf{the}(P)] : ((e,t),e)$

b. $[\![\text{†ident}]\!] = \lambda x\,[\lambda y\,[x = y]] : (e,(e,t))$

Now let's apply this setup to the example (59), repeated as (61a). For the sake of concreteness, we assume that the relative head is in the specifier position of the clause and that the determiner takes the relative clause directly as an argument, as in (33bb). The Proto-LF in (61a) is transformed into a proper LF, using the steps outlined above. First, we setup the binding configuration by applying (TCB), resulting in (61b). Second, we remove redundant copies as licensed by (DEL), resulting in (61c). Third, we apply (TCT) to arrive at the interpretable structure in (61d). Using the semantic rules introduced earlier, as indicated in the evaluation tree in (62), results in the interpretation in (63).

(61) a. $[_{DP}$ the $[_{CP}$ book $[_{CP}$ which book $[_{TP}$ Alice wrote $[_{DP}$ which book]]]]]
b. $[_{DP}$ the $[_{CP}$ book $[_{CP}$ which book $[\lambda_1$ $[_{TP}$ Alice wrote $[[_{DP}$ which book] $\_{}_1$]]]]]]
c. $[_{DP}$ the $[_{CP}$ which $[\lambda_1$ [Alice wrote [[book] $\_{}_1$]]]]]
d. $[_{DP}$ the $[_{CP}$ which $[\lambda_1$ [Alice wrote [†the [[book] [†ident $\_{}_1$]]]]]]]

(62)

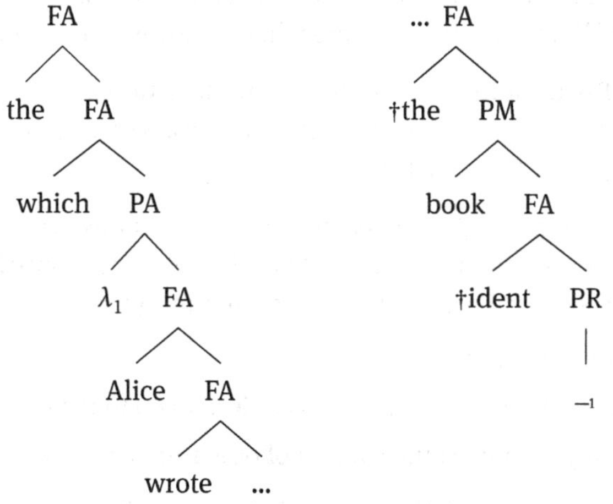

(63) **the**(λy [**wrote**(**the**(λx [**book**(x) **and** $y = x$]))(**Alice**)])

The semantic effect of interpreting the lower copy of the relative head *book* is evident if we compare (63) to (56): *book* is now interpreted in the scope of *wrote*, an important step toward capturing reconstruction effects.

3.1.3 LF with copies: Syntactic reconstruction

In the next step we use these tools to sketch how syntactic reconstruction can account for binding into the head examples like (64).

(64) The relative of his which every man admires is his mother.

The interpretation of functional relative clauses requires a few additional assumptions that go beyond what we have introduced so far. First, as already mentioned in section 2.2, the relativization site is analyzed as a *layered trace* (von Stechow

1990) that depends on both the relative head and the quantificational noun phrase that binds the pronoun inside the relative head. The indexing in (65) indicates these dependencies.

(65) the [$_{NP}$ relative of his$_1$]$_2$ [$_{CP}$ which [$_{DP}$ every man]$_1$ admires $\_{2(1)}$]

Second, in a functional reading the relative head and the relative clause, whose meanings are combined by intersection, are not predicates of type $\langle e, t\rangle$. It is usually assumed that there exists some type shifter that turns the relative head into a predicate of functions (Engdahl 1986, Jacobson 1994). This is independent of the presence of a bound pronoun in the relative head and is also required for functional relatives with simple heads like (66).

(66) the [$_{NP}$ woman] [$_{CP}$ which every man admires] is his mother

However, Heim (this volume) leverages the copy theory of movement and independently motivated mechanisms of presupposition projection to render a separate operator or rule for shifting the meaning of the relative head superfluous.

Let's return to (64). A possible Proto-LF under the copy theory of movement is given in (67a). Its transformation into a proper LF using (TCB), (DEL) and (TCT) as before results in something like (67b). The corresponding evaluation tree is shown in (68) and the target interpretation is given in (69).

(67) a. [$_{DP}$ the [$_{CP}$ relative of his [$_{CP}$ which relative of his [$_{CP}$ every man [$_{CP}$ every man admires which relative of his]]]]]

b. [$_{DP}$ the λ_2 [$_{CP}$ every man λ_1 [$_{CP}$ [†the man †ident $\__1$] admires [†the relative of his$_1$ †ident $\__{2(1)}$]]]]

(68)

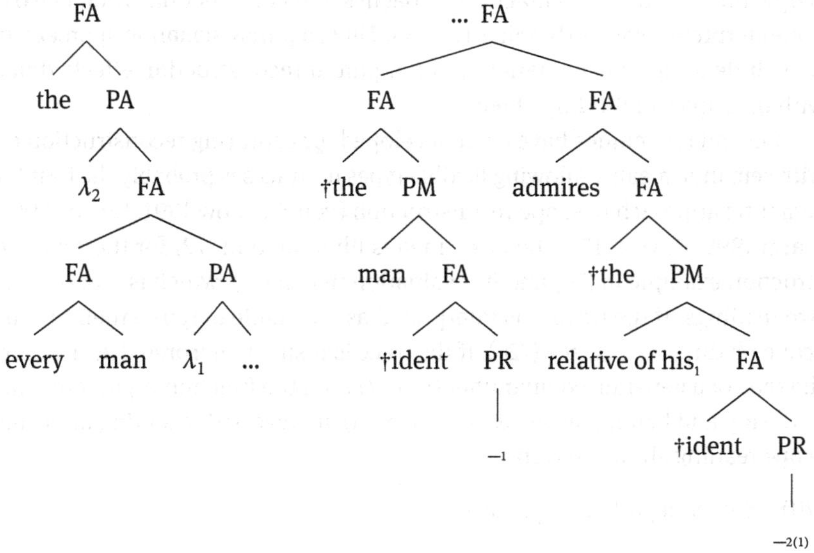

(69) $\textbf{the}(\lambda f\,[\textbf{every}(\lambda x\,[x \in \mathrm{dom}(f)])(\lambda x\,[\textbf{relative-of}(x)(f(x))])$ **and** $\textbf{every}(\lambda x\,[x \in \textbf{man}(x)])(\lambda x\,[\textbf{admire}(f(x))(x)])])$

Several variations of this approach are conceivable. For example, we have somewhat arbitrarily chosen to keep two copies of *man* (as in Fox 1999) but only the lower copy of *relative of his* (as in Heim this volume). The interpretation also depends on more general (polymorphic) lexical entries for the inserted type shifters and the definite determiner, which needs to allow for a predicate of functions as argument. Instead of going into the details of the derivation, we refer the reader to Heim (this volume) for a full account in this tradition.

Syntactic reconstruction based on the copy theory of movement is a powerful mechanism for deriving reconstruction effects. It requires, however, the adoption of a few controversial assumptions like the raising analysis of relative clauses and certain invasive refurbishing actions on LF structures to render them interpretable. Somewhat paradoxically, an elegant method of implementing the latter is by injecting semantic type shifters, which are more characteristic of semantic approaches to reconstruction.

3.2 Semantic reconstruction

Semantic reconstruction is an umbrella term for semantic approaches to reconstruction effects that do not require tampering with syntactic structures. By design, they only target interpretive reconstruction effects (pronominal binding, relative scope, idioms), unlike syntactic approaches to reconstruction, which also cover non-interpretive effects (Binding Theory). Thus, a purely semantic approach needs to include a separate explanation for apparent reconstruction effects that arise with principles of Binding Theory.

Several techniques have been developed for capturing reconstruction effects with semantic means. Allowing flexible types for traces is probably the best-known semantic approach to scope reconstruction (von Stechow 1991, Cresti 1995, Rullmann 1995, Ruys 2015). The basic idea is illustrated in (72) for the scope reconstruction example in (70) and its evaluation tree in (71), which is identical for the two readings. If the trace $\__1$ is interpreted as a variable of type e then the surface scope reading results, see (72a). If the trace is instead interpreted as a variable of the type of a generalized quantifier $((e,t),t)$ then the function-argument relations in the top and bottom instances of (FA) in (71) are reversed, resulting in the inverse scope reading shown in (72b).

(70) Someone$_1$ is likely $\__1$ to arrive.

(71)

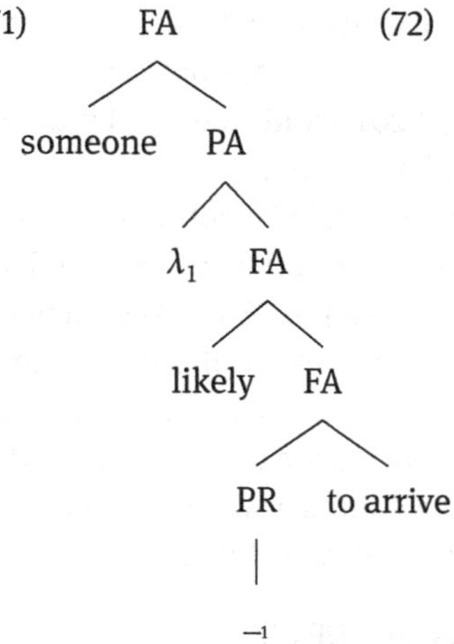

(72) Evaluation of the top node in (71)

a. with __1 of type e:
FA(**someone**, λx [**likely**(**arrive**(x))])
= **someone**(λx [**likely**(**arrive**(x))])

b. with __1 of type $((e,t),t)$:
FA(**someone**, λz [**likely**(z(λx [**arrive**(x)]))])
= **likely**(**someone**(λx [**arrive**(x)]))

Another technique that can be used to account for reconstruction effects with pronominal binding has been developed by Sternefeld (1997). Here the idea is that bound pronouns are not translated as regular variables, but as "pseudo-variables" like $\lambda g\ [g(i)]$ for *him*$_i$, where g ranges over assignment functions. Bound variables are thus treated as functions from assignments to individuals and the semantic apparatus is extended accordingly to allow abstraction over assignment functions. In this way, coindexing information can be smuggled past the standard evaluation rules for variables in the lambda calculus. In fact, Sternefeld (this volume) builds on a calculus that explicitly allows for "binding by beta reduction", a form of variable capture carefully avoided by standard lambda calculi. Büring (2005: 252) also sketches a possible implementation of this idea, using the two silent operators in (73).

(73) a. $[\![\uparrow \alpha]\!]^g = \lambda g\ [[\![\alpha]\!]^g]$
b. $[\![\downarrow \alpha]\!]^g = [\![\alpha]\!]^g\ (g)$

The idea is then to freeze the indexing information using ↑ and release it using ↓ when the local assignment function provides the desired mapping from indices to individuals, as indicated in (74). In this way, the interpretation of pronouns can be "delayed" until they reach a fitting environment.

(74) the [↑ relative of his$_1$]$_2$ that [every man]$_1$ admires ↓ __2

A similar effect is achieved in the variable-free framework by Jacobson (1999), in which pronouns are analyzed as denoting (partial) identity functions.

These semantic techniques are compatible with a polystratal derivational grammar architecture (see e.g. Ruys 2015 for a semantic approach to scope reconstruction in a Minimalist framework based on the copy theory of movement).

However, many proponents of semantic reconstruction do not see a need for a separate transformational engine in syntax and are instead committed to a grammar architecture in which form and meaning of an expression are computed in parallel. The frameworks of type-logical grammar (Moortgat 2011) and categorial grammar (Steedman & Baldridge 2011) provide elegant implementations.

In order to convey a taste of how these systems work, let's look at a very basic version of a categorial grammar. A linguistic expression can be represented as a triple of form, syntactic category and meaning, for example ⟨Alice, DP, **Alice**⟩. In many categorial frameworks it is common to represent these triples using a three-place typing relation, for example Alice $\vdash$ **Alice** : DP. When two expressions are merged to form a complex expression, their components are combined according to certain rules. These rules can be expressed in a compact way using a natural deduction notation familiar from inference rules in logic, as illustrated in (75).

(75) $$\frac{\text{Alice} \vdash \textbf{Alice} : \text{DP} \qquad \text{sleeps} \vdash \lambda x\, [\textbf{sleeps}(x)] : \text{DP}\backslash\text{CP}}{\text{Alice sleeps} \vdash \textbf{sleeps}(\textbf{Alice}) : \text{CP}}\ \backslash\text{e}$$

This sample derivation uses the backslash elimination (or backward application) rule that combines an expression or type A and an expression of type A\B to an expression of type B. Semantically, this corresponds to function application. For expressions of type A/B that are followed by expressions of type B, there is a corresponding rule of forward slash elimination (or forward application) with the same semantics. Both rules are shown in (76). They are the equivalent of the type-driven rule (FA) that was used in the section on syntactic reconstruction.

(76) $$\frac{\text{X} \vdash M : \text{A} \qquad \text{Y} \vdash N : \text{A}\backslash\text{B}}{\text{X Y} \vdash N(M) : \text{B}}\ \backslash\text{e} \qquad \frac{\text{X} \vdash N : \text{B/A} \qquad \text{Y} \vdash M : \text{A}}{\text{X Y} \vdash N(M) : \text{B}}\ /\text{e}$$

For the analysis of a simple relative clause we need two more rules: type lifting and function composition, shown in (77). Type lifting is a unary rule that shifts the meaning of a proper name to a generalized quantifier.

(77) $$\frac{\text{X} \vdash M : \text{A}}{\text{X} \vdash \lambda x\, [x(M)] : \text{B}/(\text{A}\backslash\text{B})}\ \text{l} \qquad \frac{\text{X} \vdash M : \text{A/B} \qquad \text{Y} \vdash N : \text{B/C}}{\text{X Y} \vdash \lambda x\, [M(N(x))] : \text{A/C}}\ \text{b}$$

We assume that the entries in (78) are part of our lexicon. Here we analyze *which* as providing the conjunctive link between the relative clause and the relative head. The evaluation tree for our running example (52a) is shown in (79), resulting in the target interpretation in (80).

(78) a. the $\vdash \lambda P\, [\textbf{the}(P)]$: DP/NP
b. book $\vdash \lambda x\, [\textbf{book}(x)]$: NP
c. which $\vdash \lambda P\, [\lambda Q\, [\lambda x\, [P(x)\ \textbf{and}\ Q(x)]]]$: (NP\NP)/(CP/DP)

d. Alice ⊢ **Alice** : DP

e. wrote ⊢ $\lambda x\,[\lambda y\,[\mathbf{wrote}(x)(y)]]$: (DP\CP)/DP

(79)

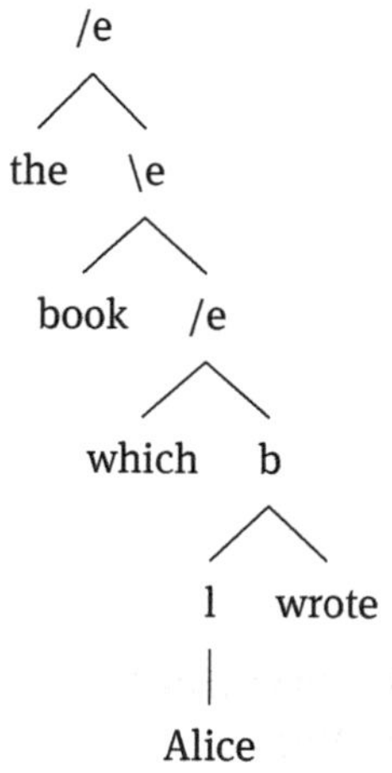

(80) **the**(λx [**book**(x) **and wrote**(x)(**Alice**)])

Jacobson (1999, 2002a, this volume) uses a variable-free semantics based on combinatory categorial grammar and demonstrates how reconstruction effects can be handled in this framework. Using a carefully motivated set of combinatory rules, it is possible to derive correct interpretations for sentences that involve apparent reconstruction effects, without assuming syntactic movement and by directly combining adjacent expressions in their surface arrangement. This is illustrated in (83) for our running reconstruction example (52b) with its target interpretation in (84). The additional combinators required for this analysis are g and z for handling pronouns and binding, shown in (81) and (82), and a decurrying rule m for functional interpretations of relative clauses. The vertical slash notation A|B for expressions of category A that need an antecedent of category B and the rule format used here are adopted from Jäger (2005: 100). For a detailed account, see Jacobson (this volume).

(81) $$\frac{\mathrm{X} \vdash M : \mathrm{A/B}}{\mathrm{X} \vdash \lambda x\,[\lambda y\,[M(x(y))]] : \mathrm{A|C/B|C}}\ \mathrm{g}$$

(82) $$\frac{\mathrm{X} \vdash M : (\mathrm{B\backslash A})/\mathrm{C}}{\mathrm{X} \vdash \lambda x\,[\lambda y\,[M(x(y))(y)]] : (\mathrm{B\backslash A})/\mathrm{C|B}}\ \mathrm{z}$$

(83)

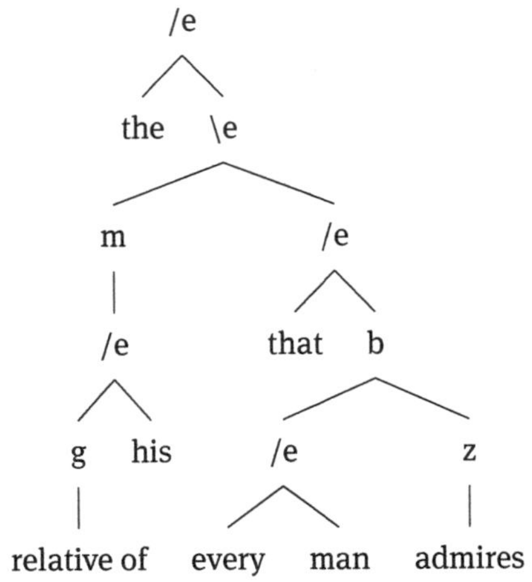

(84) $\mathbf{the}(\lambda f\,[\mathbf{every}(\lambda x\,[x \in \mathrm{dom}(f)])(\lambda x\,[\mathbf{relative\text{-}of}(x)(f(x))])\ \mathbf{and}$
$\mathbf{every}(\lambda x\,[x \in \mathbf{man}(x)])(\lambda x\,[\mathbf{admire}(f(x))(x)])])$

Barker (this volume) presents an alternative semantic approach to reconstruction phenomena on top of a continuation-based grammatical framework (Barker & Shan 2014).

4 Comparing the approaches

Having sketched both syntactic and semantic approaches to reconstruction effects, one crucial question remains: Which approach is the superior one? Are there reasons other than personal preferences and acquired habits that can objectively guide our decisions about grammar design and the architecture of the syntax-semantics interface?

In general, there are two types of arguments for deciding between competing approaches:

- Empirical arguments: Do the approaches differ in their empirical predictions? Which approach is better at correctly deriving acceptable constructions and correctly ruling out unacceptable constructions?
- Conceptual arguments: Are there conceptual or technical reasons for preferring one approach over the other, for example: simplicity, explicitness, formal precision, computability or cognitive plausibility?

First, several empirical arguments have been brought forward. On the one hand, Heycock (1995) and Fox (1999) have argued that scope reconstruction feeds Condition C, that is, that scope reconstruction is impossible in the following structural configuration (Fox 1999: 163):

(85) $[_{QP}$ ... r-expression$_1$ ...$]_2$ ... pronoun$_1$ ... $\_\_{2}$

Examples like (86) are provided as evidence: The semantics of *invent* requires scope reconstruction, but this leads to a violation of Condition C, rendering the example ungrammatical. Since scope reconstruction appears to be impossible without inducing a Condition C violation, it must involve a syntactic rather than a semantic mechanism.

(86) * $[_{DP}$ How many stories about Diana$_1$'s brother$]_2$ is she$_1$ likely to invent $\_\_{2}$?

For a detailed re-evaluation of this argument, see Krifka (this volume). In general, the analysis of interactions between different types of reconstruction effects provides a rich set of empirical facts for theories to explain. Heycock (this volume) takes a look at possible correlations between reconstruction for binding conditions, idioms and adjectival modifiers in relative clauses. Truckenbrodt (this volume) explores the interactions between stress reconstruction, idiom interpretation and Condition C effects.

On the other hand, Jacobson (2002a) presents stacked relative clauses like (87), where a quantifier in one relative clause binds a pronoun in the other, as a challenge for syntactic theories of reconstruction: There is no obvious way to (re-)construct a syntactic representation in which all bindees are in the c-command domain of their binders.

(87) The $[_{NP}$ assignment$]_3$ $[_{CP}$ that *every student*$_1$ gave $\_\_{3}$ *her*$_2]$ $[_{CP}$ that *every phonology professor*$_2$ most praised *him*$_1$ for $\_\_{3}]$ was the last one *he*$_1$ handed in to *her*$_2$.

Additional evidence in favor of a semantic approach to reconstruction comes from an empirical study on binding into the head cases in German reported by Radó, Konietzko & Sternefeld (this volume).

Second, also conceptual arguments have been voiced as a relevant factor in the controversy between syntactic and semantic reconstruction. Jacobson (2002b) compares alternative approaches to the overall organization of the grammar and the syntax-semantics interface and argues that we should prefer Direct Compositionality on conceptual grounds since it provides the simplest overall architecture. Simplicity is definitely a goal shared with practitioners of the *Minimalist* program, but to some degree even simplicity seems to be in the eye of the beholder. What is simpler: a handful of combinatory rules for constructing expressions or a fully generic merge operation coupled with a few general principles? Even when all relevant details are known, the decision could be difficult without agreed upon

Tab. 1: This simplistic view of the tradeoff between syntax and semantics is falsified by the existence of constructions like functional relative clauses: Multiple syntactic levels in a serial grammar architecture cannot compensate for the absence of polymorphic types in semantics.

grammar architecture	syntax	semantics
serial: syntax feeds semantics	poly-stratal	mono-morphic
parallel: grammar composes signs	mono-stratal	poly-morphic

objective standards for simplicity that go beyond subjective assessments, which are likely to be shaped by factors like personal familiarity.

Explicitness, formal precision and computability are additional desiderata that may be used to decide between competing theories. Jacobson (2002b: 601) noticed a “trend away from writing explicit ‘fragments’” that accompanied the shift away from Direct Compositionality. Maybe upcoming large-scale computational approaches to syntax and semantics will manage to reverse this trend. In combination with large corpora they could even allow for a quantitative comparison of the predictive success of competing theories.

5 Conclusion

Reconstruction effects in relative clauses not only constitute an interesting set of empirical facts, but also provide a useful benchmark for competing theories of grammar and the syntax-semantics interface. Accounts have been developed both in serial grammar architectures, typically involving some form of syntactic reconstruction, and in parallel grammar architectures, where richer semantic mechanisms are used to explain the same set of empirical data. There is no perfect dichotomy between syntactic and semantic approaches to reconstruction. The simplistic view in Table 1 that syntactic and semantic mechanisms are perfectly equivalent is untenable if we consider constructions like functional relative clauses. Even syntactic approaches to reconstruction will require layered traces and higher semantic types in order to arrive at correct interpretations.

The contributions in this volume search for the best balance between syntactic and semantic components in the analysis of reconstruction effects. Lechner (this volume) even argues for a hybrid theory of reconstruction in which syntactic and semantic reconstruction complement each other.

Acknowledgment: I gratefully acknowledge support by the DFG (Project *Syntax-Semantics Mismatches in Externally and Internally Headed Relative Constructions*). I would like to thank Manfred Krifka, Rainer Ludwig and Frank Sode for valuable discussions and feedback.

References

Barker, Chris & Pauline Jacobson (eds.). 2007. *Direct compositionality* (Oxford Studies in Theoretical Linguistics). Oxford: Oxford University Press.

Barker, Chris & Chung-chieh Shan. 2014. *Continuations and natural language*. Oxford: Oxford University Press.

Barss, Andrew. 2001. Syntactic reconstruction effects. In Mark Baltin & Chris Collins (eds.), *The handbook of contemporary syntactic theory*, 670–696. Oxford: Blackwell. https://doi.org/10.1111/b.9781405102537.2003.00023.x.

Bhatt, Rajesh. 2002. The raising analysis of relative clauses: Evidence from adjectival modification. *Natural Language Semantics* 10. 43–90.

Bianchi, Valentina. 2002. Headed relative clauses in generative syntax: Part 1. *Glot International* 6(7). 197–204.

Büring, Daniel. 2005. *Binding theory*. Cambridge: Cambridge University Press.

Cecchetto, Carlo. 2005. Reconstruction in relative clauses and the copy theory of traces. *Linguistic Variation Yearbook* 5(1). 5–35. https://doi.org/10.1075/livy.5.02cec.

Chomsky, Noam. 1977. On wh-movement. In Peter Culicover, Thomas Wasow & Adrian Akmajian (eds.), *Formal syntax*, 71–132. New York: Academic Press.

Chomsky, Noam. 1995. *The Minimalist Program*. Cambridge, MA: MIT Press.

Chomsky, Noam & Howard Lasnik. 1993. The theory of principles and parameters. In Joachim Jacobs, Arnim von Stechow, Wolfgang Sternefeld & Theo Vennemann (eds.), *Syntax: An international handbook of contemporary research (HSK 9)*, 506–569. Berlin: de Gruyter.

Cresti, Diana. 1995. Extraction and reconstruction. *Natural Language Semantics* 3. 79–122.

de Vries, Mark. 2002. *The syntax of relativization*. University of Amsterdam Doctoral dissertation.

Engdahl, Elisabet. 1986. *Constituent questions: The syntax and semantics of questions with special reference to Swedish*. Dordrecht: Reidel.

Fox, Danny. 1999. Reconstruction, binding theory, and the interpretation of chains. *Linguistic Inquiry* 30(2). 157–196.

Fox, Danny. 2000. *Economy and semantic interpretation*. Cambridge, MA: MIT Press.

Frey, Werner. 1993. *Syntaktische Bedingungen für die Interpretation*. Berlin: Akademie-Verlag.

Gazdar, Gerald, Ewan Klein, Geoffrey Pullum & Ivan A. Sag. 1985. *Generalized phrase structure grammar*. Cambridge, Massachusetts: Harvard University Press.

Geach, Peter T. 1968. Quine's syntactical insights. *Synthese* 19. 118–129.

Grosu, Alexander & Manfred Krifka. 2007. *The gifted mathematician that you claim to be*: Equational intensional 'reconstruction' relatives. *Linguistics and Philosophy* 30. 445–485. https://doi.org/10.1007/s10988-008-9022-5.

Heim, Irene & Angelika Kratzer. 1998. *Semantics in generative grammar*. Oxford: Blackwell.

Heycock, Caroline. 1995. Asymmetries in reconstruction. *Linguistic Inquiry* 26. 547–570.

Jacobson, Pauline. 1994. Binding connectivity in copular sentences. In Mandy Harvey & Lynn Santelmann (eds.), *Proceedings of SALT 4* (Cornell Working Papers in Linguistics), 161–178. Ithaca, NY: Cornell University.

Jacobson, Pauline. 1999. Towards a variable-free semantics. *Linguistics and Philosophy* 22. 117–184.

Jacobson, Pauline. 2002a. Direct compositionality and variable-free semantics: The case of binding into heads. In Brendan Jackson (ed.), *Proceedings of SALT 12*, 144–163. Ithaca, NY: CLS Publications.

Jacobson, Pauline. 2002b. The (dis)organization of the grammar: 25 years. *Linguistics and Philosophy* 25. 601–626.

Jäger, Gerhard. 2005. *Anaphora and type logical grammar*. Berlin & Heidelberg: Springer. https://doi.org/10.1007/1-4020-3905-0.

Kayne, Richard. 1994. *The antisymmetry of syntax*. Cambridge, MA: MIT Press.

Krifka, Manfred. 2001. Quantifying into question acts. *Natural Language Semantics* 9(1). 1–40. https://doi.org/10.1023/A:1017903702063.

Lechner, Winfried. 1998. Two kinds of reconstruction. *Studia Linguistica* 52. 276–310.

Lechner, Winfried. 2013. Diagnosing covert movement: The Duke of York and reconstruction. In Lisa Lai-Shen Cheng & Norbert Corver (eds.), *Diagnosing syntax*, 158–189. Oxford: Oxford University Press.

May, Robert. 1977. *The grammar of quantification*. Cambridge, MA: Massachusetts Institute of Technology Doctoral dissertation.

Moortgat, Michael. 2011. Categorial type logics. In Johan van Benthem & Alice ter Meulen (eds.), *Handbook of logic and language*, Second Edition, 95–179. Amsterdam: Elsevier. https://doi.org/10.1016/B978-0-444-53726-3.00002-5.

Partee, Barbara Hall. 1975. Montague grammar and transformational grammar. *Linguistic Inquiry* 6(2). 203–300.

Percus, Orin. 2000. Constraints on some other variables in syntax. *Natural Language Semantics* 8. 173–229.

Quine, Willard Van Orman. 1960. *Word and object*. Cambridge, MA: MIT Press.

Riemsdijk, Henk van & Edwin Williams. 1981. NP structure. *The Linguistic Review* 1. 171–217.

Ross, John Robert. 1967. *Constraints on variables in syntax*. Cambridge, MA: Massachusetts Institute of Technology Doctoral dissertation.

Rullmann, Hotze. 1995. *Maximality in the semantics of wh-constructions*. Amherst, MA: University of Massachusetts Doctoral dissertation.

Ruys, Eddy G. 2011. Three constraints on scope reconstruction. In Ingo Reich, Eva Horch & Dennis Pauly (eds.), *Proceedings of Sinn und Bedeutung 15*, 515–529. Saarbrücken: universaar, Universitätsverlag des Saarlandes.

Ruys, Eddy G. 2015. A minimalist condition on semantic reconstruction. *Linguistic Inquiry* 46(3). 453–488. https://doi.org/10.1162/LING_a_00189.

Ruys, Eddy G. & Yoad Winter. 2011. Quantifier scope in formal linguistics. In Dov M. Gabbay & Franz Guenthner (eds.), *Handbook of philosophical logic, volume 16*, Second Edition, 159–225. Berlin & Heidelberg: Springer. https://doi.org/10.1007/978-94-007-0479-4_3.

Safir, Ken. 1999. Vehicle change and reconstruction in A'-chains. *Linguistic Inquiry* 30. 587–620.

Salzmann, Martin. 2006. *Resumptive prolepsis: A study in indirect A'-dependencies*. Leiden University Doctoral dissertation.

Schachter, Paul. 1973. Focus and relativization. *Language* 49(1). 19–46.

Sharvit, Yael. 1999. Functional relative clauses. *Linguistics and Philosophy* 22. 447–478.

Sportiche, Dominique. 2006. Reconstruction, binding and scope. In Martin Everaert & Henk van Riemsdijk (eds.), *The Blackwell companion to syntax*, vol. 4, 35–93. Oxford: Blackwell.
Stabler, Edward P. 1997. Derivational minimalism. In Christian Retoré (ed.), *Logical aspects of computational linguistics (LACL 1996)*, 68–95. Berlin & Heidelberg: Springer. https://doi.org/10.1007/BFb0052152.
Steedman, Mark J. & Jason Baldridge. 2011. Combinatory categorial grammar. In Robert D. Borsley & Kersti Börjars (eds.), *Non-transformational syntax: Formal and explicit models of grammar*, 181–224. Oxford: Blackwell. https://doi.org/10.1002/9781444395037.ch5.
Sternefeld, Wolfgang. 1997. *The Semantics of Reconstruction and Connectivity*. Arbeitspapiere des SFB 340, Bericht 97. University of Stuttgart, University of Tübingen.
von Stechow, Arnim. 1990. *Layered Traces*. Presentation given at Revfülöp, Hungary. http://www.sfs.uni-tuebingen.de/~astechow/Aufsaetze/Revfueloep90.pdf (10 October, 2018).
von Stechow, Arnim. 1991. Syntax und Semantik. In Arnim von Stechow & Dieter Wunderlich (eds.), *Semantics: An international handbook of contemporary research (HSK 6)*, 90–148. Berlin: de Gruyter.

Manfred Krifka

A Direct Compositionality approach to Condition C effects under reconstruction and their exceptions

Condition C effects under reconstruction, as the lack of a co-referring reading of *Mary wondered* [[*which stories about Tom*$_i$] *he*$_{*i}$ *knew* _], have been discussed as evidence for an LF account in which the moved expression is reconstructed in the position of its trace (cf. Fox 1999). This paper develops an alternative explanation under a Direct Compositionality account, which assumes competition with structures that involve syntactically bound readings, e.g. [[*which stories about himself*] *Tom knew* _], in line with Reinhart (1983). It shows that a number of exceptions to Condition C effects under reconstruction are due to factors that mitigate against syntactically bound readings, and hence weakens the competitive structure. The conclusion of this paper is that Condition C effects should not be conceived as an argument for the LF account, but are fully compatible with a Direct Compositionality account.

1 Condition C effects and the Syntax/Semantics interface

1.1 Surface Interpretation, LF Interpretation, and Reconstruction

This article is concerned with a set of phenomena related to the way how syntactic structures are interpreted. There are two general strategies. The first approach, called "Direct Compositionality", or "Surface Interpretation", assumes that syntactic rules, independently motivated by syntactic constituency tests, create strings of words; these syntactically structured strings are then interpreted by semantic rules that are guided by the syntactic structure. The second approach assumes that the input to semantic interpretation is a derived or enriched syntactic structure. The enrichment may be formulated in different ways, e.g. the surface structure may

Manfred Krifka, Humboldt University of Berlin & Leibniz-Centre General Linguistics (ZAS) Berlin

https://doi.org/10.1515/9783050095158-002

be mapped to distinct syntactic structures following certain rules, called “Logical Forms”, or “LFs”, or syntax may generate additional structure, like phonologically empty nodes with semantic interpretation, that are not strictly required for the description of well-formed syntactic structures. Semantic interpretation then uses such enriched syntactic structures as input, and hence I will call this strategy “Enriched Surface Interpretation.”

There is ongoing controversy about which approach should be preferred (cf. e.g. Barker & Jacobson 2007). There is a certain tradeoff between the two strategies: Surface Interpretation assumes a simpler syntactic component, but needs more complex semantic interpretation rules; Enriched Surface Interpretation allows for a straightforward semantic interpretation, but requires a more complex syntax with rules that relate visible syntactic structures to a form to LF or assumes an enriched syntactic structure. Therefore, complexity measures that would lead to a preference of one theory over the other are not easy to apply.

In this situation it is important to consider phenomena that one strategy cannot handle in a natural way, whereas the other does. The current article discusses one such phenomenon that involves so-called Reconstruction, which was brought forward as an argument against the Surface Interpretation approach most prominently in Fox (1999).

Reconstruction concerns cases in which a constituent α occurs in one position in the syntactic string but is related to another position, resulting in a structure $[\ \alpha\ [...\ t_\alpha\ ...]]$, where α is the syntactic constituent in its surface position, and t_α is the other, or “base” position. Reconstruction phenomena are cases in which the constituent α appears to be interpreted in its base position, t_α; they suggest that the input to semantic interpretation is not the surface structure $[\ \alpha\ [...\ t_\alpha\ ...]]$, but rather a derived structure $[\ \_\ [...\ \alpha\ ...]]$ in which α is interpreted in its “reconstructed” position. While the term “reconstruction” is motivated by the LF variant of the Enriched Surface approach, it is used here as a theory-neutral term that should cover the relevant phenomena of the syntax/semantics interface in general.

This article will discuss a particular reconstruction phenomenon, namely Condition C effects, as they have been acknowledged to pose a serious problem for Surface Interpretation even by the proponents of that approach (cf. Jacobson 2004). I will discuss these effects, which are notoriously difficult to judge, and can be present or absent depending on a number of factors that are quite unclear in their nature. I will argue for an explanation of these effects following a suggestion in Jacobson’s paper, and earlier proposals by Sharvit (1999), Sternefeld (2001) and Cecchetto (2001) rooted in work by Reinhart (1983), that analyzes Condition C effects as caused by a competition with syntactic structures involving bound pronouns. The novel contribution of the current paper is an explanation of the various exceptions to these apparent Condition C effects. It takes inspiration from the last line of Jacobson's article: "a faith in direct compositionality should inspire us to look for a more explanatory account of things like Condition C effects," and I hope that it contributes to an understanding of these effects beyond the architectonical issues concerning the syntax/semantics interface.

But first we will have a more detailed look at the two approaches towards reconstruction, which we will call the "semantic" vs. the "syntactic" account, respectively.

1.2 Reconstruction: Syntactic Accounts

Consider again the structure $[\,\alpha\,[\ldots\, t_\alpha \ldots]]$, where α is a syntactic constituent in surface position, and t_α is the related base position of α in the underlying structure. After reconstruction, under the syntactic account, α will be interpreted in its base position. That is, the syntactic expression α would figure in the computation of the meaning of $[\ldots\, \alpha \ldots]$. This means that purely structural features of α could be of relevance for the interpretation, and even for the grammaticality, of the expression $[\,\alpha\,[\ldots\, t_\alpha \ldots]]$. In the Minimalist Framework, this approach is presented in the copy theory of movement (cf. Chomsky 1993, Corver & Nunes 2007). In this theory, a structure $[\,\alpha\,[\ldots\, \alpha \ldots]]$ is generated, with two copies of the string α. It is then assumed that in the phonological realization, the second copy is deleted, resulting in $[\,\alpha\,[\ldots$ ~~α~~ $\ldots]]$, whereas a structure in which the first copy is deleted, [~~α~~ $[\ldots\, \alpha \ldots]]$, serves as the input to semantic interpretation.

For the purpose of this paper, I will present the syntactic account of reconstruction within the first framework, as it comes with a worked-out treatment for model-theoretic, semantic interpretation (Heim & Kratzer 1998). However, this choice should not affect the general argument. As an example, consider the following sentence and its two possible interpretations:

(1) *Someone from New York is likely to win the lottery.*
 a. 'There is a person from New York, and this person is likely to win the lottery.'
 b. 'It is likely that there is a person from New York that will win the lottery.'

The phrase *someone from New York* can be understood as specific, referring to a particular person that can be identified beforehand – either by the speaker or by the assumption that there exists some other identification procedure (cf. e.g. Yeom 1998). For example, if there is a person from New York that bought 90% of the lottery tickets, and the speaker knows that and knows who this person is, (1) is true under reading (a). The phrase can also be understood as non-specific, not referring to a particular person. For example, if 90% of the lottery tickets have been bought by New Yorkers, (1) is true under reading (b). Of course, (1)(b) would also be true in the first scenario, but the second scenario does not verify reading (1)(a).

The two readings can be generated by assuming that the syntactic structure of (1) is mapped to two distinct Logical Forms, which are given schematically below.

(2) a. $[_{QP}$ *someone from NY*] [1 [*is likely* [t_1 *to win the lottery*]]]

b. __ *is likely* [$[_{QP}$ *someone from NY*]$_1$ *to win the lottery*]

We first consider (2)(a). This corresponds to the surface form, which records the fact that the quantifier phrase *someone from New York* is both the subject of the raising predicate, *likely*, and the subject of the infinitive construction. The mechanism of relating the quantifier phrase to the subject position of the infinitive construction follows the textbook account in Heim & Kratzer (1998). That is, if a constituent α is moved, this is indicated by an indexed trace at the base position and at the sister constituent of α; the sister constituent of α at the site where α is moved to is marked by the index of the trace. The semantic interpretation rules would lead to a wide-scope interpretation of *someone from New York*, relative to the modal adverb *likely*. This is illustrated in the sketch of a derivation in (3), which follows the convention that $[\![\cdot]\!]$ is a recursive interpretation function, where $[\![...]\!]^{i \rightarrow x}$ means that expressions with the index i in [...] are to be interpreted as the variable x. In our case, this affects the interpretation of the trace, t_i.

(3) $[\![$[*someone from NY*] [1 [*be likely* [t_1 *to win the lottery*]]]$]\!]$

a. $=$ $[\![$*someone from NY*$]\!]$($[\![$[1 [*be likely* [t_1 *to win the lottery*]]]$]\!]$)

b. $=$ $[\![$*someone from NY*$]\!]$($\lambda x_1 [\![$*be likely* [t_1 *to win the lottery*]$]\!]^{1 \rightarrow x_1}$)

c. $=$ $[\![$*someone from NY*$]\!]$($\lambda x_1 [[\![$*be likely*$]\!]^{1 \rightarrow x_1}([\![t_1$ *to win the lottery*$]\!]^{1 \rightarrow x_1})]$)

d. $= \lambda P \exists x[\text{Person}(x) \wedge \text{from NY}(x) \wedge P(x)](\lambda x_1[\text{LIKELY}(x_1 \text{ wins lottery})])$

e. $= \exists x[\text{Person}(x) \wedge \text{from NY}(x) \wedge \text{LIKELY}(x \text{ wins the lottery})]$

In the transition from (a) to (b), a rule is applied that interprets an indexed expression [1 [... t_i ...]] as $\lambda x_i [\![[...\ t_i\ ...]]\!]^{i \rightarrow x_i}$, a function from x_i to the meaning of [... t_i ...], where all expressions with index i are interpreted as x_i. The raising predicate *be likely* is interpreted here for simplicity as an operator that scopes over a clausal structure, an infinitive construction with a trace in its subject position.

In (2)(b), the subject phrase is reconstructed into its base position. Applying standard semantic rules would lead to a narrow-scope interpretation with respect to the modal.

(4) $[\![$[*be likely* [[*someone from NY*] [*to win the lottery*]]]$]\!]$

a. $=$ $[\![$*be likely*$]\!]$($[\![$*someone from NY*$]\!]$($[\![$*win the lottery*$]\!]$))

b. $= \text{LIKELY}(\lambda P \exists x[\text{Person}(x) \wedge \text{from NY}(x) \wedge P(x)](\lambda x[x \text{ wins lottery}]))$

c. $= \text{LIKELY}(\exists x[\text{Person}(x) \wedge \text{from NY}(x) \wedge x \text{ wins lottery}])$

In the copy-theory of movement (cf. Chomsky 1995, Sauerland 1998), the subject appears in two copies, and can be interpreted either in the higher or in the lower position, cf. (5)(a,b). For the wide-scope reading, we would have to assume that the lower copy is interpreted as a bound variable, which would involve a type change from a quantifier to an entity. We then can assume similar semantic interpretation rules as above.

(5) a. [*someone from NY*]$_1$ *is likely* [[~~*someone from NY*~~]$_1$ *to win the lottery*]

b. [~~*someone from NY*~~]$_1$ *is likely* [[*someone from NY*]$_1$ *to win the lottery*]

What both versions of the syntactic approach have in common is that the input to semantic interpretation is enriched, in some way or other: The reconstructed version of the LF in (2)(b) is not a possible surface form, and neither are the syntactic structures generated by the copy theory of movement in (5). Their only raison d'être is to allow for the generation of the observed readings.

1.3 Reconstruction: Semantic Accounts

We now turn to Surface Interpretation, of which there are also various implementations. Here, I will assume a version that assumes syntactic traces, in order to make possible a direct comparison with Enriched Surface Interpretation. This means that we assume a structure $[\ \alpha\ [...\ t_\alpha\ ...]]$, but now this structure is interpreted directly: Its meaning $[\![[\ \alpha\ [...\ t_\alpha\ ...]]]\!]$ is computed compositionally from the meanings of the intermediate parts $[\![\alpha]\!]$ and $[\![[...\ t_\alpha\ ...]]\!]$. Under this architecture of semantic interpretation, it is not the syntactic expression α that is related to the base position t_α in the computation of $[\![[...\ t_\alpha\ ...]]\!]$. Rather, it is the meaning of α, rendered as $[\![\alpha]\!]$, that is related to the way how the base position t_α is interpreted, rendered as $[\![t_\alpha]\!]$. The interpretation cannot refer to purely structural syntactic features of α within the interpretation of $[...\ t_\alpha\ ...]$, only to the meaning, $[\![[...\ t_\alpha\ ...]]\!]$.

It is important to realize that the semantic approach is more restrictive, in the following sense. In general, a syntactic expression α contains more information than its meaning, $[\![\alpha]\!]$, as distinct expressions α, α' with $\alpha \neq \alpha'$ can have the same meaning: $[\![\alpha]\!] = [\![\alpha']\!]$. So, formal differences between α and α' might result in differences of acceptability between $[\ \alpha\ [...\ t_\alpha\ ...]]$ and $[\ \alpha'\ [...\ t_\alpha\ ...]]$ in the syntactic account – after syntactic reconstruction, $[...\ \alpha\ ...]$ might be grammatical, but $[...\ \alpha'\ ...]$ may fail to be grammatical. But such purely formal differences cannot result in differences of acceptability in the semantic account, simply because they are not reflected in the meanings $[\![\alpha]\!]$, $[\![\alpha']\!]$, and these meanings are all that the semantic approach to reconstruction has access to. As a consequence, with the semantic account we have to assume that all differences between expressions α, α' that lead to differences in grammaticality judgements in reconstruction contexts $[\ldots \mathrm{t}_\alpha \ldots]$ must have a reflex in the semantic interpretation, that is, it must hold that $[\![\alpha]\!] \neq [\![\alpha']\!]$.

After these methodological clarifications, let us consider how the readings of (1) are derived. For our discussion we should assume a slightly more liberal way of combining meanings, which makes reference to the semantic types of the meanings to be combined:

(6) $[\![[\alpha\ \beta]]\!] = \{[\![\alpha]\!], [\![\beta]\!]\}, = [\![\alpha]\!]([\![\beta]\!])$ or $[\![\beta]\!]([\![\alpha]\!])$, whichever is well-formed.

One implementation of the readings of (1) is that the base position of the subject, represented as a trace in (2)(a), is semantically interpreted in an ambiguous way: It is either of the type of entities, *e*, or of the type of quantifiers, *(et)t* (cf. Strigin 1994, Sternefeld 2001). This can be expressed by assuming type-ambiguous traces in syntax, e.g. $\mathrm{t_i}$ for traces of type *e*, and $\mathrm{T_i}$ for traces of type *(et)t*. Alternatively, we could assume that the base positions are not ambiguous, but underspecified; they are compatible with either a type *e* interpretation, or a type *(et)t* interpretation. However, then the interpretation $[\![\cdot]\!]$ would not be a function anymore, but a relation, leading to a more complex architecture of the syntax/semantics interface. Also, we would then predict that in cases of VP ellipsis cases like (7) have a reading in which the subject quantifiers might differ in scope, which is not the case.

(7) *Someone from NY is likely to win a big price in the lottery, and someone from Philadelphia is, too.*

For these reasons, I assume the first option here, that we may have type *e* traces and type *(et)t* traces. The wide-scope interpretation can be derived as in (8), whereas the narrow-scope interpretation can be derived as in (9).

(8) $[\![[\textit{someone from NY}]\ [1\ [\textit{be likely}\ [\mathrm{t_1}\ \textit{to win the lottery}]]]]\!]$

a. $= \{[\![\textit{someone from NY}]\!], [\![[1\ [\textit{be likely}\ [\mathrm{t_1}\ \textit{to win the lottery}]]]]\!]\}$

b. $= \{[\![\textit{someone from NY}]\!], \lambda\xi_1[\![[\textit{be likely}\ [\mathrm{t_1}\ \textit{to win the lottery}]]]\!]^{1\to\xi_1}\}$

c. $= \{[\![\textit{someone from NY}]\!], \lambda\xi_1[\{[\![\textit{be likely}]\!]^{1\to\xi_1}, [\![[\mathrm{t_1}\ \textit{to win the lottery}]]\!]^{1\to\xi_1}\}]\}$

d. $= \{[\![\textit{someone from NY}]\!], \lambda\xi_1[\{\textsc{likely}, \{[\![\textit{to win the lottery}]\!]^{1\to\xi_1}, [\![\mathrm{t_1}]\!]^{1\to\xi_1}\}\}]\}$

e. $= \{[\![\textit{someone from NY}]\!], \lambda\mathrm{x_1}[\{\textsc{likely}, \{[\![\textit{to win the lottery}]\!]^{1\to\mathrm{x_1}}, \mathrm{x_1}\}\}]\}$

f. $= \{[\![\textit{someone from NY}]\!], \lambda\mathrm{x_1}[\{\textsc{likely}, \{\lambda\mathrm{x}[\text{win-lottery}(\mathrm{x})], \mathrm{x_1}\}\}]\}$

g. $= \{[\![\textit{someone from NY}]\!], \lambda\mathrm{x_1}[\{\textsc{likely}, \lambda\mathrm{x}[\text{win-lottery}(\mathrm{x})](\mathrm{x_1})\}]\}$

h. $= \{[\![\textit{someone from NY}]\!], \lambda\mathrm{x_1}[\{\textsc{likely}, \text{win-lottery}(\mathrm{x_1})\}]\}$

i. $= \{\lambda P \exists x[\text{Person}(x) \wedge \text{from NY}(x) \wedge P(x)], \lambda x_1[\text{LIKELY}(\text{win-lottery}(x_1))]\}$

j. $= \lambda P \exists x[\text{Person}(x) \wedge \text{from NY}(x) \wedge P(x)](\lambda x_1[\text{LIKELY}(\text{win-lottery}(x_1))])$

k. $= \exists x[\text{Person}(x) \wedge \text{from NY}(x) \wedge \text{LIKELY}(\text{win-lottery}(x))]$

In contrast to (3), which uses the type *e* variable x_1, this derivation uses a variable ξ_1 that is initially undetermined with respect to its type. The variable is determined as of type *e* at the transition from (d) to (e), as the trace t_1 is of type *e*. As a consequence, the quantifier in subject position, which is of type *(et)t*, is applied to the resulting predicate, and gets wide scope over the operator LIKELY.

The narrow-scope reading of the quantifier is achieved with a trace T_1 of type *(et)t*:

(9) $[\![$[*someone from NY*] [1 [*be likely* [T_1 *to win the lottery*]]]$]\!]$

a. $= \{[\![\textit{someone from NY}]\!], [\![[1\ [\textit{be likely}\ [T_1\ \textit{to win the lottery}]]]]\!]\}$

b. $= \{[\![\textit{someone from NY}]\!], \lambda\xi_1[\![[\textit{be likely}\ [T_1\ \textit{to win the lottery}]]]\!]^{1\to\xi_1}\}$

c. $= \{[\![\textit{someone from NY}]\!], \lambda\xi_1[\{[\![\textit{be likely}]\!]^{1\to\xi_1}, [\![[T_1\ \textit{to win the lottery}]]\!]^{1\to\xi_1}\}]\}$

d. $= \{[\![\textit{someone from NY}]\!], \lambda\xi_1[\{\text{LIKELY}, \{[\![\textit{to win the lottery}]\!]^{1\to\xi_1}, [\![T_1]\!]^{1\to\xi_1}\}\}]\}$

e. $= \{[\![\textit{someone from NY}]\!], \lambda Q_1[\{\text{LIKELY}, \{[\![\textit{to win the lottery}]\!]^{1\to Q_1}, Q_1\}\}]\}$

f. $= \{[\![\textit{someone from NY}]\!], \lambda Q_1[\{\text{LIKELY}, \{\lambda x[\text{win-lottery}(x)], Q_1\}\}]\}$

g. $= \{[\![\textit{someone from NY}]\!], \lambda Q_1[\{\text{LIKELY}, Q_1(\lambda x[\text{win-lottery}(x)])\}]\}$

h. $= \{[\![\textit{someone from NY}]\!], \lambda Q_1[\text{LIKELY}(Q_1(\lambda x[\text{win-lottery}(x)]))]\}$

i. $= \{\lambda P \exists x[\text{Person}(x) \wedge \text{from NY}(x) \wedge P(x)],$
$\lambda Q_1[\text{LIKELY}(Q_1(\lambda x[\text{win-lottery}(x)]))]\}$

j. $= \lambda Q_1[\text{LIKELY}(Q_1(\lambda x[\text{win-lottery}(x)]))]$
$(\lambda P \exists x[\text{Person}(x) \wedge \text{from NY}(x) \wedge P(x)])$

k. $= \text{LIKELY}(\lambda P \exists x[\text{Person}(x) \wedge \text{from NY}(x) \wedge P(x)](\lambda x[\text{win-lottery}(x)]))$

l. $= \text{LIKELY}(\exists x[\text{Person}(x) \wedge \text{from NY}(x) \wedge \text{win-lottery}(x)])$

The distinct semantic type of the trace as T_1 leads to a different way in which the meanings are combined. In the transition from line (d) to (e), the variable ξ_1 is specified as Q_1, a variable of type *(et)t*. Due to type-driven interpretation, Q_1 does not satisfy the argument of $\lambda x[\text{win-lottery}(x)]$, but rather is applied to that predicate in line (g). Further down in line in (j) the meaning of *likely to win the lottery* is applied to the quantifier, which then results in a narrow-scope interpretation of the quantifier.

Notice that in (9) reconstruction happens, in a sense, in semantics: As the trace is of a higher type, it enforces a different way of combining the meaning of syntactically moved item and the expression out of which it is moved: Now, the meaning of the constituent out of which the movement happened is applied to the meaning of the moved constituent, not the other way round. Effectively, lambda conversion brings it about that the moved item is interpreted in its base position. But notice that no syntactic reconstruction is required. In the current version of semantic theory, all that syntax has to afford is two distinct types of traces.

1.4 Overview: What is to come?

In the subsequent part of this paper I will develop an argument that apparent Condition C effects under reconstruction can be accounted for within the Surface Interpretation approach. I will not argue against Extended Surface Interpretation except for a minor conceptual point at the very end; the main point is that Condition C effects should not count as an argument for Extended Surface Interpretation. The argument will involve several steps. In section 2, I will distinguish between different ways in which pronouns can find their reference, in particularly discourse-bound pronouns and syntax-bound pronouns, and discuss implementations of syntactic binding within syntactic structures or within semantic interpretation. In section 3, I will discuss the known observations concerning the presence or absence of Condition C effects under reconstruction. Section 4 will then develop a theory in which Condition C effects can be captured within Surface Interpretation, and will in particular explain the various cases in which such effects are absent. Section 5 concludes.

2 Binding of Pronouns and Reconstruction

Before we discuss Condition C phenomena in reconstruction contexts, we will first consider the binding of pronominal expressions – that is, Condition A, which deals with reflexives and reciprocals, and Condition B, which deals with other pronouns.

2.1 Types of pronouns

Pronominal expressions get their meaning in three distinct ways. First, pronouns sometimes have no linguistic antecedent at all. For example, at a police interview, a speaker might point to a man and utter (10), referring with *he* to the man, and with *it* to a an event that is salient in the situation of utterance. I call such pronouns **situation-bound**.

(10) *He did it.*

Secondly, pronouns may be **discourse-bound**, as in intra-sentential pronouns, but also within a sentence in pronouns occurring in different non-subordinated subclauses, as in donkey sentences:

(11) *A man*$_1$ *came in. He*$_1$ *sat down.*

(12) *Always, when a man*$_1$ *came in, he*$_1$ *sat down.*

In (11), the pronoun *he* picks up the discourse referent introduced by *a man* in the first clause. The text is interpreted under a general existential closure, stating that there is a mapping of the discourse referents to entities in the actual world such that the properties of the discourse referents expressed in the sentence are true. For (11), this means that the discourse referent d_1 must have the properties of being a man, of having come in, and of having sat down. In (12), the indefinite *a man* also introduces a discourse referent that is picked up by *he*, but now this is bound under the scope of the universal quantifier *always*. This means that the actual world must support it that for all ways of mapping d_1 to an entity such that d_1 is a man and d_1 came in, it also must hold that d_1 sat down.

The third way of interpreting pronouns is as bound by an antecedent that stands in a particular syntactic configuration to the pronoun. This syntactic configuration includes, most prominently, syntactic c-command. I will call such pronouns **syntax-bound** because syntactic configuration of binder and bindee is essential. In this case, the antecedent may also be a quantifier that binds the pronoun as a variable:

(13) *John*$_1$ */ Every man*$_1$ *talked to a woman that smiled at him*$_1$.

See Reinhart (1983) and Grodzinsky & Reinhart (1993), who distinguish between syntactic binding in cases like (13) and what they call "co-reference" in cases like (12). Quantifier binding is not possible in the discourse-bound case in which the antecedent does not c-command the pronoun:

(14) *# Every man*$_1$ *came in. He*$_1$ *sat down.*

However, this statement has to be qualified. There are cases in which a quantifier appears to discourse-bind a pronoun, which are treated as modal subordination (cf. Kadmon 1987, Sells 1987), as in (15). Such cases require special treatment, and we ignore them here.

(15) *Every farmer owns a donkey. He uses it to plough the fields.*

Particular pronominal forms may correlate with syntactic binding or discourse binding, but this correspondence is not one-to-one. The best-known case are reflexive and reciprocal pronouns, which are typically understood as syntactically bound by a c-commanding expression that is a co-argument:

(16) *John*$_1$ / *Every man*$_1$ *talked to himself*$_1$.

One piece of evidence for syntactic binding is that we necessarily find the sloppy reading in ellipsis contexts in coordinated structures, cf. (17). (For the strict reading in subordinated structures see Hestvik 1995).

(17) *John talked to himself, and Bill did, too.*
'John talked to John, and Bill talked to Bill'

However, there are syntactically bound pronouns that are not reflexive:

(18) *Every man*$_1$ *thinks that there is a woman that loves him*$_1$.

And there are so-called logophoric reflexives as complements of representational nouns like *picture* that seem to allow for discourse binding to express a perspective shift (cf. Pollard & Sag 1992), as in (19). For the purpose of this paper, such uses of reflexives will be ignored.

(19) *The mayor*$_1$ *was furious. A picture of himself*$_1$ *in the museum had been mutilated.*

On the other hand, there are pronominal elements that cannot be syntactically bound. I take it that epithets like *the guy* or *the bum* belong to this class, cf. (20).

(20) *Every man*$_1$ *thinks that there is a woman that loves the guy*$_{*1}$.

Dubinsky & Hamilton (1998) have argued that epithets can be bound provided that they are not logophoric, referring to the carrier of a perspective from which a proposition is reported, as in (21)(a). However, binding does not work in this case with quantified antecedents, cf. (b), and hence we should assume that (a) is a case of discourse binding.

(21) a. *John*$_1$ *ran over a man who was trying to give the idiot*$_1$ *directions.*
b. *Every player*$_1$ *ran over a man who was trying to give the idiot*$_{*1}$ / *him*$_1$ *directions.*

Another type of pronoun that resists syntactic binding are d-pronouns in German, cf. Patel-Grosz & Grosz (2010); this will be taken up below.

(22) *Jeder Mann*$_1$ *denkt, dass es eine Frau gibt, die ihn*$_1$/*den*$_{*1}$ *liebt.*
'Every man thinks that there is a woman that loves d-PRON'

The generally assumed condition for syntactic binding is that the antecedent c-commands the anaphoric expression. However, there are cases in which quantifiers can bind pronouns that they do not c-command, e.g. from the position of a specifier of a DP, cf. (23)(a), or from an of-phrase of an indefinite DP, cf. (b), but also less well-known ones, e.g. from within a tensed clause, for quantifiers headed by each (cf. c):

(23) a. *Everyone*$_1$*'s mother thinks that he*$_1$ *is a genius.*
b. *One page of every*$_1$ *book has something written on it*$_1$.
c. *The grade that each student*$_1$ *receives is recorded in his*$_1$ *file.*

This has lead Barker (2012) to give up syntactic c-command as a condition, and assume that the only condition is that a quantifier must have semantic scope over a pronoun in order to be able to bind it. This leads to the question how syntactic scope is related to syntactic configuration. If one wants to stick with c-command for conceptual reasons, one would have to assume that the quantifier is moved to a position in which it c-commands the pronoun in the LF account. In Surface Interpretation, one would have to assume other ways in which the quantifier can achieve a wide-scope interpretation, and in which binding of the pronoun is guaranteed. It also may be that the cases in (23) do not represent syntactic binding, but discourse binding, as in donkey sentences; for example, they allow for epithets (Lasnik 1989), and for d-pronouns in German:

(24) a. *Every boy*$_1$*'s mother thinks that the little darling*$_1$ *is flawless.*
b. *Die Mutter jedes Jungen*$_1$ *glaubt, dass dieser*$_1$ *ohne Fehler ist.*
'every boy's mother thinks that d-PRON is without flaws'

I will leave the issue of non c-commanding antecedents open, but return to it shortly in section 4.3.

2.2 Syntactically bound pronouns, syntactic approach

Let us concentrate here on syntactically bound pronouns, as in the following examples:

(25) a. *Diana*$_1$ *remembered her*$_1$ *brother.*
b. *Every girl*$_1$ *remembered her*$_1$ *brother.*

The pronoun in (25)(a) could be discourse-bound or syntactically bound, whereas the pronoun in (b), with a quantifier as antecedent, can only be syntactically bound. Let us consider the textbook treatment in Heim & Kratzer (1998: chapter 10), who assume that syntactic binding is like the variable binding we have considered in example (3). That is, it is mediated by a coindexed trace:

(26) [*Diana* [1 [t_1 *remembered her*$_1$ *brother*]]]

The variable assignment serves not only for the interpretation of traces, but also for the interpretation of syntactically bound pronouns:

(27) $[\![she_1]\!]^{1\to x_1} = x_1$, provided that x_1 is female, otherwise undefined.

The possessive pronoun in our example is derived from that; we assume the following representation, where R is a relation of type *eet*:

(28) $[\![her_1]\!]^{1\to x_1} = \lambda R\iota z[R([\![she_1]\!]^{1\to x_1})(z)]$

We then get the following derivation of *her brother*, given in a bottom-up fashion, somewhat simplified:

(29) a. $[\![brother]\!]^{1\to x_1}$ = brother, type *eet*
b. $[\![her_1\ brother]\!]^{1\to x_1} = [\![her_1]\!]^{1\to x_1}([\![brother]\!]^{1\to x_1})$
$= \iota z[\text{brother}(x_1)(z)]$, x_1: female

This is the unique z such that z is brother of x_1, where x_1 is restricted to females. The derivation of (25)(a) then is as follows:

(30) $[\![[Diana\ [1\ [t_1\ remembered\ [her_1\ brother]]]]]\!]$
a. $= [\![[1\ [t_1\ remembered\ [her_1\ brother]]]]\!]([\![Diana]\!])$
b. $= \lambda x_1[[\![[t_1\ remembered\ [her_1\ brother]]]\!]^{1\to x_1}](\text{Diana})$
c. $= \lambda x_1[[\![remembered]\!]^{1\to x_1}([\![her_1\ brother]\!]^{1\to x_1})([\![t_1]\!]^{1\to x_1})](\text{Diana})$
d. $= \lambda x_1[\text{remember}(\iota z[\text{brother}(x_1)(z)])(x_1)](\text{Diana})$
e. $= \text{remember}(\iota z[\text{brother}(\text{Diana})(z)])(\text{Diana})$

We assume that the subject, *Diana*, is moved, leaving a trace. This is interpreted as usual, as a functional expression. If the pronoun is coindexed with the trace, syntactic binding ensues: The trace and the pronoun covary. Notice that, if the subject is a quantifier, we get a bound variable reading:

(31) $[\![[every\ girl\ [1\ [t_1\ remembered\ [her_1\ brother]]]]]\!]$
$= [\![every\ girl]\!]([\![[1\ [t_1\ remembered\ [her_1\ brother]]]]\!])$
$= [\![every\ girl]\!](\lambda x_1[\![[t_1\ remembered\ her_1\ brother]]\!]^{1\to x_1})$
$= \lambda P\forall x[\text{girl}(x) \to P(x)](\lambda x_1[\text{remember}(\iota z[\text{brother}(x_1)(z)])(x_1)])$
$= \forall x[\text{girl}(x) \to \text{remember}(\iota z[\text{brother}(x)(z)])(x)]$

Let us now consider cases in which we find syntactic binding of pronouns under reconstruction.

(32) [*Which story about her*$_1$ *brother*]$_2$ *did Diana*$_1$ / *every girl*$_1$ *remember* t_2?

LF interpretation would assume that the moved constituent, *which story about her*$_1$ *brother*, is reconstructed in its trace position, in which *Diana* or *every girl* would c-command the pronoun *her*$_1$. From this position, syntactic binding is obviously possible.

(33) [_ *did* [*Diana* / *every girl* [1 [t_1 *remember* [*which story about* *her*$_1$ *brother*]]]]]

This illustrates the treatment of reconstruction effects in the LF version of Enriched Surface Interpretation, where the moved constituent can be inserted and interpreted in its original position. We now consider two versions of the semantic approach.

2.3 Syntactically bound pronouns, semantic approach I

Does the way of treating pronoun binding also work for the Surface Interpretation approach? It does not. To see this, let us consider the same example as before, but under the assumption that the trace of the *wh*-phrase is of a higher type T_2 that leads to semantic reconstruction via lambda-conversion.

(34) [*which story about her*$_1$ *brother*] [2 [*did* [*Diana* / *every girl* [1 [t_1 *remember* T_2]]]]]

The meaning of the moved phrase, ⟦*which story about her*$_1$ *brother*⟧, is interpreted via lambda-conversion in the position of the trace T_2. Can the pronoun *her* get bound then? Let us consider this in detail. (35) is the interpretation of the noun phrase of the *wh*-constituent. It contains a free variable x_1, by virtue of the indexed pronoun *her*$_1$.

(35) ⟦*story about her*$_1$ *brother*⟧ $= \lambda y[\text{story}(y) \wedge \text{about}(\iota z[\text{brother}(x_1)(z)])(y)]$

I assume a standard Hamblin semantics for *wh*-constituents. This means that for *which* in direct object position we can assume the following interpretation; we disregard here that we would have to work with intensional representations to get the meaning right.

(36) ⟦*which*$_{DO}$⟧ $= \lambda P \lambda R \lambda x \exists p \exists y[P(y) \wedge p = R(y)(x)]$

(37) ⟦*which*$_{DO}$ *story about her*$_1$ *brother*⟧
$=$ ⟦*which*$_{DO}$⟧(⟦*story about her*$_1$ *brother*⟧)
$= \lambda P \lambda R \lambda x \exists p \exists y[P(y) \wedge p = R(y)(x)]$
$(\lambda y[\text{story}(y) \wedge \text{about}(\iota z[\text{brother}(x_1)(z)])(y)])$
$= \lambda R \lambda x \exists p \exists y[\text{story}(y) \wedge \text{about}(\iota z[\text{brother}(x_1)(z)])(y) \wedge p = R(y)(x)]$

For the interpretation of the remnant clause we get the following meaning, where I will work with the variant with a referring subject, *Diana*, and will neglect the auxiliary *did*. I also will assume the correct function-argument structure that is consonant with the type of the traces right from the start, to simplify the derivation.

(38) $[\![[2\ [\textit{Diana}\ [1\ [t_1\ [\textit{remember}\ T_2]]]]]]\!]$
a. $= \lambda\xi_2\ [\![[\textit{Diana}\ [1\ [t_1\ [\textit{remember}\ T_2]]]]]\!]^{2\to\xi_2}$
b. $= \lambda\xi_2\ [[\![[1\ [t_1\ [\textit{remember}\ T_2]]]]\!]^{2\to\xi_2}([\![\textit{Diana}]\!]^{2\to\xi_2})]$
c. $= \lambda\xi_2\ [\lambda\xi_1[\![[t_1\ [\textit{remember}\ T_2]]]\!]^{2\to\xi_2,1\to\xi_1}(\text{Diana})]$
d. $= \lambda\xi_2\ [\lambda\xi_1[[\![\textit{remember}\ T_2]\!]^{2\to\xi_2,1\to\xi_1}([\![t_1]\!]^{2\to\xi_2,1\to\xi_1})](\text{Diana})]$
e. $= \lambda\xi_2\ [\lambda x_1[[\![\textit{remember}\ T_2]\!]^{2\to\xi_2,1\to\xi_1}(x_1)](\text{Diana})]$
f. $= \lambda\xi_2\ [[\![\textit{remember}\ T_2]\!]^{2\to\xi_2,1\to\xi_1}(\text{Diana})]$
g. $= \lambda\xi_2\ [[\![T_2]\!]^{2\to\xi_2,1\to\xi_1}([\![\textit{remember}]\!]^{2\to\xi_2,1\to\xi_1})(\text{Diana})]$
h. $= \lambda Q_2\ [Q_2(\text{remember})(\text{Diana})]$

When we now combine the meaning of the moved *wh*-constituent (37) with the remnant clause (38) we see that binding cannot be achieved:

(39) $[\![[2\ [\textit{Diana}\ [1\ [t_1\ [\textit{remember}\ T_2]]]]]]\!]([\![\textit{which story about her}_1\ \textit{brother}]\!])$
$= \lambda Q_2[Q_2(\text{remember})(\text{Diana})]\ (\lambda R\lambda x\exists p\exists y[\text{story}(y) \wedge$
$\text{about}(\iota z[\text{brother}(x_1)(z)])(y) \wedge p = R(y)(x)])$
$= \lambda R\lambda x\exists p\exists y[\text{story}(y) \wedge \text{about}(\iota z[\text{brother}(x_1)(z)])(y) \wedge$
$p = R(y)(x)](\text{remember})(\text{Diana})$
$= \exists p\exists y[\text{story}(y) \wedge \text{about}(\iota z[\text{brother}(x_1)(z)])(y) \wedge p = \text{remember}(y)(\text{Diana})]$

The problem is that the semantic representation does not record the presence of a bound pronoun in the meaning of the *wh*-constituent. We have to assume a slightly more detailed meaning representation in order to achieve that, and we have to take care that the remnant expression is sensitive to this additional meaning component.

One could object to this move, as it appears to enrich the notion of meaning in such a way as to include aspects that seem to come for free in the syntactic approach, which allows us to scan expressions for the occurrence of indexed pronouns. However, the occurrence of a free pronoun is essential for semantic interpretation, as it signals that a meaning is unsaturated, depending on the setting of a parameter. The standard way of indicating this dependency on a parameter is by a functional expression.

2.4 Syntactically bound pronouns, semantic approach II

The suggestion at the end of the last section can be implemented along the lines of Hepple (1990), cf. also Jacobson (1999, 2004); see Sternefeld (2001) for a different way. In this approach, syntactically bound personal pronouns denote identity functions of type *ee*, that is, functions from entities to entities. For example, the meaning of *she* is a function from female persons u to u:

(40) $[\![she]\!] = \lambda$u:female[u]

To accommodate such meanings of type *ee*, we have to allow, in addition to the regularly expected type *e*, for a more flexible way of meaning combination. Whenever we have two meanings of type $\sigma\tau$ and σ that can be combined via function composition to a meaning of type τ, then we also can combine two meanings of type $\sigma\tau$ and $\omega\sigma$, and we can combine two meanings of type $\omega\sigma\tau$ and σ, in both cases resulting in a meaning of type $\omega\tau$. The additional argument of type ω is projected from the functor $\sigma\tau$ or the argument σ to the resulting meaning, τ. We can express this combination rule as follows, which is equivalent to the Geach rule in Jacobson (1999).

(41) in addition to (6):
$[\![[\alpha\ \beta]]\!] = \lambda u[[\![\alpha]\!](u)([\![\beta]\!])]$ or $\lambda u[[\![\alpha]\!]([\![\beta]\!](u))]$ or
$\lambda u[[\![\beta]\!](u)([\![\alpha]\!])]$ or $\lambda u[[\![\beta]\!]([\![\alpha]\!](u))]$,
where u is a variable of type *e*.

Rule (41) is restricted to meanings where the additional argument ω is of type *e*, as this is all we need for the current purposes. The rule could be extended for what happens if both the functor and the argument have an additional argument; the additional arguments can either both project, or they can be combined. We will not deal with such cases here.

Example (25) then is derived as follows:

(42) a. $[\![her]\!] = \lambda$u:female λR ιz[z is R of u], type *e(eet)e*
b. $[\![brother]\!]$ = brother, type *eet*
c. $[\![[her\ brother]]\!] = \lambda u[[\![her]\!](u)([\![brother]\!])]$
$= \lambda$u:female ιz[brother(u)(z)], type *ee*
d. $[\![remember]\!] = \lambda y\lambda x$[remember(y)(x)], type *eet*
e. $[\![[remember\ [her\ brother]]]\!] = \lambda u[[\![remember]\!]([\![[her\ brother]]\!](u))]$
$= \lambda$u:female λx[remember(ιz[brother(u)(z)])(x)], type *eet*

This is a point at which the projected argument u can be bound to the subject argument of *remember*. There are several ways to express this binding. For example, we could assume that the binder, *Diana*, has in addition to a quantifier meaning (43)(a) a meaning in which both the projected pronominal argument and the subject argument argument are bound, as in (43)(b).

(43) a. $[\![\textit{Diana}]\!] = \lambda P[P(\text{Diana})]$

b. $[\![\textit{Diana}]\!] = \lambda R[R(\text{Diana})(\text{Diana})]$

Alternatively, the binding can be expressed by an operator B, defined as follows:

(44) $B(R) = \lambda x[R(x)(x)]$

(45) $B(\lambda u{:}\text{female}\ \lambda x[\text{remember}(\iota z[\text{brother}(u)(z)])(x)])$
$= \lambda x{:}\text{female}\ [\text{remember}(\iota z[\text{brother}(x)(z)])(x)]$, type *et*

By the B operator, the projected argument u is identified with the subject argument, x. In the last step, the subject argument is supplied. B can be seen as an operator that applies freely; here, I will assume that it has a reflex in syntax, for perspicuity of presentation.

(46) $[\![[\textit{Diana}\ [\text{B}\ [\textit{remember her brother}]]]]\!]$
$= [\![[\text{B}\ [\textit{remember her brother}]]]\!]([\![\textit{Diana}]\!])$
$= \lambda x{:}\text{female}\ [\text{remember}(\iota z[\text{brother}(x)(z)])(x)](\text{Diana})$
$= \text{remember}(\iota z[\text{brother}(\text{Diana})(z)])(\text{Diana})$, type *t*,
provided that Diana is female.

With *every girl* as subject, we get the following interpretation, which gives us the right result.

(47) $[\![[\textit{every girl}\ [\text{B}\ [\textit{remember her brother}]]]]\!]$
$= [\![\textit{every girl}]\!]([\![[\text{B}\ [\textit{remember her brother}]]]\!])$
$= \lambda P\forall x[\text{girl}(x) \rightarrow P(x)](\lambda x{:}\text{female}\ [\text{remember}(\iota z[\text{brother}(x)(z)])(x)])$
$= \forall x[\text{girl}(x) \rightarrow \text{remember}(\iota z[\text{brother}(x)(z)])(x)]$, type *t*;
notice that x: female is satisfied.

The subject, *Diana* or *every girl*, does not really "bind" *her* in an ordinary way. Rather, a binding relation exists between an argument position and the interpretation of the pronoun, mediated by the projection of the additional argument of the pronoun and by the B operator. Notice, also, that no movement of *Diana* or *every girl* is required to express this type of binding, in contrast to the account in section 2.2.

While indices are not required to express syntactic binding, they can be used for other kinds of binding phenomena, in particular discourse binding (if they are not treated as covert descriptions, as in Elbourne 2005). One version of this is to assume dynamic interpretation, where meanings are given with respect to input assignments and output assignments, as e.g. in Rooth (1987). Without going into detail, this can be illustrated with the following example:

(48) $[\![$[*Diana*$_1$ [B [*remembered* [*her brother*]$_2$]]]$]\!]$:
a pair of an input assignment g and an output assignment g′
such that g′ differs from g insofar as it is defined for the indices 1 and 2,
such that g′(1) = Diana, g′(2) = ιz[brother(Diana)(z)], and
remember(ιz[brother(Diana)(z)])(Diana).

This allows to pick up these discourse referents in subsequent clauses, as in *She*$_1$ *hates him*$_2$. What is important for current purposes is that *her* in (48) does not carry an index. It is a syntactically bound pronoun, not a discourse-bound pronoun.

The possessive pronoun can also be interpreted as discourse-bound, in which case we would have the following input to semantic interpretation:

(49) [*Diana*$_1$ [*remembered* [*her*$_1$ *brother*]$_2$]]

Here, *Diana* binds the pronoun *her*, and no binding operator B should be required. While (48) and (49) happen to be truth-conditionally equivalent, they are different, and the differences show up in certain cases. For example, for sentences with quantified subjects such as *every girl remembered her brother*, discourse binding of *her* is not possible, as *every girl* does not introduce an index. And under ellipsis, we get the sloppy vs. strict interpretation, cf. (50)(a) and (b), respectively.

(50) *Diana remembers her brother, and Ariana does, too.*
a. [*Diana*$_1$ [B [*remembers her brother*]]
and Ariana does ~~[B [*remember her brother*]]~~ *too*]
b. [*Diana*$_1$ [*remembers her*$_1$ *brother*]
and Ariana ~~[*remembers her*$_1$ *brother*]~~ *too*]

Reflexive and reciprocal pronouns differ from regular pronouns insofar as they only have a syntactically bound reading, with a locality requirement for their antecedent. This can be expressed within the present account by assuming that they introduce a specialized variable that cannot be passed across a clause. In (51), this allows for *herself* to co-refer to *Diana* as in (a), but excludes co-reference with *Ariana* as in (b), for which a regular pronoun must be used, as in (c). The use of regular pronouns as in (d) for local co-reference is not possible, presumably due to a blocking effect by the reflexive pronoun.

(51) a. *Ariana thinks* [*that Diana* [B *likes herself*]]
b. *Ariana* [B *thinks* [*that Diana likes herself*]]
c. *Ariana* [B *thinks* [*that Diana likes her*]]
d. *Ariana thinks that Diana* [B *likes her*]

However, as we have seen with picture nouns in (19), reflexives can also refer to the person from whose perspective an event is depicted, which requires the introduction of a perspective parameter that can also bind the variable introduced by the reflexive. I will not go into further details of reflexive and reciprocal pronouns here.

We now consider what happens with syntactically bound pronouns under reconstruction. I will use the same format to handle syntactic movement as above, even though we could model dependency on traces with the same mechanism as syntactic binding: A trace (of type *e*, or of other types) could create an identity function from entities of its type, where the argument is projected, and ultimately filled by the moved item. This would be the overall more homogenous approach, but in order to keep things as comparable as possible with the LF movement account, I will not pursue this option here.

Let us now reconsider our example:

(52) [*which story about her brother*] [1 [*did Diana* [B [*remember* $\mathrm{T_1}$]]]]

Assuming that the anaphoric component of *her* is interpreted as an identity function λu:female[u] that is projected in semantic composition using the rules in (41), we get the following interpretation for the moved *wh*-constituent:

(53) $[\![\textit{which}_{\mathrm{DO}}\ \textit{story about her brother}]\!] =$
$\lambda\mathrm{u}{:}\mathrm{female}\ \lambda\mathrm{R}\lambda\mathrm{x}\exists\mathrm{p}\exists\mathrm{y}[\mathrm{story(y)} \wedge \mathrm{about}(\iota\mathrm{z}[\mathrm{brother(u)(z)}])(\mathrm{y}) \wedge$
$\mathrm{p} = \mathrm{R(y)(x)}]$, type *e(eet)et*

In contrast to (37), this representation records the presence of a pronoun that is to be bound syntactically by the argument λu:female[...].

The semantic type of the trace must correspond to this meaning. That is, it is also a function from entities *e* to the type of object quantifiers, *(eet)et*, where the entity argument is projected and ultimately bound by the B operator. Instead of (38), we now have the following derivation:

(54) $[\![[2\ [\textit{Diana}\ [\mathrm{B}\ [\textit{remember}\ \mathrm{T_2}]]]]]\!]$
a. $= \lambda\xi_2[\![[\textit{Diana}\ [\mathrm{B}\ [\textit{remember}\ \mathrm{T_2}]]]]\!]^{2\to\xi_2}$
b. $= \lambda\xi_2[[\![[\mathrm{B}\ [\textit{remember}\ \mathrm{T_2}]]]\!]^{2\to\xi_2}([\![\textit{Diana}]\!]^{2\to\xi_2})]$
c. $= \lambda\xi_2[\mathrm{B}([\![[\textit{remember}\ \mathrm{T_2}]]\!]^{2\to\xi_2})(\mathrm{Diana})]$
d. $= \lambda\xi_2[\mathrm{B}(\lambda\mathrm{u}[[\![\mathrm{T_2}]\!]^{2\to\xi_2}(\mathrm{u})([\![\textit{remember}]\!]^{2\to\xi_2})])(\mathrm{Diana})]$
e. $= \lambda\xi_2[\mathrm{B}(\lambda\mathrm{u}[\xi_2(\mathrm{u})(\lambda\mathrm{y}\lambda\mathrm{x}[\mathrm{remember(y)(x)}])(\mathrm{Diana})])]$

Due to the presence of the B operator, the variable ξ_2 must be a function from entities, *e*. As it further combines with a relation, type *eet*, and returns a property, type *et*, it must be of type *e(eet)et*. This is the type provided by the moved constituent, which now can be combined with the meaning of its remnant clause:

(55) $[\![[[\textit{which}_{DO}\ \textit{story about her brother}]\ [2\ [\textit{Diana}\ [B\ [\textit{remember}\ T_2]]]]]]\!]$

a. $= [\![[2\ [\textit{Diana}\ [B\ [\textit{remember}\ T_2]]]]]\!]([\![\textit{which}_{DO}\ \textit{story about her brother}]\!])$

b. $= \lambda\xi_2[B(\lambda u[\xi_2(u)(\lambda y\lambda x[\text{remember}(y)(x)])(\text{Diana})])]$
$(\lambda u{:}\text{female}\ \lambda R\lambda x\exists p\exists y[\text{story}(y) \wedge$
$\text{about}(\iota z[\text{brother}(u)(z)])(y) \wedge p = R(y)(x)])$

c. $= [B(\lambda u[\lambda u{:}\text{female}\ \lambda R\lambda x\exists p\exists y[\text{story}(y) \wedge$
$\text{about}(\iota z[\text{brother}(u)(z)])(y) \wedge p = R(y)(x)](u)$
$(\lambda y\lambda x[\text{remember}(y)(x)])(\text{Diana})])]$

d. $= [B(\lambda u{:}\text{female}\ \lambda R\lambda x\exists p\exists y[\text{story}(y) \wedge$
$\text{about}(\iota z[\text{brother}(u)(z)])(y) \wedge p = R(y)(x)]$
$(\lambda y\lambda x[\text{remember}(y)(x)])(\text{Diana})]$

e. $= [B(\lambda u{:}\text{female}\ \lambda x\exists p\exists y[\text{story}(y) \wedge \text{about}(\iota z[\text{brother}(u)(z)])(y) \wedge$
$p = \text{remember}(y)(x)]))(\text{Diana})]$

f. $= [\lambda x{:}\text{female}\exists p\exists y[\text{story}(y) \wedge \text{about}(\iota z[\text{brother}(x)(z)])(y) \wedge$
$p = \text{remember}(y)(x)](\text{Diana})]$

g. $= \exists p\exists y[\text{story}(y) \wedge \text{about}(\iota z[\text{brother}(\text{Diana})(z)])(y) \wedge$
$p = \text{remember}(y)(\text{Diana})]$

In (55)(a) the meaning of the remnant clause, (54), is applied to the meaning of the *wh*-constituent, (53). By lambda-conversion, the meaning of the *wh*-constituent enters the computation at the place of the meaning of the trace, T_2. This is of a semantic type that introduces a pronoun that is to be bound syntactically, which is achieved by the operator B. In this way, the pronoun *her* in the moved phrase is interpreted as the referent of the subject, Diana.

2.5 Binding into the head of relative clauses

In the section above we have seen how binding under reconstruction can be handled in a Surface Interpretation account, using movement of a *wh*-constituent as an example. Other cases of binding under reconstruction can be explained in a similar way (cf. e.g. Jacobson 1999, 2004). Let us take as an example binding into the head of a relative clause, as in the following example:

(56) [*the* [[*story about her brother*] [*that* [2 [*Diana* [B [*remembered* T_2]]]]]]]

An LF approach that would try to express the binding of the pronoun *her* by *Diana* would have to resort to the head-raising analysis of relative clauses (Vergnaud 1974, Kayne 1994). But this is not necessary. We get a working analysis under Surface Interpretation as well.

For the relative clause, we assume that the type of the trace T_2 is *ee*, a function from entities to entities. This leads to the following interpretation, in which T_2 is an argument of the relation $\lambda y \lambda x[\text{remember}(y)(x)]$:

(57) ⟦[*that* [2 [*Diana* [B [*remember* T_2]]]]]⟧

a. $= \lambda\xi_2[\text{B}(\lambda u[\lambda y\lambda x[\text{remember}(y)(x)](\xi_2(u))])(\text{Diana})]$

b. $= \lambda\xi_2[\text{B}(\lambda u[\lambda x[\text{remember}(\xi_2(u))(x)]])(\text{Diana})]$

c. $= \lambda f[\text{B}(\lambda u[\lambda x[\text{remember}(f(u))(x)]])(\text{Diana})]$

d. $= \lambda f[\text{remember}(f(\text{Diana}))(\text{Diana})]$, type *(ee)t*

The type-unspecific variable ξ_2 turns out to be a variable of functions from entities to entities, type *ee*, in step (b), and hence I replaced it by a variable f. The resulting meaning is a predicate of functions f such that Diana remembers whatever the function maps Diana to. This means, of course, that Diana must be in the domain of the function.

The head NP [*story about her brother*] is interpreted as follows; the syntactically bound pronoun *her* is projected, as usual.

(58) ⟦[*story about her brother*]⟧
$= \lambda u{:}\text{female}\ \lambda y[\text{story}(y) \wedge \text{about}(\iota z[\text{brother}(u)(z)])(y)]$, type *eet*

The semantic types of these meanings are slightly different: (57) is a function from functions from entities to entities that maps such functions into truth values (a predicate on functions), (58) is a function from entities to a function from entities to truth values (a two-place relation). Following Winter (2004), we assume a general type change mechanism from two-place relations of type *eet* to predicates over functions of type *(ee)t*, which is defined as follows:

(59) $\text{F}(R) = \lambda f\ \forall u{\in}\text{DOM}(f)\ [R(f(u))(u)]$

This maps every function f of type *ee* to truth iff for every u in the domain of f, the relation R holds between u and f(u). In the case at hand we get the following interpretation, where we again assume that the F operator is represented in syntax, for perspicuity.

(60) ⟦F[*story about her brother*]⟧
$= \text{F}(\lambda u{:}\text{female}\ \lambda y[\text{story}(y) \wedge \text{about}(\iota z[\text{brother}(u)(z)])(y)])$
$= \lambda f\ \forall u{\in}\text{DOM}(f)\ [u{:}\ \text{female} \wedge \text{story}(f(u)) \wedge \text{about}(\iota z[\text{brother}(u)(z)])(f(u))]$

This is the set of functions f that map entities u to entities f(u) such that u is female, f(u) is a story and f(u) is about the brother of u.

Combining the head noun and a restrictive relative clause is generally by intersection. We assume the following rule, where ξ is a variable of an appropriate type.

(61) $[\![[_{NP}\ [_{NP}\ \alpha]\ [_{RelCL}\ \beta]]]\!] = \lambda\xi[[\![\alpha]\!](\xi) \wedge [\![\beta]\!](\xi)]$

Combining the two meanings of (60) and (57) gives us the following result:

(62) ⟦[NP [NP F [*story about her brother*]] [RelCL *that* [2 [*Diana* [B *remember* T_2]]]]]⟧

a. = λξ[⟦[*that* [2 [*Diana* [B *remember* T_2]]]]⟧(ξ) ∧
⟦[F [*story about her brother*]]⟧(ξ)]

b. = λξ[λf [remember(f(Diana))(Diana)](ξ) ∧
λf ∀u∈DOM(f)[u: female ∧ story(f(u)) ∧
about(ιz[brother(u)(z)])(f(u))](ξ)]

c. = λf [remember(f(Diana))(Diana) ∧
∀u∈DOM(f)[u: female ∧ story(f(u)) ∧
about(ιz[brother(u)(z)])(f(u))]]

This is a predicate on functions f such that Diana remembers f(Diana), where f(Diana) is a story about Diana's brother, by the second conjunct. Notice that the interpretation of *her* by Diana is achieved in a rather indirect way here: The pronoun is used to define a function in the NP meaning [F [*story about her brother*]] that then is applied to Diana in the relative clause.

A minimal function f that satisfies this description would be one that maps Diana to the unique story about her brother that she remembers. In this case, the definite article *the* can be applied to the meaning of (62) to single out that function. The standard meaning of the definite article as the iota operator, which is defined if uniqueness is satisfied, has to be slightly amended, however: If f = {⟨Diana, s⟩} is such a function (where s is the unique story about Diana's brother that Diana remembers), then f′ = {⟨Diana, s⟩, ⟨Ariane, s′⟩} is an appropriate function as well, if s′ is a story about Ariana's brother that Ariana remembers. Grosu & Krifka (2007) argue for a minimization operation on the functions that a restrictive relative construction applies to, which in this case would only leave f as the unique minimal function; when such a unique minimal function exists, the definite article can be applied. We have also showed that the same reasoning leads to an explanation of the readings in the following case, where instead of a pronominal binding the index at which *gifted mathematician* is evaluated corresponds to the index introduced by the modal element *claim*.

(63) *the gifted mathematician that you claim to be*

The proposed treatment also works when the relative clause contains a quantifier, as in the following case:

(64) [[F [*story about her brother*]] [*that* [2 [*every girl* [B [*remembers* T_2]]]]]]

Here, the first conjunct in the function description of (62)(c) changes, resulting in the following meaning:

(65) $\lambda f [\forall x[\text{girl}(x) \rightarrow \text{remember}(f(x))(x)] \wedge \forall u \in \text{DOM}(f)[u: \text{female} \wedge \text{story}(f(u)) \wedge \text{about}(\iota z[\text{brother}(u)(z)])(f(u))]]$

The minimal function f that satisfies this is one that maps every girl x (and nothing else) to the unique story about x's brother.

The derivation proposed here might appear rather complicated, in particular as it involves the operator F that changes a relation to a predicate of functions. However, it gives us precisely the right result. Also, it should be pointed out that the head-raising analysis in an LF framework has its complications as well. For example, if we indeed want to reconstruct the NP *story about her*$_1$ *brother* in the position of the trace, then this is of the wrong syntactic category; it is an NP that is interpreted as a predicate, but we require a DP to satisfy the categorial requirements.

(66) [$_{DP}$ *the* [$_{NP}$ [$_{NP}$ *story about her*$_1$ *brother*] [$_{RelCL}$ *that* [*Diana*$_1$ [*remembers* _]]]]]

This problem can be solved, cf. e.g. Sauerland (2003) and Hulsey & Sauerland (2006). But it appears that the added complexity corresponds to the type changer F that the Surface Interpretation account has to assume.

3 Condition C effects and reconstruction

3.1 Condition C effects: A test case?

After having worked through viable accounts of syntactically bound pronouns for semantic reconstruction, and hence for Surface Interpretation, we will consider referential expressions. Their behavior was perceived as an argument against surface interpretation by Fox (1999), and was recognized as a problem even by the proponents of surface interpretation as a potential problem (cf. Jacobson 2004). The argument is based on Condition C of binding theory, in the following form:

(67) Condition C: A referential expression (r-expression), i.e. a proper name, definite description, or specific indefinite, cannot be in the scope of (be c-commanded by) a co-referential expression, especially if this c-commanding expression is a pronoun.

For example, Condition C rules out that *he* or *John* is co-referent with *John*, *the man* or *someone from New York* in the following examples:

(68) *John / He told Mary*
[*that John / the man / someone from New York won the lottery*]

This does not mean that *he* and the r-expression cannot refer to the same individual, e.g., in the unlikely event that the subject referent referred to by *he* forgot that he is actually John, or if he presents himself to Mary as another person to hide the fact that he is actually John. Condition C just rules out that the expressions are forced to co-refer. This forced co-reference is of course possible for syntactically bound pronouns, as in the following examples:

(69) *John / the man / someone from New York / every dancing partner told Mary that he won the lottery.*

These examples clearly have two readings, one in which the subject binds the pronoun *he* and enforces a co-referring reading, and one in which it doesn't, and strongly invites a reading in which *he* refers to a distinct person instead. The bound reading is especially obvious with quantified antecedents.

In reconstruction configurations, Condition C effects are relevant because it appears that they can be used to check where a constituent is interpreted, at is surface position or at its "reconstructed" position. Consider the following structure:

(70) $[_{DP}$ ... r-expression$_1$ ...] [2 [... pronoun$_1$ ... [... t_2 ...] ...]]

If Condition C is checked on Surface Structure, no violation should arise, as the pronoun does not c-command the r-expression. If it is checked on the reconstructed position, however, Condition C should result in ungrammaticality, as then the pronoun will c-command the co-indexed r-expression:

(71) * [... pronoun$_1$ ... [... $[_{DP}$ ... r-expression$_1$ ...$]_2$ ...] ...]

So, LF Interpretation is, prima facie, compatible with both outcomes: If Condition C is checked on Surface Structure, (70) should be grammatical; if it is checked in the reconstructed position, it should be ungrammatical.

In contrast, Surface Interpretation appears to predict that there should not be a problem with reconstruction if Condition C is checked on Surface Structure, which is the only option that Surface Interpretation can consider if Condition C is a syntactic principle. Under the version of the semantic account that assumes traces of different types, we assume the following syntactic structure and interpretation:

(72) $[\![[_{DP}$ ... r-expression$_1$ ...] [2 [... pronoun$_1$ ... [... T_2 ...] ...]]$]\!]$
= $[\![$[2 [... pronoun$_1$ ... [... T_2 ...] ...]]$]\!]$($[\![[_{DP}$ ... r-expression$_1$ ...]$]\!]$)

The meaning $[\![[_{DP}$ ... r-expression$_1$ ...]$]\!]$ is a semantic function for which it cannot be recorded that it contains an r-expression. Hence, if it gets interpreted in the position of T_2, nothing can cause the clause to be ruled out because of the linguistic form of an expression within $[_{DP}$ ... r-expression$_1$ ...]. To record the presence of an r-expression in the meaning $[\![[_{DP}$ ... r-expression$_1$ ...]$]\!]$, which might allow us to check

Condition C violations in semantics, would be an otherwise unmotivated move. This is in contrast with signaling the presence of bound pronouns in semantic representation, as proposed in section 2.4, as bound pronouns plausibly lead to meanings that are functionally incomplete, a semantic property that should arguably be recorded in the semantic interpretation of such expressions.

3.2 Condition C effects and reconstruction: Initial observations

Now, what are the facts? They turn out to be rather less straightforward than one would wish. Chomsky (1995) considers examples like (73), for which a co-referring reading of *he* and *Tom* is difficult to achieve.

(73) [*John wondered* [[*which picture of Tom*] [*he liked* _]]]

Chomsky states that "reconstruction appears to be forced" (p. 191; however, the example is fully acceptable under this reading for the anonymous reviewer). From Chomsky's judgement it follows that Condition C would rule out the coindexed reading:

(74) [*John wondered* [_ [*he*$_1$ *liked* [*which picture of Tom*$_1$]]]]

Chomsky assumes a "preference principle" for reconstruction: "Do it when you can (i.e. minimize the restriction on the operator position)". If this is a principle that can be violated, it might well motivate why sentences like (73) are not quite so bad as expected, cf. the hedge in Chomsky's statement that reconstruction "seems" to be forced. However, the motivation of the preference principle – to minimize the restriction in the operator position – is not really clear. See Sauerland (2000) for further empirical motivation for reconstruction, and Sportiche (2006) for an overview of research from the view of LF Interpretation.

There is a potential problem with the idea of a principle that forces reconstruction. This is because it is acknowledged that for Condition A, which governs reflexive and reciprocal pronouns, such a principle would not always hold. For example, Chomsky (1995) observes that (75) has, in addition to the reading in which *himself* is bound by *Bill*, a reading in which *himself* is bound by *John*; for this reading, it is plausible that the *which* phrase does not reconstruct.

(75) [*John wondered* [*which picture of himself*] [*Bill saw* _]]

However, we do not have to assume reconstruction of the *which* phrase in order to explain that reading. Recall that reflexives can also be bound by the person from whose perspective a state of affairs is reported, especially with picture nouns. Hence, even after reconstruction, *John* might bind *himself*. This explanation is viable if *John* can also bind the reflexive in cases in which there is no movement involved, as in (76):

(76) *John believes that Bill saw a picture of himself.*

The reading where *John* binds *himself* might be less prominent than in (75) as a matter of processing: In (76) *Bill* both precedes and c-commands *himself*. But the reading is certainly available, which can be seen when *Bill* is replaced by *Mary*.

Let us wrap up. The initial observation clearly speaks in favor of a version of LF Interpretation, as in this account, we can motivate why Condition C effects arise. To be precise, with a structure like (73) LF interpretation could either not allow for co-reference of *Tom* and *he* (in case the *which*-phrase is interpreted in its surface position), or it could allow for it (in case the *which*-phrase is interpreted in the position of the gap). The remaining problem is to come up with a convincing motivation for the preference principle, that is, why the second option is possible. In contrast, Surface Interpretation predicts that Condition C should not be violated, regardless whether the *which* phrase is interpreted in surface position or after "semantic" reconstruction by functional application gets the meaning of *which picture of Tom* to be fed into the meaning composition at the position of the gap. In the first case, *Tom* does not c-command *he*, and in the second, it is not "visible" for *he* that the meaning of *which picture of Tom* contains a referential expression.

3.3 Exceptions to Condition C effects under reconstruction

As indicated in the last section, the data concerning Condition C effects in reconstruction contexts are less clear than proponents of LF Interpretation may wish for. This is because there are a number of cases that are generally received to be exceptions. Unfortunately, there is no empirical study of the phenomena beyond introspective judgements of the researchers, and in this article I will also not be able to provide a more thorough empirical basis either. However, while the judgements of data in isolation are often unclear, the judgements of minimal pairs of sentences often are quite clear-cut, and should constitute a sufficient basis for initial attempts at an explanation.

One important class of exceptions is the argument/adjunct asymmetry (cf. Riemsdijk & Williams 1981, Freidin 1986, Lebeaux 1990).

(77) a. [*Which claim that Mary had offended John*] *did he repeat?*
b. [*Which claim that offended John*] *did he repeat?*

Notice that in (77)(a), the *that*-clause is an argument of *claim*, whereas in (b), it is an adjunct. The received judgement of such sentences is that in (a) *he* cannot co-refer with *John*, whereas in (b), *he* can. The received explanation, due to Lebeaux (1990), is that adjuncts enter the syntactic and semantic recursion late, which for some reason exempts them from being reconstructed.

But in addition to r-expressions that occur in adjuncts to heads, Condition C effects are sometimes absent if the r-expression occurs within an argument of the head. These exceptions often are of somewhat reduced grammaticality, but they have been recorded by authors in spite of the fact that they are not predicted by the proposed theories, which we should take as serious evidence that they are a real phenomenon.

Safir (1999) has collected a number of such judgements in the literature that were deemed grammatical – the following examples are by Ross, Higginbotham, Kuno, Postal, Culicover and Heycock, respectively. He calls this the "anti-reconstruction" effect.

(78) a. *That* Ed_1 *was under surveillance* he_1 *never realized.*
b. *Which biography of* $Picasso_1$ *do you think* he_1 *wants to read?*
c. *Most articles about* $Mary_1$*, I am sure* she_1 *hates.*
d. *Whose allegation that* Lee_1 *was less than truthful did* he_1 *refute vehemently?*
e. *That* $John_1$ *had seen the movie* he_1 *never admitted.*
f. *Which picture of* $John_1$ *does* he_1 *like best?*

Under Surface Interpretation, such anti-reconstruction cases can be easily explained, but we would have to explain why examples like (73), which are taken to represent the base case, do not have the bound reading. Under LF interpretation, we can assume that Condition C can be checked on surface structure, but again we would have to explain why checking is sometimes on the surface position, and sometimes on the reconstructed position.

Safir assumes that Condition C is always checked in the reconstructed position, but that there is the phenomenon of "vehicle change" (cf. Fiengo & May 1994). This allows that in the lower copy of the reconstructed expression, the r-expression in replaced by a pronoun. Using (78)(a) as example, we can represented this as follows under the copy theory of movement:

(79) [~~*That* Ed_1 *was under surveillance*~~ [he_1 *never realized* [*that* he_1 *was under surveillance*]]]

In the lower copy, the r-expression *Ed* is changed to the pronoun *he*, which avoids Condition C violation. Presumably, the second occurrence of *he* is motivated by the fact that the pronoun *he* has an antecedent, *Ed*, to which it can refer. This change from a name to a pronoun is motivated in Fiengo & May (1994) by data concerning ellipsis, as in the following example, in which the referring expression *Sol* has to be replaced by *him* in the elided clause to get the intended binding right.

(80) *Lara* [*loves* Sol_1] *and* he_1 *thinks that Sara does* [~~*love him*~~$_1$] *too.*

With this move, what we have to explain is not when reconstruction applies or not, or whether Condition C is checked at the first position or at the second, but when the r-expression is changed to a pronoun, and when it remains an r-expression.

Safir (1999) mentions as one potential factor Kuno's Logophoric NP constraint (published in Kuno 2006), which blocks co-reference between a c-commanding expression α and a name in a constituent that represents the thoughts or an utterance of the referent of α. This should explain why co-reference in (73) is not possible, as *wonder* is a predicate denoting a thought. But this argument implies that examples (78) do not involve utterance or thought predicates, and therefore should be good. However, these very examples involve predicates like *realize, want, hate, refute, admit* that presumably all fall under Kuno's Logophoric NP constraint. One may argue that for some examples, negation prevents a logophoric reading, but, presumably (81) does not differ in grammaticality from (78)(a).

(81) *That Ed was under surveillance he certainly realized.*

Also, the Logophoric NP constraint should not be applicable to (78)(f), as liking involves a thought concerning the liked object. It also cannot explain the contrast to the following example, as recognized by Safir.

(82) ?? *Which picture of John does he like?*

Hence we conclude that the exceptions to Condition C effects under reconstruction are not explained in Safir (1999).

3.4 The role of verbs of creation

Fox (1999) considers a different set of data that lack Condition C effects, and argues that there is no reconstruction in the first place. His argument elaborates on Heycock (1995).

Heycock shows that the nature of the predicate of a clause sometimes enforces a reconstructed reading. For example, *invent* implies that the object of invention does not exist independently of the invention effect, favoring a narrow-scope reading, whereas *reinvent* or *recall* presuppose that the object of invention does exist independently, allowing for a wide-scope reading. That is, *invent* is a verb of creation, whereas *reinvent* is not. This leads to different interpretations with quantifier phrases headed by *how many* that result in determiner phrases in which asking for the number and the scope of an existential determiner can be dissociated. Consider the following examples and their possible readings:

(83) [*How many stories*] *is Diana likely to invent?*

a. 'What's the number n such that Diana is likely to invent n-many stories?'

b. * 'What's the number n such that there are n-many stories that Diana is likely to invent?'

(84) [*How many stories*] *is Diana likely to reinvent / recall?*

a. 'What's the number n such that Diana is likely to reinvent n-many stories?'

b. 'What's the number n such that there are n-many stories that Diana is likely to reinvent?'

Notice that the reading (83)(b) is unavailable, as the existential quantifier has wide scope over a proposition even though it originates as the object of the narrow-scope enforcing predicate *invent*.

Now, if we construct examples that involve a potential Condition C violation under reconstruction, examples like (83) that enforce reconstruction should turn out to be bad. This is indeed the case:

(85) * *How many stories about Diana*$_1$*'s brother is she*$_1$ *likely to invent?*

(86) *How many stories about Diana*$_1$*'s brother is she*$_1$ *likely to reinvent / recall?*

b. 'What's the number n such that there are n-many stories about Diana's brother that Diana is likely to re-invent?'

Example (85), which enforces reconstruction of the quantified subject, leads to ungrammaticality due to Condition C violation. Example (86), which allows for the non-reconstructed reading, is grammatical, or at least much better than (85), but only under the non-reconstructed reading.

A word about data: Heycock's original example was the following, with her own grammaticality judgement:

(87) ? *How many stories about Diana*$_1$ *was she*$_1$ *really upset by?*

Example (86) is due to Fox (1999), and it appears to be better than (87), presumably because *Diana* is in a more subordinated position. We will come back to this point.

Example (85) differs from cases in which no Condition C violation can occur even under reconstruction such as (88). Here, the reconstructed reading reappears, even though the pronoun *her* linearly precedes its antecedent.

(88) *How many stories about her$_1$ brother is Diana$_1$ likely to invent?*

a. 'What is the number n such that Diana is likely to invent n-many stories about her (= Diana's) brother?'

We find similar differences with other verbs of creation, as the following examples show, where (89)(a) is due to Fox (1999). While these examples are not always perfect, the versions with a creation verb are clearly much worse.

(89) a. *How many houses in John$_1$'s city does he$_1$ think should be *built / demolished?*

b. *How many proofs for John$_1$'s innocence is he$_1$ likely to *fabricate / bring up again?*

c. *How many poems of Sue$_1$ is she$_1$ likely to *write / get published?*

d. *How many of this couple's children will they$_1$ *have / manage to nourish?*

The constructions we have considered so far were concerned with wh-movement. The same point can be made with relative clauses, under the assumption of the head-raising analysis (cf. Vergnaud 1974, Kayne 1994).

(90) * *the (dozens of) stories about Diana$_1$'s brother that she$_1$ is likely to invent*

As *invent* enforces a narrow-scope reading of quantificational phrases, the head of the relative clause construction, *(dozens of) stories about Diana's brother*, must reconstruct into the object position of *invent*. This results in a Condition C violation, resulting in ungrammaticality. This contrasts with cases like (91), in which the verb does not enforce a narrow-scope interpretation.

(91) *the dozens of stories about Diana$_1$'s brother that she$_1$ is likely to reinvent / recall*

Here the head of the relative clause does not have to reconstruct into the object position, allowing for a reading without Condition C violation.

The same asymmetries with relative clauses show up with other verbs of creation:

(92) *the houses in John$_1$'s city that he$_1$ thinks should be *build / demolished*

Fox (1999) also points out that tense can make a difference. Present or future tense with verbs of creation implies that the object being created does not exist yet, whereas past tense does not imply that. This explains the following difference, in which the verb of creation appears within the relative clause:

(93) *How many papers that John$_1$ *writes / *will write / wrote does he$_1$ think will be published?*

(94) [*the dozens of papers of John$_1$*] *that he$_1$ *will write / wrote*

We can summarize the findings of this section as follows: If in a configuration like (95) the referent of the moved constituent α that contains an r-expression is not claimed to come into existence by the event denoted in the clause β, then this does not result in a Condition C violation, or at least the Condition C violation is much weaker.

(95) $[_{\alpha}$ ... r-expression$_1$ ...$]_2$ $[_{\beta}$ ... pronoun$_1$ [... t_2 ...] ...]

3.5 Idiomaticity in Condition C violations?

Before we investigate these exceptions to Condition C violations more closely, we should have a look at a class of examples that has been suggested by Munn (1994). He contrasts examples like the following:

(96) *the picture of Bill$_1$ that he$_1$ *took / likes* _

Munn explains this contrast within a copy theory of movement, as follows:

(97) a. [*the picture of Bill$_1$*] [[*which picture of Bill$_1$*]
[*he$_1$ took* [*which picture of Bill$_1$*]]]

b. [*the picture of Bill$_1$*] [[*which picture of Bill$_1$*]
[*he$_1$ likes* [~~*which picture of Bill$_1$*~~]]]

According to Munn, in (97)(a) he idiomatic expression *take a picture* enforces spelling out the lowest copy, resulting in a Condition C violation, and hence, ungrammaticality. In (b), however, there is no need to spell out the lower copy, which then can be deleted, with the result that a Condition C violation can be avoided. The intermediate position of *which picture of Bill$_1$* would be turned into an operator, by an independent rule.

But notice that *take*, in its idiomatic meaning in *take a picture*, is a verb of creation; it means the same as *make a (photographic) picture*. Hence the Condition C violation might be attributable to the same factors as with examples like (90). Notice that we have the same effect with the non-idiomatic way of expressing this notion:

(98) * *the picture of Bill$_1$ that he$_1$ made*

And for idioms or collocations that do not imply creation, we find that they pattern with non-idiomatic cases. In examples (99) the bound readings are possible.

(99) a. *the picture of $Bill_1$ that he_1 touched up / framed*
b. *the impression about $Bill_1$ that he_1 thinks counts most*
c. *the old-standing grievances about $Bill_1$'s enemies that he_1 aired again*

So it appears that idiomaticity is not an independent reason that leads to Condition C effects after all.

3.6 Taking Stock

In this section, we arrived at certain intermediary results concerning the issue what Condition C violations tells us about the nature of semantic interpretation.

Let us first take LF interpretation. Recall that LF Interpretation allows for the interpretation of an expression $[\ldots \alpha_i \ldots]_j$ with a referential term α_i either in surface position or in the reconstructed position with respect to an expression $[\beta_i [\ldots t_i \ldots]]$. Depending on general principles where $[\ldots \alpha_i \ldots]$ is interpreted, Condition C effects either do not arise, or do arise, or sometimes arise. What we found is that Condition C effects sometimes arise. This is consonant with LF interpretation; hence the tasks would be to determine under which conditions we find reconstruction (and hence Condition C violations), and under which conditions we don't.

Under Surface Interpretation, we should generally not expect Condition C violations in this configuration, as it is the meaning $[\![[\ldots \alpha_i \ldots]]\!]$ that ends up being interpreted in the position of the trace, t_j. As Condition C violation effects sometimes seem to arise, this appears to be a problem for Surface Interpretation.

However, in the next section I will argue that the cases that look like Condition C violations actually can be explained in another way, a way which can characterize the class of these cases well. It will turn out that the apparent Condition C violations do not distinguish between LF Interpretation and Surface Interpretation, after all, and cannot be used as an argument against LF interpretation. The result will be interesting for LF interpretation accounts as well, as it helps to characterize the exceptions to what this account takes to be Condition C violations.

4 A Competition Account for Apparent Condition C effects

4.1 A preference for syntactic binding

The alternative explanation for apparent Condition C effects under reconstruction contexts follows a suggestion in footnote 13, attributed to Gennaro Chierchia and Yael Sharvit, in Fox (1999), as well as proposals by Sharvit (1999), Cecchetto (2001) and Sternefeld (2001), with various extensions. It makes use of the competition account for Condition C effects going back to Reinhart (1983).

Let us consider the following minimal pair:

(100) a. ?? *What kind of stories about Diana*$_1$*'s brother is she*$_1$ *likely to invent _ ?*

b. *What kind of stories about her*$_1$ *brother is Diana*$_1$ *likely to invent _ ?*

Under Surface Interpretation, the intended co-reference in (100)(b) can be expressed as a case of a syntactically bound pronoun, as in (101): *her* creates a functional reading for the *wh*-phrase, the *wh*-phrase is interpreted by lambda-conversion in the position of the trace T_2, and the binding operator B ensures that the meaning of *Diana* ends up co-referent with the meaning of *her*. The derivation is exactly as proposed for (52).

(101) [*what kind of stories about her brother*] [2 [*is Diana* [B [*likely to invent* T_2]]]]

Now, if (100)(a) were grammatical, this co-reference could not be expressed by a syntactically bound pronoun. The reason is that the referential expression *Diana* does not generate a functional reading, hence the B operator could not be applied:

(102) [*what kind of stories about Diana's brother*] [2 [*is she* [*B [*likely to invent* T_2]]]]

But syntactic binding is not the only option available. Co-reference can also be expressed by discourse binding, as in antecedent – anaphor relations across sentences in discourse, or in donkey sentences, cf. (11) and (12). This is a distinct kind of binding that follows different rules, as outlined in Discourse Representation Theory (e.g., Kamp & Reyle 1993) and Centering Theory (e.g., Walker, Joshi & Prince 1998). In discourse binding, the antecedent need not c-command the anaphoric expression, but it typically precedes it. So, discourse binding should be possible for structures like (100)(a). In particular, under the plausible assumption that a sentence like (100)(a) is uttered in a context in which Diana is already given, and even salient, *Diana* should be able to refer to the person Diana, and *she* should be able to pick up the discourse referent that is already given. Nevertheless, even in such contexts (100)(a) appears to be degraded, and (100)(b) is at least more acceptable, though not quite as acceptable as (c) in which *Diana* is picked up by a pronoun.

(103) A: *I have a friend, Diana, who comes up with weird stories about her brother.*
B: a. ?? *What kind of stories about Diana's brother is she likely to invent?*
b. ? *What kind of stories about her brother is Diana likely to invent?*
c. ✓ *What kind of stories about her brother is she likely to invent?*

I would like to propose that the reason for the degraded status of (100)(a) is not due to a Condition C violation, but rather to a competition with sentence (100)(b). The reason is that (100)(b) expresses co-reference in a more grammaticalized way, by syntactic binding, than (100)(a). The general pragmatic rule underlying this reasoning can be stated as follows:

(104) If there is a constituent [... α ... β ...] in which α and β are intended by the speaker to refer to the same entity, then it is better to express this co-reference by syntactic binding than by discourse binding.

This means that if syntactic binding can be used to express co-reference, then it should be used. As a consequence, if it is avoided, then a reading in which α and β do not co-refer results, by implicature; this is the reading that (100)(a) actually gets, with *she* referring to a different person than Diana. Of course, (100)(b) has a discourse-bound reading as well if there is a salient discourse referent not anchored to Diana that can be picked up by *her*.

The proposal to explain the lack of the indicated co-referring reading of (100)(a) is in line with other competition theories of anaphoric choice, as proposed in Reinhart (1983). Reinhart distinguishes bound anaphora, which might be reflexive/reciprocal or pronominal, and non-bound, or referential expressions, which might be non-pronominal or pronominal expressions (but not reflexive/reciprocal). She states:

(105) When syntactically permitted, bound anaphora, whether of [reflexive/reciprocal] pronouns or non-[reflexive/reciprocal] pronouns, is the most explicit way available in the language to express co-reference, as it involves referential dependency. So, when co-reference is desired, this should be the preferred way to express it. (Reinhart 1983: 76)

Reinhart's "so" conventionally implicates an important point: The most explicit way is the most preferred way. Cf. Grodzinsky & Reinhart (1993) for refinements of this argument, and Safir (2004) for a particular implementation, the FTIP principle, which states that if an antecedent c-commands a pronoun, the "most dependent" form of the pronoun must be used. With Reinhart, we could explain why (100)(a) is of reduced grammaticality because (after reconstruction, by syntactic or semantic means), co-reference could not be expressed because the pronoun cannot be syntactically bound by *Diana*, and there is an alternative way, (b), by which co-reference can be expressed. While the possibility for this type of explanation has been disregarded by Safir (2004) in his own competition theory, it was suggested in work such as Sharvit (1999), Cecchetto (2001) and Sternefeld (2001).

The picture developed here is slightly more complex than in Reinhart's original account. In that account, two conditions were considered: expressions that indicate co-reference, and expressions that don't. Here, there are three conditions: expressions that indicate co-reference by syntactic binding, expressions that indicate co-reference by discourse binding, and expressions that do neither. But Reinhart's argumentation can apply to the present case as well when we assume that syntactic binding is the most explicit way to express co-reference, followed by discourse bound pronouns. The reason for this ranking is that the conditions for syntactic binding are defined most narrowly, involving a syntactic configuration between binder and bindee, whereas the conditions for discourse binding are defined more broadly, including binding across sentences; in theories like Elbourne (2005), discourse pronouns would not express binding at all, but co-reference by covert descriptions.

Sportiche (2013) explicitly argues against a competition account as proposed in the previous section. One of his arguments is that there should be a reason why the winning candidate is the winning candidate, and he fails to see one. This argument can be answered by pointing out that we have a subset relationship between the application domains of two devices, syntactic binding and discourse binding; wherever the first can apply, the second can apply as well, but not vice versa. This is a typical situation where pragmatic rules would force language users to choose the more restrictive device, if applicable. For example, a definite DP should be used if its conditions – in particular, uniqueness of reference – is satisfied, which results with indefinite DPs as having a non-uniqueneness implicature.

4.2 When syntactic binding is not optimal

Reinhart (1983) has stated a number of cases in which the pragmatic preference (105) is superseded by other factors, and she considers it a remarkable strength of her theory over standard Binding Theory that she can explain configurations where the preference in (105) seems not to hold and relations obtain that are ruled out by standard binding theory (relations as the ones discussed by Evans 1980). For example, in statements like *He is John*, the speaker wants to express an identity that is not established yet. So, co-reference between *he* and *John* is "desired" in this case. It is not presupposed, but asserted in the very sentence. Syntactic binding does not assert co-reference, but presupposes it, and hence cannot be relied on in this case.

We have seen in section 3 that there are a number of exceptions to apparent Condition C violations under reconstruction, and we will have to explain why in these cases syntactic binding is not the best option, and discourse binding succeeds. For example, we will have to explain why example (86), here repeated, allows for a discourse-bound reading that is not surpassed by the syntactically bound reading.

(106) *How many stories about Diana$_1$'s brother is she$_1$ likely to recall?*

It should be pointed out that discourse binding does not necessarily mean that *Diana* introduces a discourse referent that is then picked up by *she*. Rather, we should assume that there is already a salient discourse referent for Diana that is picked up first by the name, and then by the pronoun. This is the typical context for such sentence. To see this, observe that if we change the name to an indefinite that introduces a new discourse referent, the resulting sentence is bad:

(107) * *What kind of stories about the brother of [a friend of yours]$_1$ is she$_1$ likely to recall?*

Only indefinites that are very clearly interpreted as specific allow for such sentences:

(108) *What kind of stories about a certain friend of yours does he prefer to forget?*

Notice that global givenness did not help much to improve cases like (103)(a), and we will have to explain why verbs of creation are different.

Another point to consider here is that in order for apparent Condition C effects to arise, the available competitor is indeed better than the alternative that it blocks. It is instructive to consider an example by Lebeaux (1990) involving intermediate traces that is refined by Fox (1999) to argue for syntactic reconstruction (with indicated judgements).

(109) a. [*Which (of his) paper(s) that he$_1$ gave to Ms. Brown$_2$*]
did every male student$_1$ hope t *that she$_2$ will read* t′ ?

b. * [*Which (of his) papers that he$_1$ gave to Ms. Brown$_2$*]
did she$_2$ hope *t *that every male student$_1$ will revise* t′ ?

Fox assumes two potential trace positions, one as the trace of cyclic wh-movement in SpecCP of the embedded clause, one as object of *read*. Reconstruction must be such that the pronoun *he* ends up being bound by the quantifier *every student*. In

(109)(a), reconstruction (or spell-out for interpretation) in t is possible, in which case the name *Ms. Brown* c-commands the pronoun. In (b), reconstruction must be at the lower trace t′, as otherwise the pronoun *he* could not be bound by *every male student*, in which case a Condition C violation ensues. This is the story for syntactic reconstruction.

From the viewpoint of semantic reconstruction, we can again assume that syntactic binding between *Ms. Brown* and *she* is preferred, where possible. Let us, for the purpose of checking the alternatives, exchange the occurrences of the name and the pronoun:

(110) a. [*Which (of his) paper(s) that* he_1 *gave to* her_2]
did every male $student_1$ *hope* t *that Ms. Brown will read* t′?

b. [*Which (of his) paper(s) that* he_1 *gave to* her_2]
did Ms. Brown hope t *that every male* $student_1$ *will revise* t′?

If we assume, with Fox, that for semantic reasons the moved phrase is associated with both traces, t and t′, then the alternative (110)(a) does not lead to an improvement over (109)(a): The moved *wh*-expression would have to be reconstructed in the position of the first trace, and in the position of the first trace, *her* would still not be in a position to be syntactically bound by *Ms. Brown.* Hence the coreference between *her* and *Ms. Brown* can only be expressed by discourse binding, to a discourse referent for Ms. Brown that is already given in the global context. As syntactic binding is not a competitor in this case, both alternatives, (109)(a) and (110)(a), are fine – but under discourse binding. The situation is different for (109)(b). Here, the alternative (110)(b) allows for syntactic binding of *her* by *Ms. Brown* in both trace positions, and in particular for the low trace position t′ that is forced as the quantifier *every student* has to bind *he.* Hence, the availability of an alternative involving syntactic binding blocks (109)(b).

We will now have a closer look where the general preference for syntactic binding does not obtain, and discourse binding draws level with it, or even overtakes it. This will be done in two sections: In section 4.3 we will consider structural features that make syntactic binding problematic, and in 4.4 we will turn to information-structural features, in particular, to topichood as a factor in the competition.

4.3 Structural exemption from preference to syntactic binding

The position of the binder. Sportiche (2013) has argued against the competition account by pointing out that there are configurations in which both competing forms are possible. For this situation he presents an example that is of intrinsic interest even though it does not involve reconstruction, (111) in contrast to (112):

(111) a. *John$_1$'s mother told Bill about him$_1$.*

b. *His$_1$ mother told Bill about John$_1$.*

(112) a. *John$_1$ told Sue about his$_1$ mother.*

b. * *He$_1$ told Sue about John$_1$'s mother.*

A plausible explanation of this difference is as follows: From the position of the specifier of a DP as in (111), syntactic binding is possible, as we have seen with quantifier antecedents as in (23)(a), but it requires a scope extension that is computationally costly. Hence the advantage of syntactic binding over discourse binding is not as evident anymore so that it would be able to block (111)(b) (even though this is presumably still less acceptable, in an appropriate context where *John* is given, than (a)).

A similar point can be made with examples involving reconstruction like the following, in which the potential binder in an apparent Condition C reconstruction configuration is in a SpecCP position:

(113) a. *the stories about Diana's brother that her uncle is likely to invent*

b. *the stories about her brother that Diana's uncle is likely to invent*

Here, example (113)(a) appears to be grammatical, even though syntactic binding from a SpecCP position is possible. The reason is that syntactic binding, as expressed in (b), is more costly from the position of a DP specifier, and hence does not outcompete discourse binding, as in (a).

It might be questioned whether the implementation of syntactic binding in section 2.4 could deal with cases like (113)(b) at all. Consider here cases like the following:

(114) a. *Diana's uncle likes her.*

b. *Every girl's uncle likes her.*

In a first step, quantifiers like *every girl's uncle* are generated by a meaning where the genitive attached to the quantifier, *every girl*, introduces an argument for a functional meaning that is then filled by the meaning of *uncle*, resulting in a complex quantifier *every girl's uncle*. We first illustrate this without pronoun binding:

(115) a. $[\![$*every girl*$]\!] = \lambda P \forall x[\text{girl}(x) \rightarrow P(x)]$

b. $[\![$*'s*$]\!] = \lambda Q \lambda f \lambda P[Q(\lambda x[P(f(x))])]$

c. $[\![$*every girl's*$]\!] = \lambda f \lambda P \forall x[\text{girl}(x) \rightarrow P(f(x))]$

d. $[\![$*every girl's uncle*$]\!] = \lambda P \forall x[\text{girl}(x) \rightarrow P(\text{uncle}(x))]$

e. $[\![$*every girl's uncle is happy*$]\!] = \forall x[\text{girl}(x) \rightarrow \text{happy}(\text{uncle}(x))]$

Syntactic binding of a pronoun *her* exist, cf. Jacobson (1999). One technique that is reminiscent of the second quantifier meaning in (43)(b) is sketched in (116); here the quantifier ends up with a meaning (d) that expects a relational expression like (a), yielding the right interpretation.

(116) a. ⟦*likes her*⟧ = λu:female λx[x likes u]
b. ⟦'s⟧ = λQλfλR[Q(λx[R(x)(f(x))])]
c. ⟦*every girl's*⟧ = λfλR∀x[girl(x) → R(x)(f(x))]
d. ⟦*every girl's uncle*⟧ = λR∀x[girl(x) → R(x)(uncle(x))]
e. ⟦*every girl's uncle likes her*⟧ = ∀x[girl(x) → uncle(x) likes x]

Again, one can assume that this derivation of a form that allows for syntactic binding is overly complex, and once again (113)(b) is would not be a strong competitor to (113)(a).

The position of the bindee. We should expect that in a situation in which the potential bindee, the pronoun, is in a less-than-optimal position, this form loses competitiveness against discourse binding. This is what happens with examples (86) vs. (87), and perhaps more obviously with the following examples:

(117) a. ?? *the stories about Diana that she is likely to invent*
b. *the stories about herself that Diana is likely to invent*

(118) a. *the stories about the castle of Diana's husband that she is likely to invent*
b. *the stories about the castle of her husband that Diana is likely to invent*

Here, (117)(a) is considerably worse than (118)(a). This can be explained by the fact that the competitor of (117)(a), namely (117)(b), allows for a natural syntactic binding relation, whereas this is not the case for the competitor of (118)(a), namely (118)(b). The reason is that in the latter case, the syntactically bound pronoun is relatively deeply embedded, which means in the implementation of syntactically bound pronouns developed in section 2.4 that the argument of the functional variable representing the pronoun would have to be projected a number of steps in the semantic competition.

The argument/adjunct asymmetry. A related argument may help to explain the well-known argument/adjunct asymmetry, the observation that referring expressions that occur in adjuncts within the moved phrase do not as easily lead to apparent Condition C violations, as in the received judgements for (119).

(119) a. ?? [*Which claim that Mary had offended John*$_1$] *did he*$_1$ *repeat* _ ?
b. [*Which claim that had offended John*$_1$] *did he*$_1$ *repeat* _ ?

Under the current line of argumentation, we should assume that the variant of with pronoun in the *which*-clause (120)(a) outcompetes (119)(a), whereas (120)(b) does not outcompete (119)(b):

(120) a. *Which claim that Mary had offended him*$_1$ *did John*$_1$ *repeat_ ?*
b. *Which claim that had offended him*$_1$ *did John*$_1$ *repeat_ ?*

We would arrive at this result if it can be shown that syntactic binding is more costly into adjuncts, as in (121)(a), than into arguments, as in (b) (here shown under syntactic reconstruction):

(121) a. *John*$_1$ *repeated [which claim [*$_{Adjunct}$ *that Mary had offended him*$_1$*]]*
b. *John*$_1$ *repeated [which claim [*$_{Argument}$ *that hat offended him*$_1$*]]*

Now, argument/adjunct asymmetries are well-known for syntactic movement, and so it would not be unexpected that syntactic binding, which involves the projection of a functional dependency from a subconstituent, is more costly when it originates from an adjunct, as adjuncts are less tightly syntactically integrated.

Another contrast may be found with picture nouns and reflexive anaphors, which presumably are syntactically bound. Under this condition, (122)(a) should be better than (b).

(122) a. *John recalled the rumor that Mary had mutilated a picture of himself.*
b. *John recalled the rumor that caused Mary to mutilate a picture of himself.*

At the end of the next section I will discuss another line of argument that helps to explain the difference between adjuncts and arguments.

4.4 Topicality as exemption from preference to syntactic binding

We now turn to a type of exemption from syntactic binding to information structure. Consider cases like (123), where (A) sets up a the context in which stories about Diana's brother become a topic of conversation. In this context, sentence (100)(a), here given as (123)(B:a), is remarkably good, presumably of similar status as (100)(b), here given as (123)(B:b), and (123)(B:c).

(123) A: *Do you remember Diana? She has this interesting brother. People make up weird stories about him. Even she herself participates in that sometimes.*
B: a. *What kind of stories about Diana's brother is she likely to invent?*
b. *What kind of stories about her brother is Diana likely to invent?*
c. *What kind of stories about her brother is she likely to invent?*

We can explain this as follows: As the stories about Diana's brother are topical, they can be referred to directly by either *stories about Diana's brother*, or by *stories about her brother*. In particular, in the latter case, *her* does not need to be syntactically bound. There is a competition between *Diana* and *her*, as Diana was previously mentioned, and one should see a preference for the pronoun, *her*. But as the topic has shifted from Diana to stories about Diana's brother, it is plausible that full-name reference is as felicitous as the use of a pronoun.

I should mention here that topicality may also be responsible for certain known exceptions to Condition C called "instantiation contexts" by Safir (2004) (Ken Safir, pers. communication). In the context of (124)(A), John is highly salient, hence *John* can outcompete a bound pronoun in (B).

(124) A: *There are no people who like John.*
B: *Well, John is someone who likes John.*

Evidence for the role of salient discourse referents, or topicality, can also be gained by looking at sentences in which no reference to a topical entity is intended. In this situation, apparent Condition C violations under reconstruction should become more prominent. And this is what we find in (125), a case with a predicate like *recall* that is known not to lead to Condition C violations under reconstruction:

(125) *the* / ??*any stories about* $Diana_1$'s *brother that she is likely to reinvent / recall*

A number of the observed exceptions to apparent Condition C effects under reconstruction can be explained by the topicality effect, to which I will now turn.

Verbs of Creation. We start with Heycock's observation that the verb meaning plays a role; in particular, apparent Condition C violations occur more reliably with verbs of creation, cf. section 3.4. With verbs of creation, the referent of the moved phrase, e.g. *stories about Diana's brother*, does not exist independently. This makes it less easy to come up with contexts in which this concept is contextually given, and hence it leads more easily to the judgement of such sentences as bad. However, as we have seen with example (123), there are contexts in which even concepts that are objects of verbs of creation are contextually given, and in such contexts the grammaticality of sentences with apparent Condition C violations increase.

Topic marking. Salzmann (2006), working on German, observed that stressing improves acceptability in cases of apparent Condition C violations under Reconstruction, as in the following example:

(126) *die Nachforschungen über* PETER, *die er mir lieber verschwiegen hätte*
'the investigations about Peter that he would rather have concealed from me'

On closer examination, it seems that it is not stressing the antecedent that is at stake. Rather, it is stressing the final constituent of the head noun, which indicates a prosodic boundary:

(127) *die Nachforschungen über Peter$_1$ in WIEN, die er$_1$ mir lieber verschwiegen hätte*
'the investigations about Peter in Vienna that he would rather have concealed from me'

I assume that the prosodic boundary marked by stress indicates the information-structural notion of topic. According to the argument developed above, this should improve sentences with preceding referential expressions, as this allows for a bound reading. This is shown in the following examples, where in addition to stress, other means like the contrastive topic particle *jedoch* or topic marking by *was betrifft* or *was angeht* ("as for") make it clear that the head of the relative clause is a topic.

(128) *die Geschichten über Diana$_1$'s Bruder jedoch, die sie$_1$ wahrscheinlich erfinden wird, darf man nicht für ernst nehmen*
'the stories about Diana's brother PARTICLE, which she will probably invent, one should not take serious'

(129) a. *was die Geschichten über Diana$_1$'s Bruder betrifft, die sie$_1$ wahrscheinlich erfinden wird*
'as for the stories about Diana$_1$'s brother that she$_1$ is likely to invent'
b. *was das Foto von Bill$_1$ angeht, das er$_1$ gerne aufnehmen würde*
'concerning the picture of Bill$_1$ that he$_1$ would like to take'

Focus marking. Sophie Repp (pers. comm.) pointed out that focus in the relative clause improves acceptability as well, as in the following example:

(130) a. *the picture of Bill [that he took / plans to take in VIENNA]$_F$*
b. *the picture of Bill [that he took / plans to take himSELF]$_F$*

We can explain this as follows: Focus, as usual, indicates the presence of alternatives that are relevant for the interpretation of expressions. In the current case, focus in the restrictive relative clause indicates that there are several sets of entities that fall under the head noun that are present in the context, here, *picture of Bill* (e.g., those that he took in Vienna and those that he took in Venice). One of these sets is selected, here those that he took in Vienna. Consequently, the concept referred to by the head noun, here, *picture of Bill*, is presupposed to be given in the global context. In such a context, the bound pronoun version, *the picture of him that the took in Vienna*, does not outcompete the form *the picture of Bill that the took in Vienna*, as the latter can refer to the given concept, *picture of Bill.*

Specificity of the head. Bianchi (2004) has identified as a factor that decreases apparent Condition C violation effect the specificity of the head of relative clauses. The more specific the head, the milder Condition C violation effect become; they are lacking with appositive relative clauses.

(131) *L'imagine di Gianni che* pro *cerca de transmettere*
'the image of John that he tries to project'

(132) *ho comprato una scultura di Defendi que* pro *dicono que* pro *che abbia realizzato*
'I bought a sculpture by Defendi that they say he had carved'

(133) *ha telefonata a i due student, que ogni medico visitera domani*
'I phoned up the two students, which all doctors will visit tomorrow'

Specificity in this sense directly relates to topicality of the head, which creates the configuration in which the two expressions do not compete with each other.

Factive complement clauses. Several exceptions that Safir (1999) mentions involve factive complement clauses, as the following ones:

(134) a. *That* Ed_1 *was under surveillance* he_1 *never realized.*
b. *That* $John_1$ *had seen the movie* he_1 *never admitted.*

Factive clauses are presupposed in the context. That is, their presuppositions can be derived from the common ground, and hence have to be given. For this reason, it might be important to identify the factive proposition in the context, which is easier if this proposition is not functionally dependent on some antecedent, that is, does not contain a syntactically bound pronoun. This is the reason why forms like (134) survive, in addition to those in which binding is expressed syntactically:

(135) a. *That* he_1 *was under surveillance* Ed_1 *never realized.*
b. *That* he_1 *had seen the movie* $John_1$ *never admitted.*

Existing vs. hypothetical entities. Another one of Safir's examples can be explained by the fact that under a plausible interpretation, the set of entities referred to should be given, and hence are better identified by a non-functional concept.

(136) *Which biography of* $Picasso_1$ *do you think* he_1 *wants to read?*

For (136) it is likely that the meaning of *biography of Picasso* is contextually salient, that is, that the speaker refers to a given set of biographies. This is even more obvious with the variant (137), in which reference to a given set is made clear by the definite description in the *which*-phrase.

(137) *Which of the biographies of Picasso$_1$ do you think he$_1$ would have liked to read?*

If *biography* means 'type of biography', that is, if the speaker does not refer to a given set of biographies, then (136) becomes considerably less grammatical, and the variety with a syntactically bound pronoun is preferred:

(138) a. ?? *Which type of biography of Picasso$_1$ do you think he$_1$ would have liked to read?*

b. *Which (type of) biography of himself do you think Picasso$_1$ would have liked to read?*

The answer to (138)(b) could be, e.g. *A biography that stresses his Spanish roots, but such a biography does not exist yet.*

Ken Safir (pers. comm.) suggested that the topicality argument only applies in case the r-expression precedes the pronoun, but not in cases like (139), which appears to disallow for a reading in which *he* refers to Picasso.

(139) *Do you think he would have liked to read one of the biographies of Picasso?*

I am not convinced that a co-referent reading is excluded. In a context like (140), which makes both *Picasso* and *biographies of Picasso* salient, (139) appears to be fine.

(140) *As of today, there are twenty biographies of Picasso on the market, fifteen biographies of Cezanne, twelve of Gauguin. Imagine Picasso were still alive, ...*

Topical vs. non-topical quantifiers. Yet another example of Safir (1999) involves the quantifier *most*. This is a topical quantifier, expressing a quantification over a salient set, and so we should expect violations of apparent Conditon C effects in reconstruction contexts. When we change *most* to a non-topical quantifier like unstressed *some*, we arrive at a clear contrast:

(141) a. *Most articles about Picasso, I am sure he hated.*

b. ?? *Some articles about Picasso, I am sure he hated.*

We should also expect differences in the following contrast, which pitches the topical quantifier *each* against the not necessarily topical *nearly every*. But the difference, if existing, appears to be slight.

(142) a. *Each article about Picasso that he authorized increased the prices of his paintings.*

b. ? *Nearly every article about Picasso that he authorized increased the prices of his paintings.*

***Which* vs. *what*.** These *wh*-words differ insofar as *which* asks for a particular instantiation out of a set that is typically given, whereas *what* asks for an entity with a certain property, typically of an open-ended list. This makes *which*-constituents more easily to be constructed as topical, which in turn should lead to to differences in acceptability in cases like the following:

(143) a. *Which stories about Diana's brother did she invent before the age of seven?*

b. ?? *What stories about Diana's brother did she invent before the age of seven?*

Uniqueness. Heycock (1995: fn. 13) discusses the following contrast, with her grammaticality judgements:

(144) a. ? *Which picture of* $John_1$ *does* he_1 *like _ best?*

b. ?? *Which picture of* $John_1$ *does* he_1 *like _?*

Again, topicality is at stake here. In order to answer which picture satisfies a certain description in the *best* way, the range of pictures under consideration must to be given, due to the requirements of the superlative. This makes it plausible that the speaker refers to it with an expression that is not functionally dependent. On the other hand, with *like*, it is easier to assume a more open class that is not topical.

Topicality of antecedent expression. The following example is difficult to interpret even though it comes with at least two features that would make it easy: the predicate *like best* and the *wh*-expression *which.*

(145) ?? *Which picture of a man does he like best?*

The problem is the indefinite expression *a man*, which presupposes that the discourse referent for *a man* is not given. This makes it impossible that the concept of pictures of that man is topical (cf. the discussion of (107)). However, it seems that sentences like (145) improve if *a man* is read generically:

(146) A: *Which picture of a man does he like best?*

B: *His wedding picture, of course.*

This is predicted, as *picture of a man* can be read as referring to a stereotypical class of pictures, and *a man* as referring to the exemplars of a given kind.

Givenness of functions. Above, I have argued that examples like (109)(b) are bad because there is a viable competitor that involves syntactic binding. Here, I would like to argue that the need to refer to topical concepts might improve such sentences as well. In such a context, the following example appears fine:

(147) *I know that each student has to write a phonology paper, a syntax paper, and a semantics paper in Ms. Brown's class. Now, [which of his papers that he gave Ms. Brown] did she hope that every student would revise?*

The reason is that the first sentence makes salient a set of papers for each (male) student that can be defined functionally, as the student's phonology, syntax and semantics paper. This is sufficient to offset the general tendency for syntactic binding between *Ms. Brown* and *she*.

The nature of the binder. It turns out that the choice of the binding expression in the main clause influences the strength of the apparent Condition C effects as well. These effects are particularly strong when the expression that c-commands the referential expression is a pronoun; sometimes Condition C is formulated in these terms (e.g., Sportiche 2013: "A pronoun cannot c-command a co-referential name"). Indeed, sentence (148) appears better with the epithet *that devil* than with *she*.

(148) *What kind of stories about Diana$_1$'s brother will she$_{*1}$ / that devil$_1$ invent_ ?*

The reason for this difference may be that epithets resist syntactic binding, cf. (21), and hence (148) does not have a clearly better competitor with the same linguistic material (the same enumeration of expressions). Furthermore, as epithets are discourse bound and must refer to salient antecedents, a context is invoked in which Diana is given, and hence the first occurrence of *Diana* can already refer to that discourse referent.

In German, we can make a similar observation with d-pronouns, which also resist syntactic binding. And indeed, violations appear much weaker in this case.

(149) *die Geschichten über Dianas$_1$ Bruder welche sie$_{*1}$ / die(se)$_1$ wieder erfinden wird*
'the stories about Diana's brother that she / d-PRON invent again'

This difference can be explained as follows. As we have seen in (22), d-pronouns resist syntactic binding; they are typically discourse bound. This means that a salient discourse referent must be already established that the d-pronoun can pick up. Hence, d-pronouns suggest a context in which the referent, here *Diana*, is discourse salient. This makes the syntactically bound alternative (150) less likely to count as competitor

(150) *die Geschichten über ihren Bruder, welche Diana wieder erfinden wird*
'the stories about her brother that Diana is likely to invent again'

The same contrast can be repeated in a pro-drop language like Italian with non-overt subjects and overt subject pronouns, which lack a Condition C effect (D. Delfitto, pers. comm.):

(151) *Nella casa di John,* pro_{*1} / *lui*$_1$ *a invitato ogni professore*
'In the house of John, pro / he invited every professor'

Arguments vs. Adjuncts, again. In section 4.3 I have argued that adjuncts may constitute an exception for the general preference for syntactic binding, as there are reasons to assume that syntactic binding is more costly into adjuncts, and hence allows for discourse binding to emerge as a co-optimal form. I would like to take up the argument/adjunct asymmetry again. Consider the following example:

(152) a. ?? *The claims that Mary had offended John*$_1$ *that he*$_1$ *remembered*
b. *The claims that had offended John*$_1$ *that he*$_1$ *remembered*

Adjuncts typically serve to identify one entity or a set of entities out of a larger class. In order for this to work, the larger class of entities has to be given. Also, the property that is used to single out a particular entity or a smaller set of entities should be known. This makes it likely that (152)(b) evokes a context in which claims that had offended John are given. Now the general reasoning pattern of this section applies: To identify this class, it is better to use a non-functional meaning, that is, to avoid syntactically bound pronouns, against the general tendency that prefers such pronouns whenever possible. The prime function of arguments is different; arguments are typically not used to restrict a class of given entities. For example, (153)(a) appears to be more natural than (b).

(153) a. *We were informed of claims that Mary had offended John.*
b. *We were informed of claims that had offended John.*

As a consequence, (152)(a) invokes less natural a context in which claims that Mary had offended John are topical, and therefore the general preference for syntactically bound pronouns leads to suboptimality of this expression with respect to its rival using syntactic binding, *The claims that Mary had offended him that John remembered.*

5 Concluding remarks

The question addressed in this article concerned the general architecture of the syntax/semantics interface, by Surface Interpretation or by Logical Form. Contexts which involve syntactic reconstruction (under the LF approach) are treated differently under these general perspectives, and lead to different predictions. In particular, while the two approaches make the same prediction for the syntactic binding of pronouns of reconstructed constituents, they differ when it comes to the reconstruction of r-expressions. The LF approach predicts that in this case reconstruction can result in so-called Condition C violations, while the Surface Interpretation approach seems not to predict that (cf. Fox 1999).

In this paper I developed an argument against this line of reasoning. Taking up initial suggestions by Reinhart (1983), and following a reasoning pattern similar to Sharvit (1999), Cecchetto (2001) and Sternefeld (2001), I argued that there is a general preference for syntactic binding, which can explain why apparent Condition C violations under reconstruction occur even within the Surface Interpretation perspective: The structure that allows for the expression of syntactic binding is preferred, and hence the structure that does not use this device is degraded.

In a second step, I looked at the numerous exceptions to apparent Condition C violations under reconstruction, and explained them by counteracting principles. First, the frequently discussed argument/adjunct asymmetry could plausibly be explained by the greater costs for syntactic binding into adjuncts, which makes syntactic binding a less viable competitor to discourse binding. Second, I argued that the need to refer to a given, topical concept can counterbalance the general preference for syntactic binding: This reference is better accomplished with non-functional meanings, that is, with expressions that avoid syntactic binding.

To be sure, the two classes of "exceptions" to apparent Condition C violations in reconstruction contexts can also be used to explain these exceptions within the Logical Form perspective. However, the general methodological point is that a potentially fatal problem for Surface Interpretation turned out to be not a problem after all.

As far as I can see, there are two main desiderata that this article leaves open. First, the subtle judgements concerning Condition C violations under reconstruction would have to be tested in a more rigid way than by introspection. It is unlikely that linguistic corpora will be very helpful here; rather, experimental evidence would have to be collected by manipulating the binder – bindee relation, and especially the context of sentences. Second, I have proposed an intricate competition model in which subtle factors can shift the balance in this way or that way. To make this line of reasoning predictive, a model that allows for the evaluation of competing forms, for example an optimality-theoretic model with ranked constraints, would have to be constructed.

There is also a larger issue here concerning the two accounts discussed here. Under a Surface Interpretation, Condition C cannot be properly formulated on the level of semantic interpretation, even for cases that do not involve reconstruction. Consider the following example, which involves a Condition C violation:

(154) ⟦[*Diana* [*likes Diana's brother*]]⟧
= ⟦*Diana*⟧(⟦[*likes Diana's brother*]⟧)

There is nothing in the meaning ⟦*likes Diana's brother*⟧, = λx[likes(ιz[brother(Diana)(z)])(x)], that would reveal that its description contains an r-expression; the constant 'Diana' cannot be retrieved from this meaning. Hence Condition C cannot be checked on this level. How, then, can it be compared with the bound variable reading, where the predicate has the meaning λx[likes(ιz[brother(x)(z)])(x)]?

(155) ⟦[*Diana* [B [*likes her brother*]]]]⟧
= ⟦*Diana*⟧(⟦[B [*likes her brother*]]⟧)

The difference is in the computation of this meaning: While in the computation of (154), a second reference to ⟦*Diana*⟧ is necessary when computing the meaning of ⟦*likes Diana's brother*⟧, no such repeated interpretation of constants is involved in the computation of (155). Assume that reference to entities by regular interpretation is costly, especially for the addressee, whereas syntactic binding is cheap; as a consequence, (155) would be preferred over (154) if reference to the same person Diana is intended. Notice that under this argument, Condition C in the usual formulation is not required anymore (where the elimination of Condition C has been proposed by a number of authors, including Safir 2004). Adding discourse binding leads to a certain refinement of this argument: We can assume that reference to entities by regular interpretation is costly, reference to meanings expressed by salient discourse referent is cheaper, and syntactically bound variables are cheaper yet, especially for the addressee; speakers would factor these differences in the way how they formulate their propositions.

Acknowledgment: I gratefully acknowledge support by the DFG (Project *Syntax/Semantics Mismatches on Externally and Internally Headed Relative Clauses*) and by the Bundesminsterium für Bildung und Forschung (Projektförderung Zentrum für Allgemeine Sprachwissenschaft, Berlin, Förderkennzeichen 01UG0711). I would like to thank an anonymous reviewer and Mathias Schenner, Rainer Ludwig, Alex Grosu, Chris Barker, Pauline Jacobson, Uli Sauerland, Hubert Truckenbrodt, Ken Safir, Anthony Koch, Haihua Pan, as well as the audiences at presentations at ZAS (2011), at the University of Pennsylvania (2013) and at the Language and Culture University in Beijing (2015).

References

Barker, Chris. 2012. Quantificational binding does not require c-command. *Linguistic Inquiry* 43(4). 614–633. https://doi.org/10.1162/ling_a_00108.
Barker, Chris & Pauline Jacobson (eds.). 2007. *Direct compositionality* (Oxford Studies in Theoretical Linguistics). Oxford: Oxford University Press.
Bianchi, Valentina. 2004. Resumptive relatives and LF chains. In Luigi Rizzi (ed.), *The structure of CP and IP* (The Cartography of Syntactic Structures 2), 76–114. Oxford: Oxford University Press.
Cecchetto, Carlo. 2001. Syntactic or semantic reconstruction? Evidence from pseudoclefts and clitic left dislocation. In Carlo Cecchetto, Gennaro Chierchia & Maria Teresa Guasti (eds.), *Semantic interfaces: Reference, anaphora and aspect*, 90–144. Stanford: CSLI Publications.
Chomsky, Noam. 1993. A minimalist program for linguistic theory. In Kenneth Hale & Samuel Keyser (eds.), *The view from building 20: Essays in linguistics in honor of Sylvain Bromberger*, 1–52. Cambridge, MA: MIT Press.
Chomsky, Noam. 1995. *The minimalist program*. Cambridge, MA: MIT Press.
Corver, Norbert & Jairo Nunes (eds.). 2007. *The copy theory of movement*. Amsterdam: John Benjamins. https://doi.org/10.1075/la.107.
Dubinsky, Stanley & Robert Hamilton. 1998. Epithets as antilogophoric pronouns. *Linguistic Inquiry* 29. 685–693.
Elbourne, Paul. 2005. *Situations and individuals*. Cambridge, MA: MIT Press.
Evans, Gareth. 1980. Pronouns. *Linguistic Inquiry* 11. 337–362.
Fiengo, Robert & Robert May. 1994. *Indices and identity*. Cambridge, MA: MIT Press.
Fox, Danny. 1999. Reconstruction, binding theory, and the interpretation of chains. *Linguistic Inquiry* 30(2). 157–196.
Freidin, Robert. 1986. Fundamental issues in the theory of binding. In Barbara Lust (ed.), *Studies in the acquisition of anaphora*, 151–188. Dordrecht: Reidel.
Grodzinsky, Yosef & Tanya Reinhart. 1993. The innateness of binding and co-reference. *Linguistic Inquiry* 24. 69–101.
Grosu, Alexander & Manfred Krifka. 2007. *The gifted mathematician that you claim to be*: Equational intensional 'reconstruction' relatives. *Linguistics and Philosophy* 30. 445–485. https://doi.org/10.1007/s10988-008-9022-5.
Heim, Irene & Angelika Kratzer. 1998. *Semantics in generative grammar*. Oxford: Blackwell.
Hepple, Mark. 1990. *The grammar and processing of order and dependency: A categorial approach*. University of Edinburgh Doctoral dissertation.
Hestvik, Arild. 1995. Reflexives and ellipsis. *Natural Language Semantics* 3. 211–237.
Heycock, Caroline. 1995. Asymmetries in reconstruction. *Linguistic Inquiry* 26. 547–570.
Hulsey, Sarah & Uli Sauerland. 2006. Sorting out relative clauses. *Natural Language Semantics* 14. 111–137.
Jacobson, Pauline. 1999. Towards a variable-free semantics. *Linguistics and Philosophy* 22. 117–184.
Jacobson, Pauline. 2004. *Direct Compositionality: Is there any reason why not?* Workshop in Philosophy and Linguistics, University of Michigan. http://web.eecs.umich.edu/~rthomaso/lpw04/jacobson.pdf (10 October, 2018).
Kadmon, Nirit. 1987. *On unique and non-unique reference and asymmetric quantification*. Amherst, MA: University of Massachusetts Doctoral dissertation.

Kamp, Hans & Uwe Reyle. 1993. *From discourse to logic: Introduction to modeltheoretic semantics of natural language, formal logic and discourse representation theory*. Dordrecht: Kluwer. https://doi.org/10.1007/978-94-017-1616-1.
Kayne, Richard. 1994. *The antisymmetry of syntax*. Cambridge, MA: MIT Press.
Kuno, Susumu. 2006. Empathy and direct discourse perspectives. In Laurence R. Horn & Gregory Ward (eds.), *The handbook of pragmatics*, 315–343. Malden: Blackwell Publishing.
Lasnik, Howard. 1989. On the Necessity of Binding Conditions. In *Essays on Anaphora*, 149–167. Dordrecht: Kluwer. https://doi.org/10.1007/978-94-009-2542-7_9.
Lebeaux, David. 1990. Relative clauses, licensing and the nature of the derivation. In *Proceedings of NELS 20*, 318–332. Amherst, MA: GLSA, University of Massachusetts.
Munn, Alan. 1994. A Minimalist account of reconstruction asymmetries. In Mercè Gonzàlez (ed.), *Proceedings of NELS 24*, 397–410. Amherst, MA: GLSA.
Patel-Grosz, Pritty & Patrick Grosz. 2010. On the typology of donkeys: Two types of anaphora resolution. In Martin Prinzhorn, Viola Schmitt & Sarah Zobel (eds.), *Proceedings of Sinn und Bedeutung 14*, 339–355. Vienna.
Pollard, Carl & Ivan Sag. 1992. Anaphors in English and the scope of Binding Theory. *Linguistic Inquiry* 23. 261–303.
Reinhart, Tanya. 1983. Coreference and bound anaphora: A restatement of the anaphora questions. *Linguistics and Philosophy* 6(1). 47–88. https://doi.org/10.1007/BF00868090.
Riemsdijk, Henk van & Edwin Williams. 1981. NP structure. *The Linguistic Review* 1. 171–217.
Rooth, Mats. 1987. Noun phrase interpretation in Montague Grammar, File Change Semantics, and Situation Semantics. In Peter Gärdenfors (ed.), *Generalized quantifiers: Linguistic and logical approaches*, 237–268. Dordrecht: Kluwer.
Safir, Ken. 1999. Vehicle change and reconstruction in A'-chains. *Linguistic Inquiry* 30. 587–620.
Safir, Ken. 2004. *The syntax of anaphora*. Oxford: Oxford University Press.
Salzmann, Martin. 2006. Reconstruction for principle C in German relative clauses: In favor of the Matching Analysis. In Jakub Dotlačil & Berit Gehrke (eds.), *Proceedings of the second Syntax AiO meeting*, 65–79. Utrecht: UiL OTS Working Papers.
Sauerland, Uli. 1998. *The meaning of chains*. Cambridge, MA: Massachusetts Institute of Technology Doctoral dissertation.
Sauerland, Uli. 2000. *Obligatory reconstruction and the meaning of traces*. Arbeitspapiere des SFB 340, Bericht 153. Tübingen.
Sauerland, Uli. 2003. Unpronounced heads in relative clauses. In Kerstin Schwabe & Susanne Winkler (eds.), *The interfaces: Deriving and interpreting omitted structures*, 205–226. Amsterdam: John Benjamins.
Sells, Peter. 1987. Binding resumptive pronouns. *Linguistics and Philosophy* 10. 261–298.
Sharvit, Yael. 1999. Connectivity in specificational sentences. *Natural Language Semantics* 7. 299–339.
Sportiche, Dominique. 2006. Reconstruction, binding and scope. In Martin Everaert & Henk van Riemsdijk (eds.), *The Blackwell companion to syntax*, vol. 4, 35–93. Oxford: Blackwell.
Sportiche, Dominique. 2013. Binding theory — structure sensitivity of referential dependencies. *Lingua* 130. 187–208. https://doi.org/10.1016/j.lingua.2012.11.005.
Sternefeld, Wolfgang. 2001. Semantic vs. syntactic reconstruction. In Christian Rohrer, Antje Roßdeutscher & Hans Kamp (eds.), *Linguistic form and its computation*, 145–182. Stanford, CA: CSLI Publications.
Strigin, Anatoli. 1994. Topicalization, scrambling and argument scope in German: Integrating semantic and syntactic information. *Journal of Semantics* 11. 311–363.

Vergnaud, Jean-Roger. 1974. *French relative clauses*. Cambridge, MA: Massachusetts Institute of Technology Doctoral dissertation.

Walker, Marilyn A., Aravind K. Joshi & Ellen F. Prince (eds.). 1998. *Centering theory in discourse*. Oxford: Clarendon Press.

Winter, Yoad. 2004. Functional quantification. *Research on Language and Computation* 2. 331–363.

Yeom, Jae-Il. 1998. *A presuppositional analysis of specific indefinites: Common grounds as structured information states*. New York & London: Garland Publishing.

Vergnaud, [illegible] Cambridge [illegible]
[illegible]
Walker, [illegible]
[illegible]
Wheeler, [illegible] significance [illegible]
[illegible]
Yackel, E. [illegible] New York: [illegible]

Caroline Heycock

Relative reconstructions

Can we arrive at a unified picture?

1 Introduction

Reconstruction phenomena in relative clauses have been accruing at least since Schachter (1973). Among the most widely-cited, often as part of the evidence in favour of a "head-raising" analysis of relatives in which at least the NP "head" of the relative originates within the relative clause, are variable binding, anaphor binding, idiom interpretation, and low scope readings:

(1) a. The book on her_i desk that every $professor_i$ liked best concerned model theory. (Sauerland 1998)
   b. The portrait of $himself_i$ that $John_i$ painted is extremely flattering. (Schachter 1973)
   c. The headway that we made was satisfactory. (Schachter 1973)
   d. No linguist would read the many books Gina will need for vet school. (need > many) (Sauerland 1998, attributed to Irene Heim)

To these, Bhatt (2002) added the interpretation of certain nominal modifiers, including *only*, *first*, *last*, and other superlatives. Thus (2), from Bhatt (2002), can have a "low" reading where *first* is within the scope of *say*, alongside its "high" reading:

(2) the first book that John said Tolstoy had written
"High" reading: In 1990, John said that Tolstoy had written *Anna Karenina*; in 1991, John said that Tolstoy had written *War and Peace*. Hence the book referred to is *Anna Karenina* (i.e. order of *saying* matters, order of *writing* is irrelevant).
"Low" reading: John said that the first book that Tolstoy had written was *War and Peace*. Hence the book referred to is *War and Peace* (i.e. order of *writing* matters, order of *saying* is irrelevant).

Although Bhatt explicitly declined to treat as a case of reconstruction the reading of other adjectives (or even head nouns) where the description is taken as attributable

Caroline Heycock, University of Edinburgh

https://doi.org/10.1515/9783050095158-003

not to the speaker, but to the holder of some attitude mentioned in the relative, this move is made in Hulsey & Sauerland (2006), the source of the following example:

(3) The wonderful books that Siouxsie said that Lydia had written turned out to be just a bunch of one-page leaflets.

In the literature on reconstruction in questions, a central argument for reconstruction having a syntactic basis has been that reconstruction effects (in particular, scope reconstruction and the Binding Conditions) pattern together. As far as relative clauses are concerned, Sauerland (2003) discusses reconstruction for variable binding, idiom interpretion, and scope. He argues that in each case the reconstruction can be shown to interact with the Binding Conditions, more specifically Condition C (the requirement that an R-expression—a non-pronominal, non-quantificational noun phrase—should not be c-commanded by a coreferential noun phrase). This paper mainly aims to explore whether similar arguments can be made for the type of reconstruction effects exemplified in (2) and (3) above. I also revisit the interaction of idioms with Condition C, arriving at a rather different conclusion from the one in Sauerland (2003), and conclude with a preliminary discussion of how these results might be reconciled with those for the reconstruction phenomena that are not the focus of this paper (scope reconstruction and variable binding).

2 An argument that reconstruction is/can be syntactic

In the literature from the 1990s on reconstruction in questions, there was a debate concerning whether reconstruction should be a syntactic operation of some kind, or whether reconstructed readings could be delivered by some alternative means, given an appropriate type for the trace of movement (see for example Cresti 1990, Rullmann 1995, Sternefeld 2001). A crucial argument in favour of a syntactic treatment was that scope reconstruction feeds Condition C (Heycock 1995, Fox 1999).

As summarised by Fox: if reconstruction takes place in the syntax (whether by "undoing" movement, or by the choice to interpret a lower rather than a higher copy in a chain), scope reconstruction should be impossible in the structural configuration in (4) if pronoun$_1$ c-commands t_2.

(4) $[_{QP}$ ... R-expression$_1$ ... $]_2$ ... pronoun$_1$ ... t_2

If the QP is reconstructed to the position of the trace t_2 in some syntactic representation, this would bring the R-expression within the c-command domain of the coreferential pronoun, where it will induce a Condition C violation. Heycock and Fox argued that is exactly what happens—hence supporting the idea that reconstruction is a syntactic operation—as illustrated by the following paradigm.

(5) a. How many stories does she want you to invent t?
*(want > many; *many > want)*

b. How many stories does she want you to reinvent t?
(want > many; many > want)

(6) a. * [How many stories about $\text{Diana}_1]_2$ does she_1 want you to invent t_2?

b. [How many stories about $\text{Diana}_1]_2$ does she_1 want you to reinvent t_2?

High scope for the existential is anomalous with a verb of creation like *invent*, in contrast to a verb like *reinvent*. Hence only the low "reconstructed" scope is available with *invent*, as shown in (5a), while both readings are available with *reinvent* in (5b). As a result, the example in (6a) is an instance of the schema in (4), as illustrated in (7).

(7) $[_{QP}$ how many stories about $\text{Diana}_1\ ]_2$ ... does she_1 want you to invent t_2

That is, the only coherent interpretation for the existential quantifier in *how many stories about Diana* is one in which it is reconstructed to a position below *she*$_1$, bringing *Diana* within the c-command domain of the coreferential pronoun. As predicted, the result is a Condition C effect: coreference is indeed impossible.

The contrast between (6a) and (6b) (and other similar cases) thus shows that reconstruction feeds Condition C. Condition C has an irreducibly syntactic component, as evidenced by the role of c-command illustrated in (8).

(8) a. * She_i was unaware that Natasha_i had been denounced.

b. Her_i mother was unaware that Natasha_i had been denounced.

We now have evidence that the "reconstructed" low scope reading must also be due to the same syntactic configuration, and hence that reconstruction for scope takes place in the syntax.

The evidence for syntactic reconstruction just reviewed comes from *wh*-questions; Fox (1999) also presents data from A-movement in raising construction. Now our question is: can we find similar cases for the reconstruction effects in relative clauses that we are focussing on here? In the next section I will review a case that has been proposed (Bhatt 2002, Bhatt & Sharvit 2005) to have exactly these properties, involving the interaction of NPI licensing (also a phenomenon implicating c-command) and the "low" reading of superlatives. I will argue, however, that here the relevant evidence is at best consistent with syntactic reconstruction, rather than being an argument for it over available alternatives.

3 Interactions between reconstruction effects in relatives

3.1 NPIs, Neg-Raising, and low readings for superlatives and *only*

As discussed above, Bhatt (2002) proposed that the "low" readings for *only* and superlative adjectives (interpreted within the scope of a predicate inside the relative) are due to reconstruction of the noun+modifier(s). In a response to that work (Heycock 2005) I argued that this account leaves as a mystery the fact that the low readings are blocked in a range of environments, some of which are recapitulated below:

- Low reading blocked by intervening negation (Bhatt 2002):

(9) a. This is the first book that John didn't think that Antonia wrote. ≠
This is the book that John didn't think that Antonia wrote first.

b. That is the first book that few people said she read. ≠
That is the book that few people said she read first.

- Low reading blocked by intervening adverb:

(10) a. This is the first book that we mistakenly thought that Antonia had written. ≠
This is the book that we mistakenly thought that Antonia had written before writing all the other books.

b. This is the first book that people have occasionally thought that Antonia wrote. ≠
This is the book that people have occasionally thought that Antonia wrote before writing all the other books.

- Low reading unavailable with various predicates, including factives (11a), implicatives (11b), weak and strong (as opposed to midscalar) deontic operators (11c):

(11) a. That is the only book that I know she likes. ≠
That is the book that I know is the only one that she likes.

b. Those are the only people that he managed to insult. ≠
Those are the people such that he managed to insult only them (he successfully avoided insulting others).

c. That is the only offence that he could / needed to claim to have committed. ≠
That is the offence such that he could/needed to claim not to have committed an offence other than that.

The generalization proposed in Heycock (2005) was that the only environments that allow a "low" reading are those that support "Neg Raising" (NR).[1] The low reading then arises because of the "Excluded Middle" presupposition carried by NR predicates (Gajewski 2005). That is, if P is an NR predicate embedding a clause S, the Excluded Middle means that the following is necessarily true: $P(S) \vee P(\neg S)$. This informal proposal can be implemented as follows, borrowing from the exposition in Bhatt & Sharvit (2005): if *Anna Karenina* is the longest book that John believes Tolstoy wrote, there is a degree d such that John believes that *Anna Karenina* is d-long, but he doesn't believe of any other member of the comparison set that it is d-long. Because of the excluded middle presupposition, it follows that John believes that every member of the comparison set is shorter than *Anna Karenina*. This yields the low reading. Of relevance here is that this account does not rely on syntactic reconstruction of the head+modifier(s).

Bhatt & Sharvit (2005) present a counter-argument in favour of syntactic reconstruction that has exactly the property described in Section 2. That is, they argue that the low reading interacts with a phenomenon that, like Condition C, relies on c-command: Negative Polarity licensing. In this case, the relevant structure involves an NP relative head containing a downward-entailing modifier that in turn licenses an NPI within the relative. If the low reading (below the position of the NPI) for the head+modifier depends on syntactic reconstruction, it will be blocked in this configuration, since such reconstruction would bring the licensor of the NPI into a non-c-commanding position.

(12) $[_{NP}$ modifier$_{DE}$ N $]_1$ ... NPI ... t_1

1 The notable exception to this is that *say* also allows this reading, while it is not a Neg-raiser. In Heycock (2005) it is argued that this is possible just where *say* can be read as a kind of evidential, but Bhatt & Sharvit (2005), Hulsey & Sauerland (2006) take this exception to invalidate the generalization. Bhatt & Sharvit (2005) argue that there are other exceptions, such as *hope* and *agree*, but here their judgments and mine differ; this remains a matter for more thorough empirical investigation.

In the relevant examples, the downward-entailing modifier that licenses the NPI is a superlative; the NPI is *ever*:

(13) $[_{NP}$ ADJ-est_{DE} N $]_1$ ... *ever* ... t_1

Bhatt & Sharvit (2005) show that in this configuration the low reading for the superlative is indeed unavailable; that is, reconstruction is blocked. The scenarios in (14) are set up to show a truth-conditional difference between low and high readings for the superlative *longest* in the noun phrase *the longest book that John said Tolstoy had written*:

(14) *Anna Karenina* is the longest book that John said Tolstoy had written.
Scenario A ("High" reading true, "Low" reading false):
John: "Tolstoy wrote *Huckleberry Finn*, *Anna Karenina* and *Tom Sawyer*. *Tom Sawyer* is the longest of these."
Anna Karenina is actually the longest among those books.

Scenario B ("High" reading false, "Low" reading true):
John: "*Anna Karenina* is the longest book Tolstoy wrote. He also wrote *War and Peace* and some other shorter books."
War and Peace is actually longer than Anna Karenina.

Bhatt and Sharvit then point out that when the NPI *ever* is in the embedded clause within the relative—as in (15)—only the low reading is possible. Conversely, and more crucially, when *ever* is in the higher clause within the relative—as in (16)—only the high reading is possible.

(15) *Anna Karenina* is the longest book that John said Tolstoy had ever written.
High reading: *; Low reading: OK

(16) *Anna Karenina* is the longest book that John ever said Tolstoy had written.
High reading: OK; Low reading: *

Bhatt and Sharvit give an explanation for the absence of the high reading when the NPI is in the embedded clause, as in (15), in terms of the pragmatic theory of NPI licensing of Kadmon & Landman (1993). It should be noted that given this explanation, the licensing of the NPI and the unambiguous low reading for the superlative are compatible with syntactic reconstruction, but they do not actually require it.[2]

---

2 This account differs from the earlier proposal in Bhatt (2002) that the unambiguous low reading in this context is due to a locality requirement on the licensing of *ever*; see Heycock (2005) for discussion of that proposal.

The absence of the low reading when the NPI is in a higher clause in the relative, as in (16), on the other hand, *does* depend on syntactic reconstruction on Bhatt and Sharvit's account. The proposal is that the low reading is lacking because the superlative that is the licensor for the NPI *ever* would no longer c-command it from the reconstructed position. Thus Bhatt and Sharvit argue that this is evidence for syntactic reconstruction, and hence evidence against the proposal in Heycock (2005). And the same argument would extend to any proposal that did not involve syntactic reconstruction of the licensing superlative to a position below the NPI. Their essential point is that unless the low reading involves syntactic reconstruction there is no explanation for the absence of the low reading in examples like (16).

However, a consideration of a wider range of facts shows that it is not only the NPI *ever* that prevents the low reading. The same effect arises if we substitute pretty much any adverb, e.g. *once*, *occasionally*, or even *mistakenly*, *foolishly* or *confidently*, as illustrated in (17)—and see also (10) above.

(17) *Anna Karenina* is the longest book that John/people {once / occasionally / mistakenly / foolishly / confidently} said/thought Tolstoy had written.
High reading: OK; Low reading: *

This is as expected if the low reading arises from the same mechanism that underlies NR, since NR is also blocked by these interveners, as shown in (18). An account of this effect in NR is given in Hegarty (2013).

(18) a. No one thought [that Tolstoy would publish until he got an advance].
b. * No one {once / occasionally / mistakenly / foolishly / confidently} thought [that Tolstoy would publish until he got an advance].

On the other hand, it is not clear why reconstruction should be blocked by intervening adverbs; certainly for the ones just cited there is no possible account in terms of a requirement for licensing by the putatively reconstructed element. We may also note that it has been independently observed that *ever* blocks NR (Lakoff 1969, Prince 1976, Gajewski 2005). (19) is from Lakoff (1969), cited in Gajewski (2005: 19):

(19) * I didn't ever think that Bill would leave until tomorrow.

But if this is the case, the NR account does predict that the low reading will be unavailable in (15). Thus the lack of the low reading in this configuration, while compatible with a syntactic reconstruction account (as we have seen) no longer constitutes evidence for it.

3.2 Low readings for superlatives and *only* and the interaction with Binding Conditions

One possible way to reconcile the constraints on the low reading pointed out in Heycock (2005) with a syntactic account of these reconstruction effects in relatives would be to posit that the low reading requires both syntactic reconstruction and whatever mechanism is responsible for NR readings (Bhatt & Iatridou 2012). That hypothesis would be completely consistent with what we have seen so far. However, since even under this revised hypothesis the low reading involves syntactic reconstruction, we expect it to correlate with other phenomena.

First, we can investigate the interaction of postulated superlative reconstruction with Condition C instead of with NPI licensing. For this we need a case in which the NP containing the modifier that is getting a low reading also contains material that would induce a Condition C violation in the reconstructed position. This is again a version of the configuration in (4).

(20) $[_{NP}$ superlative/*only* ... R-expression$_1$ ... $]_2$ ... pronoun$_1$ ... t_2

The prediction is thus that the examples in (21), which have only the low reading for *best*/*only*, should be ungrammatical with the coindexation, as instances of the schema in (20).

(21) a. That is the best picture of Moss$_i$ that she$_i$ thought she would ever see.
b. That is the only picture of Kahlo$_i$ that she$_i$ thought her mother would ever be willing to have in the house.

They should contrast both with (22), where (only) the "high" reading for the NP+modifier is available, and with (23), where the pronoun would not c-command the reconstructed NP. The prediction does not, however, seem to be borne out; the examples in (21) are not degraded with respect to their counterparts in (22) and (23).

(22) a. That is the best picture of Moss$_i$ that she$_i$ ever thought she would see.
b. That is the only picture of Kahlo$_i$ that she$_i$ ever thought her mother would be willing to have in the house.

(23) a. That is the best picture of Moss$_i$ that her$_i$ agent thinks they will ever find.
b. That is the only picture of Kahlo$_i$ that her$_i$ mother thought they should ever have in the house.

We find the same lack of correlation with the Binding Conditions if we consider reflexives. It was already noted in Heycock (2005) that reflexive binding by an antecedent within the relative—like idiom interpretation and variable binding—is not restricted to NR environments, in contrast to the low interpretation of *only* and superlatives. In all the examples in (24) there is some element in the relative that we know prevents the creation of an NR environment—the negative in (24a), the quantifier *few* in (b), the verb *deny* in (c) (see the discussion at the beginning of Section 3.1 relating to examples (9)–(11)). Hence the low reading for a modifier in these cases would not be possible (and indeed the only reading for *only* in (24a) is the high one). But the binding of the anaphor *himself* in (24a), the interpretation of the idiom in (b), and the binding of the pronoun in (c) by the universal quantifier *every* are all possible, and all suggest that reconstruction in this context *is* available.

(24) a. This is the only picture of himself$_i$ that Mary didn't think John$_i$ should show to his mother.

b. That is the kind of headway that few people thought we would be able to make.

c. The picture of his$_i$ mother that every boy$_i$ denied even existed was always discovered eventually in some drawer.

However, if the low readings for *only*/superlatives depend on NR in *addition* to reconstruction, this is not necessarily problematic; the examples in (24) would all involve reconstruction even though the low reading for *only*/superlative would be ruled out by the additional requirement for an NR environment.

What is still unexpected is that reflexive binding from outside the relative can co-exist with the low reading of *only* or a superlative. That is, the prediction is that (26b) should be ungrammatical, contrasting both with (26a) (different only in having a non-reflexive pronoun) and with (25b) (different only in not requiring reconstruction, under the assumptions of Bhatt 2002, Bhatt & Sharvit 2005). This prediction that there should be a "trapping effect" induced by the relative-external antecedent for the anaphor is not borne out: (26b) does not appear less grammatical than its counterparts where there is no putative conflict between the low reading for the modifier and external binding for the reflexive.

(25) a. I finally saw the only/best picture of me that John has ever painted.

b. I finally saw the only/best picture of myself that John has ever painted.

(26) a. I finally saw the only/best picture of me that my mother thinks John has ever painted.

b. I finally saw the only/best picture of myself that my mother thinks John has ever painted.

Similarly, (27) is grammatical even though the adverb *ever* forces a high reading of the superlative, while the reflexive has to be bound by an element that only c-commands the low, reconstructed position:

(27) That is the only/first picture of himself$_1$ that I ever thought Freud$_1$ might sell.

A possible counter to the evidence concerning reflexives is that it is by now well-known that reflexives quite frequently allow binding without c-command; this point is already made in Bhatt's original work, and has also been stressed, again specifically with respect to the use of reflexive binding as a diagnostic for reconstruction, in Bianchi (2000), Cecchetto (2006), Donati & Cecchetto (2011), among others. This counterargument is perhaps weakened by the acceptability of examples like (28), where the anaphor is a reciprocal rather than a reflexive—reciprocals are not generally considered to allow the kind of logophoric binding that may account for some cases of non-c-commanded reflexives, although see Pollard & Sag (1992: 264) and Reinhart & Reuland (1993: footnote 7) for evidence that even reciprocals do not require c-command:[3]

(28) They$_i$ showed me the best pictures of each other$_i$ that I believe we will ever see.

Even if we do accept this alternative account for the grammaticality of e.g. (26b) and (27), of course this comes at the cost of removing reflexive (and reciprocal) binding as evidence for syntactic reconstruction. The conflict with the evidence from Condition C also remains.

3.3 De dicto readings (low binding of world variables)

As discussed above, Hulsey & Sauerland (2006) argue that *de dicto* readings of modifiers and even of the nouns heading relative clauses should be handled by syntactic reconstruction—in fact, as they treat these readings as arising through binding of a world variable associated with the relevant item, this is just a special case of scope reconstruction.

Again unlike the low readings for *only* and superlatives, *de dicto* readings are not restricted to NR contexts:

(29) That is the last/biggest picture that I fervently hope he will paint.
No low interpretation for *last/biggest*

(30) The beautiful picture that I fervently hope he will paint may never come to be.

3 The example in (28) should, on the other hand, freely allow a reading where the reciprocal is bound, under reconstruction, by *we*. I find this reading hard to get; certainly it is not more prominent than the one where it is bound by matrix *they*.

In (30) the modifier *beautiful* and even the noun *picture* would, I assume, be taken to have *de dicto* readings involving scope-taking below the predicate *hope*; but as (29) shows, the intervening adverb *fervently* blocks low readings for superlatives.

As with *only* and superlatives we should however ask whether these *de dicto* readings force Condition C violations, and/or block anaphor binding by a higher antecedent.[4] Again the answer appears to be no. The example in (31) would be predicted to yield a Condition C violation if the NP including the modifier *flattering* has to be reconstructed below *hear* if it is to get the *de dicto* reading that the context requires, but it appears grammatical even with the coreference:[5]

(31) The "flattering" portrait of Moss_1 that she_1 heard Hirst had painted shocked her when she actually saw it, it made her look so ugly.

The contrasts that need to be considered as far as the interaction of *de dicto* readings and reflexive binding is concerned are exemplified in (32)–(35). The crucial prediction if reflexive-binding and *de dicto* readings in relatives depend on syntactic reconstruction is that the examples in (35) should contrast with all the others, since the external binder for the reflexive and the *de dicto* reading for the head NP would prevent and require reconstruction, respectively.

---

4 It would also be nice to be able to test the interaction of low readings for *only*/superlatives with *de dicto* readings. However, it turns out that nothing can be concluded from such a comparison. As binding of world variables is not local, de dicto readings are not expected to be obligatory even if there is reconstruction, so there is no prediction that the low reading of e.g. a superlative should force a *de dicto* reading. Conversely, if high readings for *only*/superlatives may arise not because of a failure of reconstruction but because NR conditions are not met, the possible *de dicto* reading for an example like (i) with a high reading for the superlative is also not excluded.

(i) That was the last attack on the Queen that they ever accused me of having planned.

5 Hulsey & Sauerland (2006) argue that the "scare quote" intonation favoured in examples like (31) arises when there is contra-indexing of world variables between the head noun and the adjective. I do not think that the results concerning interaction with Conditions A and C are any different if there is no such contra-indexing, however; the following examples seem to me on a par with (31) and (35).

(i) a. When I heard about the portrait of Moss_1 that she_1 thought her agent was commissioning from Hirst, I was very surprised. And indeed, it turned out that what was commissioned was something completely nonfigurative.

b. When I learned about the portrait of myself that my sister said she was about to start painting, I was very surprised. And indeed, it turned out, as I suspected, that she was actually planning something completely nonfigurative.

(32) No binding; no adjective to reconstruct

a. I saw the portrait of me that my sister said she had taken a year to paint, and I loved it.

b. When Will saw the portrait of him that Freud claimed to have spent a year painting, he was not that impressed.

(33) External binding; no adjective to reconstruct

a. I saw the portrait of myself that my sister said she taken a year to paint, and I loved it.

b. When Will saw the portrait of himself that Freud claimed to have spent a year painting, he was not that impressed.

(34) No binding; reconstruction for adjective interpretation

a. I saw the 'flattering' portrait of me that my sister said she had painted, and thought it made me look like a witch!

b. When Will saw the 'sympathetic' portrait of him that Freud claimed to have painted, he almost blew a fuse.

(35) *External binding; reconstruction for adjective interpration*

a. I saw the 'flattering' portrait of myself that my sister said she had painted, and thought it made me look like a witch!

b. When Will saw the 'sympathetic' portrait of himself that Freud claimed to have painted, he almost blew a fuse.

In my own judgment, the examples in (35) are not appreciably worse than their counterparts without the conflict, even with the relevant reading where the modifier is attributed to the embedded subject (*my sister* and *Freud*).

In order to get some sense of how representative my own judgments are, I also constructed a questionnaire that included these examples, and collated responses from 21 participants (all linguists, from various subfields, but none to my knowledge working on this issue). The items of interest were mixed with fillers, and presented in a randomized order; there was a minimum amount of counterbalancing, in that there were two versions of the questionnaire, such that no one saw the minimal pair of the same example differing only as to the presence of a reflexive/non-reflexive pronoun. Because there were two versions of the questionnaire, each example was seen by between 9 and 11 participants. The participants were asked to judge the acceptability of the sentences on a scale of 1–5, with 5 being completely acceptable, and 1 being completely unacceptable. A graph showing the mean ratings is given in Figure 1.

I do not present any figures for significance given the small number of participants, but the means appear consistent, at least, with my own judgment that

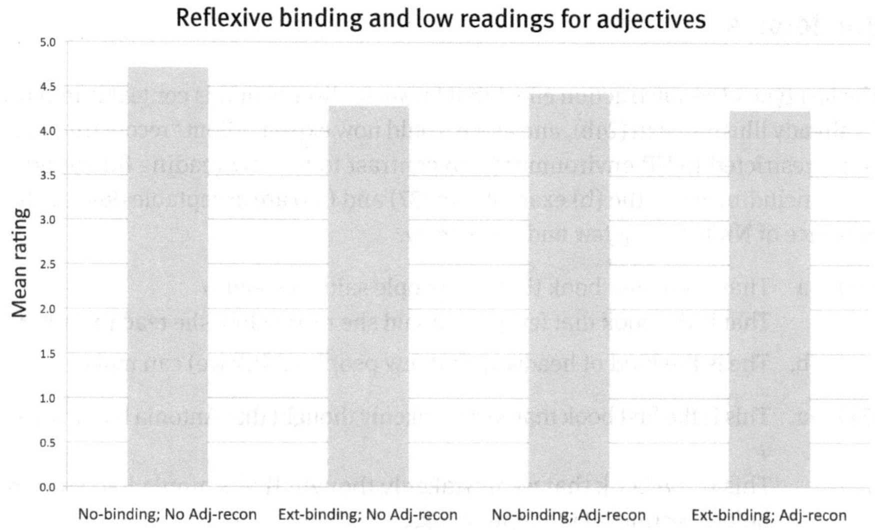

Fig. 1: Interaction of reflexive binding and low reading for adjectives

a conflict between a "reconstructed" *de dicto* reading and a non-reconstructed anaphor-binding does not engender ungrammaticality. This conflict would arise only in the last case (*External Binding; Reconstruction for Adjective*, illustrated in (35) above); thus if this was a syntactic conflict examples of this last type ought to be judged less acceptable than the other three cases. But this is not what we see in Figure 1: the judgments for this case are on a par with all the others.

In Heycock (2005) I argued that the *de dicto* readings were probably not a good diagnostic for reconstruction since apparently very similar readings can be licensed without the syntactic environment that has been crucially assumed to be required in the relative examples, as illustrated in (36):

(36) a. When I saw the 'flattering' portrait of me by my sister, I was furious: she made me look like a witch!

b. Freud's 'sympathetic' portrait of Will was really a hatchet job, in my opinion.

See also Harris & Potts (2009) on non-speaker oriented readings of expressives outside attitude predications. So here again we have the situation that we can defuse the apparently wrong predictions of a syntactic reconstruction account, but again we have to jettison *de dicto* readings as a source of evidence in favour of such an account.

3.4 Idioms

The last type of reconstruction effect that I want to discuss in this context is idioms. As already illustrated in (24b), and as we would now expect, idiom "reconstruction" is not restricted to NR environments, in contrast to the low reading for superlatives (including *first*): the (b) examples in (37) and (38) are acceptable despite the presence of NR-blocking *few* and *mistakenly*.

(37) a. That is the first book that few people said she read. ≠
That is the book that few people said she read before she read the others.
b. The is the kind of headway that few people (think we) can make.

(38) a. This is the first book that we mistakenly thought that Antonia had written. ≠
This is the book that we mistakenly thought that Antonia had written before writing all the other books.
b. We were foolishly delighted by the headway that we mistakenly thought we had made.

It is worth noting that idioms can also be used to argue for the availability of a non-head-raising analysis, given that e.g. *headway* can equally be licensed by the relative-external context (Bhatt 2002: 47):[6]

(39) a. We made headway that was sufficient.
b. She kept the kind of tabs on him that would not have disgraced Philip Marlowe.

For a much more detailed discussion of the relevance of idioms to the analysis of relatives, and the problems that they pose for the head-raising analysis, see Webelhuth et al. (this volume).

Given the limited flexibility of idioms, not every possible interaction can be tested. If *take pictures* is treated as an idiom, as for example in Sauerland (2003), we can however again test the hypothesis that relatives built on it should not allow external binding of a reflexive:

(40) Lucy$_i$ admired the picture of herself$_i$ on the beach that Bill had taken with his ancient polaroid camera.

6 The correct analysis of NPs with *kind* is not at all obvious; see Zamparelli (1998) for one account, the full ramifications of which for this type of relative clause there is not space to go into here. Discussions of idiom interpretation and reconstruction are also often quite nonspecific about at exactly which point of the derivation the idiom has to form a "unit."

(40) seems to me completely unobjectionable with the indicated coreference, despite the predicted trapping effect from the upstairs binding of the reflexive.

What about Condition C? My judgment is that (41) is acceptable, despite the fact that idiom interpretation is predicted to require reconstruction of the head NP *headway on Lucy's problem* to a position where it would be c-commanded by *she*:

(41) This represents the only headway on Lucy$_i$'s problem that she$_i$ thinks they have made so far.

The judgment that (41) shows no Condition C effect appears to be in conflict both with the data and conclusions of Sauerland (2003), where the following minimal pair is presented as evidence of idiom interpretation inducing a Condition C violation:

(42) a. * The headway on Mary$_i$'s project she$_i$ had made pleased the boss.
b. The headway on her$_i$ project Mary$_i$ had made pleased the boss.

Bhatt & Iatridou (2012) add a variant of the example in (41) that makes it more parallel to the one in (42a); they judge this example to be unacceptable with coreference, and to contrast with (41).[7]

(43) * This represents the only headway on Lucy$_i$'s problem that they think she$_i$ has made so far.

Bhatt and Iatridou suggest a generalization that the disjoint reference effect appears only when the pronoun and the R-expression are clausemates under reconstruction. They point out that this suggests a Condition-B style explanation, but note that this does not sit easily with the grammaticality of (44).

(44) She$_i$ has made headway on her$_i$ project.

An alternative, however, is that constructions where the object nominal denotes something that is inalienably connected to the subject (a person making headway, or progress for that matter, makes only their own headway/progress, not someone else's), the object may include a PRO possessor that is obligatorily bound to the subject. This PRO will always induce a Condition C effect with a co-referential nominal inside the idiom.[8]

---

7 In the handout of Bhatt & Iatridou (2012) the example is annotated with the asterisk in parentheses, but the text indicates that the authors consider that the example does not allow coreference, like (42a) and in conrast to (41).

8 In a footnote, Sauerland (2003) in fact mentions exactly this possibility, attributed to Chomsky (1986: 167); it was also raised by Edwin Williams with respect to discussion of reconstruction in questions (see Heycock 1995: 558 for discussion).

(45) * [PRO$_i$ headway on Lucy$_i$'s problem]

If the binding of PRO itself does not require syntactic reconstruction, this would make the correct predictions for the cases we have just been considering. (41) does not show a disjoint reference effect between *Lucy* and *she* if reconstruction for idiom interpretation is not forced, because the PRO within the fronted NP is bound not by *she*, but by *they*; in the examples in (42a) and (43) on the other hand the fronted NP would carry with it a PRO bound by *she* that would induce the Condition C violation. And examples like (45) would also be expected to be grammatical, just as an example like (46) is grammatical.

(46) She$_i$ has made her$_i$ usual headway on her$_i$ project.

There is thus in fact no conflict between the data in (41) and those presented in Sauerland (2003). However, the analysis suggested above would conflict with the conclusions drawn in that paper: the analysis only accounts for the data if syntactic reconstruction is *not* required for idiom interpretation (otherwise nothing could rescue (41)), so that the ungrammaticality of (42a) and (43) is again explained without syntactic reconstruction.

4 Reconstruction effects and extraposition

In the last section we have considered some cases where a reconstruction effect is predicted to be absent because of a conflict with some other requirement internal to the relative. Hulsey & Sauerland (2006) argue that there is another context in which reconstruction effects should be absent: relative extraposition. They assume an analysis of head-raised relatives and of extraposition that would make these two phenomena incompatible; hence, they argue, only the "matching" analysis is available for such cases. Their examples in (47)–(52), as reported in Hulsey & Sauerland (2006), bear out this prediction and hence constitute an indirect argument that many relatives are derivationally ambiguous:

- Idioms:

  (47) a. Mary praised the headway that John made.
  b. Mary praised the potroast that John made.

  (48) a. * Mary praised the headway yesterday that John made.
  b. Mary praised the potroast yesterday that John made.

– Reflexive binding:

(49) a. I saw the picture of himself$_i$ that John$_i$ liked.
b. I saw the picture of Clinton that John liked.

(50) a. * I saw the picture of himself$_i$ yesterday that John$_i$ liked.
b. I saw the picture of Clinton yesterday that John liked.

– Superlatives:

(51) a. I read the first novel that John said that Tolstoy had ever written.
b. I read the first novel that John ever said that Tolstoy had written.

(52) a. * I read the first novel last week that John said that Tolstoy had ever written.
b. I read the first novel last week that John ever said that Tolstoy had written.

Again here I believe that the judgments are very delicate. The questionnaire already mentioned therefore included examples that were intended to explore this paradigm further, involving *de dicto* readings of modifiers, idioms (with an attempt to make the comparison with non-idiomatic readings as minimal as possible), and anaphor binding (here simply recapitulating the paradigm in (49)–(50) but with different examples).

– De dicto (reconstruction) / De re (no reconstruction) readings of adjectives

(53) No reconstruction; Relative in situ
a. Yesterday I read the savage review that you told me Smith had written, and to be honest I thought it should never have been printed.
b. This morning I did a read-through of the 30,000-word thesis that your student claimed to have written without assistance, and I'm afraid it looked suspiciously familiar.

(54) No reconstruction; Relative extraposed
a. I read the savage review yesterday that you told me Smith had written, and to be honest I thought it should never have been printed.
b. I did a read-through of the 30,000-word thesis this morning that your student claimed to have written without assistance, and I'm afraid it looked suspiciously familiar.

(55) Reconstruction; Relative in situ

a. Yesterday I read the 'savage review' that you told me Smith had written, and actually I thought it was quite fair.

b. This morning I did a word-count of the '30,000 word thesis' that your student claimed to have submitted, and it came in at 40,000 words.

(56) *Reconstruction; Relative extraposed*

a. I read the 'savage review' yesterday that you told me Smith had written, and actually I thought it was quite fair.

b. I did a word count of the '30,000-word thesis' this morning that your student claimed to have submitted, and it came in at 40,000 words.

– Anaphor binding (reconstruction) / pronominal (no reconstruction)

(57) No reconstruction; Relative in situ

a. I had to laugh when I read this morning the anecdote about his wife that he put in his column.

b. I love Tracey's work! I was so pleased when at last I got to see the sketch of a tiger that she had once painted on the wall of her house.

(58) No reconstruction; Relative extraposed

a. I had to laugh when I read the anecdote about his wife this morning that he put in his column.

b. I love Tracey's work! I was so pleased when I got to see the sketch of a tiger at last that she had once painted on the wall of her house.

(59) Reconstruction; Relative in situ

a. I had to laugh when I read this morning the anecdote about himself that he put in his column.

b. I love Tracey's work! I was so pleased when at last I got to see the sketch of herself that she had once painted on the wall of her house.

(60) *Reconstruction; Relative extraposed*

a. I had to laugh when I read the anecdote about himself this morning that he put in his column.

b. I love Tracey's work! I was so pleased when I got to see the sketch of herself at last that she had once painted on the wall of her house.

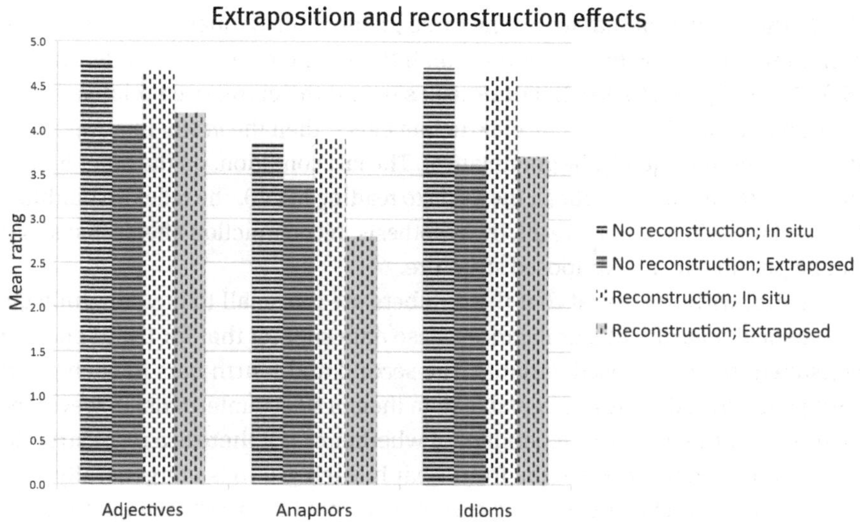

Fig. 2: Interaction of extraposition and reconstruction effects

– Idioms (reconstruction) / nonidioms (no reconstruction)

(61) No reconstruction; Relative in situ
   a. Describe to me all the habits that you dislike in a partner.
   b. Describe to me the progress that you observed.

(62) No reconstruction; Relative extraposed
   a. Describe all the habits to me that you dislike in a partner.
   b. Describe the progress to me that you observed.

(63) Reconstruction; Relative in situ
   a. Describe to me all the habits that you want to kick.
   b. Describe to me the headway that you think you have made this year.

(64) *Reconstruction; Relative extraposed*
   a. Describe all the habits to me that you want to kick.
   b. Describe the headway to me that you think you have made this year.

The means from the 21 participants (9–12 for each example, as there were two different versions of the questionnaire) are given in Figure 2. The crucial assumptions of Hulsey and Sauerland are (a) that these three phenomena derive from syntactic reconstruction within a raising structure for relatives and (b) that the raising structure is unavailble in extraposed relatives. These assumptions derive the prediction that for all the three phenomena in question the first three conditions should be fully grammatical. If there is no reconstruction effect, as in (53)/(54), (57)/(58), (61)/(62), both the *in situ* and the extraposed relative should be grammatical. If there is a reconstruction effect, then the *in situ* relatives in (55), (59), (63) should, equally, be grammatical. The last condition, on the other hand, is predicted to be ungrammatical; the *de dicto* reading in (56), the reflexive binding in (60) and the idiom in (64) are all, by hypothesis, reconstruction effects that should not be possible in an extraposed structure.

Again, with the caveat that the numbers are too small to meaningfully give a statistical measure of significance, these data suggest that for the 21 speakers consulted, the extraposed variants (the second and fourth bars in each group) were generally judged less acceptable than their *in situ* counterparts. However they also suggest that this is independent of whether or not there is a reconstruction effect in the relative clause: the fourth bar in each group is not generally lower than the second. The one possible exception is that the extraposed relatives with reflexives—(60)—were judged worse than would be expected on the basis of similar sentences with no issue of reflexive binding—(58)—or with the relatives *in situ*—(59). The reflexive data are therefore to some extent at least consistent with the data and discussion in Hulsey & Sauerland (2006); this deserves to be looked at more carefully, given that we have up to now seen that we might want rather to assume that reflexive binding in relatives is not dependent on syntactic reconstruction. Given that we have also seen that *de dicto* readings are available rather freely, the fact that they persist in extraposition is not surprising (but may be interpreted as further evidence that such readings cannot be treated as evidence for syntactic reconstruction).

What can we make of the discrepancy between the data for idioms in Hulsey & Sauerland (2006), repeated here as (65)–(66), which the authors argue crucially show a degradation when a relative headed by part of an idiom is extraposed, and the idiom cases in (61)–(64) in the questionnaire, where there did not seem to be such an effect?

(65) a. Mary praised the headway that John made.
b. Mary praised the potroast that John made.

(66) a. * Mary praised the headway yesterday that John made.
b. Mary praised the potroast yesterday that John made.

One possibility is that there is more going on in (65)–(66) than just a contrast between idiomatic and non-idiomatic heads. It is relatively easy to accommodate a concrete, non-relational definite like *the potroast*; the non-idiomatic heads in the questionnaire (*habits* and *progress*) were chosen to be more like the idiomatic heads in not being concrete and being hard to accommodate without a rich context. Compare the naturalness of (67a) to the awkwardness out of context of (67b–c):

(67) a. Mary praised the potroast.
b. Mary praised the habits. (*cf.* Mary praised his/these habits.)
c. Mary praised the progress. (*cf.* Mary praised his/this progress.)

Thus it could be that there is some kind of garden-path effect when we reach what could be the end of the sentence (*yesterday*) without having been able to even begin to resolve the reference of a definite object. But if there is such an effect, it would mean that we do not have to attribute the degradation in (66a) to failure of idiom reconstruction in particular. This is of course only speculation, but it points to a need for particularly careful investigation of the delicate judgments that form the empirical basis for reconstruction analyses.

5 Directions

In our investigation of reconstruction effects in relatives thus far we have seen that

- Reconstruction for anaphor binding, *de dicto* readings for heads and modifiers, and idiom interpretation can be to positions where low readings for *only* and superlatives are excluded.
- Low readings for *only* and superlatives, *de dicto* readings for heads and modifiers, and idiom interpretation do not induce Condition C effects or disrupt "high" binding of anaphors.
- Extraposition does not exclude idiom interpretation (arguably) or *de dicto* readings.

In earlier discussions of reconstruction effects in interrogatives, Condition C effects (obviation effects with full noun phrases) were crucially relied on as evidence for syntactic reconstruction because of the structural component in the defining configuration for Condition C. Alternative analyses of reconstruction in terms of higher order traces could capture e.g. scope reconstruction, but not the association with the syntactic effect. Condition A effects (anaphor binding) could in principle have been used in the same way, but the non-structural aspects of at least reflexive binding make such data more problematic.

As far as reconstruction effects in relatives are concerned, Sauerland (2003), Hulsey & Sauerland (2006) are more inclined to rely on both types of data. They take the fact that, in relatives, reconstruction for Condition A is possible, while reconstruction for (violation of) Condition C is not in general forced, as evidence for two possible derivations for relatives: a "matching" analysis, in which the mechanism of vehicle change predicts the absence of Condition C effect, and a "raising" analysis.

(68) a. I met the friend of $Lucy_i$'s that she_i admires most.
b. I saw the picture of $herself_i$ that $Lucy_i$ admires most.

A central part of this argument, however, is that there are contexts in which only the raising derivation analysis is available and in which reconstruction is forced: in such contexts, they argue Condition C effects emerge even in relative clauses.

As we have seen however, and as just summarised, Condition C effects seem to be absent from relative clauses even in contexts where they are predicted to appear, if the low scope of superlatives and *only*, *de dicto* readings, and idiom interpretation are all diagnostic for syntactic reconstruction. On the other hand, Sauerland (2003) has argued that Condition C effects always accompany two other diagnostics for syntactic reconstruction, low scope and variable binding.[9] The examples in (69) and (70), with the judgments, are cited from that paper:

(69) a. * The many books for $Gina_i$'s vet school that she_i needs will be expensive. (need > many)
b. * The few coins from $Bill_i$'s pocket he_i could spare weren't enough for all the needy. (could > few)

(70) a. * The letters by $John_i$ to her_j that he_i told every $girl_j$ to burn were published.
b. The letters by him_i to her_j that $John_i$ told every $girl_j$ to burn were published.

If we can rely on the distinction between the two sets of putative reconstruction effects—on the one hand, low scope of superlatives and *only*, *de dicto* readings, and idiom interpretation, and on the other low scope readings for quantified heads (e.g. with *many*, *few*) and the bound variable reading of pronouns—this gives us a nicely differentiated empirical landscape against which to develop our theories of the syntax-semantics interface. In particular, we would want to have a theory where only the second subset of "reconstruction" effects actually derives from syntactic reconstruction, and where the first subset can be derived in some other way or way(s); some possibilities have been suggested in the text.

However, it seems to me that some caution is required, as the empirical foundation for this distinction is based on judgments that are extremely delicate. As

9 As discussed above, Sauerland actually makes this claim also for idiom interpretation; as these data have already been discussed above I set this aside here.

indicated, the questionnaire data that I gathered with respect to some of the phenomena in this paper remain limited; if any of the judgments appear questionable to the reader, further investigation would be very welcome. With respect to the data concerning reconstructed bound variable readings and low scope both inducing Condition C effects, I find the judgments very difficult. For example, I agree that (70a) is severely degraded; what is less clear to me however is whether it is worse than a minimally contrasting example without scope reconstruction:

(71) The letters by John$_i$ to her$_j$ that he$_i$ told my sister$_j$ to burn were published.

The interaction of scope reconstruction in relatives with Condition C poses similar challenges. As just discussed, Sauerland (2003) provides the examples in (69) as evidence that scope reconstruction has the same effect of inducing Condition C violations as is also found in amount questions. On the other hand, Bhatt & Iatridou (2012) point out a possible contrast between amount questions and corresponding relatives. The correlation between the low scope reading and Condition C in the amount question is illustrated in (72). Bhatt and Iatridou suggest that there may not be a parallel correlation in the corresponding relative in (73); crucially, it is not clear that there is a disjoint reference (Condition C) effect in (73a).

(72) a. * [How many stories about Diana$_1$]$_2$ does she$_1$ want you to invent t$_2$?
b. [How many stories about Diana$_1$]$_2$ does she$_1$ want you to reinvent t$_2$? (only *many* > *want*)

(73) a. The five stories about Diana$_i$ that she$_i$ wants you to invent are five too many for any self-respecting journalist!
(non-specific five stories)
b. The five stories about Diana$_i$ that she$_i$ wants you to reinvent are the ones that are politically the most explosive.
(specific five stories)

It is hard to imagine a theory that will make a different prediction for (73a) and (69a). So we may well first want to try to find ways to test the relevant effects and configurations even more thoroughly and systematically. As Bhatt and Iatridou indicate, if there is indeed a difference between questions and relatives, then not only do we need a mechanism that will deliver the correct scope reading without syntactic reconstruction, we need to be able to block its application in questions.[10]

To conclude: this paper has been an attempt to pull together some of the diverse "reconstruction effects" that have been adduced for relative clauses, and

10 Bhatt and Iatridou point out that a disjoint reference effect does seem to obtain even in relatives when the gap in the relative is a clause-mate of the coreferential pronoun, a similar phenomenon to the effect they pointed out for idioms (see Section 3.4).

to check whether or not they correlate, as predicted if they are all underlain by a single mechanism of syntactic reconstruction.[11] We have seen that this is not in fact the case for all hypothesized reconstruction effects. What remains to be firmly established is whether there is a remaining well-defined set of cases that do behave as predicted by a syntactic account of reconstruction, and whether we already have the alternative mechanisms in hand that can derive the observed readings where syntactic reconstruction is excluded, without overgeneration.

Acknowledgment: I wish to thank to the organisers and participants in the 2011 workshop on Reconstruction Effects in Relative Clauses (ZAS, Berlin), and the 2012 workshop on resumptive pronouns (Hebrew University of Jerusalem); in particular I am grateful to Rajesh Bhatt and Sabine Iatridou for their thorough and insightful commentary on the version of this work that was presented at the latter event. I would also like to express my thanks to the colleagues and friends who took the time to go through my questionnaires, and to the two anonymous referees for their valuable feedback and advice.

(i) * The five stories about Diana$_i$ that she$_i$ wants to invent are five too many for any self-respecting journalist!

This could be handled in the same way as was proposed for the idioms in Section 3.4. Note that the question in (72a) is parallel to (73a), rather than to (i).
Bhatt and Iatridou further suggest that disjoint reference obtains also in (ii). This would be unexpected.

(ii) * The five stories about Diana$_i$ that she$_i$ wants to reinvent are the ones that are politiclly the most explosive.

The judgment is as given by Bhatt and Iatridou. It actually seems to me that there is no obviation effect in this case, but I have not had the chance to investigate this more thoroughly.

11 In the account of Donati & Cecchetto (2011) it is only the head N that raises out of the relative clause (and reconstructs); any modifiers are late-adjoined, when the head N is in a relative-external position. Much of the data presented here are compatible with their account, to the extent that they predict no syntactic reconstruction effects for modifiers; I am not certain what their account would predict for cases like (70). Donati and Cecchetto assume that idiom interpretation in relatives involves reconstruction (since in their account the head N does raise and reconstruct), but this does not appear to be crucial for them. In fact they might not want to maintain this assumption, as examples where part of the idiom appears to be within a PP adjoined to the head (*I admired the kind of headway that she was making*) might be incorrectly predicted to be out—but see footnote 6 concerning the complexities of *kind*-nominals.

References

Bhatt, Rajesh. 2002. The raising analysis of relative clauses: Evidence from adjectival modification. *Natural Language Semantics* 10. 43–90.

Bhatt, Rajesh & Sabine Iatridou. 2012. Comments on "Reconstructing reconstruction." Handout from the Resumptive Pronouns Workshop held at the Hebrew University of Jerusalem, July 2012.

Bhatt, Rajesh & Yael Sharvit. 2005. A note on intensional superlatives. In Efthymia Georgala & Jonathan Howell (eds.), *Proceedings of SALT XV*, 62–78. Ithaca, NY: Cornell University.

Bianchi, Valentina. 2000. The raising analysis of relative clauses: A reply to Borsley. *Linguistic Inquiry* 31(1). 123–140.

Cecchetto, Carlo. 2006. Reconstruction in relative clauses and the copy theory of traces. In Pierre Pica & Johan Rooryck (eds.), *Linguistic variation yearbook 5*, 73–103. Amsterdam: John Benjamins.

Chomsky, Noam. 1986. *Knowledge of language: Its nature, origins and use*. New York: Praeger.

Cresti, Diana. 1990. Extraction and reconstruction. *Natural Language Semantics* 3. 79–122.

Donati, Caterina & Carlo Cecchetto. 2011. Relabeling heads: A unified account for relativization structures. *Linguistic Inquiry* 42(4). 519–560.

Fox, Danny. 1999. Reconstruction, binding theory, and the interpretation of chains. *Linguistic Inquiry* 30(2). 157–196.

Gajewski, Jon Robert. 2005. *Neg-Raising: Polarity and presupposition*. Cambridge, MA: Massachusetts Institute of Technology Doctoral dissertation.

Harris, Jesse A & Christopher Potts. 2009. Perspective-shifting with appositives and expressives. *Linguistics and Philosophy* 32(6). 523–552.

Hegarty, Michael. 2013. Neg-raising and duals. In Jacques François, Pierre Larrivée, Dominique Legallois & Franck Neveu (eds.), *La linguistique de la contradiction*, vol. 17 (GRAMM-R. Études de linguistique française). Brussels: Peter Lang.

Heycock, Caroline. 1995. Asymmetries in reconstruction. *Linguistic Inquiry* 26.4. 547–570.

Heycock, Caroline. 2005. On the interaction of adjectival modifiers and relative clauses. *Natural Language Semantics* 13. 359–382.

Hulsey, Sarah & Uli Sauerland. 2006. Sorting out relative clauses. *Natural Language Semantics* 14. 111–137.

Kadmon, Nirit & Fred Landman. 1993. Any. *Linguistics and Philosophy* 16. 353–422.

Lakoff, Robin. 1969. A syntactic argument for negative transportation. In Robert I. Binnick et al. (eds.), *Proceedings of CLS 5*, 149–157. University of Chicago.

Pollard, Carl & Ivan Sag. 1992. Anaphors in English and the scope of binding theory. *Linguistic Inquiry* 23.2. 261–303.

Prince, Ellen. 1976. The syntax and semantics of neg-raising, with evidence from French. *Language* 52. 404–426.

Reinhart, Tanya & Eric Reuland. 1993. Reflexivity. *Linguistic Inquiry* 24.4. 657–720.

Rullmann, Hotze. 1995. *Maximality in the semantics of Wh-constructions*. Amherst, MA: University of Massachusetts Doctoral dissertation.

Sauerland, Uli. 1998. *The meaning of chains*. Cambridge, MA: Massachusetts Institute of Technology Doctoral dissertation.

Sauerland, Uli. 2003. Unpronounced heads in relative clauses. In Kerstin Schwabe & Susanne Winkler (eds.), *The interfaces: Deriving and interpreting omitted structures*, 205–206. Amsterdam: Benjamins.
Schachter, Paul. 1973. Focus and relativization. *Language* 49(1). 19–46.
Sternefeld, Wolfgang. 2001. Semantic vs. syntactic reconstruction. In Hans Kamp, Antje Rossdeutscher & Christian Rohrer (eds.), *Linguistic form and its computation*, 145–182. Stanford, CA: CSLI Publications.
Zamparelli, Roberto. 1998. A theory of Kinds, Partitives and OF/Z Possessives. In Artemis Alexiadou & Chris Wilder (eds.), *Possessors, predicates and movement in the determiner phrase*, vol. 22 (Linguistics Today), 259–301. Amsterdam: John Benjamins.

Winfried Lechner

A calculus for reconstruction and anti-reconstruction

1 Introduction

Dislocation is known to systematically affect aspects of truth conditional interpretation. On the one hand, movement affords quantificational terms with new scope options (*Ever movie seemed to some critic to be interesting*), isolates pied-piped referential DPs from disjoint reference requirements (*Which picture near $John_2$ did he_2 like?*), and provides variables with new binders (A-scrambling). On the other hand, natural language expressions that do not reside in their canonical environments retain interpretive properties of positions they have previously occupied in the syntactic representation. Reconciling these two faces of movement represents the main desideratum of the theory of reconstruction. Moreover, if it turns out that the analysis of the phenomena includes timing effects, providing evidence for a sequencing of discrete derivational steps in the analysis, the theory of reconstruction should also predict at which point of the derivation relevant subsets of these properties emerge.

The present contribution pursues two interrelated objectives pertaining to the theory of reconstruction. In the first part, I will briefly review arguments for the view that movement can indeed be undone at two different points of the derivation, either in syntax or in the semantic component. In Lechner (1996, 1998) (see also Sharvit 1998), this observation has been taken to indicate that the grammar includes two separate reconstruction mechanisms, a syntactic one, usually implemented in terms of Copy Theory and a semantic one which can be modeled by β-conversion into higher type traces (*semantic reconstruction*; Cresti 1990, Rullmann 1995, Ruys 2015, i.a.). While the resulting hybrid theory of reconstruction accounts for dissociations between quantifier scope and binding domains that prove recalcitrant for Copy Theory, it also leads to overgeneration (Romero 1998, Fox 1999). As a result, the system needs to be supplemented by two independently motivated assumptions regulating the distribution of higher type traces and the internal make up of copies. The condition on higher type traces will further be

Winfried Lechner, National and Kapodistrian University of Athens

https://doi.org/10.1515/9783050095158-004

seen to have important, more general consequences for the representation of scope inversion.

The second goal of this paper consists in presenting a calculus, that is a complete formal system operating on purely syntactic representations, which derives the basal scope and (anti-)reconstruction properties of canonical word orders in English and German, and scrambled word orders in German. In line with previous research (Hornstein 1995, Johnson & Tomioka 1998), scope inversion in transitive clauses of flexible scope languages will be argued to be the result of reconstruction and short type driven object QR. The typological difference between free scope languages (English) and scope rigid ones like German can then be reduced to the timing of overt movement. While in German, all movement operations apply in overt syntax, possibly by Overt Covert Movement, English has the option of postponing QR to LF. Moreover, a small adjustment in the theory of anti-reconstruction proposed in Takahashi (2006) and Takahashi & Hulsey (2009) will be seen to account for the fact that short scrambling reconstructs for scope but not for binding. Together, these analyses represent the first algorithmic account of the central characteristics of scope, scope rigidity, reconstruction and anti-reconstruction.

The paper is structured as follows. In section 2, I review two arguments from the literature for the claim that scope reconstruction is not necessarily accompanied by binding reconstruction and introduce two conditions on reconstruction from Lechner (2011, 2013). Section 3 explores empirical ramifications of one of these conditions for analyzing the scope potential of subjects and small clauses subjects (Johnson & Tomioka 1998; for consequences of the other condition see Lechner 2011, 2013). In section 4, I integrate the analysis of scope into a theory of anti-reconstruction.

2 Dissociations between scope and binding

There are at least two environments demonstrating that the scope of quantificational determiners does not necessarily coincide with the positions in which their restrictor arguments are interpreted (see also Keine & Poole 2018). One context is extensional, manifesting itself, among others, in the shape of short object-over-object scrambling in languages like German and attests to the fact that scope reconstruction is not dependent upon reconstruction for variable binding (Lechner 1996, 1998). The second class of constructions implicates intensional contexts in which a quantifier is construed referentially transparent with respect to predicates outside its scope domain. Moreover, in such constellations, the domain of referential opacity tracks the domain in which the principles of Binding Theory are computed

(Sharvit 1998). Together, these findings support two conclusions. First, the system evaluating quantifier scope is distinct from the system which is responsible for the evaluation of binding, coreference and referential opacity, in support of a hybrid theory of reconstruction which includes semantic reconstruction in addition to syntactic Copy Theory. Second, the hybrid theory must be properly constrained in order to account for the synchronicity between binding and referential opacity.

Turning to the extensional contexts first, scope ambiguity in scope rigid languages like German, Japanese or Mandarin is dependent upon overt movement of the lower quantifier over the higher one (Hoji 1985, Frey 1993, Aoun & Li 1993, Büring 1997, Krifka 1998, Bobaljik & Wurmbrand 2012). To exemplify, the scrambled word order in German (1)a admits a distributive, narrow scope reading which is absent from the canonical serialization (1)b. Moreover, while the direct object in (1)a optionally reconstructs for scope, the reciprocal inside the scrambled DP cannot be bound by the dative it has crossed over (Lechner 1996, 1998; individual observations due to Frey 1993), indicating that scope reconstruction does not entail binding reconstruction.

(1) *Short scrambling: scope reconstruction, no binding reconstruction*

a. weil wir$_1$ [einige Freunde von *einander*$_{1/*3}$]$_2$ *allen Kollegen*$_3$ t_2/T_2
since we some friends$_{ACC}$ of each other all colleagues$_{DAT}$
vorstellen wollten
introduce wanted
"since we wanted to introduce some friends of each other to every colleague" $(\exists > \forall \,/\, \forall > \exists)$

b. weil wir$_1$ [einigen Kollegen$_3$] [alle Freunde von *einander*$_{1/3}$]
since we some colleagues$_{DAT}$ all friends$_{ACC}$ of each other
vorstellen wollten
introduce wanted
"since we wanted to introduce to some colleagues all friends of each other" $(\exists > \forall \,/\, {*}\forall > \exists)$

A natural explanation of (1)a resides with the hypothesis that the overtly moved quantifier optionally binds a generalized quantifier type variable which is valued by the object in semantics by β-conversion (T_2), resulting in semantic reconstruction (SemR). Since in the syntacto-centric T-model adopted here (Chomsky 1995) scope diminishment by SemR in (1)a applies subsequent to the verification of binding relations at LF, the analysis yields the effect of scope reconstruction without binding reconstruction.

Intensional contexts add two further facets to the analysis. To begin with, it has been observed that Binding Theory reconstruction co-varies with referential opacity and not scope, as stated by the two generalizations in (2) (Sharvit 1998, Romero 1998, Lechner 2009):

(2) *Two restrictions on SemR*

a. If a moved DP is construed referentially opaque with respect to a lower predicate P, it reconstructs into the c-command domain of P for the evaluation of Binding Theory.

b. If a dislocated DP reconstructs for Binding Theory into the c-command domain of a predicate P, it is construed referentially opaque with respect to P.

Evidence for (2)a comes from the raising paradigm in (3), which introduces logical consistency as an additional condition reacting to the LF-position of the subject (Lechner 2009, 2011, 2013). While (3)a can, on the intended coreferential interpretation for the pronouns, either express a consistent *de dicto* or a contradictory *de re* proposition, sentence (3)b, in which *his* has been substituted by *John*, only admits the latter construal:

(3) a. [*His*$_2$ height] seemed to *him*$_2$ to exceed his actual height.
(consistent *de dicto*/contradictory *de re*)

i. *de dicto* construal of *his height*: "It seemed to John that John is taller than he actually is."

ii. *de re* construal of *his height*: "John obtained the impression: I am in actuality taller than I actually am."

b. [*John*$_2$'s height] seemed to *him*$_2$ to exceed his actual height.
(*consistent *de dicto*/contradictory *de re*)

Before proceeding, two remarks regarding the semantic system are in order. The discussion to follow presupposes an extensional Ty2 meta language (Gallin 1975) enriched with explicit object language representation for situation variables (Percus 2000). I will moreover adopt the widely held view that the contrast between referentially opaque, *de dicto* and transparent, *de re* subjects in (3) is determined by the choice of binder for these situation arguments inside the subject restrictor, such that *de dicto* readings are the product of the s-variable being bound by the λ-abstractor associated with the raising predicate, while *de re* results from long distance binding by a higher λ-operator (Percus 2000, Heim & von Fintel 2005, Anand 2006, i.a).[1]

---

1 For a non-structural, presuppositional account of the *de dicto*/*de re* distinction see e.g. Maier (2009).

For present purposes, (3)b is of particular interest because it reveals the systematic link between scope and Binding Theory expressed by (2)a. If the subject *John's height* is construed *de dicto*, the restrictor must, as detailed by the LF-representation (4)a, reconstruct to a position c-commanded by the λ-binder of *seem* (λ_1), which in turn induces a disjoint reference effect between *John* and *him*.[2] By contrast, the intended coreference pattern is compatible with the transparent, contradictory reading, relevant parts of which are given in (4)b, because a *de re* subject is interpretable in its surface position and therefore remains outside the c-command domain of the experiencer:

(4) a. *de dicto reading of (3)b*
λ_0 [seemed-in-s_0 [to *him*$_2$ $\underline{\lambda_1}$ [$_{TP}$ [*John*$_2$'s height-in-$\underline{s_1}$] exceeds-in-s_1 his height-in-s_0]]]

b. *de re reading of (3)b*
$\underline{\lambda_0}$ [$_{TP}$ [*John*$_2$'s height-in-$\underline{s_0}$]$_3$ seemed-in-s_0 [to *him*$_2$ λ_1 [$_{TP}$ t_3 exceeds-in-s_1 his height-in-s_0]]]

Similar structures can be employed in testing generalization (2)b. In (5), the presence of the reciprocal inside the fronted DP triggers subject reconstruction into the embedded clause.[3] Moreover, the observation that the sentence lacks the contradictory *de re* reading (cf. (3)a) signals that the s-variable inside the lower subject copy must be identified locally, below *seem*:

(5) [*Each others*$_2$'s height] seemed to *the boys*$_2$ to exceed their actual height.
(consistent *de dicto*/*contradictory *de re*)

a. *de dicto* construal of *each other's height*: "It seemed to each boy that the others are taller than they actually are."

b. *de re* construal of *each other's height*: "Each boy had the impression: the other boys are in actuality taller than they actually are."

---

2 Details orthogonal to the discussion are suppressed. First, the raising predicate is generated below the experiencer, from where it moves to its surface position, as in (i):

(i) [seem$_3$ [to him$_2$ [t_3 [λ_1 ...]]]]

Second, *to*-PPs are assumed to be transparent for c-command (Bruening 2014). Finally, *res* movement and concept generators will be ignored throughout (for recent discussion see Charlow & Sharvit 2014).

3 The situation is more complex, as the experiencer is merged above the base position of *seem* (see fn. 2). This leaves the option that the subject reconstructs below the experiencer, but above the raising verb. I assume, as is common, that such an intermediate VP-internal landing site for movement is not available.

In Lechner (2011, 2013), it is suggested to explain the two conditionals in (2) as the consequence of two general principles. The first requirement ensures that binding relations out of movement copies are always maximally local, as maintained by the *Condition on Extraction from Copies* (*CEC;* for independent motivation and an attempt to derive the CEC see Lechner 2011, 2013):

(6) *Condition on Extraction from Copies (CEC)*
Extraction out of movement copies is local.

Applied to (5), the CEC eliminates the reconstructed *de re* reading by blocking LF representation (7), in which the s-variable of the lower subject is bound across *seem*:

(7) $\underline{\lambda s_0}$ [seemed-in-s_0 [to *the boys*$_2$ [λs_1 [*each others*$_2$'s height-in-$\underline{s_0}$] to exceed-in-$\overline{s_1}$ their height-in-s_0]]]

In what follows, I will focus on the second axiom, spelled out in (8) as a restriction on the type of a subset of the logical, permutation invariant vocabulary:[4]

(8) *Extensional Traces and Antecedents (ETA)*
The denotation of quantificational DPs and their traces do not include situation variables.

The ETA postulates that ⟨et,t⟩ is a possible type for generalized quantifiers and that traces can be mapped into individual or ⟨et,t⟩-type variables, but that ⟨⟨e,st⟩,st⟩ and ⟨s,⟨et,t⟩⟩, for instance, are beyond the boundaries of the expressivity of natural language. Limiting the prohibition in (8) to permutation invariant expressions is motivated by two factors. First, it exempts non-quantificational, property denoting indefinites (⟨e,st⟩-type), sanctioning their occurrence in the object position of intensional transitive verbs like *seek*. Second, the qualification ensures that the ETA does not conflict with movement of predicates or clauses, which are standardly given denotations that include s-arguments (⟨e,st⟩ or ⟨s,et⟩ and ⟨s,t⟩, respectively).[5]

Returning to the case at hand, one immediate prediction of the ETA is that it forces SemR invariably to result in narrow scope *de re* interpretations (Heim & von Fintel 2005, Lechner 2009). This is so because according to (8), higher type traces lack an argument slot for situations, with the result that s-variables have to be bound in a movement copy – instead of a higher type trace – at LF. For instance,

4 Keshet (2010) advances a similar proposal: "Avoid reference to times/worlds in the lexical definitions, if possible". The assumption that generalized quantifiers are extensional is orthodox (Peters & Westerståhl 2006).

5 Whether predicates and clauses reconstruct in syntax or semantics is immaterial for present purposes. See Takano (1995), Lechner (1998) and Moulton (2013a) for discussion.

the silent situation pronoun in the schematic derivation (9) can be bound by the superordinate λ_0, as in (9)a, but not by the lower λ_1 subsequent to SemR ((9)b). Consequently, the restrictor of a DP which has moved across an intensional operator and is restored into its pre-movement position by SemR is to be interpreted *de re* with respect to this operator:

(9) a. LF:

$[\lambda_0 \ldots \quad [[_{DP} \ldots s_{0/*}s_1 \ldots]_2 \ldots [\textit{seem}\ [\lambda_1 \ldots T_{2,\langle et,t\rangle} \ldots \quad]]]]$

b. After SemR:

$[\lambda_0 \ldots \quad [\ldots \quad [\textit{seem}\ [\lambda_1 \ldots [_{DP} \ldots s_{0/*}s_1 \ldots]_2]]]]$

(**de dicto*/*de re*)

The sample derivation (9) makes explicit relevant details of the derivation for the narrow scope *de re* reading by SemR. (R_{seem} is the accessibility relation which collects for each situation s the set of situations compatible with the evidence available to the speaker in s.)

(10) a. A friend seemed to be sick.

b. $[\lambda_0 [_{TP2} [\text{a friend-}s_0] [\lambda_2 [_{VP} \text{seem} [_{\langle s,t\rangle} \lambda_3 [_{TP} T_{2,\langle et,t\rangle}$
$[_{\langle e,t\rangle} \lambda_1 [_{vP,t}\ t_1 \text{ to be sick-}s_3]]]]]]]]$

c. $[\![TP_2]\!] = \lambda_2.\forall s[R_{seem}(s_0)(s) \rightarrow T_2(\lambda_1.\text{sick}(s)(t_1))$
$(\lambda Q.\ \exists x[\text{friend}(\underline{s_0})(x) \wedge Q(x)])$
$= \forall s[R_{seem}(s_0)(s) \rightarrow \lambda Q.\ \exists x[\text{friend}(\underline{s_0})(x) \wedge Q(x)]\ (\lambda_1.\text{sick}(s)(t_1))]$
$= \forall s[R_{seem}(s_0)(s) \rightarrow \exists x[\text{friend}(\underline{s_0})(x) \wedge \lambda_1.\text{sick}(s)(t_1)(x)]]$
$= \forall s[R_{seem}(s_0)(s) \rightarrow \exists x[\text{friend}(\underline{s_0})(x) \wedge \text{sick}(s)(x)]]$

Another direct consequence entailed by (8) is that since SemR restores quantifier scope but does not affect referential opacity, narrow scope *de dicto* readings must be derived by syntactic reconstruction and Copy Theory. But as (6) requires movement out of copies to proceed locally, binding reconstruction never produces *de re* readings. Thus, the combination of the locality principle (6) and the ETA in (8) has the effect of establishing a close link between referential opacity, expressed in terms of s-variables binding, and the syntactic domain of Binding Theory. Reconstruction by SemR always results in *de re* interpretations, and syntactic reconstruction systematically produces *de dicto* readings, deriving what has become known as the *Scope Trapping* generalization (Romero 1998, Fox 1999, among others). Providing an explanation for this link is crucial as it eliminates a potential source of overgeneration and thereby a serious challenge for any theory that incorporates SemR. Note that the combination of (6) and (8) still admits dissociations like (1), in which extensional quantifier scope is decoupled from syntactic reconstruction.

Intensional contexts also afford a second, new insight apart from exposing (parts of) the Scope Trapping phenomenon. Sharvit (1998) observed that in amount interrogatives, binding scope correlates with referential opacity. If the fronted degree predicate *n-many* in (11) is construed with narrow scope, the availability of a coreferential link between *Anton* and *he* is contingent upon the relative clause *who hate Anton* being interpreted transparently, i.e. *de re*, with respect to *hope*.

(11) How [[many students] who hate *Anton*$_1$]$_2$ did *he*$_1$ hope [t_2/T_2 will buy him$_1$ a beer]? (**de dicto*/*de re*)

a. * *Narrow scope 'n-many', restrictor de dicto:* "For which number n and for all of Anton's bouletic alternatives s_1 in s_0: there are n-many students who hate Anton in s_1 that will buy him a beer in s_1."

b. *Narrow scope 'n-many', restrictor de re:* "For what number n, and for all of Anton's bouletic alternatives s_1 in s_0: there are n-many students who hate Anton in s_0 that will buy him a beer in s_1."

The hybrid theory of reconstruction captures this correlation by assuming a higher type trace below the pronoun and the intensional predicate, which generates a transparent *de re* reading without triggering a disjoint reference effect. Thus, (11) demonstrates that the effects of SemR are visible in intensional contexts, as well as in extensional constructions ((1)a).

Recapitulating briefly, it was seen that there are good reasons for adopting two different mechanisms for scope diminishment: SemR and Copy Theory. In order to contain overgeneration, two mechanisms were introduced guaranteeing that (i) reconstructed opaque, *de dicto* readings for moved DPs are always the product of reconstruction in syntax, and that (ii) situation variables in lower movement copies are locally bound. Together, these two conditions result in a theory of Trapping Effects as they ensure that dissociations between scope and binding emerge only in contexts where a narrow scope quantificational DP is construed transparently, *de re*, while Binding Theory is evaluated in a higher copy.

The next section explores further consequences of the ban on intensional traces, proceeding from there to the presentation of a calculus which derives the differences between scope rigid and flexible scope languages.

3 Subject reconstruction

Combining the ETA (8), which bans traces and quantificational DPs from bearing s-arguments, with a routine semantics for one-place predicates, on which VPs denote relations between individuals and eventualities (⟨e,st⟩)[6], imposes an empirically non-trivial restriction on the logical type of *in-situ* subjects. Concretely, these two assumptions ensure that only individual denoting subjects, that is individual DPs or traces/copies of such, are compositionally interpretable in their thematic position (SpecvP). If, on the other hand, SpecvP is occupied by a higher type trace (⟨et,t⟩) or (the copy of) a generalized quantifier, as in (12)a, a type mismatch ensues. Finally, intensional versions (⟨⟨e,⟨st⟩⟩,t⟩), which would in principle be type-compatible in SpecvP, are blocked by (8). The only strategy for integrating low, quantificational subjects into the semantic computation consists in supplying the vP-denotation with a situation variable first, as in (12)b, in order to create a suitable landing site for short subject movement.

(12) a. *Subject* in-situ *(type mismatch)* b. *Subject interpreted* ex-situ

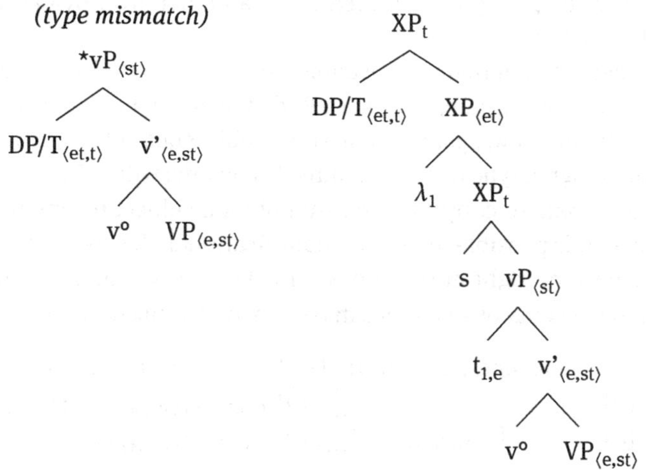

The system above ensures that quantificational subjects are never interpreted *in-situ*, regardless whether they undergo total reconstruction in syntax or in semantics. A similar requirement, prohibiting DPs from reconstructing into their Θ-position, was postulated on independent grounds in Johnson & Tomioka (1998). There, the condition had to remain an axiom unrelated to other properties of the system, though.

A first desirable empirical consequence of the ban on quantificational *in-situ* subjects comes from its ability to contribute to a better understanding of the phenomenon of scope rigidity. In scope rigid languages, inverse object scope is contingent upon overt inversion (see (1), Frey 1993, Aoun & Li 1993, i.a.). Now,

6 If the external argument is introduced by an applicative v°, then the minimal node comprising v° and VP is of type ⟨e,st⟩. Nothing bears on the choice, as far as I can see.

if subjects are always interpreted in a derived position ((13)a), and if it can be ensured that object QR indiscriminately lands *below* the subject, as in (13)b, it can be deduced that canonical word order configurations only yield surface scope. A condition which guarantees the locality of object QR in the sense intended above will be introduced momentarily. (Abstraction operators and irrelevant details will be omitted from now on.)

(13) *Scope rigid languages, non-inverted orders*

a. $[_{XP}$ $\mathit{QP}_{\mathit{Subject}}$ $[_{XP,\,t}$ s $[_{vP,\,\langle st\rangle}$ t_{Subject} $[_{VP,\,\langle e,st\rangle}$ … QP_{Object} …]]]]

b. $[_{XP}$ $QP_{Subject}$ $[_{XP}$ $\mathit{QP}_{\mathit{Object}}$ $[_{XP,\,t}$ s $[_{vP,\,\langle st\rangle}$ $t_{Subject}$ $[_{VP,\,\langle e,st\rangle}$ … t_{Object} …]]]]]

(Subject > Object)

Crucially, the prohibition on total subject reconstruction is an integral component of the analysis of scope rigidity outlined above and thereby provides additional motivation for the ETA.

Next, consider the alternative derivation (14), which is based on the (admittedly somewhat implausible) assumption that VPs denote individual predicates instead of properties. On this view, spelled out in (14)a, subject quantifiers, as well as their copies and their higher type traces, can directly combine with VP-denotations (*DP* symbolizes a movement copy, i.e. the result of total subject reconstruction). As a consequence, it is possible to assign quantificational objects wide scope even if they surface to the right of the subject. In (14)b, this is obtained by subject reconstruction in syntax or semantics in conjunction with short object QR:

(14) *Scope rigid languages, non-inverted orders (incorrect analysis)*

a. $[QP_{Subject}$ $[_{vP,\,t}$ $\mathit{DP}/\mathit{T}_{\mathit{Subject}}$ $[_{VP,\,\langle et\rangle}$ … QP_{Object} …]]]

b. $[QP_{Subject}$ $[_{vP}$ $\mathit{QP}_{\mathit{Object}}$ $[_{vP,\,t}$ $DP/T_{Subject}$ $[_{VP,\,\langle et\rangle}$ … t_{Object} …]]]]

(Object > Subject)

Thus, alternative systems which do not include the ETA or object language situation arguments in modeling VPs generate the false prediction that in scope rigid languages, scope inversion can also be obtained in absence of changes in overt word order.

As mentioned above, the analysis of scope rigidity has a second part to it, which limits the scope of object QR in German (see (13)b). What is essential is that this component is flexible enough to admit non-local, scope feeding object QR for English, but not for German. I suggest that the relevant typological asymmetry separating scope flexible from scope rigid languages is anchored to an independent factor which has been productively used in explaining cross-linguistic variation in other domains: the timing of displacement operations. While there are languages which move all *wh*-phrases in overt syntax (Bulgarian), others do not overtly mark the interpretive position of some *wh*-phrases (English, German) or even all of them

(Chinese). Following this strategy, it is proposed that the factor discriminating between English and German consists in a single criterion that restricts all movement operations in German to the overt component (in the spirit of Diesing 1992), but tolerates post-syntactic dislocation in English. English accordingly has the option of delaying QR to LF, while in German, all overt and covert displacement proceeds overtly by what has come to be known as *Overt Covert Movement* (OCM; Bobaljik 1995, Groat & O'Neil 1996, Pesetsky 2000, on OCM and scope see also Bobaljik & Wurmbrand 2012). In order to be able to define a deterministic procedure for multiple applications of QR, I will moreover adopt the standard pair of axioms in (15) for non-feature driven movement. Overt movement will be taken to subsume audible, overt displacement as well as OCM.

(15) a. Extension Condition (Chomsky 1995):
All overt movement extends the tree.
b. The Strict Cycle:
Movement proceeds bottom up, affecting lower nodes first.

Implementing the assumptions above, consider the derivation of scope rigidity for a transitive German clause like (1)b first. Representation (16)a depicts the point at which the two quantificational arguments still reside *in-situ*, where they cannot combine with their sister nodes due to type mismatch. Further up in the tree, an s-variable has been merged, generating a suitable landing site (XP) for OCM of the two argument QPs. Given that both the subject and the object need to undergo type-driven QR, a decision must be made about the order and scope of movement. The Strict Cycle (15)b determines that the lower node (the object) raises first, while the Extension Condition (15)b ensures that it attaches to the root node (XP), resulting in (16)b.[7] Next, the subject moves, again abiding by the Extension Condition, yielding (16)c. This subtree for the first time locates both quantifiers in type-compatible, interpretable positions. (Scope positions are typographically marked by double underline.) Moreover, since neither the subject nor the object can bind a higher type trace in, nor fully reconstruct into their respective base positions, the calculus predicts that canonical word orders always translate into surface scope orders.

(16) *Scope rigid languages, non-inverted orders*

a. $[_{XP,\,t}\ s\ [_{vP,\,\langle st\rangle}\ QP_{Sub}\ [_{VP,\,\langle e,st\rangle}\ \ldots\ QP_{Obj}\ \ldots\ ]]]$

b. $[_{XP}\mathit{QP}_{\mathit{Obj}}\ [_{XP,\,t}\ s\ [_{vP,\,\langle st\rangle}\ QP_{Sub}\ [_{VP,\,\langle e,st\rangle}\ \ldots\ t_{Obj}\ \ldots\ ]]]]$

c. $[_{XP}\ \underline{\underline{\mathit{QP}}}_{\mathit{Sub}}\ [_{XP}\ \underline{\underline{QP}}_{Obj}\ [_{XP,\,t}\ s\ [_{vP,\,\langle st\rangle}\ t_{Sub}\ [_{VP,\,\langle e,st\rangle}\ \ldots\ t_{Obj}\ \ldots\ ]]]]]$

(Subject > Object)

7 As will be seen in section 4, OCM of the object in (16)b does not affect a full DPs, but just the determiner, the restrictor is merged in a higher position.

In a step not represented separately, the subject is attracted to SpecTP. Finally, (16)d/e illustrate the emergence of an additional scope option by overt subject-object inversion, either by scrambling or some other overt dislocation operation. Once the object has been overtly shifted across the subject in SpecTP into a TP-adjoined position, it can either bind individual traces ((16)d) or reconstruct below the subject into XP in syntax or by SemR ((16)e), resulting in the signature ambiguity characteristic of inverted contexts in scope rigid languages:

(16) *Scope rigid languages, inverted orders*

d. $[_{TP}\ \underline{\underline{QP}}_{Obj}\ [_{TP}\ \underline{\underline{QP}}_{Sub}\ [_{XP}\ t_{Sub}\ [_{XP}\ t_{Obj}\ [_{XP,\,t}\ S\ [_{vP,\,\langle st\rangle}\ t_{Subj}\ [_{VP,\,\langle e,st\rangle} \dots t_{Obj} \dots]]]]]]]$

(Object > Subject)

e. $[_{TP}\ QP_{Obj}\ [_{TP}\ \underline{\underline{QP}}_{Sub}\ [_{XP}\ t_{Sub}\ [_{XP}\ \underline{DP/T}_{Obj}\ [_{XP,\,t}\ S\ [_{vP,\,\langle st\rangle}\ t_{Sub}\ [_{VP,\,\langle e,st\rangle} \dots t_{Obj} \dots]]]]]]]$

(Subject > Object)

The relations depicted in (16) generalize to double object constructions and short object-over-object scrambling in these contexts. In canonical structures with two non-inverted quantificational objects, (15) dictates that both internal arguments land in an order preserving manner in specifiers of XP, resulting in surface word order. Further displacement of the lower indirect object (IO) across the higher, direct one (DO), as in (17), feeds ambiguity (intermediate subject traces suppressed). The relations are for all means and purposes identical to those between the subject and the object in (16)d/e.[8]

(17) *Scope rigid languages, double object constructions, inverted orders*

$[_{XP}\ \underline{\underline{QP}}_{DO}\ [_{XP}\ \underline{\underline{\mathit{IO}}}\ [_{XP}\ t/\underline{T}_{DO}\ [_{XP,\,t}\ S\ [_{vP,\,\langle st\rangle}\ t_{Subject}\ [_{VP,\,\langle e,st\rangle} \dots [t_{IO} \dots [t_{DO} \dots]]]]]]]]$

(DO > IO / IO > DO)

English differs from German in that QR is delayed to LF. This has the important consequence that the principles regulating the scope options for canonical word orders do not only sanction order preserving movements. Specifically, in English, subjects are attracted to a higher position in overt syntax and quantifiers move at LF. This entails that subject raising may – unlike in German – precede object QR, essentially canceling the effects of the Strict Cycle condition ((15)b). Moreover, suppose that quantificational subjects pass, just like in German, through an intermediate position (XP) on their way to TP. This step is either driven by a syntactic locality metric favoring short movement paths, or the need to render trees compositionally interpretable as soon as possible ((18)b). Since the Extension Condition

8 The question why DO cannot syntactically reconstruct below IO will be addressed in section 4.

((15)a) does not impose any requirement on the landing site of LF-movement, nothing prevents then the object from QRing across the intermediate subject copy (XP), legitimizing the passage from (18)b to the two possible representations (18)c and (18)d. In the surface scope parse (18)c, the subject is interpreted in TP from where it binds an individual variable in XP. By contrast, (18)d translates into inverse scope, because the subject reconstructs, either by SemR or by Copy Theory.

(18) *Scope flexible languages, non-inverted orders*

a. $[_{XP,\,t}\ s\ [_{vP,\,\langle s,t\rangle}\ QP_{Sub}\ [_{VP,\,\langle e,st\rangle}\ \ldots\ QP_{Obj}\ldots]]]$

b. $[_{XP}\ QP_{Sub}\ [_{XP,\,t}\ s\ [_{vP,\,\langle s,t\rangle}\ t_{Sub}\ [_{VP,\,\langle e,st\rangle}\ \ldots\ QP_{Obj}\ldots]]]]$

c. $[_{TP}\ \underline{QP}_{Sub}\ [_{XP}\ \underline{QP}_{Obj}\ [_{XP}\ t_{Sub}\ [_{XP,\,t}\ s\ [_{vP,\,\langle s,t\rangle}\ t_{Sub}\ [_{VP,\,\langle e,st\rangle}\ \ldots\ t_{Obj}\ldots]]]]]]$ (Subject > Object)

d. $[_{TP} QP_{Sub}\ [_{XP}\ \underline{QP}_{Obj}\ [_{XP}\ \underline{DP/T}_{Sub}\ [_{XP,\,t}\ s\ [_{vP,\,\langle s,t\rangle}\ t_{Sub}\ [_{VP,\,\langle e,st\rangle}\ \ldots\ t_{Obj}\ldots]]]]]]$ (Object > Subject)

In sum, the present analysis locates the difference between scope rigidity and scope flexibility in the timing of object QR. If the object QRs in overt syntax, by OCM, it moves prior to the subject (Strict Cycle; (15)b). Given the Extension Condition (15)a, the subject therefore needs to land above the lowest interpretable object position. By contrast, languages which admit post-syntactic object QR such as English also generate LF-representations in which the object is higher than the subject. In section 4, it will be seen how the scope algorithm can be integrated into the analysis of (anti-)reconstruction phenomena. Before doing so, I will briefly expand on another favorable corollary of the ban on intensional traces (ETA, (8)), though.

The additional benefit comes in shape of a new perspective on a long standing puzzle regarding the interpretation of small clause subjects. Small clause subjects can – with a notable exception I will return to below – only be construed transparently with respect to the small clause selecting predicate (Stowell 1991, Williams 1983). To illustrate, while the indefinite subject of (19)a can be used to identify an individual, regardless of whether it meets the description of being a doctor, this reading is absent from (19)b. As a result, only (19)a is felicitous when followed by the context (20), which explicitly revokes the credentials of the antecedent DP, forcing a *de re* construal (context based on an allegedly true story)

(19) *Small clauses, no wide scope for subject*

a. A doctor in the audience seemed to be nervous. (*de dicto/de re*)

b. A doctor in the audience seemed nervous. (**de dicto/de re*)

(20) It is obvious why. He was the imposter Dr. Moos, who performed plastic surgery using kitchen utensils in his kitchen in Dubai.

According to a widely held view, also to be adopted here, small clauses are 'small' in that they comprise of a predicate but exclude higher functional structure. Since s-variables which turn predicates into suitable landing sites for generalized quantifiers are part of the functional skeleton (they are hosted outside vP), it follows that small clauses lack the position designated for reconstructed quantificational subjects (XP). (19)b can therefore be parsed into the tree (21)a, which encodes the logical syntax underlying a *de re* proposition, whereas the *de dicto* representation (21)b is barred by the prohibition on intensional traces (ETA).

Thus, the ETA in (8) provides a natural, minimally invasive analysis for the prohibition on scope reconstruction into small clauses.

Moulton (2013b) noticed that the wide scope requirement for small clause subjects is revoked in contexts in which the subject serves as the argument of an intensional predicate. In contrast to what was seen above, (22)a also supports the narrow scope *de dicto* interpretation (22)b, which does not commit the speaker to having a particular fridge in mind. For (22)a to come out as true, fridges can also vary across situations.[9] (R_{nec} is an accessibility relation that returns for each situation s those situations that are compatible with what is necessary in s.)

(21) a. *Small clause subject* de re

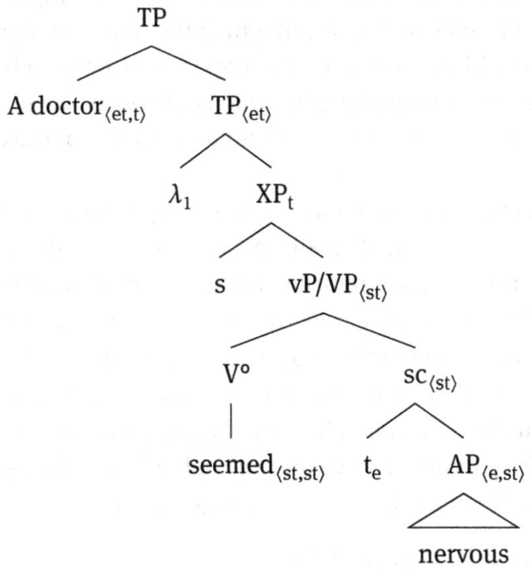

9 (22)a is also not falsified by scenarios in which the speaker misidentifies some non-fridge entity as a 'fridge', providing further confirmation for the *de dicto* character of the descriptive content.

(21) b. *Small clause subject* de dicto

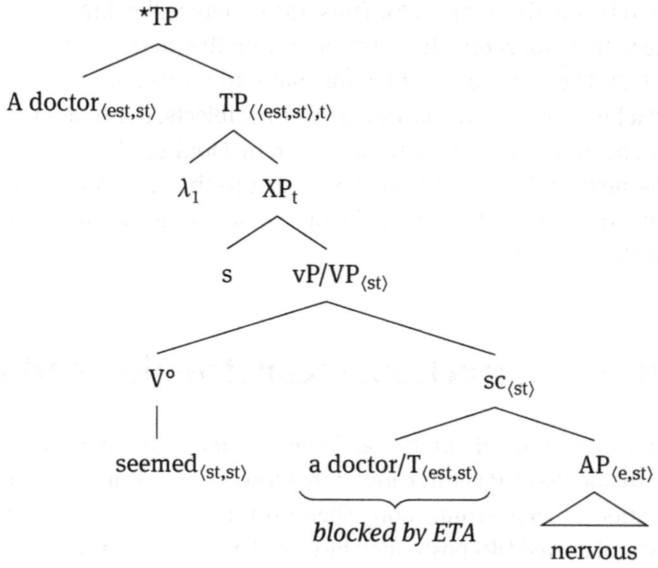

(22) a. A new fridge seems necessary. (*seem* > ∃ / ∃ > *seem*)

b. $\lambda s. \forall s' \forall s'' [R_{seem}(s)(s') \land R_{nec}(s')(s'') \rightarrow \exists x [\text{new\_fridge}(x)(s'')]$

Moulton proposes that (22) is instructive about the lexical properties of intensional predicates. If *necessary* is assigned the denotation in (23), it can directly combine with a property type argument which is existentially closed off either by the lexical meaning of *necessary* or, alternatively, a higher operator (Moulton 2013b: (17)):[10]

(23) $[\![\text{necessary}]\!] = \lambda P_{\langle e,st \rangle} . \lambda s. \forall s' [R_{nec}(s)(s') \rightarrow \exists x [P(x)(s')]]$ (Moulton 2013b: (9))

As far as I can see, the availability of exceptional narrow scope in (22) is directly compatible with the present system. Notably, the ETA only blocks situation variables in the denotation of permutation invariant expressions of the logical vocabulary, among them generalized quantifiers.

10 It is not clear how the account can be generalized to other subjects admitting *de dicto* readings (*two fridges*, *exactly seven fridges*,....). Speculatively, different quantifiers could be associated with different types of existential closure operators ($\exists_2$, $\exists_{!7}$, ...) which would have to be made to agree with their morphological exponents (*two*, *exactly seven*, ...) by a syntactic feature sharing mechanism.

Property type expressions are not permutation invariant and are accordingly not affected by the ETA (see fn. 4). Thus, the system is flexible enough to provide a suitable vehicle for scope diminishment from the matrix clause into the small clause in (22). The two analyses therefore naturally complement each other. While the ETA excludes maximally narrow scope for subjects, it also admits exceptional narrow scope in the environments identified by Moulton.[11]

In the next and final section, I will turn to the relation between ETA and other syntactic principles responsible for regulating the binding scope options of displaced DPs.

4 Anti-reconstruction, reconstruction and scope

The discussion up to this point has been restricted to environments in which an entire dislocated DP is interpreted in a lower chain link, resulting in radical reconstruction either in syntax (Copy Theory) or semantics (SemR). But not all lower occurrences of moved DPs postulated by Copy Theory enter into the computation of licit binding and coreference patterns. The central class of these *anti-reconstruction* phenomena relevant for present purposes is exemplified by Principle C obviation in A-movement environments (Lebeaux 1990):

(24) Every picture of *John*$_2$ seems to *him*$_2$ to be great.

An explicit theory of anti-reconstruction is presented in Takahashi (2006: chapter 3) and Takahashi & Hulsey (2009) who propose that a disjoint reference effect is absent from (24) because the name has actually never been part of the embedded clause. Rather, the subject starts out as a bare determiner (*every*) and raises into the higher subject position ((25)a), where it is combined with its restrictor *picture of John* ((25)b) by *Whole Sale Late Merge* (WLM).[12] Since the name *John* is merged above the point at which the coreferential pronoun is introduced, the WLM analysis derives the anti-reconstruction effect. (The position of restrictor insertion is marked by underline.)

11 A question which will have to await another occasion is to which extent binding scope and referential opacity coincide in property type DPs.

12 The lower copy of *every* is turned into an expression semantically equivalent to a variable by Trace Conversion ((i); Fox 2002, Sauerland 1998, 2004). Applying (i) to (25)b yields (ii). See discussion below and Fox (2003), i.a. for further elaboration.

(i) *Trace Conversion*: (Det)(Pred)$_n$ $\rightsquigarrow$ the ([(Pred) $\lambda x.x = n$]) (where 'n' is the index)

(ii) [Every picture of *John*$_2$]$_1$ seems to *him*$_2$ [[the $\lambda x.x = 2$] to be great]

(25) a. Every$_1$ seems to him$_2$ [~~every~~$_1$ to be great]. (Move *every*)
b. [Every picture of *John*$_2$]$_1$ seems to *him*$_2$ [~~every~~$_1$ to be great]. (WLM of restrictor)

Unlike A-movement, Ā-movement obligatorily reconstructs for Principle C (Lebeaux 1990):

(26) *Which picture of *John*$_2$ does *he*$_2$ [$_{VP}$ like best t].

This contrast falls out from the additional requirement articulated in (27) that countercyclic WLM of restrictors has to apply before the minimally containing DP is assigned Case.

(27) *Case Constraint on WLM* (adopted from Takahashi 2006)
A restrictor argument R can be merged with a determiner D only if R is within the c-command domain of its Case-assigning head.

In essence, (27) defines an upper bound on WLM. Provided that objects receive Case from v°, (27) dictates that the object restrictor in (26) is merged VP-internally, prior to movement. Accordingly, condition (27) is satisfied if (26) is assembled as in (28), with the restrictor NP being added below v° ((28)a), such that low attachment of the restrictor accounts for the disjoint reference effect:

(28) a. [$_{vP}$ v°$_{[ACC]}$ [$_{VP}$ like best which picture of *John*$_2$]]
b. * [Which picture of *John*$_2$ does *he*$_2$ [$_{vP}$ v°$_{[ACC]}$ [$_{VP}$ like best ~~which picture of *John*$_2$~~]]]

Conversely, (27) blocks the alternative derivation (29), which abides by Principle C because the restrictor has been counter-cyclically merged outside the c-command domain of the case assigning head v°$_{[ACC]}$:

(29) *[Which picture of *John*$_2$ does [$_{TP}$ *he*$_2$ [$_{vP}$ v°$_{[ACC]}$ [$_{VP}$ like best ~~which~~]]]]

Thus, the WLM analysis offers a natural explanation for the fact that Principle C does not treat A and Ā-movement alike.[13]

In what follows, I will extend Takahashi's WLM account to short (i.e. object-over-object) and medium (object-over-subject) scrambling in German. As it will turn out, the intricacies of these contexts do not fit the reconstruction typology established by A- and Ā-movement in English since the reconstruction options of

13 The availability of WLM does not affect the conclusions drawn on the basis of the scope-binding dissociation in (11). In (11), the case position of the moved object is below the pronoun to be construed coreferentially with *Anton*.

scrambled word orders are less permissive than those of displacement in English. I will therefore propose a minor modification of the licensing conditions on lexical insertion which, while leaving the basic insights of Takahashi (2006) intact, imposes an additional requirement on the lower bound of WLM in inverted contexts. The resulting system will be seen to account for the full range of scope and binding reconstruction.

Scrambling in German displays complex reconstruction properties. On the one hand, pronominal variables inside scrambled DPs can be bound by subjects to their right, both in transitive contexts (30)c and double object constructions ((31)d). On the other hand, (31)c documents that short scrambling of an accusative object across a dative cannot be undone for the computation of binding relations (Frey 1993, Haider 1993):

(30) *Medium scrambling, reconstruction for variable binding*

a. weil $jeder_2$ [$seinen_2$ Vater] liebt
since everone his $father_{ACC}$ loves
"since everyone loves his father" (base order)

b. * weil [$sein_2$ Vater] $jeden_2$ liebt
since his father $everone_{ACC}$ loves
"since his father loves everyone" (base order, WCO violation)

c. weil [$seinen_2$ $Vater]_1$ $jeder_2$ t_1 liebt
since his $father_{ACC}$ everyone loves
"since everyone loves his father" (medium object scrambling)

(31) *Short scrambling, no reconstruction for variable binding*

a. weil wir $jedem_2$ [$seinen_2$ Vater] zeigten
since we $everyone_{DAT}$ his $father_{ACC}$ showed
"since we showed everyone his father" (base order)

b. * weil wir [$seinem_2$ Vater] $jeden_2$ zeigten
since we his $father_{DAT}$ $everyone_{ACC}$ showed
"since we showed his father everyone" (base order, WCO violation)

c. * weil wir [$seinen_2$ $Vater]_1$ $jedem_2$ t_1 zeigten
since we his $father_{ACC}$ $everyone_{DAT}$ showed
"since we showed everyone his father"
(short DO scrambling, WCO violation)

d. weil uns [$seinen_2$ $Vater]_1$ $jeder_2$ t_1 zeigen wollte
since us_{DAT} his $father_{ACC}$ everyone show wanted
"since everyone wanted to show us his father"
(medium scrambling of DO)

This suggests that there is a lower bound for the position in which c-command sensitive properties of direct object (such as variable binding) are evaluated. More specifically, this lower bound is set by the left edge of the indirect object.

It is not possible to test the effects of scrambling on Principle C, because in the relevant contexts, schematized in (32), a full DP containing a name would have to precede a coreferential pronoun, and such constellations are barred for independent, prosodic reasons.

(32) *[[$_{DP}$ ... *name*$_2$ ...]$_1$ ....[*pronoun*$_2$ ... [... t_1 ...]]] (where DP_1 is scrambled)

The generality of the phenomenon is corroborated by the behavior of names inside topicalized constituents, though. While names embedded within fronted accusatives do not reconstruct below pronouns they have crossed over ((33)b), suspending a Principle C violation, the pair in (34) demonstrates that movement across a subject pronoun preserves the original coreference relations (Frey 1993). These paradigms confirm the generalization that the binding scope of (material inside) direct objects is evaluated below the subject but above the indirect object position:

(33) *Topicalization of DO, no reconstruction below IO*

a. * Ich brauchte *ihm*$_2$ [diesen alten Freund von *Peter*$_2$] nicht
I needed him$_{DAT}$ this old friend of Peter$_{ACC}$ not
vorzustellen. (base order)
to introduce

b. [Diesen alten Freund von *Peter*$_2$]$_1$ brauchte ich *ihm*$_2$ t_1 nicht
this old friend of Peter$_{ACC}$ needed I him$_{DAT}$ not
vorzustellen. (topicalization of DO)
to introduce
"I didn't need to introduce him this old friend of Peter's."

(34) *Topicalization of DO, reconstruction below subject*

a. * *Er*$_2$ brauchte uns [diesen alten Freund von *Peter*$_2$] nicht
he needed us$_{DAT}$ this old friend of Peter$_{ACC}$ not
vorzustellen. (base order)
introduce

b. * [Diesen alten Freund von *Peter*$_2$]$_1$ brauchte *er*$_2$ t_1 uns nicht
this old friend of Peter$_{ACC}$ needed he us$_{DAT}$ not
vorstellen. (topicalization of DO)
introduce
"He did not need to introduce to us this old friend of Peter's."

Finally, the behavior of A/Ā-movement under reconstruction in German parallels that of English (for data, discussion and references see also Salzmann 2006).

Combining the findings above, it can be concluded that DO reconstruction targets a node in the tree which is located directly below TP, the surface position of the subject. (35) makes visible how this condition translates into the WLM framework: the lower bound for the insertion of direct object restrictors is α, where α is immediately contained within TP.

(35) $[[_{DO}$ D° restrictor] ... $[_{TP}$ subject $[_{\alpha}$ $[_{DO}$ D° restrictor] ...
$[$IO ... $[_{VP}$ $[_{DO}$ D° *restrictor]]]]]]

Evidently, the pattern (35) poses a challenge for the WLM analysis, which only sets an upper bound for restrictor insertion, because objects are assigned case *in-situ* and nothing should therefore block objects from already being fully assembled within the VP. The task accordingly consists in defining an algorithm which preserves the results of Takahashi (2006) for A/Ā-movement, while at the same time ensuring that fronted direct objects acquire their restrictors only once they have passed over the indirect object.

A solution presents itself in form of a slight change in the licensing conditions on the first-merge position of restrictors. Suppose that WLM is not subject to Case but the requirement that the NP-complement resides within the c-command domain of an abstract head with agreeing Φ-features (henceforth 'Φ-head'). Variants of such Φ-heads are well-established in the literature. Kratzer (2009), for one, postulates a verbal functional head – a variety of v° – that serves as the link between nominal and verbal Φ-features. In a different domain, Φ-heads above v° have been used in the analysis of co-occurrence restrictions on dative and accusative arguments that fall under the Person Case Constraint (Anagnostopoulou 2003). Following this tradition of encoding Φ-feature relations in designated positions of the tree, I suggest that Φ-heads are also implicated in the licensing of WLM.

As for the details, it will be assumed that Φ is identical to α in (35), located inbetween TP and the landing site of short scrambling, which will, without ontological commitment, be referred to as ScrP.[14] Together with the deliberations of section 3, which revealed that the lowest interpretable position for quantificational arguments is XP, i.e. the point at which the s-variable is added, this yields the clausal structure in (36). While short srambling targets ScrP, medium srambling adjoins to TP:

(36) $[_{TP}$ ... $[_{\Phi P}$ ... $[_{ScrP}$ ... $[_{XP,\,t}$... s-variable $[_{vP,\,\langle st\rangle}$ ... $[_{VP}$ ...]]]]]]

14 In other languages, this position has been suggested to host clitics (*Clitic Voice* in Sportiche 1995). A related idea (Agr∀P) has been explored in Richards (1997: 92).

Furthermore, I propose (37) as the updated condition on WLM of nominal restrictors:

(37) *Φ-Constraint on Restrictor Insertion*
A restrictor argument R can be merged with a determiner D at stage S of a derivation only if R is within the c-command domain of a Φ-head at S.

The revised version differs from Takahashi's original (27) in two respects. First, (37) makes restrictor insertion contingent upon an (agreeing) higher head bearing Φ-features, instead of Case features. Second, for reasons to be explicated below, I will adhere to a strictly derivational model of the grammar, according to which restrictors can be inserted only if their licensing Φ-heads are already included in the representation. This view departs from Takahashi's (2006: 125f) valuation based feature system in which it is possible to merge restrictors at an early stage of the derivation and defer licensing to a point at which a suitable feature has been introduced.

Turning to the analysis, consider first regular, non-inverted transitive clauses, relevant parts of which are schematically exposed in (38). (37) demands that restrictors are inserted only in the presence of a c-commanding agreeing Φ-head. Given that such Φ-heads are generated VP-externally, the object starts out as a bare determiner ((38)a). In the next relevant step ((38)b), the Φ-head bearing agreeing object features is added, which in turn makes it possible to insert the restrictor in (38)c:

(38) *Restrictor insertion, canonical word order*

a.		$[_{VP}$ … $[_{DO}$ D°	…]]
b.	$[_{\Phi P}$ $\Phi_{[F]}$ …	$[_{VP}$ … $[_{DO}$ D°	…]]]
c.	$[_{\Phi P}$ $\Phi_{[F]}$ …	$[_{VP}$ … $[_{DO}$ D° $\underline{\text{restrictor}_{[F]}}$	…]]]

Note on the side that restrictor insertion in (38)c 'reaches' into the tree to a certain extent, in that the restrictor is merged below the root node. But since such a stipulation is the very defining characteristic of counter-cyclic merge, it is independently required by any theory that espouses WLM or late merge of adjuncts (*Which picture near John$_2$ did he$_2$ like*), and is therefore innocuous (on structural limits to late merge see Nissenbaum 2000).

In scrambled environments, the object undergoes an additional movement step to ScrP, which by assumption resides below ΦP. Since restrictors can only be merged if their licensing heads are already present, short scrambling in (39)b again solely affects the determiner. Once Φ is inserted in (39)c, D° is combined with its restrictor, resulting in (39)d:

(39) *Restrictor insertion, short scrambling*

a.			$[_{VP}$ IO … $[_{DO}$ D° …]]
b.		$[_{ScrP}$ $[_{DO}$ D°]	$[_{VP}$ IO … $[_{DO}$ D° …]]]
c.	$[_{\Phi P}$ $\Phi_{[F]}$ …	$[_{ScrP}$ $[_{DO}$ D°]	$[_{VP}$ IO … $[_{DO}$ D° …]]]]
d.	$[_{\Phi P}$ $\Phi_{[F]}$ …	$[_{ScrP}$ $[_{DO}$ D° $\underline{\text{restrictor}_{[F]}}$]	$[_{VP}$ IO … $[_{DO}$ D° …]]]]

Thus, the lowest node containing a full object copy is located right below ΦP, deriving the descriptive generalization (35). A contending derivation, in which restrictor insertion precedes movement is blocked by the Extension Condition, since scrambling would fail to target the root node. This view aligns well with an emerging consensus in derivational models according to which counter-cyclicity is a phenomenon which is characteristic of external merge, but which is not found with (overt) movement.

Applying the system outlined above to the empirical findings of section 3 finally provides an explanation of the reconstructive options for constellations in which a quantificational direct object has scrambled over an indirect object quantifier. Relevant details are represented by the tree in (40).

In the lowest section of (40), the direct object starts out as a determiner and moves to XP, the first position in which generalized quantifiers are interpretable. Next, movement to ScrP shifts the DO to the left of the indirect object. Scrambling optionally strands a higher type trace in XP, sanctioning scope reconstruction by SemR. Crucially, the revised WLM condition (37) ensures that the DO-restrictor is joined with its determiner no lower than in ScrP. From this, it follows that while the DO may be assigned narrow scope with respect to the indirect object by SemR, its descriptive content is not accessible below ScrP. Short scrambling leads, as desired, to scope ambiguity, but fails to reconstruct for the evaluation of binding relations. Thus, the calculus successfully derives the central generalizations about the interpretive options of short scrambling.

Two aspects of the theory deserve further attention. First, it was assumed that bare determiner movement in (40) optionally results in binding of generalized quantifier type traces.[15] While a rule for translating determiners into second order property variables, formulated in (41)a, is not part of the standard inventory for rendering movement copies interpretable, it can be seen as a member of the same family of operations as Trace Conversion ((41)b; Fox 1999). Such an extension is also not without precedent in the literature. For instance, Takahashi (2011) employs an ⟨et,e⟩-version of Trace Conversion (see (41)c) in implementing a choice function analysis of Weak Crossover (Ruys 2000, Sauerland 2004).

15 I disagree here with Takahashi (2006: 88), who pursues the idea that determiners are always translated as individual variables; see (41)c for discussion.

(40) *Reconstructive options for moved QPs*

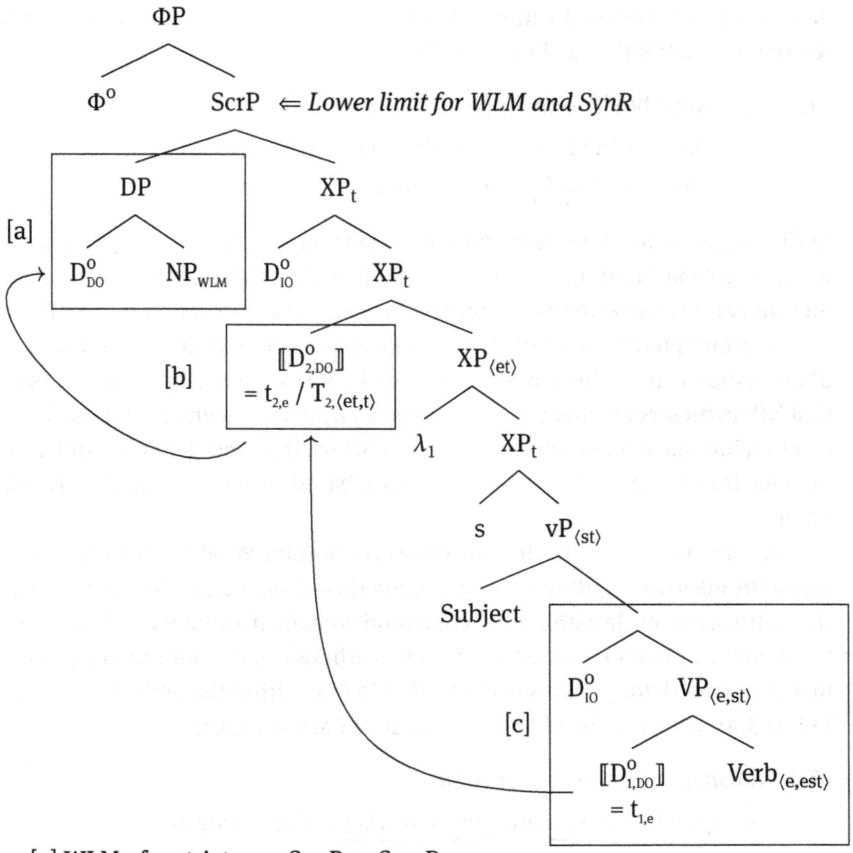

[a] WLM of restrictor ⇒ SynR or SemR
[b] No restrictor ⇒ SemR, but no SynR
[c] D^o_{IO} and D^o_{DO} translate into individual variables

(41) *Trace Conversion (generalized)*

a. $\text{Det}_n \rightsquigarrow \text{the}\ (\lambda\wp_{\langle et,t\rangle}[\wp = \lambda Q_{\langle et\rangle}[Q = \lambda x[x = n]]])$
$\equiv T_n$, where $T \in D_{\langle et,t\rangle}$ (Generalized Quantifier version)

b. $[(\text{Det})\ (\text{Pred})]_n \rightsquigarrow \text{the}\ ([(\text{Pred})\ \lambda x[x = n]])$ (Standard e-type version)

c. $\text{Det Pred} \rightsquigarrow f_{ch} \in D_{\langle et,e\rangle}\ (\text{Pred})$ (Choice function version)

On the present conception, the translation for copies is not rigidly determined by a stipulative device, but may yield a number of different values, depending on the local context.[16] The quantificational determiner *some* can then be converted into an individual variable, a variable of type ⟨et,t⟩ or – if the copy includes an overt restrictor argument[17] – a choice function:

(42) a. $[\text{some boy}]_3 \rightsquigarrow \text{the } (\text{boy and } \lambda x[x = n])$

b. $\text{some}_3 \rightsquigarrow \text{the } (\lambda\wp_{\langle et,t\rangle}[\wp = \lambda Q_{\langle et\rangle}[Q = \lambda x[x = 3]]]) \equiv T_{3,\ \langle et,t\rangle}$

c. $\text{some}_3\ (\text{boy}) \rightsquigarrow f_{ch} \in D_{\langle et,e\rangle}\ (\text{boy})$

In this way, a natural liberalization of the system which renders syntactic copies interpretable at the syntax-semantics interface also makes it possible to use bare quantificational determiners as targets for scope reconstruction by SemR.

A second point in need of clarification concerns the technical implementation of the syntactic licensing condition on restrictor insertion. Above, it was assumed that NP-restrictors are merged counter-cyclically once a licensing Φ-head has been inserted into the tree. As will be explicated below, this view generates different predictions from the ones projected by the Case based system advanced in Takahashi (2006).

Observe to begin with that the Case criterion for WLM in (27) does not make restrictor insertion contingent upon *actual* Case assignment, but merely requires the restrictor to reside within the c-command domain of a *potentially* Case assigning head. Such a proviso is essential, because otherwise, it would not be possible to merge the restrictor *pictures of each other* in (43) within the embedded infinitival TP1 ((43)a), whose T°-head lacks nominative Case features:

(43) *Raising, subject reconstruction*

a. $[_{TP1}$ T1° these pictures of *each other*$_2$ to be boring]]]

b. $[_{TP2}$ These pictures of *each other*$_2$ [T2°$_{[NOM]}$ seem to the *children*$_2$ $[_{TP1}$ T1° ~~these pictures of each other~~$_2$ to be boring]]]

This signals that the Case criterion (27) is either evaluated globally or that the link between Case assignment and WLM is indirect. Takahashi (2006: 125) avoids both complications by assuming that restrictors bear an unvalued, uninterpretable Case feature which is licensed under Agree by a c-commanding higher Case head. The restrictor of (43) can therefore be inserted early, in the lower clause ((44)a) and Case-licensed later on, once the DP has moved into the higher clause ((44)b).[18]

16 'the' in (41) is a type flexible maximalization operator.

17 This requirement is essential for capturing WCO effects. See Takahashi (2011) for details.

18 If raising subjects are driven into their surface position by Case, the [NOM]-feature has to be valued under specifier head agreement, and not by c-command. This introduces a second

(44) a. [T2°$_{[NOM]}$ seem to the *children*$_2$
[$_{TP1}$ [these pictures of *each other*$_2$]$_{[NOM]}$ ...]]

b. [$_{TP2}$ [these pictures of *each other*$_2$]$_{[NOM]}$
[T2°$_{[NOM]}$ seem to the *children*$_2$ [$_{TP1}$ ...]]]

The above solution is not compatible with the analysis advanced here, though, at least not in its present incarnation. If restrictor insertion is modeled in terms of features, and if features can be legitimized retroactively at a later point in the derivation, it should be possible to merge a complete copy of the object VP-internally ((45)a) and subsequently move that DP to its scrambled surface position (ScrP in (45)b), followed by valuation of the restrictor feature upon insertion of the Φ-head ((45)c):

(45) *Short scrambling, reconstruction (derivation overgenerates)*

a. [$_{VP}$ IO ... [$_{DO}$ [D° restrictor$_{[F]}$] ...]]

b. [$_{ScrP}$ [D° restrictor$_{[F]}$] [$_{VP}$ IO ... [$_{DO}$ [D° restrictor$_{[F]}$] ...]]]

c. [$_{\Phi P}$ Φ$_{[F]}$ [$_{ScrP}$ [D° restrictor$_{[F]}$] [$_{VP}$ IO ... [$_{DO}$ [D° restrictor$_{[F]}$] ...]]]]

However, it is evident that such an algorithm fails to derive obligatory late restrictor insertion in German, because it would legitimize direct object restrictors – to be converted into interpretable expressions by standard Trace Conversion – below indirect objects. If (45) were admitted, short scrambling should, contrary to fact, reconstruct for the purposes of Binding Theory. One way to avoid this shortcoming consists in stipulating that the relevant set of Φ-features needs to be valued immediately upon insertion. Without further pursuing this idea, note in passing that a related condition has, for similar reasons, been pursued in Takahashi & Hulsey (2009: fn. 12).[19]

But anchoring late insertion to Case features also comes at the cost of losing an important correlation between feature valuation and structural relations. While the Case-based criterion on WLM (27) states a *non-local* relation, which in raising contexts like (43) obtains between an embedded subject restrictor and a higher,

---

structural condition for Agree relations, possibly an undesirable redundancy. Alternatively, the subject could be assumed to check Case in vP-adjoined position, and move to its final destination to eliminate a EPP-feature.

19 Takahashi and Hulsey note that the prepositional complement of (i) must be merged cyclically in order to induce a disjoint reference effect. They suggest that this falls out from a requirement that Case heads need to value their features immediately upon insertion.

(i) * [In which corner of John$_2$'s room] was he$_2$ sitting?

Transposed to the present context, the condition would have to impose a similar condition on the (Φ-)features of the restrictor, instead of the Φ-head.

superordinate T°-head, Case assignment or Case valuation is usually taken to be *local*. Raising subjects are, after all, not valued for Case by lower non-finite T°-heads. Hence, (27) obfuscates the nature of the dependency of WLM on Case. By contrast, linking restrictor insertion to Φ-features, as suggested here, makes it possible to model the relations entirely locally, at least if it can be shown that the locality conditions which define Φ-relations are sufficiently similar to those attested with Case.

That Φ-features indeed pattern with Case features in being subject to a local licensing requirement can be seen in languages, among them Greek and Rumanian, in which raising subjects agree with infinitival embedded predicates in Φ-features. On a prominent interpretation, (46) indicates that raising subjects enter into local, cyclic Φ-relations with the embedded infinitive before being attracted by the higher finite T° (Alexiadou & Anagnostopoulou 1999):

(46) Ta pedia archizun na pezoun. (Raising, Greek)
the children $start_{[3pl]}$ C° $play_{[3pl]}$
"The children start to play."

This result dovetails with the local account of restrictor licensing in terms of Φ-feature (37), but is not compatible with the Case-based solution (27).

On the present conception, the fact that the insertion point for restrictors of raising subjects is variable (anti-reconstruction effect by WLM in (25)b vs. reconstruction in (43)b, both repeated below) can then be traced back to the natural assumption that each non-finite clause contains an agreeing Φ-head for subjects, which can, but does not have to, trigger restrictor insertion:

(25)b [Every picture of *John*$_2$]$_1$ seems to *him*$_2$ [~~every~~$_1$ to be great].

(43)b [$_{TP2}$ These pictures of *each other*$_2$ [T2°$_{[NOM]}$ seem to the *children*$_2$
[$_{TP1}$ T1° ~~these pictures of *each other*~~$_2$ to be boring]]]

Furthermore, since the Φ-constraint (37) introduces the requirement to be c-commanded by a Φ-head existentially ("if [the restrictor] is within the c-command domain of *a* Φ-head [...]"), a restrictor can be merged in any position inside the c-command domain of a Φ-head. Provided that subject Φ-features are hosted by T° (but see below), these nodes include the thematic base SpecvP, as well as all intermediate landing sites below matrix T°, among them adjunct positions to vP and XP:

(47) [$_{TP}$ [D° restrictor]$_{[NOM, Φ]}$ T°$_{[NOM, Φ]}$ ... [$_{vP}$ [$_{Subject}$ D° {restrictor}]
[$_{VP}$ seem [$_{TP}$ T°$_{[Φ]}$ ... [$_{vP}$ [$_{Subject}$ D° {restrictor}]...]]]]]

Hence, the Φ-variant of Takahashi's WLM analysis equally guarantees the flexibility of restrictor insertion with A-movement.

Finally, the hypothesis that Φ-features are responsible for restrictor insertion has a further consequence for the analysis of anti-reconstruction effects with Ā-movement, which happens to align well with independent, recent ideas about where Φ-relations are encoded in the tree. The starting point of these concluding remarks comes from the observation that at first sight, the system appears to overgenerate in one particular context. Notably, it admits the derivation for German object Ā-movement schematized in (48), which mimics the scrambling derivation (39), the only, immaterial, difference being that in (48), the object stops in an outer specifier of vP on its way to SpecCP, instead of ScrP. As can be seen from representation (48)b, the restrictor of the Ā-moved object has been merged *above* the thematic position of the subject:

(48) *Ā-movement, reconstruction (derivation overgenerates)*
a. $[_{\Phi P}$ $\Phi_{[F]}$... $[_{vP}$ D° $[_{vP}$ Subject $[_{VP}$ ... $[_{DO}$ D° ...]]]]
b. $[_{\Phi P}$ $\Phi_{[F]}$... $[_{vP}$ [D° restrictor$_{[F]}$] $[_{vP}$ Subject $[_{VP}$ ... $[_{DO}$ D° ...]]]]

But such a derivation wrongly leads one to expect that *wh*-movement has the option of making disjoint reference effect disappear if the subject is an individual term that can undergo full reconstruction into SpecvP. This prediction is incorrect, the German equivalent of **Which picture of John$_2$ does he$_2$ like* behaves just like its English counterpart.[20]

The problem turns out to be only apparent, though, once the details of how subject restrictors are licensed are taken into consideration.[21] In particular, subject related Φ-features are commonly held to be located above object Φ-heads, that is either in T° or, as recently suggested in Chomsky (2008), even as high as in C° (see also Pesetsky & Torrego 2001). Adopting for expository reasons the latter assumption, it follows that subject restrictors are never merged in their thematic base, but are fully assembled only once the subject has reached SpecTP. Consequently, subjects cannot reconstruct below TP, and late merge of object restrictors as in (48) has never a discernable effect on the binding and coreference relations between terms inside subjects and objects. This modification does not affect scope

20 The same problem does not arise for English, where object Φ-features are arguably not introduced in a high Φ-head, as in German, but in v°. Hence, object restrictors are always merged below SpecvP in English. This language specific difference can furthermore be related to the parametric difference between free word order languages like German and Icelandic on the one hand, which possess a more articulated functional field, and English on the other hand, where all functional heads are collapsed in a single positions (cf. Bobaljik & Thráinsson's (1998) *Split Infl Parameter*).

21 I assume with Takahashi & Hulsey (2009) that pronouns and names are hidden definite descriptions. Hence, subject pronouns start out as definite determiners and acquire their assignment dependent component only once the restrictor is merged.

reconstruction, because scope relations can of course still be reversed by SemR into XP (see derivation (18)). In sum, the analysis delivers correct results also for the reconstructive properties of subjects.

5 Conclusion

This paper addressed two questions pertaining to the study of reconstruction phenomena. Is it necessary to admit additional mechanisms for reconstruction apart from those provided by the Copy Theory? And if so, is it possible to contain overgeneration which is well-known to arise from these mechanisms? Both questions were answered in the positive. More concretely, the additional requirements that reconstruction needs to satisfy were seen to fall into two groups: a syntactic locality condition on binding into copies (which was not further pursued at the present occasion) and a condition on the logical type of quantificational DPs and their traces, repeated in (49)a.

(49) a. ETA: Traces and quantificational DPs are extensional

b. In German, all movement operations apply in the overt component. English admits post-syntactic dislocation at LF.

c. (Counter-cyclic) Insertion of restrictors is regulated by Φ-features, instead of Case.

Together with two additional components, listed in the (49)b and (49)c, the proposal offered a unified and natural explanation for five sets of data: (i) the scope rigidity of German; (ii) the scope flexibility of English; (iii) the absence of scope reconstruction into small clauses; (iv) the absence of syntactic reconstruction into short scrambling chains; (v) the availability of scope reconstruction in short scrambling chains. To my knowledge, this is the first algorithmic account of these phenomena to date which makes explicit the relations between syntactic representations and their transparent logical forms.

The present contribution can also be seen as an attempt at supporting a broader claim about the division of labor between syntax and semantics. Concretely, I believe that a theory which makes use of the mechanisms provided by a properly constrained syntactic system in tandem with semantic mechanisms is better equipped to provide an adequate description of the multifarious properties of reconstruction phenomena than a theory which relegates these explanation to a single component, either syntax or semantics.

Acknowledgment: I am indebted to the organizers of the *Berlin Workshop on Reconstruction* at ZAS in July 2011 for their support, to Wolfgang Sternefeld for valuable comments, and to the audience of GLOW 2011, Vienna, and Elena Anagnostopoulou for helpful feedback.

References

Alexiadou, Artemis & Elena Anagnostopoulou. 1999. Raising without infinitives and the nature of agreement. In S. Bird, A. Carnie, J. Haugen & P. Norquest (eds.), *The proceedings of WCCFL 18*, 14–26. Somerville, MA: Cascadilla Press.

Anagnostopoulou, Elena. 2003. *The syntax of ditransitives: Evidence from clitics*. Berlin & New York: Mouton de Gruyter.

Anand, Pranav. 2006. *De de se*. Cambridge, MA: Massachusetts Institute of Technology Doctoral dissertation.

Aoun, Joseph & Yen-hui Audrey Li. 1993. *Syntax of scope* (Linguistic Inquiry Monograph 21). Cambridge, MA: MIT Press.

Bobaljik, Jonathan D. 1995. *Morphosyntax: The syntax of verbal inflection*. Massachusetts Institute of Technology Doctoral dissertation.

Bobaljik, Jonathan D. & Höskuldur Thráinsson. 1998. Two heads aren't always better than one. *Syntax* 1. 37–71.

Bobaljik, Jonathan D. & Susi Wurmbrand. 2012. Word order and scope: Transparent interfaces and the 3/4 signature. *Linguistic Inquiry* 43(3). 371–421.

Bruening, Benjamin. 2014. Precede-and-command revisited. *Language* 90. 342–388. https://doi.org/10.1353/lan.2014.0037.

Büring, Daniel. 1997. The great scope inversion conspiracy. *Linguistics and Philosophy* 20(2). 175–194.

Charlow, Simon & Yael Sharvit. 2014. Bound 'de re' pronouns and the LFs of attitude reports. *Semantics and Pragmatics* 7(3). 1–43. https://doi.org/10.3765/sp.7.3.

Chomsky, Noam. 1995. *The minimalist program*. Cambridge, MA: MIT Press.

Chomsky, Noam. 2008. On phases. In Robert Freidin, Carlos Otero & Maria Luisa Zubizarreta (eds.), *Foundational issues in linguistic theory: Essays in honor of Jean-Roger Vergnaud*, 133–166. Cambridge, MA: MIT Press.

Cresti, Diana. 1990. Extraction and reconstruction. *Natural Language Semantics* 3. 79–122.

Diesing, Molly. 1992. *Indefinites*. Cambridge, MA: MIT Press.

Fox, Danny. 1999. Reconstruction, binding theory, and the interpretation of chains. *Linguistic Inquiry* 30(2). 157–196.

Fox, Danny. 2002. Antecedent contained deletion and the copy theory of movement. *Linguistic Inquiry* 33(1). 63–96.

Fox, Danny. 2003. On logical form. In Randall Hendrick (ed.), *Minimalist syntax*, 83–123. Oxford: Blackwell.

Frey, Werner. 1993. *Syntaktische Bedingungen für die Interpretation*. Berlin: Studia Grammatica.

Gallin, Daniel. 1975. *Intensional and higher-order modal logic. With applications to Montague semantics*. Amsterdam: New-Holland.

Groat, Erich & John O'Neil. 1996. Spell-out at the LF interface. In Werner Abraham, Samuel David Epstein, Höskuldur Thráinsson & Jan-Wouter Zwart (eds.), *Minimal ideas*, 113–139. Amsterdam: John Benjamins. https://doi.org/10.1075/la.12.07gro.

Haider, Hubert. 1993. *Deutsche Syntax – Generativ*. Tübingen: Gunter Narr Verlag.

Heim, Irene & Kai von Fintel. 2005. *Intensional Semantics*. Lecture Notes, MIT.

Hoji, Hajime. 1985. *Logical form constraints and configurational structures in Japanese*. University of Washington Doctoral dissertation.

Hornstein, Norbert. 1995. *Logical Form: From GB to Minimalism*. Cambridge, MA: Basil Blackwell.

Johnson, Kyle & Satoshi Tomioka. 1998. Lowering and mid-size clauses. In Graham Katz, Shin-Sook Kim & Heike Winhart (eds.), *Reconstruction. Proceedings of the 1997 Tübingen workshop*, 185–206. SFB 340 Bericht 127. Universität Tübingen.

Keine, Stefan & Ethan Poole. 2018. *Reconstruction beyond English*. Talk presented at GLOW 41, April 13, Budapest.

Keshet, Ezra. 2010. Situation economy. *Natural Language Semantics* 18. 385–434.

Kratzer, Angelika. 2009. Making a pronoun: Fake indexicals as windows into the properties of pronouns. *Linguistic Inquiry* 40(2). 187–237.

Krifka, Manfred. 1998. Scope inversion under the rise-fall contour in German. *Linguistic Inquiry* 29(1). 75–112.

Lebeaux, David. 1990. Relative clauses, licensing and the nature of the derivation. In *Proceedings of NELS 20*, 318–332. Amherst, MA: GLSA, University of Massachusetts.

Lechner, Winfried. 1996. On semantic and syntactic reconstruction. *Wiener Linguistische Gazette* 57-59. 63–100.

Lechner, Winfried. 1998. Two kinds of reconstruction. *Studia Linguistica* 52(3). 276–310.

Lechner, Winfried. 2009. *Criteria for diagnosing covert movement (and some remarks on the Duke of York)*. Talk presented at Diagnosing Syntax, Utrecht University/Leiden University, January 29-31. http://users.uoa.gr/~wlechner/Diagnostics%202009.pdf (10 October, 2018).

Lechner, Winfried. 2011. *Some formal conditions on logical syntax*. Talk presented at GLOW 34, April 26-30, University of Vienna. http://users.uoa.gr/~wlechner/GLOW%202011.pdf (10 October, 2018).

Lechner, Winfried. 2013. Diagnosing covert movement with the duke of york and reconstruction. In Lisa Cheng & Norbert Corver (eds.), *Diagnosing syntax*, 158–190. Oxford: Oxford University Press.

Maier, Emar. 2009. Presupposing acquaintance: A unified semantics for *de dicto*, *de re* and *de se* belief reports. *Linguistics and Philosophy* 32(3). 429–474.

Moulton, Keir. 2013a. Not moving clauses: Connectivity in clausal arguments. *Syntax* 16(3). 250–291.

Moulton, Keir. 2013b. Small clause subjects do reconstruct. In Yelena Fainleib, Nicholas LaCara & Yangsook Park (eds.), *Proceedings of NELS 41*, 27–40. Amherst, MA: GLSA.

Nissenbaum, Jon. 2000. *Investigations of covert phrase movement*. Massachusetts Institute of Technology Doctoral dissertation.

Percus, Orin. 2000. Constraints on some other variables in syntax. *Natural Language Semantics* 8(3). 173–231.

Pesetsky, David. 2000. *Phrasal movement and its kin*. Cambridge, MA: MIT Press.

Pesetsky, David & Esther Torrego. 2001. T-to-C movement: Causes and consequences. In Michael Kenstowicz (ed.), *Ken Hale: A life on language*, 355–427. Cambridge, MA: MIT Press.

Peters, Stanley & Dag Westerståhl. 2006. *Quantifiers in logic and language*. Oxford: Oxford University Press.
Richards, Norvin W. III. 1997. *What moves where when in which language?* Massachusetts Institute of Technology Doctoral dissertation.
Romero, Maribel. 1998. *Focus and reconstruction effects in wh-phrases*. Amherst, MA: University of Massachusetts Doctoral dissertation.
Rullmann, Hotze. 1995. *Maximality in the semantics of Wh-constructions*. Amherst, MA: University of Massachusetts Doctoral dissertation.
Ruys, Eddie G. 2000. Weak crossover as a scope phenomenon. *Linguistic Inquiry* 31(3). 513–539.
Ruys, Eddie G. 2015. A minimalist condition on semantic reconstruction. *Linguistic Inquiry* 46(3). 453–488.
Salzmann, Martin. 2006. *Resumptive prolepsis. A study in indirect A'-dependencies*. Leiden University Doctoral dissertation.
Sauerland, Uli. 1998. *The meaning of chains*. Cambridge, MA: Massachusetts Institute of Technology Doctoral dissertation.
Sauerland, Uli. 2004. The interpretation of traces. *Natural Language Semantics* 12(1). 63–128.
Sharvit, Yael. 1998. Possessive wh-expressions and reconstruction. In Pius Tamanji & Kiyomi Kusumoto (eds.), *Proceedings of the 28th meeting of the North Eastern Linguistic Society (NELS)*. Amherst, MA: University of Massachussetts GLSA Publications.
Sportiche, Dominique. 1995. Clitic constructions. In L. Zaring & J. Rooryck (eds.), *Phrase structure and the lexicon*, 213–276. Dordrecht: Kluwer Academic Publishers.
Stowell, Timothy. 1991. Small clause restructuring. In Robert Freidin (ed.), *Principles and parameters in comparative grammar*, 182–218. Cambridge, MA: MIT Press.
Takahashi, Shoichi. 2006. *Decomposition and identity*. Massachusetts Institute of Technology Doctoral dissertation.
Takahashi, Shoichi. 2011. *The Composition and Interpretation of Tough Movement*. Talk at GLOW 34. Vienna.
Takahashi, Shoichi & Sarah Hulsey. 2009. Wholesale late merger: Beyond the A/A'-distinction. *Linguistic Inquiry* 40(3). 387–426.
Takano, Yuji. 1995. Predicate fronting and internal subjects. *Linguistic Inquiry* 26(2). 327–340.
Williams, Edwin. 1983. Against small clauses. *Linguistic Inquiry* 14(1). 287–308.

Hubert Truckenbrodt

Notes on stress reconstruction and syntactic reconstruction

1 Overview

This paper offers a new analysis of the interaction of movement with stress-assignment from Bresnan (1971, 1972), mostly using examples from German. The interaction is analyzed as stress reconstruction, a PF-effect of the copy left behind by movement according to the copy theory of movement in Chomsky (1993) and the later development of internal merge in Chomsky (2008). This paper also offers an analysis of the interaction of this phenomenon with LF-reconstruction such as idiom chunk reconstruction and reconstruction of Condition C effects. The observations support an analysis that integrates stress reconstruction and LF-reconstruction into a coherent picture, with the following properties. (i) First, movement by internal merge leads to a representation of multi-dominance of the moved element (Chomsky 2008). This leads to obligatory stress reconstruction and to the option of LF-reconstruction, the latter as suggested by Chomsky (1993). (ii) Second, topic-comment structures do not tolerate multiple association of the topic with a position inside of the comment; there are two ways of fixing this when it arises: (a) Retaining the topic and converting its copies (i.e. its associations to positions in the comment) to bound empty categories during the syntax. Scrambling, I argue, has only this option, which blocks both LF-reconstruction and stress reconstruction; examples of wh-movement that test for Condition C reconstruction are also typically construed this way to avoid a reconstructed Condition C violation; (b) Operator-variable structures in which the operator is a topic seem to additionally allow splitting of multi-dominance structures into a copy for the operator that is a topic and a separate copy for the variable; this allows for a limited amount of LF-reconstruction for wh-phrase topics, without stress reconstruction. Topics apart, however, the normal result of movement is multi-dominance, as derived by internal merge; this is confirmed by the application of stress reconstruction.

The paper is structured as follows. Section 2 reviews Bresnan's observation about English. Section 3 discusses the effect in German in the context of a detailed prosodic analysis of German. Section 4 shows the analysis of the effect in the copy

Hubert Truckenbrodt, Leibniz-Centre General Linguistics (ZAS) Berlin

https://doi.org/10.1515/9783050095158-005

theory of movement. Section 5 addresses interactions of stress reconstruction with topics, with scrambling, and with idiom chunk reconstruction, among other things. Section 6 addresses the interaction of stress-assignment with reconstruction for Condition C, with some remarks on reconstruction for anaphor binding. Section 7 sums up the results.

2 Bresnan's observation

Bresnan (1971, 1972) employed the Nuclear Stress Rule (NSR) of Chomsky & Halle (1968), which (leaving aside cyclic effects) assigns stress rightmost as in (1a). As Bresnan notes, final pronouns must be exempt from the NSR as in (1b,c). This paper employs the term *sentence stress* (nuclear stress) and marks its position by double underlining.

(1) a. Mary teaches engineering.
    b. Mary teaches it.
    c. The boy bought some.

Throughout this paper, the concern is with stress-patterns that are not affected by narrow focus, since narrow focus on any of the elements in (1) will attract the sentence stress to the focused item. The sentences in (1) and other sentences we will be concerned with may be thought of as entirely new (Selkirk 2008). They are either focused in their entirety or are not carrying focus at all.

Bresnan's cases involve another class of systematic exceptions to the NSR, next to pronouns. This involves cases of syntactic movement from sentence-final position. She credits (2) to Newman (1946). The a.-examples of (2)–(7) are the exceptions from the NSR. These all involve movement from final position. In Bresnan's analysis the structure before movement involved a lexical object that would receive the sentence stress, for example *to leave plans* in (2a) or *had written what books* in (6a). The (b)-examples are cases for minimal comparison that do not involve this configuration and that show the final stress that is predicted by the NSR. In (2) and (3) the comparison cases do not involve movement from final position. In (4)–(7) the comparison cases are examples with movement of a pronominal element from final position. For example, in (6b) the underlying structure is *had written what.* Here it is plausible that the final pronoun, like the ones in (1b,c), is independently exempt from the NSR. Thus movement only interferes with the NSR if the element that moves from final position would receive sentence stress before movement, as in the (a)-examples in Bresnan's analysis.

(2) a. George has plans to leave t.
b. George has plans to leave.

(3) a. Mary liked the proposal that George left t.
b. Mary liked the proposal that George leave.

(4) a. George found some friends he'd like you to meet t.
b. George found someone he'd like you to meet t.

(5) a. Let me tell you about something strange I saw t.
b. Let me tell you about something I saw t.

(6) a. John asked what books Helen had written t.
b. John asked what Helen had written t.

(7) a. I can't help noticing how serene he is t.
b. I can't help noticing how he is t.

The effect will be cast in terms of stress reconstruction in this paper. The following formulation is a starting point that brings the relevant descriptive generalization into view:

(8) *Stress reconstruction*
For the rules of stress-assignment, stress on an element coindexed with a trace counts as stress in the position of the trace.

The examples (2)–(7) are repeated in (9)–(14) with coindexing and bracketing of the coindexed element. *Op* stands for an empty relative pronoun operator. This is coindexed with the head NP preceding the clause in the relative clause examples (10)–(13). Even though this head NP is outside of the relative clause, its stress reconstructs into the trace position in the relative clause.

(9) a. George has [[plans]$_1$ to leave t_1].
b. George has plans to leave.

(10) a. Mary liked the [proposal]$_1$ Op_1 that George left t_1.
b. Mary liked the proposal that George leave.

(11) a. George found some [friends]$_1$ Op_1 he'd like you to meet t_1.
b. George found [someone]$_1$ Op_1 he'd like you to meet t_1.

(12) a. Let me tell you about something [strange]$_1$ Op_1 I saw t_1.
b. Let me tell you about [something]$_1$ Op_1 I saw t_1.

(13) a. John asked [what books]$_1$ Helen had written t_1.
b. John asked [what]$_1$ Helen had written t_1.

(14) a. I can't help noticing [how serene]$_1$ he is t_1.
b. I can't help noticing [how]$_1$ he is t_1.

As (8) brings out, in all cases of non-final stress, the stress that should be in final position by the NSR is instead found on an element earlier in the clause that is coindexed with the final trace.

Bresnan's analysis of her observation involves a cyclic application of the NSR, which in her time was formulated in terms of weakening of the non-final elements. The NSR thus applied to a fully stressed structure akin to (15a). At that stage there is still a copy of the relevant element in final position. In the first application of the NSR this final element retains its strength while the preceding elements of the first cycle are weakened as in (15b). The final object is made non-overt in (15c), leaving all remaining material from the first cycle with subordinated stress. When the NSR reapplies at the highest cycle in (15d), it reduces everything except for the rightmost element among the strongly stressed elements, and thus derives the correct position of strongest stress.

(15) a. Helen left directions [for George to follow directions]
b. Helen left directions [for George to follow directions] NSR 1st cycle
c. Helen left directions [for George to follow Ø] syntax
d. Helen left directions [for George to follow Ø] NSR 2nd cycle

Lakoff (1972) and Berman & Szamosi (1972) criticized Bresnan's suggestion. A reply to the criticism can be found in Bresnan (1972). I believe that some of the factors that were difficult to tease apart then can be teased apart today, and that, when we do, Bresnan's observation remains correct; see Truckenbrodt (2013) for discussion. Further, the current paper differs from the authors in the 1970s in not assessing the preferred stress-pattern. Instead, the German judgments below assess the felicity of the reconstructed and the non-reconstructed stress patterns separately. The fact of interest is that the reconstructed stress-pattern is possible (in the absence of givenness of the verb). We will see that it is almost always optionally alternating with the non-reconstructed stress-pattern.

3 Bresnan's effect in German

In this section different aspects of the effect and its analysis in German are established. Section 3.1. shows an analysis of the effect in the context of a general prosodic analysis of German. Section 3.2. shows a restriction on the effect. Section 3.3. provides an additional argument for stress reconstruction from relative clauses.

3.1 The effect in German in a cross-linguistic prosodic analysis

In German, the effect plays out in the stress placement on the verb. It is here illustrated using the theory of stress-assignment in (16) and (17).[1] The account is a modification of that of Gussenhoven (1983, 1992) which was first applied to German in Uhmann (1991). Stress-XP is from Truckenbrodt (1995).

(16) Stress-XP: Each overt XP must contain a beat of phrasal stress (accent).[2]

(17) NSR-I: The rightmost phrasal stress (accent) in the intonation phrase is strengthened.

There are two levels of prosody-assignment above the prosodic word. At the lower of these two levels, Stress-XP requires a beat of phrasal stress in each overt XP. This is here marked by single underlining. Consider (18). The arguments and adjuncts contain such XPs, DP and NP (and sometimes PP) as in *[$_{DP}$ die [$_{NP}$ Lena]]* 'Lena', *[$_{DP}$ ein [$_{NP}$ Lama]]* 'a llama' or *[$_{PP}$ im [$_{DP}$ [$_{NP}$ Januar]]]* 'in January'. I assume for concreteness that the article is stress-rejecting like a pronoun. In each case stress on the noun satisfies Stress-XP for the NP, it simultaneously satisfies Stress-XP for the DP and for a higher PP. The NSR-I in (17) strengthens the rightmost of these stressed nouns. This is shown by double underlining in (18b).

1 This account builds on the two-level theory of Selkirk (1984, 1995) and Gussenhoven (1983, 1992) and ties this theory to the use of XPs in the prosodic structure of other languages (Chen 1987, Hale & Selkirk 1987, Selkirk 1986, Selkirk & Shen 1990, Truckenbrodt 1999, 2006, 2007a). The account was previously applied to the interaction of movement and stress in Truckenbrodt & Darcy (2010). Stress-XP is from Truckenbrodt (1995) and was also applied to Italian in Samek-Lodovici (2005) and to English in Féry & Samek-Lodovici (2006). The NSR-I desends from the NSR of Chomsky & Halle (1968) and the understanding of nuclear stress as being relative to the intonation phrase in Pierrehumbert (1980). For the formulation that strengthens the last accent of the intonation phrase, see Uhmann (1991) for German and Selkirk (1995) for English. In its application to German the account builds on, and captures results of early important work like Höhle (1982), Krifka (1984), von Stechow & Uhmann (1986), Uhmann (1991) and Jacobs (1993).

2 The reason that Stress-XP applies only to overt XPs will become apparent below. I have elsewhere used the formulation that the XPs in question need to be lexical as opposed to functional. I here generalize Stress-XP to functional projections, including *v*P, which will be crucial below. One of the main reason to exclude functional projection earlier, the lack of stress on pronouns, is better handled by a separate statement that function words are stress-rejecting, I believe, as suggested by Bresnan (1971), Kratzer & Selkirk (2007) and Truckenbrodt (2007a).

(18) a. Die Lena will dem Werner im Januar ein Lama malen.
b. Die Lena will dem Werner im Januar ein Lama malen.
the Lena wants the Werner in January a llama paint
'Lena wants to paint a llama for Werner in January.'

Here and throughout this paper, stress in the English translation, where indicated, shows the stress assigned by the same rules and same analytical assumptions, rather than word-by-word transfer of stress from the German example. Stress-XP and NSR-I (like Gussenhoven's account on which they build) are intended to also work for English, without parameterization. Stress reconstruction applies in both languages. Stress effects of focus and givenness are likewise comparable.

In German, an unmarked rendition of (18b) shows typically rising (L*+H) accents on non-final syllables with phrasal stress, as in Figure 1.[3]

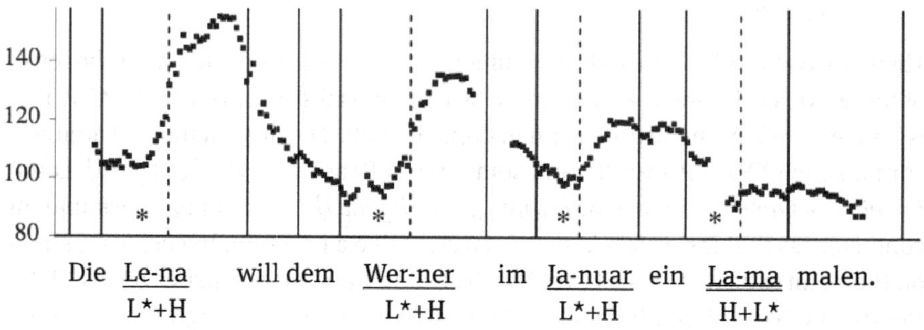

Fig. 1: F0 contour for *Die Lena will dem Werner im Januar ein Lama malen*, 'Lena wants to paint a llama for Werner in January.' Speaker TL from Baden-Württemberg. The sentence was read as an answer to the question *Was gibt's Neues?* 'What's new?'. Adapted from Truckenbrodt (2007b).

The claim that the final accent is the strongest of the sentence is based primarily on the intuitions of native speakers and connects this account to earlier reports of sentence stress that did not employ the two-level model (e.g. Höhle 1982, Cinque 1993).

The crucial issue for stress reconstruction is when the verb receives stress. Let us therefore begin by establishing in some detail when it receives stress independently of stress reconstruction. The verb is typically final in the German head-final VPs. The verb does not receive stress when preceded by an (unscrambled) direct object, as in (19a). However, it receives stress when preceded by an adjunct as

3 The successive phonetic lowering among the peaks (downstep) is a phonetic process that does not reflect relative strength of stress, see e.g. Truckenbrodt (2007b).

in (19b). See Gussenhoven (1983, 1992), Krifka (1984) and Jacobs (1993) on the argument-adjunct contrast.

(19) a. sein Fahrrad putzen
one's bicycle clean
'to clean his/one's bicycle'

b. am Wochenende putzen
on-the weekend clean
'to clean on the weekend'

In (20a), I adopt the classical analysis of the word-order between the adjunct and the argument: The adjunct is not genuinely inside of VP, the direct object is genuinely inside of VP for reasons of theta-role assignment, and must therefore be closer to the verb. A structure with only the object is therefore as in (20b), a structure with only the adjunct is as in (20c).

(20) a.	am	Wochenende	[$_{VP}$	sein	Fahrrad	putzen	]
b.			[$_{VP}$	sein	Fahrrad	putzen	]
c.	am	Wochenende	[$_{VP}$			putzen	]
	on-the	weekend		one's	bicycle	clean	
	'to clean (one's bicycle) (on the weekend)'						

The stress contrast between arguments and adjuncts is captured in the application of Stress-XP to VP. In (20a,b) the object receives phrasal stress independently on [$_{NP}$ Fahrrad]. Now, this phrasal stress also has the effect that the VP satisfies Stress-XP, since the word *Fahrrad* is within the VP. Therefore the VP contains phrasal stress in (20a,b) and there is no need to assign phrasal stress to the verb. (It is not detrimental that the same phrasal stress satisfies Stress-XP for NP and VP, and the effect is also not cumulative in this account.) In (20c), however, the phrasal stress assigned on the adjunct is not genuinely within the VP.[4] The application of Stress-XP to VP requires phrasal stress genuinely inside of VP, which is therefore assigned to the verb. (The effects of the subsequently applying NSR-I are not shown in (20). It strengthens the object in (20a,b) and the verb in (20c).) Another way of putting this analysis of the argument-adjunct asymmetry is that the verb does not invoke Stress-XP in (20a,b) where it is just a syntactic head, but that the verb invokes Stress-XP in (20c), where it is a VP, hence an XP.

A further relevant observation is discussed in Kratzer & Selkirk (2007) and Truckenbrodt (2012). In the configuration [*argument pronoun verb*] in wide focus

4 The account assumes that theta-role assignment and Stress-XP use the same strict standard for inclusion in the VP. Assuming that the adjunct is adjoined to VP, it counts as outside of VP for both theta-role and stress assignment.

contexts, the verb always requires stress in addition to stress on the argument. In other words, an argument separated from the verb by an overt pronoun cannot exempt the verb from requiring stress. (21) shows this for indefinite pronouns:

(21) a. dass vorhin ein Kind etwas essen wollte

b. # dass vorhin ein Kind etwas essen wollte (unless *essen* is given)
that earlier a child something eat wanted
'that a while ago a child wanted to eat something'

c. dass du einem Kind etwas vorgelesen hast

d. # dass du einem Kind etwas vorgelesen hast (unless *vorgelesen* is given)
that you a child something read have
'that you have read something to a child'

The analysis of this restriction requires a syntactic structure like (22) in which the direct object and the verb are joined in a VP that excludes higher arguments. (These are in higher verbal projections.) In such a structure the stressed argument is outside of the VP that contains the pronoun and the verb. Stress on that higher argument is not stress inside of the lowest VP. Satisfaction of Stress-XP for the lowest VP requires phrasal stress in this VP. It is assumed here, as in Bresnan's account, that pronouns are inherently stress-rejecting. The phrasal stress of the VP is then assigned to the verb.

(22) dass vorhin ein Kind [$_{\text{VP}}$ etwas essen] wollte
that earlier a child something eat wanted

We will refine this picture in considering the interaction of verb raising with stress reconstruction below.

A further relevant case is that of multiple final verbs. A stressed object of the inner verb exempts all following verbs from requiring accent as in (23a). Where no such stressed object is present, as in (23b), the lowest verb receives phrasal stress. The current analysis assumes successively embedded VPs.

(23) a. [$_{\text{VP}_1}$ [$_{\text{VP}_2}$ ein [$_{\text{NP}}$ Fahrrad] reparieren$_{\text{V}_2}$] wollen$_{\text{V}_1}$]
a bicycle fix want
'to want to fix a bicycle'

b. [$_{\text{VP}_1}$ [$_{\text{VP}_2}$ etwas reparieren$_{\text{V}_2}$] wollen$_{\text{V}_1}$]
something fix want
'to want to fix something'

[$_{NP}$ Fahrrad] receives stress by Stress-XP in (23a). Stress on *Fahrrad* satisfies Stress-XP also for VP_2 and for VP_1, since both contain the word *Fahrrad*. VP_2 in particular (and the word *Fahrrad* with it) is contained in VP_1 as the complement of V_1. Therefore the verbs do not separately receive stress in (23a). In (23b) *reparieren* receives

the phrasal stress of VP_2. This being the case, *reparieren* also satisfies Stress-XP for VP_1 since VP_1 then also contains the stressed word *reparieren*.

With the basics of this stress-account in place, let us turn to the interaction of stress-assignment and movement in German. The effect is found with wh-movement as in (24) and with relative clauses as in (25). Note that all German relative clauses have an overt relative pronoun.

(24) a. Ich frage mich [was für Bücher$_1$ sie t_1 geschrieben hat].
I ask myself what for books she written has
'I wonder what books she has written.'

b. Ich frage mich [was$_1$ sie t_1 geschrieben hat].
I ask myself what she written has
'I wonder what she has written.'

(25) a. Ich kenne alle Bücher$_1$ [die$_1$ sie t_1 geschrieben hat].
I know all books which she written has
'I know all the books she has written.'

b. Ich kenne alles [was$_1$ sie t_1 geschrieben hat].
I know all which she written has
'I know everything she has written.'

In all four preceding examples, the VPs are $[_{VP_1} [_{VP_2} t_1 \textit{geschrieben}_{V_2}] \textit{hat}_{V_1}]$. We find the expected stress-pattern for these VPs in (24b) and (25b): Both VP_2 and VP_1 require stress by Stress-XP and they both satisfy this condition by assignment of phrasal stress on the lower verb *geschrieben*.

The unexpected cases are (24a) and (25a). They show interaction with syntactic movement. We expect stress on the inner verb by Stress-XP; empirically, however, it is not required. In both cases *Bücher* is related to the trace in the VPs $[_{VP_1} [_{VP_2} t_1 \textit{geschrieben}_{V_2}] \textit{hat}_{V_1}]$. It is as though the stress on *Bücher* counts as stress in the position of the trace. In other words, stress in the structure (26) counts as though *Bücher* was in the position of the trace as in (27). In (27) the VPs contain stress on *Bücher* and Stress-XP is satisfied without stress on the verb.

(26) [... Bücher]$_1$ (...) sie $[_{VP_1} [_{VP_2} t_1 \text{ geschrieben}_{V_2}] \text{ hat}_{V_1}]$
books she written has

(27) sie $[_{VP_1} [_{VP_2}$ [... Bücher] geschrieben$_{V_2}] \text{ hat}_{V_1}]$
she books written has

In that sense we can think about this phenomenon as a case of stress reconstruction.

Notice that the argument cannot be undermined by postulating that the expression containing *Bücher* can have this effect from its surface position, without the mediating effect of the trace. Informally, as we have seen, such a stress-exempting effect is not normally possible across a pronoun. Formally, it is also ruled out: In (24a), for example, the wh-phrase is in Spec,CP and thus clearly outside of the VP to which it contributes its stress.

In sum, we account for the assignment of phrasal stress and sentence stress in German in terms of Stress-XP and NSR-I (rightmost strengthening). Narrow focus may override their effects (though this is not discussed here). As in Bresnan's English cases, syntactic movement creates a class of exceptions to this default stress pattern. These exceptions can be looked upon in terms of stress reconstruction: Stress-XP is satisfied for a VP (allowing a stressless verb) when there is a trace in direct object position that is coindexed with a stressed element earlier in the structure. For the purpose of Stress-XP, it is as though this earlier stress was within the VP.

Notice that Bresnan's English examples are analyzed in very similar terms in the current account. In *Mary teaches engineering*, Stress-XP assigns stress to the two NPs *Mary* and *engineering* and NSR-I strengthens the rightmost of these. In *Mary teaches* or *Mary teaches it*, stress on the verb is required by the application of Stress-XP to the VP. Likewise for the interaction with movement. In *[what books$_1$ she has written t$_1$]* the unexpected observation is that the VP *[written t]* does not show the stress expected due to Stress-XP. Stress reconstruction is observed insofar the stressed *what books* acts prosodically as though it was still inside of that VP, allowing a stressless verb.

Notice also that the stress pattern that shows stress reconstruction is typically optional (Truckenbrodt & Darcy 2010). What is interesting about it is that it is available at all in the presence of a contextually new VP. However, a stress-pattern that looks like stress is not reconstructing is typically available in addition. This is true both for wh-questions and relative clauses. For example, next to (25a), the stress-pattern in (28) is also possible.

(28) Ich kenne alle Bücher$_1$ [die$_1$ sie t$_1$ geschrieben hat].
I know all books which she written has
'I know all the books she has written.'

This additional option is analyzed in connection with topics in section 5.

3.2 A restriction on the effect

The effect shows an interesting prosodic restriction, which is mentioned here for completeness. The restriction is that *stress reconstruction is blocked by an intervening element with phrasal stress*. In Bresnan's cases stress reconstruction obtains in (11a), (12a) and (14a) across intervening unstressed pronouns and unstressed verbs. In (10a) and (13a) it obtains across a name, which, being an NP, would normally carry phrasal stress by Stress-XP. As mentioned by Selkirk (1995), stress reconstruction in the sense of the current paper only works in these cases if the name is contextually given and thus stressless. Also the detailed observations of Gussenhoven (1983, 1992), who seeks an account without interaction with movement, show that the effect only obtains in the absence of intervening stressed (accented) material. The examples in (29) illustrate the blocking effect. In (29a) we see stress reconstruction across an unstressed pronoun. In (29b) there is an intervening stressed element, *am Wochenend* 'on the weekend'. It receives phrasal stress by Stress-XP and it is stressed by NSR-I. If there was an unobstructed effect of stress reconstruction, the stress on *was für Fahrräder* should still reconstruct into the VP and license stressless final verbs. Empirically, however, this stress-pattern is not a neutral stress-pattern. It is possible only where *am Wochenende* 'on the weekend' is contrastive or where *gemietet* 'rented' is contextually given. (29c) is the only possible neutral stress-pattern in this case. It is a stress-pattern without stress reconstruction: The VP contains stress on the verb, as required by Stress-XP and regardless of the trace it contains.

(29) a. Ich frage mich [was für Fahrräder ihr t_1 gemietet habt].
I ask myself what for bicyles you rented have
'I wonder what bicycles you rented.'

b. # Ich frage mich [was für Fahrräder ihr am Wochenende t_1
I ask myself what for bicyles you on.the weekend
gemietet habt].
rented have
'I wonder what bicycles you rented on the weekend.'

c. Ich frage mich [was für Fahrräder ihr am Wochenende t_1 gemietet habt].

Cases like these motivate the conclusion that an intervening stressed element like am *Wochenende* 'on the weekend' in (29b) blocks the effect of stress reconstruction.

An analysis of this blocking effect is developed in Truckenbrodt and Büring (in preparation). The analysis is compatible with the current paper. It involves (a) an effect of stress reconstruction and (b) additional restrictions on the syntax-prosody mapping, which are not crucial in other ways for the current paper. The relevance of this restriction for this paper is thus only that we need to choose examples in which the intervening material is stressless.

3.3 An argument for stress reconstruction from relative clauses

The examples in (30a) and (31a) are here analyzed in terms of stress reconstruction in relative clauses. The b.-examples employ pronominal heads of the relative clauses that are not assigned any stress that could be reconstructed into the relative clause. Of particular interest are then the c.-examples. In these examples sentence stress reverts to the closest non-pronominal element preceding the relative clause. This element, however, is here not part of the nominal head that might be reconstructed into the relative clause. A 'reconstructing' stress-pattern is empirically not available for these examples, as shown.

(30) a. Hier ist eine Liste einiger Bücher [die ich t verkauft habe].
here is a list some books' which I sold have
'Here is a list of some books I sold.'

b. Hier ist eine Liste von dem [was ich verkauft habe].

c. # Hier ist eine Liste von dem [was ich verkauft habe].
here is a list of that which I sold have
'Here is a list of what I sold.'

(31) a. Hier ist eine Liste der Gäste [die ich t gewinnen konnte].
here is a list the guests which I win could
'Here is a list of the guests I could to win.'

b. Hier ist eine Liste derer [die ich t gewinnen konnte].

c. # Hier ist eine Liste derer [die ich t gewinnen konnte].
here is a list those which I win could
'Here is a list of those I could win.'

This shows that the VP in the relative clause, for containing a new yet unstressed verb, really requires a stressed XP that can be reconstructed into the VP of the relative clause.

4 Analysis of stress reconstruction

Section 4.1. provides an analysis of stress reconstruction in wh-questions using the copy theory of movement. Section 4.2. extends the analysis to relative clauses.

4.1 Stress reconstruction in the copy theory

Consider reconstruction for reflexive binding as in (32). Chomsky (1993: 34ff) suggested to analyze reconstruction of wh-movement in terms of a *copy theory (of movement and reconstruction)*. An underlying structure for the embedded question before movement is shown in (33a). Movement creates a copy of the wh-phrase in clause-initial position as in (33b), the structure at spell-out (the branching point to LF and PF). The lower copy is deleted at PF as in (33c). At LF, the operator *which* is separated as in (33d) and either the lower copy is retained as in (33e) or the upper copy as in (33f). The sentence in (32) allows two options of binding the reflexive as shown. Binding theory applies at LF, so that a lower copy at LF in (33e) leads to *Bill* as the antecedent of *himself*. Retention of the upper copy as in (33f) leads to *John* as the antecedent of *himself* in (32).

(32) John_1 wondered [which picture of $\text{himself}_{1/2}$] Bill_2 saw

(33)	a.		Bill saw [which pictures of himself]
	b.	[which picture of himself]	Bill saw [which pictures of himself]
	c. PF:	[which picture of himself]	Bill saw
	d. LF:	*which x* [*x* picture of himself]	Bill saw [*x* pictures of himself]
	e. →	*which x*	Bill_2 saw [*x* pictures of himself_2]
	or f. →	*which x* [*x* picture of himself_1]	Bill_2 saw t

The copy theory of movement and reconstruction is appealing insofar as it makes reconstruction sit comfortably in the theory of syntax. It is assumed for independent reasons that the wh-phrase originates in object position (in this case). The copy theory retains a silent copy of this original structure and employs it to account for 'reconstruction' effects of different kinds like reflexive binding in the example (32). The syntactic account of reconstruction is strengthened by phenomena in which reconstruction for one phenomenon entails reconstruction for another phenomenon, as shown in Chomsky (1993), Heycock (1995), Fox (1999) and others.

Let us employ the development of this theory in the form of Chomsky (2000, 2001, 2008): rather than two separate copies, there is in fact only one copy that is merged in different positions: first in object position and then again, as part of the formalization of movement, in Spec,CP. This is shown in the simplified structure in (34).

Let us assume that the multi-dominance structure is interpreted at LF and in the semantics along the lines of the suggestions of Chomsky (1993) illustrated in (33). At spell-out, then, where the structure is transferred to LF and PF, the multiply linked structure is intact and is the input to the mapping to PF. In the terms of Chomsky (1993: 35), the lower copies are deleted at PF. In the terms of Fox & Pesetsky (2005), linearization at PF will spell out the highest copy only.

(34)

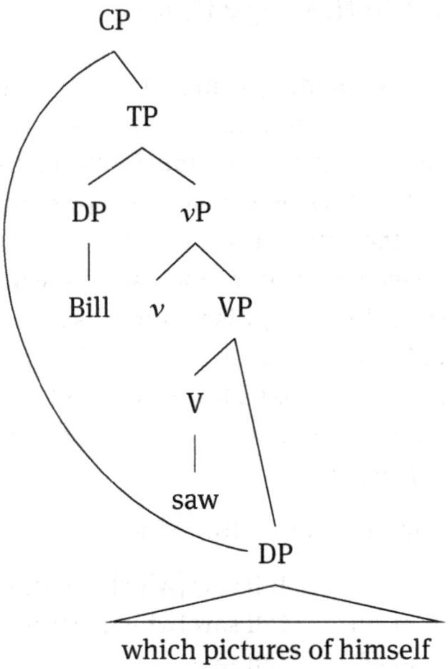

I here put aside some details of how this plays out in a cyclic derivation. There may be an additional link with which the wh-phrase is also adjoined to *v*P. This is orthogonal to the following discussion.

What is crucial is that when the structure in (34), or a part of it such as *v*P or VP, is subject to the syntax-prosody mapping, the object DP is still also dominated by VP. We want to maintain that this allows that stress on the DP still allows satisfaction of Stress-XP for the VP. I employ the more precise formulation of Stress-XP in (35), revised from (16), which derives this result quite explicitly.

(35) Stress-XP: Each overt XP must dominate an element α in the syntax such that the correspondent of α in the phonology carries a beat of phrasal stress.

Since the VP in (34) dominates the word *picture* in the DP object, stress on *picture* will count as stress in the VP for Stress-XP.

Apart from this more precise formulation of Stress-XP, we do not need to add any assumptions to the account. The copy-theory correctly predicts Bresnan's effect of movement on stress in wh-questions. Crucial to this result is the presence of the copy at spell-out, as shown in (36).

On accounts of LF-reconstruction before the copy-theory, it was not possible to derive this result. As shown in (37), the DP was inside of VP at d-structure (it originates there) and it was put back at LF, but it was not present there at s-structure. The input to the mapping to PF did not contain a copy of DP inside of VP.

(36)

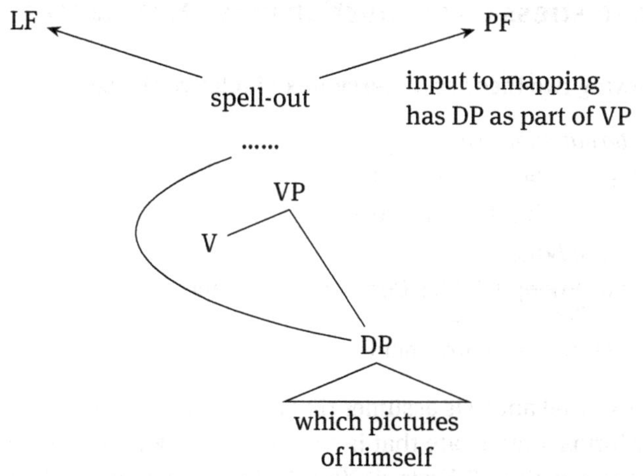

(37)

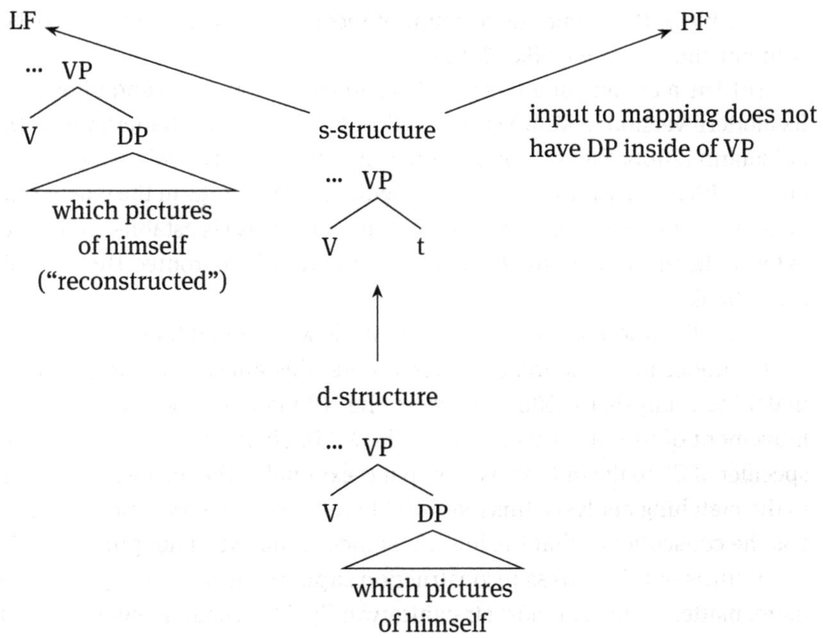

In that sense stress reconstruction provides support for the copy-theory. Stress reconstruction provides evidence that the object wh-phrase is not only in the VP underlyingly and at LF ("reconstructed" into the position of the trace), but also in between at spell-out, as postulated in the copy theory.

4.2 Approach to stress reconstruction in relative clauses

Consider the following two theories of the syntax of relative clauses:

(38) a. *head-external analysis:*
Buch [das$_1$ ich ~~das~~$_1$ gekauft habe]
book that I that bought have

b. *matching analysis:*
Buch$_1$ [[das ~~Buch~~]$_1$ ich [~~das Buch~~]$_1$ gekauft habe]
NP-matching DP-movement

(a) The head-external analysis assumes that a relative pronoun moves alone and semantically forms a predicate that is set-intersected with the head NP, in (38a) *Buch* 'book' (see e.g. Heim & Kratzer 1998). As Salzmann points out, this does not lead to a theory of syntactic reconstruction in relative clauses. It is, however, compatible with a semantic account of reconstruction as shown in Krifka (this volume) and Grosu & Krifka (2007).

(b) The matching analysis goes back to Lees (1960, 1961) and Chomsky (1965). Its modern version in Munn (1994), Citko (2001), Hulsey & Sauerland (2006), and Salzmann (2006, this volume) is illustrated in (38b). The relative pronoun is an article with an NP complement, i.e. a regular DP that fronts in the relative clause. A matching relation (originally: deletion under identity) is established between the external head NP (here *Buch* 'book') and the NP of the fronted DP (here likewise *Buch* 'book').

A modification of the matching analysis was argued for by Vergnaud (1974). In the modernized version considered here, this analysis is essentially like the matching analysis in (38b); however, the NP-matching relation is replaced by movement of the NP. Thus, in (38b), the NP *Buch* 'book' moves from within the specifier of CP to the initial position that is external to the relative clause. Similarly to the matching analysis, this requires identity of the two instances of the NP and has the consequence that the lower instance of that NP is not pronounced.

It turns out that stress reconstruction supports the analysis in (38b). Furthermore, matters come out most straightforwardly if Vergnaud raising of the NP *Buch* is assumed. This is shown in two steps in the following. First, (39a) shows movement of the DP *das Buch* 'the book' internal to the relative clause.

(39) a.

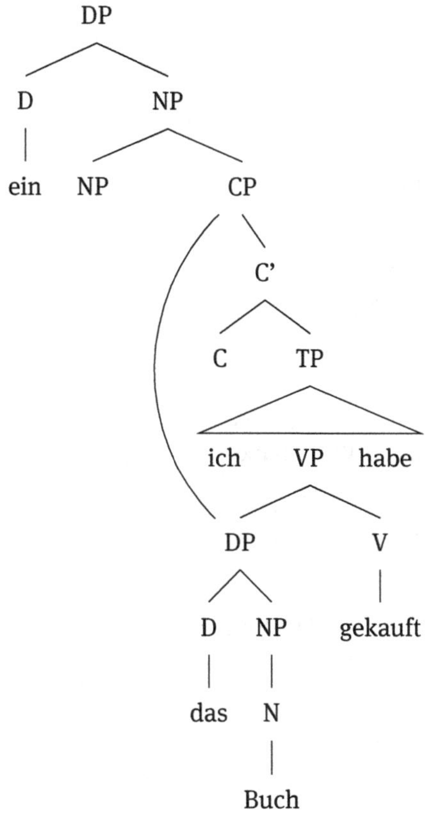

The second step is illustrated in (39b) on the following page. In this second step, the NP *Buch* 'book' is raised out of the relative clause. As a result, the relative clause external head *Buch* has an attachment inside of the VP of the relative clause. Stress on this NP thus constitutes stress on an element dominated by the VP of the relative clause as relevant to Stress-XP in (35).

If we employed the head external analysis in (38a), we would not be able to account for stress reconstruction in relative clauses. If we employed the matching analysis without Vergnaud raising, we would need to require that the matching procedure includes matching for stress, so that the elided lower instance of the NP carries stress. This raises questions about whether an empty category can carry stress. In section 5.4, a case is discussed where it is useful to assume that this is not possible.

(39) b.

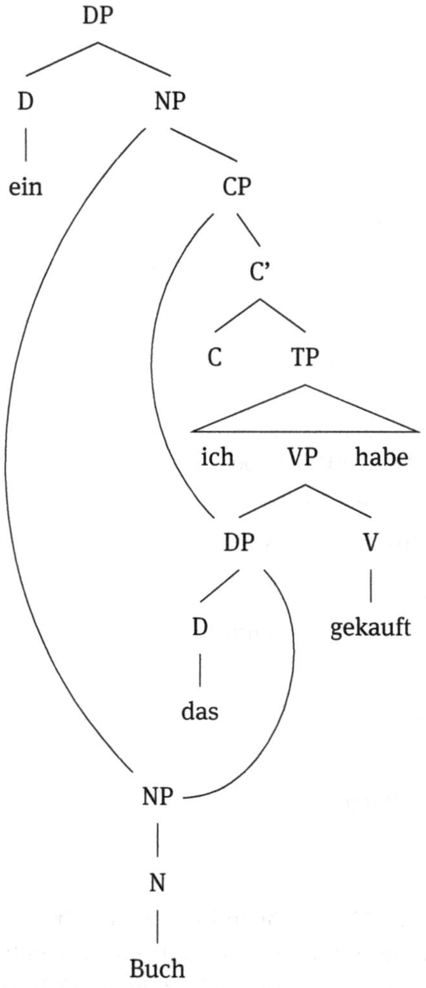

5 Syntactic restrictions on stress reconstruction

This section addresses the interaction of stress reconstruction with LF-reconstruction (primarily idiom chunk reconstruction) and with topics and scrambling. Section 5.1 introduces the prosodic effect of topics. Section 5.2 shows the absence of LF and PF reconstruction for scrambling, using idiom chunks for LF-reconstruction. Section 5.3 discusses the stress-pattern of idioms in situ. Section 5.4 addresses LF- and stress-reconstruction under wh-movement and relativization, for idiom chunks, reflexive binding and scope reconstruction.

5.1 Topics do not reconstruct for stress

As discussed in Truckenbrodt & Darcy (2010), not all instances of movement show Bresnan's interaction of stress with movement; in the current terms: not all instances of movement reconstruct for stress. This section discusses that topics do not reconstruct for stress.

For concreteness, let us follow Frey (2004) in assuming that German clauses can have a high position (here: outside of *v*P), though still below C, for aboutness-topics. These topics are also close to what Diesing (1992) sees as material outside of the VP and close to the topics of Jäger (2001) adopted also in Kratzer & Selkirk (2007). Jäger (2001) suggests that every clause requires such a topic, and that in thetic clauses, the reported event can be the topic.

Consider first (40a). With an initial topic preceding the subject, a stress pattern with a stressless verb is preferred. Without the adverb, the most natural stress pattern is one in which sentence stress is assigned to the verb (in addition to the phrasal stress on the subject). Why is this so?

(40) a. dass draußen ein <u>Mann</u> gegeigt hat
b. dass ein <u>Mann</u> <u>gegeigt</u> hat
that (outside) a man fiddled has
'that (outside) a man has fiddled'

Building on the suggestions of Jacobs (1993) and Frey (2004) and following Jäger (2001) and Kratzer & Selkirk (2007), the difference is here analyzed as shown in (41) and (42). In (41) the initial adverb is the topic and the rest of the sentence the comment, as shown. In (42), on the other hand, there is no initial adverb and so the sentence will tend to take the subject as its topic, as shown. On this understanding, the structure in (41) shows the default stress pattern between the subject and the intranstive verb within the comment: the subject is stressed and the verb is not. We derive this in terms of Stress-XP if the verb heads *v*P as in *[$_{vP}$ [$_{DP}$ ein [$_{NP}$ <u>Mann</u>]] gegeigt]*: Stress-XP is satisfied for *v*P by the stress on the subject, so the verb does not require phrasal stress.

(41)

		topic	comment	
	dass	draußen	[$_{vP}$ ein <u>Mann</u> gegeigt]	hat
	that	outside	a man fiddled	has

(42)

		topic	comment
	dass	ein <u>Mann</u>	<u>gegeigt</u> hat
	that	a man	fiddled has

In (42), on the other hand, the topic-comment structure is responsible for the different stress-pattern. In Kratzer & Selkirk (2007) this is related to the structurally higher position that topics plausibly have in German. This higher position is assumed here as well. In the current account, however, when the topic moves to a higher position as in (42), stress reconstruction will still exempt the verb from being stressed. We thus require an account over and above a higher topic position of why stress does not reconstruct in a topic-comment structure.

Notice then that it will not do to add the overwriting stress-requirement in (43).

(43) *Topic-stress* (rejected)
In a topic-comment structure the topic must not contain stronger stress than the comment.

In (42), this will require that stress is added to the comment. The problem with this account is that it wrongly predicts that stress could be added to either of the two verbs, *gegeigt*, or *hat*. However, stress on *hat* is possible only with verum focus, not otherwise. The problem cannot be circumvented by postulating that the auxiliary *haben* is stress-rejecting because it is functional. There is no independent evidence for such a distinction among the German verbs in their stress-behavior. Also, similar examples with a bona fide full verb still show the same behavior: *dass [ein Mann]$_{TOP}$ singen gesehen wurde* 'that a man was seen sing', but not *#dass [ein Mann]$_{TOP}$ singen gesehen wurde* or (apart from verum focus) *#dass [ein Mann]$_{TOP}$ singen gesehen wurde*. This wrong prediction arises because the stress on the subject would, on this account, still be reconstructed into the lowest *v*P, where it satisfies Stress-XP for both the lowest VP and the higher VP. Since Stress-XP is thus satisfied, it would have no influence on the distribution of the stress among the verbs. (43) would then enforce additional stress on either of the verbs, wrongly with no preference for the lowest verb. The fact that this stress obligatorily occurs on the lowest verb is evidence that Stress-XP is still at work: Placing the stress on the lowest verb satisfies Stress-XP for the lowest VP as well as for higher VP, which also contain the stress on the lowest verb, since they contain the lower VPs. We have evidence, then, that in topic-comment structures, the default stress is not overwritten by a statement like (43), but that, instead, stress fails to reconstruct. If it fails to reconstruct, Stress-XP, in its application to the VPs, will require stress on the VPs, and will correctly choose stress on the lowest among the verbs. This intermediate result is highlighted in (44).

(44) In topic-comment structures, stress fails to reconstruct. It seems not to be the case that stress reconstruction is overwritten by a stress-constraint relating to the topic-comment structure.

We are thus led to hypothesize a structural distinction that sets apart topic-comment structures. The particular suggestion developed here for this is motivated in connection with idiom chunk reconstruction in the following sections.

5.2 No idiom chunk reconstruction with scrambling

There is a complex literature on the syntactic properties of scrambling in German, including suggestions about reconstruction in scrambling. I will address some of their results on binding reconstruction in section 6.2. In the current section I take my cue from the behavior of idioms under scambling.

In German, scrambled idiom chunks do not reconstruct.

(45) a. dass der Peter *Eulen* *nach Athen* *trägt*
that the.NOM Peter owls.ACC to Athens carries
'that Peter is doing something unneccessary'
b. dass *Eulen* der Peter *nach Athen trägt* (no idiom-reading)

(46) a. dass die Maria *einen Frosch im* *Hals* *hat*
that the.NOM Maria a.ACC frog in.the neck has
'that Maria has difficulties speaking'
b. dass *einen Frosch* die Maria *im Hals hat* (no idiom-reading)

(47) a. dass der Peter *in einen sauren Apfel* *gebissen* hat
that the.NOM Peter in a sour apple bitten has
'that Peter has swallowed a bitter pill'
b. dass *in einen sauren Apfel* der Peter *gebissen* hat (no idiom-reading)

(48) a. dass Marias Leben *an einem seidenen Faden* *hängt*
that Maria's life.NOM on a silken thread hangs
'that Maria's life is in danger'
b. dass *an einem seidenen Faden* Marias Leben *hängt* (no idiom-reading)

(49) a. dass wir der Maria *einen Bären* *aufgebunden* haben
that we the.DAT Maria a.ACC bear tied.onto have
'that we lied to Maria as a prank'
b. dass wir *einen Bären* der Maria *aufgebunden* haben (no idiom-reading)

In fact, where the idiom consists of a subject and a verb, a non-idomatic accusative or dative object is required to scramble across the subject:

(50) a. dass den Peter *der* *Hafer* *sticht*
that the.ACC Peter the.NOM oat stings
'that Peter feels up to something'
b. dass *der Hafer* den Peter *sticht* (no idiom-reading)

(51) a. dass der Maria *eine Laus über die Leber gelaufen ist*
that the.DAT Maria a.NOM louse across the liver walked is
'that Maria is in a bad mood'

b. dass *eine Laus* der Maria *über die Leber gelaufen ist* (no idiom-reading)

Following Jäger (2001), I assume that scrambled constituents are always topics. I will work with the hypotheses in (52) and (53).

(52) A topic must not have an additional link into the comment (the scope of the topic) as part of a multiply linked structure.

(53) A way of changing a multiply linked structure into one compatible with (52) is to transform the lower links into bound empty categories.

Notice that the reduction of the lower copy by (53) may be viewed as the anticipation, during the syntax, of the PF-deletion of the lower copy suggested as part of the copy theory by Chomsky (1993).

For the idiom chunks, I furthermore adopt the suggestion of Chomsky (1993) in (54).

(54) An idiom needs to be a unit at LF (Chomsky 1993: 39).

We can now derive the observations above. First, if an idiom chunk is scrambled, it cannot be syntactically reconstructed to satisfy (54) because of delinking following (52) and (53). Second, for the idiom to be a unit at LF, non-idiomatic accusative and dative objects need to scramble above a subject that is part of the idiom. They will leave behind a bound empty category by (52)/(53), which we may take to be not interfering with (54).

The account has the correct consequences for stress reconstruction: Scrambling does not reconstruct for stress-assignment. Consider for example scrambling across the adverb *oft* 'often' in the following examples. Without scrambling the stress on the object *den Peter* is sufficient to satisfy Stress-XP for the VP in (55). The stress-pattern in (56) is possible only if the verb *besucht* is contextually given. If stress-reconstruction of the scrambled object *den Peter* were an option, then (56) should be the regular stress-pattern, with stress reconstruction of the stress on object back into the VP. The verb would not then need to be given in this stress-pattern. This is not the case. Instead, (57) is the regular stress-pattern for such scrambled constituents: There is no stress-reconstruction and therefore Stress-XP, applying to the VP, requires a stressed verb.

(55) dass sie oft [$_{VP}$ den Peter besucht] hat
that she often the.ACC Peter visited has

(56) dass sie den Peter oft [$_{VP}$ besucht] hat (only if *besucht* is given)

(57) dass sie den Peter oft [$_{VP}$ besucht] hat (regular stress pattern)

Parallel stress-patterns are found systematically in the examples of Diesing (1992): LF-Interpretation inside of VP corresponds to a stressless verb, LF-interpretation outside of VP (here: scrambling) corresponds to a stressed verb. In the current account, the absence of stress reconstruction follows from (52) and (53), which also prevent LF-reconstruction of scrambling: VP no longer dominates a scrambled DP after the requirement (52) is fulfilled as in (53).

We can now also account for the stress-pattern in (42). The subject is a scrambled topic, so that (52) leads to reduction of the link of the subject in the VP to a bound empty category. There is therefore no stress reconstruction. The stress required by Stress-XP for the VP is assigned to the verb.

Before turning to the stress in idiom chunks with wh-movement, it is useful to establish the baseline for this discussion: the stress pattern of the idioms without wh-movement.

5.3 Stress on idioms in situ

The preceding account has the correct consequence that the idioms show the stress derived by Stress-XP unobstructed by scrambled topics, i.e. the idiom chunks always show VP-internal behavior for stress. For example, a non-idiomatic example like (58) has the standard stress-option in (58a) with the VP-internal object, but also the topic-comment stress-option in (58b), here derived by string-vacuous scrambling: the object is a topic.

(58) a. Ich glaube, dass sie den Peter gesehen hat.
I think that she the.ACC Peter saw has
b. Ich glaube dass sie den Peter gesehen hat.

This second option is not available for idioms, since it would require (string-vacuous) scrambling of an idiom chunk:

(59) a. Ich glaube, dass sie mit ihm noch *ein Hühnchen zu rupfen hat.*
I believe that she with him still a chicken to pluck has
'I believe that she will want to have a serious conversation with him.'
b. # Ich glaube, dass sie mit ihm noch *ein Hühnchen zu rupfen hat.*

(60) a. Ich glaube, dass sie dir *einen Bären aufgebunden* haben.
I believe that they you a bear tied.onto have
'I believe they have lied to you as a prank.'

b. # Ich glaube, dass sie dir *einen Bären aufgebunden* haben.

This logic extends to other instances of stress-assignment in idioms, and in fact the idioms help us sort between default stress and topic-induced stress in some other cases. For example, in a non-idiomatic sentence in which the object of a transitive verb has moved across the subject, stress on the subject has the consequence that no stress on the verb is required (where the verb is not given), see Kratzer & Selkirk (2007).

(61) Ich weiß, dass dieses Haus$_1$ [Maffiosi e$_1$ besitzen].
I know that this house Maffiosi own
'I know that Maffiosi own this house.'

Using different examples, Truckenbrodt (2012) pointed out that this stress-pattern is often optional and that stress on the verb is also possible. The idioms now confirm the assessment of Kratzer & Selkirk (2007) that there is only one default stress pattern, the one with stress on the subject. Thus, an idiom only allow this stress-pattern, as in (62).

(62) a. Ich glaube, dass dich *der Hafer sticht.*
I think that you.ACC the.NOM oat stings
'I think you are feeling up to something.'

b. # Ich glaube, dass dich *der Hafer sticht.*

The additional option of stressing the verb in this configuration, discussed by Truckenbrodt (2012), must thus be derived by the subject being a topic (e.g. by string-vacuous scrambling of the subject below the moved object), with the consequences defined in (52) and (53).

For deriving the default pattern of this case, let us follow Kratzer & Selkirk (2007) and Truckenbrodt (2012) in assuming raising of the verb to *v*: *dieses Haus$_1$ [$_{vP}$ Mafiosi [$_{VP}$ e$_1$ t$_V$] besitzen].* Stress-XP is then satisfied for *v*P by stress on the subject *Mafiosi.* In its formulation in (16) and (35), Stress-XP need not be satisfied for categories that do not contain overt material like the VP in this structure.

Notice that these assumptions also correctly derive the related but different case of a pronominal object intervening between the subject and the verb in (21)–(23). Here we have *dass [$_{vP}$ ein Kind [$_{VP}$ etwas ~~essen~~] essen] wollte* with raising of V to *v* by internal merge. In this case, the VP is overt because of the presence of the overt pronoun. The VP therefore invokes Stress-XP by its formulation in (35). The VP must thus contain stress. This is satisfied if the raised verb is stressed, since technically, the VP still dominates the raised verb. Put differently, Stress-XP is satisfied for VP by a stressed raised verb with the help of stress reconstruction of that verb.

A further case of interest concerns locative or directional PPs that are predicated over the internal argument. These can be stressless even if they are not contextually given, as in (63) (see Uhmann 1991, Kratzer & Selkirk 2007, Truckenbrodt 2012).

(63) Maria hat einen <u>Nagel</u> *in ein Brett* geschlagen.
Maria has a nail into a board hit
'Maria hit a nail into a board.'

The account in terms of Stress-XP here requires the assumption of untypical syntax, in particular it requires treating the PP as pseudo-incorporated into the verb (Truckenbrodt 2012). This, together with the assumption that the verb (with the pseudo-incorporated PP) strives to be a prosodic word, provide an approach to the stressless nature of these PPs. See Kratzer & Selkirk (2007) for a different account not invoking untypical syntax for this case, but with therefore more complex assumptions about the mapping, than Stress-XP. The point of interest here is that the default rules derive only a stressless option for the PP according to Kratzer & Selkirk (2007) while this stress-pattern is treated as optional in Truckenbrodt (2012). The following stress-pattern of the words in (63) is also allowed:

(64) Maria hat einen <u>Nagel</u> *in ein <u>Brett</u>* geschlagen.
Maria has a nail into a board hit

Once again, the idioms confirm the assessment of Kratzer & Selkirk (2007): When it is part of an idiom, such a PP is obligatorily stressless. This is shown in (65) and (66) for a direct object preceding the PP and in (67) for a subject preceding the PP where the direct object of the idiom is obligatorily scrambled.

(65) a. Ich glaube, dass du <u>Eulen</u> *nach Athen* trägst.
I believe that you owls to Athen carry
'I believe that you are doing redundant things.'

b. # Ich glaube, dass du <u>Eulen</u> *nach <u>Athen</u>* trägst.

(66) a. dass Maria einen <u>Frosch</u> *im Hals* hatte
that Maria a frog in.the neck had
'that Maria had difficulties speaking'

b. # dass Maria einen <u>Frosch</u> *im <u>Hals</u>* hatte

(67) a. Ich glaube, dass ihm eine Laus über *die Leber* gelaufen ist.
I believe that him a louse across the liver walked is
'I believe that he is in a bad mood.'

b. # Ich glaube, dass ihm eine Laus über *die Leber* gelaufen ist.

Thus, the optional alternative in (64) must be derived by topic-status of the direct object (e.g. by string-vacuous scrambling of the direct object), which is not available for idiom chunks.

In sum, idioms show the default stress-pattern (here derived by Stress-XP) that cannot be distorted by a topic-comment structure derived by scrambling. This allows us to separate default stress-assignment from scrambling/topic-induced stress in a number of cases, confirming the way Kratzer & Selkirk (2007) separate default stress from topic-induced stress. The discussion also established the stress patterns of idioms as a baseline for the discussion of idioms in the following section.

5.4 Wh-movement and topics

Wh-movement and relatizivation of idiom chunks require a minimal amount of transparency of the idioms to begin with, so as to allow questioning or relativizing of an idiom chunk. Some idioms do not have this minimal amount of transparency and thus do not allow wh-movement or relativization:

(68) a. Sie haben ihm *den Garaus gemacht.*
they have him the "Garaus" made
'They killed him.'

b. * Ich frage mich, welchen *Garaus* sie ihm *gemacht* haben.
I ask myself which "Garaus" they him made have

c. * der *Garaus*, den sie ihm *gemacht* haben, ...
the "Garaus" that they him made have

Let us call these *absolutely opaque idioms*. Many other idioms have this minimal amount of transparency and allow wh-movement and relativization, sometimes with a small amount of markedness as indicated, which is here tolerated in the discussion. As far as the stress-pattern, the idioms here fall into two classes. (Speakers may differ which class they assign an idiom to.)

In one class of idioms, here called *more opaque idioms*, stress obligatorily reconstructs under wh-movement and relativization:

(69) a. ? Ich frage mich, welcher *Hafer* dich *sticht.*

b. ??/* Ich frage mich, welcher *Hafer* dich *sticht.*
I ask myself which oat you stings
lit. 'I wonder which oat is stinging you.'

(70) a. Wir kennen alle den Hafer, der dich *sticht*.
b. ?? Wir kennen alle den *Hafer*, der dich *sticht*.
we know all the oat which you stings
lit. 'We all know the oat that stings you.'

(71) a. Ich frage mich, was für eine Laus ihm *über die Leber gelaufen ist*.
b. ?? Ich frage mich, was für eine Laus ihm *über die Leber gelaufen ist*.
I ask myself what for a louse him across the liver walked is
lit. 'I wonder what kind of louse walked across his liver.'

(72) a. Wir wundern uns über die Laus, die dir *über die Leber gelaufen ist*.
b. ?? Wir wundern uns über die Laus, die dir *über die Leber*
we wonder ourselves about the louse which you across the liver
gelaufen ist.
walked is
lit. 'We are wondering about the louse that walked across your liver.'

(73) a. Es gibt da noch ein Hühnchen, das ich mit ihm *zu rupfen habe*.
b. ?? Es gibt da noch ein Hühnchen, das ich mit ihm *zu rupfen habe*.
it exists there also a chicken that I with him to pluck have
lit. 'There is still a chicken that I have to pluck with him.'

(74) a. Wir staunen alle über die Eulen, die du *nach Athen trägst*.
b. ?? Wir staunen alle über die Eulen, die du *nach Athen trägst*.
we maze all about the owls which you to Athens carry
lit. 'We are all amazed about the owls you are carrying to Athens.'

(75) a. Nicht von ungefähr kommt der Frosch, den du *im Hals hast*.
b. ?? Nicht von ungefähr kommt der Frosch, den du *im Hals hast*.
not from broadly comes the frog which you in-the neck have
'No accident is the frog you have got in your neck.' (dictionary translation)

In the second class of idioms, here called *less opaque idoms*, stress reconstruction is not obligatory. While the structure with stress reconstruction is an option, stress on the verb is also a possibility:

(76) a. ? Ich frage mich, *in* welchen *sauren Apfel* er *gebissen hat*.
b. ? Ich frage mich, *in* welchen *sauren Apfel* er *gebissen hat*.
I ask myself in which sour apple he bitten has
lit. 'I wonder in which sour apple he has bitten.'
'I wonder which bitter pill he swallowed.'

(77) a. Ich frage mich, was für *einen* Bären sie ihm *aufgebunden haben.*

b. ? Ich frage mich, was für *einen* Bären sie ihm *aufgebunden* *haben.*
I ask myself what for a bear they him tied.onto have
lit. 'I wonder what bear they tied onto him.'
'I wonder what lie they told to him.'

(78) a. Sehr dünn ist der *seidene* Faden, an dem das *hängt.*

b. Sehr dünn ist der *seidene* Faden, an dem das *hängt.*
very thin is the silken thread on which this hangs
lit. 'The thread of silk on which this hangs is very thin.'
'This might easily go wrong.'

Before accounting for the idioms, let us return to the optionality of stress reconstruction that was illustrated in (28) for a relative clause. It is illustrated with wh-movement in (79) and (80). Alongside the reconstructing stress-pattern (79) (repeated from (24a)) the non-reconstructing stress-pattern in (80) is also possible. The original site of the wh-phrase is here marked with "__".

(79) Ich frage mich [was für Bücher sie __ geschrieben hat].
I ask myself what for books she written has
'I wonder what books she has written.'

(80) Ich frage mich [was für Bücher sie __ geschrieben hat].
I ask myself what for books she written has

This non-reconstructing alternative in (80) is now analyzed in terms of a topic-comment structure as in (81).

(81) Ich frage mich [[was für Bücher]$_{TOP}$ sie __ geschrieben hat].
I ask myself what for books she written has

Following Krifka (this volume) I assume that a wh-phrase can be a topic. I analyze the non-reconstructed stress-pattern in (81) in terms of the topic-hood of the wh-phrase. It may be derived by first scrambling the wh-phrase or it may be derived by making the wh-phrase into a topic in Spec,CP. In the account as developed up to here, (52) will require dismantling the multi-dominance structure, making stress-reconstruction into the VP impossible. Stress-XP will need to be satisfied for VP by stressing the verb. Let us now refine this picture with the help of the observations about the idioms we saw.

First, for all idioms in wh-movement and relativization, stress reconstruction is an option, as expected: The structure derived by internal merge leads to stress reconstruction and allows idiom chunk reconstruction at LF.

Second, the non-reconstructing stress-pattern is now analyzed in terms of topic-comment structures. The more opaque idioms are the expected case: topic-comment structures do not reconstruct for idiom chunks or for stress due to (52) and (53) in the account formulated so far.

The less opaque idioms are the unexpected case: they do not allow idiom chunk reconstruction under scrambling, but they allow idiom chunk reconstruction where the wh-phrase (or relative clause operator) is a topic that does not reconstruct for stress. We can represent this if wh-movement (and relativization) have an additional way of satisfying (52), as formulated in (82).

(82) An additional option for satisfying (52) in operator-variable structures is that operator and variable are turned into separate but split copies, no longer multiply linked.

This plays out in the less opaque idioms as follows: First, their lesser opacity allows the idiom chunk wh-phrase to be a topic in Spec,CP. Furthermore, if their topic-representation is derived as allowed in (82), there are then two split copies, one for the wh-phrase topic, one for the position inside of the VP in situ. The copy in the VP allows for a reconstructed idiom interpretation. However, since the representation is split into two separate copies, there is conceivably no stress reconstruction: the upper, overt, copy can be stressed, but is not dominated by the VP. Let us assume that stress is not shared among split copies, but is a property only of the overt copy. Stress-XP will then need to be satisfied for the *v*P or VP by stress on the verb.

This picture is compatible with the division between the more opaque idioms and the less opaque idioms. Consider the structure now assumed for a less opaque idiom in (83), in which the two bracketed instances of the idiom chunk should be taken to be separate copies:

(83) [in welchen sauren Apfel]$_{TOP}$ er [*in welchen sauren Apfel*] *gebissen* hat
in which sour apple he in which sour apple bitten has
'what unpleasant event happened to him'

We can make sense of this semantically as follows. The idiom chunk in question in (76)–(78) has a metaphorical meaning in which it stands for another referent and in this regard the idiom is more transparent: the sour apple in (76) transparently stands for something that happened to the referent of *er* 'he'. The bear in (77) transparently stands for the lie that was told to the referent of *ihm* 'him'. The silken thread in (78) may transparently stand for what keeps the referent of *das* 'that' from breaking. If we allow these metaphorical idiom chunks to refer to such actual referents, it is not unreasonable that they can constitute topics: the comment is about the non-metaphorical referent of these metaphorical idiom chunks.

For the more opaque idioms, this is, by hypothesis, not an option:

(84) * [der Hafer]$_1$ ... dich [der Hafer]$_1$/e$_1$ sticht
the oat you the oat stings
'you feel compelled to do something'

Here we are led to take the position that the idiom chunk does not have the possibility of metaphorically referring in a way that allows it to serve as a topic. This is not unreasonable for the more opaque idioms. However, we are postulating a subtle division: these idiom-chunks must be transparent enough to be questioned or relativized, yet not transparent enough for serving as topics. More extensive research on idiom chunks, beyond of the scope of this paper, would be useful for substantiating the right kind of analysis of this divide. For now, the analysis just formulated appears to be reasonable.

The picture we arrive at, then, is that there is a simple standard case, multiple linking by internal merge with stress reconstruction and the possibility of LF reconstruction as discussed in section 4. This option is available to the more and the less opaque idioms. In addition, topics require not to be multiply linked with a position in the comment. For wh-movement and relativization, split copies are a way of satisfying the topic requirement. This allows idiom chunk reconstruction without stress reconstruction for the less opaque idioms. The more opaque idioms do not allow the separate copy of an idiom chunk. For scrambling topics, by assumption not operator-variable structures, the only available option is the reduction of the lower link to a bound empty category. This blocks LF-reconstruction, so that the more and the less opaque idioms do not allow scrambling.

Let us then also consider the stress-patterns of some other phenomena of LF-reconstruction. Reconstruction for anaphor binding allows both stress patterns:

(85) a. Ich frage mich was für Bilder von sich sie mag.
b. Ich frage mich was für Bilder von sich sie mag.

a. 'I wonder what pictures of herself she likes.'
b. 'I wonder what pictures of herself she likes.'

Reconstruction for anaphor binding will be briefly addressed in section 6.2. The account there correctly predicts that there is no interaction with whether the moved element is a topic or not.

Consider then also scope reconstruction. Heycock (1995) pointed out reconstruction effects in connection with verbs of creation, which are further discussed by Fox (1999); see also Heycock (this volume). I employ examples that provide a test case for stress assignment below. While (86) has the two scope readings shown, only one of them is possible with a verb of creation as in (87). The a.-paraphrases render readings in which *n-many* scopes over *want*. In the b.-paraphrases *want* scopes over *n-many*. Heycock and Fox argue with the help of interaction of this phenomenon with Condition C that there is obligatory reconstruction in readings involving creation as in (87).

(86) Wie viele Geschichten will sie erzählen?
how many stories wants she tell
'How many stories does she want to tell?'
What is the number n such that
a. there are n-many stories and she wants to tell them. (n-many > want)
b. she wants to tell n-many stories. (want > n-many)

(87) Wie viele Geschichten will sie sich ausdenken?
how many stories wants she herself invent
'How many stories does she want to invent?'
What is the number n such that
a. * there are n-many stories and she wants to invent them. (*n-many > want)
b. she wants to invent n-many stories (want > n-many)

However, we do not see obligatory stress reconstruction entailed by this syntactic reconstruction:

(88) a. Ich frage mich, wie viele Geschichten sie sich ausdenken will.
b. Ich frage mich, wie viele Geschichten sie sich ausdenken will.
a. 'I wonder how many stories she wants to invent.'
b. 'I wonder how many stories she wants to invent.'

The analysis of these examples with stress reconstruction is as in section 4: multiple dominance at spell-out allows stress reconstruction as well as LF-reconstruction. The analysis of these examples without stress reconstruction invokes a topic as the higher copy, with splitting of the copies for operator and variable by (82). Thus, putting aside details of the resulting LFs, it seems that the current account correctly allows a representation employing LF reconstruction of scope with or without stress reconstruction.

Let us then finally turn to reconstruction for Condition C effects.

6 Condition C effects and stress reconstruction

6.1 Stress-assignment and Condition C reconstruction

I begin with wh-movement. There are predicates that reconstruct for Condition C like the typical example from the English literature in (89a), here in its German translation. Other predicates as in (90a) and (91a) do not seem to reconstruct for Condition C as readily. As noted in Krifka (this volume) we will normally judge these on stress-patterns and contextual assumptions that ameliorate the judgments as much as possible. Such stress-patterns are employed in these a.-examples. Even the bad ones are far from reaching the unacceptability we find with Condition C violations that do not involve reconstruction as in (92)–(94). As we shift the sentence stress to the offending r-expression and employ a pattern of stress reconstruction, as in (89b), (90b) and (91b), we get a strong Condition C effect, comparable to (92)–(94). The c.-examples are controls that show that the problem with the b.-examples is really a Condition C violation.

(89) a. ?(?) Ich frage mich welche Bilder von $Maria_1$ sie_1 mag.
b. * Ich frage mich welche Bilder von $Maria_1$ sie_1 mag.
c. Ich frage mich welche Bilder von $Maria_1$ du_2 magst.
I ask myself which pictures of Maria she/you like(s)
a. 'I wonder which pictures of $Mary_1$ she_1 likes.' (?(?))
b. 'I wonder which pictures of $Mary_1$ she_1 likes.' (*)
c. 'I wonder which pictures of $Mary_1$ you_2 like.'

(90) [Let us return to the case of $Vischnevsky_1$]
a. Wir müssen rauskriegen, welche Bilder von $Maria_1$ sie_1 gesehen hat.
b. * Wir müssen rauskriegen, welche Bilder von $Maria_1$ sie_1 gesehen hat.
c. Wir müssen rauskriegen, welche Bilder von $Maria_1$ *er*$_2$ gesehen hat.
we must find-out which pictures of Maria she/he seen has
a. 'We must find out which pictures of $Mary_2$ she_2 saw.'
b. 'We must find out which pictures of $Mary_2$ she_2 saw.' (*)
c. 'We must find out which pictures of Mary he_1 saw.'

(91) a. Ich frage mich, welche von $Marias_1$ Bildern sie_1 mag.
b. * Ich frage mich, welche von $Marias_1$ Bildern sie_1 mag.
I ask myself which of Marias pictures she likes
a. 'I wonder which of Mary's pictures she likes.'
b. 'I wonder which of Mary's pictures she likes.'

(92) * Sie_1 mag alle Bilder von $Maria_1$.
'She_1 likes all pictures of $Maria_1$.' (*)

(93) * Sie_1 hat alle Bilder von $Maria_1$ (schon) gesehen.
'She_1 (already) saw all pictures of $Maria_1$.' (*)

(94) * Sie_1 hat alle von Marias_1 Bildern gesehen.
'She_1 saw all of Maria_1's pictures.' (*)

A similar, though weaker, effect obtains in (95) and (96). Here stress reconstruction is favored by an element in the NP that is different from the r-expression. These seem to still be degraded, even though the same sentences without a reconstructing stress pattern in (90a) and (91a) are acceptable.

(95) ?(?) Wir müssen rauskriegen, welche <u>Bilder</u> von Maria_2 sie_2 gesehen hat.
we must find-out which pictures of Maria she seen has
'We must find out which pictures of Mary_2 she_2 has seen.'

(96) ?? Ich frage mich, welche von Marias_1 <u>Bildern</u> sie_1 mag.
I ask myself which of Maria's pictures she likes
'I wonder which of Mary's pictures she likes.'

I turn to a first conceivable explanation. Safir (1999) has argued that a mechanism of *vehicle change* affects reconstructed representations. In applying this, Safir assumes that the upper copy and the lower one are retained at LF. Vehicle change is an independently motivated analytical device due to Fiengo & May (1994). Applied to reconstruction, it allows that an r-expression is replaced by a pronoun in the reconstructed copy. This goes a long way towards explaining the difference in acceptability between, on the one hand, (89a), (90a), and (91a), and on the other (92)–(94). For example, after reconstruction with vehicle change in (91a), we obtain, *sie_i mag welche von $ihren_i$ Bildern* 'she likes which of her pictures', which, due to vehicle change (*Marias Bildern* ⟶ *ihren Bildern*), is not a violation of Condition C. However, vehicle change fails to account for the strong ill-formedness of the b-examples in (89)–(91): Here, too, we expect that vehicle change can deflect the Condition C effect, yet it cannot. The effects in the b-examples are as strong as the regular Condition C effects without reconstruction in (92)–(94). Vehicle change is therefore not adopted here.

Consider then a second approach. Krifka (this volume) argues in some detail that topic-status of a moved wh-phrase removes or ammeliorates Condition C violations relating to the reconstruction of the wh-phrase. This descriptive point is adopted here. It follows from the account of the current paper: Where the wh-phrase is a topic, it must not retain its link into the comment due to (52). If this link is removed in the way that (53) allows, the original position of the wh-phrase contains only a bound empty category and there is then no reconstruction for Condition C effects. This now predicts that the a-examples of (89)–(91) do not show reconstruction for Condition C, since the wh-phrase has topic intonation here. It further predicts that the b-examples of (89)–(91) are deviant since the wh-phrase is not a topic here: the wh-phrase shows a reconstructing stress-pattern which is a cue for the presence of multiple linking of the original position of the wh-phrase and its derived position. In these cases, then, Condition C is violated, since the pronoun c-commands the coreferent name via the lower link of the multiply linked structure. These consequences are adopted here. I return to the deviance of (89a) in section 6.2. Furthermore, we also predict some deviance for (95) and (96): Since their stress-patterns do not support topic-hood of the moved wh-phrase but stress reconstruction, we expect multidominance and hence a Condition C effect. Concerning the partial ammelioration in (95) and (96), I follow related remarks in Krifka (this volume). I hypothesize that the contextual givenness of *Maria* that is compatible with these stress-patterns (see e.g. Féry & Samek-Lodovici 2006, Ladd 1983) may help with marginally assigning topic-status to the wh-phrase after all.

Krifka (this volume) sees the ammelioration of Condition C reconstruction by topic-status of the wh-phrase in different terms. Krifka uses the competition account of Condition C by Reinhart (1983), which I adopt here as well. Krifka sees the competition between an r-expression and a pronoun as becoming less important inside of a topic in connection with the link that the topic has to the preceding discourse. I think that a problematic aspect of this approach is that it predicts that the topic-effect is not specific to reconstruction and should also occur without movement and reconstruction in examples like (92)–(94). However, this does not seem to be the case. This is shown in more detail in (97). Here the r-expression is discourse anaphoric and the object containing it is discourse-anaphoric, and both are destressed accordingly. However, the Condition C effect is fully in force and not ameliorated.

(97) Wir haben mit Maria über die Bilder von ihr gesprochen. Ich finde, dass sie nochmal aufgenommen werden sollten. Aber ...
 * sie$_1$ mag die Bilder von Maria$_1$.
 'We talked with Maria about the pictures of her. I think they should be redone. However,
 she$_1$ likes the pictures of Maria$_1$.'

On the other hand, in the current implementation of Krifka's observation, topic-status of the wh-phrase is relevant only where reconstruction is at issue, since topic-status interferes with multi-dominance.

What, then, of the deviance of examples like (89a)? This is addressed in the following section.

6.2 Reconstruction for anaphor binding and apparent Condition C effects

The remarks in this section are tentative. I begin by backing up a bit. I will work my way to an outline of an account in a number of steps.

Müller & Sternefeld (1994) showed that anaphor binding reconstructs under scrambling. This is shown in (98).

(98) dass [Bilder von $sich_1$] (nur) die $Maria_1$ aufgehängt hat
that pictures of herself (only) the.NOM Maria put.up has
'that (only) $Maria_1$ put up pictures of $herself_1$'

I here reconcile this with the idiom chunk facts and the current account as follows. Let us construe anaphor-binding as a syntactic process before spell-out. This move shares elements with the suggestion of Kuno (1987, 2006) that Conditions A and B apply cyclically while Condition C applies postcyclically. This move will allow anaphor-binding to precede scrambling in (98). Anaphor binding, on this account, may apply early or late. If it applies early, it shows apparent reconstruction effects. However, they do not relate to the retention of a lower copy. They simply reflect early application of anaphor binding. This kind of reconstruction effect is now taken to be different from reconstruction for idiom interpretation, for Condition C, and for stress assignment. These processes apply late – at LF for idiom interpretation and for Condition C, as is standardly assumed, and at spell-out for stress-assignment, likewise a standard assumption. This late application requires the retention of a low copy for reconstruction. Consequently, scrambling, which does not retain a low copy, does not reconstruct for idiom interpretation, Condition C or for stress-assignment. However, scrambling reconstructs for anaphor binding, since anaphor binding may simply apply before scrambling.

Frank, Lee & Rambow (1996) show that Condition C effects with picture nouns do not reconstruct under scrambling, except where binding from the subject position is at issue (see (100) and (101) below). To accommodate this, let us adopt a comparison-based account of anaphor- and pronoun-binding (Safir 2004, Rooryck & Wyngaerd 2011): an anaphor (rather than a pronoun or an r-expression) must be used where it can be bound. Observe that picture nouns with anaphors also accord a special place to the subject: they are obligatory and fully natural only where the subject is their antecedent:

(99) a. Die $Maria_i$ hat [Bilder von $sich_1$/??ihr_1] aufgehängt.
the.NOM Maria has pictures of herself/her put.up
'Maria put up pictures of herself.'

b. Ich habe der Maria$_1$ [Bilder von ihr$_1$/*sich$_1$] gezeigt.
I have the.DAT Maria pictures of her/herself shown
'I showed Maria pictures of her.'

c. Ich habe die Maria$_1$ [einigen Fans von ihr$_1$/*sich$_1$] vorgestellt.
I have the.ACC Maria some fans of her/herself introduced.to
'I introduced Maria to some fans of her.'

We can now analyze the apparent effects of Condition C reconstruction with scrambling of Frank, Lee & Rambow (1996) in (100) as follows: One must not use an r-expression instead of the anaphor *sich*. This is because doing so would be skipping the opportunity to use a bound anaphor, as in the alternative (98) with the structure before scrambling as in (99a). This is prohibited by the competition account of anaphor- and pronoun-binding.

(100) * dass [Bilder von Maria] die Maria aufgehängt hat
that pictures of Maria the.NOM Maria put.up has
'that Maria has put up pictures of Maria'

Different facts obtain with binding to an object. If the bracketed constituents in (99b,c) are scrambled across *die Maria*, the pronoun *ihr* in them can be replaced with an r-expression as in (101).

(101) ? dass ich [Bilder von Maria$_1$] der Maria$_1$ gezeigt habe
that I pictures of Maria the.dat Maria shown have
'that I showed pictures of Maria to Maria'

The current account is that in these cases, there is no alternative with a bound anaphor, as shown in (99b,c).

In the preceding analysis, we analyzed what appears to be Condition C reconstruction for scrambling in (100) in different terms, namely in terms of the missed chance to use an anaphor, using an r-expression instead. We find reconstruction under scrambling because the anaphor, had it been used, would have had the option of undergoing anaphor binding before scrambling.

Let us then extend this account to (89a). An anaphor could have been used instead of the r-expression *Maria* (cf. also (85)) and could have been bound during the syntax under our assumptions. This approach is confirmed by the absence of a similar reconstruction effect in (91a): In German, as in English, possessive pronouns do not have a reflexive alternative in the lexical inventory of pronouns. The competition with the use of an anaphor does not arise in this case and the structure is predicted to be fine.

(90a) is a case of the well-known variability in judgements about Condition C reconstruction. It is structurally similar to (89a), though without the apparent

Condition C reconstruction. The context here supports a referentially independent reading of the wh-phrase topic, which also makes the use of an anaphor instead of *Mary* more marked than in (89a).

In sum, we obtain a coherent picture that integrates stress reconstruction with Condition C reconstruction. Where the wh-phrase is not a topic, we find both stress reconstruction and Condition C reconstruction. Where the wh-phrase is a topic, the account requires neither stress reconstruction nor Condition C reconstruction. For the most part, this leads to the correct results. A remaining apparent Condition C effect was analyzed as an interactions with anaphor binding. In the tentative account of anaphor binding employed here, anaphor binding is a syntactic process that can apply before the putatively reconstructed movement, thus showing a different kind of reconstruction effect. It can interact with the deployment of names if the use of a name amounts to a missed opportunity to use a bound anaphor.

7 Summary

The discussion in this paper supports the following points.

First, stress-assignment shows effects of reconstruction, as first shown in different terms by Bresnan (1971, 1972). This phenomenon occurs both in wh-questions and in relative clauses.

Second, when we consider stress reconstruction side by side with syntactic reconstruction effects, a coherent picture emerges: scrambled constituents do not reconstruct for idiom chunks, for Condition C (interaction with anaphor binding apart), or (importantly) for stress, while wh-movement with a non-topic wh-phrase reconstructs for idiom chunks, for Condition C, and, crucially, for stress.

Third, stress reconstruction provides a new source of evidence for the copy left behind by moving elements in the copy theory of movement and reconstruction, here adopted in the form of the theory of internal merge: The copy of the moved element at spell-out will trigger these effects in the mapping to PF, during which stress is assigned. These effects are interesting support for the copy theory (or its successor in terms of internal merge), as previous accounts of LF-reconstruction would not derive stress reconstruction.

Fourth, topics (including all scrambled constituents) require the destruction of the multi-dominance representation. One alternative that they seem to generally allow is the conversion of the lower links of multi-dominance into bound empty categories (akin to the classical traces) during the syntax. Scrambling seems to have only this option, thus blocking both idiom chunk reconstruction at LF and stress reconstruction in the mapping to PF. Operator-variable structures in which the operator is also a topic seem to have the further option of representing operator and variable as separate, split, copies. This allows for an understanding of why operator topics allow for some amount of LF-reconstruction in the absence of stress reconstruction with weakly opaque idioms and in scope reconstruction.

Fifth, it was shown that the account is compatible with specific assumptions about anaphor binding, i.e. the local binding of reflexives. Their binding reconstructs in scrambling, though neither idiom chunks nor Condition C nor stress reconstruct in scrambling. This suggests that anaphor binding is a syntactic process that may apply prior to the putatively reconstructed movement and does not depend on the lower "copy" for reconstruction later in the derivation. It is thus different from the other phenomena, which require the lower "copy": idiom chunks are interpreted at LF, Condition C applies at LF, and stress is assigned to the structure at spell-out. Further, the account is compatible with the assumption that anaphor binding can interfere with the use of a name if the use of a name is a missed opportunity to use a bound anaphor instead.

Acknowledgment: I would like to thank two anonymous reviewers, Daniel Büring. Manfred Krifka, Uli Sauerland, and Mathias Schenner for helpful comments and support. All errors are of course my own. This work was supported by the German Federal Ministry of Education and Research (BMBF), grant 01UG1411.

References

Berman, Arlene & Michael Szamosi. 1972. Observations on sentential stress. *Language* 48(2). 304–325. https://doi.org/10.2307/412137.

Bresnan, Joan W. 1971. Sentence stress and syntactic transformations. *Language* 47(2). 257–281. https://doi.org/10.2307/412081.

Bresnan, Joan W. 1972. Stress and syntax: A reply. *Language* 48(2). 326–342. https://doi.org/10.2307/412138.

Chen, Matthew Y. 1987. The syntax of Xiamen Tone Sandhi. *Phonology Yearbook* 4. 109–149.

Chomsky, Noam. 1965. *Aspects of the theory of syntax*. Cambridge, MA: MIT Press.

Chomsky, Noam. 1993. A minimalist program for linguistic theory. In Kenneth Hale & Samuel Keyser (eds.), *The view from building 20: Essays in linguistics in honor of Sylvain Bromberger*, 1–52. Cambridge, MA: MIT Press.

Chomsky, Noam. 2000. Minimalist inquiries: The framework. In Roger Martin, David Michaels & Juan Uriagereka (eds.), *Step by step: Essays on minimalism in honor of Howard Lasnik*, 89–155. Cambridge, MA: MIT Press.

Chomsky, Noam. 2001. Derivation by phase. In Michael Kenstowicz (ed.), *Ken Hale: A life in language*, 1–52. Cambridge, MA: MIT Press.

Chomsky, Noam. 2008. On phases. In Robert Freidin, Carlos Otero & Maria Luisa Zubizarreta (eds.), *Foundational issues in linguistic theory: Essays in honor of Jean-Roger Vergnaud*, 133–166. Cambridge, MA: MIT Press.
Chomsky, Noam & Morris Halle. 1968. *The sound pattern of English*. New York: Harper & Row.
Cinque, Guglielmo. 1993. A null theory of phrase and compound stress. *Linguistic Inquiry* 24. 239–297.
Citko, Barbara. 2001. Deletion under identity in relative clauses. *Proceedings of NELS* 31. 131–145.
Diesing, Molly. 1992. *Indefinites*. Cambridge, MA: MIT Press.
Féry, Caroline & Vieri Samek-Lodovici. 2006. Focus projection and prosodic prominence in nested foci. *Language* 82(1). 131–150.
Fiengo, Robert & Robert May. 1994. *Indices and identity*. Cambridge, MA: MIT Press.
Fox, Danny. 1999. Reconstruction, binding theory, and the interpretation of chains. *Linguistic Inquiry* 30(2). 157–196.
Fox, Danny & David Pesetsky. 2005. Cyclic linearization of syntactic structure. *Theoretical Linguistics* 31. 1–45.
Frank, Robert, Young-Suk Lee & Owen Rambow. 1996. Scrambling, reconstruction and subject binding. *Rivista di Grammatica Generativa* 21. 67–106. http://hdl.handle.net/11707/339 (10 October, 2018).
Frey, Werner. 2004. A medial topic position for German. *Linguistische Berichte* 198. 153–190.
Grosu, Alexander & Manfred Krifka. 2007. *The gifted mathematician that you claim to be*: Equational intensional 'reconstruction' relatives. *Linguistics and Philosophy* 30. 445–485. https://doi.org/10.1007/s10988-008-9022-5.
Gussenhoven, Carlos. 1983. Focus, mode and the nucleus. *Journal of Linguistics* 19. 377–417.
Gussenhoven, Carlos. 1992. Sentence accents and argument structure. In Iggy M. Roca (ed.), *Thematic structure: Its role in grammar*, 79–106. Berlin: Foris.
Hale, Kenneth & Elisabeth Selkirk. 1987. Government and tonal phrasing in Papago. *Phonology Yearbook* 4. 151–183.
Heim, Irene & Angelika Kratzer. 1998. *Semantics in generative grammar*. Oxford: Blackwell.
Heycock, Caroline. 1995. Asymmetries in reconstruction. *Linguistic Inquiry* 26. 547–570.
Höhle, Tilman N. 1982. Explikation für "normale Betonung" und "normale Wortstellung". In Werner Abraham (ed.), *Satzglieder des deutschen*, 75–153. Tübingen: Narr.
Hulsey, Sarah & Uli Sauerland. 2006. Sorting out relative clauses. *Natural Language Semantics* 14. 111–137.
Jacobs, Joachim. 1993. Integration. In Marga Reis (ed.), *Wortstellung und Informationsstruktur*, 63–116. Tübingen: Max Niemeyer Verlag.
Jäger, Gerhard. 2001. Topic-comment structure and the contrast between stage level and individual level predicates. *Journal of Semantics* 18. 83–126.
Kratzer, Angelika & Elisabeth Selkirk. 2007. Phase theory and prosodic spellout: The case of verbs. *The Linguistic Review* 24(2-3). 93–135. https://doi.org/10.1515/TLR.2007.005.
Krifka, Manfred. 1984. *Fokus, Topik, syntaktische Struktur und semantische Interpretation*. Unpublished Ms.
Kuno, Susumu. 1987. *Functional syntax: Anaphora, discourse and empathy*. Chicago: University of Chicago Press.
Kuno, Susumu. 2006. Empathy and direct discourse perspectives. In Laurence R. Horn & Gregory Ward (eds.), *The handbook of pragmatics*, 315–343. Malden: Blackwell Publishing.

Ladd, D. Robert. 1983. Even, focus, and normal stress. *Journal of Semantics* 2(2). 157–170. https://doi.org/10.1093/semant/2.2.157.
Lakoff, George. 1972. The global nature of the nuclear stress rule. *Language* 48(2). 285–303. https://doi.org/10.2307/412136.
Lees, Robert B. 1960. *The grammar of English nominalizations*. The Hague: Mouton.
Lees, Robert B. 1961. The constituent structure of noun phrases. *American Speech: A Quarterly of Linguistic Usage* 36. 159–168.
Müller, Gereon & Wolfgang Sternefeld. 1994. Scrambling as A-bar movement. In Norbert Corver & Henk van Riemsdijk (eds.), *Studies on scrambling: Movement and non-movement approaches to free word-order phenomena*, 331–386. Berlin: Mouton.
Munn, Alan. 1994. A Minimalist account of reconstruction asymmetries. In Mercè Gonzàlez (ed.), *Proceedings of NELS 24*, 397–410. Amherst, MA: GLSA.
Newman, Stanley S. 1946. On the stress system of English. *Word* 2. 171–187. https://doi.org/10.1080/00437956.1946.11659290.
Pierrehumbert, Janet Breckenridge. 1980. *The phonology and phonetics of English intonation*. Massachusetts Institute of Technology Doctoral dissertation. http://hdl.handle.net/1721.1/16065 (10 October, 2018).
Reinhart, Tanya. 1983. Coreference and bound anaphora: A restatement of the anaphora questions. *Linguistics and Philosophy* 6(1). 47–88. https://doi.org/10.1007/BF00868090.
Rooryck, Johan & Guido Vanden Wyngaerd. 2011. *Dissolving binding theory*. Oxford: Oxford University Press.
Safir, Ken. 1999. Vehicle change and reconstruction in A'-chains. *Linguistic Inquiry* 30. 587–620.
Safir, Ken. 2004. *The syntax of anaphora*. Oxford: Oxford University Press.
Salzmann, Martin. 2006. *Resumptive prolepsis: A study in indirect A'-dependencies*. Leiden University Doctoral dissertation.
Samek-Lodovici, Vieri. 2005. Prosody–syntax interaction in the expression of focus. *Natural Language and Linguistic Theory* 23(3). 687–755. https://doi.org/10.1007/s11049-004-2874-7.
Selkirk, Elisabeth. 1984. *Phonology and syntax: The relation between sound and structure*. Cambridge, MA: MIT Press.
Selkirk, Elisabeth. 1986. On derived domains in sentence phonology. *Phonology Yearbook* 3. 371–405.
Selkirk, Elisabeth. 1995. Sentence prosody: Intonation, stress, and phrasing. In John Goldsmith (ed.), *The handbook of phonological theory*, 550–569. Cambridge, MA: Blackwell.
Selkirk, Elisabeth. 2008. Contrastive focus, givenness, and the unmarked status of "discourse new". *Acta Liguistica Hungarica* 55. 331–346.
Selkirk, Elisabeth & Tong Shen. 1990. Prosodic domains in shanghai chinese. In Sharon Inkelas & Draga Zec (eds.), *The phonology-syntax connection*, 313–337. Chicago: University of Chicago Press.
Truckenbrodt, Hubert. 1995. *Phonological phrases: Their relation to syntax, focus, and prominence*. Massachusetts Institute of Technology Doctoral dissertation.
Truckenbrodt, Hubert. 1999. On the relation between syntactic phrases and phonological phrases. *Linguistic Inquiry* 30. 219–255.
Truckenbrodt, Hubert. 2006. Phrasal stress. In Keith Brown (ed.), *The encyclopedia of languages and linguistics*, 2nd edn., vol. 9, 572–579. Oxford: Elsevier.
Truckenbrodt, Hubert. 2007a. The syntax-phonology interface. In Paul de Lacy (ed.), *The Cambridge handbook of phonology*, 435–456. Cambridge: Cambridge University Press.

Truckenbrodt, Hubert. 2007b. Upstep on edge tones and on nuclear accents. In Carlos Gussenhoven & Tomas Riad (eds.), *Tones and tunes. Volume 2: Experimental studies in word and sentence prosody*, 349–386. Berlin: Mouton.

Truckenbrodt, Hubert. 2012. Effects of indefinite pronouns and traces on verb stress in German. In Toni Borowsky, Shigeto Kawahara, Takahito Shinya & Mariko Sugahara (eds.), *Prosody matters: Essays in honor of Elisabeth Selkirk*, 487–513. London: Equinox Publishing.

Truckenbrodt, Hubert. 2013. An analysis of prosodic F-effects in interrogatives: Prosody, syntax and semantics. *Lingua* 124. 131–175.

Truckenbrodt, Hubert & Isabelle Darcy. 2010. Object clauses, movement, and phrasal stress. In Nomi Erteschik-Shir & Lisa Rochman (eds.), *The sound patterns of syntax*, 189–216. Oxford: Oxford University Press.

Uhmann, Susanne. 1991. *Fokusphonologie. Eine Analyse deutscher Intonationskonturen im Rahmen der nicht-linearen Phonologie*. Tübingen: Niemeyer.

Vergnaud, Jean-Roger. 1974. *French relative clauses*. Cambridge, MA: Massachusetts Institute of Technology Doctoral dissertation.

von Stechow, Arnim & Susanne Uhmann. 1986. Some remarks on focus projection. In Werner Abraham & Sjaak de Meij (eds.), *Topic, focus, and configurationality*, 295–320. Amsterdam: John Benjamins.

Martin Salzmann

A new version of the Matching Analysis of relative clauses

Combining deletion under recoverability with vehicle change

1 Introduction: Analyses of relative clauses

The biggest analytical challenge posed by relative clauses is arguably the so-called connectivity problem, viz., the double role of the head noun: it is a constituent of the matrix clause but is also related to a position inside the relative clause.

In the current syntactic literature on relative clauses, there are three basic derivations that are still entertained to solve the connectivity problem: the Head External Analysis (HEA), the Head Raising Analysis (HRA) and the Matching Analysis (MA):[1]

(1) a. the book$_i$ [$_{CP}$ [$_{DP}$ Op$_i$/which$_i$]$_1$ John likes __$_1$] HEA
b. the [$_{CP}$ [$_{DP}$ book$_2$ Op/which __$_2$]$_1$ John likes __$_1$] HRA
c. the book$_i$ [$_{CP}$ [$_{DP}$ Op/which ~~book$_i$~~]$_1$ John likes __$_1$] MA

The Head External Analysis (HEA) is the classical analysis based on A′-movement of a relative pronoun/operator (overt or covert) to the left periphery of the relative clause and adjunction of the relative clause to the head NP; the relationship between the head NP an the operator is handled by means of co-indexation or simply follows from the compositional interpretation of such structures (including predicate abstraction and predicate modification). The HEA seems to go back to Quine (1960) and is explicitly adopted in Montague (1973), Partee (1975), Chomsky (1977) and Jackendoff (1977); it was the standard analysis in the Government and

1 In most accounts the HRA and the MA are combined with adjunction of the relative clause to the head noun while in the raising analysis the relative clause is merged as a complement (usually of the matrix determiner); alternative proposals (HRA/MA with complementation and raising with adjunction) can be found as well, though. There are in my view hardly any decisive arguments in favor of either complementation or adjunction; the choice between complementation and adjunction will therefore not play a role in what follows except in section 3.6 below. See Salzmann (2017: 40–55) for detailed discussion of this issue.

Martin Salzmann, University of Leipzig

https://doi.org/10.1515/9783050095158-006

Binding period. The Head Raising Analysis goes back to Brame (1968), Schachter (1973) and Vergnaud (1974) and was revived in Kayne (1994); it captures the double role of the head noun by means of a direct movement relationship from within the relative clause to its surface position, which is either taken to be a position at the periphery of the RC as in (1b), the structure proposed by Kayne (1994) and in the implementations by Bianchi (1999) and de Vries (2002), or a position outside of the relative clause as in Bhatt (2002), Donati & Cecchetto (2011), Cecchetto & Donati (2015). As a consequence of this movement operation there is a full representation of the external head inside the relative clause. The Matching Analysis, going back to Lees (1960, 1961), Chomsky (1965), and revived in Munn (1994), Sauerland (1998, 2003), Citko (2001) and Salzmann (2006), can be considered a compromise between the two other analyses: While there is A′-movement to the left periphery but no movement out of the relative clause, there is a full representation of the external head inside the relative clause because the relative operator/pronoun is reanalyzed as a determiner taking an NP-complement; the relationship between the two is mediated by deletion of the NP-complement of the operator under identity with the external head.

In the GB-era there was surprisingly little discussion about the structure of relative clauses. Since Kayne's revival of the Raising Analysis, however, discussions about the syntax of relative clauses have become very prominent. Kayne's proposal has been extremely influential and it seems fair to say that the HRA is considered by many the standard analysis of relative clauses nowadays. This is somewhat surprising since the HRA has been subject to very serious criticism, starting with Borsley (1997). Some of the issues were addressed in Bianchi (2000), but many of the problems are left unsolved, and additional problems have been identified in Borsley (2001), Heck (2005), Salzmann (2006: 13–19), Boef (2012), Salzmann (2017) and Webelhuth, Bargmann & Götze (this volume). In my view, the high cost associated with the adoption of the HRA can only be justified if it can be shown to be indispensable in a very central part of grammar. This indeed seems to characterize the majority view in the field: The shortcomings are either ignored or tacitly accepted because it is assumed that the HRA is the only possible derivation to model reconstruction effects. This is to some extent a historical coincidence in that the revival of the HRA coincided with the introduction of the copy theory of movement in early Minimalism, which led to a different view on reconstruction: Instead of literally undoing a movement operation at LF to bring back a constituent into the position where it is interpreted, reconstruction could be handled by simply interpreting the lower copy of a movement chain. Under the copy theory, reconstruction for variable binding in wh-movement as in (2a) is accounted for by the (simplified) LF in (2b):

(2) a. [Which gift of his$_i$ wife]$_1$ does every man$_i$ like best [which gift of his$_i$ wife]$_1$?
b. [Which x] does every man$_i$ like best [x gift of his$_i$ wife]?

Note that the copies are modified according to the Preference Principle, cf. Chomsky (1995: 209), which prefers minimally restricted operators. As a consequence, only the bottom copy is retained (the copy of the operator is replaced by a variable) while the copy in the final landing site is reduced to the operator.[2] The major motivation for the Preference Principle comes from reconstruction for Principle C in wh-movement as in (3):

(3) * Which picture of John$_i$ did he$_i$ buy __?

If reconstruction, i.e. the interpretation of the lower copy, were optional, this fact could not be derived. Importantly, this default can be overriden if the interpretation of the higher copy instead of the lower one leads to a semantic effect, i.e. provides different scope or binding possibilities, see Heycock (1995) and Fox (1999).

I will argue in this paper that the advantage of the HRA with respect to capturing reconstruction effects is only apparent. Rather, I will propose a new version of the matching analysis that not only captures the basic facts just as well but additionally accounts for various intricate reconstruction data that neither the raising analysis nor previous versions of the matching analysis can handle.

The paper is organized as follows: In section two, I present an overview of the major reconstruction effects in relative clauses and how they have been captured in the various analyses. In section three, I will introduce a new version of the matching analysis and show that it can account for the entire range of reconstruction effects. Section four argues that the mechanism at the heart of the matching analysis, viz., deletion under identity, is also at work in resumptive relatives and in ATB-movement. Section five concludes.

2 Reconstruction effects in relative clauses

In this section I will provide an overview of the most prominent reconstruction effects that have been discussed in the literature. I will first address instances of reconstruction before discussing cases of non-reconstruction. In the last subsection, I will briefly discuss reconstruction effects that arguably do not provide conclusive evidence for the presence of a relative clause-internal representation of the external head.

2 Fox (1999, 2002) provides a more elaborate Trace Conversion mechanism, but since the differences do not matter for my present purposes, I will stick to the older notation.

2.1 Reconstruction of the external head

The following examples illustrate reconstruction for idiom interpretation, Principle A and scope reconstruction ((4a) is from Schachter 1973: 32, (4b) from Salzmann 2006: 99, and (4c) from Sauerland 1998: 68; for reconstruction of bound variables and superlative adjectives, see section 2.4; the external head is henceforth enclosed in brackets):[3,4]

(4) a. The [*careful track*] [that she's *keeping* __ of her expenses] pleases me.

b. Der [Wesenszug von sich$_i$], [den Peter$_i$ noch nicht __ kannte],
the trait of self which Peter still not know.PST.3SG
störte niemanden.
annoy.PST.3SG no one.ACC
'No one was annoyed by the side of himself$_i$ that Peter$_i$ did not know yet.'

---

3 Reconstruction for Principle A requires some care because many of the examples that have been discussed in the literature contain confounds and thus do not provide conclusive evidence for reconstruction. The first issue concerns the presence of an implicit PRO: While the choice between reflexive and pronoun is normally free in picture nouns, cf. Reinhart & Reuland (1993: 685f.), Salzmann (2006: 24–28), there are cases where only the reflexive is acceptable:

(i) a. Lucie$_i$ saw a picture of her$_i$/herself$_i$.

b. Lucie$_i$ took a picture of *her$_i$/herself$_i$.

Cases like (i-b) involve verbs whose semantics entails that the agent of the verb must be identical to the agent/producer of the nominal predicate. One way of accounting for this is to postulate an implicit PRO inside the NP representing the agent: [PRO$_i$ picture of herself$_i$] (there are alternative proposals in the literature that would also work for my purposes, cf. Reinhart & Reuland 1993: 685f.). Many examples in the literature do not control for this so that they arguably do not constitute reliable evidence for reconstruction. To avoid the possibility of an implicit PRO acting as a binder example (4b) contains an unaccusative noun that does not take an external argument. For related discussion, see Bianchi (1999: 118–119) and Cecchetto (2005: 16–18).
Second, one has to make sure that what looks like local anaphor binding does not in fact constitute logophoric binding. Since English allows for logophoric binding, cf. Reinhart & Reuland (1993: 681–685), many of the examples in the literature putatively illustrating reconstruction for Principle A may thus be irrelevant. For this reason, an example from German is used in the text, where logophoric binding is not a possibility, see Kiss (2001: 186). Other languages that do not allow for logophoric binding and thus can be used to test reconstruction for Principle A are e.g. Italian, see Bianchi (1999: 116), and Dutch, see de Vries (2002: 80–82). See Salzmann (2017: 66–71) for more detailed discussion of these issues.

4 As has been pointed out in de Vries (2002: 79), relativization is restricted to collocations while it is blocked with completely opaque idioms like *kick the bucket*. For arguments against treating the interpretation of idioms/collocations as evidence for reconstruction see Sternefeld (this volume) and Webelhuth, Bargmann & Götze (this volume); for further discussion, see also Salzmann (2017: 71–72).

c. No linguist would read the [*many books*] [Gina will *need* __ for vet school]. (many > need); need > many

Under the HEA it never became clear how the information in the external head in examples like (4) could be made available inside the relative clause through mediation of the relative operator. The HRA, however, offers a straightforward solution: Reconstruction effects simply result from interpreting the lower copy of the raised head, which leads to the following LF-representations/-interpretations (after application of the Preference Principle; note that amount readings as in (4c) involve abstraction over a degree; I will use English words in all LFs for ease of representation):

(5) a. the λx. that she is keeping [x, careful track] of her expenses
b. the λx. Peter$_i$ did not know [x, trait of himself$_i$]
c. the λd. Gina will need [d, many books] for vet school

Crucially, it has been argued that only the raising analysis can provide an account of reconstruction effects in relative clauses, cf. Bhatt (2002: 52), Hulsey & Sauerland (2006). This is why reconstruction effects have become the prime diagnostic for the correct analysis of RCs. Although the MA also features a representation of the external head inside the RC, the above-mentioned authors argue that it cannot easily capture reconstruction effects because the external head also has to be interpreted. This becomes problematic once it contains material that cannot receive a proper interpretation in this position as in (4a/b): it is unclear how the idiomatic NP in (4a) can be interpreted if it normally only receives an interpretation together with the verb; similarly, the reflexive pronoun in (4b) seems to remain unbound. Furthermore, in (4c), retaining both the external head and the relative clause-internal copy would lead to contradictory scope readings. Given that the external head is not part of a movement chain, it cannot be deleted at LF (unlike in the HRA where the top copy is deleted as a consequence of the Preference Principle). Consider the following simplified LF-structure/-interpretation of (4a) under the MA:

(6) a. the [careful track]$_i$ [$_{CP}$ [Op careful track$_i$]$_1$ that she is keeping [Op careful track]$_1$ of her expenses]
b. the careful track λx. that she is keeping [x, careful track] of her expenses

However, this argument only applies to a particular implementation of the MA, viz. that by Sauerland (1998, 2003).

Munn (1994) and Citko (2001) propose a version of the matching analysis where deletion of the external head is possible as long as it can be recovered from the relative clause-internal context. Since this is the case in the reconstruction examples above, they can be accommodated by this theory as well. The LFs of the examples in (4) thus look as under the raising analysis (next to deletion of the external head, the Preference Principle applies inside the relative clause; the authors do not explicitly discuss amount readings, but nothing should rule them out as far as I can tell if the upper copy can be deleted under identity with the lower one):

(7) a. the [~~careful track~~] [$_{CP}$ [λx. ~~careful track~~]$_1$ she is keeping [x careful track]$_1$ of her expenses]

b. the [~~trait of himself$_i$~~] [$_{CP}$ [λx. ~~trait of himself$_i$~~]$_1$ Peter$_i$ did not know [x trait of himself$_i$]$_1$]

c. the [~~many books~~] [$_{CP}$ [λd. ~~many books~~]$_1$ Gina will need [d many books]$_1$ for vet school]

To summarize up to this point, regular reconstruction effects in relative clauses can be captured both by the raising and by the matching analysis given certain assumptions.

2.2 Non-reconstruction

Proponents of the raising analysis (e.g. Bhatt 2002, Sauerland 2003) generally admit that it cannot be applied to all restrictive relatives. It cannot be available in those instances where reconstruction of the external head does not seem to take place. The case discussed most frequently are Principle C effects, which are absent in relative clauses unlike in wh-movement (Sauerland 2003: 211):

(8) a. * [Which report on Bob's$_i$ division]$_1$ will he$_i$ not like __$_1$?

b. I have a [report on Bob's$_i$ division] [he$_i$ won't like __].

It must be pointed out that there is no perfect consensus in this debate. While many agree on the contrast, some, e.g. Safir (1999) and Henderson (2007), argue that Principle C effects are absent in wh-movement as well. I will follow the majority view here, not the least because the contrast seems quite clear in other languages, e.g. in German. The issue is somewhat more complex in that the argument–adjunct distinction and factors like embedding and perspective play a certain role. But I believe that once these factors are carefully controlled for, robust contrasts can be obtained. See Salzmann (2006: 28–34) and Salzmann (2017: 134ff.) for a detailed overview of the discussion.

At any rate, if the HRA is applied to (8b), the top copy is reduced according to the Preference Principle while the lower copy is retained. This incorrectly predicts

Principle C effects in relative clauses (i.e. (9) should have the same status as (3) above):

(9) * I have a λx. he$_i$ won't like [x, report on Bob$_i$'s division]

Proponents of the raising analysis (e.g. Bhatt 2002, Sauerland 2003) generally assume that the matching analysis is used in these configurations. There are two types of explanations for the absence of Principle C effects in relative clauses: The version proposed by Sauerland (1998, 2003) capitalizes on the deletion operation involved in the matching analysis. He argues that since ellipsis is involved, we expect properties of ellipsis to be visible in relative clauses as well. One such property are systematic mismatches between antecedent and ellipsis site, so-called vehicle change effects first described in Fiengo & May (1994). Consider the following example from VP-ellipsis:

(10) a. * John likes Mary$_i$ and she$_i$ does, too.
b. John likes Mary$_i$, and she$_i$ knows that I do, too.

This contrast is mysterious if the ellipsis site is identical to the antecedent, viz. consists of *like Mary*. The pattern can be made sense of, however, if the ellipsis site contains a pronoun instead of an R-expression:

(11) a. * John likes Mary$_i$ and she$_i$ does (~~like her$_i$~~), too.
b. John likes Mary$_i$, and she$_i$ knows that I do (~~like her$_i$~~), too.

While the pronoun still triggers a Principle B violation in (11a), the additional level of embedding in (11b) improves the example to full grammaticality. Simplifying somewhat, it is generally assumed that the mismatch is licensed because antecedent and ellipsis site are semantically identical (cf. e.g. Merchant 2001). Sauerland (1998, 2003) then applies the same reasoning to relative clauses: In (8b) the R-expression *Bob* corresponds to the personal pronoun *he* in the relative clause-internal representation of the external head (since *Bob* occupies the possessor position, it surfaces as *his*):[5]

---

5 I assume that vehicle change is not an operation as such but rather describes certain types of mismatch that are licensed under ellipsis. I further assume that vehicle change is restricted to ellipsis and thus not freely available (unlike Safir 1999 and Henderson 2007, who assume that vehicle change can freely affect bottom copies in A′-movement).
Note that while Sauerland (1998: 76) assumes that in a relative clause like *the picture of John that he likes* the representation inside the the relative clause contains a personal pronoun, viz., *picture of him*, he proposes in Sauerland (2003: 222) that it actually contains the NP-anaphor *one* (because he assumes that pronouns coreferential with the subject are not licensed inside picture

(12) I have a [report on Bob$_i$'s division] [$_{CP}$ [λx. ~~report on his$_i$ division~~]$_1$ he$_i$ won't like [x report on his$_i$ division]$_1$].

This derives the correct result because the relative thus corresponds to a simple clause like *He$_i$ won't like a report on his$_i$ division* where no violation of the Binding Theory obtains. To account for the entire reconstruction pattern, proponents of the raising analysis like Bhatt (2002), Sauerland (1998, 2003) and Hulsey & Sauerland (2006) therefore assume that the grammar includes both the raising analysis and Sauerland's version of the MA.

In the implementations of the MA by Munn (1994) and Citko (2001), the absence of Principle C effects is accounted for differently: While the external head is retained, the internal head is deleted under identity with the external one. As a consequence no offending R-expression is present within the relative clause. This leads to the following LF:

(13) I have a [report on Bob$_i$'s division] [$_{CP}$ [λx. ~~report on Bob$_i$'s division~~]$_1$ he$_i$ won't like [x ~~report on Bob$_i$'s division~~]$_1$].

In this theory, recoverability thus plays a crucial role. Either the external head or the relative clause-internal copy can be deleted as long as it can be recovered. Deleting the external head is needed to account for reconstruction effects. Deletion of the RC-internal copy is required to model the absence of reconstruction effects.

2.3 Intermediate summary

Table 1 provides an overview of the reconstruction phenomena discussed so far and shows which theory can account for them to what extent. The table shows that the frequent claim that the HRA is indispensable because it is the only theory that provides an account of reconstruction effects must be reconsidered: It cannot be applied to all configurations, the absence of Principle C effects requires a version of the MA. The consequence of adopting the HRA is thus that the grammar necessarily contains two derivations for relative clauses. Given certain assumptions however, the MA can provide an account of both regular reconstruction effects and cases where there is no reconstruction as with Principle C. It thus has better empirical coverage than the HRA. Since in addition it is not confronted with the many independent problems that the HRA is (see the references in section 1), the MA already emerges as superior.

NPs, contrary to Reinhart & Reuland 1993, recall fn. 3). I will assume in what follows that vehicle change involves a mismatch between an R-expression and a pronoun. See section 3.3 for two further types of vehicle change.

Tab. 1: Reconstruction phenomena and analyses of relative clauses

	Raising	MA: Sauerland	MA: Munn/Citko
Idioms	+	–	+
Principle A	+	–	+
Amount readings	+	–	+
non-reconstruction Principle C	–	+	+

In the rest of this paper, I will strengthen this claim by showing that there are more reconstruction effects that require the MA. I will also show that previous versions of the MA are not sufficient to capture the entire range of facts. I will therefore propose a new version of the MA that combines insights from Citko (2001) and Sauerland (2003).

Before presenting my own analysis, I will briefly address reconstruction diagnostics that have played a prominent role in the discussion but which upon closer inspection arguably do not provide strong evidence for a relative clause-internal representation of the external head.

2.4 Problematic reconstruction diagnostics

Reconstruction for variable binding has figured quite prominently in the discussion. Consider the following examples ((14a) is from Safir 1999: 613, (14b) is from Hulsey & Sauerland 2006: 121, (14c) a translation of an Italian example by Bianchi 1999: 124):

(14) a. John generally has an [opinion of his$_i$ book] [that every novelist$_i$ respects __].
b. The [picture of himself$_i$] [that everybody$_i$ sent __ in] annoyed the teacher.
c. The [period of his$_i$ life] [which nobody$_i$ is willing to speak about __] is adolescence.

In much of the literature (e.g. Åfarli 1994: 87, Safir 1999: 613, Bianchi 1999: 124, Bhatt 2002: 52, Aoun & Li 2003: 113), reconstruction for variable binding has been taken as evidence for a relative clause-internal representation of the external head. However, this view has been challenged for two reasons. First, Cecchetto (2005: 19–21) has observed that for many speakers reconstruction for variable binding is only fully acceptable in equative sentences but degraded in subject predicate sentences.[6] He suggests that this is not accidental and proposes that reconstruction

6 He argues that the same pattern can be observed for cases of scope reconstruction where quantifiers interact.

for variable binding as in (14c) can be subsumed under classical cases of indirect binding as in (15) (cf. Cecchetto 2005: 19, 22):

(15) The woman every man$_i$ loves __ is his$_i$ mother.

Such examples cannot easily be accounted for by means of interpreting a relative clause-internal copy of the external head. Rather, simplifying somewhat, the interpretation of such examples results from the fact that two functions are equated with each other. Given this possibility, the interpretation of examples like (14c) does not require a relative clause-internal copy of the external head. Although I tend to share Cecchetto's judgments, it should be pointed out that there is no consensus in the literature. While it is indeed remarkable that many of the examples in the literature involve equatives (cf. (14c)), there are also several examples with subject-predicate structures (cf. (14a/b)).

Even if we set the confound with equatives aside, simply interpreting the lower copy inside the relative clause in the examples in (14) will not be sufficient to derive the most salient interpretation of these examples; in (14b), for instance, *picture* covaries with *everybody*, i.e. everyone sent in a different picture showing only himself. As discussed in Hulsey & Sauerland (2006: 121), since the determiner has scope over the RC, we would expect a different interpretation, viz., one where there is a single picture that shows every student. To derive the salient distributive interpretation, something else is needed, e.g. QR of the QP out of the relative clause as proposed in Hulsey & Sauerland (2006) (but see Sharvit 1999 and Sternefeld this volume for critical discussion). Whatever will turn out to be the best solution, it should be clear that reconstruction for variable binding cannot be considered a strong argument in favor of interpreting a relative clause-internal copy. I will consequently set it aside in the rest of this paper.

Another controversial issue are the low readings of superlative adjectives, first discussed in Bhatt (2002):

(16) the *first* book that John said that Tolstoy had written

Under the so-called low reading, the superlative adjective applies to the lower verb, this interpretation is thus about the first book Tolstoy actually wrote. Under the high reading, the superlative adjective applies to the matrix verb and is thus about the first book about which John made the claim that Tolstoy wrote it. Heycock (2005) argues that a syntactic reconstruction account overgenerates and argues instead that there is a link between low readings and neg-raising (the verbs supporting the low reading also allow neg-raising). Bhatt & Sharvit (2005) and Hulsey & Sauerland (2006) on the other hand argue that the low readings do constitute evidence for syntactic reconstruction. Given the complexities involved, I will set the low readings of superlative adjectives aside as well.

Facts like those discussed in this subsection and reconstruction in pseudo-clefts where a solution in terms of the copy theory is even less likely have led Cecchetto (2005) and Boef (2012) to the conclusion that reconstruction effects do not provide any insight into the structure of relative clauses (see also Salzmann 2017: 177, fn. 136). Even though I agree that the range of reconstruction effects that have to be accounted for without recourse to syntax is larger than previously thought, I believe that the data discussed in this paper do provide interesting insights for the (syntactic) analysis of relative clauses.[7]

3 A new version of the MA

In this section, I will propose a new version of the MA that can account for all the data discussed so far as well as additional ones that have received little attention in the literature and which prove problematic for both the HRA and previous versions of the MA.

3.1 Basic assumptions

The version of the MA I am about to introduce combines ingredients of both the recoverability approach proposed in Munn (1994) and Citko (2001) as well as the vehicle-change approach by Sauerland (1998, 2003).[8] As in other versions of the MA, I assume that there is A′-movement of the operator phrase to Spec, CP. The relative pronoun/operator takes a full NP complement which is PF-deleted under identity with the external head, leading to the following PF-representation:

(17) the book$_i$ [$_{CP}$ [$_{DP}$ Op/which ~~book$_i$~~]$_1$ John likes __$_1$]

The LF-representation is basically derived according to the Preference Principle (thus as in wh-movement): the restriction of the wh-operator is deleted in the operator copy but retained in the lower copy inside the relative clause where the

7 For reasons of space, I will not be able to discuss the semantic literature in any detail; this is not intended to mean that semantic accounts for reconstruction are misguided; rather, what I intend to show is that if a syntactic approach to reconstruction is to be adopted, then the MA is clearly superior to the HRA. For semantic accounts of reconstruction, see e.g. Sharvit (1999), Sternefeld (2001, this volume).

8 An earlier version appeared in Salzmann (2006: chapter 2); for a more detailed version, see Salzmann (2017: 134–179).

copy of the operator is replaced by a variable; additionally, the external head is also retained:

(18) the book λx. John likes [x book]

In other words: both reconstruction and retention of the external head are the default. Furthermore, both defaults can be overridden in well-defined circumstances: if the external head or the lower copy inside the relative clause contains an element with a so-called positive licensing requirement, it can be exceptionally LF-deleted if the material is not licensed in that particular position. By "positive licensing requirement" I mean that a given element is dependent on another element. Two types of elements are relevant in the present discussion: anaphors and idiomatic NPs: anaphors require a local c-commanding antecedent and idiomatic NPs have to be adjacent to the idiomatic verb to receive an interpretation. Importantly, this exceptional deletion operation is subject to a recoverability requirement: the external head may only be deleted if its content is recoverable from the copy inside the relative clause and vice versa. Next to elements with a positive licensing requirement there are elements with a "negative licensing requirement". Such elements have to be free in a certain domain. The prime examples of this category are pronouns and R-expressions. By assumption neither one can be exceptionally deleted. This division will turn out to be crucial for the analysis of Principle C effects and cases where only the external head is interpreted. This is also where I crucially differ from the recoverability approaches by Munn (1994) and Citko (2001), where exceptional deletion of either the external head or the relative clause-internal copy is in principle always possible if it rescues an otherwise ungrammatical structure. I will argue instead that cases where reconstruction of elements with a negative licensing requirement fails to be observed are due to vehicle change.

3.2 Regular reconstruction effects

The reconstruction effects in (4) above are repeated in (19) for convenience:

(19) a. The [*careful track*] [that she's *keeping* __ of her expenses] pleases me.

b. Der [Wesenszug von $sich_i$], [den $Peter_i$ noch nicht __ kannte],
the trait of self which Peter still not know.PST.3SG
störte niemanden.
annoy.PST.3SG no one.ACC
'No one was annoyed by the side of $himself_i$ that $Peter_i$ did not know yet.'

c. No linguist would read the [*many books*] [Gina will *need* __ for vet school].
(many > need); need > many

Under the present analysis, (19a/b) receive the LFs in (20), which are identical to those proposed by Munn (1994) and Citko (2001), cf. ex. (7), and those of the HRA:

(20) a. the [~~careful track~~] [$_{CP}$ [λx. ~~careful track~~]$_1$ she is keeping [x, careful track]$_1$ of her expenses]

b. the [~~side of himself~~$_i$] [$_{CP}$ [λx. ~~side of himself~~$_i$]$_1$ Peter$_i$ did not know [x, side of himself$_i$]$_1$]

While the Preference Principle modifies the copies inside the relative clause in the by now familiar way, the external head is deleted as well. In (20) this happens because the external head contains elements with a positive licensing requirement that are not licensed there (no idiomatic verb, no local binder for the anaphor); due to the RC-internal copy, deletion of the external head is recoverable. Deletion of the external head is also necessary to capture the amount reading in (19c). However, the deletion must be motivated differently because the quantified external head is not subject to a positive licensing requirement. Deletion can be motivated by the fact that retaining both copies would lead to contradictory scope readings. I propose that in such a situation either copy can be privileged to yield the respective meanings. Importantly, this option is limited to scopal elements because it yields a difference in interpretation (as we will see in the next subsection, this option is crucially unavailable in the case of Principle C).

(21) a. the [~~many books~~] [$_{CP}$ [λd. ~~many books~~]$_1$ Gina will need [d many books]$_1$ for vet school]

b. the [many books] [$_{CP}$ [λx. ~~many books~~]$_1$ Gina will need [x ~~many books~~]$_1$ for vet school]

So far, the present proposal has the same coverage as the previous versions of the MA. In the next subsections, I will discuss data that only my version can account for.

3.3 Obligatory non-reconstruction

As shown in section 2.2 above, the MA provides two different accounts of the absence of Principle C effects: either it is due to vehicle change as in Sauerland (1998, 2003) or it results from the deletion of the copy inside the relative clause as in Munn (1994) and Citko (2001). Regular Principle C data do not distinguish between these two options. The Crossover data from Safir (1999: 611) (indirectly) show, however, that vehicle change is the correct solution:

(22) a. * [Pictures of anyone$_i$] which he$_i$ displays __ prominently are likely to be attractive ones.

b. [Pictures of anyone$_i$] [which __ put him$_i$ in a good light] are likely to be attractive ones.

The contrast clearly suggests that there is reconstruction because the position of the trace with respect to the coreferential pronoun matters. (22a) thus displays a Crossover effect. If offending copies could be freely deleted, deleting the relative clause-internal copy should lead to a well-formed structure, contrary to fact. Munn (1994) and Citko (2001) thus wrongly predict the following LF-representation for (22a):

(23) [Pictures of anyone$_i$][$_{CP}$ [λx. ~~pictures of anyone$_i$~~]$_1$ he$_i$ displays [x ~~pictures of anyone$_i$~~]$_1$ prominently] are likely to be attractive ones.

Under my approach where elements with a negative licensing requirement cannot undergo exceptional deletion, the Crossover effect is expected. However, it remains to be explained why the example cannot be saved by vehicle change. Here I follow Safir (1999: 605ff.), who shows that vehicle change cannot freely apply to (copies of) quantifiers (or their variables).[9] Consequently, there is a full copy of *anyone* inside the relative clause, leading to a Principle C violation in (22a) due to c-command by *he*, but not in (22b), where the quantifier is not c-commanded by *him*. The LF of (22a) under the present analysis is shown in (24):

(24) * [Pictures of anyone$_i$] [$_{CP}$ λx. ~~pictures of anyone$_i$~~]$_1$ he$_i$ displays [x pictures of anyone$_i$]$_1$ prominently] are likely to be attractive ones.

The Crossover data thus provide an argument for my approach and against that of Munn (1994) and Citko (2001).[10]

9 For a different view, see Sauerland (2003: 222f.). For more discussion, see Salzmann (2017: 151–154).

10 The inapplicability of vehicle change also accounts for Strong Crossover Effects in relative clauses:

(i) a. * the man who$_i$ he$_i$ likes __

b. * the man whose$_i$ sister he$_i$ likes __

The relative clause-internal representation under the MA is *who man* and *who man's sister*. Vehicle change, which targets DPs, cannot apply here: the only DP available is the entire operator phrase, but given that it contains a quantifier, it cannot be vehicle changed so that a Principle C violation is unavoidable; cf. Salzmann (2006: 65–70) for further discussion.

Regular cases of non-reconstruction for Principle C as in (8b) above, repeated in (25a), follow under vehicle change in the present account, as shown by the LF in (25b):[11]

(25) a. I have a [report on Bob's$_i$ division] [he$_i$ won't like __].
b. I have a [report on Bob$_i$'s division] [$_{CP}$ [λx. ~~report on his$_i$ division~~]$_1$ he$_i$ won't like [x, report on his$_i$ division]$_1$].

While unrestricted exceptional deletion is thus too powerful, there are cases of non-reconstruction that can be handled straightforwardly if elements with a positive licensing requirement must be deleted in positions where they are not licensed. While the problem of obligatory non-reconstruction is usually discussed on the basis of Principle C facts, the issue is more general: There are cases where the external head must be interpreted while the internal head must not. The following examples illustrate this for idiom interpretation and Principle A, see McCawley (1981: 137) for (26a):

(26) a. Parky pulled the [strings] [that __ got me my job].
b. but Hawking has endorsed The Theory of Everything, so he$_i$ must like the [portrait of himself$_i$] [that it presents __]
http://www.spectator.co.uk/2015/01/what-the-theory-of-everything-doesnt-tell-you-about-stephen-hawking/, accessed October 10, 2018

The following German examples make the same point (for Dutch data, see Boef 2012: 161f.):

(27) a. Hier werden die [Fäden] gezogen, [die __ anschließend zu
here become.3PL the strings pull.PTCP which later to
Toren führen].
goals lead.3PL
'This is where the strings are pulled that later lead to goals.'
http://www.kicker.de/news/fussball/bundesliga/startseite/608708/2/slideshow_ein-koeniglicher-weltmeister-geht-voran.html, accessed October 10, 2018

11 Further evidence that copies containing elements with a negative licensing requirement cannot be deleted comes from examples like (i), where retention of the external head is crucial to account for the Principle C effect:

(i) * He$_i$ likes the picture of John$_i$ that I bought.

Vehicle change could turn *John* into *him*, avoiding the Principle C effect inside the relative clause; if additionally the external head could be deleted, the Principle C effect would also be voided in the matrix clause, contrary to fact.

b. Schicken Sie$_i$ uns ein [Foto von sich$_i$], [das __ beweist], dass Sie
send.IMP you us a picture of self which prove.3SG that you
ein wahrer Ferrari-Anhänger sind.
a true Ferrari-fan be.3PL
'Send us a picture of yourself which proves that you are a true Ferrari-fan.'
https://web.archive.org/web/20051227190131/http://www.vodafone-racing.de/pda/f_fancontest.html, accessed October 10, 2018

Examples of this type are a problem for the HRA (like the absence of Principle C effects), where the lower copy is interpreted by default.[12] Here the recoverability aspect of the MA I have proposed becomes important: Interpreting the idiom or the anaphor in the external head is no problem under the MA because the external head is retained by default. The bottom copy inside the relative clause, however, contains material with a positive licensing requirement that is not licensed there (the anaphor is too far away from its antecedent and the idiomatic NP is not adjacent to the idiomatic verb). Consequently, the bottom copy undergoes LF-deletion under identity with the external head. The LF of (26a) thus looks as follows:

(28) John pulled the strings [$_{CP}$ [λx. ~~strings~~] that [x ~~strings~~] got him the job].

Vehicle change is arguably not sufficient to capture both cases of non-reconstruction: it can deal with the anaphor example because ellipsis has been shown to

12 A variant of (27b) can be found in Kayne (1994: 87, ex. 8), which suggests that reconstruction for anaphor binding is optional (see de Vries 2002: 82, ex. 26 for a Dutch example):

(i) John$_i$ bought the picture of himself$_{i/j}$ that Bill$_j$ saw

This recalls facts from wh-movement, where it is usually assumed that although the Preference Principle is the default, it can be overridden if additional binding options obtain:

(ii) John$_i$ wondered [which picture of himself$_{i,j}$]$_1$ Bill$_j$ saw __$_1$.

It is conceivable that the Preference Principle can also be overruled under the raising analysis in the binding case. However, while this may work for English, it arguably does not for languages like German where anaphors cannot be bound when located in Spec, CP (see Kiss 2001: 186 and Salzmann 2006: 140–141):

(iii) Hans$_i$ fragt sich, [[welches Foto von *sich$_i$/ihm$_i$]$_1$ ich am liebsten __$_1$ mag].
John asks self which picture of self/him I the best like
'John$_i$ was wondering which picture of himself$_i$ I like best.'

Even if privileging the higher copy were possible under the raising analysis, this would not be sufficient to account for German cases of non-reconstruction of anaphors as in (27b) above, at least not in those implementations where the external head remains inside the relative clause (as in Kayne 1994, Bianchi 1999 and de Vries 2002). Things may be different in the implementation by Bhatt (2002), where the external head moves out of the relative clause.

license a mismatch between reflexives and pronouns, as in the following VP-ellipsis example from Fiengo & May (1994: 206–214):

(29) John$_i$ believes himself$_i$ to be heroic, and he$_i$ said that Mary does, too ⟨ believe him$_i$ to be heroic ⟩.

Applied to the relative clause in (26b), the relative clause-internal copy would appear as *portrait of him$_i$*, leading to a well-formed result.[13] The idiom example in (26a), however, cannot be accounted for this way. Bhatt (2002: 47f., note 1) speculates that the MA could perhaps handle such cases if the external head is matched not against the literal form of the idiom but its semantic interpretation. But this certainly goes beyond regular cases of vehicle change and it is not clear what the consequences of such an extension would be. I thus conclude that some cases of non-reconstruction require a recoverability perspective.

A case where vehicle change is necessary under the present assumptions are non-reconstruction examples with NPIs discussed in Citko (2001: 134ff.). The example in (30a) would be predicted to be as ungrammatical as (31) if the external head were interpreted within the relative clause as in (30b) because another quantifier would intervene between the negative quantifier and the NPI (thereby violating the Immediate Scope Constraint by Linebarger 1987: 338):[14]

(30) a. Nobody found [a picture of *anybody*] that everybody liked
b. * Nobody found [a ~~picture of *anybody*~~] that everybody liked [picture of *anybody*]

(31) John didn't give a red cent to *every charity.
(at LF: *not > every charity > a red cent)

Munn (1994) and Citko (2001) can handle such cases straightforwardly since the relative clause-internal copy can be freely deleted. In my system this is not possible

13 Note that nothing so far prevents application of vehicle change in cases of reconstruction for Principle A like (4b). If the external head is deleted and there is vehicle change from anaphor to pronoun, a well-formed representation obtains inside the RC, viz. *side of him*. Importantly, examples where only the anaphor is grammatical show that vehicle change must be optional:

(i) Peter$_i$ took a picture of himself$_i$ that he$_i$ should not have taken.

Recall from fn. 3 that in picture NPs of this semi-idiomatic type, only the reflexive is grammatical while the pronoun is not, cf. *He$_i$ took a picture of himself$_i$/*him$_i$* (arguably because of an implicit PRO). Consequently vehicle change must not apply in (i) and therefore must in principle be optional.

14 The argument is weakened by the frequent observation that NPI-licensing is sensitive to surface structure.

because *pictures of anybody*, an element with a positive licensing requirement, is in principle licensed within the relative clause as it is in the c-command domain of *nobody*. Consequently, exceptional deletion is not an option. Rather, I argue that vehicle change comes to the rescue as ellipsis allows mismatches between *some* and *any*: *John drank some milk, but Bill didn't ⟨drink any milk⟩*. Consequently, the relative clause-internal representation will be *a picture of somebody*, which avoids a violation of the Immediate Scope Constraint and thus leads to a well-formed result:

(32) Nobody found a picture of anybody λx. that everybody liked [x picture of *somebody*].

As in the Principle C cases, both the external head and the relative clause-internal copy are thus retained.

3.4 Conflicting requirements

The data discussed in the previous subsection represent an argument in favor of the MA and against the HRA because they require the interpretation of the external head and the non-interpretation of the internal head. The data discussed in this subsection will provide additional evidence for the MA because they require the interpretation of relative clause-internal as well as relative clause-external material. Additionally, they provide more evidence for vehicle change. Consider the following example, which involves conflicting requirements (the English data have been verified by native speakers):[15]

(33) a. I will never forget Somi, his sunken eyes, and the way he crawled into my arms as he$_i$ showed me the [picture of himself$_i$] [$_{CP}$ that one of my fellow students took __].
http://www.textbooksforafrica.org/19438.html, accessed in 2005

b. Peyton$_i$ bekommt per Email ein [Foto von sich$_i$], [das Derek __ gemacht hat].
P. receives by e-mail a picture of self which D. taken has
'Peyton receives by mail a picture of himself that Derek took.'
http://www.myfanbase.de/one-tree-hill/episodenguide/?eid=2596, accessed October 10, 2018

15 For data with variable binding see Heck (2005) and Salzmann (2006: 42, 118).

The examples are challenging for two reasons: the reflexive is only licensed in the highest copy/in the external head, but for the idiomatic interpretation the external head also has to be inside the relative clause. I don't see a possibility to derive this example with the HRA. Even if both copies were retained at LF, there would be two problems: First, the reflexive would not be licensed relative clause-internally as the binder in the matrix clause is too far away. Second, since in *take a picture* only the reflexive is grammatical, it contains an implicit PRO. Inside the RC this must be coreferential with *one of my fellow students*, but then the reflexive inside the RC should be bound by *one of my fellow students*, contrary to fact, and the reflexive inside the higher copy cannot be bound by *he* because PRO intervenes. Since picture NPs in English may also allow for logophoric binding (even though this may be blocked in this case because of the PRO, cf. Reinhart & Reuland 1993: 686, note 29), data from English must be taken with care. German is more reliable in this respect, logophoric use being impossible (recall from fn. 3 above and see Salzmann 2006: 85–94). The problem posed by examples like (33) is thus real.

The MA is better equipped to handle such cases because the interpretation of both the external and the internal copy is generally possible. However, this is not yet sufficient. First, the implicit PRO inside the picture NP that is disjoint from the reflexive will block binding of the anaphor inside the relative clause. Second, if this PRO is also present inside the external head, Principle A will also be violated in the matrix clause. In other words, such examples cannot be captured by the recoverability approach by Munn (1994) and Citko (2001) because both copies would have to be retained and there is no possibility to modify either of them. The present approach, however, provides a solution by means of vehicle change: The anaphor in the matrix clause can correspond to a personal pronoun inside the relative clause (recall (29)) so that we obtain *[PRO$_j$ picture of him$_i$]*. Additionally, since the picture NP does not receive an idiomatic interpretation in the matrix clause there is arguably no implicit PRO (which is also suggested by the fact that the reflexive could be substituted by a pronoun). I thus propose that the external head does not contain an implicit PRO and that vehicle change licenses the mismatch between an NP with a PRO and one without. The resulting LF-representation of (33b) thus looks as follows:

(34) Peyton$_i$ received a [picture of himself$_i$] [$_{CP}$ λx. Derek$_j$ took [x, PRO$_j$ picture of him$_i$]]

The present analysis is thus superior to both the raising analysis and previous versions of the MA.[16]

3.5 Re-emergence of Principle C?

A frequent argument in favor of syntactic reconstruction is based on the observation that reconstruction effects usually go together, see Heycock (1995), Romero (1998: 90–101) and Fox (1999: 164–178) for wh-movement. The same observation has been made for relative clauses. Crucially, it has been argued that Principle C effects re-emerge in relatives once reconstruction (and thus head-raising) is forced for variable binding, idiom interpretation or scope, cf. Munn (1994: 402, ex. 15), Citko (2001); the following data are from Sauerland (2003: 213–215):

(35) a. * The [letters by John$_i$ to her$_j$] that he$_i$ told every girl$_j$ to burn __ were published.

b. * the [picture of Bill$_i$] that he$_i$ took __

c. * The [headway on Mary's$_i$ project] that she$_i$ had made __ pleased the boss.

d. * The [many books for Gina's$_i$ vet school] that she$_i$ needs __ will be expensive.

---

16 Henk van Riemsdijk (p.c.) has pointed out to me a related (but less problematic) case where the head noun receives an idiomatic interpretation both in the matrix clause and relative clause-internally (cf. also fn. 13):

(i) John never pulled [the strings] [that his mother told him should be pulled __].

Such examples are a problem for the raising analysis if the higher copy is obligatorily deleted or if only one copy can be retained for principled reasons. No problem arises for the matching analysis since usually there are always two occurrences that are interpreted.

The same issue arises with anaphor binding if the anaphor is licensed both in the matrix and inside the RC-clause (note that the subject containing the relative clause starts out below the experiencer object):

(ii) Das [Spiegelbild von sich$_i$], [das er$_i$ an der Wand __ sah], beunruhigte ihn$_i$.
the reflection of self which Peter on the wall see.PST.3SG disquiet.PST.3SG him
'The reflexion of himself that Peter saw on the wall made him nervous.'

Next to the problem of having to interpret both copies, such examples pose an additional challenge for those implementations of the raising analysis where the head of the relative remains inside the relative clause as this would require binding in an A′-position, which German generally disallows, recall the discussion in fn. 12 above.

Note that such examples are unproblematic for the present account as well as for previous versions of the MA since unlike the examples in the main text the retention of both instances of the head is sufficient.

e. * I visited all [the relatives of Mary's$_i$] that she$_i$ said there are __ left.

These facts follow straightforwardly under the raising analysis. Since reconstruction for variable binding, cf. (35a), idiom interpretation, cf. (35b/c), and scope, cf. (35d/e), requires a relative clause-internal copy, that copy will also contain the R-expression so that one correctly expects Principle C effects as well.

These facts also follow under the version of the MA proposed by Munn (1994) and Citko (2001) because reconstruction requires a full copy inside the relative clause (the external head can be deleted without violating recoverability).

However, the facts seem to constitute a serious problem for the present account because vehicle change should void the Principle C effects: If the R-expression can correspond to a pronoun, the examples in (35c–e) would thus correspond to the following well-formed simple sentences (on (35a/b) see below):

(36) a. She$_i$ made headway on her$_i$ project.
b. She$_i$ needs many books for her$_i$ vet school.
c. She$_i$ said that there are relatives of hers$_i$ left.

I will show in the remainder of this subsection that upon closer inspection the argument from the examples in (35) actually turns out to be an argument in favor of the present vehicle change-based account: Most of the data discussed in the previous literature are ungrammatical for independent reasons and once the examples are properly constructed, Principle C effects indeed vanish. They thus argue against the HRA and the accounts by Munn (1994) and Citko (2001).

3.5.1 Irrelevant cases

First of all, I will disregard examples with variable binding as in (35a) given the objections raised in section 2.4.[17] Second, (35b) is semi-idiomatic and thus arguably contains an implicit coreferential PRO (note that the pronoun is ungrammatical inside the picture NP). Consequently, even if vehicle change applies, the pronoun substituted for *Bill* will trigger a Principle B violation inside the picture NP as the lower copy contains *[PRO$_i$ picture of him$_i$]*. Note that once a level of embedding is added, the example becomes grammatical: *the picture of Bill$_i$ that he$_i$ thinks I took.*[18]

---

17 See Salzmann (2006: 108f.) for German equivalents of (35a) that do not show Principle C effects. I do not know what causes this crosslinguistic difference.

18 This objection applies to most of the data in the literature suggesting that there are Principle C effects in relatives, cf. e.g. Schachter (1973: 32).

There thus remain the cases in (35c–e). Examples with existential *there* like (35c) are generally assumed to require reconstruction as they involve amount readings (cf. e.g. Bhatt 2002). The ungrammaticality of examples of this type is unclear, though. Safir (1999: 613, note 22), for instance, judges the following example acceptable:

(37) the [number of pictures of Diana$_i$] [that she$_i$ thought there were __ in the envelope]

I will thus assume that these are only putative counter-examples. The grammaticality of (37) is due to vehicle change, with *Diana* corresponding to *her* inside the relative clause. See the next subsection for more examples of this type.

The examples (35c) and (35d) are ungrammatical for independent reasons: the external head is not a proper constituent. In fact it consists of two independent constituents. In the idiom case (35c), *headway on Mary's project* is simply not a possible constituent. In the expression *make headway on Mary's project* the PP *on Mary's project* is not dependent on *headway* as it would yield the wrong semantics: *on Mary's project* does not restrict *headway*; rather, the PP depends on the entire expression *make headway*. One can test this syntactically: if the PP *on Mary's project* were a complement of *headway*, one would expect it to be inextractable when *headway* is headed by a definite determiner because definite DPs normally disallow extraction of their complements. But this prediction is not borne out: wh-moving the allegedly dependent PP is unproblematic:

(38) On which tasks did Peter make the most significant headway?

Conversely, in cases where *headway* is used without the idiomatic verb it can take complements and then bars extraction of complements if the DP is definite:

(39) * On which tasks did the boss praise the significant headway?

Similarly, if we passivize such sentences, moving *headway* + PP leads to strong degradedness, it is much more natural to just move *headway* without the PP (for unclear reasons not all speakers find (40a) completely ungrammatical):

(40) a. ?? Much headway on this project was made.
b. Much headway was made on this project.

This strongly suggests that *headway* + PP cannot form a nominal constituent in (35c). Consequently, (35c) is simply ungrammatical because it contains a non-constituent as external head. Note that when the PP restricts *headway*, passivization is unproblematic:

(41) The headway on her project was considered sufficient.

However, this reanalysis seems to be refuted by the observation in Sauerland (2003: 214, ex. 24b) that (35c) becomes grammatical if the R-expression is replaced by a pronoun:

(42) The [headway on her$_i$ project] [Mary$_i$ had made __] pleased the boss.

However, I have found several speakers who find this sentence still strongly degraded, arguably for the above-mentioned reasons. The much more acceptable way of saying this is by leaving the PP inside the relative clause:

(43) The [headway] [that Mary$_i$ had made __ on her$_i$ project] pleased the boss.

The contrast is very clear in German, consider the following pair (for unclear reasons, (44a) is not fully ungrammatical for all speakers):

(44) a. ?? Die [Fortschritte bei ihrem Projekt], [die Maria __ machte], waren
the progress at her project which Mary made were
beträchtlich.
remarkable
'The progress that Mary made on her project was remarkable.'

b. Die [Fortschritte], [die Maria __ bei ihrem Projekt machte], waren
the progress which Mary at her project made were
beträchtlich.
remarkable

Alain Rouveret and Nicolas Guilliot have pointed out to me that the same holds for French.

I therefore conclude that (35c) does not provide any evidence for a full relative clause-internal representation of the external head.[19]

The same explanation can be given for the ungrammaticality of (35d): the external head simply is a non-constituent. The string *need something for something* as such is structurally ambiguous; *for something* can be dependent on the first noun and restrict it or it can be independent, i.e. a VP-adjunct, in which case it

---

19 The empirical facts have recently been challenged to some extent. Heycock (2012: 9, ex. 42, this volume) gives the following as grammatical (which under our assumptions would be expected to be ungrammatical as it contains an illicit external head):

(i) This represents the [only headway on Lucy$_i$'s problem] [that she$_i$ thinks they made __ so far].

Bhatt & Iatridou (2012: 6, ex. 22) on the other hand give a minimally different version of (i) (where *she* and the reconstruction site are clause-mates) as ungrammatical. German equivalents of their examples and of (i) all seem equally degraded as equivalents of (35c).

describes the purpose/goal of the NP. Depending on the context, both construals are felicitous or just one of them. Consider the following sentence:

(45) I still need a present for Mary.

The sentence is ambiguous: the speaker either needs a present, and this present is for Mary so that the PP is independent or the speaker needs a present of a particular type, namely one that is characterized by being for Mary. Consider now the following base sentence of the relative in (35d):

(46) Gina still needs many books for her vet school.

The obvious construal of this sentence is that Gina needs many books and she needs them for her vet school while the other construal with the PP dependent on *books* is highly unlikely here. But the constituency underlying (35d) corresponds to the unlikely (if not unavailable) reading. Independent evidence that the ungrammaticality of (35d) is due to an illicit external head comes from the fact that the sentence remains strongly degraded if the R-expression is replaced by a pronoun (since the judgments are murky, I only assign two question marks):

(47) ?? the [many books for her$_i$ vet school] [that she$_i$ needs __] will be expensive

Again, the only really natural way of expressing such a content would be to leave the modifier inside the relative clause:

(48) the [many books] [that she$_i$ needs __ for her$_i$ vet school] will be expensive

Similarly, if we passivize the sentence, moving just *many books* is much more acceptable than moving *many books* + the *for*-PP:[20]

20 The same reanalysis is possible for examples based on verbs of creation like *build*, which force a reconstructed reading, cf. Heycock (1995), Fox (1999). They have been used in the literature to show that Principle C effects pattern with scope reconstruction in *wh*-movement, but in my view, like the examples in the main text, many of them are ungrammatical because of an illicit external head; the same holds for the corresponding relatives:

(i) * the [many houses in John$_i$'s city] [that he$_i$ thinks you should build __]
think > many; *many > think

In (i), *John's city* cannot restrict *many houses* because the houses do not exist yet. Passivization as in (ii) shows again that *many houses in John's city* cannot form a constituent under this reading:

(ii) a. * Many houses in John's city should be built this year.
b. Many houses should be built in John's city this year.

Furthermore, replacing the R-expression by a pronoun does not lead to an improvement. There is a clear preference to keep the PP-modifier inside the RC:

(iii) a. ?? the [many houses in his$_i$ city] [that John$_i$ thinks you should build __]
b. the [many houses] [that John$_i$ thinks you should build __ in his$_i$ city]

(49) a. Many books are needed for vet school these days.
b. * Many books for vet school are needed these days.

Under the construal where the PP is dependent on the NP, however, passivization is unproblematic:[21]

(50) Many books for vet school are sold in this bookshop.

Having reassessed the examples that putatively provide evidence for Principle C effects, I will now show that once the examples are constructed properly, Principle C effects are still absent even if reconstruction of the external head is forced otherwise.

3.5.2 Further evidence for vehicle change

I will now discuss examples that require reconstruction for idiom interpretation; crucially, even though the idiomatic NP contains an R-expression, Principle C effects still do not obtain if there is a coreferential pronoun inside the relative clause. Consider first the following pair from German, cf. Salzmann (2006: 134–137):

(51) a. * Der [Streit über Maria$_i$], [den sie$_i$ __ vom Zaun gebrochen
the fight about Mary which she off.the fence break.PTCP
hat], nervt mich.
have.3SG annoy.3SG me
lit.: 'The fight about Mary$_i$ that she$_i$ started annoys me.'

b. Der [Streit über Peters Kritik an Maria$_i$], [den sie$_i$ __ vom
the fight about Peter's criticism of Mary which she off.the
Zaun gebrochen hat], nervt mich.
fence break.PTCP have.3SG annoy.3SG me
lit.: 'The fight about Mary's criticism of Peter$_i$ that he$_i$ started annoys me.'

The idiom *einen Streit vom Zaun brechen*, lit. 'break a fight off the fence', meaning 'start a fight' arguably contains an implicit PRO because in simple sentences only the reflexive is possible within the NP, while the pronoun is ungrammatical:

Bhatt & Iatridou (2012: p. 8, ex. 28–29) present an example similar to (i) as grammatical and minimally different ones (where the binder and the reconstruction site are clause-mates) as ungrammatical. I find the German equivalents of their examples strongly degraded.

21 Similarly, in variants of (35d) where there are no problems with the external head, no Principle C effects occur. See Salzmann (2006: 115–116) and Salzmann (2017: 163) for German examples.

(52) Sie$_i$ hat einen [PRO$_i$ Streit über *sie$_i$/sich$_i$] vom Zaun gebrochen.
she have.3SG a fight about her/self off.the fence break.PTCP
'She$_i$ started a fight about *her$_i$/herself$_i$.'

The implicit PRO will lead to a Principle C effect in (51a) irrespective of vehicle change, i.e. even if *Maria* corresponds to *sie* 'her' because that would correspond to the ungrammatical variant of (52). If, however, the R-expression is further embedded as in (51b), the example becomes grammatical. This is expected under the vehicle change account because (51b) then essentially corresponds to the following simple sentence where the pronoun is grammatical:

(53) Sie$_i$ hat einen [PRO$_i$ Streit über Peters Kritik an ihr$_i$] vom
She have.3SG a fight about Peter's criticism of her off.the
Zaun gebrochen.
fence break.PTCP
'She$_i$ started a fight about Peter's criticism of her$_i$.'

Importantly, the contrast in (51) does not follow under the raising analysis because it would always posit a full copy of the R-expression inside the relative clauses and thus predicts both examples to be ungrammatical. The same goes for the approach by Munn (1994) and Citko (2001), who would also assume a full copy of the external head inside the relative clause. The present vehicle change-based account, however, derives the contrast straightforwardly. The LFs of the two sentences thus look as follows (note that there is no implicit PRO inside the external head because that NP does not receive an idiomatic reading, vehicle change thus licenses this mismatch as well):[22]

22 Citko (2001: 144) tries to argue against vehicle change by means of a semi-idiomatic example with an implicit PRO coreferential with the subject:

(i) * He$_i$/Picasso$_i$ painted [PRO$_i$ self-portraits of him$_i$] in the Blue period.

There is no doubt that this sentence is ungrammatical. In a next step, she uses such an idiomatic DP with an R-expression instead of a pronoun and tests reconstruction for Principle C. According to her, the following sentence is grammatical:

(ii) The [self-portraits of Picasso$_i$] [that he$_i$ had painted __ in the Blue period] are in the Met now.

She argues that under a Vehicle Change approach, (ii) should be equally ungrammatical as (i): the lower copy inside the relative clause is retained and *Picasso* would be turned into *him*, but would still be c-commanded by the implicit PRO so that a Principle B effect should obtain as in (i), which is not the case according to her:

(iii) % The [self-portraits of Picasso$_i$]$_j$ [[Op [PRO$_i$ self-portraits of him$_i$]$_j$]$_1$ that he$_i$ had painted [x PRO$_i$ self-portraits of him$_i$]$_1$ in the Blue period] are in the Met now.

(54) a. * the fight about Mary$_i$ λx. she$_i$ started [x, PRO$_i$ fight about her$_i$] off the fence

b. the fight about Peter's criticism of Mary$_i$ λx. she$_i$ started [x, PRO$_i$ fight about Peter's criticism of her$_i$] off the fence

The correlation data, which were originally intended as an argument for the raising analysis, thus actually turn out to be an argument in favor the the MA proposed here with deletion under recoverability and vehicle change. See also Heycock (2012, this volume) for more evidence that reconstruction effects can be dissociated (she discusses dissociation of low readings of adjectives with Principle C and anaphor binding).[23]

Under her recoverability approach, however, things are different because the lower copy can be deleted under identity with the external head so that not even a Principle B effect obtains:

(iv) The [self-portraits of Picasso$_i$]$_j$ [[Op [~~PRO$_i$ self-portraits of Picasso$_i$~~]$_j$]$_1$ that he$_i$ had painted [x ~~PRO$_i$ self-portraits of Picasso$_i$~~]$_1$ in the Blue period] are in the Met now.

This seems indeed to argue in favor of Citko's approach. However, I do not think that the argument goes through because the speakers I have consulted do not share the judgment that (ii) is grammatical. Rather, the example patterns with (51a) above.
For the speakers that find the sentence acceptable, *of Picasso* is arguably treated as an adjunct and can thus be merged late (see the next subsection). Note also that the interpretation of *of Picasso* does not seem to be identical in the baseline sentence and in the relative. In the relative, only a possessor/creator but not a theme interpretation seems possible.

23 There are aspects of reconstruction for Principle C that remain ill-understood. On the one hand, there is a non-syntactic component affecting the acceptability: For instance, stress on the coreferential pronoun within the relative clause or focus particles associated with it makes coreference much more acceptable, even in wh-movement, see Salzmann (2006: 29) for German and English and Bianchi (1999: 109–115) for Italian; see Krifka (2011, this volume) for more discussion of information structural factors.
On the other hand, there are cases where vehicle change does not seem to be sufficient. Consider the following examples involving possessors (cf. Krifka 2011: p. 2, ex. 15; p. 4, ex. 44b):

(i) a. * the [responsible guardian of Bill$_i$'s sister] [that he$_i$ claims to be __]

b. * the [(dozens of) stories about Diana$_i$'s brother] [that she$_i$ is likely to invent __]

The external head should not be problematic in either of these examples as the PP restricts the head noun. Under vehicle change, the R-expressions would correspond to possessive pronouns inside the relative clause so that the Principle C effect should be bled, contrary to fact:

(ii) a. he$_i$ claims to be [$_{XP}$ PRO$_i$ [$_{X'}$ [$_{DP}$ guardian of his$_i$ sister]]]

b. she$_i$ is likely to invent dozens of stories about her$_i$ brother.

Interestingly, both examples improve if a level of embedding is added:

(iii) a. John is not the [responsible guardian of Mary$_i$'s daughter] [that she$_i$ was hoping he would be __].

3.6 Late merged relative clauses and reconstruction

The last type of configuration I will discuss here provides both evidence for the MA as well as for a recoverability component. It involves instances of wh-movement with a relative clause modifying the wh-phrase; one can construct cases where the restriction of the wh-word must reconstruct into that relative clause while the relative clause itself does not reconstruct together with the wh-phrase, see Henderson (2007: 214) (equivalent data are discussed in Sportiche 2006: 65 and Takahashi & Hulsey 2009):

(55) a. [What headway] [that John$_i$ made __] did he$_i$ later regret [what headway]$_1$?
  b. [Which picture of himself$_j$]$_1$ [that John$_j$ gave __ to Mary$_i$] did she$_i$ take home [which picture of himself$_j$]$_1$?

Reconstruction of *headway* and *picture of himself* requires a representation of them within the relative clause. The fact that there is no Principle C violation suggests that the relative clause does not reconstruct. The non-reconstruction of the RC can be accounted for by assuming that it is merged late, like other adjuncts, cf. e.g. Lebeaux (1991). This creates an interesting paradox for the HRA: The reconstruction facts seem to require a raising analysis and thus complementation; late merger, however, implies adjunction on standard assumptions (but see Takahashi & Hulsey 2009 and Stanton 2016 for a different view and Salzmann 2017: 110–118, 168–172

---

b. Noone will want to hear the [(dozens of) stories about Diana$_i$'s brother] [that she$_i$ thinks people will invent __].

This may at first suggest the presence of an implicit PRO, and at least in cases with verbs of creation like (iii-b), this has been argued for, see Fox (1999: 167, fn. 24) (cf. *he invented stories about himself/*him*, but see Heycock 1995: 558, note 15 for a different view). However, an implicit PRO would still not cause a Binding violation under vehicle change in (i) since the possessive pronoun can be bound locally:

(iv) She$_i$ invented [PRO$_i$ stories about her$_i$ father].

Consequently, a different explanation must be found.
The Principle C effect in the intensional context in (i-a) may perhaps be due to independent reasons since there seems to be no possibility to turn the fragment into a full sentence without *Bill* or *he* as the subject so that the Principle C effect already obtains in the matrix clause:

(v) He$_i$/Bill$_i$ is not the responsible guardian of Bill$_i$'s sister that he$_i$ claims to be.

Consequently, while (i-a) may eventually turn out to be irrelevant, (i-b) remains unaccounted for under the present approach. The facts thus suggest that embedding plays an important role in ways that are not fully understood yet. See Fischer (2002) for an interesting proposal in this respect.

for critical discussion of these proposals). Henderson (2007) attempts to solve the paradox by adopting sideward movement and proposes the following derivation:[24]

1. A head-raising relative is constructed, the RelDP moves to the left periphery:

(56) [$_{CP}$ headway$_1$ that John made headway$_1$]

2. Sideward movement of *headway* to an unconnected *wh*-determiner applies:

(57) [$_{CP}$ headway$_1$ that John make headway$_1$]   what + headway$_2$

Sideward Movement

3. *what headway* is merged as a complement of *regret*

(58) regret + [what headway$_2$]

4. The root clause is constructed including wh-movement of [what headway]

(59) [what headway$_2$]$_3$ did he$_i$ later regret [what headway$_2$]$_3$

5. Then, the RC is late-merged, i.e. adjoined to NP:

(60) [What [[headway$_2$] [headway$_1$ that John$_i$ made headway$_1$]]]$_3$ did he$_i$ later regret [what headway$_2$]$_3$?

Finally, chain reduction PF-deletes the lower copy of wh-movement and the relative clause-internal copies.

While ingenious, there are two problems with this approach: First, as the author points out himself (p. 212, fn. 16), his approach is not fully compatible with the chain formation algorithm developed for sideward movement in Nunes (2004) – the external head noun does not c-command into the adjoined relative clause so that chain reduction should not be possible on standard assumptions. Second, the bottom copy of wh-movement contains unlicensed material, viz., an idiomatic NP without the corresponding verb or an anaphor without a local binder.

An MA is more promising in this respect: it can handle reconstruction effects by exceptional deletion of the external head and late merger is, of course, not a problem given that the RC can be an adjunct. However, as just pointed out, the examples in (55) contain an extra complication in that the bottom copy of the wh-phrase contains unlicensed material. This is where the recoverability component becomes crucial again: I argue that exceptional LF-deletion of material with a positive licensing requirement should be extended to wh-movement: Deletion is exceptionally possible here because it is recoverable from inside the relative clause.

24 For a different raising derivation based on sideward movement, see Nunes (2001: 318).

Normally, such deletion is not possible in wh-movement as this would mean that no copy of the restriction survives. But once it is additionally modified by a relative clause, an additional copy is available for the purposes of recoverability.[25]

25 My treatment of the data in (55) seems to make the wrong prediction for extraposed relatives: As pointed out in Hulsey & Sauerland (2006: 114), reconstruction effects vanish if the relative clause is extraposed:

(i) a. * Mary praised the [headway] last year [that John made __].

b. * I saw the [picture of himself$_i$] yesterday [that John$_i$ liked __].

On their account, this follows because adjunct extraposition involves QR of the head noun and late merger of the relative clause. Since late merger requires adjunction, only the MA is a possibility, which under their assumptions cannot handle reconstruction. The resulting structure for (i-a) will thus be as follows, where *headway* is not licensed inside the external head:

(ii) Mary praised [the headway]$_1$ last year [[the headway]$_1$ [[λx. ~~headway~~] that John made [x headway]]]

With my assumptions so far, reconstruction should not be a problem since *headway* is licensed within the relative clause and given the treatment of (55), LF-deletion of *headway* in the theta-position should also be possible.

Henderson (2007: 215) observes that the examples in (i-a/b) improve once the copy in the theta-position is also licensed by a binder or a verb with which it can form an idiomatic expression. It thus seems that the offending copy is the one in the theta-position. Why it can be deleted in wh-movement as in (55) but apparently not under extraposition as in (i) is unclear (note that the problem also obtains if relative clause extraposition simply involves movement of the relative CP). However, there are also reasons to be skeptical about the data in Hulsey & Sauerland (2006): First, reconstruction of idiomatic NPs under extraposition is unproblematic in German, cf. (iii):

(iii) weil er sich über den [Streich] ärgerte, [den wir ihm __ gespielt haben]
because he self about the trick be annoyed.PST.3SG which we he.DAT play.PTCP have.1PL
'because he was annoyed about the trick we played on him'

Similarly, Heycock (2012, this volume) has argued that extraposition does not always block reconstruction in English either (at least not reconstruction of low readings of adjectives and reconstruction of idioms, perhaps not even reconstruction of anaphors):

(iv) Describe all the [habits] to me [that you want to kick __].

Reconstruction for binding in German is strongly degraded under extraposition, see Salzmann (2006: 147–148, fn. 123). This may be related to the fact that binding reconstruction is best if the head noun occurs sentence-initially, a fact that holds in Dutch as well, see de Vries (2002: 82). Claiming that reconstruction is generally blocked under extraposition is thus too strong. Further research is needed to tease apart the factors that affect the acceptability. At the moment, the present account certainly does not fare worse than the other approaches. See Salzmann (2017: 172–174) for further discussion of these issues.

3.7 Overview

Table 2 provides an overview of the relevant reconstruction (and non-reconstruction) effects in restrictive relative clauses and shows the coverage of the various theories discussed in this paper. It shows very clearly that the raising analysis only covers a rather small part of the data. Even if the grammar were to contain both the raising analysis and Sauerland's version of the MA (a combination that is opted for in Bhatt 2002 and Sauerland 2003), its coverage would still not exceed that of the MA proposed by Munn (1994) and Citko (2001). The version of the MA proposed in this paper that combines recoverability with vehicle change clearly has the best

Tab. 2: Reconstruction phenomena and analyses of relative clauses

	Raising	MA Sauerland	MA Munn/Citko	MA Salzmann
Idioms	+	–	+	+
Principle A	+	–	+	+
Amount readings	+	–	+	+
non-reconstruction Principle C	–	+	+	+
Crossover	+	+	–	+
non-reconstruction idiom	–	–	+	+
non-reconstruction Principle A	–	+	+	+
non-reconstruction NPI	–	+	+	+
conflicting requirement	–	+	–	+
no correlation idiom/Principle C	–	–	–	+
late merger	+/–	–	+	+

coverage in that it accounts for all the relevant reconstruction diagnostics that have been discussed in the literature (to my knowledge).[26,27]

---

26 This section has shown that reconstruction effects eventually do not provide evidence in favor of the HRA. The same holds in my view for most of the evidence unrelated to reconstruction that is often said to require the HRA. There is some evidence for a special relationship between the external determiner and the relative clause; but this may only be evidence for complementation (which is also compatible with the MA) if not simply an interpretive dependency that need not be modeled by means of syntactic selection.
Perhaps the strongest remaining evidence for the HRA are head-internal relative clauses like the following, cf. Bianchi (1999: 61ff.):

(i) [Nuna bestya-ta ranti-shqa-n] alli bestya-m ka-rqo-n.
man horse-ACC buy-PFV-3 good horse-EVD be-PST-3
'The horse that the man bought was a good horse.' *Ancash Quechua*

Under the HRA, such relatives can be analyzed as simply involving PF-realization of the lower copy instead of the higher one as in externally headed relative clauses. The difference thus reduces to spell-out differences at PF and allows for a unified treatment of these superficially very different constructions. Under the HEA where there is just an operator relative clause-internally, it is not clear how such structures can be derived. It seems that a completely different approach is needed to accommodate this type of relative clause. The HRA with its unified treatment of both head-internal and head-external relative clauses is thus certainly superior. I believe, though, that the MA can handle head-internal relatives as well because a. it has a relative clause-internal representation of the external head, which can be PF-realized, and b. the necessary PF-deletion of the external head can be understood from the recoverability perspective I have taken here: Deletion of the external head is possible because its content is recoverable from the relative clause-internal copy. What I postulated at LF for the reconstruction data is thus mirrored on the PF-side.
Interestingly, there are also languages where relatives have both an internal and an external head, cf. the following example from Tibetan, cf. Keenan (1985: 152):

(ii) [PeemE *coqtsee* waa-la kurka thii-pe] *coqtse* the na noo-qi yin
Peem.ERG table.GEN under-DAT cross.ABS write-PART table the.ABS I.ABS buy-PRS be
'I will buy the table under which Peem made a cross.' *Tibetan*

The existence of such structures is directly predicted by the MA but not necessarily by the HRA under which it would require the realization of multiple copies, which is normally subject to very strict conditions. Note though that Cinque (2011) has shown that double-headedness is often quite restricted with the external head frequently having classifier-like properties; furthermore, the two heads sometimes differ, which may suggest that the phenomenon eventually does not provide strong evidence for the MA. For detailed discussion of all these issues see Salzmann (2017: 17f., 56–60, 147–150).

27 One unsatisfactory aspect of the MA that it shares with the HRA is that it has to assume that the relative pronoun always is a transitive determiner; this will lead to rather strange configurations in adverbial relatives: A sentence like *the reason why he did not come* will contain a representation like *why reason* inside the relative clause; one thus loses the generalization that wh-relativizers are surface-homophonous with interrogative pronouns. Similarly, in German, by treating the relative pronoun as a determiner one looses the generalization that it inflects like the demonstrative pro-

4 Further evidence for the role of ellipsis in reconstruction

In this section I will briefly discuss two other configurations where an ellipsis/matching perspective has proved to be fruitful to account for reconstruction effects.

The first one concerns reconstruction under resumption/base-generation: In the more recent literature on resumption it has been found that reconstruction is also observed in configurations where movement is unavailable, i.e. within (strong) islands, so that reconstruction cannot be modeled by means of interpreting the bottom copy of a movement chain. Consider the following example from French wh-movement where the wh-phrase is related to a resumptive within an adjunct island, cf. Guilliot & Malkawi (2006: 170):

(61) Quelle photo$_i$ de lui$_j$ es-tu fâché ⟨ parce que chaque prof$_j$ l$_i$' a
which picture of him are-you furious because every prof it has
déchirée? ⟩
tear.apart.PTCP
'lit.: 'Which picture of him are you furious because each teacher tore it?'

The bound variable interpretation suggests that an instance of the wh-phrase occupies the position of the resumptive. Since direct movement cannot be at stake, a different solution is necessary. The authors propose, adapting the NP-ellipsis theory of pronouns of Elbourne (2005), that weak resumptives can be analyzed as transitive determiners whose complement is elided under identity with an antecedent. This is sufficient to get the reconstruction effect in (61), where the representation of the resumptive is actually [$_{DP}$ the [photo de lui$_i$]].

Another configuration where an ellipsis/matching perspective has proved fruitful is ATB-movement. As argued in Salzmann (2012a,b), there are non-identity effects between the gap in the first conjunct and that in the second. While there is always reconstruction into the first conjunct, reconstruction into the second is – apparently – only found with idioms, scope and variable binding as in (62) but not e.g. with Principle C as in (63):

---

noun *der* rather than the demonstrative determiner. See Heck (2005), Salzmann (2006), Salzmann (2017: 93–96, 174f.), Webelhuth, Bargmann & Götze (this volume) for critical discussion of these issues. But see also Wiltschko (1998) for arguments that both D- and relative pronouns involve an elided NP and that morphological differences between the "pronominal" and the determiner use are due to ellipsis licensing.

(62) [Which picture of his$_i$ mother] did [you give __ to every Italian$_i$] and [sell __ to every Frenchman$_i$]?

(63) a. * [Which picture of John$_i$] did [he$_i$ like __] and [Mary dislike __]?

b. [Which picture of John$_i$] did [Mary like __] and [he$_i$ dislike __]?

I cannot go into the details here, but the core of the analysis involves an ellipsis operation of the ATB-moved constituent in the second conjunct under identity with the ATB-moved constituent in the first. Since ellipsis is involved, we expect the possibility of mismatches. The lack of Principle C effects in (63b) can then be related to vehicle change. A Simplified LF-representation of (63b) looks as follows:

(64) [$_{CP}$ [$_{DP}$ Which x] C [$_{\&P}$ [$_{TP}$ Mary like [x picture of John$_i$]] & [$_{TP}$ he$_i$ dislike [$_{DP}$ x picture of him$_i$]]]]]

These two phenomena clearly show that ellipsis plays an important role in accounting for reconstruction patterns quite generally and thus provide indirect support for a deletion/matching analysis of relative clauses.[28]

5 Conclusion

In this paper I have argued against the mainstream view that reconstruction in relative clauses requires the Head Raising Analysis. I have shown that a slightly modified version of the Matching Analysis that includes a recoverability component as well as vehicle change not only accounts for cases of reconstruction but can also handle instances of obligatory non-reconstruction in a straightforward way. It thus achieves better empirical coverage than the HRA and previous versions of the MA. Given that it is not subject to the severe criticism that has been directed against the HRA, it emerges as superior. Since we no longer need both the HRA and the MA as in the mainstream accounts but just one analysis of relative clauses, we arrive at a simpler and theoretically more satisfactory result that also does justice to Occam's razor. The postulation of a matching operation in relativization receives additional support from other reconstruction configurations where ellipsis plays a crucial role as well.

28 Further evidence for ellipsis can be found in Salzmann (2006, 2017), where I show that prolepsis and *tough*-movement basically display the same reconstruction pattern: while there is systematic reconstruction for variable binding, Principle A and idiom interpretation, there is no reconstruction for Principle C. I argue that the matching analysis can be fruitfully extended to these constructions.

Acknowledgment: Earlier versions of these ideas have been presented at various occasions over the years which are too numerous to mention here. I am grateful to the respective audiences for helpful discussion. I would also like to thank the two anonymous reviewers whose comments have led to a signification improvement of the paper. The usual disclaimers apply. Finally, this work has been supported by the SNSF-grant PA00P1_136379/1 and the DFG-grant SA 2646/1-1.

References

Åfarli, Tor. 1994. A promotion analysis of restrictive relative clauses. *The Linguistic Review* 11(1). 81–100.

Aoun, Joseph & Yen-hui Audrey Li. 2003. *Essays on the representational and derivational nature of grammar: The diversity of wh-constructions*. Cambridge, MA: MIT Press.

Bhatt, Rajesh. 2002. The raising analysis of relative clauses: Evidence from adjectival modification. *Natural Language Semantics* 10(1). 43–90.

Bhatt, Rajesh & Sabine Iatridou. 2012. *Comments on Reconstructing Reconstruction*. Paper presented at the Workshop on resumptive pronouns, Hebrew University of Jerusalem.

Bhatt, Rajesh & Yael Sharvit. 2005. A note on intensional superlatives. In Efthymia Georgala & Jonathan Howell (eds.), *Proceedings of SALT XV*, 62–78. Ithaca, NY: Cornell University.

Bianchi, Valentina. 1999. *Consequences of antisymmetry: Headed relative clauses*. Berlin: Mouton de Gruyter.

Bianchi, Valentina. 2000. The raising analysis of relative clauses: A reply to Borsley. *Linguistic Inquiry* 31(1). 123–140.

Boef, Eefje. 2012. *Doubling in relative clauses. Aspects of morphosyntactic microvariation in Dutch*. Utrecht: LOT.

Borsley, Robert. 1997. Relative clauses and the theory of phrase structure. *Linguistic Inquiry* 28(4). 629–647.

Borsley, Robert. 2001. *More on the Raising Analysis of Relative Clauses*. Ms., University of Essex.

Brame, Michael. 1968. A new analysis of the relative clause: Evidence for an interpretive theory. Ms., MIT.

Cecchetto, Carlo. 2005. Reconstruction in relative clauses and the copy theory of traces. In Pierre Pica, Johan Rooryck & Jeroen van Craenenbroeck (eds.), *Linguistic variation yearbook 2005*, 3–35. Amsterdam: John Benjamins.

Cecchetto, Carlo & Caterina Donati. 2015. *(Re)labeling*. Cambridge, MA: MIT Press.

Chomsky, Noam. 1965. *Aspects of the theory of syntax*. Cambridge, MA: MIT Press.

Chomsky, Noam. 1977. On wh-movement. In Peter Culicover, Thomas Wasow & Adrian Akmajian (eds.), *Formal syntax*, 71–132. New York: Academic Press.

Chomsky, Noam. 1995. *The minimalist program*. Cambridge, MA: MIT Press.

Cinque, Guglielmo. 2011. On double-headed relative clauses. *Linguística: Revista de Estudos Linguísticos da Universidade do Porto* 6(1). 67–91.

Citko, Barbara. 2001. Deletion under identity in relative clauses. *Proceedings of NELS* 31. 131–145.

de Vries, Mark. 2002. *The syntax of relativization*. Utrecht: LOT.

Donati, Caterina & Carlo Cecchetto. 2011. Relabeling heads: A unified account for relativization structures. *Linguistic Inquiry* 42(4). 519–560.
Elbourne, Paul. 2005. *Situations and individuals*. Cambridge, MA: MIT Press.
Fiengo, Robert & Robert May. 1994. *Indices and indentity*. Cambridge, MA: MIT Press.
Fischer, Silke. 2002. Reanalyzing reconstruction effects: An optimality-theoretic account of the relation between pronouns and R-expressions. In Marjo van Koppen, Erica Thrift, Erik Jan van der Torre & Malte Zimmermann (eds.), *Proceedings of Console IX*, 68–81. Leiden: SOLE.
Fox, Danny. 1999. Reconstruction, binding theory, and the interpretation of chains. *Linguistic Inquiry* 30(2). 157–196.
Fox, Danny. 2002. Antecedent-contained deletion and the copy theory of movement. *Linguistic Inquiry* 33(1). 63–96.
Guilliot, Nicolas & Nouman Malkawi. 2006. When resumption determines reconstruction. In Donald Baumer, David Montero & Michael Scanlon (eds.), *Proceedings of the 25th West Coast Conference on Formal Linguistics*, vol. 25, 168–176. Somerville, MA: Cascadilla.
Heck, Fabian. 2005. *Gegen Kopfanhebung in deutschen Relativsätzen*. Paper presented at GGS 31, Tübingen.
Henderson, Brent. 2007. Matching and raising unified. *Lingua* 117(1). 202–220.
Heycock, Caroline. 1995. Asymmetries in reconstruction. *Linguistic Inquiry* 26(4). 547–570.
Heycock, Caroline. 2005. On the interaction of adjectival modifiers and relative clauses. *Natural Language Semantics* 13(4). 359–382.
Heycock, Caroline. 2012. *Reconstructing reconstruction: Can we arrive at a unified picture?* Paper presented at the Workshop on resumptive pronouns, Hebrew University of Jerusalem.
Hulsey, Sarah & Uli Sauerland. 2006. Sorting out relative clauses. *Natural Language Semantics* 14(2). 111–137.
Jackendoff, Ray. 1977. *X′ syntax. A study of phrase structure*. Cambridge, MA: MIT Press.
Kayne, Richard. 1994. *The antisymmetry of syntax*. Cambridge, MA: MIT Press.
Keenan, Edward. 1985. Relative clauses. In Timothy Shopen (ed.), *Language typology and syntactic description. Vol 2: Complex constructions*, 141–170. Cambridge: Cambridge University Press.
Kiss, Tibor. 2001. Anaphora and exemptness. A comparative treatment of anaphoric binding in German and English. In Dan Flickinger & Andreas Kathol (eds.), *Proceedings of the 7th international conference on Head-Driven Phrase Structure Grammar*, 182–197. Stanford: CSLI Publications.
Krifka, Manfred. 2011. *An explanation of Condition C effects under apparent reconstruction*. Paper presented at the Workshop on Reconstruction Effects in Relative Clauses, ZAS Berlin.
Lebeaux, David. 1991. Relative clauses, licensing, and the nature of the derivation. In Susan Rothstein (ed.), *Syntax and semantics 25. Perspectives on phrase structure: Heads and licensing*, 209–239. New York: Academic Press.
Lees, Robert B. 1960. *The grammar of English nominalizations*. The Hague: Mouton.
Lees, Robert B. 1961. The constituent structure of noun phrases. *American Speech: A Quarterly of Linguistic Usage* 36. 159–168.
Linebarger, Marcia C. 1987. Negative polarity and grammatical representation. *Linguistics and Philosophy* 10(3). 325–387.
McCawley, James D. 1981. The syntax and semantics of English relative clauses. *Lingua* 53. 99–149.
Merchant, Jason. 2001. *The syntax of silence. Sluicing, islands, and the theory of ellipsis*. Oxford: Oxford University Press.

Montague, Richard. 1973. The proper treatment of quantification in ordinary English. In Jaakko Hintikka, Julius Moravcsik & Patrick Suppes (eds.), *Approaches to natural language*, 221–242. Dordrecht: Reidel.

Munn, Alan. 1994. A minimalist account of reconstruction asymmetries. *Proceedings of NELS* 24. 397–410.

Nunes, Jairo. 2001. Sideward movement. *Linguistic Inquiry* 32(2). 303–344.

Nunes, Jairo. 2004. *Linearization of chains and sideward movement*. Cambridge, MA: MIT Press.

Partee, Barbara. 1975. Montague grammar and transformational grammar. *Linguistic Inquiry* 6(2). 203–300.

Quine, Willard Van Orman. 1960. *Word and object*. Cambridge: MIT Press.

Reinhart, Tanya & Eric Reuland. 1993. Reflexivity. *Linguistic Inquiry* 24(4). 657–720.

Romero, Maribel. 1998. *Focus and reconstruction effects in wh-phrases*. University of Massachusetts Doctoral dissertation.

Safir, Ken. 1999. Vehicle change and reconstruction in A′-chains. *Linguistic Inquiry* 30(4). 587–620.

Salzmann, Martin. 2006. *Resumptive prolepsis: A study in indirect A′-dependencies*. Utrecht: LOT.

Salzmann, Martin. 2012a. A derivational ellipsis approach to ATB-movement. *The Linguistic Review* 29(3). 397–438.

Salzmann, Martin. 2012b. Deriving reconstruction asymmetries in ATB-movement by means of asymmetric extraction + ellipsis. In Peter Ackema, Rhona Alcorn, Caroline Heycock, Dany Jaspers, Jeroen van Craenenbroeck & Guido Vanden Wyngaerd (eds.), *Comparative Germanic syntax: The state of the art*, 353–386. Amsterdam: John Benjamins.

Salzmann, Martin. 2017. *Reconstruction and resumption in indirect A′-dependencies. On the syntax of prolepsis and relativization in (Swiss) German and beyond*. Berlin & Boston: De Gruyter Mouton.

Sauerland, Uli. 1998. *The meaning of chains*. Massachusetts Institute of Technology Doctoral dissertation.

Sauerland, Uli. 2003. Unpronounced heads in relative clauses. In Kerstin Schwabe & Susanne Winkler (eds.), *The interfaces: Deriving and interpreting omitted structures*, 205–226. Amsterdam: John Benjamins.

Schachter, Paul. 1973. Focus and relativization. *Language* 49(1). 19–46.

Sharvit, Yael. 1999. Functional relative clauses. *Linguistics and Philosophy* 22(5). 447–478.

Sportiche, Dominique. 2006. Reconstruction, binding and scope. In Martin Everaert & Henk van Riemsdijk (eds.), *The Blackwell companion to syntax*, 35–94. Oxford: Blackwell.

Stanton, Juliet. 2016. Wholesale late merger in A′-movement: Evidence from preposition stranding. *Linguistic Inquiry* 47(1). 89–126.

Sternefeld, Wolfgang. 2001. Semantic vs. syntactic reconstruction. In Christian Rohrer, Antje Roßdeutscher & Hans Kamp (eds.), *Linguistic form and its computation*, 145–182. Stanford, CA: CSLI Publications.

Takahashi, Shoichi & Sarah Hulsey. 2009. Wholesale late merger: Beyond the A/A′ distinction. *Linguistic Inquiry* 40(3). 387–426.

Vergnaud, Jean-Roger. 1974. *French relative clauses*. Massachusetts Institute of Technology Doctoral dissertation.

Wiltschko, Martina. 1998. On the syntax and semantics of (relative) pronouns and determiners. *The Journal of Comparative Germanic Linguistics* 2(2). 143–181.

Gert Webelhuth, Sascha Bargmann, and Christopher Götze

Idioms as evidence for the proper analysis of relative clauses

1 Introduction

Relative clauses (RCs)[1] form a core phenomenon of English grammar and have been the subject of intense theoretical analysis both in traditional and formal approaches to grammar. In Generative Grammar, their analysis has followed the fluctuating ups and downs of the various theoretical assumptions that have characterized the major frameworks and their dialects over the decades.

Three approaches to RCs have dominated the theoretical literature: (i) the Modification Analysis, commonly ascribed to Quine (1960), (ii) the Raising Analysis, suggested in an unpublished paper by Michael Brame and argued for in a publication for the first time in Schachter (1973), and (iii) the Matching Analysis, proposed in early Generative Grammar. With occasional exceptions (e.g. Vergnaud 1974 or Carlson 1977), the Raising and Matching approaches receded along with the trend towards base-generating pronouns, including relative pronouns, in the so-called interpretive semantics of the 1970s (see, for example, Jackendoff 1972). As a consequence, the Modification Analysis reigned the field both syntactically and semantically during the 1980s.

The pendulum began to swing back, however, at the beginning of the 1990s, when Kayne (1994) brought Antisymmetry to the table. Since (i) Antisymmetry is incompatible with the rightward adjunction analysis of RCs, which was perceived to be closely connected to the Modification Analysis,[2] and since (ii) the Modification Analysis has difficulties with reconstruction phenomena, Modification became unfashionable. Instead, Kayne revived the Raising Analysis, which was subsequently

1 When we speak of RCs in this paper, we refer to *restrictive* RCs (unless explicitly indicated otherwise).

2 It is important to note that the Modification Analysis and rightward adjunction are not at all inter-dependent and that there have been proposals to combine Modification with an analysis of RCs as complements. See, for example, Schmitt (2000) or Boef (2012).

Gert Webelhuth, Goethe University Frankfurt am Main
Sascha Bargmann, Goethe University Frankfurt am Main
Christopher Götze, Georg-August University Göttingen

https://doi.org/10.1515/9783050095158-007

developed in book-length treatments in Bianchi (1999) and de Vries (2002), as well as a number of shorter influential works, e.g. Bhatt (2002) and Sauerland (2003).

Sauerland (2003) argues that the full range of reconstruction phenomena can only be captured if RCs are derivationally ambiguous between Raising and Matching. This claim is contested in Salzmann (2006), where Matching is considered to be sufficient, and in Henderson (2007), who argues the same for Raising. As a result, we find a bewildering disparity of assumptions about the analysis of RCs in the recent research literature:

1. Chomsky (1977): Modification only
2. Kayne (1994): Raising only
3. Sauerland (2003): Raising and Matching
4. Salzmann (2006): Matching only
5. Henderson (2007): Raising only

It is clearly desirable to compare the competing RC-analyses and to only keep the most promising candidate(s). This is the raison d'être of this paper, in which we will first sketch the three analyses (Section 2) and then point to a large number of pivotal linguistic generalizations that are missed by grammars that analyze RCs in terms of Raising and/or Matching (Section 3). We will in effect argue that the loss of generalizations is both so systematic and so immense that by usual standards of argumentation in Generative Grammar, both the Raising and the Matching Analysis of RCs are effectively disqualified from further consideration. This, however, leaves us with the challenge that a few grammatical phenomena, practically all involving reconstruction of one kind or another, have been shown to be difficult to capture without Raising and/or Matching.

We will turn to one such thorny issue in Section 4: the behavior of idiomatic expressions in RCs. We will show that idioms in RCs can be licensed without recourse to literal reconstruction of the RC-head. Our conclusion will be that this effectively removes idioms as evidence for the existence of Raising and/or Matching derivations of RCs, which constitutes another step towards showing that such derivations are superfluous in general.

2 The Modification, Raising, and Matching Analyses of Relative Clauses

In this section, we will sketch the three major approaches to the analysis of RCs.

2.1 The Modification Analysis

The Modification Analysis is pervasive in the literature.[3] It is implicit in Quine (1960) and assumed in Montague (1974), Partee (1975), Chomsky (1977), and Heim & Kratzer (1998). This approach analyzes a DP like the one in (1) as in (2):[4]

(1) the house which I bought

(2) $[_{DP}$ the $[_{NP}$ house$]_i$ $[_{RC}$ $[_{RelPro}$ *which*$_i]$ $[_{IP}$ I bought $t_{RelPro}]]]$

The intuition underlying the Modification Analysis in its standard form is that the RC-head (here *house*) and the RC itself denote predicates that combine semantically via intersective modification. The head originates outside the RC and stays external to it throughout the whole derivation. Therefore, it is not ever reconstructed into an RC-internal position. As in traditional grammar, *which* is treated as a relative pronoun (RelPro). There is only one movement operation in Modification: The RelPro moves from its base position into the specifier position of the RC, sometimes pied-piping other material in the process.

2.2 The Raising Analysis

The Raising Analysis was originally proposed in an unpublished paper by Michael Brame as well as in Schachter (1973) and Vergnaud (1974).[5] It was revived by Kayne (1994), Bianchi (1999), and de Vries (2002). All forms of the Raising Analysis in the literature propose variants of the derivation in (3) for our example DP in (1):

3 What we call *Modification Analysis* in this paper has, among many other things, often been dubbed *Head-External Analysis* in the literature (see, for example, Bhatt 2002, Salzmann 2006). We prefer the term *Modification* over *Head-External* to prevent any confusion with the Matching Analysis, which also involves an external head.

4 In (2) and the other numbered examples in Section 2, italics indicate that the string has been moved.

5 Parts of this section are also part of our contribution to the *Festschrift* for David Pesetsky in celebration of his 60th birthday.

(3) Base: $[_{DP_1}$ the$_{ext}$ e $[_{RC}$ $[_{IP}$ I bought $[_{DP_2}$ which$_{int}$ $[_{NP}$ house]]]]]
Step 1: $[_{DP_1}$ the$_{ext}$ e $[_{RC}$ $[_{DP_2}$ *which*$_{int}$ $[_{NP}$ *house*]] $[_{IP}$ I bought t_{DP_2}]]]
Step 2: $[_{DP_1}$ the$_{ext}$ $[_{NP}$ *house*] $[_{RC}$ $[_{DP_2}$ *which*$_{int}$ t_{NP}] $[_{IP}$ I bought t_{DP_2}]]]

The intuition of this analysis is that the head of the RC takes on a double role. In the base, it appears inside the RC in the relativized position determined by the *wh*-word *which*. In contrast to both traditional grammar and the Modification Analysis, the Raising Analysis does not treat *which* as a relative pronoun but as a relative determiner, namely the int(ernal) determiner, which takes the head of the RC as an NP-complement and forms a DP with it (DP_1). The surface position of the RC-head is empty at the beginning of the derivation. The word order in (1) is the result of two subsequent movements. First, the entire DP_2 *which house* is preposed to the beginning of the RC (Step 1) and then the NP *house* is moved to the left into a position where it enters into a grammatical relation with the ext(ernal) determiner *the*, which selects the RC and the head (Step 2). Because of this derivational history, the head can easily be reconstructed into the RC.

Given that the RC can be linearly separated from the head NP, see (4),

(4) Sue wanted to talk about the $[_{NP}$ house] again $[_{RC}$ which I bought].

it is most plausible to assume that the head NP leaves the RC and moves into the complement position of the external determiner, as shown in (3) above.[6]

6 An anonymous reviewer states that whether or not sentences like the one in (4) can be taken to be arguments for the head leaving the RC within Raising approaches is "completely dependent on the analysis of extraposition one assumes", which, she says, entails that "extraposition does not seem to provide evidence in favor of any analysis of RCs." While we generally agree with the first statement, we disagree with the second one, as most, if not all, of the analyses of extraposition that avoid moving the head out of the RC (RC-internal Raising) face major problems. Two examples of such an analysis can be found in Kayne (1994) and de Vries (2002). In Kayne (1994)'s original stranding account of extraposition, for instance, it is not only the head NP *house* that moves to the left, as suggested in (4), but the entire DP *the house*. As several authors have observed (e.g. Büring & Hartmann 1997, Koster 2000, and de Vries 2002), this analysis is problematic, as the DP does not form a constituent under Kayne's analysis. This issue, as well as the problem that complex heads with an additional complement pose for this theory (as in *A picture has been issued of the suspect*) is among the numerous problems that Sheehan (2010) points out. She concludes that "additional movements would need to be posited to make *a picture* into a derived constituent. This would presumably involve extraction of the complement PP/CP, followed by remnant movement of DP (meaning that the PP/CP is not, strictly speaking, stranded)." It is fair to say that those additional movements are stipulated for theory-internal reasons only. Furthermore, as Webelhuth, Sailer & Walker (2013) show, de Vries (2002)'s extraposition theory, which relies on specifying coordination and ellipsis and, according to the reviewer, is in principle compatible with any of the three analyses of RCs, runs into serious difficulties.

It is important to observe that in movement step 2 of the derivation in (3) *house* moves out of the RC, despite the fact that RCs are syntactic islands. In order to avoid this, there are also versions of the Raising Analysis (such as Kayne 1994 or de Vries 2002) that do not extract the head NP from the RC, thereby circumventing an island violation. Instead of moving the head out, it is stipulated to move RC-internally. Kayne (1994), for instance, suggests for *wh*-relatives that the head NP moves from the complement position of the RC-internal DP to the specifier position of that DP, see (5).[7]

(5) $[_{DP_1}$ the$_{ext}$ $[_{RC}$ $[_{DP_2}$ $[_{NP}^{SpecDP_2}$ *house*] *which*$_{int}$ t_{NP}] $[_{IP}$ I bought t_{DP_2}]]]

We will refer to these versions of the Raising Analysis as *RC-internal Raising*. RC-internal Raising analyses face several difficulties. Among these difficulties are case and agreement facts (see Section 3.2 below). To account for them, even proponents of RC-internal Raising have to admit some kind of movement out of the RC, such as covert head incorporation (Bianchi 1999) or feature movement (de Vries 2002). Boef (2012: 147) comes to the conclusion that these additional mechanisms are "all (to a greater or lesser extent) stipulative and not particularly explanatory." Further difficulties for RC-internal Raising, as we will now show, are head NPs with a complement, the 'Big Mess' construction, and extraposition. For the case of head NPs with a complement, consider the sentences in (6):

(6) a. $[_{PP}$ *Von welchem Popstar*] wurden $[_{RC}$ $[_{NP}^{SpecRC}$ *Nacktbilder* t_{PP}],
of which pop star were *nude-pictures*
die t_{NP} gestohlen waren], ins Internet gestellt?
RelPron stolen were in-the Internet put
'Of which pop star were nude pictures that had been stolen put on the Internet?'

b. This is the pop star $[_{PP}$ *of whom*] $[_{RC}$ $[_{NP}^{SpecRC}$ *nude pictures* t_{PP}] that had been stolen t_{NP}] were put on the Internet.

In (6a), the head NP *Nacktbilder von welchem Popstar* is moved into SpecRC. Hence, no island violation is incurred. In the next step, however, the PP *von welchem Popstar* is *wh*-moved out of the RC into the left periphery of the matrix sentence. We judge the sentence grammatical, yet the RC-internal Raising Analysis still requires material to move out of the RC island. In (6b), the head NP *nude pictures of whom* is only moved into the Spec of the most deeply embedded RC, so that, again, no island violation is incurred. But then the PP *of whom* (the complement to the relational noun *pictures*) undergoes subsequent movement out of this RC into the

7 Superscripts in the bracket notation indicate the structural position of an expression.

higher RC. This should induce an island violation, but the sentence is grammatical (judgment due to Bob Levine, p.c.). Note that a Modification Analysis of sentences like those in (6) causes no comparable problems because there the head always remains external to the RC, so that material extracted out of the head is in no way forced to move out of an RC island.

Let us now consider the interaction of the RC-internal Raising Analysis with the 'Big Mess' construction (Berman 1974, van Eynde 2007) or, to use the more descriptive terminology of Kay & Sag (2009), the 'complex pre-determination phenomenon.'

(7) [$_{\text{AP}}$ *How expensive*] [$_{\text{DP}}$ a [$_{\text{RC}}$ [$^{\text{SpecRC}}_{\text{NP}}$ t_{AP} *car*] that t_{NP} works]] can we afford?

In the Raising Analysis sketched in (7), the head NP *how expensive car* is moved to SpecRC and no island violation is incurred. In the next step, the AP *how expensive* is fronted to the left of the DP. Again, this requires the AP to be extracted out of the RC if one assumes that the RC head stays within the confines of the RC.

Finally, consider extraposition (judgments due to Bob Levine, p.c.).

(8) a. The police showed [$_{\text{RC}}$ [$^{\text{SpecRC}}_{\text{NP}}$ *color pictures* t_{PP}] that had been taken t_{NP}] to every witness [$_{\text{PP}}$ *of everybody who had been at the crime scene*].

b. We should mention just those [$_{\text{RC}}$ [$^{\text{SpecRC}}_{\text{NP}}$ *attempts* t_{CP}] $t_{\text{R'}}$] to Mary [$_{\text{CP}}$ *PRO to break into the Bank of England*] [$_{\text{R'}}$ *that were successful* t_{NP}].

In (8a), the relativized head NP consisting of the relational noun *color pictures*, which takes the PP *of everybody who had been at the crime scene* as its complement, has been moved into SpecRC. Subsequently, the PP is extraposed. Under the RC-internal Raising Analysis, this last movement step should incur an island violation, contrary to fact. In (8b), the relativized head NP consisting of the plural noun *attempts*, which takes an infinitival CP as its complement, has been moved into SpecRC. In this case, the infinitival complement as well as the RC have been extraposed. According to the logic of the RC-internal Raising Analysis, this should again undermine the islandhood status of RCs and the corresponding sentences should be ungrammatical, which, however, is not the case. Furthermore, the island violations caused by the movements to the right in (8) are violations of Ross (1967)'s Right Roof Constraint, an otherwise exceptionless constraint in both German and English, as far as we are aware.

2.3 The Matching Analysis

The Matching Analysis was originally proposed by Lees (1960, 1961) and Chomsky (1965) and extended by Sauerland (1998). Under a Matching Analysis, the derivation of the DP in (1) is as follows:

(9) Base: $[_{DP_1}$ the$_{ext}$ $[_{NP}$ house$]_i$
$[_{RC}$ $[_{IP}$ I bought $[_{DP_2}$ which$_{int}$ $[_{NP}$ house$]_i]]]]$
Step 1: $[_{DP_1}$ the$_{ext}$ $[_{NP}$ house$]_i$
$[_{RC}$ $[_{DP_2}$ *which*$_{int}$ $[_{NP}$ *house*$]_i]$ $[_{IP}$ I bought $t_{DP_2}]]]$
Step 2: $[_{DP_1}$ the$_{ext}$ $[_{NP}$ house$]_i$
$[_{RC}$ $[_{DP_2}$ *which*$_{int}$ $[_{NP}$ ~~*house*~~$]_i]$ $[_{IP}$ I bought $t_{DP_2}]]]$

Intuitively, the Matching Analysis is a hybrid between the Modification and the Raising Analysis. As in Modification, the head originates and remains external to the RC during the entire derivation. In contrast to Modification, however, the head has an RC-internal counterpart, the so-called internal head. We indicate this by co-indexation. Since the relation between the external and the internal head is not established via a movement chain, each head has to be considered individually. The internal head is obligatorily deleted under "identity" with the external head.[8] Instead of the R-expression of the external head, the internal head may also contain a pronoun co-referential with that R-expression (see "vehicle change" in Fiengo & May 1994). As in the Raising Analysis, the relativizer is treated as a relative determiner.

3 Empirical Motivations and Problems for Raising and Matching

3.1 Two Pro(blematic) Arguments: Idiom Licensing and Binding Theory

3.1.1 Idiom Licensing

A standard argument in favor of the Raising Analysis is idiom licensing. An idiom (e.g. *make headway* ≈ 'make progress') is licensed, so the argument goes, if all of

8 Note that for the motivation of this kind of deletion, most Matching accounts usually only hint at a possibly existing analogy with comparative deletion, which, however, is not very well understood either.

its parts form a constituent at D-structure/the point of merge.[9] Note the following data from Schachter (1973: 31):[10]

(10) a. We *made headway*.

b. * (The) *headway* was satisfactory.

c. The *headway* that we *made* was satisfactory.

In (10a), this licensing requirement is met since *headway* is base-generated in the complement position of *make*. In (10b), in contrast, this is not the case (as there is no form of *make*), so that the idiomatic reading of *headway* is unavailable. In order to account for the grammaticality of (10c), the Raising Analysis assumes that *headway* is base-generated in the complement position of *make*, just as in (10a), and only later raised to its surface position:

(11) The [$_{NP}$ *headway*] [$_{RC}$ that we *made* t_{NP}] was satisfactory.

Note that the Matching Analysis cannot account for (10c) since it postulates two copies of *headway*, but only the RC-internal one is licensed:

(12) The [$_{NP}$ *headway*] [$_{RC}$ that we *made* [$_{NP}$ ~~*headway*~~]] was satisfactory.

Even though idiom licensing was (and still is) one of the major motivations for Raising, the grammaticality of the sentence in (13) from Salzmann (2006: 43, example due to Henk v. Riemsdijk) is problematic for this approach, as the "D-structure" licensing requirement is not fulfilled for the upper occurrence of *pulled*.

(13) John never *pulled* the [$_{NP}$ *strings*] [$_{RC}$ that his mother told him should be *pulled* t_{NP}].

Here, Matching needs to come to the rescue. Under Matching, both occurrences of *pulled* have a copy of *strings* in their respective complement position:

9 A reviewer wonders why the licensing requirement on idioms should be met at D-structure/the point of merge rather than at LF. The formulation of the licensing requirement in terms of D-structure/the point of merge is a traditional one. It can be found, for instance, in Chomsky (1981: 146, fn. 94), where D-structure is considered to be the "natural place for the operation of idiom rules." Similarly, Bhatt (2002) claims that idioms need to appear "in the relevant environment at some point in the derivation (minimally point of Merge, maybe also at LF)." With the advent of the Minimalist Program and its move to abandon D-structure, the licensing requirement is often reformulated as a condition on LFs, for "the unitary nature of the idiom must be captured at some other level. In a minimalist theory, the only level available for this is LF, as only this level affects semantic interpretation" (Hornstein, Nuñes & Grohmann 2005), see Munn (1994) or Boef (2012: 163), among many others. As far as we are aware, however, none of these authors attempts to work out a theory detailed enough to handle all the cases discussed in the present work.

10 In (10) and Section 3.1.1 in general, italics indicate that the string is part of an idiom.

(14) John never *pulled* the [$_{NP}$ *strings*] [$_{RC}$ that his mother told him should be *pulled* [$_{NP}$ ~~*strings*~~]].

Note, however, that neither Raising nor Matching can explain cases in which there is obligatory non-reconstruction, as, for example, in the sentence in (15) from McCawley (1981: 137) and Alexiadou et al. (2000: 12).

(15) Parky *pulled* the [$_{NP}$ *strings*] [$_{RC}$ that t_{NP}/[$_{NP}$ ~~*strings*~~] got me the job].

Under Matching, the RC-internal occurrence of *strings* lacks its idiomatic counterpart at the point of merge. Either the RC-internal occurrence of *strings* is not licensed, or it is non-idiomatic. If it is not licensed, the derivation crashes at this point. If it is non-idiomatic, the RC-external occurrence of *strings* cannot be idiomatic either since it is supposed to be identical with RC-internal *strings*. This, of course, causes a severe licensing problem for idiomatic *pull*.

Under Raising, the situation is even worse: It is not only *strings* that lacks its idiomatic counterpart at the point of merge, but also *pull*. So, both idiom parts end up unlicensed from the very beginning of the derivation.

3.1.2 Binding Theory

Let us now turn to the second standard argument for Raising and Matching: binding-theoretic reconstruction. According to Chomsky (1981), anaphors, including reflexives and reciprocals, must be locally bound (Principle A of the Binding Theory). In (16) taken from Schachter (1973), the anaphor *each other*, in its surface position, is not c-commanded by and hence not bound by its antecedent *John and Mary*.[11]

(16) The [$_{NP}$ interest in *each other$_i$*] [$_{RC}$ that *John and Mary$_i$* showed t_{NP}] was fleeting.

Whereas Raising can resolve the issue by resorting to reconstruction of the head into the complement position of *showed* inside the RC, Matching runs into the problem that the anaphor *each other* in the external copy of the head induces a Principle A violation.

Salzmann (2006: 117) shows that while Raising has problems with (17), a Matching account is technically feasible.

11 In (16) and Section 3.1.2 in general, italics, on top of the usual co-indexation, indicate that two strings are either co-referential or that one is bound by the other.

(17) Schicken *Sie*$_i$ uns [ein Foto von *sich*$_i$], das beweist, dass Sie ein
Send you us a photo of REFL that proves that you a
wahrer Ferrari-Anhänger sind!
real Ferrari enthusiast are
'Send us a photograph of yourself that proves that you are a real Ferrari enthusiast!'

In (17), the reflexive *sich* needs to get bound by the matrix pronoun *Sie* in order to satisfy Principle A. This is not possible under Raising, as the head, including *sich*, would get reconstructed into the RC, which results in the disruption of the binding relation between *sich* and its antecedent, given that German does not seem to have exempt anaphors, as demonstrated in Kiss (2001). Matching, on the other hand, deletes the RC-internal copy of the head while the external one remains in its initial position, so that Principle A is not violated.

In (18), taken from Sauerland (2003), the head of the RC contains the variable *his*, which, according to standard assumptions and under the given indexing, needs to be bound by the quantifier *everybody* within its c-command domain.[12]

(18) The [$_{NP}$ relative of *his*$_i$] [$_{RC}$ that *everybody*$_i$ likes t_{NP}] lives far away.

Under Raising, this structural requirement is met since the head is reconstructed into the complement position of *likes*. Matching, on the other hand, is forced to opportunistically delete the upper occurrence of the head including the pronoun and to reconstruct the lower occurrence back into the c-command domain of the subject of the RC.

Last but not least, let us turn to Principle C effects as discussed in Munn (1994) and Sauerland (2003). Consider the minimal pair in (19):[13]

(19) a. the picture of *Bill*$_i$ that *he*$_i$ likes
b. * the picture of *Bill*$_i$ that *he*$_i$ took

In order to explain the grammaticality contrast between (19a) and (19b), Sauerland (2003), following Carlson (1977), argues for the coexistence of Raising and Matching within one and the same grammar:

---

12 Barker (2012) casts doubt on those standard assumptions. Based on "a wide variety of systematic counterexamples", Barker shows "that in English, quantificational binding does not require c-command"; see Barker (2012) for details.

13 Sauerland (2003) points to significant speaker variation. For a discussion of the corresponding German data, see Salzmann (2006).

(20) a. * the [$_{NP}$ picture of *Bill$_i$*] [$_{RC}$ that *he$_i$* likes t_{NP}] (Raising)
b. the [$_{NP}$ picture of *Bill$_i$*] [$_{RC}$ that *he$_i$* likes [$_{NP}$ ~~one~~]] (Matching)

(21) a. * the [$_{NP}$ picture of *Bill$_i$*] [$_{RC}$ that *he$_i$* took t_{NP}] (Raising)
b. * the [$_{NP}$ picture of *Bill$_i$*] [$_{RC}$ that *he$_i$* took [$_{NP}$ ~~one~~]] (Matching)

Sauerland claims that (19a) is grammatical because (at least) one of the two approaches (Matching in this case) can generate it: Whereas Raising in (20a) causes a Principle C violation (after reconstruction), Matching in (20b) relies on vehicle change and, thereby, avoids that very problem. (19b), in contrast, is ungrammatical since neither Raising nor Matching are available: Raising in (21a) yields a Principle C violation. Matching in (21b), on the other hand, does not license the idiom *take a picture*.

Let us sum up our discussion of the idiom and binding arguments for the Raising and Matching analyses of RCs: We have seen that neither theory can actually claim to be able to capture all the data that needs to be accounted for. Moreover, Matching draws on arguably undesirable conceptual devices, namely vehicle change and opportunistic deletion.

3.2 Morpholexical Generalizations Lost with Raising and/or Matching

Having discussed the major arguments for Raising and Matching, we will now turn to pivotal linguistic generalizations that are missed by grammars containing one or both of these approaches to RCs.[14] We will start off with morpholexical generalizations and then move on to syntax.

As has already been mentioned, both Raising and Matching crucially take relativizers to be determiners rather than pronouns. As will be shown, this assumption results in the loss of at least the following five morpholexical generalizations:[15]

1. In German, the *d*-relativizer is paradigmatically isomorphic to personal pronouns, NOT to determiners.
2. In English and German, *wh*-relativizers are surface-homophonous with interrogative pronouns, NOT with determiners.
3. In English, relativizers and personal pronouns, but NOT determiners, are characterized by animacy and case distinctions.

14 Most of the arguments in this and the next section stem from Borsley (1997, 2001) and Heck (2005).

15 A generalization followed by a superscript *R* is only violated by Raising.

4. A DP heading an A′-chain carries the case assigned to the foot of the chain.[R]
5. In German, determiners govern the declension class of nouns and adjectives they co-occur with.[R]

We will now go through these generalizations one by one and demonstrate with the help of German and English data how they are missed by Raising and/or Matching.

3.2.1 Paradigm Isomorphy between German *d*-Relativizers and Personal Pronouns

Consider the following data taken from Heck (2005):

(22) a. Ich vertraue *den*$_{\text{det}}$/**denen*$_{\text{pron}}$ Freunden.
I trust the/*them friends
'I trust the friends.'

b. Ich vertraue **den*$_{\text{det}}$/*denen*$_{\text{pron}}$.
I trust *the/them
'I trust them.'

c. die Freunde, **den*/*denen* ich vertraue
the friends whom I trust
'the friends who(m) I trust'

In (22a), *Freunden* can only be specified by the determiner *den*, not by the personal pronoun *denen*. In (22b), on the other hand, it is the determiner that cannot function as the complement of the verb, whereas the pronoun of course works perfectly well. As can be observed in (22c) then, the German *d*-relativizer morphologically patterns with the personal pronoun *denen*, NOT with the determiner *den*. These empirical facts are unexpected from the perspective of Raising and Matching, which, as mentioned above, take the relativizer to unambiguously be a determiner.

3.2.2 Systematic Surface Homophony of *wh*-Relativizers and Interrogative Pronouns

As the embedded question in (23) and the adverbial RC in (24) exemplarily illustrate for German *wo*,

(23) Ich fragte, [$_{Q}$ *wo* du geboren bist].
I asked where you born are
'I asked where you were born.'

(24) der Ort, [$_{RC}$ *wo* du geboren bist]
the place where you born are
'the place where you were born'

wh-relativizers are systematically surface-homophonous with interrogative pronouns, see Table 1 for German and Table 2 for English.

Tab. 1: German Relativizers and Interrogatives

Relativizers	Interrogatives	Gloss
wo	*wo*	where
was	*was*	which
womit	*womit*	with what
wieso	*wieso*	why
weshalb	*weshalb*	why
warum	*warum*	why
wie	*wie*	how

Tab. 2: English Relativizers and Interrogatives

Relativizers	Interrogatives
who(m)	*who(m)*
where	*where*
why	*why*

Despite the fact that *wh*-interrogative pronouns and *wh*-relativizers are systematically identical in surface form, Raising and Matching predict the former to be syntactically simplex and the latter to be syntactically complex. Within these approaches the *wh*-relativizer *wo* in (24) would be analyzed as in (25) and (26) respectively.

(25) der [$_{NP}$ *Ort*], [$_{RC}$ [*wo* t_{NP}] du geboren bist]

(26) der [$_{NP}$ *Ort*], [$_{RC}$ [*wo* [$_{NP}$ ~~*Ort*~~] du geboren bist]

This variable degree of syntactic complexity between *wh*-interrogative pronouns and *wh*-relativizers enforces a number of additional stipulations. Kayne (1994: 154, fn.12), for instance, suggests that "*who* could be taken to be a form of *which* that appears under spec-head agreement with a [+ human] NP."

3.2.3 Animacy and Case Distinctions of Relativizers and Personal Pronouns

English relativizers behave like personal pronouns, and unlike determiners, in that their morphological paradigms are characterized by animacy and case distinctions:

Tab. 3: Animacy Distinctions

	animate	**inanimate**
personal pronouns	*he/she*	*it*
relativizers	*who*	*which*
determiners	*a/the*	

Tab. 4: Case Distinctions

	nominative	**accusative**
personal pronouns	*I, he, she, we, they*	*me, him, her, us, them*
relativizers	*who*	*whom*
determiners	*a, the*	

As the first line of Table 3 indicates, English 3rd-person-singular personal pronouns display a distinction between the animate forms *he/she* and the inanimate *it*. An analogous distinction holds between the relativizers *who* and *which* in line 2. The determiners *a* and *the* in line 3, in contrast, do not show this distinction. In a parallel fashion, see Table 4, English animate relativizers and 1st- and 3rd-person animate personal pronouns display a form distinction between nominative and accusative case, which the determiners *a* and *the* do not. Again, these empirical facts are ignored by Raising and Matching.

3.2.4 Case Assignment

As is well-known, a DP heading an A′-chain always carries the case assigned to the foot of the chain. This becomes evident in languages with overt case marking such as German, see (27) and (28).

(27) Sie fragte, $[_{Q}$ $[_{DP}$ welchen^{acc} Jungen$^{acc}]$ du $t_{DP}{}^{acc}$ kennst].
she asked which boy you know
'She asked which boy you know.'

(28) a. * Sie fragte, [$_Q$ [$_{DP}$ welcher^{nom} Junge^{nom}] du $t_{DP}{}^{acc}$ kennst].
b. * Sie fragte, [$_Q$ [$_{DP}$ welcher^{nom} Jungen^{acc}] du $t_{DP}{}^{acc}$ kennst].
c. * Sie fragte, [$_Q$ [$_{DP}$ welchen^{acc} Junge^{nom}] du $t_{DP}{}^{acc}$ kennst].

Since all of the analyses presented in Section 2 (Modification, Raising, and Matching) involve A′-movement, they should all respect the above generalization. Under Raising, however, non-subject RCs should display a clash between the case assigned to the RC-head at the bottom of the chain and the case assigned to the RC-head at the top of the chain:

(29) Der^{nom} [$_{NP}$ Junge]^{nom}, [$_{RC}$ [$_{DP}$ den^{acc} t$_{NP}{}^{acc}$] du t$_{DP}{}^{acc}$ kennst], kommt
the boy whom you know comes
auch.
also
'The boy who(m) you know will also come.'

While the RC-head in (29) is assigned accusative case in its base position (the complement position of the internal determiner *den*, together with which it forms the DP *den Jungen* in the complement position of *kennst*), it should also be assigned nominative case by the verb in the main clause. It is thus unexplained why (29) is grammatical but (30) is not, since there should be a case clash in both structures:

(30) * Der^{nom} [$_{NP}$ Jungen]^{acc}, [$_{RC}$ [$_{DP}$ den^{acc} t$_{NP}{}^{acc}$] du t$_{DP}{}^{acc}$ kennst], kommt
the boy whom you know comes
auch.
also
'The boy who(m) you know will also come.'

While Kayne (1994) and Henderson (2007) offer no account whatsoever of these facts, Bianchi (1999)'s approach violates cyclicity (see de Vries 2002: 115) and the ones in Bhatt (2002) and de Vries (2002) are based on ad hoc assumptions and thus lack explanatory force (see Salzmann 2006, Section 1.2.3). Salzmann (2006), Section 1.2.3.3, concludes: "The case problem ... certainly remains one of the strongest arguments against the HRA [Head Raising Analysis]."

3.2.5 Declension Class

In German, determiners govern the declension class of nouns and adjectives they are in construction with. As can be seen in (31) and (32) respectively, the indefinite article *ein* is followed by the mixed declension, whereas the definite article *der* requires the weak declension.

(31) **ein** [$_{NP}$ jung**er**^{mixed} Angestellt**er**^{mixed}]
a young employee
'a young employee'

(32) **der** [$_{NP}$ jung**e**^{weak} Angestellt**e**^{weak}]
the young employee
'the young employee'

This also holds when the NP consisting of the noun and the adjective forms the head of an RC, see (33) and (34):

(33) **ein** jung**er** Angestellt**er**, **der** befördert wurde
a (young) employee who promoted became
'a (young) employee who was promoted'

(34) a. * **ein** jung**e** Angestellt**e**, **der** befördert wurde
b. **der** jung**e** Angestellt**e**, **der** befördert wurde
c. * **der** jung**er** Angestellt**er**, **der** befördert wurde

Under Raising, however, (33) and (34a) contain a clash between the weak declension required by the definite internal determiner and the mixed declension required by the indefinite external determiner, see (35a) and (35b) respectively:

(35) a. **ein** [$_{NP}$ jung**er** Angestellt**er**], [**der** t_{NP}] befördert wurde
b. * **ein** [$_{NP}$ jung**e** Angestellt**e**], [**der** t_{NP}] befördert wurde

3.3 Syntactic Generalizations Lost with Raising and/or Matching

As we have shown in the previous section, Raising and Matching, due to their commitment to treat relativizers as determiners (rather than pronouns), cannot cope with a number of MORPHOLEXICAL generalizations in both German and English.

In the current section, we will show in a parallel fashion that there is a whole range of SYNTACTIC generalizations that Raising and/or Matching miss. Many of these facts have been at the heart of Generative Grammar ever since its inception and fall under the empirically well-investigated rubric of island constraints. To be exact, Raising and/or Matching miss the following seven robust syntactic generalizations:[16]

---

16 Once again, a generalization followed by a superscript *R* is only violated by Raising.

1. In English, external arguments are extraction islands.^{R}
2. In German, no part of a genitive specifier of a DP can be extracted.^{R}
3. In German, no part of a dative specifier of a DP can be extracted.^{R}
4. In English, non-pronominal specifiers of a DP are marked with 's.
5. In German, the DP complement of an adjunct PP is an extraction island.^{R}
6. In German, *mit*-class adpositions are prepositional with an inanimate PHRASAL complement and postpositional with an inanimate PRONOMINAL complement.
7. In German, restrictive and non-restrictive RCs are typically identical in form.

Just as with the morphological generalizations, Raising violates every single one of these constraints. Matching fares better but still misses generalizations 4, 6, and 7.

3.3.1 The Subject Condition

As is well-known, external arguments are extraction islands in English (see Chomsky 1973, Huang 1982):

(36) * [$_{DP}$ *Who(m)*] did [$_{SUBJ}$ pictures of t_{DP}] give Mary a headache?

In (36), the interrogative pronoun *who* is moved out of the subject. This movement step violates the Subject Condition and, as a result, leads to the ungrammaticality of the sentence. In the Raising Analysis of RCs, however, extraction from the subject of an RC must be able to result in perfectly grammatical DPs like the one in (37):

(37) the [$_{NP}$ *person*] [$_{SUBJ}$ who t_{NP}] gave Mary a headache

Here, the head NP *person* moves out of the subject, even though this step represents a clear violation of the Subject Condition. It is not obvious how the contrast between this violation and the grammaticality of the DP in (37) could be explained without recourse to ad hoc stipulations exempting the subjects of RCs from the Subject Condition. Thus, the Raising Analysis leads to the loss of a robust empirical generalization of English syntax.

3.3.2 The Left Branch Condition – Part 1

Let us now turn to the Left Branch Condition (LBC). The following is a modernized version of Ross (1967: 207)'s original definition:

(38) Left Branch Condition
No DP (or any of its parts) that is the leftmost constituent of a larger DP can be reordered out of this DP by a transformational rule.

While it is known that some languages allow for left branch extraction, German respects the LBC: In German, no part of a genitive specifier of a DP can be extracted:

(39) * *Wessen*$_{wh}$ hat [$_{DP}$ t_{wh} Tochter] das Pulver erfunden?
whose has daughter the gunpowder invented
'Whose daughter invented gunpowder?'

In (39), the extraction of *wessen* from the DP *wessen Tochter* incurs a violation of the LBC, which consequently leads to the ungrammaticality of the sentence. Now compare (39) to the Raising derivation in (40).

(40) der [$_{NP}$ *Mann*] [$_{DP}$ *dessen*^{gen} t_{NP} Tochter] das Pulver erfand
the man whose daughter the gunpowder invented
'the man whose daughter invented gunpowder'

The analysis in (40) is a case of sub-extraction where part of the genitive specifier, namely the head NP *Mann*, is subject to movement, thereby violating the LBC (see also Bhatt 2002: 76). Yet, *der Mann, dessen Tochter das Pulver erfand* is perfectly grammatical. This loss of an otherwise well-respected generalization of German is an unwelcome consequence of the Raising Analysis of RCs.

3.3.3 The Left Branch Condition – Part 2

In German, no part of a dative specifier of a DP can be extracted:

(41) * *Wem*$_{wh}$ hat [$_{DP}$ t_{wh} seine Tochter] das Pulver erfunden?
who has his daughter the gunpowder invented
'Whose daughter invented gunpowder?'

In (41), *wem* is moved out of the DP *wem seine Tochter*, which yields a straightforward LBC-violation and rules (41) out as ungrammatical. In the Raising Analysis in (42), *Mann* is moved out of the DP *dem Mann seine Tochter*, thereby incurring the same kind of LBC-violation. Yet the DP in (42) is grammatical in certain varieties of German.

(42) der [$_{NP}$ *Mann*] [$_{DP}$ *dem*^{dat} t_{NP} seine Tochter] das Pulver erfand
the man who his daughter the gunpowder invented
'the man whose daughter invented gunpowder'

Again, Raising leads to the loss of an otherwise exceptionless generalization.

3.3.4 The Mysterious Disappearance of the Possessive *'s*

We now turn to an argument due to Alexander Grosu (p.c.). In English, non-pronominal DP specifiers like *the woman* in (43) are marked with the possessive 's:

(43) [$_{DP}$ [$_{DP}$ the woman's] car] was stolen

Building on this generalization and the fact that Raising and Matching have an internal head and analyze relativizers as determiners, (44b) and (44c) should be plausible Raising/Matching derivations for the genitive RC in (44a).

(44) a. the woman whose car was stolen
b. * the [$_{NP}$ *woman*] [$_{DP}$ [$_{DP}$ whose t_{NP}'s/[$_{NP}$ ~~*woman*~~]'s] car] was stolen
c. * the [$_{NP}$ *woman's*] [$_{DP}$ [$_{DP}$ whose t_{NP}/[$_{NP}$ ~~*woman's*~~]] car] was stolen

While the head NP *woman* is severed from the possessive marker 's in (44b), the two remain adjacent to one another in (44c). Whichever way you go, though, the result is ungrammatical. It seems that the 's has to inexplicably disappear from the structure during the course of the derivation in order for Raising and/or Matching to yield (44a).

3.3.5 The Condition on Extraction Domains

In German, the DP complement of an adjunct PP is an extraction island. This is an immediate corollary of Huang (1982: 505)'s Condition on Extraction Domains, see (45):

(45) Condition on Extraction Domains (CED)
A phrase A may be extracted out of a domain B only if B is properly governed.

Here, we understand the CED as a descriptive generalization, not in terms of its technical implementation. As is well-known, the concept of (proper) government has long been superseded in Minimalism. Yet there remains an empirical difference between domains that allow for extraction, and those that do not. A prototypical example for the latter are adjuncts. Consider the following minimal pair:

(46) * [$_{DP}$ Welchem Tag] hatte Petra [$_{PP}$ an t_{DP}] Urlaub?
which day had Petra on vacation
'Which day did Petra take off?'

(47) der [$_{NP}$ *Tag*], [$_{PP}$ an dem t_{NP}] Petra t_{PP} Urlaub hatte
the day on which Petra vacation had
'the day that Petra took off'

In (46), *welchem Tag* has been extracted from a temporal PP adjunct, which is a straightforward CED violation. Consequently, the sentence becomes ungrammatical. Next consider (47), an adverbial RC pied-piping the temporal preposition *an*: Under the Raising Analysis, the PP is moved into the left periphery of the RC. Subsequently, the head NP *Tag* is extracted from the adjunct PP, a clear violation of the CED. Hence, (47) should be banned, yet it is grammatical. Again there is an incompatibility between the facts and the predictions of the Raising Analysis, the adoption of which results in the immediate loss of a uniform explanation for CED effects in German adverbial RCs.

The situation is even worse, however: If Huang's CED is cross-linguistically valid, then the structural type *adverbial RC* should be universally unavailable. Even a cursory look at English reveals that this is not the case; (48) gives two grammatical examples of English adverbial RCs: locative and reason.

(48) a. the [$_{\text{NP}}$ *place*] [$_{\text{RC}}$ [$_{AdvP}$ where t_{NP}] I would like to be buried one day]
b. the [$_{\text{NP}}$ *reason*] [$_{\text{RC}}$ [$_{AdvP}$ why t_{NP}] I can't come]

In both cases, a Raising derivation is committed to moving the head *place/reason* out of an AdvP, which *qua* adjunct fails to satisfy the CED. Both examples, however, are grammatical. The situation is virtually identical in German. Compare the two adverbial RCs of English in (48) with their German equivalents in (49) and (50):

(49) der [$_{\text{NP}}$ *Ort*] [$_{\text{RC}}$ [$_{AdvP}$ wo t_{NP}] ich mal begraben werden möchte]
the place where I sometime buried be want
'the place where I want to be buried one day'

(50) der [$_{\text{NP}}$ *Grund*] [$_{\text{RC}}$ [$_{AdvP}$ warum t_{NP}] ich nicht kommen kann]
the reason why I not come can
'the reason why I will not be able to come'

3.3.6 The Syntax of Adpositions

German *mit*-class adpositions are prepositional when combined with an inanimate phrasal complement and postpositional when the inanimate complement is pronominal:

(51) Wir hatten [$_{\text{PP}}$ *mit* dem Anruf (**mit*)] gerechnet.
we had with the call (with) expected
'We had expected the phone call.'

(52) Wir hatten [$_{PP}$ (*mit) da *mit*] gerechnet.
we had (with) it with expected
'We had expected the phone call.'

In (51), *mit* takes the inanimate DP *dem Anruf* as its complement. In this case, *mit* must obligatorily precede its complement; the use of *mit* as a postposition results in ungrammaticality. This establishes the first half of the above generalization. Next, we combine *mit* with the inanimate R-pronoun *da* as its complement. In this case, as (52) shows, *mit* may only be used as a postposition, not as a preposition. This establishes the second half of the generalization. Interrogative clauses respect this generalization:

(53) [$_{PP}$ (*mit) Wo *mit*] hattet ihr nicht gerechnet?
(with) what with had you not expected
'What did you not expect?'

The fronted PP in (53) contains the inanimate R-pronoun *wo*. In accordance with the above generalization, only a postpositional use of *mit* yields a grammatical interrogative clause. Now consider the case of alleged Raising in (54):

(54) etwas [$_{NP}$ *Schreckliches*], [$_{PP}$ (*mit) [wo t_{NP}] *mit*] man nicht
something terrible (with) what with one does-not
rechnet
expect
'something terrible that one does not expect to happen'

Note that the RC-head *Schreckliches* is inanimate. Hence both Raising and Matching assume that, in its base position, *mit* combines with an inanimate phrasal complement (the DP headed by *wo*). The above generalization, therefore, predicts *mit* in (54) to have its prepositional use only. But the opposite is true: Only the use of *mit* as a postposition makes the sentence grammatical.

So, if the above generalization is valid, then this provides strong evidence for the claim that *wo* in (54) has the status of a pronoun, not that of a determiner. This is irreconcilable with the assumption (common to Raising and Matching) that relativizers, in general, are to be treated as determiners rather than pronouns.

3.3.7 Formal Identity of Restrictive and Non-restrictive Relative Clauses

In German, restrictive and non-restrictive RCs are typically identical in form. Consider the following DP:

(55) das Bild, das im Wohnzimmer hängt
the picture which in the living room hangs
'the picture(,) which is hanging in the living room'

The RC in (55) is ambiguous between a restrictive and a non-restrictive reading. One would expect this uniformity to be reflected in a generative analysis of German RCs, as Generative Grammar was developed for the very purpose of capturing this kind of generalization. However, Raising and Matching have largely been limited to restrictive RCs.

Kayne (1994) claimed that appositives show reconstruction effects and, consequently, proposed to extend the Raising analysis to cover appositives as well. Bianchi (1999: chapters 4 and 5) questioned the validity of these reconstruction effects and put forth a non-Raising analysis for appositives, as did de Vries (2002: chapter 6). Assigning those two types of RC different derivations misses a generalization. Yet, general conditions of economy suggest that, *ceteris paribus*, this formal identity should be captured by giving (at the level of form) a unitary analysis to restrictive as well as appositive RCs.

3.3.8 Conclusion

In the balance, the adoption of the Raising and Matching theories of RCs leads to a systematic loss of empirical generalizations about English and German. What is particularly damning is that these missed generalizations are not of a theory-internal nature, but represent robust empirical generalizations in syntax and morphology that have been the subject of formal grammar for decades. This is particularly true of the island constraints. In our view, this disqualifies both Raising and Matching from further consideration.

This leaves us with the problem that these theories have a measure of success in accounting for reconstruction phenomena, even though, as we have shown above, neither theory is perfect on this front either. Clearly, though, if we discard Raising and Matching, as the systematic counterevidence provided above suggests we should, we will have to find different solutions for the apparent reconstruction effects in RCs involving idioms and bound elements. In the remainder of the paper, we will tackle the first issue and show that the behavior of idioms in RCs can be captured without postulating an RC-internal occurrence of the head at any point of the derivation.

4 Idioms within and outside of Relative Clauses

Idioms do not form a homogeneous class. There seem to be at least two different subclasses:[17]

- syntactically frozen idioms
- syntactically flexible idioms

We will structure this section accordingly: Subsection 4.1 deals with syntactically frozen idioms, Subsection 4.2 with syntactically flexible idioms. The parts of syntactically flexible idioms can be separated by an RC and other clause boundaries. Such idioms have been used to argue for the Raising Analysis of RCs.

In light of the above-mentioned arguments against the Raising Analysis, we are in need of an account that avoids raising the head NP out of the RC in the course of the syntactic derivation. We will work out the guiding ideas of such an account.

4.1 Syntactically Frozen Idioms

The following are typical examples of syntactically frozen idioms:[18]

- *kick the bucket* (≈ 'die')
- *saw logs* (≈ 'snore')
- *shoot the breeze* (≈ 'chit-chat')

We will take *kick the bucket* as our standard example here.

---

17 See, for example, Nunberg, Sag & Wasow (1994) or Sailer (2003). Initially, following Horn (2003) and the judgments in the literature, we thought that there were at least three idiom classes, with *pull strings* and *spill the beans* being in different classes. Having looked into the data situation ourselves, however, including corpus searches and feedback from native speakers, there was no indication for having two separate idiom classes on the basis of a difference between *pull strings* and *spill the beans*. We thank an anonymous reviewer for reinforcing this point even further. Please note in this context that *spill the beans* should actually rather be cited as *spill beans*, as the definite determiner is not an obligatory part of the idiom. Neither is the plural of the idiomatic noun, by the way. This also holds for the idiomatic noun in *pull strings*. Both nouns can also occur in their singular form, as for instance in *pull a string or two* or *spill bean after bean*. See Bargmann (2015) for details.

18 See Fraser (1970: 32), Wasow, Sag & Nunberg (1980: 89), and Nunberg, Sag & Wasow (1994: 497), respectively.

4.1.1 Data

The syntactic behavior of *kick the bucket* is very straightforward: The idiom always occurs contiguously; a form of the verb *kick* directly precedes the noun phrase *the bucket*.[19] As this condition is met under embedding under an auxiliary, VP-preposing, and VP-clefting, the idiomatic VP (VP_{id}) can occur in each of these constructions, as illustrated below:[20]

(56) a. He might [$_{VP_{id}}$ *kick the bucket*].
b. ... and [$_{VP_{id}}$ *kick the bucket*] he did.
c. It was [$_{VP_{id}}$ *kick the bucket*] that he did last week.

The difference between verbal and nominal gerunds in (57), which was pointed out by Fraser (1970: 32), falls out from the stated generalization as well, as the syntactic pieces of the idiom are contiguous in the verbal gerund, whereas they are illicitly interrupted by *of* in the nominal gerund.

(57) a. Your friend's [$_{VP_{id}}$ *kicking the bucket*] caused great concern.
b. * Your friend's *kicking* **of** *the bucket* caused great concern.

Finally, the idiom is incompatible with all constructions in which its nominal part would appear to the left of its verbal part. Thus, passivization is impossible:[21]

(58) * *The bucket* was *kicked*.

The same holds for DP-preposing, DP-clefting, RCs, and *wh*-movement:[22]

(59) a. * *The bucket* Pete *kicked*.
b. * It was *the bucket* that Pete *kicked*.
c. * *The bucket* John *kicked* was astonishing.
d. * Which *bucket* did John *kick*?

4.1.2 Analysis

A construction-based analysis of syntactically frozen idioms is rather simple. Besides a lexicon for words, a construction-based grammar also provides a lexicon

19 We ignore cases of external modification, in which a domain-delimiting adjective inserted in-between *the* and *bucket* semantically modifies the idiom as a whole, see Ernst (1981).
20 The examples are due to Dianne Jonas.
21 See Bargmann & Sailer (2018), though.
22 From Schenk (1995: 254).

for phrases. A syntactically frozen idiom is listed in this phrasal lexicon as a single, contiguous, and mostly fixed syntactic tree structure, which, as a whole, is assigned the idiomatic meaning, whereas the subconstituents of the phrasal lexical entry are meaningless. In the case of *kick the bucket*, we are looking at the structure of a standard VP and the idiomatic meaning *die'*:[23]

(60) The phrasal lexical entry of idiomatic *kick the bucket*:[24]
SYN: $[_{VP}$ $[_{V}$ kick-] $[_{DP}$ the bucket]]
SEM: *die'*

The constraints in (60) must be met at the single syntactic representation level that our grammar licenses for a given string: its surface representation or spell-out. The grammaticality pattern of *kick the bucket* in (56)–(59) follows straightforwardly from these simple assumptions.

The point that phrasal lexical entries are *surface* lexical entries is worth elaborating, as it reveals an important gap in the idiom argument for the Raising Analysis of RCs: Idioms differ from one another with regard to the surface configurations they allow. Therefore, idiom licensing at the point of merge is at best incomplete, because by itself it makes no predictions about the observable surface forms that can be derived from the merged structures. This issue is highlighted by the existence of idioms restricted to occurring in non-canonical sentence forms. The following examples are from Wasow, Sag & Nunberg (1980: 89) and Nunberg, Sag & Wasow (1994: 516):

(61) a. *Passive:* fit to be tied
b. *Tough-movement:* hard to take, play hard to get
c. *Imperative:* Break a leg!
d. *Yes-no question:* Is the Pope catholic?

For the topic of the present article, an idiom like *kill the goose that lays the golden egg* is particularly noteworthy, as it obligatorily contains an RC, highlighting again that an adequate theory of idioms needs to encompass a theory of surface forms that allow idiomatic interpretations, not merely a theory of how the pieces of idioms must be merged.[25]

---

23 There is another option: Lichte & Kallmeyer (2016), Bargmann & Sailer (2018), and Kay, Sag & Flickinger (2016) analyze *kick the bucket* in terms of individual word entries.

24 The hyphen in the SYN-value allows for verbal inflection.

25 The treatment of idioms at the point of merge is problematic in other respects as well. Radford (2009: 242), for instance, still maintains the claim that “only a string of words which forms a unitary constituent can be an idiom” and hence concludes (as originally claimed in Marantz 1984)

Like word entries, phrasal entries are permitted to show different degrees of specificity. The classical *What's X doing Y* construction analyzed in Kay & Fillmore (1999), for instance, requires the presence of a sentence-initial expression *what's*, a lexically flexible subject, the progressive main verb form *doing*, and a lexically flexible predicate:

(62) a. *What's* Jill *doing* sleeping?
b. *What's* that fly *doing* in my soup?

One limiting case of such listed phrases consists of those entries that do not make reference to specific words but merely specify grammatical (and semantic) configurations. Examples of this are the classical X-bar configurations, e.g. the phrase that combines a head with its complements or the phrase that combines a (lexical or phrasal) head and its subject. Complete sentences are not built up with the use of merge in this theory but as the spelling out of parts of constructions by other phrasal constructions and/or words. Thus, in addition to realizing the flexible subject slot as the proper name *Jill* in (62a) above, other instantiations of the DP-construction are possible realizations of the subject in the *What's X doing Y* construction as well, as is illustrated below:

(63) a. What's [$_{DP}$ she] doing sleeping?
b. What's [$_{DP}$ the cat] doing sleeping?
c. What's [$_{DP}$ my cat] doing sleeping?
d. What's [$_{DP}$ my neighbor's cat] doing sleeping?
e. ...

4.2 Syntactically Flexible Idioms

Let us start off with two examples:

(64) a. spill beans ('divulge secrets')
b. pull strings ('use connections')

We will use *pull strings* to exemplify the behavior of syntactically flexible idioms.

that "we don't find idioms of the form subject+verb where the verb has a complement which isn't part of the idiom." Idioms like *What's eating X, The bottom fell out of X*, and *A little birdy told X that Y* clearly falsify this claim.

4.2.1 Data

The idiom *pull strings* may, of course, form a surface VP, as in the canonical sentence in (65).

(65) Kim's family *pulled strings* on her behalf.
(based on example (10c) in Nunberg, Sag & Wasow 1994: 502)

However, it may also occur non-contiguously – for instance in the passive voice:

(66) *Strings* seem to be *pulled* every time he applies for a promotion.
(Horn 2003: 261)

The example in (66) also shows that the nominal part of the idiom can undergo raising into the subject position of a raising verb like *seem*. Moreover, *pull strings* permits its nominal part to undergo A′-movement, which (67) demonstrates for preposing and (68) for *wh*-movement.

(67) Those *strings*, he wouldn't *pull* for you. (Gazdar et al. 1985: 238)

(68) How many *strings* did he *pull* to get the promotion? (Horn 2003: 261)

There are at least two more surface variants of the idiom that need to be captured. First, the verbal part of the idiom can undergo VP-ellipsis:

(69) I was worried that *strings* might be *pulled*, but *they* weren't __.

In (69), the elided passive participle after *weren't* in the second conjunct is anaphoric to *pulled* in the first conjunct. And second, the nominal part does not have to be realized by the surface phrase *strings* but can be pronominalized. The following examples illustrate this even more clearly:

(70) a. Kim's family *pulled* some *strings* on her behalf, but *they* weren't enough to get her the job. (Nunberg, Sag & Wasow 1994: 502)

b. I would not want you to think that we are proud of our ability to *pull strings*, such as *the ones* we *pulled* to get you down here. (Nunberg, Sag & Wasow 1994: 502)

c. We need to *pull* some *strings* to get Mary the job and we need to *pull them* fast. (Dianne Jonas, p.c.)

Being discourse-anaphoric processes, ellipsis and pronominalization rely on the meaning, not the form, of the expressions they apply to. Consequently, idiomatic *pull* and idiomatic *strings* must both have a meaning (see Nunberg, Sag & Wasow 1994). The example in (70a) is noteworthy because in the second conjunct the anaphoric continuation *they* of *some strings* occurs as the argument of a verb other than *pull*. This shows that the nominal part of the idiom not only carries a meaning, but that this meaning is compatible with predicates differing in both form and meaning from idiomatic *pull*. The theoretical relevance of this observation was pointed out by Wasow, Sag & Nunberg (1980: 94).

Let us now look at the behavior of this idiom class in RCs. Structures comparable to the one in (71) have typically been cited as motivation for the Raising Analysis of RCs:[26]

(71) We were surprised at [$_{DP}$ the *strings* [$_{RC}$ that were *pulled*]] to get Joe's promotion. (Horn 2003: 261)

The argument goes as follows: Idioms are licensed at the point of merge. Hence, *strings* must be merged into the complement position of *pulled* inside the RC of (71) and then raised into its surface position, where it serves as the head of the RC.

This argument gets repeated in the literature to this day, even though, in its simplest form, it was already refuted by McCawley in the early eighties with the example in (15) and later by van Riemsdijk with the example in (13), both repeated here for convenience:

(72) Parky *pulled* the [$_{NP}$ *strings*] [$_{RC}$ that t_{NP} got me the job].

(73) John never *pulled* the [$_{NP}$ *strings*] [$_{RC}$ that his mother told him should be *pulled* t_{NP}].

Under the Raising Analysis, *strings* would appear inside the RC at the point of merge in both cases. This robs the verb *pulled* in the main clause of its idiomatic licensing context and should make both sentences ungrammatical in the idiomatic reading, contrary to fact. The grammaticality of McCawley's sentence in (72) is particularly unexpected, since *strings* would be merged into an argument position of *got* in the RC, which does not contain *pull* at all. Any theory of *pull strings* will have to handle similar "argument to the wrong verb" sentences from the literature:

(74) a. Pat *pulled strings* that Chris had no access to.
(Wasow, Sag & Nunberg 1980: 93)

b. The *strings* that Pat *pulled* helped Chris get the job.
(Wasow, Sag & Nunberg 1980: 93)

And it gets even worse. The final two examples in (70) showed that *pull* can occur in its idiomatic meaning without being syntactically linked to *strings*. Wasow, Sag & Nunberg (1980: 93f) provide the following discourse to show that

26 See our earlier discussion of *make headway* and *pull strings* in Section 3.1.1.

the reverse is true as well, i.e. *strings* can occur in its idiomatic meaning without being syntactically linked to *pull*:

(75) Pat and Chris graduated from law school together with roughly equal records. Pat's uncle is a state senator, and he *pulled strings* to get Pat a clerkship with a state supreme court justice. Chris, in contrast, didn't have access to any *strings*, and ended up hanging out a shingle.

Here is a similar example of *make headway*:[27]

(76) We have two to three weeks left before we move to Utah and only this week have we *made* any *headway* on the things that we have to get done before then. Though our *headway* was late it was however every (sic!) effective.

Wasow, Sag & Nunberg (1980) claim that (75) is grammatical because idiomatic *strings* can occur without *pull* in a discourse where the whole idiom has already been introduced. We will incorporate this idea into our analysis of *pull strings*, to which we now turn (albeit in a different fashion from Wasow, Sag & Nunberg 1980, who offer a processing account).

4.2.2 Analysis

The analysis of syntactically flexible idioms is more involved than the analysis of syntactically frozen idioms because there is no (obvious) way to analyze a syntactically flexible idiom as a single and contiguous phrase-level lexical entry. In a syntactically flexible VP-idiom, the internal argument of the verb is not restricted to the latter's object function, so that the relationship between the two subconstituents of the idiom cannot be hardwired as that of head and complement in a listed VP.

In view of its syntactic flexibility and the fact that *pull* can occur without *strings* being in the same sentence and vice versa, we will follow Wasow, Sag & Nunberg (1980) and take *pull strings* to be composed of two separate lexical entries: the idiomatic verb *pull* and the idiomatic plural noun *strings*:[28]

---

27 From https://web.archive.org/web/20090414024229/http://www.jacobboyle.com/eventide/?p=192, last accessed on 2018-10-10.

28 As already mentioned towards the end of footnote 17, it is a simplification that the second word-level lexical entry of the idiom *pull strings* consists of the idiomatic plural noun *strings*.

(77) Lexical entry of idiomatic *pull*:
SYN: [$_V$ pull-]
SEM: $pull'_{id}$
Co-occurrence constraint: Idiomatic *pull* is licensed iff (after a discourse update) the variable in the second argument position of its SEM-value $pull'_{id}$ is predicated over by the SEM-value of idiomatic *strings*, i.e. $strings'_{id}$.

(78) Lexical entry of idiomatic *strings*:
SYN: [$_N$ strings]
SEM: $strings'_{id}$
Co-occurrence constraint: Idiomatic *strings* is licensed iff
(i) its SEM-value $strings'_{id}$ predicates over the variable in the second argument position of the SEM-value of idiomatic *pull*, i.e. $pull'_{id}$ or
(ii) $strings'_{id}$ is already present and salient in the discourse.

Neither of these two lexical entries refers to the syntax (SYN) of the other, and they combine according to standard syntactic rules. However, both entries contain a specific co-occurrence constraint on the semantic representation (SEM) of the linguistic context containing them, where each entry can be identified on the basis of its unique SEM-value, which basically functions like a genetic code or fingerprint.

The two co-occurrence constraints – which, except for the additional licensing option for *strings* in (ii), include essentially the same licensing condition formulated from two different perspectives – ensure that neither of the two idiom parts can occur without the other one being in the discourse as well: Any occurrence of *pull* requires an instance of the semantic representation of *strings*, and any occurrence of *strings* requires an instance of the semantic representation of *pull*, both of which, we assume, can eventually only be introduced into the overall semantic representation by the lexical entries in (77) and (78).

Specifically, it follows from the co-occurrence constraint in (77) that idiomatic *pull* must occur in the context of idiomatic *strings*, because the second argument of *pull*'s SEM-value $pull'_{id}$ must be predicated over by the SEM-value $strings'_{id}$, which can only be introduced into the overall semantic representation by idiomatic *strings*. The proviso "after a discourse update" allows for the cross-sentential anaphora in (70): *pull* need not be syntactically linked to *strings*, but it must be syntactically linked to an anaphoric element whose meaning is determined by *strings*.

Conversely, it follows from the co-occurrence constraint in (78) that idiomatic *strings* must occur in a linguistic context containing idiomatic *pull*. This is the case since the SEM-value of *strings* (i.e. $strings'_{id}$) must either (i) predicate over the second argument of $pull'_{id}$, which we assume can ultimately only be contributed by idiomatic *pull*, or (ii) occur in a linguistic context where $strings'_{id}$ is already present and salient. In the latter case, the latest occurrence of $strings'_{id}$ can predicate over the semantic argument of predicates other than $pull'_{id}$, allowing for examples such as (72), (74), and (75). However, $strings'_{id}$ must have been entered into the discourse by some prior occurrence of *strings*, and in the semantic representation of the discourse including that prior occurrence of *strings*, $strings'_{id}$ must predicate over the idiomatic argument of $pull'_{id}$, which can only be contributed by some occurrence of *pull*. Consequently, each occurrence of *strings* is required to occur in a discourse that contains at least one occurrence of *pull*.

Let us now go through the *pull strings* examples from Section 4.2.1 and illustrate how they are licensed on the basis of the co-occurrence constraints in the lexical entries in (77) and (78). We will start off with a shortened version of the (canonical) example in (65), see (79a), for which a semantic representation would roughly look like (79b).[29]

(79) a. Kim's family *pulled strings*.

b. $\exists x[strings'_{id}(x)](pull'_{id}(kim's\text{-}family', x))$

Since both idiomatic *pull* and idiomatic *strings* occur in (79a), their respective co-occurrence constraint must be fulfilled in order for them to be licensed. This is the case. The constraint on *pull* is fulfilled because the variable in the second argument position of $pull'_{id}$ (here x) is predicated over by $strings'_{id}$, and the constraint on *strings* is fulfilled because $strings'_{id}$ predicates over the variable in the second argument position of $pull'_{id}$ (x again).

The same holds for the passive and raising sentence in (66), see (80a) and (80b) for a shortened version of (66) and its semantic representation.

(80) a. *Strings* seem to be *pulled*.

b. $seem'(\exists x[strings'_{id}(x)](\exists y.pull'_{id}(y, x)))$

As in (79a), both *pull* and *strings* are present, so both constraints have to be fulfilled. And as in (79a), this is the case.

The preposing and *wh*-movement examples in (67) and (68), repeated below as (81a) and (81b),

(81) a. Those *strings*, he wouldn't *pull* for you.

b. How many *strings* did he *pull* to get the promotion?

are well-formed since in both cases the moved constituent containing idiomatic *strings* (*those strings* in (81a) and *how many strings* in (81b)) is interpreted as the

29 For the purposes of exposition, we will use some form of predicate logic and ignore tense information, but readers should feel free to use their favorite semantic representation language and include more details.

internal argument of idiomatic *pull*, so that the relevant parts of the semantic representations of (81a) and (81b) look like they did in (79b).

In the example in (69), repeated below as (82), we observed two anaphoric relations: The pronoun *they* is anaphoric to idiomatic *strings* and the elided passive participle after *weren't* to idiomatic *pulled*.

(82) I was worried that *strings* might be *pulled*, but *they* weren't __.

All that is necessary for the second conjunct to be well-formed is for the pronoun and the ellipsis site to be licensed by the idiomatic meaning of *strings* and *pull* in the first conjunct. This is the case, because the relevant parts of the semantic representation of the first conjunct look just like in (80b).

With (70), repeated below as (83), we gave more examples for the pronominalizability of *strings* and demonstrated with (70a), repeated below as (83a), that an anaphoric continuation of *some strings* (here the pronoun *they*) can occur as the argument of a verb other than *pull*.

(83) a. Kim's family *pulled* some *strings* on her behalf, but *they* weren't enough to get her the job.
b. I would not want you to think that we are proud of our ability to *pull strings*, such as *the ones* we *pulled* to get you down here.
c. We need to *pull* some *strings* to get Mary the job and we need to *pull them* fast.

The first parts of these sentences are all unproblematic, because idiomatic *pull* and idiomatic *strings* co-occur locally, as in (79a). So let us focus on the second parts.

In (83a), the second conjunct contains neither idiomatic *pull* nor idiomatic *strings*, as it was the case in (82). In consequence, neither of the constraints in (77)–(78) applies. The pronoun *they* adopts the idiomatic meaning of idiomatic *strings* in the first conjunct, and the meaning of *strings* is compatible with the meaning of the VP *weren't enough to get her the job*.

In (83b), the *such*-phrase only contains *pull* but not *strings*, hence only the constraint on idiomatic *pull* needs to be fulfilled, which it is since the anaphoric expression *the ones* is licensed by the idiomatic meaning of *strings* in the first conjunct, just as the pronoun *they* in (83a). We will get to the details of how *the ones* and *pulled* interact when we turn to the analysis of the RCs in (71)–(74) in just a moment.

In (83c), the second conjunct again only contains *pull* but not *strings*, so that, again, only the constraint on idiomatic *pull* needs to be fulfilled, which it is: The variable in the second argument position of $pull'_{id}$ is predicated over by $strings'_{id}$ since the pronoun *them* is co-indexed with the DP *some strings* in the first conjunct and, therefore, obtains the meaning of idiomatic *strings*.

Wasow, Sag & Nunberg (1980)'s example (75), whose relevant parts are repeated below as (84), contains an occurrence of *strings* that is not syntactically linked to *pull*. This is possible since the latest occurrence of *strings* is licensed by the previous occurrence of *strings* (see clause (ii) of the co-occurrence constraint of *strings*), which, in turn, is locally licensed by *pull* (see clause (i) of the co-occurrence constraint of *strings*).

(84) Pat's uncle *pulled strings* to get Pat a clerkship. Chris, in contrast, didn't have access to any *strings*.

Let us now finally come the sentences in (71)–(74), repeated below in a different order as (85a)–(89a). What these sentences have in common is that each of them contains an RC whose head is idiomatic *strings*. They differ, however, with respect to whether idiomatic *pull* is part of the RC, as in (85a) and (86a), or the host clause, as in (87a) and (88a), or both, as in (89a). These differences are directly mirrored in the semantic representations in (85b)–(89b), which include only those (= underlined) parts of the sentences that are relevant for licensing *pull strings*.

In (85b) and (86b), the quantifier restricted by $strings'_{id}$ binds the variable in the second argument position of $pull'_{id}$ within its restrictor (delineated by the square brackets). In (87b) and (88b), the quantifier restricted by $strings'_{id}$ binds the variable in the second argument position of $pull'_{id}$ within its scope. And in (89b), the quantifier restricted by $strings'_{id}$ binds the variable in the second argument position of $pull'_{id}$ within both its restrictor and its scope.

(85) a. We were surprised at <u>the *strings* that were *pulled*</u> to get Joe's promotion.

b. $the\, x[strings'_{id}(x)\ \&\ \exists y.pull'_{id}(y, x)]$

(86) a. <u>The *strings* that Pat *pulled*</u> helped Chris get the job.

b. $the\, x[strings'_{id}(x)\ \&\ pull'_{id}(pat', x)]$

(87) a. <u>Parky *pulled* the *strings*</u> that got me the job.

b. $the\, x[strings'_{id}(x)](pull'_{id}(parky', x))$

(88) a. Pat <u>*pulled strings*</u> that Chris had no access to.

b. $\exists x[strings'_{id}(x)](pull'_{id}(pat', x))$

(89) a. <u>John never *pulled* the *strings* that his mother told him should be *pulled*</u>.

b. $\neg\exists x[strings'_{id}(x)\ \&\ tell'(john\text{'s-}mother', john', should'(\exists y.pull'_{id}(y, x)))]\ (pull'_{id}(john', x))$

As can easily be seen now, *strings*$'_{id}$ always predicates over the variable in the second argument position of *pull*$'_{id}$, so that the co-occurrence constraints in (77) and (78) are always fulfilled.

5 Conclusion

At the outset of the paper, we showed that the theoretical literature offers at least three different approaches to the analysis of restrictive RCs (Modification, Raising, Matching) and that it would be desirable to pare down the list of contenders. We went on to show that Raising and Matching both lead to the loss of linguistically significant generalizations. In the case of Raising, we take this loss to be so intolerable in terms of both amount and nature that we consider this to be one of those relatively rare cases where a linguistic theory must actually be viewed as refuted by the evidence. Matching avoids some of the problems of Raising, yet the problems that remain for Matching are sufficiently significant for us to want to go down a different avenue.

Of the original three contenders, this only leaves Modification in play. It is not affected by the disqualifying objections to Raising and Matching but faces serious problems of its own, apparently all involving reconstruction of one form or another. We presented data from idiom licensing and binding theory that have been argued to require Raising and/or Matching and illustrated that the solutions that Raising and/or Matching offer for these issues are not completely free of problems. We then set out to look for an analysis of the idiom data that is compatible with Modification.

Drawing on the previous literature, we illustrated that not all idioms behave alike. It appears that grammatical theory needs to capture at least two cases: syntactically frozen idioms and syntactically flexible idioms. We showed that it is insufficient to require the pieces of syntactically flexible idioms to be merged locally, since idioms differ from each other in the kinds of observable surface configurations they permit. In fact, as Nunberg, Sag & Wasow (1994) emphasize, some idioms can only appear in transformationally derived structures. We sketched analyses for the two classes of idioms and demonstrated that these analyses capture the empirical differences between them.

A syntactically frozen idiom like *kick the bucket* is analyzed as a single and contiguous entry in the phrasal lexicon, which explains why its pieces have to stay adjacent in phrase structure. A syntactically flexible idiom like *pull strings* consists of two separate parts in the word lexicon that are semantically linked. Under the right circumstances, this permits a degree of syntactic flexibility that allows the two pieces of the idiom to be separated by RC-boundaries or even main clause boundaries, as long as the meanings of the pieces are appropriately connected in the semantic representation of the discourse. We believe that all grammatical cases of idioms in RCs can be handled within our approach. As the theory we have sketched avoids representing the head of the RC inside the RC at any point of the syntactic derivation, it is compatible with Modification. Better yet, the combination of Modification with our treatment of idioms not only accounts for the data that have traditionally been taken to motivate Raising and/or Matching, but it also captures examples that neither of the latter two theories can handle, in particular the "argument to the wrong verb" cases, and it does all of the above in a uniform fashion.

Acknowledgment: We would like to thank Anne Abeillé, Doug Arnold, Chris Barker, Andreas Blümel, Olivier Bonami, Patricia Cabredo-Hofherr, Berthold Crysmann, Mary Dalrymple, Berit Gehrke, Jonathan Ginzburg, Caroline Heycock, Dianne Jonas, Éric Laporte, Bob Levine, Timm Lichte, Philip Miller, Frank Richter, Manfred Sailer, Susanna Salem, three anonymous reviewers, and the audience at the Workshop "Reconstruction Effects in Relative Clauses" in Berlin in 2011 for discussing the contents of this paper with us. Moreover, we are particularly grateful to our colleagues in the Research Unit "Relative Clauses" at the Goethe University Frankfurt am Main. The Research Unit is funded by the German Research Foundation, and the research that this paper is based on was entirely carried out within that framework. Any mistakes in the text are ours.

References

Alexiadou, Artemis, Paul Law, André Meinunger & Chris Wilder. 2000. Introduction. In Artemis Alexiadou, Paul Law, Andre Meinunger & Chris Wilder (eds.), *The syntax of relative clauses*, 1–51. Amsterdam & Philadelphia: John Benjamins.

Bargmann, Sascha. 2015. *Syntactically Flexible VP-Idioms and the N-after-N Construction*. Poster presented at the PARSEME 5th General Meeting at Alexandru Ioan Cuza University, Iasi, Romania. http://typo.uni-konstanz.de/parseme/images/Meeting/2015-09-23-Iasi-meeting/WG1-BARGMANN-poster.pdf (10 October, 2018).

Bargmann, Sascha & Manfred Sailer. 2018. The syntactic flexibility of semantically non-decomposable idioms. In Stella Markantonatou & Manfred Sailer (eds.), *Multiword expressions: Insights from a multi-lingual perspective*, 1–29. Berlin: Language Science Press. https://doi.org/10.5281/zenodo.1182587.

Barker, Chris. 2012. Quantificational binding does not require c-command. *Linguistic Inquiry* 43(4). 614–633.

Berman, Arlene. 1974. *Adjectives and adjective complement constructions in English*. Vol. 29. Department of Linguistics, Harvard University.

Bhatt, Rajesh. 2002. The raising analysis of relative clauses: Evidence from adjectival modification. *Natural Language Semantics* 40. 43–90.
Bianchi, Valentina. 1999. *Consequences of antisymmetry: Headed relative clauses*. Berlin & New York: Mouton de Gruyter.
Boef, Eefje. 2012. Doubling in relative clauses. *Aspects of Morphosyntactic Variation in Dutch. Utrecht: LOT.*
Borsley, Robert D. 1997. Relative clauses and the theory of phrase structure. *Linguistic Inquiry* 28(4). 629–647.
Borsley, Robert D. 2001. More on the raising analysis of relative clauses. Unpublished manuscript.
Büring, Daniel & Katharina Hartmann. 1997. Doing the right thing. *The Linguistic Review* 14(1). 1–41.
Carlson, Greg N. 1977. Amount relatives. *Language* 53. 520–542.
Chomsky, Noam. 1965. *Aspects of the theory of syntax*. Cambridge: MIT Press.
Chomsky, Noam. 1973. Conditions on transformations. In Paul Kiparsky Stephen R. Anderson (ed.), *A Festschrift for Morris Halle*. Holt, Reinhart & Winston.
Chomsky, Noam. 1977. On wh-movement. In Peter W. Culicover, Thomas Wasow & Adrian Akmajian (eds.), *Formal syntax*, 71–132. New York, NY: Academic Press.
Chomsky, Noam. 1981. *Lectures on government and binding*. Dordrecht: Foris.
de Vries, Mark. 2002. *The syntax of relativization*. University of Amsterdam Doctoral dissertation. http://www.let.rug.nl/dvries/pdf/proefschrift-mdevries.pdf (10 October, 2018).
Ernst, Thomas. 1981. Grist for the linguistic mill: Idioms and "extra" adjectives. *Journal of Linguistic Research* 1(3). 51–68.
Fiengo, Robert & Robert May. 1994. *Indices and identity*. Linguistic Inquiry Monographs 24. Cambridge: MIT Press.
Fraser, Bruce. 1970. Idioms within a transformational grammar. *Foundations of Language* 6(1). 22–42.
Gazdar, Gerald, Ewan Klein, Geoffrey Pullum & Ivan A. Sag. 1985. *Generalized phrase structure grammar*. Cambridge, MA: Harvard University Press.
Heck, Fabian. 2005. *Gegen Kopfanhebung in deutschen Relativsätzen*. Handout, 31. Tagung zur GGS.
Heim, Irene & Angelika Kratzer. 1998. *Semantics in generative grammar*. Oxford: Blackwell.
Henderson, Brent. 2007. Matching and raising unified. *Lingua* 117. 202–220.
Horn, Georg M. 2003. Idioms, metaphors and syntactic mobility. *Journal of Linguistics* 39. 245–273.
Hornstein, Norbert, Jairo Nuñes & Kleanthes Grohmann. 2005. *Understanding Minimalism*. Cambridge University Press.
Huang, C. T. James. 1982. *Logical relations in Chinese and the theory of grammar*. Massachusetts Institute of Technology Doctoral dissertation.
Jackendoff, Ray. 1972. *Semantic interpretation in generative grammar*. Cambridge: MIT Press.
Kay, Paul & Charles J. Fillmore. 1999. Grammatical constructions and linguistic generalizations: The *What's X Doing Y?* construction. *Language* 75.1. 1–33.
Kay, Paul & Ivan A Sag. 2009. How hard a problem would this be to solve? In Stefan Müller (ed.), *Proceedings of the 16th International Conference on Head-Driven Phrase Structure Grammar*, 171–191. Stanford, CA: CSLI.
Kay, Paul, Ivan A. Sag & Dan Flickinger. 2016. A lexical theory of phrasal idioms. Unpublished manuscript, to be published as a book.

Kayne, Richard. 1994. *The antisymmetry of syntax*. Cambridge, MA: MIT Press.
Kiss, Tibor. 2001. Anaphora and exemptness: A comparative treatment of anaphoric binding in German and English. In Dan Flickinger & Andreas Kathol (eds.), *Proceedings of the 7th International Conference on Head-Driven Phrase Structure Grammar*, 182–197. Stanford, CA: CSLI.
Koster, Jan. 2000. Extraposition as parallel construal. *Ms., University of Groningen*.
Lees, Robert B. 1960. *The grammar of English nominalizations*. Massachusetts Institute of Technology Doctoral dissertation.
Lees, Robert B. 1961. The constituent structure of noun phrases. *American Speech* 36. 159–168.
Lichte, Timm & Laura Kallmeyer. 2016. Same syntax, different semantics: A compositional approach to idiomaticity in multi-word expressions. In Christopher Piñón (ed.), *Empirical issues in syntax and semantics*, vol. 11, 111–140. Paris: CSSP.
Marantz, Alec. 1984. *On the nature of grammatical relations*. Cambridge: MIT Press.
McCawley, James D. 1981. The syntax and semantics of English relative clauses. *Lingua* 53. 99–149.
Montague, Richard. 1974. English as a formal language. In Richmond H. Thomason (ed.), *Formal philosophy: Selected papers of Richard Montague*, 188–226. Originally published in 1970. New Haven: Yale University Press.
Munn, Alan. 1994. A Minimalist account of reconstruction asymmetries. In Mercè Gonzàlez (ed.), *Proceedings of NELS 24*, 397–410. Amherst, MA: GLSA.
Nunberg, Geoffrey, Ivan A. Sag & Thomas Wasow. 1994. Idioms. *Language* 70(3). 491–538.
Partee, Barbara H. 1975. Montague grammar and transformational grammar. *Linguistic Inquiry* 6(2). 203–300.
Quine, Willard Van Orman. 1960. *Word and object*. Cambridge: MIT Press.
Radford, Andrew. 2009. *Analyzing English sentences: A Minimalist approach*. Cambridge: Cambridge University Press.
Ross, John R. 1967. *Constraints on variables in syntax*. Massachusetts Institute of Technology Doctoral dissertation.
Sailer, Manfred. 2003. *Combinatorial Semantics and Idiomatic Expressions in Head-Driven Phrase Structure Grammar*. Arbeitspapiere des SFB 340, Number 161. Universität Tübingen.
Salzmann, Martin. 2006. *Resumptive prolepsis. A study of indirect A'-dependencies*. Utrecht: LOT.
Sauerland, Uli. 1998. *The meaning of chains*. Cambridge, MA: Massachusetts Institute of Technology Doctoral dissertation.
Sauerland, Uli. 2003. Unpronounced heads in relative clauses. In Kerstin Schwabe & Susanne Winkler (eds.), *The interfaces: Deriving and interpreting omitted structures*, 205–226. Amsterdam & Philadelphia: John Benjamins.
Schachter, Paul. 1973. Focus and relativization. *Language* 49(1). 19–46.
Schenk, Andreé. 1995. The syntactic behavior of idioms. In Martin Everaert, Erik-Jan van der Linden, André Schenk & Rob Schreuder (eds.), *Idioms: Structural and psychological perspectives*, 253–272. Hillsdale, NJ: Lawrence Erlbaum Associates.
Schmitt, Cristina. 2000. Some consequences of the complement analysis. In Artemis Alexiadou, Paul Law, André Meinunger & Chris Wilder (eds.), *The syntax of relative clauses*, 309–348. Amsterdam: John Benjamins.
Sheehan, Michelle. 2010. Extraposition and antisymmetry. *Linguistic Variation Yearbook* 10(1). 201–251.

van Eynde, Frank. 2007. The Big Mess Construction. In Stefan Müller (ed.), *Proceedings of the 14th International Conference on Head-Driven Phrase Structure Grammar*, 415–433. Stanford, CA: CSLI.

Vergnaud, Jean-Roger. 1974. *French relative clauses*. Cambridge, MA: Massachusetts Institute of Technology Doctoral dissertation.

Wasow, Thomas, Ivan A. Sag & Geoffrey Nunberg. 1980. Idioms: An interim report. In *Preprints of the XIIIth international congress of linguists*, 87–96. Tokyo.

Webelhuth, Gert, Manfred Sailer & Heike Walker. 2013. Introduction. In Gert Webelhuth, Manfred Sailer & Heike Walker (eds.), *Rightward movement in a comparative perspective*, 1–60. Amsterdam & Philadelphia: John Benjamins.

Maribel Romero

Some notes on connectivity and predicational copular sentences

1 Introduction

There are (at least) two types of copular sentences: predicational copular sentences and specificational copular sentences (Akmajian 1970, Higgins 1973). The first type is illustrated in (1), where the postverbal XP intuitively predicates the property "being large" of the object denoted by the subject. The second type is illustrated in (2), where, intuitively, the postverbal XP identifies or specifies the value or denotation of the subject. We will use the terms 'predicational subject' and 'predicate' to refer to the pre-verbal and post-verbal XPs respectively in (non-inverse) predicational sentences like (1), and the terms 'specificational subject' and 'pivot' to refer to the pre-verbal and post-verbal XPs respectively in (non-inverse) specificational sentences like (2).

(1) The number of planets is large. PREDICATIONAL

(2) The number of planets is eight. SPECIFICATIONAL

These two types of copular sentences are known to display different grammatical patterns. On the one hand, in predicational copular sentences – as in regular sentences –, an element embedded in a predicational complex NP subject cannot scope over or c-command material that is outside that complex NP at surface structure. Hence, the quantificational NP *no woman* cannot bind the pronoun *her* in (3); *a centaur* cannot be interpreted de dicto with respect to the verb *look for* in (4); and, under the predicational reading "The (most salient) property P that John has – e.g. being the dean of the school – is a nuisance to John", Principle A is violated in (5a) and Principles B and C are spared in (5b,c), as expected from the fact that the first coindexed expression *John*$_1$/*he*$_1$ does not c-command the second one (see Chomsky 1981).

(3) Variable binding:
* [The person *no woman*$_1$ hates t] is nice to *her*$_1$.

Maribel Romero, University of Konstanz

https://doi.org/10.1515/9783050095158-008

(4) Opacity:
[What John is *looking for* t] is important to *a centaur*.
* *[a centaur]* as de-dicto

(5) Binding Theory under the predicational reading:
a. Principle A: * [What *John*$_1$ is t] is a nuisance to *himself*$_1$.
b. Principle B: [What *John*$_1$ is t] is a nuisance to *him*$_1$.
c. Principle C: [What *he*$_1$ is t] is a nuisance to *John*$_1$.

On the other hand, in specificational sentences, the grammar behaves as if an element embedded in the specificational complex NP subject could scope over material that is outside the island at surface structure, as if some material was "put back together" or "reconstructed" (Akmajian 1970, Higgins 1973, Halvorsen 1978, i.a.). These reconstruction effects, also known as 'connectivity effects', are illutrated in (6)–(8): *no woman* can bind the pronoun *her* in (6); *a centaur* can be interpreted de dicto under *look for* in (7); and, under the specificational reading "John is a nuisance to John (i.e., to himself)", the judgments on Binding Theory are reversed from (5), as if the first coindexed expression could now c-command the second one.

(6) Variable binding connectivity:
[The person *no woman*$_1$ hates t] is *her*$_1$ mother.

(7) Opacity connectivity:
[What John is *looking for* t] is [*a centaur*]$_{\text{de-dicto}}$.

(8) Binding Theory connectivity under the specificational reading:
a. Principle A: [What *John*$_1$ is t] is a nuisance to *himself*$_1$.
b. Principle B: * [What *John*$_1$ is t] is a nuisance to *him*$_1$.
c. Principle C: * [What *he*$_1$ is t] is a nuisance to *John*$_1$.

Connectivity effects have intrigued researchers for decades, giving rise to two main lines of analysis: a syntactic line and a semantic line.

Within the syntactic line, we will concentrate on the **Question plus deletion account (Q+D).**[1] This approach maintains that the pre-copular constituent is either syntactically an interrogative clause (Ross 1972, den Dikken, Meinunger & Wilder 2000, Ross 2000) or syntactically an NP and semantically a question (Schlenker 2003, Romero 2005). The post-copular constituent is a partially elided clause. It is

1 For an alternative syntactic line based on movement, see Akmajian (1970), Culicover (1977), Grosu (1973), Bošković (1997).

from the underlying syntax of this partially elided clause that connectivity arises. This is illustrated in (9)–(11).

(9) Variable binding connectivity:
$[_{CP/NP}$ The person no woman$_1$ hates t] is $[_{IP}$ ~~no woman hates~~ her$_1$ mother].

(10) Opacity connectivity:
$[_{CP/NP}$ What John is looking for t] is $[_{IP}$ ~~John is looking for~~ a centaur]

(11) Binding Theory connectivity under the specificational reading:
a. Principle A:
$[_{CP/NP}$ What John$_1$ is t] is $[_{IP}$ ~~John$_1$ is~~ a nuisance to himself$_1$]
b. Principle B:
* $[_{CP/NP}$ What John$_1$ is t] is $[_{IP}$ ~~John$_1$ is~~ a nuisance to him$_1$]
c. Principle C:
* $[_{CP/NP}$ What he$_1$ is t] is $[_{IP}$ ~~he$_1$ is~~ a nuisance to John$_1$]

The semantic line is championed by the **'As is' account**. This approach takes the pre- and post-copular constituents to be as seen in surface structure. Specificational *be* expresses identity ('=') crosscategorially. Connectivity follows from the resulting semantics (opacity connectivity, as in (12)) enhanced with skolem functions (for variable binding connectivity, as in (13)) and with Reinhart's (1983) rule I (for Binding Theory connectivity) (Jacobson 1994, Sharvit 1999, Cecchetto 2000, Heller 2002).

(12) Variable binding connectivity:
a. $[_{NP}$ The person no woman$_1$ hates t] is $[_{NP}$ her$_1$ mother].
b. $\lambda w.\ \iota f_{\langle e,e\rangle}\ [\forall x\ [\text{woman}(x,w) \rightarrow \neg\text{hate}(x,f(x),w)]]$
$= \lambda y_e.\ \iota z_e[\text{mother-of}(z,y,w)]$

(13) Opacity connectivity:
a. $[_{NP}$ What John is looking for t] is $[_{NP}$ a centaur]
b. $\lambda w.\ \iota P_{\langle e,st\rangle}[\text{look-for}(j,P,w)] = \lambda y_e.\ \lambda w'_s[\text{centaur}(y,w')]$

With this background in mind, let us turn to the focus of the present paper. In an interesting article, Sharvit (2009) makes two important claims: (i) Predicational sentences also exhibit connectivity: *the only N'* examples; (ii) the Q+D account cannot derive connectivity in predicational sentences, while the 'as is' account can derive it straightforwardly. The goal of the present paper is to reexamine these claims. It will be argued that:

i. *The only N'* examples do not show that predicational sentences exhibit connectivity.

ii. If there is connectivity in predicational sentences – and this may in fact be the case –, the Q+D analysis can easily be extended to cover these cases.

The rest of the paper is organized as follows. Section 2 presents Sharvit's data, which exhibit connectivity under what she argues to be a predicational reading. We will show that the intended reading of *the only N'* is found also in specificational sentences and, thus, that it does not show that the original sentences under that reading are being used predicationally. Section 3 shows how the Q+D approach can be extended to allow for connectivity in predicational sentences if connectivity is indeed found in them. Section 4 concludes.

2 *The only N'* examples

Sharvit (2009) argues that sentences like (14), with an NP of shape *the only N'* in post-copular position, are ambiguous between a specificational reading and a predicational reading. The point she wants to make is that, under the predicational reading, the sentence exhibits connectivity too, more concretely, backwards connectivity (from right to left):[2]

(14) A parody of her_1 mother is the only thing no woman_1 wants to be.

Sharvit presents two main sets of data, which we will discuss in turn.

In the first set of data, to detect the predicational reading in *the only N'* examples, Sharvit (2009) compares them to their *the N'* counterparts without *only* in negative contexts. She argues that the former but not the latter allow for a reading where uniqueness is not presupposed but asserted. In (15), the context guarantees uniqueness (i.e., it guarantees that ⟦N'⟧ is a singleton) and negation in the test sentences is understood as negating something other than uniqueness. As expected, both the sentence with *the only N'* and the one with *the N'* are felicitous. In (16), the context guarantees non-uniqueness (i.e., the cardinality of ⟦N'⟧ is said to be greater than 1) and negation in the test sentences is to be understood precisely as negating uniqueness. Here a contrast arises: sentence (16b) with *the N'* is infelicitous, but, interestingly, sentence (16a) with *the only N'* is perfectly acceptable.

2 (14) under the intended predicational reading should be distinguished from inverse specificational sentences like (i), which carry special focus intonation on the fronted NP:

(i) A NUIsance to himself_1 is what John_1 is.

(15) Context guaranteeing uniqueness:
John went out with only one woman last night. I thought it was Sue, but then I found out that Sue was with Fred last night ...

a. ... so it seems that Sue was not *the only woman John went out with.*

b. ... so it seems that Sue was not *the woman John went out with.*

(16) Context guaranteeing non-uniqueness:
John went out with Sue and some other woman last night ...

a. ... so it seems that Sue was not *the only woman John went out with.*

b. # ... so it seems that Sue was not *the woman John went out with.*

Hence, besides a reading where uniqueness is presupposed, sentences with post-copular *the only N'* allow for a second reading that asserts – rather than presupposes – uniqueness. Sharvit (2009) claims that, in this second reading, *the only N'* is an ⟨e, ⟨(s), t⟩⟩-predicate and the sentence is predicational. She proposes that the definite article in post-copular position can be optionally treated as invisible to semantic interpretation in *the only N'* whereas it is mandatorily interpreted in *the N'*. When *the* is interpreted, *the only N'* is of type e, it combines with be_{SPEC} in (17a) (saturating its λy_e argument) and the sentence is specificational. When *the* is invisible to semantic interpretation, *the only N'* is of type ⟨e, ⟨(s), t⟩⟩, it combines with be_{PRED} in (17b) (saturating its $\lambda P_{\langle e,t\rangle}$ argument) and the sentence is predicational. Since only the first possibility is an option for *the N'*, the sentence is always specificational. This analysis is sketched in (18).

(17) a. $[\![be_{\text{SPEC}}]\!] = [\, \lambda y_e.\ \lambda x_e.\ x = y\,]$ (Sharvit 2009: (10))

b. $[\![be_{\text{PRED}}]\!] = [\, \lambda P_{\langle e,t\rangle}.\ \lambda x_e\!: x \in \text{Dom}(P).\ P(x) = 1\,]$

(18) Sharvit's analysis:

the only N':	*the N'*:
[the only N'] ⇐ SPECIF	[the N'] ⇐ SPECIF
[~~the~~ only N'] ⇐ PRED	* [~~the~~ N'] ⇐ * PRED

The judgments in (15)–(16) follow, then, from the standard lexical entries for *the* (presupposing uniqueness) and *only* (asserting uniqueness) given in (19). Both *the N'* and *the only N'* can be interpreted as presupposing uniqueness – as in (20a,b) respectively – and, thus, are felicitous in (15). But only *the only N'* allows for a parse where uniqueness is simply asserted ((20c)) and, thus, only *the only N'* can express the intended reading in (16).

(19) Lexical entries:

a. $[\![the]\!] = [\ \lambda P_{\langle e,t\rangle}: |P| = 1.$ that unique x]
$= [\ \lambda P_{\langle e,t\rangle}.\ \iota x\ [P(x) = 1]\ ]$

b. $[\![only]\!] = [\ \lambda P_{\langle e,t\rangle}.\ \lambda x_e: P(x) = 1.\ \forall y[P(y) = 1 \rightarrow y = x]\ ]$[3]

(20) Composed meanings:

a. $[\![the\ N']\!] = \iota x_e\ [[\![N']\!](x) = 1]$

b. $[\![the\ only\ N']\!] = \iota x_e\ [\forall y[[\![N']\!](y) = 1 \leftrightarrow y = x]]$[4]

c. $[\![$~~the~~ *only N'*$]\!] = [\ \lambda x_e: [\![N']\!](x) = 1.\ \forall y[[\![N']\!](y) = 1 \rightarrow y = x]\ ]$

Crucially, this means that, according to Sharvit's (2009) analysis, the following conditional relation holds between the status of the uniqueness implication and the type of copular sentence:

(21) In a copular sentence, if the uniqueness implication arising from the NP *the only N'* is not presupposed but at-issue information, then *the only N'* is being used as an ⟨e, ⟨s, t⟩⟩-predicate and that the sentence is predicational.

With this empirical generalization at hand, she goes back to sentences like (14) that exhibit connectivity effects. In (22), a negative version of (14) is used in which uniqueness is at-issue (it is part of what is being negated) rather than presupposed information. According to (21), this makes the sentence predicational. Backward connectivity is licensed in (22). Therefore, so goes the argument, connectivity is allowed in predicational sentences as well.

(22) Look, there are many things that no woman wants to be. So, a parody of her_1 mother is not the only thing no $woman_1$ wants to be.

I will argue that the conditional relation in (21) does not hold and that, thus, sentences like (22) do not show that connectivity is allowed in predicational sentences. While (16a) convincingly shows that *the only N'* has a non-presuppositional reading with respect to uniqueness, I argue that, from this, it does not follow that *the only N'* is being used as an ⟨e, ⟨s, t⟩⟩-predicate and that the sentence is, thus, predicational.

---

3 For Sharvit's (2009) purposes and for the present paper, it suffices to consider examples with singular NPs. To deal with sentences with plural NPs, as in (i), (19b) should be modified along the lines of (ii):

(i) Sue and Mary were not the only women John went out with.

(ii) $[\![only]\!] = [\ \lambda P_{\langle e,t\rangle}.\ \lambda x_e: P(x) = 1.\ \forall y[P(y) = 1 \rightarrow y \leq_i x]\ ]$

4 *The only N'* in (20b) presupposes that there is an x such that $P(x) = 1$ and $\forall y[P(y) = 1 \rightarrow y = x]$ (i.e., $\forall y[P(y) = 1 \leftrightarrow y = x]$) and, redundantly, that that x is unique. It denotes that unique x.

I note that the same pattern observed for the post-copular phrase in (15)–(16) is also found in specificational subjects in standard specificational sentences. Consider the following examples.

In (23)–(24), we use negation to detect whether uniqueness is at-issue content or a presupposition. The contrast between (23B') and (24B') shows that the reply *That's not true* cannot negate uniqueness with respect to ⟦*N'*⟧ when the specificational subject is *the N'*, but it can when the specificational subject is *the only N'*. Thus, *the only N'* functioning as a specificational subject allows for a reading where uniqueness is asserted rather than presupposed:

(23) A: The person that John danced with last night was Mary.
B: That's not true. It was Sue.
B': # That's not true. He danced with Sue as well.

(24) A: The only person that John danced with last night was Mary.
B: That's not true. It was Sue.
B': That's not true. He danced with Sue as well.

In (25), the context sets up the question under discussion "Who, if anybody, called the victim that evening?", making clear that it is not presupposed that exactly one person called. In this context, the answer (25A) with *the N'* is deviant whereas (25A') with *the only N'* is perfectly fine. Again, this means that the specificational subject *the only N'* in (25A') allows for a non-presuppositional reading of uniqueness:

(25) Q: Did anybody call the victim that evening? I need the complete list of callers.
A: #? Inspector, the person that called the victim that night was John.
A': Inspector, the only person that called the victim that night was John.

Finally, in (26), we text whether the uniqueness implication is semantically embeddable under *because*. In (26A) with *the N'*, uniqueness is not naturally understood as part of the reason for being upset. Rather, the most natural reading is one in which exactly one present was expected to begin with and the speaker is disappointed that that present was a simple greeting card. This suggests that the uniqueness implication is presupposed. Compare this to (26A') with *the only N'*. Here, uniqueness is easily understood as part of the reason for being upset and, thus, it is part of the asserted content of the clause.[5]

5 All the infelicitous replies in (23)–(26) with *the N'* can of course be rescued if the presupposition is locally accommodated. The point is that (23)–(26) show a contrast between *the N'* and *the only N'*, the latter of which is perfectly fine without rescuing.

(26) Q: Why are you so upset at your uncle from Chile?
A: Because the thing he sent me for my birthday was a greeting card.
A': Because the only thing he sent me for my birthday was a greeting card.

Hence, in all these sentences *pre*-copular *the only N'* has a reading that asserts – rather than presupposes – uniqueness. But, as we saw, these are standard specificational sentences. Recall that, according to Sharvit's (2009) lexical entry for be_{SPEC} in (17a), *the only N'* in sentences (24)–(26) saturates be_{SPEC}'s λx_e slot and thus it should be of type e. But this means that, in these cases, *the only N'* asserts uniqueness but it has type e and the sentence is specificational. This shows that the fact that *the only N'* is used non-presuppositionally with respect to uniqueness in a copular sentence does not guarantee that it is acting as an ⟨e, ⟨s, t⟩⟩-predicate and that the sentence is predicational, contra the empirical generalization in (21).[6,7]

I turn now to the second set of data presented from Sharvit (2009), which concentrates precisely on the behavior of *the only N'* in specificational subject position. The sentences are now in an interrogative context and, to identify the presupposed content, the 'wait-a-minute' test is used (von Fintel 2004), illustrated in (27).

6 If we treated *the only N'* in (23)–(26) as an ⟨e, ⟨s, t⟩⟩-predicate, the sentences would be inverse predicational sentences comparable to (i), which intuitively belongs to a different, poetic register of English. See Williams (1983, 1994) for an inverse predicational analysis of specificational sentences and Heycock & Kroch (1999) for arguments against it.

(i) Tender is the night.

7 Coppock & Beaver (2012) observe that *the only N'* can be understood as asserting rather than presupposing uniqueness in certain argumental, non-predicative positions, as exemplified in (i). Unlike Sharvit (2009), they propose that the definite article *the* is always visible to semantic interpretation but that it does not presuppose uniqueness, as in (19a), but weak uniqueness, as in (ii). Additionally, when *the only N'* appears in argumental position, an IOTA-shift or an A-shift applies. Their analysis covers (i) as well as simple predicational uses like (iii), and it may be extendible to the specificational sentences in (23)–(26). Again, this shows that the fact that a definite NP is used as not presupposing (regular) uniqueness does not entail that it is being used predicatively.

(i) Q: How many people gave invited talks at SALT?
A: Well, I know Anna didn't give the only invited talk.

(ii) $[\![the]\!] = [\, \lambda P_{\langle e,t\rangle} : |P| \leq 1 \,.\, P \,]$

(iii) We know that France is not a monarchy. Thus, John is not the king of France.

(27) Q: Is the king of France bald?

A: Wait a minute! You are assuming something I am not: that France has a king!

Consider first the two implications in (28). Parallel to the presuppositional and non-presuppositional readings under negation, *the only N'* in post-copular position allows for these two readings under the question operator: (29Q) with post-verbal *the only N'* can be understood as presupposing (28a) and questioning the uniqueness implication (28b), as the reply in (30A) suggests, or as questioning (28a) and presupposing the uniqueness implication (28b), as the reply in (29A') indicates. Now consider *the only N'* in specificational subject position, as in (30Q). Sharvit notes that (30Q) allows for the second reading – questioning (28a) and presupposing the uniqueness implication (28b) – but, crucially, not for the first reading – presupposing (28a) and questioning the uniqueness implication (28b) –, witness the infelicity of (30A). This is exactly what Sharvit's analysis in (17)–(18) would expect: *the only N'* used as specificational subject is predicted to be of type e to saturate the λx slot of be_{SPEC} and, thus, to allow only a presuppositional reading of uniqueness.

(28) a. Identity implication: "that John is dating Sally".

b. Uniqueness implication: "that John is dating exactly one person".

(29) Q: Is Sally (really) the only woman John is dating?

A: Wait a minute! You are assuming something I'm not: that John is dating Sally!

A': Wait a minute! You are assuming something I'm not: that John is dating one woman only!

(30) Q: Is the only woman John is dating (really) Sally?

A: ## Wait a minute! You are assuming something I'm not: that John is dating Sally!

A': Wait a minute! You are assuming something I'm not: that John is dating one woman only!

The contrast between (29A) with *the only N'* in post-copular position and (30A) with *the only N'* in precopular position is taken by Sharvit (2009) as further evidence for the empirical generalization (21): If a copular sentence with *the only N'* conveys uniqueness as part of the at-issue content, the sentence is predicational, as in (29A); conversely, if the sentence is clearly not predicational but specificational, only a presuppositional reading of uniqueness is possible, as in (30A).

Assuming that the context in (29Q-A) guarantees that the sentence is being used predicationally, it can be tested whether connectivity is permitted in this context. The answer is 'yes', as shown in (31). Again, this leads Sharvit (2009) to conclude that predicational sentences exhibit connectivity effects.

(31) Q: Is a parody of her_1 mother (really) the only thing no $woman_1$ wants to be?

A: Wait a minute! You are assuming something that I'm not: that no $woman_1$ wants to be a parody of her_1 mother.

Clearly, the second set of data (29)–(30) from Sharvit (2009) is at odds with our data in (23)–(26). The sentences in (23)–(26) showed that *the only N'* as specificational subject allows, in fact, for a reading where uniqueness is asserted rather than presupposed. Why, then, is (30A) a deviant reply?

I argue that the unacceptability of (30A) is orthogonal to the presuppositional vs. at-issue content of the specificational subject, and that it is in fact due to the presuppositional vs. at-issue status of the information conveyed by the pivot, which in turn follows from focus.

To see this, note first that the acceptable replies above align with the position of focal intonation in the original question, as shown in (32)–(33). When *Sally* is not focused and *only* is, as in (32), the identity implication (28a) is presupposed and the uniqueness implication (28b) is at-issue:

(32) Q: Is Sally (really) the $[\text{ONly}]_F$ woman John is dating?

A: Wait a minute! You are assuming something I'm not: that John is dating Sally!

When *only* is not focused and *Sally* is, as in (33) and (34), the status of the two implications reverses:

(33) Q: Is $[\text{SALly}]_F$ (really) the only woman John is dating?

A: Wait a minute! you are assuming something I'm not: that John is dating one woman only!

(34) Q: Is the only woman John is dating (really) $[\text{SALly}]_F$?

A: Wait a minute! You are assuming something I'm not: that John is dating one woman only!

This is exactly as expected, since unfocused material tends to be projective, i.e., not at-issue, whereas focused material is non-projective, i.e., at issue. (Simons et al. 2010, among many others).

Crucially, specificational sentences have an inherent focus structure (Percus 1997, a.o.). In contrast to the free patterns found in predicational sentences, the pivot of a specificational sentence must receive focal accent, as illustrated in the declarative sentences in (35)–(36):

(35) Predicational sentences:

a. A: Who is the murderer?
B: JOHN$_F$ is the murderer.

b. A: Who is John?
B: John is the MURderer$_F$.

(36) Specificational sentences:

a. A: Who is the murderer?
B: The murderer is JOHN$_F$.

b. A: Who is John?
B: # The MURderer$_F$ is John.

This means that the specificational sentence (30Q) must be pronounced with focal accent on the pivot (besides possibly somewhere else as well). This explains the unacceptability of (30A). For this reply to be acceptable, (30Q) would have to be pronounced as in (37Q), with focus on *only* and leaving the pivot *Sally* unfocused, so that the identity implication would be understood as presupposed and the *Wait a minute!* response (37A) could be justified. But this violates the inherent focal requirements of specificational sentences.

(37) Q: ## Is the [ONly]$_F$ woman John is dating (really) Sally?

A: ## Wait a minute! You are assuming something I'm not: that John is dating Sally!

Hence, the missing reading of specificational subjects of shape *the only N'* has nothing to do with the status of the uniqueness implication (28b), but rather with the mandatory at-issue status of the identity implication (28a), which in turns follows from inherent focus restrictions on specificational sentences.

To sum up this section, the empirical evidence considered by Sharvit (2009) does not grant the empirical generalization (21), repeated below as (38). We have seen that a non-presuppositional reading of uniqueness is available too when *the only N'* functions as the specificational subject of a straightforward specificational sentence, thus falsifying (38). Cases in which a specification subject *the only N'* does not license such reading are ruled out by independent factors. All in all, this means that assertion of uniqueness by *the only N'* in (39), repeated from (14), is not evidence that the sentence is predicational. Hence, we do not have evidence that backwards connectivity is found in predicational sentences.

(38) In a copular sentence, if the uniqueness implication arising from the NP *the only N'* is not presupposed but at-issue information, then *the only N'* is being used as an ⟨e, ⟨s, t⟩⟩-predicate and that the sentence is predicational. (= (21))

(39) A parody of her$_1$ mother is the only thing no woman$_1$ wants to be. (= (14))

3 Connectivity in predicational sentences and the Q+D account

As we saw in (3)–(5), it is received wisdom that 'forward connectivity' is not possible in predicational sentences. This is sketched in (40). But *is* there 'backward connectivity' in predicational sentences, as sketched in (41)? This important question, raised for the first time – to the best of my knowledge – by Sharvit (2009), is still in want of an answer. The previous section only showed that Sharvit's examples cannot be taken as evidence that backwards connectivity in predicational sentences exists, but the possibility that other empirical data may make the point remains, of course, open.

(40) [$_{PredSu}$ ... BINDER ...] is$_{PRED}$ [$_{Pred}$ ... BINDEE ...]

×

(41) [$_{PredSu}$ ... BINDEE ...] is$_{PRED}$ [$_{Pred}$ ... BINDER ...]

???

It is beyond the scope of the present paper to empirically prove or disprove the pattern in (41). But let me briefly note that data with *become* suggest that Sharvit's suspicion might be correct. First, note that the verb *become* typically does not behave as the inchoative version of specificational *be*, but, as Higgins points out, "*[b]ecome* behaves rather like an inchoative to the verb *be* in its Predicational meaning" (Higgins 1973: 151). This can be seen in (42)–(43). Plain *be* in (42) can be used predicationally or specificationally. But the verb *become* in (43) is only used naturally in the predicational template (43a), the specificational template (43b) allowing only for a "magic" reading (where the person who happens to be the dean of SAS magically turns into John).

(42) a. John is the dean of the School of Arts and Sciences. PREDICATIONAL

b. The dean of the School of Arts and Sciences is John. SPECIFICATIONAL

(43) a. John became the dean of the School of Arts and Sciences. PREDICATIONAL

b. # The dean of the School of Arts and Sciences became John.
(Only ✓ under "magic" reading) * SPECIFICATIONAL

With the assumption that the verb *become* is only predicational, we can test backwards connectivity with variable binding. This is done in sentence (44), which is judged acceptable. This suggests that the backward connectivity pattern in (41) might, in fact, be found in natural language.[8]

(44) In the 60s, a parody of her_1 mother was what no $woman_1$ in her 20s wanted to be. Nowadays, a parody of her_1 mother has become what no $woman_1$ at all wants to be.

Be it as it may be, we turn now to Sharvit's (2009) second claim, namely, that the Q+D account cannot derive connectivity in predicational sentences. In the remainder of this section, we will show that, if backwards connectivity is indeed proven to exist in predicational sentences, the Q+D account can be easily extended to deal with the new connectivity pattern.

Let us first look at the semantics of the Q+D as it currently stands in the literature (Schlenker 2003, Romero 2005, 2007)[9]. The underlying syntax for e.g. (45a) is given in (45b). We start with the composition of the specificational subject. The specificational subject Noun Phrase is analysed in Romero (2007) as carrying a silent answer operator *ANS*, defined in (46a), that turns the intension of the

---

8 Despite the judgment in (43b), there are some uses of *become* that look like the inchoative version of specificational *be*, as in (i). This means that we cannot be entirely sure that the English sentence (44) is predicational. Spanish *convertirse en* 'become' may be a better candidate to make the point, as the Spanish version (ii) of (i) is deviant (it only has a magic reading) and the Spanish counterpart (iii) of (44) is still acceptable.

(i) [After a big explosion in outer space.]
The number of planets just became seven.

(ii) # El número de planetas se ha convertido en siete.
The number of planets SE has transformed into seven
(Only ✓ under magic reading)

(iii) En los años 60, una parodia de su_1 madre era lo que ninguna $mujer_1$ de 20 años
In the years 60, a parody of her mother was the that no woman of 20 years
quería ser.
wanted to-be

Hoy en día, un parodia de su_1 madre se ha convertido en lo que ninguna $mujer_1$
Today in day, a parody of her mother SE has transformed in the that no woman
en general quiere ser.
at general wants to-be

9 What I will present is a simplification of the current Q+D analysis, leaving aside differences in presuppositions as well as the exhaustivity implicature of the post-verbal clause. See Romero (2007) for details.

NP – in this case, the individual concept in (46b) – into a question meaning à la Groenendijk & Stokhof (1984) – here, the ⟨s, ⟨s, t⟩⟩-function in (46c).[10]

(45) a. The person that John likes best is Mary.

b. LF: [ANS The person that John likes best] is [~~John likes~~ Mary ~~best~~].

(46) Specificational subject: (Romero 2007)

a. $[\![ANS]\!] = \lambda y_{\langle s,e\rangle}.\ \lambda w.\ \lambda w'.\ y(w') = y(w)$

b. ⟦*the person that John likes best*⟧
$= \lambda w''.\ \iota x_e[\text{like}(j,x,w'')]$

c. ⟦*ANS the person John likes best*⟧
$= \lambda w.\ \lambda w'.\ \iota x_e[\text{like}(j,x,w')] = \iota x_e[\text{like}(j,x,w)]$

The post-verbal constituent is a partially elided clause, the only overt element of which is the pivot. It expresses a proposition, as illustrated in (47):

(47) Post-verbal clause including pivot:
⟦~~*John likes*~~ *Mary* ~~*best*~~⟧ $= \lambda w'.\ \text{like}(j,m,w')$

The two constituents are put together using the asymmetric lexical entry for be_{SPEC} defined in (48). The result is the truth conditions in (49), paraphrased in (50).

(48) $[\![be_{SPEC}]\!] = \lambda q_{\langle s,t\rangle}.\ \lambda p_{\langle s,\langle s,t\rangle\rangle}.\ \lambda w.\ p(w) = q$

(49) ⟦*ANS The person that John likes best is* ~~*John likes*~~ *Mary* ~~*best*~~⟧
$= \lambda w.\ [\ \lambda w'.\ \iota x_e[\text{like}(j,x,w')] = \iota x_e[\text{like}(j,x,w)] = \lambda w'.\ \text{like}(j,m,w')]$

(50) Paraphrase of (49):
'We are in a w such that: the answer to the question "Who does John like best?" in w is the proposition "that John likes Mary best"'.

Specificational sentences exhibiting (forward) variable binding connectivity are dealt with in the same way. To see just one example, (51a) is assigned the underlying structure in (51b). As mentioned in section 1, connectivity arises from the underlying syntax of the post-copular clause. The compositional derivation leads to the truth conditions in (52), paraphrased in (53).

(51) a. The person no $woman_1$ hates is her_1 mother.

b. $[_{NP}$ ANS The person no $woman_1$ hates t] is $[_{IP}$ ~~no $woman_1$ hates~~ her_1 mother].

10 Different *ANS* operators encapsulate the different degrees of exhaustivity, as Romero (2007) argues is needed for specificational sentences.

(52) ⟦ANS *The person no woman$_1$ hates is ~~no woman$_1$ hates~~ her$_1$ mother*⟧

$$= \lambda w.\ [\lambda w'.\ \iota f_{\langle e,e\rangle}[\forall x[\text{woman}(x,w') \rightarrow \neg\text{hate}(x, f(x), w')]] = \iota f_{\langle e,e\rangle}[\forall x[\text{woman}(x,w) \rightarrow \neg\text{hate}(x, f(x), w)]]] = \lambda w'.\ \forall x[\text{woman}(x,w') \rightarrow \neg\text{hate}(x, \iota z{:}\text{mother-of}(z,x), w')]$$

(53) Paraphrase of (52):
'We are in a w such that: the answer to the question "For which $f_{\langle e,e\rangle}$ does no woman x hate f(x)?" in w is the proposition "that no woman x hates the mother of x".'

Now we turn to the putative examples of backward connectivity in predicational sentences. How can we extend the current Q+D analysis to cover these cases? As we will see, a parsimonious extension of the current analysis will do.

First, in order to derive backward connectivity in a way parallel to forward connectivity above, sentence (54), repeated from the second part of (44), needs to be understood as consisting of a question and its propositional answer, as paraphrased in (55). The only intuitive difference with respect to the standard cases above is that, for the putative predicational sentences, the syntactic source of the question and the propositional answer is reversed: the question arises not from the specificational subject but from the predicate, and the propositional answer is expressed by a partially elided clause containing not the pivot but the surface predicational subject. This is illustrated in (56). Note that these steps are granted by general assumptions about the grammar: the same phrase – in this case, the constituent *[ANS what no woman$_1$ (at all) wants to be]* – expresses the same meaning regardless of its syntactic position, and partial clausal ellipsis is permitted within predicational subjects, witness (57). Connectivity arises, as before, from the underlying syntax of the constituent expressing the propositional answer, namely (56b).[11]

(54) Nowadays a parody of her$_1$ mother has become (/ is) what no woman$_1$ (at all) wants to be.

(55) 'We are in a w such that: the proposition "that no woman x at all wants to be a parody of x's mother" has become in w the answer to the question "For which $P_{\langle e,(s)t\rangle}$ does no woman x at all want to be P(x)?".'

11 If (44) and (54) indeed involve predicational structures, then they need not follow the information structure constraints illustrated in (36) for specificational sentences in general (and in footnote 2, example (i), for inverse specificational sentences in particular), but instead allow for the freedom shown the predicational structures in (35). This expectation is borne out: In (44), main sentential stress easily falls on (*no woman) at all*, that is, it easily falls somewhere else than on what would be the pivot (i.e., *a parody of her mother*) if the sentence were specificational.

(56) a. LF of the predicational subject in (54):
[~~No woman$_1$ (at all) wants to be~~ a parody of her$_1$ mother]

b. LF of the predicate in (54):
[ANS what no woman$_1$ (at all) wants to be t]

(57) A: Are you going to do the homework assignment with David?
B: ~~To do the homework assignment~~ with Charlotte would be better.

Now we need the lexical entry for *become* or *be*$_{\text{PRED}}$ to combine the semantic contribution of the two constituents in (56). For simplicity, I will illustrate the derivation for *be*$_{\text{PRED}}$, but the same steps would apply to *become*. Consider first how *be*$_{\text{PRED}}$ in (58) – the intensional version of (17b) – combines in the simple sentences in (59). In (59a), the verb combines directly with the $\langle s, \langle e, t\rangle\rangle$-function expressed by the predicate *important*. But, in (59b), the predicate *the leader of the guerrilla* expresses an individual concept, i.e., a function of type $\langle s, e\rangle$. As standardly assumed since Partee (1986b), the mismatching $\langle s, e\rangle$-function is type-shifted into the appropriate $\langle e, \langle s, t\rangle\rangle$-function by the shifter in (60). The result combines with *be*$_{\text{PRED}}$, as illustrated in (61).

(58) $[\![be_{\text{PRED}}]\!] = \lambda P_{\langle e, \langle s, t\rangle\rangle}.\ \lambda x_e.\ \lambda w_s.\ P(x)(w) = 1$

(59) a. John is / became important$_{\langle e, \langle s, t\rangle\rangle}$.

b. John is / became [the leader of the guerrilla]$_{\langle e, \langle s, t\rangle\rangle}$.

(60) $[\![SHIFT^{\langle s, e\rangle \rightarrow \langle e, st\rangle}]\!] = \lambda P_{\langle s, e\rangle}.\ \lambda z_e.\ \lambda w_s.\ P(w) = z$

(61) John is$_{\text{PRED}}$ the leader (of the guerrilla).

a. $[\![\textit{the leader}]\!] = \lambda w''.\ \iota y[\text{leader}(y,w'')]$

b. $[\![\textit{SHIFT the leader}]\!] = \lambda z_e.\ \lambda w'.\ \iota y[\text{leader}(y,w')] = z$

c. $[\![\textit{is}_{PRED}\ \textit{SHIFT the leader}]\!] = \lambda x_e.\ \lambda w.\ \iota y[\text{leader}(y,w)] = x$

d. $[\![\textit{John is}_{PRED}\ \textit{SHIFT the leader}]\!] = \lambda w.\ \iota y[\text{leader}(y,w)] = j$

Now we turn to the more complex example (54). To combine the two constituents in (56), we just need a derivation parallel to the one we just saw. We simply need a crosscategorial version of *be* (Partee 1986a, Jacobson 1994, Sharvit 1999), as in (62), and the corresponding crosscategorial type-shifter, as in (63).

(62) $[\![be_{\text{PRED},crosscat.}]\!] = \lambda P_{\langle \sigma, \langle s, t\rangle\rangle}.\ \lambda x_\sigma.\ \lambda w_s.\ P(x)(w) = 1$

(63) $[\![SHIFT^{\langle s, \sigma\rangle \rightarrow \langle \sigma, st\rangle}]\!] = \lambda P_{\langle s, \sigma\rangle}.\ \lambda z_\sigma.\ \lambda w_s.\ P(w) = z$

With these tools at hand, the derivation of the putative predicational sentence with connectivity effects proceeds as in (64):

(64) A parody of her_1 mother has become / is_{PRED} what no woman_1 wants to be.

a. LF: [~~No woman_1 wants to be~~ a parody of her_1 mother] is_{PRED} [SHIFT ANS what no woman_1 wants to be t]

b. ⟦*what no woman wants to be t*⟧ =
$\lambda w''.\iota P_{\langle e,\langle e,st\rangle\rangle}: \forall x[\text{woman}(x,w'') \rightarrow \neg\text{want}(x,[\lambda w'''.\,P(x)(x)(w''')],w'')]$

c. ⟦*ANS*⟧ = $\lambda y_{\langle s,\sigma\rangle}.\,\lambda w.\,\lambda w'.\,y(w') = y(w)$

d. ⟦*ANS what no woman wants to be*⟧ = $\lambda w.\,\lambda w'.$
$\iota P_{\langle e,\langle e,st\rangle\rangle}: \forall x[\text{woman}(x,w') \rightarrow \neg\text{want}(x,[\lambda w'''.\,P(x)(x)(w''')],w')] =$
$\iota P_{\langle e,\langle e,st\rangle\rangle}: \forall x[\text{woman}(x,w) \rightarrow \neg\text{want}(x,[\lambda w'''.\,P(x)(x)(w''')],w)]$

e. ⟦*SHIFT ANS what no woman wants to be*⟧ =
$\lambda p_{\langle st\rangle}.\,\lambda w.\,[\,p = \lambda w'.$
$\iota P_{\langle e,\langle s,et\rangle\rangle}: \forall x[\text{woman}(x,w') \rightarrow \neg\text{want}(x,[\lambda w'''.\,P(x)(x)(w''')],w')] =$
$\iota P_{\langle e,\langle s,et\rangle\rangle}: \forall x[\text{woman}(x,w) \rightarrow \neg\text{want}(x,[\lambda w'''.\,P(x)(x)(w''')],w)]\,]$

f. ⟦*is_{PRED} SHIFT ANS what no woman wants to be*⟧ =
$\lambda p_{\langle st\rangle}.\,\lambda w.\,[\,p = \lambda w'.$
$\iota P_{\langle e,\langle s,et\rangle\rangle}: \forall x[\text{woman}(x,w') \rightarrow \neg\text{want}(x,[\lambda w'''.\,P(x)(x)(w''')],w')] =$
$\iota P_{\langle e,\langle s,et\rangle\rangle}: \forall x[\text{woman}(x,w) \rightarrow \neg\text{want}(x,[\lambda w'''.\,P(x)(x)(w''')],w)]\,]$

g. ⟦~~*No woman_1 wants to be*~~ *a parody of her_1 mother*⟧ =
$\lambda w'.\,\forall x[\text{woman}(x,w') \rightarrow$
$\neg\text{want}(x,\,[\lambda w'''.\,\text{parody}(x,\text{the.mother.of}(x),w''')],w')]$

h. ⟦~~*No woman_1 wants to be*~~ *a parody of her_1 mother is_{PRED} SHIFT ANS what no woman wants to be*⟧ = $\lambda w.$
$[\,\lambda w'.\,\forall x[\text{woman}(x,w') \rightarrow$
$\neg\text{want}(x,[\lambda w'''.\,\text{parody}(x,\text{the.mother.of}(x),w''')],w')]$
$= \lambda w'.\,\iota P_{\langle e,\langle s,et\rangle\rangle}: \forall x[\text{woman}(x,w') \rightarrow$
$\neg\text{want}(x,[\lambda w'''.\,P(x)(x)(w''')],w')] =$
$\iota P_{\langle e,\langle s,et\rangle\rangle}: \forall x[\text{woman}(x,w) \rightarrow$
$\neg\text{want}(x,[\lambda w'''.\,P(x)(x)(w''')],w)]\,]$

To sum up this section, the question whether backward connectivity exists in predicational sentences remains open. If connectivity is indeed found in predicational sentences, this connectivity effect can be derived in the Q+D account by parsimoniously generalizing the shifting operation $\langle s,e\rangle \rightarrow \langle e,st\rangle$ to its crosscategorial version $\langle s,\sigma\rangle \rightarrow \langle\sigma,st\rangle$.

4 Conclusions

In this paper, we have considered the three potential patterns of variable binding connectivity sketched in (65)–(67). The 'forward' binding patterns in (65) and (66) have been long discussed in the literature, where the former has been established as not being allowed by the grammar and the latter as being allowed. The paper has focused on the 'backward' pattern (67), considering its empirical attestation and its potential repercussions for two of the main approaches to connectivity, namely, the 'question plus deletion' (Q+D) approach and the 'as is' approach.

(65) Forward connectivity in predicational sentences: IMPOSSIBLE
$[_{PredSu}$ ... BINDER ...] is_{PRED} $[_{Pred}$ ... BINDEE ...]
×

(66) Forward connectivity in specificational sentences: POSSIBLE
$[_{SpecSu}$ ... BINDER ...] is_{SPEC} $[_{Pivot}$ ... BINDEE ...]
✓

(67) Backwards connectivity in predicational sentences: ???
$[_{SpecSu}$ ... BINDEE ...] is_{SPEC} $[_{Pivot}$ ... BINDER ...]
???

The present paper has argued for the following points.

First, Sharvit (2009) claimed, based on examples with *the only N'*, that the backward connectivity pattern in predicational sentences (67) is empirically attested. We have shown that the intended reading of sentences with *the only N'* – one where uniqueness is asserted rather than presupposed – cannot be taken as a sign that the sentence under this reading is predicational. Hence, the important question whether or not backward connectivity exists in predicational sentences remains an open issue.

Second, if backward connectivity is found in predicational sentences – and this may in fact be the case –, we have shown how the Q+D approach can be minimally extended to cover the new pattern by simply generalizing Partee's (1986b) shifting operation $\langle s, e\rangle \rightarrow \langle e, st\rangle$ to its crosscategorial version $\langle s, \sigma\rangle \rightarrow \langle \sigma, st\rangle$.

As the reader will have noted, there is in principle a fourth potential pattern of variable binding connectivity, involving backward connectivity in (non-inverse) specificational sentences. This is sketched in (68). We leave this potential pattern and its implications for the theoretical debate for future research.

(68) Backwards connectivity in specificational sentence:

[$_{\text{SpecSu}}$ ... BINDEE ...] is$_{\text{SPEC}}$ [$_{\text{Pivot}}$ ... BINDER ...]

???

Acknowledgment: I would like to thank the audience of the workshop "Reconstruction Effects in Relative Clauses" (ZAS, July 8-9, 2011) and two anonymous reviewers for their useful comments and suggestions. Remaining errors are mine.

References

Akmajian, Adrian. 1970. On deriving cleft sentences from pseudo-cleft sentences. *Linguistic Inquiry* 1(2). 149–168.

Bošković, Željko. 1997. Pseudoclefts. *Studia Linguistica* 51(3). 235–277. https://doi.org/10.1111/1467-9582.00022.

Cecchetto, Carlo. 2000. Connectivity and anti-connectivity in pseudoclefts. In M. Hirotani, A. Coetzee, N. Hall & J.-Y. Kim (eds.), *Proceedings of NELS 30*, 137–151. Amherst, MA: GLSA.

Chomsky, Noam. 1981. *Lectures on government and binding*. Dordrecht: Foris.

Coppock, Elizabeth & David Beaver. 2012. Weak uniqueness: The only difference between definites and indefinites. In Anca Chereches (ed.), *Proceedings of SALT 22*, 527–544. LSA.

Culicover, Peter. 1977. Some observations concerning pseudo-clefts. *Linguistic Analysis* 3. 347–375.

den Dikken, Marcel, André Meinunger & Chris Wilder. 2000. Pseudoclefts and ellipsis. *Studia Linguistica* 54. 41–89. https://doi.org/10.1111/1467-9582.00050.

Groenendijk, Jeroen & Martin Stokhof. 1984. *Studies on the semantics of questions and the pragmatics of answers*. University of Amsterdam Doctoral dissertation.

Grosu, Alexander. 1973. On the status of the so called right roof constraint. *Language* 49. 294–311.

Halvorsen, Per-Kristian. 1978. *The syntax and semantics of cleft constructions*. Austin: University of Texas Doctoral dissertation.

Heller, Daphna. 2002. On the relation of connectivity and specificational pseudoclefts. *Natural Language Semantics* 10. 243–284. https://doi.org/10.1023/A:1022152007523.

Heycock, Caroline & Anthony Kroch. 1999. Pseudocleft connectedness: Implications for the LF interface level. *Linguistic Inquiry* 30. 365–397. https://doi.org/10.1162/002438999554110.

Higgins, Francis Roger. 1973. *The pseudo-cleft construction in English*. Revised version published by Garland, New York, 1979; page references are to this version. Massachusetts Institute of Technology Doctoral dissertation.

Jacobson, Pauline. 1994. Binding connectivity in copular sentences. In Mandy Harvey & Lynn Santelmann (eds.), *Proceedings of SALT 4* (Cornell Working Papers in Linguistics), 161–178. Ithaca, NY: Cornell University.

Partee, Barbara Hall. 1986a. Ambiguous pseudoclefts and unambiguous be. In S. Berman, J.-W. Choe & J. McDonough (eds.), *Proceedings of NELS 16*, 354–366. Amherst MA: GLSA.

Partee, Barbara Hall. 1986b. Noun phrase interpretation and type-shifting principles. In Jeroen A. G. Groenendijk, Dick de Jongh & Martin B. J. Stokhof (eds.), *Studies in discourse representation theory and the theory of generalized quantifiers*, 115–144. Dordrecht: Foris.
Percus, Orin. 1997. Prying open the cleft. In K. Kusumoto (ed.), *Proceedings of NELS 27*, 337–351. Amherst MA: GLSA.
Reinhart, Tanya. 1983. *Anaphora and semantic interpretation*. London: Croom Helm.
Romero, Maribel. 2005. Concealed questions and specificational subjects. *Linguistics and Philosophy* 28. 687–737.
Romero, Maribel. 2007. Connectivity in a unified analysis of specificational subjects and concealed questions. In Chris Barker & Pauline Jacobson (eds.), *Direct compositionality*, 265–305. Oxford: Oxford University Press.
Ross, John Robert. 1972. Act. In D. Davidson & G. Harman (eds.), *Semantics of natural language*, 70–126. Dordrecht: Reidel.
Ross, John Robert. 2000. *The Frozenness of Pseudoclefts: Towards an Inequality-based Syntax*. Ms. University of North Texas.
Schlenker, Philippe. 2003. Clausal equations (a note on the connectivity problem). *Natural Language Semantics* 21. 157–214.
Sharvit, Yael. 1999. Connectivity in specificational sentences. *Natural Language Semantics* 7. 200–339.
Sharvit, Yael. 2009. Revisiting connectivity in copular sentences. In Ed Cormany, Satoshi Ito & David Lutz (eds.), *Proceedings of SALT 19*, 427–455. LSA.
Simons, Mandy, Judith Tonhauser, David Beaver & Craige Roberts. 2010. What projects and why. In Nan Li & David Lutz (eds.), *Proceedings of SALT 20*, 309–327. LSA.
von Fintel, Kai. 2004. Would you believe it? The king of France is back! Presuppositions and truth-value intuitions. In Marga Reimer & Anne Bezuidenhout (eds.), *Descriptions and beyond: An interdisciplinary collection of essays on definite and indefinite descriptions*, 315–341. Oxford: Oxford University Press.
Williams, Edwin. 1983. Against small clauses. *Linguistic Inquiry* 14(1). 287–308.
Williams, Edwin. 1994. *Thematic structure in syntax*. Cambridge MA: MIT Press.

Irene Heim

Functional readings without type-shifted noun phrases

Engdahl (1986) proposes that the interrogative *which*-phrase in (1) ranges not over pictures but over picture-valued functions.

(1) Which picture of herself did no girl submit?

(1) expresses the question 'which function f from girls to pictures of them is such that no girl submitted what f maps her to?' In this paper, I essentially agree with Engdahl about the denotation of (1) as a whole, but not about its compositional derivation. In particular, I show how functional question meanings can be derived without interpreting the restrictor of *which* as a predicate of functions, and without assuming that pronouns in the *which*-phrase are bound within that *which*-phrase. The analysis exploits the fact that the restrictor of *which* is in a low ("reconstructed") position at Logical Form (LF), and it relies on the presuppositional semantics of *which*-phrases or their traces that was developed by Rullmann & Beck (1998) and Fox (2000).

1 Engdahl's three innovations

I begin with a version of Engdahl's proposal. Engdahl built on Karttunen (1977), in whose theory (here simplified and syntacticized) a plain non-functional *which*-question received the following analysis.

(2) Which student did John invite?
LF: λ_p. which student$_@$ λ_x. Q(p) λ_w. John invite$_w$ t_x

Q encodes Karttunen's "proto-question" formation; **which** is an existential determiner.

(3) $[\![\mathbf{Q}]\!] = \lambda p_{st}.\ \lambda q_{st}.\ p = q$

(4) $[\![\mathbf{which}]\!] = \lambda P_{et}.\ \lambda Q_{et}.\ \exists x_e\ [P(x)\ \&\ Q(x)]$

To render unnecessary a special rule for quantifying into proto-questions, a covert propositional argument for **Q** is represented in the syntax in (2) and abstracted over

Irene Heim, Massachusetts Institute of Technology

https://doi.org/10.1515/9783050095158-009

at a higher point.[1] World-arguments are also made explicit in the object language. These can be either variables bound by a lambda-abstractor or an indexical @ that refers to the utterance world. The LF in (2) denotes the (characteristic function of the) set of propositions (5).[2]

(5) $\{p: \exists x\, [\text{student}_@(x)\ \&\ p = \lambda w.\ \text{invite}_w(j, x)]\}$

Turning now to functional readings, the denotation that Engdahl proposes for example (1) is the set of propositions in (6).[3]

(6) $\{p: \exists f_{\langle e,e\rangle}\, [\forall x.\ \text{picture-of}_@(f(x), x)\ \&\ p = \lambda w.\ \neg\exists x\, [\text{girl}_@(x)\ \&\ \text{submit}_w(x, f(x))]]\}$

The LF from which Engdahl computes this denotation is essentially (7).

(7) $\lambda_p.$ which E_y [picture$_@$ of herself$_y$] $\lambda_f.$ Q(p) $\lambda_w.$ no girl$_@$ $\lambda_x.$ t_x submit$_w$ $t_{f(x)}$

E is a covert variable-binder and type-shifter which corresponds to Engdahl's rule of Closure.[4]

1 Fox (2010) suggests that this structure may result from movement of an Answer operator in the sense of Dayal (1996).

2 I use a semi-formal meta-language as in Heim & Kratzer (1998), with additional notational conventions that should be self-explanatory. (E.g., *student*$_@$*(x)* means 'x is a student in the utterance world.')

3 For expository simplicity, I construe all nouns rigidly or *de re* (hence the indexical subscripts on both *picture* and *girl*). The general version of the theory – both Engdahl's and mine – also generates *de dicto* readings, i.e., LFs in which the world-arguments in (some or all) NPs are bound. For example, in addition to LF (7) with denotation (6), Engdahl's theory generates LF (i) with denotation (ii).

(i) $\lambda_p.$ which $E_{y,w'}$ [picture$_{w'}$ of herself$_y$] $\lambda_f.$ Q(p) $\lambda_w.$ no girl$_w$ $\lambda_x.$ t_x submit$_w$ $t_{f(x)(w)}$

(ii) $\{p: \exists f_{\langle e,se\rangle}\, [\forall x \forall w'.\ \text{picture-of}_{w'}(f(x)(w'), x)\ \&\ p = \lambda w.\ \neg\exists x\, [\text{girl}_w(x)\ \&\ \text{submit}_w(x, f(x)(w))]]\}$

(i)/(ii) is arguably a better rendition of the intuitively salient functional reading of (1) than (7)/(6). Answers to functional questions typically name functions-in-intension and do not (even in conjunction with contextual information) determine the extensions of these functions in the utterance world. Relatedly, (iii) is judged true when John knows that no man invited his mother-in-law but doesn't know anything about who the men are, who is whose mother-in-law, and who invited whom.

(iii) John knows which of his relatives no man invited.

It is therefore an unrealistic simplification to restrict attention to rigid readings, as I will throughout the main body of this paper. We want to be sure, of course, that the paper's lessons are not dependent on the simplification. See footnote 11 below.

4 Definition (8) covers just one special case of a family of **E**-operators that can bind any number of individual and/or world variables. See previous footnote and examples in Engdahl (1986) for other special cases. I refer to the literature for formal treatment of the general case, as well as for

(8) $[\![\mathbf{E_x}\zeta]\!]^g = \lambda f_{\langle e,e\rangle}.\ \forall x.\ [\![\zeta]\!]^{g^{x/x}}(f(x)) = 1$

Compare (7) to the LF for a non-functional reading of the same sentence, which would be (9).

(9) λ_p. which $\text{picture}_@$ of herself_y λ_z. Q(p) λ_w. no $\text{girl}_@$ λ_x. t_x submit_w t_z

There are three important differences: First, *herself*$_y$ is free in (9) but bound by the covert operator E_y in (7). Second, the sister of the *which*-DP is a predicate of individuals in (9) but a predicate of functions in (7). Accordingly *which* in (7) is of type ⟨⟨ee,t⟩,⟨⟨ee,t⟩,t⟩⟩ rather than the standard determiner type ⟨et,⟨et,t⟩⟩ that it has in (9) and (4). Third, the wh-trace is a simple individual variable in (9) but a complex of a function-variable and its argument in (7). The argument in this complex is a variable bound by *no girl*.

We can thus summarize Engdahl's analysis of functional readings as a package of three innovations:

(i) pronoun binding within NP:
a covert operation at the edge of the NP restricting *which*, which both binds pronouns inside the NP and shifts the type of the NP from a predicate of individuals to a predicate of functions;

(ii) polymorphic *which*:
a type-flexible meaning for *which*, which allows it to quantify not only over individuals (type e) but also over functions to individuals (e.g. type ⟨e,e⟩);

(iii) layered traces:[5]
the option of introducing covert arguments into traces, so that the trace as a whole can consist of one part that is bound in the usual way by the moved phrase, plus another part which may be bound from elsewhere.

The analysis put forth in this paper will contain versions of innovations (ii) and (iii) (polymorphic *which* and layered traces), but no counterpart of innovation (i) (pronoun-binding within NP).

---

proposals to break down the job of **E** into more elementary separate operations such as lambda abstraction (variable-binding) and further type-shifting (e.g. from ⟨e,et⟩ to ⟨ee,t⟩). See e.g. von Stechow (1990), Jacobson (1994, 2002).

5 I borrow this label from von Stechow (1990).

2 Partial functions and presupposition projection

Before I embark on the new analysis, I would like to amend a detail of Engdahl's proposal that is typically glossed over. This concerns the domains of the functions. According to (6) above, the interrogative quantifier ranges over functions f that satisfy the condition $\forall x.\ \text{picture-of}_{@}(f(x), x)$. Taken literally, this describes total functions on the domain D_e, mapping every individual to a picture of it. Since many individuals don't have pictures, no such total functions realistically exist. The functions that functional readings are typically about are *partial* functions. But which partial functions exactly, and how can their partiality be made explicit in the analysis? This pedantic-sounding question turns out to be pertinent to the agenda of this paper.

In order to admit partial functions, we want to change the definition of the **E**-operator from (8) to (10).

(10) $[\![\mathbf{E_x}\zeta]\!]^{g} = \lambda f_{\langle e,e\rangle}.\ \forall x\ [x \in \text{dom}(f) \rightarrow [\![\zeta]\!]^{g^{x/\mathbf{x}}}(f(x)) = 1]$

But functions whose domain is too small won't do. Intuitively, (1) asks for functions that are defined for (at least) all the girls. We cannot encode this directly in the meaning of **E**, since we don't have compositional access to the NP **girl** at this point in the structure. Fortunately, we don't need to. The issue takes care of itself through standard mechanisms of presupposition projection.

Let us see what happens in the step-by-step compositional calculation for the LF in (7), paying close attention to any denotation gaps that arise from partiality. We start with the layered trace.

(11) $[\![t_{f(x)}]\!]^{g}$ is defined only if $g(\mathbf{x}) \in \text{dom}(g(\mathbf{f}))$;
where defined, $[\![t_{f(x)}]\!]^{g} = g(\mathbf{f})(g(\mathbf{x}))$

The clause $t_x\ submit_w\ t_{f(x)}$ thus has a truth-value under only some assignments, and when we lambda-abstract over the variable **x** we obtain a partial function.[6]

(12) $[\![\lambda_x.\ t_x\ \text{submit}_w\ t_{f(x)}]\!]^{g} = \lambda x\text{: } x \in \text{dom}(g(\mathbf{f})).\ \text{submit}_{g(\mathbf{w})}(x, g(\mathbf{f})(x))$

For the next node up, we need to assume something about how presuppositions project from the nuclear scope of a quantifier. A standard assumption for **no**-DPs

6 This step is based on Heim & Kratzer's (1998) "pedantic" version of the Predicate Abstraction rule, which turns the presuppositions of the abstracted clause into restrictions on the domain of the function:

(i) $[\![\lambda_1\alpha]\!]_{g} = \lambda x\text{: } \alpha \in \text{dom}([\![\cdot]\!]^{g^{x/1}}).\ [\![\alpha]\!]^{g^{x/1}}$

is that they project universal presuppositions, so we get the following partial proposition after binding the world variable.

(13) $[\![\lambda_w.\ \text{no girl}_@\ \lambda_x.\ t_x\ \text{submit}_w\ t_{f(x)}]\!]^g =$
$\lambda w{:}\ \forall x\ [\text{girl}_@(x) \rightarrow x \in \text{dom}(g(\mathbf{f}))].\ \neg\exists x\ [\text{girl}_@(x)\ \&\ \text{submit}_w(x, g(\mathbf{f})(x))]$

At the end of the computation, we then have this.

(14) $[\![\lambda_p.\ \text{which}\ E_y\ [\text{picture}_@\ \text{of herself}_y]\ \lambda_f.\ Q(p)\ \lambda_w.$
$\text{no girl}_@\ \lambda_x.\ t_x\ \text{submit}_w\ t_{f(x)}]\!]^g =$
$\{p{:}\ \exists f\ [\forall x\ [x \in \text{dom}(f) \rightarrow \text{picture-of}_@(f(x), x)]\ \&$
$p = \lambda w{:}\ \forall x\ [\text{girl}_@(x) \rightarrow x \in \text{dom}(f)].\ \neg\exists x\ [\text{girl}_@(x)\ \&\ \text{submit}_w(x, f(x))]]\}$

This looks like a set of partial propositions, but upon closer inspection the propositions in this set are not genuinely partial.[7] Rather, since *w* does not occur in the domain-description of the λw-term, we always get either a total proposition or the universally undefined proposition (the empty set of world-truth-value pairs). It depends on whether or not f satisfies the condition $\forall x\ [\text{girl}_@(x) \rightarrow x \in \text{dom}(f)]$. If it does, (15) holds, otherwise (16).

(15) $\lambda w{:}\ \forall x\ [\text{girl}_@(x) \rightarrow x \in \text{dom}(f)].\ \neg\exists x\ [\text{girl}_@(x)\ \&\ \text{submit}_w(x, f(x))]$
$= \lambda w.\ \neg\exists x\ [\text{girl}_@(x)\ \&\ \text{submit}_w(x, f(x))]$

(16) $\lambda w{:}\ \forall x\ [\text{girl}_@(x) \rightarrow x \in \text{dom}(f)].\ \neg\exists x\ [\text{girl}_@(x)\ \&\ \text{submit}_w(x, f(x))]$
$= \varnothing$

This being so, we can redescribe the denotation in (14) as follows.

(17) $\{p{:}\ \exists f\ [\forall x\ [x \in \text{dom}(f) \rightarrow \text{picture-of}_@(f(x), x)]\ \&$
$\forall x\ [\text{girl}_@(x) \rightarrow x \in \text{dom}(f)]\ \&$
$p = \lambda w.\ \neg\exists x\ [\text{girl}_@(x)\ \&\ \text{submit}_w(x, f(x))]]\}$
$\cup \{\varnothing\}$

The extra pathological element ∅ looks out of place as a member of a question denotation, but its presence is arguably innocuous. It makes no difference to how such sets of propositions can be used in semantic and pragmatic theories of question-answer dialogues and of question-embedding predicates.[8] Disregarding this pathological element, then, we see that all the propositions in our question

---

7 The following reasoning depends on the idealization that all nouns are interpreted rigidly. But see footnote 11.

8 For example, the mapping to partitions that is defined in footnote 10 yields identical results with or without the pathological member in the input.

denotation are about functions whose domains include all the girls, as desired. We can simplify (17) further; the following formulation is equivalent.[9]

(18) $\{p: \exists f\ [\forall x\ [girl_{@}(x) \rightarrow x \in dom(f)\ \&\ picture\text{-}of_{@}(f(x), x)]\ \&$
$p = \lambda w.\ \neg\exists x\ [girl_{@}(x)\ \&\ submit_{w}(x, f(x))]]\}$
$\cup \{\emptyset\}$

In this section, I have gone beyond what was made explicit by Engdahl or (to my knowledge) by subsequent authors who have pursued Engdahl-style analyses of functional questions. The issue of what are the domains of the relevant functions is not normally attended to. Once it is contemplated, however, the story about partiality and presupposition projection that I just laid out seems to be the obvious story to tell. The significance of this point will become clear shortly. In a nutshell, my own proposal will rely even more extensively on presupposition projection. But in light of what we just saw, none of the machinery I must invoke will be new. If it was not machinery that figured explicitly in previous implementations of Engdahl's theory, that was only because those implementations were not fully spelled out.

3 *In situ* interpretation of the restrictor of *which*

A crucial ingredient in the analysis to be advocated now is the position of the restrictor NP of *which* at LF: it is not in its wh-moved surface position but inside the question nucleus and within the scope of the relevant non-wh quantifier (e.g., *no girl*). There are two variants of this assumption. Following Rullmann & Beck (1998), the entire *which*-DP is in the low position (henceforth "*in situ*"). Following Fox (2000), the *in situ* position contains a "converted trace." On both versions, the *in situ* DP is interpreted as a definite description that contains a free variable. This variable is existentially bound from the edge of the interrogative clause, either by a covert existential quantifier, perhaps wrapped into the Q morpheme (Rullmann & Beck), or by the determiner *which* in its wh-moved position (Fox). The choice between the two variants is immaterial to the goals of this paper. For concreteness, I spell out the Foxian version. Before I add counterparts of Engdahl's innovations (ii)

9 It is obvious that (17) is a subset of (18). Let us prove that (18) is also a subset of (17). Let p^* be a proposition in (18). Then there is a function f^* which maps every $girl_{@}$ to a $picture_{@}$ of hers such that $p^* = \lambda w.\ \neg\exists x\ [girl_{@}(x)\ \&\ submit_{w}(x, f^*(x))]$. Consider now the restriction of f^* to girls, i.e., $f^*_G := \lambda x: x \in dom(f^*)\ \&\ girl_{@}(x).\ f^*(x)$. By definition of f^*_G, the proposition p^*_G, defined as $\lambda w.\ \neg\exists x\ [girl_{@}(x)\ \&\ submit_{w}(x, f^*_G(x))]$, is in (17). Since we have $f^*(x) = f^*_G(x)$ for every $girl_{@}$ x, it follows that for all w, $\neg\exists x\ [girl_{@}(x)\ \&\ submit_{w}(x, f^*(x))] \leftrightarrow \neg\exists x\ [girl_{@}(x)\ \&\ submit_{w}(x, f^*_G(x))]$. So $p^* = p^*_G$, and we have shown that p^* is in (17).

and (iii) to cover functional readings, I illustrate the basics with a non-functional *which*-question.

Chomsky's (1995) "copy theory of movement" broke movement down into the operations Copy and Delete. Fox spelled out additional operations that are needed to obtain interpretable operator-variable structures. His mechanism of "trace conversion" interpolates a step between Copy and Delete, the insertion of a binder index (lambda operator) in the immediate scope of the higher copy and a matching variable as a sister to the lower copy. After this, he obtains an interpretable configuration by not only deleting suitable parts of either copy but also inserting the type-shifters IDENT and THE in suitable places.

These mechanisms allow the following derivation for the question *which student did John invite?*

(19) before wh-movement:
$\lambda_p.\ Q(p)\ \lambda_w.$ John invite$_w$ which student$_@$
copy:
$\lambda_p.$ which student$_@$ [Q(p) $\lambda_w.$ John invite$_w$ which student$_@$]
insert binder and variable:
$\lambda_p.$ which student$_@$ $\lambda_x.$ Q(p) $\lambda_w.$ John invite$_w$ [which student$_@$ x]
delete lower determiner and higher NP:
$\lambda_p.$ which $\lambda_x.$ Q(p) $\lambda_w.$ John invite$_w$ [student$_@$ x]
insert type-shifters THE and IDENT:
$\lambda_p.$ which $\lambda_x.$ Q(p) $\lambda_w.$ John invite$_w$ [THE student$_@$ IDENT x]

How is the LF in the final line of this derivation interpreted? The type-shifters **THE** and **IDENT** are defined in (20) and (21). **IDENT x** combines with **student$_@$** by Predicate Modification, and the "converted trace" has the meaning in (22).

(20) $[\![\textbf{THE}]\!] = \lambda P_{et}: [\exists! x_e.\ P(x)].\ \iota x_e.\ P(x)$

(21) $[\![\textbf{IDENT}]\!] = \lambda x_e.\ \lambda y_e.\ x{=}y$

(22) $[\![\text{THE student}_@\ \text{IDENT x}]\!]^g = g(\mathbf{x})$ if $\text{student}_@(g(\mathbf{x}))$, otherwise undefined

The presupposition triggered by **THE** projects and creates partial functions under lambda-abstraction. To complete the computation, the only other thing we need is an appropriate meaning for **which**.

(23) $[\![\textbf{which}]\!] = \lambda P_{et}.\ \exists x_e.\ P(x)$

(24) $[\![\lambda_p.\ \text{which}\ \lambda_x.\ Q(p)\ \lambda_w.\ \text{John invite}_w\ \text{THE student}_@\ \text{IDENT x}]\!] =$
$\{p: \exists x.\ p = \lambda w: \text{student}_@(x).\ \text{invite}_w(j, x)\}$

Two points here deserve attention. First, I chose an unrestricted meaning for *which*, which implies that the upper copy of the NP has to be deleted to obtain an interpretable LF. This contrasts with Fox's treatment of QR, which assumed the standard restricted type (⟨et,⟨et,t⟩⟩) for quantificational determiners, yielding LFs containing both upper and lower copies of the restricting NP. I might have done the same for *which*; there was so far no reason not to. My motivation for choosing an unrestricted *which* will emerge below.

The second point is that I chose a *de re* interpretation for the *which*-NP (in keeping with the general policy to consider only rigid noun denotations; but see footnotes). As a result of this, the partial propositions computed when abstracting the world-variable *w* are again not really partial. Rather, for x such that x is a student in the utterance world @, we have a total proposition, and when x is not a student in @, we have the universally undefined proposition. This is made transparent in the following reformulation of (24), which shows that we have converged essentially on the classical Karttunen semantics.[10]

(25) $[\![\lambda_p.\ \text{which}\ \lambda_x.\ Q(p)\ \lambda_w.\ \text{John invite}_w\ \textsc{the}\ \text{student}_@\ \textsc{ident}\ x]\!] =$
$\{p: \exists x\,[\text{student}_@(x)\ \&\ p = \lambda w.\ \text{invite}_w(j, x)]\} \cup \{\varnothing\}$

10 Since our new syntax also generates *de dicto* construals of the converted traces, this theory is in certain respects closer to Groenendijk & Stokhof (1982) than to Karttunen (1977). The precise relation to Groenendijk & Stokhof's proposal is a topic for a different paper. (See Rullmann & Beck 1998, Sharvit & Guerzoni 2003, for relevant discussion). Here I just observe the existence of a straightforward mapping from the question denotations generated in this paper to the partitions proposed as question denotations by Groenendijk & Stokhof (1982). We can use (i) to let our sets of (possibly partial) propositions induce an equivalence relation (cf. George 2011).

(i) $\sim_Q := \lambda w \lambda w'.\ \forall p\,[Q(p) = 1 \rightarrow [w \in \text{dom}(p)\ \&\ p(w) = 1 \leftrightarrow w' \in \text{dom}(p)\ \&\ p(w') = 1]]$

The partition based on this equivalence relation then is Groenendijk & Stokhof's denotation. For example, for the simple question *Which student did John invite?* we generate not only the *de re* LF that was shown in (25) in the text, but also the *de dicto* LF (ii), which denotes (iii), a set of genuinely partial propositions.

(ii) $\lambda_p.\ \text{which}\ \lambda_x.\ Q(p)\ \lambda_w.\ \text{John invite}_w\ [\textsc{the}\ \text{student}_w\ \textsc{ident}\ x]$

(iii) $\{p: \exists x.\ p = \lambda w: \text{student}_w(x).\ \text{invite}_w(j, x)\}$

Applying (i) to (iii), we obtain the partition which contains a proposition for every set of possible individuals, namely the proposition that all and only the members of this set are students whom John invited.

4 Functional readings

The assumptions now in place already allow us to generate an LF in which the pronoun *herself* in the *which*-phrase in (1) is bound by the quantifier *no girl* in the question-nucleus.

(26) λ_p. which λ_x. Q(p) λ_w. no girl$_@$ λ_y. t_y submit$_w$
[THE picture$_@$ of herself$_y$ IDENT x]

But this is not yet an LF that expresses a functional reading. Given that **x** is a variable of type e, each proposition in the set denoted by (26) is a proposition about an individual, not about a function as we would like it to be.

Suppose we generalize the meanings of **which**, **THE**, and **IDENT** in such a way that they do not by themselves prejudge the semantic type of the variable **x** in (26).

(27) polymorphic **which**, **THE**, and **IDENT**:

a. $[\![\textbf{which}]\!] = \lambda P_{\sigma t}.\ \exists x_\sigma[P(x)]$

b. $[\![\textbf{THE}]\!] = \lambda P_{\sigma t}\text{: } \exists! x_\sigma[P(x)].\ \iota x_\sigma[P(x)]$

c. $[\![\textbf{IDENT}]\!] = \lambda x_\sigma.\ \lambda y_\sigma.\ x{=}y$,

where σ is any type.

Even so, type e is still the only possible type for **x** which allows the entire structure in (26) to be interpreted. After all, the NP headed by **picture** is type ⟨e,t⟩ and as such can only be modified by another phrase of type ⟨e,t⟩. This in turn forces **IDENT** to be type ⟨e,et⟩ and its argument **x** to be type e.

The situation changes if we furthermore allow the insertion of covert pronouns into our LFs. Strategic placement of such covert pronouns can remedy type-mismatches that would otherwise result from exploiting the polymorphic potential of **which**. For example, if we can generate a covert pronoun of type e as sister to the variable after **IDENT**, that variable itself can be type ⟨e,e⟩. After it combines with its sister, we have a phrase of type e that the ordinary **IDENT** of type ⟨e,et⟩ can apply to. Among the numerous interpretable configurations that can be generated by means of this strategy, there is the following LF for our sentence (1).

(28) λ_p. which λ_f. Q(p) λ_w. no girl$_@$ λ_y. t_y submit$_w$
[THE picture$_@$ of herself$_y$ IDENT [f pro$_y$]]

Here **which** has type ⟨⟨ee,t⟩,t⟩, the variable it binds (now written as **f** rather than **x**) has type ⟨e,e⟩, and the complement of **IDENT** contains a covert pronoun of type e which saturates the argument position of **f**. This pronoun also happens to be bound by the quantifier **no girl**.

Needless to say, the two new tricks we have used to generate LF (28) are equivalents of Engdahl's innovations (ii) and (iii). We have a polymorphic *which* like Engdahl, except that ours is unrestricted. And we have "layered traces" (complexes of function-variables and argument-variables), except that ours are integrated into the larger structure of a Fox-style converted trace. Before we worry about the myriad of additional LFs that this enriched theory generates for our example sentence, let us verify that the particular LF in (28) expresses the desired functional reading.

The converted trace triggers a presupposition about the values of **y** and **f**, and lambda-abstraction over **y** yields a partial function.

(29) $[\![$THE picture$_{@}$ of herself$_{y}$ IDENT f pro$_{y}]\!]^{g} = g(\mathbf{f})(g(\mathbf{y}))$
if $g(\mathbf{y}) \in dom(g(\mathbf{f}))$ & picture-of$_{@}(g(\mathbf{f})(g(\mathbf{y})), g(\mathbf{y}))$,
otherwise undefined

(30) $[\![\lambda_{y}.\ t_{y}$ submit$_{w}$ THE picture$_{@}$ of herself$_{y}$ IDENT f pro$_{y}]\!]^{g} =$
λy: $y \in dom(g(\mathbf{f}))$ & picture-of$_{@}(g(\mathbf{f})(y), y)$. submit$_{g(\mathbf{w})}(y, g(\mathbf{f})(y))$

At the next node up, the quantifier **no girl** projects a universal presupposition from its nuclear scope, and we get the following partial proposition after binding the world variable.

(31) $[\![\lambda_{w}.$ no girl$_{@}$ $\lambda_{y}.\ t_{y}$ submit$_{w}$ THE picture$_{@}$ of herself$_{y}$ IDENT f pro$_{y}]\!]^{g} =$
λw: $\forall y$ [girl$_{@}(y) \rightarrow y \in dom(g(\mathbf{f}))$ & picture-of$_{@}(g(\mathbf{f})(y), y)$].
$\neg\exists y$ [girl$_{@}(y)$ & submit$_{w}(y, g(\mathbf{f})(y))$]

As before, because of the rigidity of the nouns, this is either the universally undefined proposition or a total proposition, depending on whether the value of **f** satisfies the presupposition in the actual world. The final result of the computation then is the following set of propositions.

(32) {p: $\exists f$ [$\forall y$ [girl$_{@}(y) \rightarrow y \in dom(f)$ & picture-of$_{@}(f(y), y)$] &
p = $\lambda w.\ \neg\exists y$ [girl$_{@}(y)$ & submit$_{w}(y, f(y))$]]}
$\cup \{\varnothing\}$

Apart from the pathological element, this set contains a proposition for each function that maps all girls to pictures of theirs, namely the proposition that no girl submitted what the function maps her to. It is exactly the same denotation that was derived in the amended Engdahl-theory (with partial functions) in section 2 above, cf. (18).[11]

11 What if we remove the idealization that all NPs are *de re*? As far as I can see, our predicted denotations for functional questions will still collapse into (amended) Engdahl's, though we have

The polymorphic meaning of **which** in combination with the free insertion of covert pronouns predicts countless additional interpretable LFs for the same sentence. To represent the intended functional reading in the LF (28), I picked ⟨e,e⟩ for the unspecified type σ in the entry for **which**, and I chose one covert pronoun that "matched" (i.e., was co-indexed and co-bound with) the overt pronoun in the **which**-phrase. Nothing in the theory forced these choices. σ could be any type, the number of covert pronouns could be different from the number of overt ones, and there need not be any coindexing. Does this system overgenerate readings?

Assuming that covert pronouns (indeed, pronouns generally) come only in a few basic types – let's say here e and s – the choices for σ in the entry of **which** are effectively confined to types of the form $\langle\tau_1,\langle...\langle\tau_n, e\rangle...\rangle\rangle$, where $n \geq 0$ and each τ_i is e or s. The whole type needs to end in e to ensure that the converted trace is interpretable.

---

to go about proving this in a different way. (My reasoning in the text relied on rigidity.) I don't have a general proof, but let me run through a hopefully representative example.

As noted in footnote 3, a better candidate for the LF of (1) within Engdahl's theory might be (i).

(i) λ_p. which $E_{y,w'}$ [picture$_{w'}$ of herself$_y$] λ_f. Q(p) λ_w. no girl$_w$ λ_x. t_x submit$_w$ $t_{f(x)(w)}$

Given our amendment that introduced partial functions, (i) denotes (i′). (This differs from the denotation given in footnote 3, which predated the amendment. I am also using some further abbreviations, e.g., *G(wx)* for *girl$_w$(x)*, and *xw* ∈ *dom(f)* for *x* ∈ *dom(f) & w* ∈ *dom(f(x)).*)

(i′) $\{p : \exists f\, [\forall xw\, [xw \in dom(f) \rightarrow P(w, f(xw), x)]\ \&$
$p = \lambda w{:}\ \forall x\, [G(wx) \rightarrow xw \in dom(f)].\ \neg\exists x\, [G(wx)\ \&\ S(w, x, f(xw))]]\}$

In my theory, too, I can let *which* quantify over functions of type ⟨e,se⟩, generate an additional covert pronoun of type s, and use locally-bound world-arguments for both the nouns *picture-of* and *girl*. This yields the LF in (ii), which denotes (ii′).

(ii) λ_p. which λ_f. Q(p) λ_w. no girl$_w$ λ_x. t_x submit$_w$ THE picture$_w$ of herself$_x$ IDENT f pro$_x$ pro$_w$

(ii′) $\{p{:}\ \exists f\, .\, p = \lambda w{:}\ \forall x\, [G(wx) \rightarrow xw \in dom(f)\ \&\ P(w, f(xw), x)].\ \neg\exists x\, [G(wx)\ \&\ S(w, x, f(xw))]\}$

It is easy to see that (i′) is a subset of (ii′): Given the restriction on f in (i′), the domain of p is equivalently described as in (i′) or (redundantly) as the set of worlds that satisfy $\forall x\, [G(wx) \rightarrow xw \in dom(f)\ \&\ P(w, f(xw), x)]$. It remains to show that (ii′) is also a subset of (i′).

Let p be an element of (ii′), and let f be a function such that

(iii) $p = \lambda w{:}\ \forall x\, [G(wx) \rightarrow xw \in dom(f)\ \&\ P(w, f(xw), x)].\ \neg\exists x\, [G(wx)\ \&\ S(w, x, f(xw))]$.

We can define the following restriction of f:

(iv) $f^- := \lambda x{:}\ x \in dom(f).\ \lambda w{:}\ w \in dom(f(x))\ \&\ P(w, f(xw), x)].\ f(xw)$

Since the definition in (iv) guarantees that f^- satisfies the restrictor of the existential quantifier in (i′), the following proposition p^- is contained in (i′):

(v) $p^- := \lambda w{:}\ \forall x\, [G(wx) \rightarrow xw \in dom(f^-).\ \neg\exists x\, [G(wx)\ \&\ S(w, x, f^-(xw))]$

But $p^- = p$, by the definition of f^-.

As for covert pronouns, let's first consider free covert pronouns and convince ourselves that we needn't worry about those. For example, suppose Mary is sufficiently salient in the context for her to be referred to by a zero pronoun, and the speaker utters *Which book did John read?* Our liberal syntax predicts, oddly, that one possible parse for this surface string could be the LF in (33), which – assuming that the contextually given assignment maps **x** to Mary – denotes (34).

(33) λ_p. which λ_f. Q(p) λ_w. John read_w [THE $\text{book}_@$ IDENT [f pro_x]]

(34) $\{p: \exists f\,[m \in dom(f)\ \&\ book_@(f(m))]\ \&\ p = \lambda w.\ read_w(j, f(m))]\ \} \cup \{\emptyset\}$

Answers to this "reading" of the question should be assertions like *John read Mary's dissertation* or *John read the book that Mary gave him for Christmas*, but not e.g. *John read "War and Peace"*, unless there is some known connection between Mary and "War and Peace" (e.g., it is presupposed that Mary gave "War and Peace" to John for Christmas). The answers predicted appropriate on this reading are intuitively among the possible answers for the question, but we certainly don't feel there is a specific reading of the question that allows only answers about books related to Mary. On the other hand, if we assume, as is common, that quantifiers (including interrogative ones) can be parsed with covert contextually provided restrictors, we already predict anyway that the question has a "reading" that is about books related to Mary. So I suggest that there is nothing to worry about: the additional LFs with free covert pronouns that arise from our innovations for functional readings only duplicate meanings already expressible by simpler LFs.

What about bound covert pronouns that don't match overt bound pronouns in the *which*-NP? As Engdahl (1986) already argued, being able to generate these is desirable. Functional readings exist even in questions without overt bound pronouns. A simplified variant of our original example, *Which picture did no girl like*, still can have answers like 'her graduation picture'. This is captured by the LF in (35), which our system generates.

(35) λ_p. which λ_f. Q(p) λ_w. no $\text{girl}_@$ λ_y. t_y submit_w [THE $\text{picture}_@$ IDENT [f pro_y]]

The reverse case, of overt bound pronouns which do not have matching covert counterparts, is not supported by empirical evidence, but is there evidence that it is impossible? We have already come across a concrete example in LF (26) for sentence (1), where the bound *herself* in the *which*-NP was not matched by a covert argument of the wh-variable. If parsed as in (26), the question should elicit answers that name a particular picture which is presupposed to be a picture of each girl. In this particular example, such a reading may be unavailable for the extraneous reason that there is no such thing as a picture of each girl. (A picture that shows two or more girls is not really a picture "of" any one of them, only a picture of the plurality). Let's change the example to correct this issue and consider the dialogue in (36), which sounds unexceptional.

(36) Which institution in his hometown does every Boston schoolboy visit in first grade? – The Science Museum.

The upshot of this discussion is that I am not aware of any empirical problems with the present system's unconstrained generation of covert pronouns.

5 Comparison with Engdahl's proposal

The present analysis of functional questions is a close relative of Engdahl (1986). The main difference is in the LF-position of the *which*-NP and, relatedly, in the nature of the relation between the bound pronoun and its superficially non-c-commanding quantificational "antecedent". For Engdahl, this relation is indirect: the real binder of the pronoun is a covert operator. On my approach, it is the very same relation that obtains in ordinary cases of bound variable pronouns with c-commanding quantificational antecedents. There are reasons to think this is a good thing. Engdahl's view that *herself* in (1) is not bound by *no girl* creates puzzles which do not arise if it is. My brief discussion in this section may not convince you that the puzzles are unsurmountable, but I hope to convey at least that they are challenging.

Before I elaborate, I hasten to acknowledge that a DP strictly speaking never binds variables. When we say that a pronoun is "bound by" a DP in a run-of-the-mill case of bound-variable anaphora, this is always shorthand for the pronoun being bound by the lambda operator (binder index) which was created by the movement of that DP. Still, Engdahl's analysis denies that *herself* is bound by *no girl* in even this usual, not quite literal, sense. The **E**-operator that binds the pronoun is not the operator created by moving the quantifier; it stands in no syntactic relation with it.

One puzzle that this creates concerns the phi-features (person, number, gender) that we see on the bound pronoun. *herself* in (1) is 3rd person singular feminine, just as it would have to be if it were bound by *no girl*. If we replace *no girl* by a quantifier with different features, we see corresponding changes on the pronoun (always assuming a functional reading, of course).[12]

12 Manfred Krifka (pc) asked about the obligatoriness of this agreement and reported that some speakers also accept functional readings with a non-agreeing, generic, pronoun (e.g. *oneself*). I have not investigated this matter.

(37) Which picture of *himself* did *no boy* submit?

(38) Which relative of *theirs* did *most people* complain about?

(39) Which mistake that *we* have made will *none of us* ever forgive ourselves?

The question for an Engdahl-style approach thus is why the pronoun should agree in phi-features with a DP that doesn't bind it.

Whether this is a real problem depends on what feature agreement in bound-variable pronouns is all about in the first place. If it is all a consequence of the semantics of features (e.g., presuppositions associated with the features that will fail when they don't "agree"), then Engdahl's innovation (i) seems not to hurt. The features on the pronoun will constrain the domain of the questioned function (e.g. to females in (1)). In the nucleus of the question, this function is applied to the individuals quantified over by the pronoun's apparent antecedent, and presupposition failure ensues at this point if the function's domain is too small. There is an on-going debate in the literature about whether the semantic approach to agreement can cover all the data or must be replaced or supplemented by syntactic agreement mechanisms.[13] I cannot do justice to this literature here, but let me draw your attention to example (39) in the list above, which is modeled on cases that are especially challenging for the purely semantic approach (see Rullmann 2008). All I will say here is that, if there are cases that do require a syntactic agreement mechanism, and if these cases can be replicated in configurations of binding reconstruction, then the absence of a real binding relation between the pronoun and its apparent antecedent is problematic.

A more familiar challenge for Engdahl's analysis is the distribution of reflexive vs. non-reflexive pronoun forms. As already observed by Engdahl (1980), whether the pronoun inside the *which*-phrase is reflexive depends on the syntactic relation between the wh-trace and the apparent antecedent.[14] E.g., we can have a reflexive *herself* in (1), where the wh-trace is the object of the clause whose subject is the "antecedent" *no girl*. But if we embed the "antecedent", say, within the subject so that it no longer c-commands the wh-trace, we need a non-reflexive pronoun.

---

13 Kratzer (2009) and Heim (2008) took the latter position, but see Jacobson (2012), Sudo (2012), Sauerland (2013), Podobryaev (2014).

14 Engdahl (1980: 79) made the point with data from Swedish, which distinguishes reflexive and non-reflexive possessive pronouns.

(i) Vilken of $sina_{2,*1}$ / $hans_{1,*2,3}$ bökker trodde författaren$_1$ att alla$_2$ hade läst?
which of self's / his books thought the author that everybody had read
'Which of his books did the author think that everybody had read?'

(40) Which picture of *herself/her did no girl's father choose?

In general, the licensing of the reflexive form depends on where the pronoun was in relation to the apparent antecedent before wh-movement took it out of its scope. But if, as Engdahl's innovation (i) would have it, the apparent antecedent is not the pronoun's binder, why is its position relevant?

Responses that an advocate of Engdahl might make here go in two directions. One direction is to define a notion of "syntactic binding" that is sufficiently different from semantic binding so that the apparent antecedent can be a syntactic binder without being a semantic one. Proposals in this general spirit were elaborated in the 1980s (see e.g. Barss 1986, von Stechow 1990), but are not currently seen to compete insightfully against the more ambitious enterprise (initiated by Reinhart 1983) of basing Binding Theory on an independently established notion of binding that also plays a role in semantics. A more appealing stance for a contemporary Engdahl-advocate is to deny that reflexive pronouns which occur in moved *which*-phrases are ever genuine anaphors in the first place. Instead they may be "exempt" anaphors in the sense of Pollard & Sag (1992) or "logophors" in the sense of Reinhart & Reuland (1993). The contrast between (1) and (40) then has nothing to do with c-command but rather with the fact that (1) invokes the girls' point of view while (40) does not. Without a more precise understanding of the licensing conditions for exempt/logophoric reflexives it is difficult to assess the general viability of this approach. If we look beyond English, however, we find Engdahl-style examples with pied-piped reflexives even in languages whose reflexives don't allow exempt/logophoric uses. The German reflexive *sich* is a case in point,[15] yet we do find German functional questions parallel to (1).

(41) Welches Foto von sich hat keiner an die Wand gehängt?
which photo of self has nobody on the wall hung
'which photo of himself did nobody hang on the wall?'

Finally, denying that there is a binding relation between the pronoun and its apparent antecedent poses a problem for the formulation of the Weak Crossover constraint, if that is another constraint on well-formedness of representations. If, for example, the relevant constraint is that bound variable pronouns must be c-commanded by a binder in an A-position (as maintained by Reinhart 1983 and

15 See e.g. Büring (2005: 242f.). Regardless of the discourse factors that can license logophoric reflexives in English, *sich* without a local c-commanding antecedent is ungrammatical.

(i) John was furious. The picture of himself in the museum had been mutilated.

(ii) Hans war wütend. Das Bild von *sich/ihm im Museum war verunstaltet worden.

defended against counterexamples by Büring 2005), we do not expect the implicit operator which supposedly binds the pronoun in (1) to be capable of licensing it. The formulation of the constraint will need to be revised, and it remains to be seen if this is possible without sacrificing simplicity, and without making it a mere accident that the apparent binder must c-command the trace of the wh-phrase that contains the pronoun.

This was a quick survey of the considerations that militate against Engdahl's innovation (i) and favor instead an analysis that is able to let the pronoun in the fronted phrase of a functional question be bound by its apparent antecedent in the question nucleus.

6 Implications for relative clauses

In this final section, I point out that the current analysis of functional *which*-questions leads inevitably to a head-raising analysis of certain relative clauses. Examination of relative clauses also will help us develop a fuller picture of the distribution of covert pronouns and the structure of converted traces.

Engdahl's approach to functional *which*-questions has been generalized to certain relative-clause constructions.[16] For example, Jacobson (2011) discusses (42).

(42) Every third grade boy invited the (very) woman that no fourth grade boy would invite (namely, his mother).

Her analysis makes use of a version of Engdahl's innovation (i) and treats the head-noun *woman* as a predicate of (woman-valued) functions. Having done away with this innovation, I cannot follow this route. If the head-noun can only be of type ⟨e,t⟩, however, then it can only be modified by a type-⟨e,t⟩ relative clause, and this leads inevitably to a non-functional reading for the sentence. In the LF of the intended reading, then, there cannot be any head noun. The surface head must be interpreted inside the relative clause only. This will free up the relative clause to be a predicate of functions – provided that we permit the article *the* to be polymorphic (see (27b) above). We must moreover allow that there are two covert pronouns: one in the familiar place within the wh-trace, and a second one that is sister to the complex definite description in the matrix clause and bound by the matrix subject. The second pronoun is needed because *invite* selects for an object of type e.

16 Von Stechow (1990), Jacobson (1994, 2002, 2011).

(43) every 3rd-grader$_{@}$ λ_x. t_x invite$_{@}$ [the λ_f. no 4th-grader$_{@}$ λ_y.
t_y invite$_{@}$ THE woman$_{@}$ IDENT f(pro$_y$)](pro$_x$)

In the interpretation of this LF, we encounter an issue related to the uniqueness presupposition of *the*. The argument of *the* here is the set of (partial) functions whose domain includes (at least) the 4-th-graders and which map each 4-th-grader to a woman he didn't invite. There are very many such functions, for two reasons. First, even when we stick to functions with the minimal required domain (i.e., defined *only* for 4th-graders), there are countless ways of mapping people to women they did not invite. Second, each such function can be extended in unlimited ways to a larger domain that may include 3rd-graders and others. Evidently, contextual restriction bears a heavy burden here. This kind of utterance does not make sense unless we understand the speaker to be talking about one of a narrow range of salient or natural functions.

Head-raising and reconstruction must also be invoked in certain complex examples where relative clauses restrict the *which*-DP in a functional question.[17] (44) is a variant of another example from Jacobson (2011).[18]

(44) Which relative of his that every 3rd grade boy invited did no 4th grade boy invite?

Here we must "reconstruct" both the entire complex *which*-DP and the head-NP of the relative clause within it. The converted trace of the *which*-DP has the same internal structure as the complex definite description in the previous example, (42), except for the added **IDENT-g** that makes it a trace. The nucleus of the complete question has essentially the same structure as the matrix sentence (43), including the additional covert pronoun **pro$_x$** that fixes the type-mismatch between the converted trace and the matrix verb.

(45) a. LF of the NP *relative of his that every 3rd-grade boy invited*:
λ_f. every 3rd-grader$_{@}$ λ_y.
t_y invite$_{@}$ THE [relative$_{@}$-of-his$_y$ IDENT f(pro$_y$)]

b. LF of complete question (44), where α abbreviates the structure in (a):
λ_p. which λ_g. Q(p) λ_w. no 4th-grader$_{@}$ λ_x.
t_x invite$_w$ [THE [α IDENT g]](pro$_x$)

17 Of course, this analysis is not required for every relative clause in a *which*-DP of a functional question. We can get away with a standard head-external analysis (and relative trace of simple type e) in examples such as *Which book that he bought did every man read?*

18 Jacobson's paper is not about questions. Her version of the example is a specificational copula sentence: *The relative of his that every 3rd grade boy invited that no 4th grade boy would be caught dead inviting is his mother.*

In summary, the head-raising analysis that we applied to functional relative clauses in this section drew on the same syntactic and semantic machinery as the analysis of functional questions earlier in the paper. But it is fair to say that we had to generalize certain tools in ways that were not already motivated by the run-of-the-mill cases of functional questions that we started out with. Extending polymorphicity to the type-shifters **IDENT** and **THE** was one of these moves. More surprisingly perhaps, we had to deploy covert pronouns with some flexibility to overcome type-mismatches both in the immediate environment of function variables and higher in the structure. As for the head-raising analysis for relative clauses, it is an old idea proposed previously with other kinds of motivation. That it is also needed in the present setting may be seen as further support for it, but also raises further questions that remain to be explored. Predictions that are yet to be checked may arise particularly from the hypothesis that not all relative clauses involve raising and that raising and matching relatives coexist with subtly different properties (Sauerland 2003).

Acknowledgment: Previous versions of this material were presented at the 2005 LSA Institute (with P. Jacobson), classes at MIT over more than a decade (including a fall 2010 seminar with Kai von Fintel and Danny Fox), the Workshop on Reconstruction Effects in Relative Clauses in July 2011 at ZAS in Berlin, and the workshop "Structures of Meaning" in November 2011 at the University of Konstanz. I thank the audiences and organizers of these events for their interest, comments, and patience. I am also grateful for the hospitality and financial support of the Zukunftskolleg at the University of Konstanz, where most of this paper was written. Special thanks go to Danny Fox and Polly Jacobson for many useful questions and comments over the years, and to Polly Jacobson and an anonymous reviewer for comments on the 2012 draft which helped improve the final version.

References

Barss, Andrew. 1986. *Chains and anaphoric dependence: On reconstruction and its implications*. Massachusetts Institute of Technology Doctoral dissertation.

Büring, Daniel. 2005. *Binding theory* (Cambridge Textbooks in Linguistics). Cambridge: Cambridge University Press.

Chomsky, Noam. 1995. *The minimalist program*. Cambridge, MA: MIT Press.

Dayal, Veneeta. 1996. *Locality in wh-quantifications: Questions and relative clauses in Hindi*. Dordrecht: Kluwer.

Engdahl, Elisabet. 1980. *Constituent questions*. Amherst, MA: University of Massachusetts Doctoral dissertation.

Engdahl, Elisabet. 1986. *Constituent questions: The syntax and semantics of questions with special reference to Swedish*. Dordrecht: Reidel.

Fox, Danny. 2000. *Economy and semantic interpretation*. Cambridge, MA: MIT Press.

Fox, Danny. 2010. *Topics in Semantics: Questions*. Class notes, taught at MIT.

George, Benjamin. 2011. *Question embedding and the semantics of answers*. UCLA Doctoral dissertation.

Groenendijk, Jeroen A. G. & Martin B. J. Stokhof. 1982. Semantic analysis of wh-complements. *Linguistics and Philosophy* 5. 175–233.

Heim, Irene. 2008. Features on bound pronouns. In Daniel Harbour, David Adger & Susana Bejar (eds.), *Phi theory: Phi-features across modules and interfaces*, 35–56. Oxford: Oxford University Press.

Heim, Irene & Angelika Kratzer. 1998. *Semantics in generative grammar*. Oxford: Blackwell.

Jacobson, Pauline. 1994. Binding connectivity in copular sentences. In Mandy Harvey & Lynn Santelmann (eds.), *Proceedings of SALT 4* (Cornell Working Papers in Linguistics), 161–178. Ithaca, NY: Cornell University.

Jacobson, Pauline. 2002. Direct compositionality and variable-free semantics: The case of binding into heads. In Brendan Jackson (ed.), *Proceedings of SALT 12*, 144–163. Ithaca, NY: CLS Publications.

Jacobson, Pauline. 2011. *Deconstructing reconstruction*. Talk at workshop "Reconstruction effects in relative clauses", ZAS Berlin.

Jacobson, Pauline. 2012. Direct compositionality and 'uninterpretability': The case of (sometimes) 'uninterpretable' features on pronouns. *Journal of Semantics* 29. 305–343.

Karttunen, Lauri. 1977. Syntax and semantics of questions. *Linguistics and Philosophy* 1. 3–44.

Kratzer, Angelika. 2009. Making a pronoun: Fake indexicals as windows into the properties of pronouns. *Linguistic Inquiry* 40(2). 187–237.

Podobryaev, Alexander. 2014. *Persons, impostors, and monsters*. Massachusetts Institute of Technology Doctoral dissertation.

Pollard, Carl & Ivan Sag. 1992. Anaphors in English and the scope of Binding Theory. *Linguistic Inquiry* 23. 261–303.

Reinhart, Tanya. 1983. *Anaphora and semantic interpretation*. London: Croom Helm.

Reinhart, Tanya & Eric Reuland. 1993. Reflexivity. *Linguistic Inquiry* 24. 657–720.

Rullmann, Hotze. 2008. *Binding and person/number features*. Slides from talk at SALT 18.

Rullmann, Hotze & Sigrid Beck. 1998. *Presupposition projection and the interpretation of which-questions*. Proceedings of SALT 8.

Sauerland, Uli. 2003. Unpronounced heads in relative clauses. In Kerstin Schwabe & Susanne Winkler (eds.), *The interfaces: Deriving and interpreting omitted structures*, 205–226. Amsterdam: John Benjamins.

Sauerland, Uli. 2013. Presuppositions and the alternative tier. In Todd Snider (ed.), *Proceedings of SALT 23*, 156–173.

Sharvit, Yael & Elena Guerzoni. 2003. Reconstruction and its problems. In *Proceedings of the 14th Amsterdam Colloquium*, 205–210. Amsterdam: Universiteit van Amsterdam.

Sudo, Yasutada. 2012. *On the semantics of phi-features on pronouns*. Massachusetts Institute of Technology Doctoral dissertation.

von Stechow, Arnim. 1990. *Layered traces*. Presentation given at Revfülöp, Hungary. http://www.sfs.uni-tuebingen.de/~astechow/Aufsaetze/Revfueloep90.pdf (10 October, 2018).

Pauline Jacobson

Deconstructing reconstruction

1 Goals and Background

This paper has four (related) goals. The first is to show that there is little (if any) solid evidence for a "reconstruction" analysis in relative clauses.[1] Many of the phenomena used to motivate reconstruction have straightforward alternative accounts (within a direct compositional and variable-free framework) (see Section 4). There are others whose account remains open, but these provide no definitive case for

1 Of course one ultimately needs to address the more general question of whether reconstruction is ever needed, and so a more thorough study would concentrate on questions as well as relative clauses, but this is beyond the scope here. But a reviewer of this paper objects that limiting the (main) focus to relative clauses ignores an argument in von Stechow (1996) that potentially argues for a reconstruction analysis in *wh*-questions. A bit of context is needed here. Von Stechow was arguing against an analysis of Nishigauchi (1990) regarding the interpretation of certain Japanese *wh*-questions. In Japanese, the relevant material is – in the 'pronounced' syntax – *in situ* (and not in fronted position). Nishigauchi proposed that there is Pied-Piping at LF of material surrounding the *wh* constituent, just as there is overt Pied-Piping in English; von Stechow shows that Nishigauchi's proposal gives the wrong semantics. In English the immediate force of von Stechow's argument was not about reconstruction *per se*, but rather argued that in Japanese the interpretation of the *wh* material should be in its *in situ* (which is also its pronounced) position. Nonetheless his point naturally extends to an argument for reconstruction in English – i.e., for interpreting Pied Piped material *not* in its pronounced fronted position but in its 'pre-movement' position (in theories with movement). Thus if the Pied-Piped material in English were interpreted in its fronted position *using the type of semantics proposed by Nishigauchi*, we would get the wrong semantics for similar cases in English.
However, this argument does not directly extend to the analysis of Pied Piping given in this paper. Crucially, I will suggest (Section 4.1) that Pied-Piping in relative clauses does necessitate reconstruction since the gap can be a functional gap (i.e., a gap of type $\langle e,e \rangle$); I also will argue that this technique comes 'for free' given certain other assumptions. The use of functional gaps was not considered by either Nishigauchi or von Stechow. Space precludes working out the full semantics of Pied Piping in questions in this paper – and again a full assessment of the reconstruction situation needs to ultimately address whether the analysis extends easily to questions. Nonetheless, since von Stechow's argument against the interpretation of Pied Piped material in the fronted position was crucially directed at one particular analysis that did not make use of functional gaps, it does not directly bear on the general type of analysis being pursued here.

Pauline Jacobson, Brown University

https://doi.org/10.1515/9783050095158-010

reconstruction because reconstruction does not account for the full range of relevant facts (Section 6). The second goal is to show that there is positive evidence for a non-reconstruction analysis over reconstruction in some of the core cases (Section 5). The third goal is a bigger picture one: to demonstrate that the world-view that concludes that we need reconstruction is based on certain entrenched but unnecessary assumptions about how things work. The example of most direct relevance to this paper revolves around the vast amount of literature which assumes – either implicitly or explicitly – that the grammar must reference some relationship between "binders" and "bindees". But the job of the grammar is simply to predict the set of well-formed expressions and pair each with a meaning, and if it can do that without making any reference to such a relationship then all is well. In fact, the viewpoint to be argued for below does not even have any notion of "binders" and "bindees", and there is no reason to think that such notions have any status beyond being convenient terms for the linguist. Once we stop worrying about notions like "binders", indices, etc, the picture changes dramatically and – of relevance here – some of the traditional arguments for reconstruction fall away. Finally, one might wonder: what is wrong with reconstruction? Why go to the trouble to deconstruct it? Perhaps there is no solid evidence for it, but – all other things being equal – is it not, perhaps, just a matter of "taste" as to whether one posits reconstruction or some alternative? I will suggest (Section 2) that it is not just a matter of taste. All other things being equal, we should prefer a direct compositional view of the grammatical architecture, and such a view would lead us to be suspicious of reconstruction.

We begin with some historical background on the notion of reconstruction for relative clauses. The concept was introduced in Chomsky (1977) to account for the observation that Pied Piped material appears to make its semantic contribution in its original pre-movement position. For example, it would appear that the interpretation of (1a) should – like that of (1b) – contain at least *the mother of*__ in the position of the gap, because the object of *invite* is not the student themselves but the mother of the relevant student. (Of course this discussion is informal and depends entirely on how the interpretive procedure actually works, but the intuition is clear.)

(1) a. the student whose mother/the mother of whom Bill invited __

b. the student who Bill invited the mother of __

Chomsky's solution was that *whose mother/the mother of whom* is put back into the position of the gap at LF where it is interpreted (see his rule (38)). (Another – perhaps simpler – view of this in a framework that assumes movement would take the interpretation to precede movement, as was the case in the Generative Semantics literature of the 1960s and 1970s; see Jacobson 2002b for general discussion of this point with respect to related cases.)

Since then, the reconstruction analysis has been expanded and revised in two ways of relevance to the discussions in this volume. The first (which removes the embarrassment of positing that material moves from one position to another and then back again) is to recast reconstruction using the copy theory of movement (see Chomsky 1995, Fox 2000). Assume that when an NP (i.e., "DP") moves it leaves a copy of all of the material minus the determiner.[2] The representation of (1a) (with the version using *the mother of whom*), then, will be roughly (2):

(2) the student [[the mother of $\text{whom}_8]_7$ [Bill invited $t_{7\,-\,\text{mother of whom-8}}$]]

where $[\![t_{7\,-\,\text{mother of whom-8}}]\!]$ on any g is g(7) provided that g(7) $\in [\![\text{mother of 8}]\!]^g$; this is undefined otherwise. Second, reconstruction has also been married to the head movement analysis of relative clauses (Schachter 1973, following unpublished work of Brame 1968). The idea is that – for at least some relative clauses – the head is initially internal to the relative clause. Thus in a simple case like (3a) the trace contains a copy of the head as shown in (3b):

(3) a. the student (who) Bill saw
b. the student (who) Bill saw $t_{8\,-\,\text{student}}$

where again $[\![t_{8\,-\,\text{student}}]\!]$ on any g is g(8) provided that $g_8 \in [\![\text{student}]\!]^g$. (A number of researchers have proposed that there are both head internal and head external relative clauses (see Hulsey & Sauerland 2006 for detailed discussion) and so (3) would have another analysis in addition to the one shown above.)

The question arises as to how Pied Piped material and the head can both be the original occupants of the gap position. Take, for example, a case like (4) where the worldview under discussion here requires this to be a head internal relative clause (since there is "binding" of *his)* and yet there is also Pied-Piping:

(4) The relative of his_i whose dog every man_i hates is his brother-in-law.

In fact, a case like (5) raises the same sort of question, since normally one thinks of the relative pronoun *who* as being the original occupant of the trace position:

(5) The relative of his who every man hates (the most) is is brother-in-law.

The reconstruction story here is that the head *(relative of his* in the examples above) raises from the position of *who* (we can think of the relative pronoun as a kind

2 Following standard terminology in much of the Categorial grammar literature and that of many other theories as well, I will use the traditional term "NP" rather than "DP". Readers should be able to make the obvious translation when needed.

resumptive pronoun copy). In (5), then, the original occupant of the gap position is *relative of his* – this moves to the front of the relative clause. *Relative of his* then moves further into head position, leaving *who* (along with, perhaps, a copy of *relative of his)* in the Spec position of the relative clause. Similar remarks carry over to (4), where presumably the original occupant (and hence copy) of the trace position contains the material *relative of his's dog* (English morphology does not allow this to be represented in a way which could actually be pronounced, but the point should be clear). *Relative of his* then further moves to head position, leaving the resumptive *who* which would combine with the leftover *'s* to give *whose*; this ultimately leaves *whose dog* in Spec position in the relative clause.

2 Why not reconstruction?

Given that the copy theory of movement at least removes the obvious embarrassment of a theory in which material moves and then moves back, is there any reason to doubt reconstruction? Is it ultimately just a matter of taste or religion to try to find alternative accounts of the phenomena for which reconstruction is posited?

Obviously if the non-reconstruction accounts involve considerable complications over the reconstruction alternatives then it might seem like a tortured exercise to pursue them. But if all else is equal then arguably there are *a priori* reasons to prefer non-reconstruction accounts. (I argue below that actually all else is not equal: the non-reconstruction analysis has empirical advantages, but we postpone that discussion.) The general worldview behind these remarks is one which says that the minimal assumptions about how syntax and semantics work together is the direct compositional view (advocated in e.g., Montague 1970 and taken in much work in Categorial Grammar and related theories). Under this view, there is no "level" or representation which feeds the semantics. The syntax is a system proving expressions well-formed – often proving larger expressions well-formed on the basis of smaller ones, and the semantics works in tandem to assign a meaning to each expression as it is "built" (proven well-formed) in the syntax. Note that any theory needs a compositional syntax – i.e., some view of how expressions combine to form larger well-formed expressions and any theory needs a compositional semantics. And so having the two work together is arguably a very natural conception of the architecture of the grammar. Moreover, if this is combined with a fairly impoverished view of possible syntactic operations (one where, for example, the syntax can only concatenate expressions[3]) then the grammar never "sees" structures or representations; representations such as our familiar trees are merely for the convenience of the linguist. They represent the steps used by the grammar to prove an expression well-formed, and are (somewhat crude) representations of how the compositional semantics works, but that is all. Note, incidentally, that the rubric of "surface structure interpretation" is also a misleading characterization of the position being advocated here. The compositional semantics is computed in tandem with the compositional syntax, and it makes no sense to talk about any level that inputs the semantics.

Reconstruction – at least as it is usually conceived – is incompatible with the above picture in two ways. The first is that (whether implemented via Copy theory of movement or the earlier "put material back at LF" view) this is committed to the view that what is interpreted is some level such as LF – the syntax computes a representation which is "sent" to the semantics for interpretation. Crucially, reconstruction relies on the assumption that the actual (pronounced) position of some expression is not where it makes its semantic contribution and so needs a representation at which the relevant material is in that position. Second, at least under the reconstruction views normally posited – the syntax needs not just operations that concatenate expressions but additional movement rules – for it is the pre-movement position of some material that determines its reconstruction representation. (There may be ways to recast this without movement, but I will not explore this here.) Again – all other things being equal, a theory without movement has less apparatus than one with – and we know that for the kinds of cases of relevance here (*wh* constructions) there are well-worked out accounts that do not rely on movement. In this paper I use basically the type of Categorial Grammar account of *wh* constructions discussed in, e.g., Steedman (1987) (with modifications): similar accounts have been explored in the GPSG and HPSG literatures.

---

3 It is well known that only concatenation rules is not enough. I assume that the syntax also allows for infixation rules (dubbed "Wrap" in much of the Categorial grammar literature). This means that the syntax does need to keep track of a very small amount of structure: strings must contain some information as to where material can be infixed. See, e.g., Pollard (1984) for one proposal to this effect.

3 Background: Variable Free Semantics

3.1 Basic mechanisms

Since many of the subsequent remarks assume the account of pronominal "binding" proposed in Jacobson (1999, 2000), I provide here a brief review of the key apparatus. (A non-reconstruction analysis of some of the material here is also developed in Barker 2009, this volume and Barker & Shan 2014). Space precludes a comparison of my approach with that of Barker and Shan; I will primarily limit my remarks to a comparison of my approach to the "standard" reconstruction approach, although see footnotes 5 and 13.) Thus, the variable-free view in Jacobson (1999, 2000) makes no use of assignment functions as part of the semantic apparatus, no use of variables, and no indices in the syntax. Consider the analysis of a simple case like (6); note that the use of indices here and throughout is not meant to imply anything about the grammar but is simply a way to indicate the intended reading:

(6) a. Every 3rd grade boy_i called his_i mother.
b. Every 4th grade boy_i thinks that his_i mother lost.

A pronoun – or an expression containing a pronoun which is "unbound" within that expression – has as its meaning some function from individuals to something else. (I use the term "unbound" here only for convenience. Such a notion has no role in the grammar itself, but I believe is sufficiently clear as to be useful for expository purposes.) Thus ⟦his mother⟧ in (6) is a function of type $\langle e, e\rangle$, and is what we can informally call the-mother-of function (the function mapping each individual to the mother of that individual). I will generally ignore the contribution of the gender feature; strictly speaking this function is $\lambda x_{x \in \text{males}}[\text{the mother of } x]$. A pronoun itself is also of type $\langle e, e\rangle$, and is the identity function on individuals.

The next question to consider is how it is that expressions containing pronouns (or, pronouns themselves) combine in the semantics with others. To deal with the internal composition of an NP like *his mother* requires an irrelevant digression into the semantics of genitives, so we will simply assume that ⟦his mother⟧ is as shown above. However, we can explore the point with respect to the rest of the composition of the embedded S (*his mother lost)* in (6b). The lexical meaning of *lost* is $\langle e, t\rangle$ (here and throughout I ignore intensions), yet it combines with *his mother* of type $\langle e, e\rangle$, so something is needed to allow this. This is easily accomplished with the help of a unary ("type shift") rule that I label **g** (as it is known as the "Geach rule" in much of the Categorial Grammar literature). A unary rule is one that takes as input a linguistic expression (a triple of sound, syntactic category, and meaning) and outputs a new triple, and in this case the phonology remains the same. Here and throughout this paper I will actually ignore the syntax; the full syntax and semantics is rooted in a Categorial Grammar formalism and is spelled out in Jacobson (1999). The semantics of the **g** rule is given in (7). (My use of the notation $\langle a, b\rangle$ is not entirely the standard one; I use $\langle a, b\rangle$ to simply be the set of all functions from a to b rather than the name of a "semantic type", although when I say that some expression α "is of type $\langle a, b\rangle$" I also mean that its meaning (or, its extension) is a function in $\langle a, b\rangle$.)

(7) Given a function f in $\langle a,b\rangle$, $\mathbf{g_c}(f)$ is a function in $\langle\langle c,a\rangle,\langle c,b\rangle\rangle$, where $\mathbf{g_c}(f) = \lambda X_{\langle c,a\rangle}\ [\lambda C_c\ [f(X(C))]]$.

Note that **g** is actually a family of operations since any f in $\langle a, b\rangle$ can be mapped into a variety of functions by **g** according to what is the domain of the domain of the new function (in the above case, c is the domain of the domain $\langle c, a\rangle$ of the new function), and the subscript notates this. Most often, however, we can omit the subscript and I will in general do so. Note too that **g** is simply a unary (i.e., "Curry'ed") version of the function composition operator: $\mathbf{g}(h)(f) = h \circ f$. The idea, then, is that the grammar contains a unary rule allowing any expression to map to one via the **g** rule with no phonological change. (Again the full Categorial Grammar system in Jacobson 1999 also maps the input syntactic category to a different one in the output.)

In the example at hand, *lost* shifts from its lexical meaning of type $\langle e, t\rangle$ to a new meaning of type $\langle\langle e, e\rangle, \langle e, t\rangle\rangle$; this then combines with *his mother* (of type $\langle e, e\rangle$) to give the result below. (I will alternate between $[\![\alpha]\!]$ and α' to indicate the meaning of some expression α; the two are used entirely interchangeably here.)

(8) $[\![\text{lost}]\!] \rightarrow_{g} \lambda f_{\langle e,e\rangle}\ [\lambda x_e\ [\text{lost}'(f(x))]]$
$[\![\text{his mother}]\!] = \lambda y\ [\text{the-mother-of}'(y)]$
$[\![\text{his mother lost}]\!] =$
$\lambda f_{\langle e,e\rangle}\ [\lambda x_e\ [\text{lost}'(f(x))]](\lambda y\ [\text{the-mother-of}'(y)]) =$
$\lambda x\ [\text{lost}'(\text{the-mother-of}'(x)]$

This takes care of the mechanism needed to keep passing up "open slots" that correspond to pronouns which remain free within a given expression. But of course something is also needed to give what we intuitively think of as the "bound" readings, such as the readings indicated by the indices in (6). This is accomplished by one additional unary rule which I have dubbed **z**; the semantics is given in (9):

(9) Given a function f in $\langle a, \langle e, b\rangle\rangle$, $\mathbf{z}(f)$ is a function in $\langle\langle e, a\rangle, \langle e, b\rangle\rangle$ and is $\lambda h_{\langle e,a\rangle}\ [\lambda x_e\ [f(h(x))(x)]]$.

(Both the **g** rule and the **z** rule are given in more general forms in Jacobson (1999) to account for – among other things – the case of 3-place verbs; these generalizations will be skipped here.) Again the idea is that any expression with the right kind of meaning can map to a new one via **z** (with no phonological change but – in the full system – with a new syntactic category as well). In (6a), for example, *called* undergoes **z**. Its lexical meaning is a Curry'ed 2-place relation between individual; its meaning here is a relation between individuals and functions of type $\langle e, e\rangle$ such that to **z**-call some function f is to be an x who ordinary calls $f(x)$. The intuitive notion of "binding", then, is the "merging" of the two e-argument slots by **z**: in this case the subject slot, and the slot which is ultimately occupied by the pronoun *his*. Hence the expression ***z**-call his mother* denotes the set of self's mother callers, which is then taken as argument of the subject. The full derivation of the (6a), then, is shown in (10) (without the syntactic categories):

(10) call; $[\![\text{call}]\!] \rightarrow$ call; $\mathbf{z}([\![\text{call}]\!]) = \lambda f_{\langle e,e\rangle}\ [\lambda x\ [\text{call}'(f(x))(x)]]$
his mother; the-mother-of′
call his mother; $\lambda x\ [\text{call}'(\text{the-mother-of}'(x))(x)]$
every 3rd grade boy called his mother;
  $\text{every-third-grade-boy}'(\lambda x\ [\text{call}'(\text{the-mother-of}'(x))(x)])$

The full derivation of (6b) involves **z** on *think* and so (6b) (on the reading indicated there) ultimately has as its meaning (11):

(11) $\text{every-3rd-grade-boy}'(\lambda x\ [\text{think}'(\text{lost}'(\text{the-mother-of}'(x)))(x)])$

The full generalizations of the **g** rule and the **z** rule also allows the system to handle cases of multiple pronouns and multiple binders, again see Jacobson (1999) for full details.

Finally, note that "free pronouns" are simply instances where **z** has never applied. Take, for example, a simple sentence like *his mother lost*. We have already shown in (8) how this is put together, and this is the end of the story as far as the semantics is concerned. Hence *his mother lost* does not denote a proposition but a function from individuals to propositions; presumably the listener applies it to some contextually salient individual in order to extract propositional information. But it should not really bother us that this does not denote a proposition; on the standard account it also does not directly correspond to a proposition. Rather, it is a function from assignment functions to proposition (and of course *his* comes with an index – let us say 8) and the proposition it denotes depends on what assignment function is chosen. Hence here too the job of the listener is to pick some assignment in order to get a proposition; surely the idea of finding a contextually salient individual is at least as intuitive as is the idea that the listener picks a relevant assignment function.

There is almost no extra apparatus in this view beyond that which is also needed in the standard theory. In fact, it eliminates indices and assignment functions, and builds up the meaning of sentences in a direct compositional fashion. Note too that any theory needs something for binding – the standard account makes use of a step of λ-abstraction in order to "bind" pronouns. So both views need a "binding" rule (here it is **z**) – the difference really is simply that **z** is more local and shifts the meaning of an expression like *called* in (6b) rather than the meaning of t_8 *called* his_8 *mother* as in the standard strategy. The **g** rule is extra in the variable-free system, but it is arguably rather natural. Finally, in the interest of full disclosure, we will need two additional unary rules to be discussed below in order to account for the full range of facts of relevance here, but as will be seen these rules are also simple to state. Nothing else will be needed – no extra levels of representation, no mapping from representations and, indeed, no use at all of "representations". The approach here also has considerable empirical payoffs, to be discussed below.

But first a word about the theoretical status of the notion "binding" and the relationship between *every 3rd grade boy* and *his* in, e.g., (6a). I bring this up because it is relevant to points made in both Barker (2009, this volume) and Heim (2011). As noted earlier, under the approach here there is no actual relationship that one can directly point to in the grammar between "binders" and "bindees" – no co-indexing or any semantic relationship. But there is also no obvious reason why there should be – the truth conditions come out just fine, and this is all the grammar needs to worry about. Note that – as discussed at length in Jacobson (2007) – the standard account also has no direct semantic connection between these two. In the particular implementation of "binding" in Heim & Kratzer (1998), for example, *every 3rd grade boy* "binds" *his* in the sense that it is a sister to the node whose index "tracks" that λ-abstraction abstracts over the index of the pronoun. Certainly one can introduce a definition of "binding" but it is hardly a simple task to do so.

Nonetheless, Heim (2011) suggests that such a move and/or use of coindexation is advantageous for the purpose of feature agreement between "binders" and pronouns. If agreement is syntactic, then perhaps no semantic notion of binding is needed, but feature agreement can easily be tracked by, for example, co-indexation. But while it is true that co-indexing gives a way to accomplish agreement (in *some* cases), it is also true that if the gender on the pronoun is purely a matter of semantics then this is not needed.[4] The full set of issues regarding whether agreement can be handled in the semantics are rather complex, but three points

4 Incidentally, one can build feature agreement into the syntax of the **z** rule if one wanted to. But this does not address Heim's basic objection to the system here which centers on the fact that **z** is supplemented by another rule (**m** – to be discussed below) whose syntax would also have to "track" agreement. I agree that it would be somewhat unhappy to have two separate rules that

are worth noting here. First, it is sometimes claimed that gender features on certain bound pronouns must be done by agreement and hence not semantic (see, e.g., Kratzer 1998, von Stechow 2003, Heim 2008). But a reply to this is given in Jacobson (2012) who provides evidence (centering on paycheck pronouns) for a semantic solution over one using syntactic agreement. Second, while a semantic account of agreement is obviously more challenging for languages with "syntactic gender", it is also well known that co-indexing cannot account the fact that when speaking French and pointing to a chair (with no prior mention of the word *chaise* (*fem*)) one will say *Elle est belle* rather than **Il est beau*. For accounts of this making no use of co-indexing see Dowty & Jacobson (1989) and Culicover & Jackendoff (2005). Whatever device is used to account for the fact that agreement is with the word commonly used to refer to an object can be used for the case of pronominal agreement when the object happens to have been mentioned as well. And third (a related point), co-indexation does not account for other "agreement" facts. It is well known that in cases where a pronoun has, for example, a definite NP as antecedent (as in *The smartest 3rd grade boy loves his mother*) nothing ensures co-indexation between the subject and *his*. They can be non-coindexed (where *his* is free) and still "co-refer". They nonetheless they agree in gender. There is, then, arguably no advantage to coindexation, and thus no reason to assume that the grammar marks some sort of link between "binders" and "bindees". Moreover, the usual understanding of how such a link works – each pronoun can have only a single "binder"; I argue below that this prediction is incorrect. But multiple "binders" for a single pronoun will give us no pause if we stop worrying about a grammatical notion of "binding".[5]

---

track agreement. Fortunately, I think that anyone will need agreement to be semantic and not syntactic.

5 The system in Barker (2009) also makes use of a direct notion of "binding" between binders and pronouns. Barker (2009) contrasts this with the system in Jacobson (2002a) (and other related accounts of some of the phenomena to be discussed herein) by referring to those accounts as making use of "apparent binding". In contrast, Barker (2009) summarizes his account as follows: "the appearance of quantificational binding in reconstruction examples is in fact *genuine binding* [emphasis mine, PJ] brought about by delayed evaluation". I would contend that "apparent" vs. "genuine" binding is not some *a priori* useful notion that is motivated by empirical considerations. It is true that Barker's account uses the same mechanism for "binding" into heads of relative clauses as it does in run-of-the-mill "binding" cases while the approach here uses two different unary rules, but I do think that notions such as "genuine" and "apparent" binding are misleading. The remarks below – particularly in Section 5.2 – concerning cases where there is a single pronoun with two apparent "binders" are, as far as I can tell, problematic for Barker's account as well as for the standard account.

3.2 Some advantages of this approach

3.2.1 Functional questions and their answers

A number of empirical advantages to this approach are documented in Jacobson (1999, 2000), and several other papers; here I review just a few which will be relevant as we proceed. First and very central to the material here – the functional readings of questions and relative clauses comes (almost) "for free". Under the standard approach, the existence of functional readings is really a surprise. Here it is not; with one minor tweak, functional readings are an automatic consequence of the very mechanisms used for "binding" in general. Thus consider the functional reading of a question like (12) (where an appropriate answer is as shown):

(12) Who did every third grade boy$_i$ call (on his first day of school)?
His$_i$ mother.

Groenendijk & Stokhof (1983) and Engdahl (1986) both propose that this is a question about functions of type $\langle e, e\rangle$. Its meaning can be informally represented as in (13):

(13) what is the function f (of type $\langle e, e\rangle$) such that
$[\![$every-3rd grade boy$]\!](\lambda x\ [x \text{ call } f(x)])$

I take their insight to be correct: this is indeed a question about $\langle e, e\rangle$ functions. But notice that in a theory with traces (or some similar device such as that proposed in Engdahl 1986) the existence of this reading is truly a surprise. Recasting Engdahl's mechanisms slightly, it requires positing that there is a complex trace following *call*. We will represent its indices as a function index (where this corresponds to a variable of type $\langle e, e\rangle$) and a second index which will correspond to a variable of type *e*. I'll use *f-i* as the function index, and *x-i* as an individual index, so the trace here might for example be represented as $t_{f\text{-}8/x\text{-}7}$ where *f-8* corresponds to the 8th variable of type $\langle e, e\rangle$ and *x-7* to the 7th variable of type *e*. (One set of mechanisms is spelled out in Chierchia 1992.) Then the compositional semantics is such that the interpretation of this complex trace on any g is $g(f\text{-}8)(g(x\text{-}7))$. The variable *x-7* is then bound in the normal way that any such variable is bound (here, by λ-abstraction over 7); the variable *f-8* is presumably λ-abstracted over when or before the material *every Englishman [t_7 called $t_{f\text{-}8/x\text{-}7}$]* combines with the question word. The full details of that depend on the exact semantic composition of questions, which is beyond our scope here. But the result is that the expression *every 3rd grade boy called* $t_{f\text{-}8/x\text{-}7}$ is $\lambda f_{\langle e,e\rangle}\ [\lambda x\ [\text{every-third-grade-boy}'(\text{called}'(f(x))]]$ and this combines with *who*. Later we will revisit this using the corresponding case with relative clauses and using reconstruction. But even with reconstruction, a functional trace will be used to give the functional reading (see Heim this volume).

Note, though, that nothing in the standard view of binding predicts the existence of complex traces. Note too that Engdahl (1986) points out that the trace can be indefinitely complex, as we have cases like (14) where we would need the trace to correspond to a variable of type $\langle e, \langle e, e\rangle\rangle$ applied to two individual variables:

(14) Q: Which poem did every 3rd grade boy hope that every 4th grade girl would love the best?

A: The one he wrote for her on Valentine's day.

So here the trace would be $t_{w\text{-}8/x\text{-}7/x\text{-}9}$ for w the 8th variable of type $\langle e, \langle e, e\rangle\rangle$, etc.

The existence of functional readings thus came as somewhat of a surprise under the usual view of variables. But in the variable free view, the fact that a "gap" can correspond to a function of type $\langle e, e\rangle$ (and indeed the more complex type in (14) too) follows immediately. It is an automatic consequence of the conventions needed for "binding" in general – the surprise would have been had functional readings not existed. In the simple case in (12), the functional reading is just the result of the application of **z** on *call*. To clarify, I am assuming a movement-less traceless account of extraction along the lines of, e.g., Steedman (1987). For the ordinary (individual-seeking) reading of (12) ⟦every 3rd grade boy⟧ simply function composes with ⟦call⟧ to give λx [⟦every 3rd grade boy⟧(⟦call⟧(x))] which occurs as argument of *who*. (Again, the last step may be different as it depends on just what meaning one gives both to questions in general and exactly what part of that comes from the meaning of *who*; this will not affect the basic discussion here.) But *call* can equally well undergo **z**, and if **z**-*call* instead function composes with *every 3rd grade boy* the functional reading emerges. Hence ⟦every third grade boy call⟧ is predicted to have a second meaning of type $\langle\langle e, e\rangle, t\rangle$ which is λf [⟦every 3rd grade boy⟧(**z**⟦call⟧(x))] (this is the set of functions f that every third grade boy is an x such that x calls $f(x)$). Thus a functional "gap" in this system is an automatic consequence of the fact that the verb can undergo **z** and so expects a functional argument. Put simply, the existence of functional "gaps" is just part and parcel of the existence of "binding" in general. To be fair, we are not entirely home free for the rest of the composition depends in part on how we treat ⟦who⟧. If ⟦every man calls⟧ is argument of *who* then the latter must be polymorphic; it needs to be able to combine with expressions both of type $\langle e, t\rangle$ and of type $\langle\langle e, e\rangle, t\rangle$. But this is true under the standard account as well. (And it might also be that the "polymorphicity" of *who* follows from other facts about the system; see the discussion below about relative pronouns.) The more complex cases – such as that in (14) – is also automatic. A full discussion of these is given in Jacobson (1999); put simply the system allows for multiple binders and multiple pronouns by various applications of **g** and **z** and the interactions of these needed for ordinary pronoun cases automatically gives cases with "complex functions" such as that found in (14). Nothing new is needed for these.

Consider now the answer to a functional question. I dwell on this at some length, as it is relevant to several of the remarks below. As far as I can see, a proponent of the standard view (who also assumes that these involve functional questions) has two choices (either of which involves something extra). The first is to assume that *his mother* is really an "elliptical" utterance – i.e., that short answers are hiddenly full sentences, and so the answer here is not something which directly denotes a function (even though this is what the question asks for), but is rather *Every 3rd grade boy called his mother*. I will call this the Silent Linguistic Material (SLM) hypothesis. This of course is – in any case – quite a popular view of answers; see e.g., Morgan (1973), Merchant (2004) and many others for defense of this position.

But despite its popularity, this view is problematic. In the first place, some conventions are needed as to when material can be "silenced" or "elided"; see Merchant (2004) for one explicit modern account of this. Merchant's proposal is that *his mother* in the answer fronts, roughly (15) has the structure of the answer (I suppress several details in Merchant's full account which are not relevant here):

(15) [His$_i$ mother]$_8$ [~~every 3rd grade boy called t_8~~]

Incidentally, under the copy theory the trace would of course be more complex than shown above I will not flesh this out here as it actually engenders additional complications for the ellipsis view. The question at issue, though, is what allows the strikethrough material above to have its phonology suppressed? In just about all works maintaining the SLM hypothesis, silencing (and/or deletion) is allowed in virtue of some sort of identity with something else in the discourse context. In the case of a question/answer pair, it obviously is some kind of identity with the similar material in the question which I italicize here:

(16) Which woman did *every third grade boy call* $t_{f\text{-}8/x\text{-}7}$?

The literature has gone back and forth on whether the identity condition here (and in other ellipsis constructions) is semantic or formal. While there are reasons to believe it would have to be semantic (see, e.g., Hankamer & Sag 1984, Jacobson 2016), we can be neutral on this here. The point is that neither kind of identity is satisfied in the above pair. This is because the trace in the question is functional, but it is not functional in the answer. (One can make it functional, as will be discussed below – but this simply adds another piece of apparatus, see footnote 6.)

Second, Jacobson (2016) provides several arguments against the SLM view of "short" or "fragment" answers (such as *his mother* in (12)). To mention just one here, consider the short answer in (17b) as opposed to the long reply in (17c):

(17) a. Q: Which mathematics professor left the party at midnight?
b. A: Jill.
c. Reply: Jill left the party at midnight.

The short answer in (b) commits the responder to the belief that Jill is a mathematics professor; this is not true of (c). (In fact, (c) is most natural when preceded by *Well,* and given the FRF intonation discussed in, e.g., Ward & Hirschberg 1985 and which is used here to signal that in fact the listener is not sure that Jill is a mathematics professor.) Jacobson (2016) details that there is no obvious identity condition on ellipsis which will predict this fact about the short answer under SLM. It does, however, follow under the view of question/answer pairs first put forth in Groenendijk & Stokhof (1984) by which the short answer means nothing more than ⟦Jill⟧ and the proposition that Jill left the party at midnight is the consequence of a rule combining the meaning of the question with that of the answer.

But if the SLM solution is indeed incorrect, then *his* in the answer cannot be "directly bound" by *every man.* And so a second possibility – which is much closer to the solution to be taken here – is one suggested in von Stechow (1990), Sharvit (1999) (both for a slightly different case) and Gawron & Peters (1990). This is to allow *his mother* – which denotes an assignment dependent individual – to shift into a functional meaning where it denotes (on any assignment) the-mother-of function. This can be accomplished by a generalized lambda-abstraction rule. Whether or not one thinks that this constitutes something extra depends on just what one believes ought to trigger lambda-abstraction. Be that as it may, notice that there is no co-indexing between *every man* in the question or a copy of it in the answer and *his.* And so there is no real binding relationship, in a theory that insists that such a notion is meaningful.[6] Incidentally, this solution in the analogous case of relative clauses in specificational sentences (to be discussed below) is sometimes referred to as "indirect" or "apparent" binding – for just this reason. But as should be clear, under the variable-free view "binding" has no status of any sort, so "direct" vs. "indirect" binding is a meaningless distinction, and one that has no use.

In the variable-free view advocated here, nothing is needed to predict that *his mother* is a good answer for a functional question. Not only is the functional reading of a question automatic (modulo the open issue about the meaning of *who*) but so is the fact that *his mother* is a good answer to this question. Thus *his*

6 One could have one's cake and eat it too by positing ellipsis combined with a version of the von Stechow/Gawron and Peters/von Stechow solution which allows *his mother* to shift to a function of type $\langle e, e \rangle$ whereby it fronts and leaves a functional trace. This removes the worry about having the answer satisfy the identity condition for ellipsis, but still requires the extra step of shifting the assignment dependent individual ⟦his_8 mother⟧ to an $\langle e, e \rangle$ function.

mother – as noted above – just denotes the-mother-of function; exactly the right sort of type to answer a functional question. As mentioned above, there is good reason to believe that short answers do not contain silent material. One can adopt the view of question-answer pairs first put for in Groenendijk & Stokhof (1984) (see also Ginzburg & Sag 2000 and Jacobson 2016) whereby a question-answer pair is a linguistic unit, and the meaning of the question combines with the meaning of the answer to give a proposition. In that case the question – as already noted – is asking for some $\langle e, e \rangle$ function, and *his mother* by itself in the variable-free view automatically denotes such a function. It is thus the right object to combine with a functional question. These remarks carry over directly to the case of specificational sentences, to which we now turn.

3.2.2 Functional Relative Clauses (and specificational connectivity)

We turn now to a parallel case in the relative clause domain which domain is the central topic of this volume. Before turning in the next section to cases which have been taken to motivate reconstruction, we first look at specificational sentences where the pre-copular constituent contains a relative clause and which are analogous to the case of functional questions. Here too – with just one extra device – the variable-free apparatus provides the relevant tools with no further ado. Thus consider the unexpected "connectivity" effect in a specificational sentence like (18):

(18) The woman (who) every 3rd grade boy called (on his first day of class) is his mother.

First a word about the semantics of specificational sentences. I will be treating this as if *be* is polymorphic but simply means "=" ; it equates two things of the same type. But this is largely for expository convenience. Many authors have had the intuition that there is something akin to a question-answer pair in specificational sentences, and I agree with this. (See, for example, Ross 1985 and Schlenker 2003 among others.) The precopular constituent raises a question, is a concealed question, or names a question under discussion – and the post-copular constituent supplies an answer. For those committed to the view that answers themselves contain silent linguistic material, this means that *his mother* in (18) is elliptical (for *every 3rd grade boy called his mother)*. But as was discussed above, there is good reason to doubt the ellipsis analysis of answers in general (see Jacobson 2016), and so even though (18) may well be quite similar to a question/answer pair, the "binding" of *his* is not via some silent/deleted "binder".

But, as discussed in Jacobson (1994), Sharvit (1999) and others, this is similar to a functional question/answer pair as in (12) – here we just have a functional relative clause. Take first the ordinary individual reading for an NP like *the woman who every 3rd grade boy called* – which is brought out in an ordinary case like (19)

(19) The woman (who) every 3rd grade boy called (on his first day of class) finally decided to turn off her cell phone.

Using again the general account of extraction here, this can be put together by having *every 3rd grade boy* function compose with *call* as above. Leaving aside the contribution of the relative pronoun (more on that below), we will assume here that this combines with ⟦woman⟧ by intersection.[7] As to the functional reading that emerges in (14), this is quite similar to what we see above with functional questions. *every 3rd grade boy* can function compose with **z**-*call* to give a set of functions, exactly as in the question case. The only "trick" here is that this of course cannot directly combine with ⟦woman⟧ by intersection; the relative clause denotes a set of functions of type $\langle e, e\rangle$ while ⟦woman⟧ is a set of individuals. But this is easily remedied with the addition of one unary (type-shift) rule letting ⟦woman⟧ to shift to the set of functions whose range is ⟦woman⟧ (Jacobson 1994; Sharvit 1999). It is true that an extra rule is needed here (and one which, as will be shown below, is avoided under reconstruction). But it is sufficiently simple that this does not seem to be a serious defect in the analysis. As to the rest of the analysis, it assumes that *the* is polymorphic (as it would be in any account). Here it takes the set of functions f (of type $\langle e, e\rangle$) with range women such every 3rd grade boy z-called f, and returns a single such function – the unique or most contextually salient one. And *his mother* automatically denotes a function of the right type. Continuing to probably oversimplify the semantics of specificational sentences (in a way which is harmless here), *is* equates the two functions. (See appendix for two refinements on this.)

Again, then, the variable-free view already contains in place most of what is needed to get functional readings for the precopular NPs in specificational sentences and to get the functional reading for the postcopular NP as well. This not only provides some initial motivation for the variable-free view but – as shown below – is quite central to "reconstruction" cases with relative clauses, because those cases which involve apparent "binding" into the head are intimately tied in to the analysis of functional relatives.

---

7 Here and throughout I assume an analysis in which the relative clause combines with the head noun (rather than the noun + determiner). It is well known that a compositional semantics can be given either way (using domain restriction for the latter); nothing in my discussion really hinges on the outcome of this debate.

3.2.3 ATB Binding

One of the most elegant results of Categorial Grammar (and related theories) is its ability to handle Right Node Raising (RNR) constructions without any kind of movement, ellipsis, or mechanisms by which two separate constituents are somehow "merged" into one. (These remarks hold for ATB movement in general.) Consider (20):

(20) Every third grade boy called but every fourth grade boy ignored the principal (on the first day of summer vacation).

As discussed in Dowty (1988), *every third grade boy* can function compose with *call* to give the expression *every third grade boy called* with meaning λx [every-third-grade-boy$'$(call$'$(x))]. Similarly for *every fourth grade boy ignored*. Since each of these denote sets of individuals, they can intersect (via the meaning of *and* or *but*) and then *the principal* is taken as argument of that function.

But there are also cases with "ATB binding". Many of the examples from here on out will become more natural with the help of a running scenario: the Boys School scenario. As in the examples above, the 3rd grade boys are still quite dependent on their mothers. But boys grow up and want to break away, and so in our scenario throughout this paper the 4th grade boys all are in that breakaway phase where they think they hate their mothers or at least try to distance themselves. In our scenario, consider the following case of "Across-the-Board" binding which is discussed in von Stechow (1990), Jacobson (1996, 1999), Munn (1999) and others:

(21) Every third grade boy called but every fourth grade boy ignored his mother (on Mother's Day).

Here we seem to have one pronoun but two "binders" – something quite unexpected under any view positing some kind of grammatical relationship (of the usual kind) between binders and bindees. But (21) is straightforward under the above CG analysis of RNR combined with the variable-free apparatus sketched above. This is exactly analogous to (20) except that both *call* and *invite* have undergone **z**. Hence ⟦every third grade boy called⟧ is λf [every-third-grade-boy$'$(λx [x call $f(x)$]]) and similarly for ⟦every fourth grade boy ignored⟧. These two intersect (via the meaning of *and* or *but*) and ⟦his mother⟧ is the argument of this.

There are, of course, various things one could try in the standard theory. If there is ellipsis, there really are two different instances of *his*. Alternatively, one can extent the functional question analysis as is done in von Stechow (1990) and Munn (1999). Arguments against these strategies are detailed in Jacobson (1996, 1999). But in any case the variable-free account here provides is a good example of the kind of advantage that comes from not worrying about "binders" and "bindees";

we get the truth conditions just right with no further ado. Additional cases where there appears to be two "binders" for one pronoun will become central in Section 5.

4 Reconstruction arguments: Two initial cases

With this background, we turn to some of the classic arguments for reconstruction – both of the Pied-Piped material and of the head – and show that they are straightforward without any kind of reconstruction.

4.1 Pied Piping semantics does not require reconstruction

There is no problem getting the right semantics for (1a) without reconstruction; this was shown already both in Sharvit (1998) and in Jacobson (1998) (Sharvit's account is not framed within a variable-free semantics but embodies the same idea; I will use the variable free version here). The basic premise in this account is that a relative "pronoun" is indeed a pronoun like any other – as such it is of type $\langle e, e\rangle$ and denotes the identity function over individuals. This means that an expression like *the mother of whom* has the same meaning (modulo the gender on the pronoun) as *the mother of him/his mother* – it is a function of type $\langle e, e\rangle$ and denotes the-mother-of function. Of course a full syntax is needed to predict that this kind of expression can occur at the front of a relative clause (as also can an ordinary pronoun like *who*); I will not spell out the syntax here, but it can be modeled in large part on the treatment of relative clause syntax and *wh*-features in Gazdar et al. (1985).

The compositional semantics is unproblematic. The key point to note is that **z** is not the only operation which would allow the "gap" corresponding to the object position of *invite* to be of type $\langle e, e\rangle$. **g** could just as well apply to *invite* which also allows for an object gap of type $\langle e, e\rangle$. Notice, then that **g**(call) is of type $\langle\langle e, e\rangle, \langle e, t\rangle\rangle$. For reasons having to do with the syntax of the system **g**(invite$'$) cannot directly function compose with the type-lifted subject *Bill* of type $\langle\langle e, t\rangle, t\rangle$ (this would give a wrong meaning, but the syntax is set up in such a way that this derivation is impossible and hence there is no worry about the system overgenerating). Rather, type-lifted *Bill* itself will undergo **g** also. This is to be expected, "gaps" introduced by **g** are "passed up" by each would-be function undergoing **g**, and this is exactly what happens here. The derivation of the inner part of the relative clause is thus shown in (22).

(22) $\mathbf{g}(\text{call}') = \lambda f_{\langle e,e \rangle}\ [\lambda x\ [\text{call}'(f(x))]]$
$\text{Bill}' = \lambda P\ [P(b)]$ of type $\langle\langle e,t\rangle,t\rangle$,
hence **g** maps this to something of type $\langle\langle e,\langle e,t\rangle\rangle,\langle e,t\rangle\rangle$, where:
$\mathbf{g}(\text{Bill}') = \lambda R_{\langle e,\langle e,t\rangle\rangle}\ [\lambda y\ [\lambda P\ [P(b)](R(y))]] =$
$\lambda R\ [\lambda y\ [R(y)(b)]]$
$\mathbf{g}(\text{Bill}') \circ \mathbf{g}(\text{call}') = \lambda f\ [\lambda R\ [\lambda y\ [R(y)(b)]](\lambda x\ [\text{call}'(f(x)])] =$
$\lambda f\ [\lambda y\ [\text{call}'(f(y))(b)]]$

This then is of type $\langle\langle e,e\rangle,\langle e,t\rangle\rangle$. As noted above, *the mother of whom* is a function of type $\langle e,e\rangle$, and so if the above applies to that fronted material we get the set of individuals whose mother Bill called – exactly what we want. (This intersects with the head.) There is, then, no need to "reconstruct" the fronted material into the gap position or posit that it is ever there for the purpose of interpretation. The gap – thanks to **g** – is a "missing" object of type $\langle e,e\rangle$; the-mother-of function is right to be argument of the expression *Bill called* (when both *Bill* and *call* undergo **g**). The idea that the relative pronoun has the same semantics as an ordinary pronoun is also not particularly strange, and thus the entire analysis requires nothing additional.

This does have one interesting consequence: it means that even for a simple relative clause like *the student who(m) Bill called* we also have a "functional" gap – i.e., a gap of type $\langle e,e\rangle$. This is because *who(m)* itself is a pronoun and thus of type $\langle e,e\rangle$. But the derivation will be exactly analogous to the Pied-Piping case above. The only difference is that here *Bill called* – whose meaning is again $\lambda f\ [\lambda y\ [\text{call}'(f(y))(b)]]$ – takes as argument $[\![\text{who(m)}]\!]$ which is the identity function on individuals. In the end, the meaning of *who(m) Bill called* is $\lambda y\ [\text{call}'(y)(b)]$, as expected.

4.2 Binding into heads does not require reconstruction (of head material)

One of the main arguments given for reconstruction in *wh*-questions and in relative clauses is the "binding" of a pronoun in the wh phrase and in the head of a relative clause (note that for the relative clause case, the reconstruction account goes hand-in-hand with a head raising account of relative clauses). The standard sort of data pulled out for these discussions is cases like (23) and (24):

(23) Which picture of herself did every woman like the best?

(24) The picture of herself that every woman liked the best was her graduation picture.

But these examples actually conflate two separate issues which should be teased apart. The first is simply how to get the "bound" reading on the pronoun, and for that we could just as well use examples without a reflexive, such as those in (25) and (26) (I give here only the relative clause versions);

(25) The relative of his that every third grade boy invited (to the promotion ceremony) was his mother.

(26) The woman he once knew that no man would dream to invite to his second wedding is his ex-wife.

The second issue concerns the fact that a reflexive is found here; there is thus – under a certain set of assumptions – a question about how to satisfy the formal conditions which allow reflexives in the complement of certain relational nouns like *picture of*. Following Warshawsky (1965) I will refer to these as Picture Noun Reflexives (PNRs). It is often assumed that such reflexives require a coindexed NP which both c-commands the reflexive and is within some local relationship to the reflexive. Just exactly what is the right locality condition differs in different accounts. But the argument for reconstruction assumes that the only way *herself* can satisfy the syntactic conditions on its distribution is for it, at some level, to be locally c-commanded by *every woman* in (23) and (24). This of course happens if the condition is sufficiently generous that it does not target *herself* in its "surface" (raised) position but requires only that at some level it – or a copy of it – is in the right position and if it (or a copy of it) is in the gap position (via copy theory and head raising) at the relevant level.

I want to set aside until Section 6.1 the question of the syntactic constraints on Picture Noun Reflexives. For now we consider only the semantic issue: how to allow a pronoun in the head to have the "bound" reading. While this does not, unfortunately, come entirely for free in the variable-free program from the mechanisms sketched above, it is easy to account for the relevant reading with just one more unary ("type-shift") rule. Surely one wants to limit the number of such rules, but the rule to be proposed here is not complex; it is the minimal way that one could map a function of type $\langle e, \langle e, t\rangle\rangle$ to a set of functions of type $\langle e, e\rangle$. We will, moreover, see in the next section that there is evidence for this type of strategy over the "reconstruction" strategy.

Thus note that under the variable-free account, *relative of his* will (like *relative)* denote a function of type $\langle e, \langle e, t\rangle\rangle$; similar remarks hold for *who he loves*. (To actually show how *who he loves* is composed up to give this meaning requires a full syntax and some generalization of the rules above to give the interaction of "extraction" and pronouns; see Jacobson (1999) for the full details.) We have already seen that the head *woman* can shift to a set of functions of type $\langle e, e\rangle$, and that *who every 3rd grade boy invited* can (if *invite* undergoes **z**) also denote a set of functions of type $\langle e, e \rangle$. I am assuming that the two relative clauses are stacked and that, therefore, *who he loves* should also be a function of type $\langle e, e \rangle$. And, if *relative of his* is the head, we want the same thing. The question, then, is whether there is some obvious way to map a two place relation between individuals to a set of functions of type $\langle e, e \rangle$. Indeed there is. To see this, imagine deCurrying the $\langle e, \langle e, t \rangle \rangle$ function to a set of ordered pairs. Then take all subsets of that set which are functions. This is all that is needed: that result is exactly the set of functions of type $\langle e, e \rangle$ that gives the right semantics. In Jacobson (2002a) I dubbed this **m**, and it is spelled out formally here:

(27) Let F be a function of type $\langle b, \langle a, t \rangle \rangle$. Then $\mathbf{m}(F)$ is a function of type $\langle \langle b, a \rangle, t \rangle$ such that $\mathbf{m}(F) = \lambda h_{\langle b,a \rangle} [\forall x_{x \text{ is in domain of } h} [F(x)(h(x))]]$, where h is a partial function from b to a.

We then allow any expression whose meaning is of the right type to map to another one with no phonological change by **m** (again I ignore the syntax here). Hence an expression such as *relative of his* of type $\langle e, \langle e, t \rangle \rangle$ can map to a set of functions. Note that – if one insists on using the term "binding" – the "binding" of a pronoun by **z** is different than that which is done by **m** – but since this notion plays no role in the grammar there is nothing problematic about this result. (See the Appendix for a reply to some arguments against this strategy.)

With this apparatus, we have no difficulty giving a compositional semantics for (25) without use of reconstruction; we show this below. (I am assuming a stacking analysis of relative clauses where recursion is on the (possibly complex) N rather than NP. Other analyses are possible, but most alternatives that come to mind will not affect the main points here.)

(28) $[\![\text{relative of his}]\!] = \lambda x\, [\lambda y\, [\text{relative-of}'(x)(y)]]$

$\mathbf{m}([\![\text{relative of his}]\!]) =$

$\lambda h_{\langle e,e \rangle}\, [\forall z\, [\lambda x\, [\lambda y\, [\text{relative-of}'(x)(y)]](z)(h(z))]] =$

$\lambda h_{\langle e,e \rangle}\, [\forall z\, [\text{relative-of}'(z)(h(z))]]$

in prose: the set of (possibly partial) functions h of type $\langle e, e \rangle$ such that for all z, $h(z)$ is a relative of z (so, this includes functions like *the-mother-of* function, *the-brother-in-law-of* function, etc.)

The rest of the computation of the relative clause is straightforward. Assuming the usual stacking structure, this set will; intersect with the set of functions with range $[\![\text{woman}]\!]$; that result in turn intersects with the set of functions f such that every man z-loves f, and then this combines with *the*. (26) is similar; the interested reader can verify that or consult Jacobson (2004) for details.

4.3 The interaction of Pied piping and binding into heads does not require reconstruction

Recall the discussion in Section 1 surrounding (4):

(4) The relative of his_i whose dog every man_i hates is his_i brother-in-law.

Here we have a pronoun in the head ensuring that – under the standard view – this must be a case of a head internal relative clause. Yet we also have Pied-Piping and so – in the standard view – *whose dog* must originally be in the position of the gap. We saw that this means that the original occupant of the gap is something like *(the) relative of his's dog* where the entire phrases moves to Spec position of the relative clause, and then *relative of his* presumably raises out of this (leaving something like *whose* perhaps as a copy).

Under the view here, there is nothing special about this case. It merely involves having both a functional relative clause and Pied Piping, and there is no reason to be surprised by the existence of this combination (indeed, the surprise would be if this didn't exist). The easiest way to show the point is to walk this case backwards, for in fact all we need to say about (4) is essentially what we would say for the case of a simple functional relative clause (like (29)) once we folded in the contribution of the relative pronoun.

(29) The girl who every third grade boy called (on Valentine's Day) is his girlfriend.

Recall first that a simple relative clause (in the non-functional reading) like *the woman who Bill called* is semantically composed in much the same way as a non-functional Pied-Piping case like *the woman the mother of whom Bill called* is. ⟦the mother of whom⟧ is of type $\langle e, e\rangle$ just as is ⟦the mother of him⟧; the Pied Piping semantics is possible because *Bill invited* can undergo **g** to be of type $\langle\langle e, e\rangle, \langle e, et\rangle\rangle$. Whether it combines with *the mother of whom* or *who*, the same result will happen. The key is that relative pronouns – like other pronouns – have a lexical meaning of type $\langle e, e\rangle$ and can be the argument of something like **g**(*Bill invited*) which is of type $\langle\langle e, e\rangle, t\rangle$.

The functional case in (29) follows directly from the observation that pronouns in general (and hence relative pronouns too) can have a higher type which is needed for "paycheck" pronouns. And in fact the analysis of paycheck pronouns illustrates another advantage of the variable-free approach; for the "paycheck" reading of pronouns comes essentially for free from the general apparatus. Thus let us digress momentarily to consider a case of a paycheck pronouns as in (30) (on the relevant reading).

(30) Every 3rd grade boy loves his mother. Every fourth grade boy hates her.

Here *her* is a paycheck pronoun – a pronoun exhibiting "sloppy identity". As detailed in Jacobson (2000), the existence of paycheck readings for pronouns is another nice benefit to the variable-free apparatus. For this reading comes for free and is entirely expected. (A caveat is in order here: the syntactic conventions given in Jacobson 1999 need to be generalized to fully account for this case, but there is no difficulty in doing so; see Jacobson 2000 for discussion.) As discussed above, the lexical meaning of *her* is the identity function over individuals: it is of type $\langle e, e \rangle$. But it can undergo **g** to be of type $\langle\langle e, e \rangle, \langle e, e \rangle\rangle$, and **g** applied to the identity function over individuals yields the identity function over functions of type $\langle e, e \rangle$. So "paycheck" *her* is **g**(⟦her⟧); its meaning is $\lambda f_{\langle e,e \rangle}\ [f]$. (The interested reader can compute that this is indeed just the result of applying **g** to $\lambda x_e\ [x]$.) In the end, then *every fourth grade boy hates her* contains what we think of as a free pronoun. But here it is not an ordinary pronoun (or type $\langle e, e \rangle$) but a functional pronoun (of type $\langle ee, ee \rangle$). As with any other free pronoun a "slot" is passed up by **g** throughout, and the final meaning of *every fourth grade boy hates her* (on the paycheck reading) is a function from functions f of type $\langle e, e \rangle$ to the proposition that every fourth-grade boy **z**-hates f. In other words, everything is the same as the derivation of *every fourth grade boy hates her* with *her* a free individual pronoun modulo the higher types. Thus the semantics in this case delivers λf [every-4th-grade-boy$'$(**z**-hates$'$(f))]. As with free pronouns in general, this is applied by the listener to something salient in the context; here the discourse makes the-mother-of function salient, and the paycheck reading results.

With this in mind, we see that (29) can be derived by *who* (like any paycheck pronoun) having undergone **g** to have the higher type $\langle ee, ee \rangle$ (following the notational convention in Heim & Kratzer (1998) I will eliminate the innermost brackets when it makes things clearer). As to what happens in the derivation of *every third grade boy calls*, there is more than one equivalent derivation. Perhaps the simplest to exposit is the following. ⟦every-third-grade-boy⟧ function composes with **z**(call$'$) giving the set of functions that every third grade boy **z**-called (so this is of type $\langle ee, t \rangle$ But now that can undergo **g** in such as way as to introduce a new $\langle e, e \rangle$ slot – so this maps to something of type $\langle\langle ee, ee \rangle, \langle ee, t \rangle\rangle$. The higher ("paycheck") type for *who* is right to be argument of this. The same exact thing happens in a parallel case which happens to involve Pied Piping, such as (31) ((4) above is similar, but we will show the point with (31) to be parallel to (29)):

(31) The girl the mother of whom every third grade boy called (on Mother-in-Law Day) is his girlfriend.

We sketch the derivation of (31) in (32a) below (switching to *every boy* to reduce clutter). (29) is the same, except that the material at the front of the relative clause is the identity function of type $\langle ee, ee\rangle$; the last part of the derivation of this is given in (32b):

(32) **z**(call): is of type $\langle\langle e,e\rangle\langle e,t\rangle\rangle$ and is: $\lambda f_{\langle e,e\rangle}$ [λx [x call $f(x)$]]
every-boy **z**(call) = every-boy ∘ **z**(call) =
$\lambda f_{\langle ee\rangle}$ [every-boy$'$(λx [x call $f(x)$])]
$\mathbf{g}_{\langle ee\rangle}$ [every-boy **z**(call)] =
$\lambda T_{\langle ee,ee\rangle}$ [λg_{ee} [$\lambda f_{\langle e,e\rangle}$ [every-boy$'$(λx [x call $f(x)$])($T(g)$)]]] =
$\lambda T_{\langle ee,ee\rangle}$ [λg_{ee} [every-boy$'$(λx [x call $T(g)(x)$]]]]

a. the mother of who (with higher type of who) =
$\lambda f_{\langle ee\rangle}$ [λy [the-mother-of($f(y)$)]] (note: this of type $\langle ee, ee\rangle$)
the mother of who(m) every boy called =
$\lambda T_{\langle ee,ee\rangle}$ [λg_{ee} [every-boy$'$(λx [x call $T(g)(x)$]]]
($\lambda f_{\langle ee\rangle}$ [λy [the-mother-of($f(y)$)]]) =
λg_{ee} [every-boy$'$(λx [x call $\lambda f_{\langle ee\rangle}$ [λy
[the-mother-of($f(y)$)]](g)(x)]]] =
λg_{ee} [every-boy$'$(λx [x call the-mother-of($g(x)$)]]

b. who (higher type) = $\lambda f[f]$
who every boy called =
$\lambda T_{\langle ee,ee\rangle}$ [λg_{ee} [$every-boy'$(λx [x call $T(g)(x)$]]]($\lambda f[f]$) =
λg [every-boy$'$(λx [x call $g(x)$])]

So *the mother of whom every third grade boy called* on the functional reading is the set of function which are such that every boy is an x who called the value of that function applied to x. Then this can intersect with the set of functions whose range is ⟦girl⟧ which, when combining with *the*, is then the unique salient function with range girl which is in the set above; and the copular sentence says that the girlfriend-of function is this function. The case where the head is complex and happens to contain a pronoun, as in (4) is not different; in this case there just is an additional intersection with the set of functions mapping each person into a relative of his.

5 Problems with reconstruction

I have shown that at least two of the classic arguments for reconstruction – Pied Piping and binding into heads – are handled without reconstruction given the variable-free program for binding, a program which appears to have considerable independent motivation. Moreover, I have argued in Section 2 that – all other things being equal – there is reason to prefer the direct compositional, non-reconstruction approach. Of course, it is difficult to know for sure which approach in the end has more apparatus until full and explicit fragments are constructed for both. But on the face of it the direct compositional non-reconstruction approach certainly has no obviously more apparatus, and an arguably simpler conception of the architecture of the grammar. But there are also empirical problems with the reconstruction view of the domain here – problems which are entirely avoided under the approach suggested here; we now turn to these.

5.1 Why no individual reading?

Let us return to cases like (33); in (b) there is a pronoun but there is none in (a); similar pairs can be constructed with functional questions:

(33) a. The woman who no third grade boy would dream to call is his mother.
b. The relative of his that no third grade boy would dream to call is his mother.

The affinity between these and functional questions/answer pairs like (12) is quite clear, and I will take it for granted that a proponent of head raising/copy theory would treat (33) in analogous way such that the precopular constituent has a functional reading (We leave aside the question of how to treat the representation of *his mother*; this was discussed already in Section 3.2.2.)

I assume that the functional reading for the precopular expression is derived as follows. The trace is complex, and hence in (33a) it is $t\text{-}f(7)(x\text{-}8)_{woman}$ and in (33b) it is $t\text{-}f(7)(x\text{-}8)_{relative\text{-}of\text{-}8}$. I assume the following convention on interpretation of functional traces:

(34) $[\![t_{f\text{-}i/x\text{-}j\,-\,N}]\!]^g = g(f\text{-}i)(g(x\text{-}j))$ provided that $g(f\text{-}i)(g(x\text{-}j)) \in [\![N]\!]$
(for "*N*" some noun, possibly complex)
(undefined otherwise)

So the value of a functional trace such as $t\text{-}f(7)(x\text{-}8)_{woman}$ is $g(f\text{-}7)(g(x\text{-}8))$ provided that this individual is a member of [[woman]] and undefined otherwise. Similarly $t\text{-}f(7)(x\text{-}8)_{relative\text{-}of\text{-}8}$ is $g(f\text{-}7)(g(x\text{-}8))$ provided that individual is in the set of relatives of $g(x\text{-}8)$ and is undefined otherwise. Similarly, a complex functional trace like *relative of his-7* would be

(35) $[\![t\text{-}f_7/x_8]\!]^g = g(f\text{-}7)(g(x\text{-}8))$ provided that $g(f\text{-}7)(g(x\text{-}8)) \in [\![\text{relative-of } g(x\text{-}8)]\!]$

The "win" for this over the variable-free view is that the contribution of *woman* requires no shift on *woman* and no use of **m**. (Of course it requires the use of complex traces, along with all of the other machinery of the reconstruction analysis.)

The rest of the analysis, however, is presumably analogous to the one under the variable-free view. *Woman (who) no third grade boy would dream to call* denotes a set of functions, and *the* is polymorphic and maps this set to the unique (or most) contextually salient member.

But – while this view avoids rules shifting the meaning of the heads – there is no reason under the reconstruction view why the trace in "reconstruction" cases would have to be a functional trace. And hence there is no reason why the "binding into head" phenomena seem to go hand in hand with functional readings; this does not occur with ordinary individual readings. To clarify, consider (36a) and (36b):

(36) a. The woman that he_i invited that no 3rd grade boy liked came to the class party.
b. The relative of his that no 3rd grade boy liked came to graduation.

(36a) is not good on the "bound" reading. (This claim is discussed in detail and questioned in Kuhn 2010, but even though Kuhn does provide a semantics for the individual reading, he acknowledges that whether or not it exists is unclear. Most informants seem to think it does not.) Put differently, it cannot have the meaning given by the paraphrase in (37):

(37) The woman that no 3rd grade boy both liked and invited came to the class party.

And (36b) does not have the reading paraphrased in (38):

(38) The person that no 3rd grade boy both likes and is related to came to the class party.

Yet these readings should be available under reconstruction, as will be documented momentarily.

A caveat is in order. It is known since Doron (1982) that there are surprising cases like (39) in which *every* does appear to "bind" a pronoun in the head:

(39) The picture of herself/her dog that every woman likes the best sits on her dresser.

Under the proposals in this paper, (39) will remain unaccounted for. But it should be noted that it takes a number of special circumstances to get this phenomenon. First, the phenomenon exists with *every* but not with *no* (or at least they are considerably worse with *no*):

(40) * The picture of herself/her dog that no woman likes gets buried in her dresser drawer.

Second these are much better in generic-like sentences like (39) (which often allow for additional kinds of "binding"). Thus (41a) is worse than (39), and if one can stretch to get (40) this becomes much worse in (41b):

(41) a. ? The picture of herself/her dog that every woman liked was posted last month on her facebook page.

b. * The picture of herself/her dog that no woman liked was removed last month from her facebook page.

And finally, these almost demand a pronoun in the object; they deteriorate significantly without that

(42) ?* The picture of herself/her dog that every woman likes the best was chosen to hang in the museum.

(42) cannot mean "for every woman it is the case that her favorite picture of herself/her dog is was chosen for the museum display", even though this is a perfectly sensible and pragmatically felicitous meaning.

So consider again (36b) (*The relative of his that no third grade boy liked came to the graduation*). Suppose that the trace just happens to be an individual trace rather than a functional trace (nothing at all should force a functional trace), where (43) is the full representation:

(43) [The relative of $\text{his}_8]_7$ [that no 3rd grade boy liked $t_{7\,-\,\text{relative of his-8}}$] came to the party.

$[\![t_{7\,-\,\text{relative of his-8}}]\!]$ on any *g* is *g(x-7)* provided that *g(x-7)* is a relative of *g(x-8)*. The interpretation of the full relative clause involves λ-abstracting over *7*, such that this will denote the set of individuals which are such that no 3rd grade boy is an *x* such that *x* likes him/her restricted to relatives of *x*. The material makes no contribution in the head position (indeed it cannot because then *his* would also be interpreted as a free variable which would seem to wreak havoc with the semantics); *the* combines with this to give the unique such person. This is a perfectly sensible meaning. But it does not exist. So some convention is needed to link binding in the heads with functional traces; there is no obviously independently motivated way to do this. Notice again that this problem does not arise in the account here. The "binding" of the pronoun is tied in with the application of **m**, this creates a set of functions and this can combine sensibly with the head only when that too is a set of functions. (Independently, Barker and Heim (personal communications) have both pointed out to me that individual readings *do* seem to exist in cases like this as long as the relevant NP is in a specificational sentence, as in *The professor of hers that no student ever criticized was Jorge Hankamer*. But in fact this is still amenable to a functional analysis, where the post-copular constituent is simply a constant function, mapping everyone to Jorge.)[8]

5.2 One pronoun – two "binders"

5.2.1 Bound upstairs and down

Consider (44) – which, like the ATB binding case (20) in Section 3.2.3 – involves two different "binders" for one pronoun. (All of the material in parentheses is put here to make the sentence more natural but is irrelevant to the analysis, so will be omitted in subsequent discussion).

(44) Every third grade boy invited the (very) relative of his that no fourth grade boy would (dream to) invite (namely his mother).

Even without the addition of *namely his mother*, this sentence has a perfectly good functional reading and the *his* in the head is simultaneously bound by *every third grade boy* and by *no fourth grade boy*. Of course it also has a reading (perhaps not the most salient one) in which *his* is bound only by *every third grade boy*, and it merely says that for each mom of a 3rd grader, no 4th grade boy would invite her. But this is not the reading of interest here; the reading of interest here is where every 3rd grade boy invites his own mother, but being a self's mother inviter is something no 4th grade boy would do.

---

8 A referee points out that although my analysis does not admit of the particular individual reading under discussion here, it seems to have a somewhat parallel problem. The referee makes the point with respect to the cases under discussion here, but their point is more general and can be made with respect to a simple case like (i) that does not involve "binding" into heads

(i) The woman that no man wants to see came to the party.

The query that the referee raises is this. Since *the woman that no man wants* can – under the system discussed above – denote a function of type $\langle e, e\rangle$, and since *came to the party* can undergo **g** so as to combine with this, (i) would be a function of type $\langle e, e\rangle$ which could then be applied to some contextually salient individual, say Joe. In other words, in the right context, it would say that the function f which is such that for no man y, y wants to see $f(y)$ came to the party, $f(\text{Joe})$ came to the party.

While this is not the obvious reading for (i), it seems to me that indeed this is a possible reading. Consider he scenario in which Joe is looking very despondent, and I ask you why. You answer 'well, because the very woman that no man wants to see came to the/his party'. Let's suppose that you and I know that that function is the 'ex-wife-of' function; I can easily understand your answer and infer that Joe's ex-wife showed up at the party. It is, admittedly, easier to get if followed by something like *namely, his ex-wife*, but even if that continuation is required to bring out the functional reading, that does not change the fact that the functional reading does exist.

I don't see any obvious way to put this all together under the standard account – at least not if one is committed to the idea that there is some tight relationship between "binders" and "bindees" (and that this plays a role in, for example, agreement). The problem is that if the head is raised and leaves a complex (functional) trace – so as to have *no 4th grade boy* bind *his* – then *every third grade boy* cannot also bind *his*. In fact, before pursuing this in detail, there is an even simpler problem. Even if the head did not happen to contain a pronoun, these can have functional readings, but in standard view functions of type $\langle e, e\rangle$ cannot be the object of, e.g., *invite*. So some "hidden variable" needs to be supplied to be argument of the relevant function.

To walk through this more explicitly, consider a simpler case of a functional NP as in (45):

(45) Every third grade boy invited the (very) woman that no fourth grade boy would invite (namely, his mother).

(A related case was discussed already in Groenendijk & Stokhof 1983; they point out the existence of examples like *Every man loves someone – namely, his mother.*) Here we have a functional NP and a "variable" which is argument of that function, where that variable is bound by *every third grade boy.* Of course once again this has a reading where for each 3rd grade boy, no fourth grade boy would invite the 3rd graders' mother, but again this is not the reading at issue. The reading we are after is the functional interpretation, which entails that no fourth grade boy would invite his own mother. Focusing our attention only the object NP itself – *the woman that no fourth grade boy would invite* – we already do know how to give that a functional reading. Let the trace in the embedded clause be a complex functional trace, let the head *woman* reconstructed in the trace position, and let *the* pick a unique function from a set of functions. This is no different than what happens for the case of the precopular NP in the specificational sentence in (33a). The problem is – what allows for a function to occur as object of *invite*?

Recall that in the variable-free view this is no mystery; *invite* can be **z**(invite), allowing a functional object. But the standard view will have to assume that there is a silent pronoun which serves as argument of the function. That mechanism will indeed allow the relevant reading. But – aside from the need for an extra mechanism above and beyond what is needed for binding in general (and above and beyond the "reconstruction" mechanism) – such a move undermines any victory that can be claimed by having a correspondence between "binders" and "bindees". The "bindee" in the matrix clause is the silent pronoun that is the argument of the woman-function, while in the relative clause it is the individual variable supplied as part of the complex trace in the relative clause. Of course there is no reason to worry about that fact for (45); the catch comes in the case of (44) where the only argument for saying that *his* in the relative clause is co-indexed with its "binder" is that this accounts for agreement. But in (44), *his* would be co-indexed with (and "bound" by) the 4th grade boy, and bear no "binding" relationship to the matrix 3rd grade boy. If this is to account for, say, gender agreement, nothing in the story being told here would block the following on the relevant reading:

(46) * Every 3rd grade girl invited the (very) relative of his that no fourth grade boy would (dream to) invite.

Of course a semantic account of gender pronouns (as is being assumed here) will succeed in blocking (46) and can be maintained under the standard account. The point, though, is simply that there is no real advantage then to having a co-indexation or some other relationship between "binders" and "bindees".

5.2.2 Stacking

An even more interesting problem arises for the case of stacked relatives. We also find the 2-binders phenomena in (47):

(47) The relative of his that every 3rd grade boy invited that no 4th grade boy would be caught dead inviting is his mother.

I will assume without argument that the right structure for these is a stacking structure, where these modify the head *relative of his*. The problem here is not just there are apparently two "binders" for one pronoun, but in fact the types do not come out right in order to give a straightforward semantics for this (on the reading in question).

Here is a sketch of the problem. In order for the entire subject NP to have a functional reading (as is required by the semantics of the whole sentence), the relative clause *that no fourth grade boy invited* needs to contain a functional trace (leaving out the "copied" material, call that $t_{f\text{-}8/x\text{-}7}$). The head material which is in this trace position via head raising and copy theory of movement is *relative of his*$_7$ *that every 3rd grade boy*$_7$ *invited*. Incidentally, I have used the index 7 here both on *his* and *every 3rd grade boy* and also on the individual-argument of the functional trace. This is somewhat irrelevant; 7 will be bound entirely within the interpretation of *every man invited t* so there is actually no connection between those two occurrences of "7". In theories with indices there are complex questions about whether one can "accidentally reuse" indices (see, e.g., Heim 1997) but it does no harm to do that here. One can substitute in a different index if one prefers.

Since the trace following *no fourth grade boy invited* is a functional trace, this means that the value of that trace (which is $t_{f\text{-}8/x\text{-}7}$) is as follows. On any g, $[\![t_{f\text{-}8/x\text{-}7}]\!]^g$ is

$g(f\text{-}8)(g(x\text{-}7))$ provided that that individual is indeed a member of the set denoted by *relative of his that every third grade boy invited* on g (and it is undefined otherwise). So now let us compute the value of *relative of his that every third grade boy invited*; this is the entire head which is raised from the fourth grade boy trace position. Given what is said above, it must be of type $\langle e,t\rangle$. Indeed we can put this together such that it is of type $\langle e,t\rangle$, but only if the trace following *invite* here itself is not a functional trace. So, suppose that that trace is an individual trace. What this means is that the 3rd grade boy clause is *every third grade boy*$_7$ *invite* $t_{9\text{-}relative\ of\ his\text{-}7}$. Thus $[\![t_{9\text{-}relative\ of\ his\text{-}7}]\!]^g$ is $g(9)$ provided that $g(9)$ is a relative of $g(7)$. Thus the entire relative clause *that every third grade boy invited* $t_{9\text{-}relative\ of\ his\text{-}7}$ characterizes the set of individuals such that every 3rd grade boy is an x who invited y and y is a relative of x. This is actually then the unwanted "individual" reading that we saw above was blocked in general. Aside from the fact that this reading actually does not seem to exist (one can walk through the rest of the composition to see that it results in a nonexistent reading), it certainly is not the reading we are after here. We don't care about individuals who are relatives of every 3rd grade boy; we care about the set of functions f such that every 3rd grade boy invited the value of that function applied to himself.

And so of course what we really want is a functional trace in the third grade boy clause. That is, we want *relative of his that every third grade boy invited* to be represented as *relative of his*$_7$ *that every third grade boy*$_7$ *invited* $t_{f\text{-}8/x\text{-}7\ -\ relative\ of\ his\text{-}7}$. (Again I have recycled the index "8" on the functional trace here and in the fourth grade boy clause. This does no harm; each will be λ-abstracted over separately.) I won't repeat the details of how this is put together since this was done earlier. Basically, though, the relative clause part (*that every third grade boy ...*) will involve lambda-abstraction over the function part of the trace (and *relative of his* need not shift but will be entirely interpreted in the trace position), and this does indeed give the set of functions f such that every third grade boy is an x who invited $f(x)$. All well and good, but now this is of type $\langle\langle e,e\rangle,t\rangle$, not of type t. Since this is the head material from the fourth grade boy trace position, this is not of the right type to be a restriction on the value of the complex trace in the fourth-grade boy clause. I will not speculate here on how this can be fixed (I leave this to native speakers of reconstruction), but clearly something more is needed to get the parts to compose up properly.[9]

9 One might be tempted to posit that this is not a case of stacking but that these are conjoined relative clauses with a silent *and* between them. This, then, would reduce the problem of "two binders" with one pronoun (here, *his*) to the problem of how to do this in a case of ATB extraction in general. But there is no evidence that *and* can be silent when conjoining two relative clauses and

Notice that this is entirely unproblematic in the variable-free non-reconstruction view advocated here. The meaning of *relative of his* (after the application of **m**) is $\lambda f\ [\forall x\ [x \text{ is a relative of } f(x)]]$. The meaning of *every 3rd grade boy invited* is the set of functions that every third grade boy z-invited. And the meaning of *no fourth grade boy invited* is the set of functions that no fourth-grade boy z-invited. These all intersect, in the normal way that stacked relatives are put together, and we end up with the unique (contextually salient) such function in the intersection of these three sets. The mother-of function is then said to be that function.

5.3 Multiple relatives with multiple binding patterns

The final problem that I see for reconstruction is one that I will just sketch here; full details are spelled out in Jacobson (2002a). Consider (48):

(48) The woman who he loves who every 3rd grade boy invited (to graduation) is his mother.

In the variable free treatment each relative clause gets its meaning independently of the other. The semantics of *who he loves* involves an application of **m**, the semantics of *who every 3rd grade boy invited* involves **z** on *invite*. Both then denote sets of functions of type $\langle e, e\rangle$. The head noun *woman* shifts in the way discussed earlier to also denote a set of functions. All three sets ultimately intersect, with the set denoted by *woman* first intersecting with *who he loves* and then that result with the second relative clause (as dictated by the stacking syntax). Given the fact that each relative clause meaning composes up independently to denote a set of functions, there is no reason why their order could not be interchanged. And indeed interchanging them is fine:

---

not when conjoining (just two expressions) of any other category. Note too that stacked relative clauses in which the second relative has no *wh* word nor *that* are bad:

(i) a. The candidate that Newt voted for who/that Sarah (had) endorsed lost.
 b. * The candidate that Newt voted for Sarah (had) endorsed lost.

And sure enough the phenomenon in question here is not good if the second relative contains no overt *wh* or *that*, while parallel cases with an overt *and* are fine:

(ii) a. The relative of his that every man invited and no sane person should have invited is his most obnoxious uncle.
 b. * The relative of his that every man invited no sane person should have invited is his most obnoxious uncle.

(49) The woman who every 3rd grade boy loves who he invited to graduation was his mother.

(49) at first blush is problematic for the head raising analysis of the "binding" of *he*. As discussed earlier, head raising + copy theory is intended to account for the "binding" of *he* in the first relative clause in (48); *woman he loved* is in the position of the trace (presumably it raised by the two steps of raising to Spec position occupied by *who* and then raised from *who* to head position). But then what about *he* in (49)? There is no obvious way that head raising/copy theory accounts for this.

Now for this case there is a conceivable solution. Perhaps (49) is not a case of stacked relatives. Rather, perhaps here *who he invited* is an extraposed relative, extraposed from the position of the trace following *loves*. The full syntactic and semantic composition would need to be spelled out, but one can imagine that under such a view it is reasonable to suppose that *he* is "bound" by *every 3rd grade boy* (or it might be that extraposed relatives also leave a copy and it is the copy of *he* that is bound).

But there are more complex cases. Recall Engdahl's observation with respect to functional questions that there can be two binders and two pronouns (see the discussion surrounding (14)). These remarks carry over to functional relatives: there can be two binders and two pronouns. Interestingly, we can have a "mix and match" case where one binder is in one relative clause and the other binder in the other. To set the context and help disambiguate via the gender on the pronouns, imagine a Linguistics Department in which all of the syntax professors are female and all of the students in the syntax courses are male. Each student is taking several syntax classes, and each syntax class requires a series of squibs. In such a context (50) – while perhaps not the most elegant of sentences – is fine (I use __ as a theory neutral device to illustrate the "gap" position):

(50) The squib that every student handed in __ to her that every syntax professor gave him the highest grade on __ is the last one he handed in to her.

The reconstruction explanation for the "binding" of the pronoun in (48) combined with the extraposition explanation for (49) cannot get both pronouns bound. If the relative clauses are stacked, then *her* in the first relative clause has left a copy in the gap position following *on* – and *every syntax professor* can "bind" *her*. But then there is no way for *him* to be bound. If, on the other hand, this is a case involving an extraposed relative, then *that every syntax professor gave him a C on* is extraposed from the position of the first gap (the one following *in*) and *him* can successfully be bound. But then there is no way for *her* in the first relative clause to be bound.

The story does not quite end here: two more points need to be made before we can claim victory for the non-reconstruction story. First, Heim (2011) points out that this version of the problem uses *every* in both relative clauses. But we do know independently that there are special circumstances under which NPs with *every* have unexpected "binding" properties; see the discussion of the Doron example in (39). Heim's challenge, then, is to construct a parallel example with *no* in both NPs. But indeed I believe this is possible, as in (51):

(51) The (only) assignment that no student had handed in to her that no syntax professor was inclined to excuse him for was the one that was supposed to show that he understood her own theory.

While I grant that (51) is a bit hard to process, much of that is independent of the problem at hand here. It is difficult in any case to construct stacked cases with two *no*-NPs in subject position, and difficult in any case to construct multiple binders of the Engdahl type. But modulo those problems (51) certainly does not seem to be jibberish and seems quite understandable with enough contextual support. I see no way, though, that a reconstruction story of binding can possibly account for this sentence.

To be fair, though, we need to be sure that the variable-free account can indeed get (51). As it turns out, this is actually not automatic with only the formulation of **m** given above. So we acknowledge that more is needed. First, **m** needs to be defined recursively to apply in cases like these where there are additional "open slots". Details of this are given in Jacobson (2002a) but we can note that this type of recursion is both quite simple to state and is in any case needed throughout the system (see Jacobson 1999 and Jacobson 2014 for relevant discussion). Second (and again we leave out the full details here) **m** needs to be extended to cover 3-place relations, and so can be extended as follows:

(52) Let R be a function of type $\langle e, \langle e, \langle e, t \rangle \rangle \rangle$.
Then **extended-m**$(R) = \lambda f\ [\lambda y\ [\forall x\ [R(x)(f(x))(y)]]]$.

While this type of extension does not introduce any new type of machinery, it does admittedly add complexity into the system. Nonetheless, it is compatible with the general approach here, and under reconstruction it is not obvious as to how any analysis can be given for (51).

6 Other arguments for reconstruction

The discussion above deals with a series of examples surrounding functional readings of relative clauses (and NPs) and the binding into the heads (and also Pied-Piping) showing that these are all amenable to non-reconstruction analyses quite fine, and that for at least a group of facts the non-reconstruction story seems to do better. But there are other arguments that have been given for a reconstruction (plus head raising) analysis of relative clauses. While I cannot deal with all of these here, a brief tour through some will hopefully suffice to make the point that reconstruction is neither well motivated nor a very good solution for some of the puzzles.

6.1 Reflexives in "picture nouns"

One of the standard cases in support of reconstruction stems rests on the claim that "picture noun reflexives" (PNRs) must be locally c-commanded by a "binder". This is exemplified in (53), where it is assumed that the head must be (or have a copy) in the trace position to license the PNR:

(53) The picture of himself that Mitt liked the best was published on his website.

Note that the logic here is somewhat different from the case of pronominal "binding" (it is unfortunate that the term "binding" is used both for the syntactic conditions on the licensing of reflexives and for the completely separate semantic notion). The problem under consideration here does not revolve around how to give a meaning for (53). Rather, here the argument for reconstruction stems from the assumption that *himself* (or a copy thereof) must be locally c-commanded by *Mitt* in order to be licensed. We should also note that there are two separate potential claims: (a) that a PNR needs only to be c-commanded by a co-indexed NP, or (b) a PNR must be locally c-commanded by a coindexed NP (in some sense of local whose precise definition varies among different authors).

But there are certainly many who have argued that there simply is no c-command condition (let alone a local one) on PNRs. This is well documented in, for example, Zribi-Hertz (1989) and Pollard & Sag (1992) who support the idea first put forward in Kuno (1975) that the conditions have to do with "point-of-view" conditions within a discourse. Indeed counterexamples to a c-command condition can be found as early as Jackendoff (1972), and examples like (54) show that no co-indexed NP is necessary within the same sentence:

(54) John was really upset. That picture of himself that had hung in the museum had been stolen.

While the full set of conditions on PNRs is perhaps not completely understood, the claim that these require condition on local c-command (which would in any case be completely stipulative) is not a solid one.

Let us consider some additional facts. First, it is well known that we also get sentences like (55):

(55) John thought that the picture of himself that Mary liked the best was actually quite ugly.

A defender of the syntactic constraint approach could say one of three things about this. One is that it involves head raising but that the condition on PNRs is just c-command, not local c-command. A second is that this also involves head raising, but that the conditions are actually "anywhere" conditions (in derivational terms) or are "any member of a chain" (in representational terms). Put differently, while the copy of *picture of himself* in the trace position is not in a position for the reflexive to be licensed, the moved material *picture of himself* does enter into the relevant relationship with *John* and so the entire "chain" is licensed. A third is that not all relative clauses involve head raising; some have external heads, and this is a case of an external head. The third position is the most obvious one in light of much of the work advocated by reconstructionists, see, e.g., Hulsey & Sauerland (2006) who argue for the existence of both head internal and head external relative clauses in English.

I will not address the first two positions here; the facts below are consistent with either of these but I am not sure that there is anyone who actually maintains those positions. The third solution is probably the one more likely to be maintained by modern reconstructionists, so we turn to that here. Interestingly, this can be eliminated as a possible explanation for (55) by showing that a case like (55) can be expanded in such a way that – under the view of reconstruction – the head has to actually be a head-raised (hence head internal) case. This would be to combine it with the case of a bound pronoun. So consider (57) in context of the scenario in (56):

(56) Mary is a well known high priced prostitute with whom a number of male congressmen have liaisons. For future blackmail purposes, Mary uses a hidden camera to take pictures of herself with each of her johns. She always makes sure to take one of herself with him in her red satin bed, another of herself with him in her large swimming pool, another with herself and him on his yacht, etc. She does realize that a clever congressman might be able to cook up some explanation for some of these, but:

(57) She thinks that the picture of herself with/and him that no candidate would be able to "explain away" is the is the one (of them together) in the red satin bed.

The point should be clear: to get the "binding" of *him* this would have to be a head internal relative clause case. But then we would need a different story as to why *herself* is licensed in the head raised relative. There are, as noted above, solutions available but require some revisions to the usual assumptions. In any case, the claim that PNRs require a c-commanding 'binder' is at least controversial and hence arguments for reconstruction based on PNRs should be approached with caution.

6.2 Principle C effects

Another kind of evidence that has been used for reconstruction revolves around so-called "Principle C" violations. For the case of relative clauses, the situation is complicated by the claim that there are both head internal and head external relative clauses so we will instead consider the situation with respect to questions. Thus it is commonly claimed (see, e.g., Schachter 1973) that sentences like (58) are bad; I put a * here to reflect that common wisdom without any commitment as to the actual facts.

(58) * Which picture of John_i/John's_i mother did he_i decide to post on his Facebook page?

The logic, of course, is that under reconstruction the trace position will contain a copy of the lexical material *picture of John/John's mother*; this will be c-commanded by a co-indexed pronoun and so Principle C is violated.

There are a number of reasons to be skeptical of this argument for reconstruction. In the first place, I question the robustness to the judgment that this is bad. While all of these so-called Principle C violations depend somewhat on context, (58) certainly has none of the strangeness of something like (59) (out of context):

(59) ?* He_i decided to post the picture of John_i/John's_i mother at Base Camp on his Facebook page.

Second, although (58) is reputed to be bad, it has been known since at least as early as Postal (1970) that similar cases with a relative clause are fine:

(60) Which picture that portrays John_i/John's_i mother did he_i decide to post on his Facebook page?

There is a well-known story in the literature regarding the purported contrast between (58) and (60) (Lebeaux 1988). This is that adjuncts (such as relative clauses) can be merged in later in the derivation. If correct, this means that the grammaticality of (60) is attributed to the fact that the relative clause (*that portrays John/John's mother*) is introduced as a sister to *picture* only after the *wh* phrase *which picture* has fronted. Hence *John/John's* is never c-commanded by the pronoun. But arguments (such as the complement of a picture noun) cannot be merged in late and so *John/John's mother* in (58) must be in the base position before head raising applies, giving rise to a violation (since the copy of *John('s)* will be in the trace position). Here too, though, I believe that some systematic checking of the facts is in order. Over the years I have informally consulted with a number of students, none of whom find (58) to be significantly worse than (60). In fact, when presented with (58) and (60) in an admittedly unsystematic informant check, most people prefer (58). I don't think that there is anything significant about the fact that (58) seems *better*: I think that the improvement comes from the irrelevant fact that it is unnatural to talk about pictures "portraying" things (one would just use the more natural "picture of" construction). Nonetheless, if there were a serious syntactic principle at work. that should override the slight unnaturalness of (60), and informants should find (60) still better. (This is especially true if the reason for the awkwardness of (60) is that it competes with (58); if (58) is bad then (60) should seem less strange.) Again I leave it to future research to systematically check these facts since my own informant work has been quite unsystematic and informal, but it is hardly obvious that informants with no theory at stake get the contrasts described above.

For the sake of argument, however, suppose that the facts are as often reported. There is still a potential problem with using these purported effects as evidence for reconstruction – at least under some views of how to account for the full range of Principle C effects. The problem begins with the well-known observation that a constraint on co-indexation is not enough. Consider first a run-of-the-mill Principle C case like (59). As noted at least as early as Reinhart (1983) a constraint on co-indexation does not actually rule this out. For the pronoun here can be a "free" pronoun that happens to pick up the (contextually salient) individual John, yet still – without a lot of special circumstances – this is impossible. This would lead us to believe that the whole effect is not on structure but on some kind of information packaging – as Kuno (1975) suggested – but then there is no reason to come to the conclusion that (58) – even if it were bad – needs to share a structure with (59).

Again, though, let us assume (since the literature often seems to) that (58) really is bad and that some facts about structure are crucially involved in this. The usual solution, then, to the fact that "accidental coreference" is blocked in (59) (even without coindexing) is to posit a competition based principle. The basic idea is that the relevant reading of (59) – with or without co-indexing – would be blocked in virtue of a preferred way to say this, which is (61);

(61) John decided to post the picture of him/his mother at Base Camp on his Facebook page.

(61) allows for the relevant reading via binding; here *him/his* can be "bound" by *John*. So assume that the constraint blocks coreference (including "accidental

coreference") between a pronoun and a non-pronominal NP if there is another sentence with the same meaning/understanding which involves binding. (This is stated loosely here; indeed a full formalization is not easy and there are empirical problems with such a constraint which center on strict and sloppy readings, but the goal here is to be as charitable as possible to see if this kind of logic can lead to an argument for reconstruction.) Notice that this type of principle has to be a constraint on the processor: the grammar does not deliver the "accidental coreference" reading (under most views of where the grammar leaves off). The grammar itself only delivers an analysis of, e.g., (59) where the pronoun and *John* do not share an index. It is up to some principle of processing to access the competitor (61) and use its existence to block the relevant understanding of (59). Hence a proponent of the competition-based explanation of this domain needs to show some independently motivated facts about processing which are applicable here. To my knowledge, this has not been done; it is odd to think that a processor will care about blocking a reading that doesn't involve "binding" on the basis of the existence of a different sentence which does involve "binding". This is especially true in view of the fact that even under the standard view "binding" is a complex and derivative notion.

Leaving these worries aside, consider how this will extend to (58) (under the assumption that this really is bad). The copy theory of movement/reconstruction blocks the relevant reading with co-indexing or "accidental coreference" because of competition with (62); (62) in turn allows for "binding" of *him/his* under the reconstruction story:

(62) Which picture of him/his mother did John decide to post on his Facebook page?

The problem is that once one factors in a competition based explanation for the badness of the run-of-the-mill case (59) (and for the purported badness of the "reconstruction case" in (58)) the Lebeaux explanation for the *goodness* of (60) is undermined. The reason is that nothing in the theory in which the whole story at issue is embedded *requires* late merger; early merger is perfectly possible too. (In fact Fox (1999) gives a complex set of facts the explanation for which crucially depends on the availability of both early and late merger.) In other words, a relative clause *can* be brought in at the point where the head is still in its base position. With that in mind, consider (63):

(63) Which picture that portrays him_i/his_i mother did $John_i$ decide to post on his Facebook page?

This has an analysis in which *him/his* is bound by *John*; this can happen in the derivation in which *that portrays him/his mother* is merged in early, before fronting of *picture that portrays* ... But since this derivation exists, it should block the relevant understanding of (60). But (60) is generally acknowledged to be good. So the story under consideration here regarding (58) vs. (60) does not go through; reconstruction does not account for the facts. Now it could be that one could formulate the relevant notion of a competing derivation (with binding) in such a way as to make (63) not a competitor for (60) even given the possibility of an early merger derivation, and I leave that open. The point, though, is that competition based accounts of the full range of Principle C violations do not lead in a straightforward way to an account of the badness of (58) (requiring early merger) vs. the goodness of (60) (which allows early merger) under reconstruction, and so it is premature to take (58) as strong evidence for reconstruction.

This is not to say that I *do* have an explanation for the existence of 'Principle C' effects in general (but see Krifka this volume). But that is not the point here: the point here is that even if the facts are as they are often claimed, questions remain about reconstruction based accounts of (58) (vs. (60)).

6.3 Other arguments

This by no means exhausts the inventory of arguments that have been put forward for reconstruction, but let me briefly mention two others. The first concerns idiom chunks. Indeed, Schachter (1973) argued for the head raising analysis of relative clauses on the basis of cases like (64):

(64) The strings that he pulled got me my job.

The argument assumes that the meaning of *pull strings* is not derivable compositionally, and so *strings* (or some copy thereof) must be in the object position of *pull* for the idiomatic interpretation to be possible. I have little to add here to the extensive discussion in the literature as to whether such separable "idioms" truly are non-compositional (see e.g., Wasow, Numberg & Sag 1984) but we can note that to say they are not raises at least as many problems as it solves. The simplest such problem is that positing that these are non-compositional raises the question of just what it is in (64) that got me my job. Or, consider the following "reverse" case from McCawley 1981 (which, under the worldview in which *pull strings* is non-compositional would have to be a case of a head external relative):

(65) He pulled the strings that got me my job.

While a head external analysis might look like it gives a reasonable analysis for this, what does it mean to modify *strings* if *strings* has no meaning? How does the relative clause combine with the head? A similar point is raised by (66) (which would necessitate not just a head external analysis but some sort of copy analysis):

(66) He pulled the strings that he said he would pull.

And finally, the "modern" view of reconstruction – using the copy theory of movement – would seem to be committed to a compositional analysis. For the claim here is that the trace in the subject position of the relative clause in (64) is $[t_{i\text{ - }strings}]$ where the interpretation of this on any *g* is *g(i)* provided that *g(i)* is a member of ⟦strings⟧. Already, then, the battle to maintain a non-compositional treatment of these is lost since the interpretation of the trace given above is incoherent if *strings* doesn't have some meaning in and of itself. Reconstruction, then, does not seem to be a particularly illuminating way to solve the mystery of just how these separable idioms function in the semantics.

A second phenomenon is the "Bhatt" effect (Bhatt 2002) as in (67):

(67) The longest book that Bill believes Tolstoy ever wrote is *Anna Karenina*.

Bhatt's observation is that these can have a "low" reading for the superlative, where Bill's belief is that *Anna Karenina* is Tolstoy's longest book. He may well know that Tolstoy also wrote *War and Peace*, but he is mistaken about their relative length. (Use of *ever*, as Bhatt points out, forces the low reading.)

Again any serious discussion of the Bhatt phenomena is far beyond our current scope, but let me just mention three mysteries which reconstruction (by itself) does not help to solve. The first is documented in Heycock (2005); this occurs only with a small set of verbs. Just what verbs is controversial and although I believe that Heycock's generalization to the effect that it is just the Neg Raising verbs, authors such as Bhatt & Sharvit (2005) have disagreed. But whatever is the exact set of verbs, a head raising analysis itself does not by itself provide an explanation for the full set of facts. A second point which to my knowledge has not received much discussion is that the "low" reading of the superlative for (67) are good only in specificational sentences or as concealed questions.[10] (This is reminiscent of the fact that the "binding into heads" phenomena exists only in functional cases – most easily brought out in, e.g., in specificational sentences and questions – but I don't know how to link up these facts.) Thus (67) is fine, but (68) does not have a low reading:

(68) I just finished reading the longest book that Bill believes Tolstoy ever wrote.

10 While I don't know of anywhere that this has been discussed, I have looked through the examples cited for these and – with one exception – they always involve specificational sentences. The exception is Hulsey & Sauerland (2006) who give these in non-specificational contexts. Obviously whenever there is judgment disagreement some systematic checking is in order, but all of the informants that I have consulted agree with the generalization above.

If Bill knows that Tolstoy also wrote *War and Peace*, this cannot be a statement about *Anna Karenina*. These are alright in normal argument position if taken to be concealed questions, but not otherwise. Hence (69) has a low reading while (70) does not:

(69) I just found out the longest book that Bill believes Tolstoy ever wrote.

And notice that we can "tweak" (68) into something that conveys the low reading – but that is because we turn it into something that contains a specificational sub-piece:

(70) I just finished reading what is the longest book that Bill believes Tolstoy wrote.

Third (a point which also has not been discussed to my knowledge), the lexical head makes a semantic contribution inside the relative clause – but it *also* makes a contribution externally. (Hulsey & Sauerland 2006 discuss the first point and dispute the second, but their particular examples are quite unclear. The examples below have been checked with five informants all of whom robustly get the pattern reported below.) Thus suppose that Lee is a girl who went to Classical High School. Moreover, Tom thinks she is smarter than any of the other girls who have ever graduated from Classical High (whether the comparison class at issue here is girls in the actual world or girls in Tom's beliefs is not immediately relevant to the point at hand). But Tom mistakenly thinks that Lee is a boy. Then one cannot truthfully say (71) – which might be expected under the head raising analysis:

(71) The smartest girl that Tom thinks ever graduated from Classical High is Lee.

But now suppose that Tom thinks Lee is a girl but that he is mistaken, and she is actually a boy. Then in that case (71) is still bad. The upshot is that there are a number of complex facts surrounding this construction, but "reconstruction" by itself accounts for a small enough portion of the domain that there is no particular reason to find it a particularly promising solution.

7 Conclusion

I have not attempted to give any analysis here of some of the facts that have been used to motivate reconstruction (the Bhatt facts, idiom chunks, and – if the putative facts are even correct – the "Principle C" cases). I have, however, tried to cast doubt on reconstruction as the right approach to these. For the other domains considered in this paper – in particular the interaction of all of this material with binding – there are straightforward non-reconstruction alternatives. I have argued that these accounts are at least as simple, that they are compatible with a simpler worldview of the grammar and hence to be preferred *a priori* in any case, and that they avoid problems engendered by the reconstruction approach. Along the way to make the case there is no real reason to think of what we are used to calling "bound" readings as necessitating any relationship in the grammar between "binders" and "bindees"; indeed such a notion gets in the way. (Jacobson 2003 also addresses exactly this issue in detail and argues that some interesting facts concerning Antecedent Contained Ellipsis also require us to abandon any notion of "binders" and "bindees".)

If one is "keeping score", it is true that the approach argued for here needs a rule shifting the meaning of head nouns, and the additional rule of **m**, and generalization of that rule given in (52). But all of the other apparatus is motivated entirely independently of this domain, requires no use of levels of representation, no assignment functions, no use of indices, and – perhaps most importantly – is compatible with a direct compositional architecture.

Appendix: Responding to challenges

Problems for the general account of "binding" into heads (and the general strategy for "binding" in specificational sentences) have been noted by Heycock (personal communication) and in Barker (2009). While I do not have complete solutions to all of these, some discussion is in order.

Domain restriction

Barker's first worry centers on the semantics for cases like (72):

(72) The person that every 3rd grade boy loves the most is his mother.

The analysis here equates two functions; the first is one whose range is restricted to people and the second is the mother-of function. But the two are of course not identical; kittens have mothers too. Thus the functional analysis here – where crucially the two functions are equated – would seem to give the wrong truth conditions. But recall that the functional analysis is crucial to the "binding" facts (and ultimately of key relevance to the account in this paper of "reconstruction" effects involving binding), so this problem might seem to undermine the basic strategy taken throughout this paper.

But this is no different from any other case of domain restriction, and exactly the mechanisms used for domain restriction in general carry over straightforwardly. Because the use of the genitive in *his mother* makes the exposition lengthier, we will switch to the unnatural but presumably synonymous phrase *the mother of him*. It is well known that quantified NPs like *every student* are restricted to some domain, and the same is true with *the student*. (It is the unique student in some contextually specified domain.) Just about any account of how to do domain restriction will be sufficient to solve Barker's kitten problem, but we will chose one to make this point explicit. Thus assume that the domain restriction is part of the semantics and "comes" with the determiner (von Fintel 1994) In variable-ful terms this means that *the*, *every* etc. come with a "free variable" in their meaning. The variable-free analogue is that *the*, for example, is of type $\langle\langle e,t\rangle,\langle\langle e,t\rangle,e\rangle\rangle$ – it is a function from domains D to a function which takes some subset of D and returns the unique individual in that set. ⟦the student⟧ is a function from sets (of type $\langle e,t\rangle$) to the unique (or most salient) student in that set. (The "open" domain slot is passed up in the usual way as with an "free" pronoun – **g** applies to the material taking *the student* as argument, and so forth all the way up.) The version of *the* that takes as argument a set of functions would be no different. ⟦the mother of him⟧ is not just the unique (or most salient) function of type $\langle e,e\rangle$, but rather the unique (or most salient) such function relative to some set of functions. (I.e., it is a function from sets of functions of type $\langle e,e\rangle$ to a single such function.) And here the context happily sets the domain as only those functions with range ⟦person⟧. (The genitive case will be similar; *John's cousin* also has a domain restriction. How and where to build in the domain restriction there just depends on how one works out the details of the semantics of genitives.) Thus nothing new is needed for this case.[11]

Counting relatives

A second problem posed by Barker comes from questions, but since the same point is relevant to relative clause we will consider it with respect to the latter domain. Thus, Barker considers sentences analogous to (73):

(73) The number of relatives of hers that every woman invited to her bootcamp graduation is four.

11 Barker considers and argues against solving this problem using a domain restriction approach, but his argument is based on considering only one way to do the domain restriction and showing problems with that particular method.

Barker's worry is that the semantics here would predict that this means "the number of functions mapping each woman into a relative of hers is 4". In other words, he assumes that the semantics will have this count functions, rather than individuals. But the semantics that has this count function will be disastrous; there are far too many functions. Rather this should have a reading in which it is a function from individuals to numbers.

There are then two separate questions about these. The first is the one Barker raises: will we get the wrong reading (the "counting functions" reading) under the analysis here (and in earlier works of mine)? Second, can we get the right reading for (73) (and related cases to be discussed immediately below). The answer to the first is fairly simple; the wrong reading emerges only if one assumes that *number* is polymorphic (in the lexicon) and can count functions as well as counting atomic individuals. But there is no reason at all to assume this. (Barker's actual discussion centers on *how many* but the same point holds for this phrase.) I will assume that *(the) number of* can indeed combine with functions of type $\langle e, e\rangle$ as well as with individuals, but only after it shifts such that the result will be a function from individuals to numbers (or, sets of numbers) and not a single number. And it will not be counting the number of these functions. Ordinary *(the) number of* presumably counts atoms in a maximal plural individual; the shifted version will "count" the atoms in the plural that that individual is mapped into.

As to the more complex question of how to get the right reading for (73), we should note first that this phenomenon can clearly be tied in to functional readings. Consider, for example, a case where the reading is obviously functional, as in (74):

(74) The number of relatives of hers that every woman invited to her bootcamp graduation is the number that she had put on the form she filled out when she first joined the navy.

A sentence like this makes it clear that the pre-copular constituent is denoting a function from individuals to numbers. With that in mind, the discussion is simplified if we don't have a "binding into head" case; we can recast as (75) (the remarks for (75) will carry over directly to (74)):

(75) The number of people that every woman invited (to her bootcamp graduation) is the number she had put on the questionnaire ...

Most of what we need to get a functional analysis for these is already in place in the system here and just involves application of **g** though one open question remains. I will sketch the analysis – the full semantics of *number* and *how many* are sufficiently complex that the sketch is preliminary, but I think that the sketch here can be modified to fit whatever turns out to be the right semantics for *(the) number of* in general.

Thus an ordinary NP such as *the number of dogs that Mary owns*. Assume that *dogs that Mary owns* is both a plural noun (denoting a set of plural objects) but can also shift to an NP that denotes the maximal such plural object (i.e., for any set of objects in $\langle e^*, t\rangle$ – for e^* a plural object – then $e^{\max}$ is the individual such that for all x in the set, $x \leq e^{\max}$). Assume further that *number (of)* takes only such maximal NPs; this can be ensured in the syntax, for example by giving such NPs a special category and having *number of* subcategorize for that. It is of type $\langle e, \langle n, t\rangle\rangle$; it takes a (maximal plural) individual and returns a set of numbers – the singleton set of atoms in that individual. *The* then comes in and does its usual business (it returns the unique number in that set). Incidentally, I have had *number of* return something of type $\langle n, t\rangle$ in order to allow *the* to have its usual type, but it might be that *number of* is really just of type $\langle e, n\rangle$ and *the* combines directly with an individual.

The key is that *number (of)* can shift by the usual **g** rule to be of type $\langle\langle e, e\rangle, \langle e, \langle n, t\rangle\rangle\rangle$ (or, perhaps $\langle\langle e, e\rangle, \langle e, n\rangle\rangle$) – it takes a function from individuals to individuals and returns a function from individuals to (singleton) sets of numbers (or to a number). There is one trick needed here. We need *number of* to combine not with any function of type $\langle e, e\rangle$ but only with "maximal" such functions (to be defined momentarily). I do not see how to get this to immediately follow from the rest of the system, so leave that as open. (Ideally it should follow from the fact that ordinary *number of* combines with maximal plurals, but I do not see how to collapse the two cases.) In any case, though, defining this is no problem. Let F be some set of functions of type $\langle e, e\rangle$. Then $f^{\max}$ is that function in F such that for all x, and y, if $f(x) = y$ then for all g in F, if $g(x) = z$ then $z \leq y$. Intuitively, $f^{\max}$ is that function in F which maps each individual into the "biggest" plural individual that any function in F does. Take, for example, the set of functions in the functional version of ⟦people that every woman invited⟧. This is the set of functions (of type $\langle e, e\rangle$) whose range are people and which are such every woman z-invited f. Such functions include those mapping individuals to plurals as well as to singulars. We want to select from that set the single function $f^{\max}$ which is the one that maps each woman to the largest group that she invited.

The rest is straightforward. Our **g**(*number of*) takes that function and returns a function of type $\langle e, \langle n, t\rangle\rangle$ (or, of type $\langle e, n\rangle$). Its semantics is $\lambda f_{\langle e,e\rangle}$ [λx [number-of$'$ $(f(x))$]]. It then takes some maximal function f in the sense defined above, and returns a function from individuals to the (singleton) set of numbers (or, to a single number) which is the number of atoms in $f(x)$. This gives the functional reading. But what about (73) with which we began the discussion? I see no reason not to assume that this too is functional, and that *four* can denote the constant function mapping each individual to the number 4.

The Heycock problem

Carolyn Heycock observed the following problem with the functional analyses of "binding" (a version of this problem is also discussed in Barker 2009). Given the claim that NPs with pronouns in them can denote functions of type $\langle e, e \rangle$, and given the claim that specificational sentences can equate functions, Heycock notes that (76) should have a reading roughly the same as (77):

(76) The woman who he loves the most is his mother.

(77) The woman who every male loves the most is his mother.

Even ignoring the gender contribution of *he*, (76) should be good and should mean that the function mapping any individual to the woman he loves the most is the same as the-mother-of function. But it doesn't have this reading; *he* here can only understood as a "free pronoun" (in both NPs) and picks up one (or two) contextually salient individual(s). The same problem arises with something like (78), which does not have a reading saying that the-mother-of function is the same as the-best-friend-of function:

(78) His mother is his best friend.

It is indeed a mystery as to why (76) and (77) do not have the relevant readings, But the problem is not unique to the account here. Indeed any account that allows the post-copular constituent in (77) to denote a function of type $\langle e, e \rangle$ inherits exactly this problem. And any account that takes the answer in (79) to denote a function of type $\langle e, e \rangle$ also has this problem:

(79) Q: Which woman does no 4th grade boy call at lunchtime?
A: His mother

The advantage noted above of the variable-free account is the fact that *his mother* denotes such a function is automatic. But – leaving that aside – many variable-ful accounts have also proposed mechanisms to allow the assignment dependent individual ⟦his mother⟧ to shift to the requisite function of type $\langle e, e \rangle$. (See, e.g., von Stechow 1990, Sharvit 1999, Gawron & Peters 1990 among others.) And there is a good reason to believe (regardless of the issue of variables or not) that indeed these must denote functions of type $\langle e, e \rangle$, for it is not clear that there is any other reasonable account of the 'binding' effect in the question/answer pair such as (79). As far as I can see, there are three choices for the analysis of the answer in (79). One is the one under consideration here: it denotes a function and the question is a functional question. The second – and probably most popular one – is that ellipsis is involved and the answer is 'hiddenly' a full sentence (of the form *no 4th grade boy calls his mother at lunch)*. But we have already seen evidence above against this (see Section 3.2.1), and Jacobson (2016) provides a much more detailed set of problems for the ellipsis analysis. The third would be some notion allowing 'binding' across speakers.[12] But this would need to be spelled out, and – unlike cases that have gone under the rubric of 'dynamic' binding (or donkey binding), we would need some notion allowing binding from something like *no fourth grade boy*. Unless some such notion can be formulated, we are left with the functional analysis of (79) as the most viable analysis. If this analysis is correct, then any theory needs some mechanism allowing *his mother* to denote a function. But as long as there is such a mechanism, then (assuming that specificational sentences can equate functions), any theory will inherit the Heycock problem. It is an intriguing problem – but one which is not unique to the theory argued for here.

It is worth some very brief speculation on a hopeful solution to this problem. The problem seems insurmountable only assuming two things. One is that the pre and post-copular constituents in specificational sentences make exactly the same semantic contribution. The second is that *the woman who every male loves (the most)* (in its functional reading) means exactly the same thing as *the woman who he loves (the most)* in its functional reading. Probably neither of these is correct.

As to the first, we noted earlier that for convenience we were taking here *be* to merely assert identity, but this is almost certainly incorrect. As many have argued, specificational sentences "raise" a question (or name a question under discussion) and then provide an answer. The problem is in having a pronoun only in the question part. Notice that sentences like (80) are good but only as what have been called "reverse specificational sentences":

(80) His mother is the woman that every man loves the most.

Similarly, we do not get functional questions like (81a) (in contrast to (81b)):

(81) a. * Who does he loves the most? (as a functional question)
b. Who does every man love the most?

So the first observation is that the two parts of a specificational sentence are not the same – the "question" part (as in the case of a functional question) cannot have only a pronoun as a way to name the function. This means that if *the woman that every male loves the most* and *the woman that he loves the most* actually have

12 Jacobson (2016) – following Groenendijk & Stokhof (1984) – does advocate for an analysis of question/answer pairs which treats them as a unit, and so gives the semantics for such a pair even though each part is spoken by a different speaker. But it is still the case in this analysis that each part by itself (the question and the answer) has a meaning; I am not sure what it would mean to have a "binding" relationship that crossed speakers.

subtly different meanings, that very difference could be what is responsible for the fact that the first but not the second can "raise" or name a question. (Similarly, (81b) is a sensible functional question while (81a) is not.)

There is indeed a subtle difference between these two. It is reasonable to assume that *male* in (77) refers to the extension of ⟦male⟧ in this world. I leave open exactly how it that folds into the full compositional semantics but one possibility is that the question raised by the pre-copular constituent is one about a function whose domain is restricted to males in this world. But *the woman that he loves the most* does not have this restriction. Although *he* arguably contributes a domain restriction to males, nothing here ensures that *he* is the identity function only over males in this world. Indeed, Yanovich (2012) contains detailed discussion about the role of gender features across worlds, and notes that *he* is perfectly happy with respect to imaginary individuals, as in cases like (82):

(82) If Catherine of Aragon had had a son, he would have been ruler of England in 1548.

Thus an NP like *the woman that he loves* arguably does not have the same extensional domain restriction that *the woman that every male loves* does – even when both have functional readings. The hope, then, is that this fact makes the "question" raised by *the woman he loves* (and the corresponding functional question in (81a)) simply be a nonsensical question. But I will leave this speculation for future research. In closing, though, I should note that one might think the speculation here is undermined by the point earlier that Barker's kittens is solved by having *his mother* be a domain restricted function. While indeed my solution to Barker's kittens was to propose that there is an open slot for a a domain restriction, this does not undermine the point that the actual *meaning* of functional NPs with pronouns is different from those without. Thus the fact that there is this meaning difference should give us hope that there is a solution to the Heycock problem.[13]

Acknowledgment: Portions of this material were presented at the Workshop on Linguistics and Philosophy at the University of Michigan in 2003, at the joint course with Irene Heim at the 2005 LSA Summer Institute at MIT, and at the Berlin Reconstruction Workshop in July, 2011. I thank the audiences and commentators at these events for much helpful discussion. Moreover, this work has particularly benefited from numerous discussions over the years with both Chris Barker and

13 Barker (2009) brings up one additional problem with the variable-free account pursued here which has to do with "outbound" binding. I will not address this here as it is tied into a much larger question concerning inverse scope in NPs.

Irene Heim (among many others), and from the comments of two reviewers for this volume. The research was partially supported by NSF grant BCS 0646081.

References

Barker, Chris. 2009. Reconstruction as delayed evaluation. In Erhard Hinrichs & John Nerbonne (eds.), *Theory and evidence in semantics*, 1–28. Stanford: CSLI Publications.

Barker, Chris & Chung-Chieh Shan. 2014. *Continuations and natural language*. Oxford: Oxford University Press.

Bhatt, Rajesh. 2002. The raising analysis of relative clauses: Evidence from adjectival modification. *Natural Language Semantics* 10. 43–90.

Bhatt, Rajesh & Yael Sharvit. 2005. A note on intensional superlatives. In E. Georgala & H. Howell (eds.), *Proceedings of Semantics and Linguistic Theory 18*, 62–79. Ithaca: Cornell University CLC Publications.

Brame, Michael. 1968. *A new analysis of relative clause: Evidence for an interpretive theory.* Unpublished Ms.

Chierchia, Gennaro. 1992. Anaphora and dynamic binding. *Linguistics and Philosophy* 15. 111–183.

Chomsky, Noam. 1977. On wh-movement. In P. Culicover, T. Wasow & A. Akmajian (eds.), *Formal syntax*, 71–132. New York: Academic Press.

Chomsky, Noam. 1995. *The minimalist program*. Cambridge, MA: MIT Press.

Culicover, Peter & Ray Jackendoff. 2005. *Simpler syntax*. Oxford: Oxford University Press.

Doron, Edit. 1982. The syntax and semantics of resumptive pronouns. *Texas Linguistics Forum* 19. 1–48.

Dowty, David R. 1988. Type raising, functional composition, and non-constituent conjunction. In Richard T. Oehrle, Emmon Bach & Deirdre Wheeler (eds.), *Categorial grammars and natural language structures*, 153–197. Dordrecht: Reidel.

Dowty, David & Pauline Jacobson. 1989. Agreement as a semantic phenomenon. In J. Powers & K. de Jong (eds.), *Proceedings of the Eastern States Conference on Linguistics 8*, 95–108. Columbus: Ohio State University.

Engdahl, Elisabet. 1986. *Constituent questions*. Dordrecht: Reidel.

Fox, Danny. 1999. Reconstruction, binding theory, and the interpretation of chains. *Linguistic Inquiry* 30(2). 157–196.

Fox, Danny. 2000. *Economy and semantic interpretation*. Cambridge, MA: MIT Press.

Gawron, Mark & Stanley Peters. 1990. *Anaphora and quantification in situation semantics*. Stanford: CSLI Publications.

Gazdar, Gerald, Ewan Klein, Geoffrey K. Pullum & Ivan Sag. 1985. *Generalized phrase structure grammar*. Cambridge, MA: Harvard University Press.

Ginzburg, Jonathan & Ivan Sag. 2000. *Interrogative investigations: The form, meaning, and use of English interrogatives*. Stanford: CSLI Publications.

Groenendijk, Jeroen & Martin Stokhof. 1983. Interrogative quantifiers and skolem functions. In K. Ehlich & H. van Riemsdijk (eds.), *Connectedness in sentence, discourse, and text*, 71–110. Tilburg: Tilburg University.

Groenendijk, Jeroen & Martin Stokhof. 1984. *Studies on the semantics of questions and the pragmatics of answers*. University of Amsterdam Doctoral dissertation.
Hankamer, Jorge & Ivan Sag. 1984. Toward a theory of anaphoric processing. *Linguistics and Philosophy* 7. 325–345.
Heim, Irene. 1997. Predicates or formulas? Evidence from ellipsis. In *Proceedings of Semantics and Linguistic Theory 7*, 197–221. Ithaca: Cornell University CLC Publications.
Heim, Irene. 2008. Features on bound pronouns. In D. Adger, S. Bejar & D. Harbour (eds.), *Phi theory: Phi features across modules and interfaces*, 35–56. Oxford: Oxford University Press.
Heim, Irene. 2011. *Constructing Reconstruction*. Presented at the Workshop on Reconstruction Effects in Relative Clauses, ZAS, Berlin.
Heim, Irene & Angelika Kratzer. 1998. *Semantic interpretation in generative grammar*. Malden: Blackwell.
Heycock, Caroline. 2005. On the interaction of adjectival modifiers and relative clauses. *Natural Language Semantics* 13. 359–382.
Hulsey, Sarah & Uli Sauerland. 2006. Sorting out relative clauses. *Natural Language Semantics* 14. 111–137.
Jackendoff, Ray. 1972. *Semantics in generative grammar*. Cambridge, MA: MIT Press.
Jacobson, Pauline. 1994. Binding connectivity in copular sentences. In M. Harvey & L. Santelmann (eds.), *Proceedings of SALT IV*, 161–178. Ithaca: Cornell University CLC Publications.
Jacobson, Pauline. 1996. The locality of interpretation: The case of binding and coordination. In T. Galloway & J. Spence (eds.), *Proceedings of Semantics and Linguistic Theory 6*, 111–135. Ithaca: Cornell University CLC Publications.
Jacobson, Pauline. 1998. Antecedent contained deletion and pied-piping: Evidence for a variable-free semantics. In A. Lawson & D. Strolovich (eds.), *Proceedings of Semantics and Linguistic Theory 8*, 74–91. Ithaca: Cornell University CLC Publications.
Jacobson, Pauline. 1999. Toward a variable-free semantics. *Linguistics and Philosophy* 22. 117–184.
Jacobson, Pauline. 2000. Paycheck pronouns, bach-peters sentences, and variable free semantics. *Natural Language Semantics* 8. 77–155.
Jacobson, Pauline. 2002a. Direct compositionality and variable-free semantics: The case of binding into heads. In B. Jackson (ed.), *Proceeedings of Semantics and Linguistic Theory 12*, 144–163. Ithaca: Cornell University CLC Publications.
Jacobson, Pauline. 2002b. The (dis)organization of the grammar: 25 years. *Linguistics and Philosophy* 25. 601–626.
Jacobson, Pauline. 2003. Binding without pronouns (and pronouns without binding). In G.-J. Kruiff & R. Oehrle (eds.), *Binding and resource sensitivity*, 57–96. Dordrecht: Kluwer.
Jacobson, Pauline. 2004. *Direct Compositionality: Is there any reason why not?* Workshop in Philosophy and Linguistics, University of Michigan. http://web.eecs.umich.edu/~rthomaso/lpw04/jacobson.pdf (10 October, 2018).
Jacobson, Pauline. 2007. Direct compositionality and variable-free semantics: The case of 'Principle B' effects. In Chris Barker & Pauline Jacobson (eds.), *Direct compositionality* (Oxford Studies in Theoretical Linguistics), 191–236. Oxford: Oxford University Press.
Jacobson, Pauline. 2012. Direct compositionality and 'uninterpretability': The case of (sometimes) 'uninterpretable' features on pronouns. *Journal of Semantics* 29. 305–343.
Jacobson, Pauline. 2014. *Compositional semantics: An introduction to the syntax/semantics interface*. Oxford: Oxford University Press.

Jacobson, Pauline. 2016. The short answer: Implications for direct compositionality and vice-versa. *Language* 92. 331–375.
Kratzer, Angelika. 1998. More structural analogies between pronouns and tenses. In D. Strolovitch & A. Lawson (eds.), *Semantics and Linguistic Theory 8*, 92–110. Ithaca: Cornell Linguistics Club Publications.
Kuhn, Jeremy. 2010. *Binding from a relative clause: A second chance for the head raising analysis*. Brown University B.A. Honors thesis.
Kuno, Susumu. 1975. Three perspectives in the functional approach to syntax. In Robin E. Grossman, L. James San & Timothy J. Vance (eds.), *Papers from the parasession on functionalism*, 276–336. Chicago: Chicago Linguistic Society.
Lebeaux, David. 1988. *Language acquisition and the form of the grammar*. Amherst, MA: University of Massachusetts Doctoral dissertation.
McCawley, James D. 1981. The syntax and semantics of English relative clauses. *Lingua* 53. 99–149.
Merchant, Jason. 2004. Fragments and ellipsis. *Linguistics and Philosophy* 27. 661–738.
Montague, Richard. 1970. English as a formal language. In Bruno Visentini et al. (eds.), *Linguaggi nella società e nella tecnica*, 189–224. Milan: Edizioni di Comunità.
Morgan, Jerry. 1973. Sentence fragments and the notion 'sentence'. In Braj B. Kachru et al. (eds.), *Issues in linguistics: Papers in honor of Henry and Renée Kahane*, 719–751. Urbana: University of Illinois Press.
Munn, Alan. 1999. On the identity requirement of ATB movement. *Natural Language Semantics* 7. 421–425.
Nishigauchi, Taisuke. 1990. *Quantification in the theory of grammar*. Dordrecht: Kluwer.
Pollard, Carl. 1984. *Head grammars*. Stanford University Doctoral dissertation.
Pollard, Carl & Ivan Sag. 1992. Anaphors in English and the scope of binding theory. *Linguistic Inquiry* 23. 261–303.
Postal, Paul. 1970. On coreferential complement subject deletion. *Linguistic Inquiry* 1. 439–500.
Reinhart, Tanya. 1983. *Anaphora and semantic interpretation*. London: Croom Helm.
Ross, John R. 1985. *The source of pseudo-cleft sentences*. Handout, New York University.
Schachter, Paul. 1973. Focus and relativization. *Language* 49(1). 19–46.
Schlenker, Philippe. 2003. Clausal equations (a note on the connectivity problem). *Natural Language Semantics* 21. 157–214.
Sharvit, Yael. 1998. Possessive wh-expressions and reconstruction. In Pius Tamanji & Kiyomi Kusumoto (eds.), *Proceedings of the 28th meeting of the North Eastern Linguistic Society (NELS)*. Amherst, MA: University of Massachussetts GLSA Publications.
Sharvit, Yael. 1999. Connectivity in specificational sentences. *Natural Language Semantics* 7. 200–339.
Steedman, Mark. 1987. Combinatory grammars and parsitic gaps. *Natural Language and Linguistic Theory* 5. 403–439.
von Fintel, Kai. 1994. *Restrictions on quantifier domains*. University of Massachusetts Doctoral dissertation.
von Stechow, Arnim. 1990. *Layered traces*. Presentation given at Revfülöp, Hungary. http://www.sfs.uni-tuebingen.de/~astechow/Aufsaetze/Revfueloep90.pdf (10 October, 2018).
von Stechow, Arnim. 1996. Against LF pied piping. *Natural Language Semantics* 4. 57–110.
von Stechow, Arnim. 2003. Feature deletion under semantic binding. In M. Kadowaki & S. Kawahar (eds.), *Proceedings of the North Eastern Linguistic Society 23*, 122–157. Amherst, MA: GLSA.

Ward, Gregory & Julia Hirschberg. 1985. Implicating uncertainty: The pragmatics of fall-rise intonation. *Language* 61. 747–776.
Warshawsky, Florence. 1965. Reflexivization. In James D. McCawley (ed.), *Syntax and semantics 7: Notes from the linguistic underground*, 63–83. New York: Academic Press.
Wasow, Thomas, Geoffrey Numberg & Ivan Sag. 1984. Idioms. *Language* 70. 491–538.
Yanovich, Igor. 2012. *Indexical presuppositions of pronominal gender features*. Ms., MIT.
Zribi-Hertz, Anne. 1989. Anaphoric binding and narrative point of view: English reflexive pronouns in sentence and discourse. *Language* 65. 695–727.

Chris Barker

Evaluation order, crossover, and reconstruction

This paper explores an approach to reconstruction that falls into the general category of semantic reconstruction: the syntax and the semantics collaborate in order to account for a number of reconstruction effects, but without any syntactic movement.

The analysis developed here builds on Shan & Barker (2006), Barker & Shan (2008), and Barker (2009). It serves in turn as the basis for chapter 6 of Barker & Shan (2014), which, although published earlier, was written later. The briefer discussion in Barker & Shan (2014) relies on the current paper for a number of elaborations and more detailed discussions.

My starting point is the observation in Shan & Barker (2006: 123) that at least some reconstruction effects fall out from the interaction of their particular analyses of scope-taking, binding, and wh-interrogatives. In Barker (2009) I discuss that account of reconstruction, developing especially some of the details of the treatment of questions and higher-order pronoun meanings. These previous discussions, however, considered only a very small range of example types. One of the main goals of the current paper is to see how well the approach scales up to a wider range of reconstruction effects and example types, including quantificational binding, binding of anaphors, idiom licensing, and especially crossover phenomena, in the context of wh-interrogatives, relative clauses, and wh-relatives.

Although the analyses just mentioned differ small ways, they all share core assumptions and goals with the account presented here. I will call the general strategy they develop the *evaluation order* approach. The central goal is to explain crossover effects as following from imposing a default left-to-right evaluation order:

(1) a. Everyone$_i$ loves his$_i$ mother.
    b. * His$_i$ mother loves everyone$_i$.

If a quantifier such as *everyone* must be evaluated (in a sense to be discussed below) before any pronoun that it binds, and if evaluation proceeds from left to right, then we have an explanation for the contrast in (1): in (1b), the quantifier will not be evaluated until after we have already encountered the pronoun.

Chris Barker, New York University

https://doi.org/10.1515/9783050095158-011

Reconstruction appears at first glance to pose a sharp challenge to the evaluation-order account of crossover:

(2) a. Which of his_i relatives does $everyone_i$ love __?
(Answer: his mother)

b. the relative of his_i that $everyone_i$ loves __
(completion: ... is his mother)

In the wh-question in (2a), the pronoun precedes the quantifier, yet there is a salient interpretation of (2a) on which the pronoun varies with the person selected by the quantifier; likewise for the relative clause in (2b). We shall see that this sort of quantificational binding, as well as other types of reconstruction effects, are in fact perfectly compatible with an evaluation-order explanation for crossover.

Crucially, the possibility of backwards quantificational binding in (2) does not mean that evaluation order restrictions have been suspended. In particular, crossover effects re-emerge when the wh-trace precedes the quantifier:

(3) a. * Which of her_i relatives __ loves $everyone_i$?

b. * the relative of $hers_i$ who __ loves $everyone_i$

These expressions are ungrammatical on the indicated binding relationships. The difference between the examples in (2) and the examples in (3) is that in (3), the reconstructed position of the pronoun (marked with '__') still precedes the quantifier. The rough descriptive generalization, then, is that a quantifier can bind a pronoun just in case the quantifier is evaluated before the *reconstructed* pronoun. Given a default evaluation order of left to right, the facts above follow.

On syntactic reconstruction approaches, material including the pronoun would syntactically reconstruct (move) into the reconstruction position, or, as in some versions (e.g., Munn 1994) there would be an unpronounced copy of the syntactic material within the gap site. Instead, on the approach here, the meaning of the constituent containing the pronoun will be packaged semantically in such a way that its evaluation will be delayed. The net result will be that the evaluation of the pronoun will be timed as if the pronoun had appeared in its reconstructed position.

After explaining how the evaluation-order strategy works in detail, and how delayed evaluation works, both for wh-questions and relative clauses, I will go on to consider other kinds of reconstruction effects, including idioms, reflexive pronouns, and *each other* anaphors:

(4) a. Which strings did John pull?

b. the strings that John pulled

(5) a. Which picture of herself does Mary like?
    b. the picture of herself that Mary likes

(6) a. Which pictures of each other did they like?
    b. the pictures of each other that they liked

Although some empirical issues will remain unresolved, the conclusion I will come to is that the evaluation order strategy is a viable explanation for crossover, at the same time that it accounts for a substantial range of reconstruction effects.

1 Three key ideas

The approach here will rely heavily on three central ideas about meaning. The first idea is that natural language pronouns denote identity functions. This view of pronoun meaning has been advocated most prominently in a series of papers by Jacobson, e.g., Jacobson (1994, 1999).[1] Likewise, and not coincidentally, on the Shan/Barker fragment, not only pronouns, but wh-phrases and gaps will also denote identity functions.

The second idea is that we can think of pronouns and other bindable elements as taking scope, as suggested by Dowty (2007). On this view, a bound pronoun chooses its binder by taking scope just narrower than the quantifier that binds it. This is important here because it predicts that pronouns interact in certain ways with other scope-taking elements such as quantifiers, all within a unified system for scope-taking.

The third key idea is the notion of semantic reconstruction, as first articulated by von Stechow (in unpublished work I do not have access to), Cresti (1995), Rullmann (1995), and Sternefeld (1998, 2001). They suggest that allowing pronouns and gaps to denote higher-order functions can delay evaluation (in my terms) in a way that models reconstruction effects. The fragment here is just one specific implementation of this strategy. One point of interest is that the higher-order functions proposed by, e.g., Sternefeld, follow here without stipulation from independently motivated aspects of the semantic analysis of scope-taking, wh-question formation, and relative clause formation.

The key innovation here is to combine Jacobson's notion of pronouns as identity functions with Dowty's notion of pronouns as scope-takers in order to provide a delayed evaluation implementation of semantic reconstruction.

1 Analogously in formal languages, variables translate as identity functions in the standard elimination of variables in combinatory logic, e.g., Barendregt (1984: 152).

2 Fragment

The fragment as presented here takes the form of a combinatory categorial grammar in the style of Jacobson (1999) or Steedman (2000), in which a small number of type-shifters ("combinators") apply freely and without constraint. It is faithful both to the spirit and to many of the details of the Shan & Barker (2006) analysis, though it uses the 'tower' notation introduced in Barker & Shan (2008), rather than strings of combinators as in Shan & Barker (2006). The presentation here will provide just enough detail to understand the derivations below. A similar tower presentation, as well as additional technical details and some relevant discussion concerning reconstruction, can be found in Barker (2009). See especially Barker & Shan (2014) for a more complete development of the fragment in the context of a treatment of scope, binding, and a wide range of other phenomena.

Atomic categories include DP, S, and N. Complex categories include $B\backslash A$ and A/B, where A and B are any categories. These slashes are the normal slashes from categorial grammar. Syntactically, they correspond to the ordinary merge operation, and semantically, they correspond to function application, as usual:

(7)
$$\left(\begin{array}{cc} \mathrm{DP} & \mathrm{DP}\backslash\mathrm{S} \\ \textit{John} & \textit{left} \\ \mathbf{j} & \mathbf{left} \end{array}\right) = \begin{array}{c} \mathrm{S} \\ \textit{John left} \\ \mathbf{left}(\mathbf{j}) \end{array}$$

For instance, an expression in the category DP\S can merge with a DP to its left in order to form a complex expression of category S, with the semantics of function application.

The set of complex categories also includes $A\mathbin{\backslash\!\!\backslash} B$ and $B\mathbin{/\!\!/} A$. Syntactically, these hollow slashes correspond to in-situ scope-taking.

(8)
$$\left(\begin{array}{cc} \dfrac{\mathrm{S}\mid\mathrm{S}}{\mathrm{DP}} & \dfrac{\mathrm{S}\mid\mathrm{S}}{\mathrm{DP}\backslash\mathrm{S}} \\ \textit{everyone} & \textit{left} \\ \dfrac{\forall y.[\,]}{y} & \dfrac{[\,]}{\mathbf{left}} \end{array}\right) = \begin{array}{c} \dfrac{\mathrm{S}\mid\mathrm{S}}{\mathrm{S}} \\ \textit{everyone left} \\ \dfrac{\forall y.[\,]}{\mathbf{left}(y)} \end{array}$$

There are several elements in this derivation that need to be explained. First, as a purely notational convenience, syntactic categories of the form $C\mathbin{/\!\!/}(A\mathbin{\backslash\!\!\backslash} B)$ can be written as $\frac{C\,|\,B}{A}$ (this is the 'tower' convention). So, in particular, the syntactic category given here for *everyone* is $\frac{\mathrm{S}\,|\,\mathrm{S}}{\mathrm{DP}} \equiv \mathrm{S}\mathbin{/\!\!/}(\mathrm{DP}\mathbin{\backslash\!\!\backslash}\mathrm{S})$: something that functions locally as a DP, takes scope over an S, and returns as a result an expression of category S. Likewise, in the corresponding semantics, $\lambda\kappa.g[\kappa f]$ can by convention be written equivalently as $\frac{g[\,]}{f}$, so the denotation of *everyone* is $\frac{\forall y.[\,]}{y} \equiv \lambda\kappa.\forall y.\kappa y$.

Syntactic and semantic combination proceeds according to the following general schema:[2]

$$(9)\qquad \left(\begin{array}{cc} \dfrac{C \mid D}{A/B} & \dfrac{D \mid E}{B} \\ \textit{left} & \textit{right} \\ \dfrac{g[\;]}{f} & \dfrac{h[\;]}{x} \end{array}\right) = \begin{array}{c} \dfrac{C \mid E}{A} \\ \textit{left right} \\ \dfrac{g[h[\;]]}{f(x)} \end{array}$$

Translating from the tower notation back into linear notation, on the syntactic level we have $C /\!\!/ ((A/B) \backslash\!\!\backslash D) + D /\!\!/ (B \backslash\!\!\backslash E) = C /\!\!/ (A \backslash\!\!\backslash E)$. On the semantic level, below the horizontal line is normal function application: $f + x = f(x)$. Above the line is something resembling function composition: $g[\;] + h[\;] = g[h[\;]]$. Translating from tower notation back to linear notation, we have: $(\lambda\kappa.g[\kappa f]) + (\lambda\gamma.h[\gamma(x)]) = (\lambda\delta.g[h[\delta(fx)]])$.

Another element that needs comment in the derivation in (8) given above is that the syntax and semantics for *left* does not match that given in (7) above. The reason is that non-scope-taking elements such as *left* must be adjusted in order to combine with scope-takers, in the same way that Montague recognized that the denotations of proper names (fundamentally of type e) must be adjusted in order to match quantificational DPs (type $\langle\langle e, t\rangle, t\rangle$). In both cases, the adjustment mechanism is the same: Partee's (1987) LIFT type-shifter. In general, for all categories A and B:

$$(10)\qquad \boxed{\begin{array}{c} A \\ \textit{phrase} \\ x \end{array} \overset{\text{LIFT}}{\Rightarrow} \begin{array}{c} \dfrac{B \mid B}{A} \\ \textit{phrase} \\ \dfrac{[\;]}{x} \end{array}}$$

2 There is a variant of this schema in which the functor category (B\A beneath the line) is on the right and the argument category (B) is on the left, with the function/argument roles in the semantics reversed. In linear notation, the variant is $C /\!\!/ (B \backslash\!\!\backslash D) + D /\!\!/ ((B\backslash A) \backslash\!\!\backslash E) = D /\!\!/ (A \backslash\!\!\backslash E)$. The combination in (8) is an instance of this second schema. The need for two variants of the combination schema can be eliminated in favor of a single schema, as in Shan & Barker (2006), but doing this here would complicate exposition.

$$
(11)\quad \text{a.}\quad
\begin{array}{c} \text{DP} \\ \textit{John} \\ \mathbf{j} \end{array}
\overset{\text{LIFT}}{\Rightarrow}
\begin{array}{c} \dfrac{\text{S} \mid \text{S}}{\text{DP}} \\ \textit{John} \\ \dfrac{[\,]}{\mathbf{j}} \end{array}
\qquad \text{b.}\quad
\begin{array}{c} \text{DP}\backslash\text{S} \\ \textit{left} \\ \mathbf{left} \end{array}
\overset{\text{LIFT}}{\Rightarrow}
\begin{array}{c} \dfrac{\text{S} \mid \text{S}}{\text{DP}\backslash\text{S}} \\ \textit{left} \\ \dfrac{[\,]}{\mathbf{left}} \end{array}
$$

If x is the semantic value of A, then $\frac{[\,]}{x} \equiv \lambda\kappa.\kappa x$ is the value of LIFT(A). For instance, in (11a), LIFTing the proper name *John* into the quantifier category yields the usual generalized quantifier semantics, $\frac{[\,]}{\mathbf{j}} \equiv \lambda\kappa.\kappa(\mathbf{j})$. Likewise, when *left* undergoes the LIFT typeshifter, the result in (11b) is the verb phrase that appears above in the derivation of *everyone left*.

The final element in the derivation of *everyone left* that requires explanation is the fact that the derivation as given above ends with a multi-level syntactic category. That is, the final syntactic category is $\frac{\text{S} \mid \text{S}}{\text{S}}$ instead of a plain S. This would be appropriate if we imagined that the sentence might be embedded in a larger expression over which the quantifier might need to take scope; but since this is the complete utterance, we need a way to close off the scope domain of the quantifier. We accomplish this with the following type-shifter:

(12) For all categories A, and for all $B \neq \text{DP} \triangleright C$:

$$
\boxed{
\begin{array}{c} \dfrac{A \mid B}{B} \\ \textit{phrase} \\ \dfrac{f[\,]}{x} \end{array}
\overset{\text{LOWER}}{\Rightarrow}
\begin{array}{c} A \\ \textit{phrase} \\ f[x] \end{array}
}
$$

$$
(13)\quad
\begin{array}{c} \dfrac{\text{S} \mid \text{S}}{\text{S}} \\ \textit{everyone left} \\ \dfrac{\forall y.\,[\,]}{\mathbf{left}\ y} \end{array}
\overset{\text{LOWER}}{\Rightarrow}
\begin{array}{c} \text{S} \\ \textit{everyone left} \\ \forall y.\,\mathbf{left}\ y \end{array}
$$

If F is the semantic value of the original expression, then $F(\lambda\kappa.\kappa)$ is the value of the shifted expression. This combinator lowers the category of the sentence *everyone left* back to S. If the semantic value of *everyone* is $\lambda P \forall x.Px$, and the semantic value of *left* is **left**, then the semantic value of LOWER(*everyone* LIFT(*left*)) is $\forall x.\,\mathbf{left}(x)$. The LOWER type-shifter plays a role closely similar to Groenendijk & Stokhof's

(1991) '↓' operator. We will see in the next subsection that it is important to add the restriction that $B \neq \mathrm{DP} \triangleright C$ to account for weak crossover. (This concludes the explanation for the derivation of *everyone left* in (8).)

To see how the combination schema enforces left-to-right evaluation order, note that when a sentence contains two quantifiers, by default, the quantifier on the left takes scope over the one on the right:

$$(14)\quad \begin{array}{c}\dfrac{\mathrm{S}\,|\,\mathrm{S}}{\mathrm{DP}}\\ \textit{someone}\\ \dfrac{\exists x.\,[\,]}{x}\end{array} \left(\begin{array}{c}\dfrac{\mathrm{S}\,|\,\mathrm{S}}{(\mathrm{DP}\backslash \mathrm{S})/\mathrm{DP}}\\ \textit{loves}\\ \dfrac{[\,]}{\textbf{loves}}\end{array} \quad \begin{array}{c}\dfrac{\mathrm{S}\,|\,\mathrm{S}}{\mathrm{DP}}\\ \textit{everyone}\\ \dfrac{\forall y.\,[\,]}{y}\end{array}\right)$$

$$= \begin{array}{c}\dfrac{\mathrm{S}\,|\,\mathrm{S}}{\mathrm{S}}\\ \textit{Someone loves everyone}\\ \dfrac{\exists x.\,\forall y.\,[\,]}{\textbf{loves}\;y\,x}\end{array} \overset{\text{LOWER}}{\Rightarrow} \begin{array}{c}\mathrm{S}\\ \textit{Someone loves everyone}\\ \exists x.\,\forall y.\,\textbf{loves}\;y\,x\end{array}$$

As a result of the left-to-right bias built into the combination schema, this evaluates to $\exists x \forall y.\,\textbf{loves}\;y\,x$.

2.1 Pronouns and binding

As in Jacobson (1999), the presence of an unbound pronoun will be recorded on the category of each larger expression that contains it. In particular, a clause containing an unbound pronoun will have category $\mathrm{DP} \triangleright \mathrm{S}$ rather than plain S. In order to accomplish this, a pronoun functions locally as a DP, takes scope over an S, and turns that S into an open proposition:

$$(15)\quad \left(\begin{array}{c}\dfrac{\mathrm{DP} \triangleright \mathrm{S}\,|\,\mathrm{S}}{\mathrm{DP}}\\ \textit{he}\\ \dfrac{\lambda y.\,[\,]}{y}\end{array} \quad \begin{array}{c}\dfrac{\mathrm{S}\,|\,\mathrm{S}}{\mathrm{DP}\backslash \mathrm{S}}\\ \textit{left}\\ \dfrac{[\,]}{\textbf{left}}\end{array}\right) = \begin{array}{c}\dfrac{\mathrm{DP} \triangleright \mathrm{S}\,|\,\mathrm{S}}{\mathrm{S}}\\ \textit{he left}\\ \dfrac{\lambda y.\,[\,]}{\textbf{left}\;y}\end{array} \overset{\text{LOWER}}{\Rightarrow} \begin{array}{c}\mathrm{DP} \triangleright \mathrm{S}\\ \textit{he left}\\ \lambda y.\,\textbf{left}\;y\end{array}$$

Note that the lexical denotation of the pronoun is $\dfrac{\lambda y.\,[\,]}{y} \equiv \lambda \kappa y.\,\kappa y$, a (two-place) identity function.

If the category of a complete utterance is DP $\rhd$ S, the value of the embedded pronoun must be supplied by the pragmatic context. In order to demonstrate how an element within the utterance can bind a pronoun, we can give a variant of the quantifier *everyone* that is able to bind. It will have category $\frac{\mathrm{S} \mid \mathrm{DP} \rhd \mathrm{S}}{\mathrm{DP}}$ and semantics $\lambda\kappa\forall x.\,\kappa\, x\, x$: something that knows how to turn a sentence containing a pronoun (DP $\rhd$ S) into a plain clause (S) by semantically duplicating an individual and using the second copy to provide the value of the pronoun.[3]

We immediately have an account of quantificational binding:

(16)

$$\begin{array}{c}\dfrac{\mathrm{S} \mid \mathrm{DP} \rhd \mathrm{S}}{\mathrm{DP}} \\ \textit{everyone} \\ \dfrac{\forall x.[\,]x}{x}\end{array} \left(\begin{array}{c}\dfrac{\mathrm{DP} \rhd \mathrm{S} \mid \mathrm{DP} \rhd \mathrm{S}}{(\mathrm{DP}\backslash \mathrm{S})/\mathrm{DP}} \\ \textit{loves} \\ \dfrac{[\,]}{\mathbf{loves}}\end{array} \left(\begin{array}{c}\dfrac{\mathrm{DP} \rhd \mathrm{S} \mid \mathrm{S}}{\mathrm{DP}} \\ \textit{his} \\ \dfrac{\lambda y.\,[\,]}{y}\end{array} \begin{array}{c}\dfrac{\mathrm{S} \mid \mathrm{S}}{\mathrm{DP}\backslash \mathrm{DP}} \\ \textit{mother} \\ \dfrac{[\,]}{\mathbf{mom}}\end{array} \right)\right)$$

$$= \begin{array}{c}\dfrac{\mathrm{S} \mid \mathrm{S}}{\mathrm{S}} \\ \textit{Everyone loves his mother} \\ \dfrac{\forall x.(\lambda y.\,[\,])x}{\mathbf{loves}\,(\mathbf{mom}\; y)\; x}\end{array} \overset{\text{LOWER}}{\Rightarrow} \begin{array}{c}\mathrm{S} \\ \textit{Everyone loves his mother} \\ \forall x.(\lambda y.\mathbf{loves}\,(\mathbf{mom}\; y)\; x)x\end{array}$$

After beta reduction, the semantic value reduces to $\forall x.$ **loves** (**mom** x) x.

2.2 Crossover

Continuations are well suited to providing control over evaluation order. Shan & Barker (2006) propose explaining weak crossover as default left-to-right evaluation order: a quantifier must be evaluated before any pronoun that it binds. We've already seen how left to right evaluation gives default linear scope in (14), and also how a quantifier can bind a pronoun. Here is what happens when we try to allow a quantifier to bind a pronoun when the quantifier follows the pronoun in a classic weak crossover configuration:

3 In general, a type-shifter will derive a binding version of an arbitrary DP (see Barker & Shan 2014: chapter 2): $\lambda\kappa.g[\kappa x] : B /\!\!/ (\mathrm{DP} \backslash\!\!\backslash A) \overset{\text{BIND}}{\Rightarrow} \lambda\kappa.g[\kappa x x] : B /\!\!/ (\mathrm{DP} \backslash\!\!\backslash (\mathrm{DP} \rhd A))$.

$$(17)\quad \left(\frac{\mathrm{DP} \rhd \mathrm{S} \mid \mathrm{S}}{\substack{\mathrm{DP} \\ \textit{his}}} \quad \frac{\mathrm{S} \mid \mathrm{S}}{\substack{\mathrm{DP\backslash DP} \\ \textit{mother}}} \right) \left(\frac{\mathrm{S} \mid \mathrm{S}}{\substack{\mathrm{(DP\backslash S)/DP} \\ \textit{loves}}} \quad \frac{\mathrm{S} \mid \mathrm{DP} \rhd \mathrm{S}}{\substack{\mathrm{DP} \\ \textit{everyone}}} \right)$$

$$= \frac{\mathrm{DP} \rhd \mathrm{S} \mid \mathrm{DP} \rhd \mathrm{S}}{\substack{\mathrm{S} \\ \textit{his mother loves everyone}}}$$

Combination proceeds smoothly, and the complete string is recognized as a syntactic (and semantic) constituent; but the result is not part of a complete derivation of a clause. In particular, it can't be lowered, since the category of the expression does not match the input to the LOWER type-shifter. This means that the pronoun continues to need a binder, and the quantifier continues to need something to bind. We'll see in section 3 how reconstruction can sometimes circumvent the need for a quantifier to precede a pronoun that it binds.

2.3 Scope ambiguity

The left-to-right bias built into the combination scheme guarantees linear scope for any derivation that has a single layer of scope-taking, as we have seen. But of course sentences containing two quantifiers typically are ambiguous, having both a linear scope reading and an inverse scope reading. Clearly, then, inverse scope must require more than a single layer of scope-taking. This requires, in turn, generalizing type-shifters so that they can apply to a multi-story tower. We will do this by requiring the following: if some type-shifter maps an expression of category A into category B, then the same type-shifter also maps any expression of category $\frac{C \mid D}{A}$ into category $\frac{C \mid D}{B}$.[4] Then for any category α, we have

4 In more detail, if some combinator $\mathbf{X}$ is such that $\mathbf{X}(x{:}A) \Rightarrow (y{:}B)$, then

$$\mathbf{X}(\lambda\kappa.f[\kappa x]){:}(C /\!\!/ (A \backslash\!\!\backslash D)) \Rightarrow (\lambda\kappa.f[\kappa y]){:}(C /\!\!/ (B \backslash\!\!\backslash D)).$$

(18)
$$\begin{array}{c} \dfrac{\mathrm{S} \mid \mathrm{S}}{\mathrm{DP}} \\ \textit{everyone} \\ \dfrac{\forall x.[\;]}{x} \end{array} \overset{\text{LIFT}}{\Rightarrow} \begin{array}{c} \dfrac{\mathrm{S} \mid \mathrm{S}}{\dfrac{\alpha \mid \alpha}{\mathrm{DP}}} \\ \textit{everyone} \\ \dfrac{\forall x.[\;]}{\dfrac{[\;]}{x}} \end{array}$$

The semantics of the generalized LIFT interacts with the combination schema in such a way that within a layer, quantifiers on the left still outscope quantifiers on the right, but any quantifier in a higher layer outscopes any quantifier on a lower layer. Because the LIFTed version of *everyone* given in (18) allows the quantification introduced to take place on the top level, it will outscope the existential introduced by *someone*, which occupies the middle layer.

I will not dwell on scope ambiguities in this paper; see, e.g., Barker & Shan (2014: chapter 4) for additional discussion. What is most relevant for present purposes is that even when the lifted *everyone* is at a different layer from the pronoun, crossover is still correctly ruled out:

(19)
$$\begin{array}{c} \dfrac{\mathrm{S} \mid \mathrm{S}}{\dfrac{\mathrm{DP} \rhd \mathrm{S} \mid \mathrm{S}}{\mathrm{DP}}} \\ \textit{he} \end{array} \left(\begin{array}{c} \dfrac{\mathrm{S} \mid \mathrm{S}}{\dfrac{\mathrm{S} \mid \mathrm{S}}{(\mathrm{DP}\backslash\mathrm{S})/\mathrm{DP}}} \\ \textit{loves} \end{array} \quad \begin{array}{c} \dfrac{\mathrm{S} \mid \mathrm{DP} \rhd \mathrm{S}}{\dfrac{\mathrm{S} \mid \mathrm{S}}{\mathrm{DP}}} \\ \textit{everyone} \end{array} \right)$$

$$= \begin{array}{c} \dfrac{\mathrm{S} \mid \mathrm{DP} \rhd \mathrm{S}}{\dfrac{\mathrm{DP} \rhd \mathrm{S} \mid \mathrm{S}}{\mathrm{S}}} \\ \textit{He loves everyone} \end{array} \overset{\text{LOWER}}{\Rightarrow} \begin{array}{c} \dfrac{\mathrm{S} \mid \mathrm{DP} \rhd \mathrm{S}}{\mathrm{DP} \rhd \mathrm{S}} \\ \textit{He loves everyone} \end{array}$$

Because the LOWER type-shifter given in (13) is forbidden to match categories containing DP ⊳ S in the key positions (namely, the '*B*' position in the schema in (12)), this final category still cannot be lowered to a plain S. Since LOWERing is the way that the scope of quantifier is closed, one way to gloss this restriction on lowering would be to say 'Pronouns cannot have their value resolved by lowering'. As a result, quantifiers can only bind pronouns when they occupy the same layers of their towers; given the left-to-right bias of the combination scheme, this means that (at least, in the absence of reconstruction) a quantifier must precede any pronoun that it binds.

2.4 Gaps

In order to discuss reconstruction in wh-questions, we must provide an account of basic wh-questions such as *Who did John see __?*. The first step towards that goal is to provide an account of gapped clauses, such as *did John see __*.

A gap will be an identity function with category $X /\!\!/ X$ for some choice of X. In arithmetic, it is always legitimate to multiply by X/X, since multiplication by 1 does not change the result; likewise, in the current context it is ok to merge with a gap, since gaps are the identity category. Furthermore, since there are many possible choices for X in the category schema $X /\!\!/ X$, there are many flavors of gap. For instance, if we choose $X = \mathrm{DP}\backslash\!\!\backslash \mathrm{S}$, we can prove that LOWER(*did John see __*) has category $\mathrm{DP}\backslash\!\!\backslash \mathrm{S}$ (i.e., a clause missing a DP), with denotation $\lambda x.\mathbf{saw}\ x\ \mathbf{j}$:

$$(20)\quad \begin{array}{c} \alpha \mid \alpha \\ \hline \mathrm{S/S} \\ \textit{does} \\ [\,] \\ \hline \lambda p.p \end{array} \left(\begin{array}{c} \alpha \mid \alpha \\ \hline \mathrm{DP} \\ \textit{John} \\ [\,] \\ \hline \mathbf{j} \end{array} \left(\begin{array}{c} \alpha \mid \alpha \\ \hline (\mathrm{DP}\backslash \mathrm{S})/\mathrm{DP} \\ \textit{see} \\ [\,] \\ \hline \mathbf{see} \end{array} \quad \begin{array}{c} \mathrm{DP}\backslash\!\!\backslash \mathrm{S} \mid \mathrm{S} \\ \hline \mathrm{DP} \\ \_\_ \\ \lambda x.[\,] \\ \hline x \end{array} \right)\right)$$

$$= \begin{array}{c} \mathrm{DP}\backslash\!\!\backslash \mathrm{S} \mid \mathrm{S} \\ \hline \mathrm{S} \\ \textit{does John see}\_\_ \\ \lambda x.[\,] \\ \hline \mathbf{see}\ x\ \mathbf{j} \end{array} \overset{\text{LOWER}}{\Rightarrow} \begin{array}{c} \mathrm{DP}\backslash\!\!\backslash \mathrm{S} \\ \textit{does John see}\_\_ \\ \lambda x.\mathbf{see}\ x\ \mathbf{j} \end{array}$$

In this derivation, choose $\alpha = \mathrm{DP}\backslash\!\!\backslash \mathrm{S}$ when lifting.

To summarize, unsaturated predicates, clauses containing an unbound pronoun, and gapped clauses all denote functions from individuals to propositions, and differ only in their syntactic category (see Table 1).

Tab. 1: Unsaturated predicates, clauses containing an unbound pronoun, and gapped clauses all denote functions from individuals to propositions, and differ only in their syntactic category.

	Category	Type	Example
Predicate:	$\mathrm{DP}\backslash \mathrm{S}$	$e \to t$	*left*
Open proposition:	$\mathrm{DP} \rhd \mathrm{S}$	$e \to t$	*He left.*
Gapped clause:	$\mathrm{DP}\backslash\!\!\backslash \mathrm{S}$	$e \to t$	*does John see __*

2.5 Wh-phrases

In English, in-situ WH phrases are limited to echo questions and multiple wh-questions, though they are common cross-linguistically. Semantically, they turn the sentences that contain them into questions. Therefore the in-situ *who* will have category $\frac{\text{Q} \mid \text{S}}{\text{DP}}$: something that takes scope over a clause S and turns it into an interrogative Q. This means that the echo question *John saw WHO??* will denote $\mathbf{who}(\lambda x.\,\mathbf{saw}\,x\,\mathbf{j})$, where **who** is a function that turns the property of being seen by John into a question meaning (for instance, on some theories of questions, a set of propositions).

In order to derive English-style wh-questions, in which (the first) wh-phrase occurs at the left edge of the interrogative clause, we need a simple type-shifter that adjusts the syntactic category of a wh-phrase:

(21) $$\boxed{C_F /\!\!/ (A \backslash\!\!\backslash B) \overset{\text{FRONT}}{\Rightarrow} C/(A \backslash\!\!\backslash B)}$$

This type-shifter is purely syntactic, and does not affect the semantic value of the shifted expression in any way. Syntactically, the type-shifter replaces the hollow forward slash ('$/\!\!/$'), which says that the nuclear scope of the wh-phrase must surround it (i.e., that the wh-phrase is in-situ) into a solid slash ('/'), which says that the nuclear scope of the wh-phrase follows it (i.e., that the wh-phrase has been fronted). In addition, the type-shifter also removes the syntactic feature 'F', which controls the timing of the FRONT rule in order to manage pied-piping, as discussed shortly.

Recall that by the tower notational convention,

$$\frac{(\text{DP?S})_F \mid \text{S}}{\text{DP}} \equiv (\text{DP?S})_F /\!\!/ (\text{DP} \backslash\!\!\backslash \text{S}).$$

Then the FRONT type-shifter applies to the following lexical entry for the wh-phrase *who*:

$$\begin{array}{c} \dfrac{(\text{DP?S})_F \mid \text{S}}{\text{DP}} \\ \textit{who} \\ \dfrac{\mathbf{who}(\lambda x[\;])}{x} \end{array} \overset{\text{FRONT}}{\Rightarrow} \begin{array}{c} (\text{DP?S})/(\text{DP} \backslash\!\!\backslash \text{S}) \\ \textit{who(m)} \\ \lambda\kappa.\mathbf{who}(\lambda x.\kappa x) \end{array}$$

Making use of the derivation of the gapped clause *did John see* __ given above in (20), we now have a derivation of a complete wh-question:

(22)
$$\begin{array}{ccccc} \mathrm{(DP?S)/(DP\backslash\!\!\backslash S)} & \mathrm{DP\backslash\!\!\backslash S} & & \mathrm{DP?S} \\ \textit{who} & \textit{does John see}\_\_ & = & \textit{Who does John see}\_\_\textit{?} \\ \lambda\kappa.\mathbf{who}(\lambda x.\kappa x) & \lambda x.\mathbf{see}\;x\;\mathbf{j} & & \mathbf{who}(\lambda x.\mathbf{see}\;x\;\mathbf{j}) \end{array}$$

Pied piping is handled by delaying the application of the FRONT type-shifter until the wh-phrase has combined with additional material. For example, in order to derive questions in which *to whom* or *which man* has been fronted, we reason as follows:

(23)
$$\begin{array}{ccccc} \begin{array}{c} \alpha \mid \alpha \\ \hline \mathrm{PP/DP} \\ \textit{to} \\ [\;] \\ \hline \mathbf{to} \end{array} & \begin{array}{c} \mathrm{(DP?S)}_F \mid \mathrm{S} \\ \hline \mathrm{DP} \\ \textit{whom} \\ \mathbf{who}(\lambda x[\;]) \\ \hline x \end{array} & = & \begin{array}{c} \mathrm{(DP?S)}_F \mid \mathrm{S} \\ \hline \mathrm{PP} \\ \textit{to whom} \\ \mathbf{who}(\lambda x[\;]) \\ \hline \mathbf{to}(x) \end{array} \end{array}$$

$$\overset{\text{FRONT}}{\Rightarrow} \begin{array}{c} \mathrm{(DP?S)/(PP\backslash\!\!\backslash S)} \\ \textit{to whom} \\ \lambda\kappa.\mathbf{who}(\lambda x.\kappa(\mathbf{to}(x))) \end{array}$$

(24)
$$\begin{array}{ccccc} \begin{array}{c} \mathrm{((DP/N)?S)}_F \mid \mathrm{S} \\ \hline \mathrm{DP/N} \\ \textit{which} \\ \mathbf{which}(\lambda f.[\;]) \\ \hline f \end{array} & \begin{array}{c} \alpha \mid \alpha \\ \hline \mathrm{N} \\ \textit{man} \\ [\;] \\ \hline \mathbf{man} \end{array} & = & \begin{array}{c} \mathrm{((DP/N)?S)}_F \mid \mathrm{S} \\ \hline \mathrm{DP} \\ \textit{which man} \\ \mathbf{which}(\lambda f.[\;]) \\ \hline f(\mathbf{man}) \end{array} \end{array}$$

$$\overset{\text{FRONT}}{\Rightarrow} \begin{array}{c} \mathrm{((DP/N)?S)/(DP\backslash\!\!\backslash S)} \\ \textit{which man} \\ \lambda\kappa.\mathbf{which}(\lambda f.\kappa(f(\mathbf{man}))) \end{array}$$

In each case of pied piping, the lexical entry for the wh-word introduces an F feature, which remains part of the category of each successively larger constituent until the FRONT rule is applied, at which point the result category produced by the FRONT rule no longer contains the F feature. The net result is that a larger constituent surrounding the wh-word can appear in the fronted position:

(25)
a. [Who] did John speak to? $\mathbf{who}(\lambda x.\mathbf{speak}\,(\mathbf{to}(x))\,\mathbf{j})$
b. [To whom] did John speak? $\mathbf{who}(\lambda x.\mathbf{speak}\,(\mathbf{to}(x))\,\mathbf{j})$
c. [Which man] did John speak to? $\mathbf{which}(\lambda f.\mathbf{speak}\,(\mathbf{to}(f(\mathbf{man})))\,\mathbf{j})$
d. [To which man] did John speak? $\mathbf{which}(\lambda f.\mathbf{speak}\,(\mathbf{to}(f(\mathbf{man})))\,\mathbf{j})$

In (25a), the preposition is stranded because we applied the FRONT type-shifter to the bare wh-word *who*. In (25b), the wh-word combines with the preposition *to* before the FRONT type-shifter applies, creating a syntactic PP gap.[5]

3 Reconstructing a bound pronoun in a wh-question

All of the details above in section 2, including the analyses of in-situ scope, binding, wh-fronting and pied-piping, were determined without any view towards handling reconstruction. Nevertheless, we are now in a position to derive at least some reconstruction effects without any additional assumptions.

The essential element in the analysis that gives rise to reconstruction effects is the FRONT type-shifter. This type-shifter captures the essential similarity of the semantic scope-taking behavior of in-situ wh-phrases with the syntactic scope-taking behavior of fronted wh-phrases. Because the type-shifter does not affect semantic interpretation, it guarantees that the semantic value of the fronted wh-question will be exactly the same as if it had occurred in-situ in the wh-gap position.

For instance:

(26) Which of his_i relatives does everyone_i love __ (the most)?

In order to derive this example, we will discuss its two main syntactic constituents in turn: the fronted wh-phrase *which of his relatives*, followed by a derivation of the question body *does everyone love* __.

Recall that the category of a simple pronoun (as in (15)) is $\text{pn} \equiv \frac{\text{DP} \rhd \text{S} \mid \text{S}}{\text{DP}}$.

5 What, then, blocks **Which did John see* __ *man*? The derivation of this violation of the Left Branch island constraint would involve postulating a gap with category $\frac{(\text{DP/N}) \backslash\!\!\backslash \text{S} \mid \text{S}}{\text{DP/N}}$. We can recognize this as a violation because the gap category is looking to combine with a nominal N to its right. This particular island constraint, then, can be implemented as a constraint on the syntactic form of permissible gap categories.

$$(27)\quad \begin{array}{c} \begin{array}{c|c} ((DP/N)?S)_F & S \\ \hline \alpha & \alpha \\ \hline \end{array} \\ DP/N \\ \textit{which} \\ \mathbf{which}(\lambda f.[\,]) \\ \hline [\,] \\ \hline f \end{array} \left(\begin{array}{c} \begin{array}{c|c} S & S \\ \hline \alpha & \alpha \\ \hline \end{array} \\ N/DP \\ \textit{relative-of} \\ [\,] \\ \hline [\,] \\ \hline \mathbf{rel} \end{array} \quad \begin{array}{c} \begin{array}{c|c} S & S \\ \hline DP \rhd S & S \\ \hline \end{array} \\ DP \\ \textit{his} \\ [\,] \\ \hline \lambda z.[\,] \\ \hline z \end{array} \right)$$

$$= \begin{array}{c} \begin{array}{c|c} ((DP/N)?S)_F & S \\ \hline DP \rhd S & S \\ \hline \end{array} \\ DP \\ \textit{which rel of his} \\ \mathbf{which}(\lambda f.[\,]) \\ \hline \lambda z.[\,] \\ \hline f(\mathbf{rel}\, z) \end{array} \equiv \begin{array}{c} ((DP/N)?S)_F /\!\!/ (pn \backslash\!\!\backslash S) \\ \textit{which rel of his} \\ \text{(no change)} \end{array}$$

$$\overset{\text{FRONT}}{\Rightarrow} \begin{array}{c} ((DP/N)?S)/(pn \backslash\!\!\backslash S) \\ \textit{which rel of his} \\ \text{(no change)} \end{array}$$

For lifting purposes in this derivation, choose $\alpha = DP \rhd S$. Note that we have lifted in such a way that the main semantic effect of the wh-phrase occupies a higher layer than that of the pronoun. Translating the semantic tower back into linear notation, the semantic value of the fronted wh-phrase is $\lambda\gamma.\mathbf{which}(\lambda f.\gamma(\lambda\kappa\lambda z.\kappa(f(\mathbf{rel}\, z))))$.

We next derive the body of the question (ignoring the contribution of *does* for simplicity, see (20) for details):

$$(28)\quad \begin{array}{c} \begin{array}{c|c} \alpha & \alpha \\ \hline S & DP \rhd S \\ \hline \end{array} \\ DP \\ \textit{everyone} \\ [\,] \\ \hline \forall x.[\,]x \\ \hline x \end{array} \left(\begin{array}{c} \begin{array}{c|c} \alpha & \alpha \\ \hline \beta & \beta \\ \hline \end{array} \\ (DP\backslash S)/DP \\ \textit{love} \\ [\,] \\ \hline [\,] \\ \hline \mathbf{love} \end{array} \quad \begin{array}{c} \begin{array}{c|c} pn \backslash\!\!\backslash S & S \\ \hline DP \rhd S & S \\ \hline \end{array} \\ DP \\ \_\_ \\ \lambda\mathcal{P}.[\,] \\ \hline \mathcal{P}(\lambda y.[\,]) \\ \hline y \end{array} \right)$$

$$
\begin{array}{c}
\begin{array}{c|c} \text{pn}\backslash\!\!\backslash\text{S} & \text{S} \\ \hline \text{S} & \text{S} \\ \hline \end{array} \\
\text{S} \\
= \textit{does everyone love\_\_} \\
\lambda\mathcal{P}.[\,] \\ \hline
\forall x.(\mathcal{P}(\lambda y.[\,]))\,x \\ \hline
\textbf{love}\ y\ x
\end{array}
\quad \overset{\text{LOWER } (twice)}{\Rightarrow} \quad
\begin{array}{c}
\text{pn}\backslash\!\!\backslash\text{S} \\
\textit{does everyone love\_\_} \\
\lambda\mathcal{P}.\forall x.(\mathcal{P}(\lambda y.\textbf{love}\ y\ x))\ x
\end{array}
$$

Here, choose $\alpha = \text{pn}\backslash\!\!\backslash\text{S}$ and $\beta = \text{DP} \triangleright \text{S}$; $\mathcal{P}$ is a variable of type pn. The idea is that instead of having a simple gap in which an individual of category DP is missing, as in (20), we have a higher-order gap in which a pronoun is missing. Nevertheless, the pronoun denotation is still an identity function (see Barker 2009: 20).

Putting the two halves of the question together, we have:

(29)

$$
\begin{array}{cc}
((\text{DP}/\text{N})?\text{S})/(\text{pn}\backslash\!\!\backslash\text{S}) & \text{pn}\backslash\!\!\backslash\text{S} \\
\textit{which relative of his} & \textit{does everyone love\_\_} \\
\lambda\gamma.\textbf{which}(\lambda f.\gamma(\lambda\kappa\lambda z.\kappa(f(\textbf{rel}\ z)))) & \lambda\mathcal{P}.\forall y.\mathcal{P}(\lambda w(\textbf{love}\ w\ y))\ y
\end{array}
$$

This is a simple function/argument construction of the form $A/B + B = A$. The category of the entire question, then, will be (DP/N)?S: a question asking for a function from nominals to entities (as discussed below).

Although the derivation just given is complex, it makes use of nothing beyond what is needed for the simpler examples discussed in section 2, namely, the general combination schema, the four type-shifters (LIFT, LOWER, BIND, and FRONT), and the identity schema for gaps.

It will be instructive to consider the series of beta reductions that leads to a simplified representation of the semantic value of the question. As the reduction proceeds, the material to be reconstructed—the semantic contribution of the constituent *relative of his*—is underlined. The reconstructed material is destined to be the argument of the pronoun gap variable $\mathcal{P}$:

(30)
$$
\begin{array}{l}
(\lambda\gamma.\textbf{which}(\lambda f.\gamma(\lambda\kappa\lambda z.\kappa(f(\textbf{rel}\ z)))))(\lambda\mathcal{P}.\forall y.\mathcal{P}(\lambda w.\textbf{love}\ w\ y)\ y) \\
\rightsquigarrow \textbf{which}(\lambda f.(\lambda\mathcal{P}.\forall y.\mathcal{P}(\lambda w.\textbf{love}\ w\ y)\ y)\underline{(\lambda\kappa\lambda z.\kappa(f(\textbf{rel}\ z)))}) \\
\rightsquigarrow \textbf{which}(\lambda f.\forall y.\underline{(\lambda\kappa\lambda z.\kappa(f(\textbf{rel}\ z)))}(\lambda w.\textbf{love}\ w\ y)\ y) \\
\rightsquigarrow \textbf{which}(\lambda f.\forall y.(\lambda z.(\lambda w.\textbf{love}\ w\ y)(f(\textbf{rel}\ z)))\ y) \\
\rightsquigarrow \textbf{which}(\lambda f.\forall y.(\lambda w.\textbf{love}\ w\ y)(f(\textbf{rel}\ y))) \\
\rightsquigarrow \textbf{which}(\lambda f.\forall y.\textbf{love}(f(\textbf{rel}\ y))\ y)
\end{array}
$$

Gloss: for what choice function f is it the case that every person y loves f(y's relatives)? A possible answer for this question might be "the tallest". (In order to arrive at the traditional answer, namely, *his mother*, we need yet higher types; that derivation is somewhat more complicated, but requires no additional assumptions. Full details are provided in Barker 2009.)

It is worth emphasizing that there is no syntactic movement, nor is there any sense in which the semantic beta reductions are actually moving semantic material from one place to another. That is, the lambda calculus is an equational theory: the series of reductions are a series of equivalences, not transformations. In other words, the analysis here is directly compositional in the sense of Jacobson (2002): every syntactic constituent has a well-formed semantic interpretation that does not depend on any material outside of the constituent.

3.1 Despite reconstruction, crossover effects remain in force

In the simplest examples, crossover occurs when a pronoun precedes the quantifier that binds it, as shown in (17). In reconstruction examples, a pronoun can precede the quantifier that binds it. But this does not mean that reconstruction suspends crossover effects:

(31) ? Which of his_i relatives __ loves everyone?

In the analysis of *Which of his relatives does everyone love __?*, the binding analysis requires the quantifier *everyone* to bind the virtual pronoun inside the gap site, as illustrated above in (28). This is possible in part because the quantifier precedes the gap site, conforming to the left-to-right restrictions on binding imposed by the combination schema. In (31), in contrast, since the gap site precedes the quantifier, there is no way for the quantifier to bind into the gap, for exactly the same reason that the simple crossover binding attempts failed in (17) and (19).

In other words, even though semantic reconstruction can allow a quantifier to bind a pronoun that precedes it, crossover restrictions remain in effect even in reconstruction situations. In each reconstruction analysis below, we shall see that crossover effects remain in force.

3.2 Reconstructing binders instead of pronouns; strong versus weak crossover

In addition to reconstructing bound pronouns, we should observe reconstruction effects from reconstructing any scope-taking element. In particular, it should be possible for scope-taking quantifiers to behave as if they were evaluated in the reconstructed position. We can test this prediction by seeing which pronouns a reconstructed quantifier is able to bind:

(32) a. John had to explain the lowest grade of each student$_i$ to her$_i$ mother.
b. Which grade of each student$_i$ did John have to explain to her$_i$ mother?

In (32a), the quantifier *each student* binds the pronoun *her*. Because the quantifier is to the left of the pronoun, the binding configuration conforms to left-to-right evaluation order. (The quantifier does not c-commanding the pronoun, but c-command is not required for binding on the account here; see Barker 2012 for arguments that c-command is irrelevant for quantificational binding.)

Likewise, if we replace *the lowest* in (32a) with the wh-determiner *which*, then, factoring in pied piping, we have the corresponding wh-question in (32b). Once again, because the FRONT type-shifter does not affect semantic value, the binding potential of the quantifier will be exactly similar to the corresponding quantifier in (32a). Thus the analysis here gives a bound reading as indicated in (32b).

The account here predicts that we should be able to observe crossover effects if the reconstruction position follows the pronoun to be bound. First, consider the following non-interrogative sentences:

(33) a. * She$_i$ called several friends of each student$_i$.
[STRONG CROSSOVER]
b. ?? Her$_i$ mother called several friends of each student$_i$.
[WEAK CROSSOVER]

(34) a. * She completed some of each student's assignments.
[STRONG CROSSOVER]
b. ?? Her$_i$ mother completed some of each student's$_i$ assignments.
[WEAK CROSSOVER]

In these examples, the contrast between weak and strong crossover effects is quite dramatic.

In order to create the corresponding reconstruction examples, we replace the expressions *several* and *some* with wh-expressions:

(35) a. ? Which friends of each student$_i$ did she$_i$ call __?
b. ? Which friends of each student$_i$ did her$_i$ mother call __?

(36) a. ? How many of each student$_i$'s assignments did she$_i$ complete __?
b. ? How many of each student$_i$'s assignments did her$_i$ mother complete __?

Because the reconstruction gap follows the pronoun, the account here correctly predicts that an attempt to derive a bound reading for the pronoun will give rise to a crossover violation.

Interestingly, after pied-piping, the contrast between the strong crossover in the (a) examples versus weak crossover in the (b) examples becomes attenuated in comparison with the strength of the effects observed above in (33) and (34). Nothing in the formal system distinguishes strong crossover from weak crossover. Presumably, strong crossover is due to some factor over and above whatever characterizes weak crossover, perhaps something along the lines of Safir's (2004) Independence Principle, which entails that if a pronoun is bound by a quantifier, that pronoun cannot c-command the quantifier. If so, it is telling that the pronouns in (35a) and in (36a) do not c-command the quantifier in question. If strong crossover follows from the Independence Principle, and the Independence Principle depends on syntactic c-command relations, then we have no reason to expect that examples like those in (35a) and (36a) will qualify as strong crossover, in agreement with the comparatively weak ungrammaticality of these examples.

In any case, the examples in (35) and (36) all give rise to the kind of processing difficulty expected from weak crossover, as predicted by the account here. Thus not only can reconstruction lead to situations in which a quantifier can bind a pronoun that precedes it, it can also lead to situations in which a quantifier does linearly precede a pronoun and yet still can't bind it. Left-to-right evaluation order accounts for both of these non-default patterns automatically for semantic reconstruction as provided by the FRONT type-shifter.

3.3 Principle C

Under syntactic reconstruction, it is natural to expect Principle C effects.

(37) * Whose evaluation of John$_i$ did he$_i$ expect Mary to repudiate __?

This example and its judgment is from Safir (1999: 592). If *evaluation of John* syntactically reconstructs, then the name *John* will come to be c-commanded by the pronoun *he*. The ungrammaticality of (37) would then follow from Principle C, which says that referring expressions, including names, cannot corefer with a c-commanding expression. Note that the Independence Principle mentioned above also rules out (37), since (after syntactic reconstruction) the pronoun c-commands a coreferring expression.

The empirical status of Principle C violations in reconstruction contexts is both subtle and intricate (see Heycock 1995, Büring 2005, Sportiche 2006, Salzmann 2006, and others for comprehensive discussions). Certainly there are well-established classes of examples where reconstructed Principle C violations do not result in ungrammaticality. Safir (1999: 609) discusses a range of such exceptions, including when the referring expression is within a possessor phrase, or, more generally, within an adjunct. Here are a few of Safir's examples, which I take it are generally accepted as grammatical:

(38) a. Which of John$_i$'s friends does he$_i$ like?
b. Which biography of Picasso$_i$, do you think he$_i$ wants to read?
c. Which witness's attack on Lee$_i$ did he$_i$ try to get expunged from the trial records?
d. Whose criticism of Lee$_i$ did he$_i$ choose to ignore?

Any approach involving syntactic reconstruction must consider Principle C violations to be the default, and then explain how some examples escape through some separate mechanism. For instance, Safir suggests that reconstructed referring expressions sometimes function as if they were pronouns for the purposes of the binding constraints ('vehicle change').

In contrast, on the approach here, because reconstruction is entirely semantic, reconstruction does not have any effect on syntactic c-command relations. As a result, reconstruction is never expected to create Principle C effects. Thus it is ungrammatical cases such as (37) that must be explained through additional factors, such as Kuno's notions of discourse perspective and participant sympathy.[6]

4 Relative clauses and wh-relatives

As noted above in (2), it has long been observed that wh-questions bear a striking resemblance to some kinds of relative clauses:

(39)	a.	[Which	relative of his]	does everyone love __?
	b.	[the	relative of his]	that everyone loves __

Just as there can be a quantificational binding relationship between *everyone* and *his* in (39a), there can be the same kind of binding relationship in (39b). On the account here, this suggests that the definite determiner *the* may have a lexical entry that closely resembles the pied-piping lexical entry for the wh-determiner *which*:

6 Kuno (1987) is relevant, and there is an unpublished 1997 Harvard manuscript cited in the literature called 'Binding Theory and the Minimalist Program' that I have not been able to get hold of.

(40)

$$\frac{\dfrac{((DP/N)?S)_F \mid S}{DP/N}}{\textit{which}} \qquad \frac{\dfrac{DP_F \mid S}{DP/N}}{\textit{the}}$$

$$\frac{\mathbf{which}(\lambda f.[\,])}{f} \qquad \frac{\mathbf{the}(\lambda f.[\,])}{f}$$

If we have such a lexical entry among the analyses for *the*, we get the following analysis in parallel with the reconstruction derivation given above for wh-questions:

(41) a. Which relative of his does everyone love __?
(answer: the tallest)

b. $\mathbf{which}(\lambda f.\forall y.\mathbf{love}(f(\mathbf{rel}\ y))\ y)$

(42) a. the relative of his that everyone loves __
(completion: is always the tallest)

b. $\mathbf{the}(\lambda f.\forall y.\mathbf{love}(f(\mathbf{rel}\ y))\ y)$

This is an analysis on which the definite description receives (at least by default) a functional interpretation rather than a strictly referential one.

To see what this means, start with the denotation of the wh-question in (41b). This will be a question whose answers correspond to choice functions that pick an object out of a set of relatives. The answer will be referential ("Uncle Bob") just in case the choice function returns the same individual for each set of relatives (assume that the quantificational domain for *everyone* is contextually restricted to the participants in a family reunion).

Analogously, the denotation of the definite description in (42a) will likewise be functional. To the extent that it refers, it describes an intensional object, similar to the definite description in *the most beloved person is the one who listens most carefully*. As for the wh interrogative, the functional description can be coerced into referring to an individual just in case the relevant function returns the same individual for every set of relatives (the "Uncle Bob" reading).

Anticipating the treatment of reflexive pronouns in the next section, we can make the referential interpretation highly salient:

(43) a. the picture of herself that Mary likes

b. $\mathbf{the}(\lambda f.\mathbf{likes}(f(\mathbf{pic}\ \mathbf{m}))\ \mathbf{m})$

In order to arrive at a bound interpretation of the reflexive pronoun, the analysis here requires the reconstruction definite determiner given above in (40). Although the description in (43a) might still have a functional interpretation, a referential interpretation is much more natural. To arrive at a referent, **the** must take a property of choice functions and return an individual.

$$\textbf{the}_{\text{ref}} \equiv \lambda\kappa.\iota x.\forall f.(\forall P.Px \rightarrow (fP = x)) \rightarrow \kappa f$$

Gloss: given κ, a property of choice functions, return the unique object x such that any choice function that returns x whenever possible has property κ.

On the topic of functional (intensional) descriptions, Grosu & Krifka (2007) note that reconstruction is relevant for understanding what they call equational intensional reconstruction relatives:

(44) a. the gifted mathematician that John claims to be

b. $\textbf{the}(\lambda f.\textbf{claim}(\textbf{be}(f(\textbf{gifted-math'n}))\,\textbf{j}))$

As they note, one of the hallmarks of this construction is that the referent of the description is not entailed to be a gifted mathematician. This is exactly what we would expect by using the version of *the* from (40), since the semantic material contributed by *gifted mathematician* will be reconstructed into the gap position under the scope of *claim*. There are many special properties of this construction that I cannot explore in this paper; nevertheless, the general approach to reconstruction here may provide some hint into how the interaction of reconstruction and intensionality in this construction can be implemented in a framework that does not make use of syntactic movement.

4.1 Combining wh with relative clauses: relative pronouns with pied piping

Of course, one place where wh-phrases and relative clause formation overlap is in relative pronouns:

(45)
$$\frac{(A\backslash\!\!\backslash S)_F \mid S}{A}$$
who(se)/which
$$\frac{\lambda x.[\,]}{x}$$

Given that the feature F triggers the pied-piping mechanism, we expect that relative pronouns can participate in pied piping:

(46) a. the man [who] John saw

b. the man [whose mother] John saw

c. the man [the mother of whom] John saw

In addition, we also expect that a reconstructed pronoun can be bound by a quantifier that follows it:

(47) John is a man [[whose opinion of her$_i$] every woman$_i$ respects __]

Both of these patterns fall out from the analysis.

Finally, we predict that if the reconstruction site precedes a pronoun, a bound reading should be good, as in (47), but if the reconstruction site follows a pronoun, an attempt at binding should give rise to crossover effects:

(48) a theory [[every proponent$_i$ of which] {?he$_i$/?his$_i$ advisor} cites __]

Native speakers report that this sentence is somewhat hard to process, but the reported judgments tend to support the predicted contrast.

5 Idioms

Idiom chunks—DPs that serve as parts of idioms, such as *care* in *take good care of someone*, or *lip service*, as in *pay lip service to*—generally must occur as an argument of a limited, specific set of verbs in order to receive their idiomatic interpretation. Yet they can sometimes be separated from the relevant verb in wh-interrogatives and in relative clauses:

(49) a. How much care did (Mary say that) John took of Bill?
b. the lip service that (Mary said that) John paid to civil liberties

In order for the idiomatic interpretations to be licensed, there must be some mechanism for transmitting information about the idiom chunk from its displaced position to the rest of the idiomatic expression. This has traditionally served as an argument for syntactic reconstruction (see, e.g., Sportiche 2006), since one way to make the needed connection is to syntactically reconstruct the idiom chunk, at which point it will be reunited with the rest of its idiom.

Although the approach here is primarily semantic, nevertheless a limited amount of syntactic information does flow from the gap site to the fronted constituent, as we have seen above in pied piping examples. To handle idiom licensing, we need only provide some fine-grained syntactic features that will enable suitable syntactic bookkeeping to take place. For example, the relevant idiomatic sense of *strings* as in *to pull strings* may subcategorize for a DP_S ('*S*' for strings), and of course the noun *strings* will itself have category N_S. Then we have the following derivation for *Which strings did John pull?*:

(50)

$$\left(\begin{array}{c}\dfrac{((DP/N)?S)_F \mid S}{\begin{array}{c}DP_\gamma/N_\gamma\\ \textit{which}\\ \mathbf{which}(\lambda f.[\,])\end{array}}\\ \hline f\end{array}\quad \begin{array}{c}\dfrac{\alpha \mid \alpha}{\begin{array}{c}N_S\\ \textit{strings}\\ [\,]\end{array}}\\ \hline \mathbf{connections}\end{array}\right)$$

$$\left(\begin{array}{c}\dfrac{\alpha \mid \alpha}{\begin{array}{c}DP\\ \textit{John}\\ [\,]\end{array}}\\ \hline \mathbf{j}\end{array}\left(\begin{array}{c}\dfrac{\alpha \mid \alpha}{\begin{array}{c}(DP\backslash S)/DP_S\\ \textit{pull}\\ [\,]\end{array}}\\ \hline \mathbf{use}\end{array}\quad \begin{array}{c}\dfrac{DP_S\backslash\!\!\backslash S \mid S}{\begin{array}{c}DP_S\\ \_\_\\ \lambda x.[\,]\end{array}}\\ \hline x\end{array}\right)\right)$$

The remainder of the derivation goes exactly as in (22) except that the category of the question body is $DP_S\backslash\!\!\backslash S$ instead of $DP\backslash\!\!\backslash S$, and likewise for the category that the fronted wh-phrase is seeking to combine with. If *strings* were replaced with an ordinary nominal, or if *pull* were replaced with an ordinary transitive verb, the two halves of the derivation would not match appropriately. Because the gap faithfully transmits (via the scope-taking mechanism) the detailed syntactic category expected at the gap site to form part of the category of the entire gapped clause, further embedding the idiomatic verb (e.g., *Which strings did Mary get so upset that John pulled?*) will not disrupt the licensing connection.

6 Reflexives and *each other* anaphors

One classic reconstruction effect involves reflexives. Normally, reflexives must be bound by some less oblique coargument in the same clause:

(51) a. John liked a picture of himself.
b. * Mary liked a picture of himself.
c. * John claimed Mary liked a picture of himself.
d. * A picture of himself was liked by John.

But in reconstruction situations, the reflexive can be separated from its binder:

(52) a. Which picture of himself does John like __?
b. the picture of herself that Mary likes __

Assuming that the anaphors in (52) are grammatically bound, the analysis here requires reconstruction.

One additional wrinkle: as (53) shows, a reconstructed reflexive can even take an antecedent that is not in the same minimal clause as the reconstruction site.

(53) Which picture of himself does John claim Mary liked __?

This suggests that reconstruction somehow enables a reflexive to take advantage of a wider range of possible binders than it would have been able to if it had been generated in the reconstruction position.

The approach here follows Dowty's (2007: 97) suggestion that reflexives are scope-taking expressions. Building on Szabolcsi's (1992) proposal that reflexives express the combinator **W** = $\lambda\kappa x.\kappa x x$:

(54)
$$\begin{array}{c} \alpha \mid \alpha \\ \hline (DP\backslash S)/DP \\ \textit{saw} \\ \dfrac{[\,]}{\textbf{saw}} \end{array} \quad \begin{array}{c} DP\backslash S \mid DP\backslash S \\ \hline DP \\ \textit{himself} \\ \dfrac{\lambda x.[\,]x}{x} \end{array} \quad = \quad \begin{array}{c} DP\backslash S \mid DP\backslash S \\ \hline DP\backslash S \\ \textit{saw himself} \\ \dfrac{\lambda x.[\,]x}{\textbf{saw}\ x} \end{array}$$

$$\overset{\text{LOWER}}{\Rightarrow} \quad \begin{array}{c} DP\backslash S \\ \textit{saw himself} \\ \lambda x.\textbf{saw}\ x\ x \end{array}$$

On this view, reflexives are an in-situ VP modifier: they take scope over a VP, and return a new VP whose next argument (the subject) gets copied into the anaphor position.[7]

(55) Which picture of himself did John see?

(56)
$$\begin{array}{c} ((DP/N)?S)_F \mid S \\ \hline \alpha \mid \alpha \\ \hline DP/N \\ \textit{which} \\ \dfrac{\dfrac{\textbf{which}(\lambda f.[\,])}{[\,]}}{f} \end{array} \quad \begin{array}{c} S \mid S \\ \hline DP\backslash S \mid DP\backslash S \\ \hline N \\ \textit{picture of himself} \\ \dfrac{\dfrac{[\,]}{\lambda x.[\,]x}}{\textbf{pic}\ x} \end{array}$$

7 In general, non-subject arguments can bind reflexives in English; as Dowty comments, his strategy requires postulating a family of categories, including also, for instance, for ditransitive cases such as *Mary described Bill to himself*, a more general lexical category schema $\dfrac{\alpha/DP \mid \alpha/DP}{DP}$.

$$\begin{array}{c} ((\mathrm{DP/N})?\mathrm{S})/(\dfrac{\mathrm{DP\backslash S} \mid \mathrm{DP\backslash S}}{\mathrm{DP}} \backslash\!\!\backslash \mathrm{S}) \\ \overset{\text{FRONT}}{\Rightarrow} \quad \textit{which picture of himself} \\ \lambda \gamma.\mathbf{which}(\lambda f.\gamma(\dfrac{\lambda x.[\,]x}{f(\mathbf{pic}\ x)})) \end{array}$$

The only difference between this analysis and the one for quantificational binding of an ordinary pronoun is that the gap within the pied-pied material is a reflexive-pronoun type gap rather than a standard pronoun, with corresponding adjustments in the question body.

This approach automatically gives good results for the following examples:

(57) a. John saw no pictures of himself.
b. Which picture of himself did John claim Mary liked?

Unfortunately, this simple analysis also generates the following kind of ungrammatical examples:

(58) * John claimed Mary liked a picture of himself.

The reason that (58) is generated is that there is no way to block the reflexive from taking scope over the higher, non-local verb phrase.

The approach to reflexives explored here will only be viable if it is possible to find a way to constrain scope-taking operators. There is little agreement on how best to manage scope preferences and scope requirements in the literature at this point. One possible strategy in the approach taken here would be to impose restrictions on the categories of the towers that clause-embedding predicates can take as complements; but I leave this for future research.

Reconstruction of anaphors such as *each other* can be handled analogously:

(59) a. Which of each other's papers did they read __?
b. the descriptions of each other that they offered __

Like reflexives, *each other* must generally be c-commanded by the element that binds it. We can therefore give *each other* a scope-taking analysis on which it takes scope just equal to the scope of its binder, e.g., category $\dfrac{\mathrm{DP\backslash S} \mid \mathrm{DP\backslash S}}{\mathrm{DP}}$. The semantics will require that the binder be the kind of object that the quantificational part of *each other* can distribute over, but otherwise the derivation will proceed exactly as shown above for *himself*.

7 Conclusions

Shan & Barker (2006) propose that crossover follows under their continuation-based framework for scope-taking, given two assumptions: that pronouns find their binders by taking scope, and so participate in the same scope-taking system as their binders; and that the evaluation order that governs scope relations defaults to left-to-right.

This paper, building on Shan & Barker (2006) and Barker (2009), explores a number of reconstruction effects. A fully explicit fragment provides derivations for reconstruction effects involving bound pronouns, reconstructed binders, wh-questions, relative clauses, and wh-relatives.

The formal system involves a general combination schema, along with four freely-applied type-shifters: LIFT, LOWER, BIND, and FRONT. The resulting grammar is directly compositional, variable-free, and does not make use of QR or any syntactic movement operations. Thus a continuation-based system allows us to model crossover as a processing constraint in the competence grammar, without needing to say anything special in order to handle a respectable variety of reconstruction examples.

In each case of reconstruction, the analysis hinges on the application of the FRONT type-shifter, repeated here:

(60) $$\boxed{C_F /\!\!/ (A \backslash\!\!\backslash B) \overset{\text{FRONT}}{\Rightarrow} C/(A \backslash\!\!\backslash B)}$$

This type shifter turns what would otherwise be an in-situ scope-taker (such as a wh-phrase) into an expression that has been syntactically displaced to the left. Because it adjusts the syntactic category of an expression without adjusting its semantic value, the semantic value of the resulting expression is guaranteed to be exactly as if the displaced constituent were delayed, that is, as if it were evaluated in the position of the gap in the gapped clause. This accounts for the semantic reconstruction effects, including bindability as well as ability to bind.

Crucially, the effects due to the FRONT type-shifter are perfectly compatible with default left-to-right evaluation, so the reconstruction effects discussed to not constitute counterexamples to the Shan/Barker approach to crossover. Indeed, I have presented empirical data from a range of constructions that in fact crossover is not suspended in reconstruction situations: for instance, if a reconstructed quantifier follows a pronoun, it cannot bind the pronoun, so crossover remains in effect.

Furthermore, since the FRONT type-shifter does not involve syntactic movement, there is no syntactic reconstruction. This is why reconstruction often does not trigger Principle C violations, since there is no syntactic structure inside the reconstruction gap site.

Shan & Barker (2006) emphasize that the FRONT type-shifter is motivated entirely by a desire to give the simplest possible analysis to wh-question formation, without considering reconstruction examples. Nevertheless, it provides analyses not only of syntactic pied piping, but also a variety of reconstruction effects, in a way that remains fully compatible with a principled explanation for crossover.

References

Barendregt, Hendrik Pieter. 1984. *The lambda calculus: Its syntax and semantics*. Revised Edition (Studies in Logic and the Foundations of Mathematics 103). Amsterdam: Elsevier.

Barker, Chris. 2009. Reconstruction as delayed evaluation. In Erhard Hinrichs & John Nerbonne (eds.), *Theory and evidence in semantics*, 1–28. Stanford: CSLI Publications.

Barker, Chris. 2012. Quantificational binding does not require c-command. *Linguistic Inquiry* 43(4). 614–633. https://doi.org/10.1162/ling_a_00108.

Barker, Chris & Chung-chieh Shan. 2008. Donkey anaphora is in-scope binding. *Semantics and Pragmatics* 1(1). 1–46. https://doi.org/10.3765/sp.1.1.

Barker, Chris & Chung-chieh Shan. 2014. *Continuations and natural language*. Oxford: Oxford University Press.

Büring, Daniel. 2005. *Binding theory* (Cambridge Textbooks in Linguistics). Cambridge: Cambridge University Press.

Cresti, Diana. 1995. Extraction and reconstruction. *Natural Language Semantics* 3. 79–122.

Dowty, David. 2007. Compositionality as an empirical problem. In Chris Barker & Pauline Jacobson (eds.), *Direct compositionality* (Oxford Studies in Theoretical Linguistics), 23–101. Oxford: Oxford University Press.

Groenendijk, Jeroen A. G. & Martin B. J. Stokhof. 1991. Dynamic predicate logic. *Linguistics and Philosophy* 14. 39–100.

Grosu, Alexander & Manfred Krifka. 2007. *The gifted mathematician that you claim to be*: Equational intensional 'reconstruction' relatives. *Linguistics and Philosophy* 30. 445–485. https://doi.org/10.1007/s10988-008-9022-5.

Heycock, Caroline. 1995. Asymmetries in reconstruction. *Linguistic Inquiry* 26. 547–570.

Jacobson, Pauline. 1994. Binding connectivity in copular sentences. In Mandy Harvey & Lynn Santelmann (eds.), *Proceedings of SALT 4* (Cornell Working Papers in Linguistics), 161–178. Ithaca, NY: Cornell University.

Jacobson, Pauline. 1999. Towards a variable-free semantics. *Linguistics and Philosophy* 22. 117–184.

Jacobson, Pauline. 2002. The (dis)organization of the grammar: 25 years. *Linguistics and Philosophy* 25. 601–626.

Kuno, Susumu. 1987. *Functional syntax: Anaphora, discourse and empathy*. Chicago: University of Chicago Press.

Kuno, Susumu. 1997. *Binding Theory and the Minimalist Program*. Ms. Harvard University, Cambridge, MA.
Munn, Alan. 1994. A Minimalist account of reconstruction asymmetries. In Mercè Gonzàlez (ed.), *Proceedings of NELS 24*, 397–410. Amherst, MA: GLSA.
Partee, Barbara Hall. 1987. Noun phrase interpretation and type shifting principles. In Jeroen A. G. Groenendijk, Dick de Jongh & Martin B. J. Stokhof (eds.), *Studies in discourse representation theory and the theory of generalized quantifiers*, 115–143. Dordrecht: Foris.
Rullmann, Hotze. 1995. *Maximality in the semantics of wh-constructions*. Amherst, MA: University of Massachusetts Doctoral dissertation.
Safir, Ken. 1999. Vehicle change and reconstruction in A'-chains. *Linguistic Inquiry* 30. 587–620.
Safir, Ken. 2004. *The syntax of (in)dependence*. Cambridge, MA: MIT Press.
Salzmann, Martin. 2006. *Resumptive prolepsis: A study in indirect A'-dependencies*. Leiden University Doctoral dissertation.
Shan, Chung-chieh & Chris Barker. 2006. Explaining crossover and superiority as left-to-right evaluation. *Linguistics and Philosophy* 29. 91–134.
Sportiche, Dominique. 2006. Reconstruction, binding and scope. In Martin Everaert & Henk van Riemsdijk (eds.), *The Blackwell companion to syntax*, vol. 4, 35–93. Oxford: Blackwell.
Steedman, Mark J. 2000. *The syntactic process*. Cambridge, MA: MIT Press.
Sternefeld, Wolfgang. 1998. The proper treatment of binding in pseudo cleft sentences. In Graham Katz, Shin-Sook Kim & Heike Winhart (eds.), *Reconstruction. Proceedings of the 1997 Tübingen workshop*, 39–58. SFB 340 Bericht 127. Universität Tübingen.
Sternefeld, Wolfgang. 2001. Semantic vs. syntactic reconstruction. In Christian Rohrer, Antje Roßdeutscher & Hans Kamp (eds.), *Linguistic form and its computation*, 145–182. Stanford, CA: CSLI Publications.
Szabolcsi, Anna. 1992. Combinatory grammar and projection from the lexicon. In Ivan A. Sag & Anna Szabolcsi (eds.), *Lexical matters*, vol. 24 (CSLI Lecture Notes), 241–269. CSLI Publications.

Wolfgang Sternefeld
Telescoping by continuations

1 Overview

The term "telescoping" has first been used in Roberts (1989) to describe cases like (1) in which the pronoun in (1b) seems to be bindable by a universal quantifier occuring in the preceding clause (1a):

(1) a. Each degree candidate walked to the stage
 b. He took his diploma from the Dean and returned to his seat

These cases are not handled by standard theories of dynamic binding (cf. Groenendijk & Stokhof 1991), although the conditions on binding can be relaxed (and assimilated to the conditions for indefinites) so that at least in principle the required kind of binding becomes feasible.

Unfortunately, the exact conditions that enable anaphoric relations by telescoping have not been sufficiently explored, and this paper does not contribute much to the issue. Instead, I want to draw attention to another type of telescoping that seems even more intriguing than the original one, namely the possible binding relations in (2):

(2) The picture of his_i mother that every $soldier_i$ kept wrapped in a sock was not much use to him_i

Here, the potential binder is embedded in a relative clause, but nonetheless the universal quantifier inside that clause seems to be capable of binding the specifier of the DP *his mother*. As these relations are far from local, an analysis along the usual lines of dynamic binding seems out of reach. However, it will be shown in this paper that a certain variant of dynamic binding — one which may be called "delayed binding" — together with continuation theory as proposed by Barker (2002) can be combined in such a way as to make an *in situ* analysis of (2) at least feasible.

Before putting forth such an analysis we have to investigate the syntactic structure of (2), in particular the relation between the relative clause and its head. This immediately relates to the topic of the volume, namely so-called "internally headed relative clauses", and the question of whether assumptions entertained

Wolfgang Sternefeld, University of Tübingen

https://doi.org/10.1515/9783050095158-012

in connection with the semantics of such clauses could provide for an (at least partial) solution of the problem. We will show that this is not the case and then develop a solution of our own.

2 Introducing internally headed relative clauses

Turning first to the syntax of relative clauses, let me remark that the current success of minimalist syntactic theories seems to be proportional to their degree of abstractness and the resulting number of wrong predictions. A case in point is relative clauses in Kayne's Antisymmetric Syntax, cf. Kayne (1994). Consider the structures in (3), with "RC" short for the relative CP:

(3) a. $[_{DP}$ D $[_{NP}$ NP RC]]

b. $[_{DP}$ $[_{DP}$ D NP] RC]

c. $[_{DP}$ $[_{D'}$ D NP] RC]

None of these configurations, which have been proposed in the literature, would be compatible with Kayne's Linear Correspondance Axiom LCA. Kayne therefore resurrects Vergnaud's (1974) raising analysis by assuming that the head of the RC is positioned in the specifier of a CP and has been moved there from inside the RC, as illustrated in (4):

(4) a. $[_{DP}$ D $[_{CP}$ NP$_i$ $[_{C'}$ ... t$_i$ ...]]]

b. $[_{DP}$ the $[_{CP}$ man$_i$ $[_{C'}$ (that) $[_{IP}$ I saw t$_i$]]]]

That way, the RC becomes a C′ with the effect that now, with no adjunction to the right being involved, the structure is consistent with the LCA. This analysis has become known as the internal head analysis of RCs and the construction itself is called an internally headed RC.

Empirical motivation for this analysis has been derived from diverse domains including data from binding theory as in (5);

(5) the interest in *each other* $[_{C'}$ that *John and Mary* showed t]

data involving bound variables as in (6);

(6) The relative of *his*$_i$ $[_{C'}$ that *everybody*$_i$ likes t] lives far away

data involving idiom reconstruction as in (7);

(7) the *headway* $[_{C'}$ that we *made* t] was satisfactory

and many others. In each case it would seem that the data can easily be explained by the raising analysis because the head of the RC (i.e. the item moved to SpecCP) can be interpreted at the position of its trace.

However, the theory has to face a number of serious objections. One is the obvious fact that the morphology of the head noun does not match that of the trace. For example, in a language like German, the head noun could be nominative while the trace is accusative. Moreover, a raising analysis would have to stipulate otherwise unattested movement operations, as illustrated in (8):

(8) [$_{DP}$ der [$_{CP}$ [$_{PP}$ Tag$_i$ [$_{P'}$ an [$_{DP}$ dem t_i]]]$_j$ [er t_j ankam]]]
the day on which he arrived

In (8), one first has to move the PP *an dem Tag* into the SpecC position, but this is not sufficient because word order is still incorrect. Therefore subsequent movement of the NP *Tag* to SpecPP must apply. However, this movement is otherwise unmotivated and it appears to induce an island violation, cf.

(9) * Tag$_i$ komme ich [an dem t_i]
day come I on that

These and many additional problems are discussed in Webelhuth, Bargmann & Götze (this volume).

As a way to overcome these difficulties a modification of the raising analysis has been proposed, the idea being that there is no movement into the head position but a kind of matching between the head and some invisible material in the SpecC position – a "matching" that must explicitly be allowed to ignore morphological mismatches or island conditions, as shown in (10):

(10) [$_{DP}$ der$_{nom}$ [$_{NP}$ Tag$_{i,nom}$ [$_{RC}$ [$_{PP}$ an [$_{DP}$ dem$_{dative}$ ~~Tag$_{i,dative}$~~]]$_j$ [$_{IP}$ er t_j ankam]]]]

The details of the new theory need not concern us here, since the matching analysis still assumes that the relevant copy for interpretation is the lower one at the trace position t_j. There still remain an impressive number of counterarguments against both theories; we cannot go into the details here (cf. again Webelhuth, Bargmann & Götze this volume). Let me just mention Martin Salzmann's dissertation and the work by Caroline Heycock (this volume), where it is shown that the potential reconstruction site (the trace t_j) does not exhibit any condition C effects:

(11) That is the [only picture of *Kahlo*$_i$]$_j$ that they say *she*$_i$ was ever willing to look at t_j

(12) die [Nachforschungen über *Peter*$_i$]$_j$ die *er*$_i$ mir lieber t$_j$ verschwiegen
the investigations about Peter which he me prefer concealed
hätte
had
'the investigations about Peter$_i$ that he$_i$ would have rather concealed from me'

In both examples we would expect a condition C violation if the solution to the above problems is reconstruction (or a copy) at LF. But at LF – the only level of representation for structural conditions in a minimalist theory – no such effect can be observed: the sentences are fully grammatical. It seems, therefore, that the reconstruction site is irrelevant for Binding Theory and that the observed Principle A effects should be handled along the lines of Reinhart & Reuland (1993), i.e. as either logophoric (for *picture*-nouns) or in a semantically driven way that takes into account the argument structure of nouns like *interest*, as proposed in the early days of Binding Theory (cf. Ross 1967).

As concerns idiom reconstruction, it has been observed by Gazdar et al. (1985: 238) that the second conjuncts in (13) still carry an idiomatic meaning:

(13) a. My goose is cooked, but *yours* isn't
b. We had expected that excellent care would be taken of the orphans, and *it* was taken
c. I said close tabs would be kept on Sandy, but *they* weren't
d. We thought the bottom would fall out of the housing market, but *it* didn't.

Here, ordinary pronouns seem to "pick up" idiomatic expressions in an environment where movement or reconstruction of the idiomatic material into the position of the pronoun is impossible. But if ordinary pronouns can anaphorically point to (or copy) idiomatic material, relative pronouns can as well. Hence idioms provide no argument for syntactic reconstruction. In sum, I conclude that the traditional analysis is correct and that there is no reason to assume that the head of the RC has a syntactic copy in the trace position of the relative pronoun.

One of the things most often overlooked in the discussion of internally headed RCs is the fact that the proposed analysis for examples like (14)

(14) The picture of himself that everybody sent in annoyed the teacher

would imply that there is only one picture that depicts everybody (or only one person that is the relative of everybody in examples like (6)). But (14) also has a reading with the uniqueness presupposition embedded under *everybody*. In other words, there is a different picture for each person. The obvious conclusion must be that the internal head analysis is insufficient because the quantifier has to gain wide scope w.r.t. the determiner.

Another fact has been overlooked in the discussion of (2). The original example was (15) without an index on *him*:

(15) The picture of his_i mother that every $soldier_i$ kept t wrapped in a sock was not much use to him

(15) is taken from Safir (1999: 613), who attributes it to Bianchi and Åfarli, and it is also discussed in Salzmann (2006). None of these authors, however, seemed to be aware of the following crucial problems:

- *every soldier* must have scope over the entire subject phrase
- *every soldier* might be able to bind *him* in the matrix clause

To me it is intuitively clear that some sort of back reference of *him* to *every soldier* is possible. If this reading exists, the pronoun *him* cannot be interpreted as an E-type pronoun of sorts; rather, it must be interpreted as a genuine bound variable. This seems to be an important observation, because it shows that Kayne's theory alone cannot adequately handle the data, and at the same time it corroborates a proposal by Hulsey & Sauerland (2006) who assume QRing of *every soldier* into the root node of the matrix clause.

Hulsey and Sauerland also discuss a similar example, namely

(16) The picture of $himself_i$ $everybody_i$ sent in annoyed his_i mother

They observe that *his* is problematic in having a bound reading. "But in [(16), their ex. (70), W. St.], *his* can be analyzed as an E-type pronoun *the person on x*, where *x* is bound by the DP *the picture of himself*." (p. 135) I do not see, however, how such a move could solve the problem, because the antecedent DP itself contains a variable that must in some way be interpreted in the scope of *everybody*. I therefore see no gain in assuming an E-type analysis but instead take (16) at face value by assuming that both *himself* and *his* are to be analyzed as bound variables.

A QR-analysis for examples like these seems to have first been suggested by Doron (1982) but has widely been rejected on the grounds that QR should normally be clause-bound. In the present paper, I will propose a semantic account for the relevant binding data that does without QR. It combines two ingredients: Barker's continuation theory as developed for inverse linking, and my own theory of delayed binding (cf. Barker 2002, Sternefeld 2001, and Klein & Sternefeld 2013).

There are a number of reasons why such an in situ theory is preferable to QR, most of which follow from Heycock's contribution to this volume; in particular the restrictions on reconstruction seem to be semantic rather than syntactic in nature. On the other hand, the semantic framework I will suggest in this paper is more or less unrestricted and rather general. E.g., it does not, in and of itself, obey clause boundedness; rather, the appropriate (island) conditions still need to be built in additionally, much as in the theory of Barker (2002).

As a starting point, note that Barker's theory nicely accounts for inverse linking illustrated in (17):

(17) [$_{DP}$ [$_{DP}$ the rose][$_{PP}$ in every vase]]

Given the structure in (17), the PP can be interpreted as the so-called continuation of the predicate *rose* and thus as a further restriction of the determiner *the*; this yields the linear reading.

Or it can also be interpreted by giving wide scope to the PP and its quantifier, which means that *the rose* is merely an argument of *in* and the main quantifier now becomes *every vase*; this yields the inverse linking reading. The technical details will be developed in section 4; the important points for now are these: (1.) no movement is involved in the analysis of the two readings and (2.) the wide scope analysis of *every vase* not only works for PPs but also for RCs as in (18):

(18) die Rose, die in jedem Knopfloch steckt
the rose which in every buttonhole sticks

However, Barker's theory does not automatically guarantee that wide quantifier scope also implies the potential for the binding of pronouns. This is so because quantifiers are still Fregean relations, not real quantifiers. In the present framework, as in the classical one, quantifier expressions will take a restriction and a scope, but in contrast with Generalized Quantifier Theory will additionally be real binders. That is, they behave like expressions ($\forall x$) or ($\exists y$) in being capable of binding variables (namely x and y respectively). In addition, we assume a compositional semantics for these expressions along the lines of Henkin & Tarski (1961). For details I refer the reader to Sternefeld (2001) and Klein & Sternefeld (2013). For now, the important thing to note is that binding of a pronoun does not require QR – everything works *in situ*.

The structure in (17) and the parallel structure [$_{DP}$ DP RC] for RCs are not the ones we find in textbooks; nonetheless there is reason to believe that they are correct. A well-known argument in favor of [$_{DP}$ DP RC] comes from data called *hydras* (cf. Link 1984):

(19) [[$_{DP}$ the man and the woman][$_{RC}$ who hate each other]]

The head of the RC must be a plural phrase, which can only be formed by the conjunction of two DPs. The RC must therefore be attached to the conjoined DP (or conjoined D′s) as a whole.

Quite different evidence showing that the RC interacts closely with the determiner rather than with the NP is provided by data like (20):

(20) a. Alle Kinder haben den Arm, der dreckert war, gehoben
all children have the arm that dirty was raised

b. * Alle Kinder ham'n Arm, der dreckert war, gehoben
all children have-the arm that dirty was raised

(German)

Prinzhorn (2005) has shown that there cannot be phonological reduction of the definite article *der* (*the*) in the presence of a RC. Without such a RC, the contraction *ham'n* is fully okay. It seems that the RC requires some further accent or stress on the definite determiner. This points to a close relation between D and the RC, which can be implemented as a semantic relation between D and a further restriction of D (cf. Sternefeld 2006). Likewise, we find determiners like *derjenige* in German, that obligatorily require a relative clause as a complement (unless they are used as anaphoric DPs without any extensions):

(21) derjenige (Mann) *([$_{RC}$ der kam])
that-one (man) who came

The conclusion is that the RC is not attached to the NP but to a projection of D.

Before going into technical details, I would like to stress again that the semantics to be developed in this paper is meant to provide a general framework for telescoping rather than a linguistic theory. Its status is that of an abstraction like X-bar theory in syntax. Every such system overgenerates; we would not expect the X-bar scheme to be instantiated for all possible values of the variables in $[_{X^i}\ X^{i-1}\ Y^{max}]$. Likewise we do not expect that the full expressive power of our formal system is put to use in natural language semantics; some restrictions still have to be imposed on the semantic composition rules; I refer the reader to Barker (2002).

When considering data like (2) or (15) linguists tend to ask a number of questions that will not necessarily be answered by the formal system as such. For example, observing that there are two bound variables involved we may well ask whether there is an interaction between cataphoric and anaphoric anaphora. As far as I can see, the semantic theory proposed below does make a specific prediction, namely that forward anaphora is possible only if the cataphoric reading is. In terms of semantic processing one might then ask whether there is a difference between (21) and (22):

(22) The picture of Peter's mother that every soldier$_i$ kept t wrapped in a sock was not much use to him$_i$

In (22), the wide scope reading is not enforced by the possessive, is it therefore more difficult to get?

Another case in point is the difference between subject and object quantifiers. The syntactic reconstruction theories make a clear prediction: If reconstruction is involved, (23) should be bad on the intended reading, because the accusative object cannot have scope over the (trace of) the subject:

(23) Seine$_i$ Dozentin, die jeden$_{acc}$ Studenten$_i$ faszinierte, las seinen$_i$ Text
His lecturer who every student fascinated read his text
Korrektur
proof
'the lecturer who fascinated every student proofread his text'

If QR is involved, the picture is reversed: we would expect an LF asymmetry between subjects and objects along the lines of the ECP. Such a theory would predict that (24) is ungrammatical:

(24) Seine$_i$ Dozentin, die jeder$_{nom}$ Student$_i$ anhimmelte, las seinen$_i$ Text
His lecturer who every student adored read his text
Korrektur
proof
'the lecturer who every student adored proofread his text'

A purely semantic theory would be unable to differentiate between the two constructions. In our theory both construals would be possible, and it seems to me that intuitively this is the correct conclusion.

There are many other questions we cannot discuss here, one being the nature of the quantifiers that permit telescoping. Recently we got a panic-stricken email from our colleague Gisbert Fanselow who was horrified to find that in his introductory semantics course 50% of the students accepted a bound reading for sentences like (25):

(25) der Sohn von keiner Frau liebt ihre Schwester
the son of no woman$_i$ loves her$_i$ sister

This was not too surprising for us, because in a questionaire concerning the readings of

(26) Die Dozentin, die keinen Studenten$_i$ faszinierte, las seinen$_i$ Text
the lecturer who no student$_{acc}$ fascinated read his text
Korrektur
proof
'the lecturer who fascinated no student, proofread his text'

we also found a 50% availability of the bound reading. Again, we would like to stress that the system we propose is neutral in this respect, it may allow continuations with negative quantifiers, or it may exclude them.

Are there any grammatical restrictions and if so, what is their nature? Is the telescoping phenomenon real, or can we disregard it and explain it as a side effect of something else still to be explained? These questions call for an empirical investigation; I refer the reader to the contribution of Radó et al. in this volume.

3 Introducing continuations

We are now entering the technical part of the paper and I will briefly introduce the idea of a continuation. A continuation is basically a placeholder for material that will be supplied only at a later stage in the processing of a sentence. Every category, whether phrasal or lexical, may come with a continuation. In Dynamic Montague Grammar (cf. Groenendijk & Stokhof 1990), a sentence like *A man is walking* is represented roughly as $\lambda p \exists x(\mathbf{man}(x) \wedge \mathbf{walk}(x) \wedge p)$, where p stands in for the following sentence, this is what we call a continuation. In continuation semantics, this idea is generalized; not only propositions but any constituent can have a continuation.

In more technical terms, a continuation of a category X is a property of X; in particular, a continuation of a proposition is a property of that proposition. In this paper, we will only consider continuations of (possibly open) propositions. A sentence like *A man is walking* can, at least in principle, be represented in three different ways, depending on the position of the placeholder for the continuation:

(27) a. $\lambda c.c(\exists x(\mathbf{man}(x) \wedge \mathbf{walk}(x)))$

b. $\lambda c.\exists x(\mathbf{man}(x) \wedge c(\mathbf{walk}(x)))$

c. $\lambda c.\exists x(c(\mathbf{man}(x)) \wedge \mathbf{walk}(x))$

In all three cases, c is of type $\langle t, t\rangle$ in an extensional system; for the purposes at hand we can ignore intensionality. In (27a), we consider the possibility that the existential quantifier is in the scope of some other expression to be added later, this is the case of inversed linking discussed below. (27b) is a case where something is added to the scope of a quantifier; this would be a continuation like *He whistles* in Dynamic Montague Grammar. In (27c) something is added to the restriction of a quantifier; this could be an extraposed relative clause, e.g. *who whistles*.

For example, we simply want to add a new proposition, e.g. $\mathbf{whistle}(x)$; this addition can be interpreted as conjunction so that the combinatory rule that adds $\mathbf{whistle}(x)$ (= z) to (27) (= α) would be (28):

(28) $\alpha(\lambda r(r \wedge z))$

Thus, applying (27) to $\lambda r(r \wedge \mathbf{whistle}(x))$ yields three different outputs:

(29) a. $(\exists x(\mathbf{man}(x) \wedge \mathbf{walk}(x)) \wedge \mathbf{whistle}(x))$
b. $\exists x(\mathbf{man}(x) \wedge (\mathbf{walk}(x) \wedge \mathbf{whistle}(x)))$
c. $\exists x((\mathbf{man}(x) \wedge \mathbf{whistle}(x)) \wedge \mathbf{walk}(x))$

In Dynamic Semantics, all formulas are equivalent and could be expressed by either (30a), (30b), or (30c):

(30) a. A man is walking. He whistles.
b. A man is walking and whistling.
c. A man who is whistling is walking.

Of course, what we really want in a general theory of continuations is a recursive system where the resulting formulae in (29) themselves are capable of having continuations, i.e. are formulae beginning with λc. We will present such a system further below. The system will not use rules like (28) but instead will combine the scopal possibilities in (27) in a unified system with unambiguous lexical entries, using more complicated functions that combine via functional composition.

Barker supposes that quantifiers and determiners are grammatical signs of continuations themselves. This feature of his analysis is not really important for us. However, a crucial assumption of our analysis will be that the restriction and the scope of a quantifier may come with their own continuations and these continuations can be projected up to the DP. We thus have to assume that a determiner like *every* comes along with two possibilities of recursive continuations: first we can add and pile up continuations as restrictions (in classical theory, only one restriction is possible, here we assume a recursive process of adding restrictions) and only after this process is finished can we continue with the scope of the quantifier and recursive continuations of its scope. This forces us to combine (27b) and (27c) as will become clear below.

Before formalizing these ideas, let me explain another assumption that will become relevant below for variable binding. I will assume that every predicate P is encoded as an open proposition; for a one-place predicate P this could be the proposition $P(x)$, with the choice of the variable being immaterial (cf. Klein & Sternefeld 2017). Under this assumption, (31) below very roughly sketches different steps of a compositional derivation of the (dispreferred) linear analysis of *the rose in every vase*, whereas (32) sketches the preferred inverse linking analysis. We still assume (28) as a combinatory rule. Another simplification in (31) concerns the assumption that we exploit continuations only at one point, throughout (31) there is only one continuation concerning the expression *the rose* (= (31d)), which is assumed to have a continuation generated by the determiner's restriction. As can be seen in (31a), *every vase* in this derivation has no continuation at all. Likewise, no other lexical expression is assumed to have a continuation in the present (preliminary) derivation. A third simplification concerns the assumption that beta reduction is "unsual" in the sense that the usual restrictions for free and bound variables do no apply:

(31) the rose in every vase

a. every vase = $\lambda p \forall x(\mathbf{vase}(x) \rightarrow p)$

b. in = $\mathbf{in}(y, x)$

c. in every vase = $\forall x(\mathbf{vase}(x) \rightarrow \mathbf{in}(y, x))$

d. the rose = $\lambda c \lambda q\ \text{THE}_y(c(\mathbf{rose}(y)), q)$

e. the rose in every vase = $\lambda q.\text{THE}_y(\mathbf{rose}(y) \wedge \forall x(\mathbf{vase}(x) \rightarrow \mathbf{in}(y, x)), q)$

The notation $\text{THE}_y(p, q)$ abbreviates the Russellian quantificational paraphrase $\exists y(\forall x(p \leftrightarrow x = y) \wedge q)$. (31a) and (31b) combine via β-reduction of the unusual kind that will be commented upon below. The resulting (31c) combines with (31d) to yield (31e) by applying (28) and the same kind of unorthodox β-reduction.

For the more plausible inverse linking reading we need a continuation of the predicate *in* and a different rule for combining (32a) and (32b):

(32) a. every vase = $\lambda p \forall x(\mathbf{vase}(x) \rightarrow p)$

b. in = $\lambda c.c(\mathbf{in}(y, x))$

The rule is functional composition:

(33) $\lambda c \llbracket \text{every vase} \rrbracket (\llbracket \text{in} \rrbracket (c))$

(34) a. in every vase = $\lambda c \forall x(\mathbf{vase}(x) \rightarrow c(\mathbf{in}(y, x)))$

b. the rose = $\lambda c \lambda q\ \text{THE}_y(c(\mathbf{rose}(y)), q)$

c. the rose in every vase = $\lambda q \forall x(\mathbf{vase}(x) \rightarrow \text{THE}_y(\mathbf{rose}(y) \wedge \mathbf{in}(y, x), q))$

The rule that combines (34a) and (34b) could be something like (35):

(35) $\lambda q \llbracket \text{in every vase} \rrbracket (\lambda r \llbracket \text{the rose} \rrbracket (\lambda p.p \wedge r)(q))$

Obviously, these rules are *ad hoc* and will be replaced by only one uniform rule (namely functional composition) to which we will come back further below.

The unorthodox machinery necessitated by the above derivations concerns the binding of variables. Note that the free variable x in (32b) must end up bound in the scope of the binder $\forall x$ in (34a), and likewise when going from (34a) and (34b) to (34c), the variable y, which is free in (34a), ends up bound in the scope of the binder THE_y. We therefore need a theory where semantic composition via λ-abstraction is fully compatible with unrestricted β-reduction. In other words, we need a theory where the following equivalence holds:

(36) $\lambda p \forall x(P(x) \rightarrow p)(Q(x)) = \forall x(P(x) \rightarrow Q(x))$

But β-reduction of this sort is strictly forbidden in standard semantics: we cannot interpret a free variable (the last occurence of x on the left of =) as if it were in the scope of a binder.

Logical theory notwithstanding, we as linguists need such a new framework for independent reasons, e.g. one might want to account for data like (37) in a semantics that is fully compositional and avoids syntactic reconstruction:

(37) a. Sich selber$_i$ hasst$_j$ niemand$_i$ t$_i$ t$_j$
him self hates nobody
'nobody hates himself'

b. Seinen$_i$ Bruder hasst$_j$ niemand$_i$ t$_i$ t$_j$
his brother hates noone
'noone$_i$ hates his$_i$ brother'

It is at this point that a theory of semantic reconstruction is called for that allows for delayed interpretation of variable binding.

I have sketched such a theory in much previous work, but a general theory has been developed only recently in joint work with Udo Klein; cf. Klein & Sternefeld (2013). I refer the reader to this article, which explains a general semantics that minimally differs from the standard semantics in that it allows for beta reduction in an unrestriced way, so that the equivalence in (36) is provably valid.

4 Restricted quantifiers and continuations

As said above, each (open) proposition p that enters the computation may come along with its continuation. But in many cases, these continuations will not be exploited in actual derivations. To account for this in a uniform way we will assume that such continuations are initially generated but semantic composition can always kill or plug a continuation by "lowering", i.e., by applying $\lambda c \ldots$ to the identity function $\lambda p.p$. Up to now we have always used lexical entries without continuations in case the potential continuation are not needed and would be plugged later. From now on we will include all possible continuations but will also make all plugging operations explicit.

Let us next go into a more detailed analysis of our practice examples, namely the linear and inverse construals of *an apple in every basket*. Having derived these, we will finally analyze the telescoping example (2)/(15).

We assume that all categories are indexed in syntax, where indexing encodes the identity of variables to be bound or coordinated (see Klein & Sternefeld 2017 for the coordination of variables). In general, syntactic merge will require identity of indices, i.e. coordination of variables. Moreover, relations like *in* will be represented as open propositions $\mathbf{in}(x_i, x_j)$ whose variables will eventually be bound by appropriate binders. In order to identify the correct indices, we assume that the preposition is indexed by $\langle i, j\rangle$, the general convention being that the first argument encountered in syntax binds the last argument in this list.

This much said, we have to develop a general format of lexical entries which combines the possibilities for an item to have wide or narrow scope by using one continuation variable, here c, for continuations that will have scope over the lexical entry, and another variable, here p, which simply adds further material, possibly within the dynamic scope of the entry in question (cf. Bott & Sternefeld 2017 for an elaboration of the theory and for numerous applications). According to this scheme, a two-place relation like *in* is represented as follows:

(38) $[\![\text{ in }]\!]_{i,j} = \lambda c \lambda p.c(\mathbf{in}(x_i, x_j) \wedge p)$

Simple nouns like *vase* or *rose* are one-place relations, hence have the format in (39):

(39) $[\![\text{ N }]\!]_i = \lambda c \lambda p.c(\mathbf{N}(x_i) \wedge p)$

Turning finally to determiners, their lexical entry must provide for a continuation of both its scope and its restriction. In particular, having parsed the DP *a rose*, continuing with a PP or a relative clause will further add to the restriction *rose* (in the linear reading). Accordingly, the determiners are doubly continualized:

(40) a. $[\![\text{ every }]\!]_i = \lambda c \lambda p \lambda c' \lambda p' \forall x_i [c(p) \rightarrow c'(p')]$
b. $[\![\text{ a }]\!]_i = \lambda c \lambda p \lambda c' \lambda p' \exists x_i [c(p) \wedge c'(p')]$

The only mode of combining A and B is functional composition:

(41) a. $\lambda c A(B(c))$ (linear)
b. $\lambda c B(A(c))$ (inverse)

Let us now analyze the two readings of *an apple in every basket (is rotten).*

Functional composition of noun and determiner indexed by i and j yields (42):

(42) $[\![\text{ an apple }]\!]_i = \lambda c [\![\text{ an }]\!]_i ([\![\text{ apple }]\!]_i (c)) =$
$\lambda c \lambda p \lambda c' \lambda p' \exists x_i [c(\mathbf{apple}(x_i) \wedge p) \wedge c'(p')]$

And likewise for *every basket*:

(43) $[\![\text{ every basket }]\!]_j = \lambda c [\![\text{ every }]\!]_j ([\![\text{ basket }]\!]_j)(c) =$
$\lambda c \lambda p \lambda c' \lambda p' \forall x_j [c(\mathbf{basket}(x_j) \wedge p) \rightarrow c'(p')]$

The next step is to combine *in* with *every basket*. We assume that *every basket* is a complete DP, hence its restriction cannot have further continuations. This means that we have to plug the restriction by applying *every basket* first to the identity function $\lambda p.p$ of type $\langle t,t\rangle$ and then to the propositional constant T (= truth). The result is given in (44):

(44) $\lambda c'\lambda p'\forall x_j[\mathbf{basket}(x_j) \rightarrow c'(p')]$

This will then be applied to *in* as shown in (45):

(45) $[\![\text{ in every basket }]\!]_i = \lambda c[\![\text{ every basket }]\!]_j([\![\text{ in }]\!]_{\langle i,j\rangle}(c)) =$
$\lambda c\lambda p'\forall x_j[\mathbf{basket}(x_j) \rightarrow c(\mathbf{in}(x_i, x_j) \wedge p')]$

Now adding this to *an apple* in the linear mode means that *in every basket* restricts the restriction of *an apple*, hence we can straightforwardly combine the two:

(46) $[\![\text{ an apple in every basket }]\!]_i = \lambda c[\![\text{ an apple }]\!]_i([\![\text{ in every basket }]\!](c)) =$
$\lambda c\lambda p\lambda c'\lambda p'\exists x_i[\mathbf{apple}(x_i) \wedge \forall x_j[\mathbf{basket}(x_j) \rightarrow c(\mathbf{in}(x_i, x_j) \wedge p)] \wedge c'(p')]$

Assuming that this DP is complete and followed by the sentence predicate enforces plugging of the restriction's continuation, resulting in:

(47) $\lambda c'\lambda p'\exists x_i[\mathbf{apple}(x_i) \wedge \forall x_j[\mathbf{basket}(x_j) \rightarrow \mathbf{in}(x_i, x_j)] \wedge c'(p')]$

Adding a one-place predicate like *is rotten*$_i$ yields:

(48) $\lambda c\lambda p'\exists x_i[\mathbf{apple}(x_i) \wedge \forall x_j[\mathbf{basket}(x_j) \rightarrow \mathbf{in}(x_i, x_j)] \wedge c(\mathbf{rotten}(x_i) \wedge p')]$

If we assume that this is the end of a text, we plug the continuations in the usual way:

(49) $\exists x_i[\mathbf{apple}(x_i) \wedge \forall x_j[\mathbf{basket}(x_j) \rightarrow \mathbf{in}(x_i, x_j)] \wedge \mathbf{rotten}(x_i)]$

In the more natural inverse linking reading, *in every basket* takes wide scope over *an apple*. This presupposes that *an apple* is complete and thus has no continuations of its restriction.

(50) $[\![\text{ an apple }]\!]_i = \lambda c\lambda p\exists x_i[\mathbf{apple}(x_i) \wedge c(p)]$

We then apply *in every basket* to *an apple*:

(51) $\lambda c\,(45)((50)(c)) =$
$\lambda c\lambda p\forall x_j[\mathbf{basket}(x_j) \rightarrow \exists x_i[\mathbf{apple}(x_i) \wedge c(\mathbf{in}(x_i, x_j) \wedge p)]]$

Adding *is rotten*$_i$ and plugging the continuation gives the desired truth conditions:

(52) $\forall x_j[\mathbf{basket}(x_j) \rightarrow \exists x_i[\mathbf{apple}(x_i) \wedge (\mathbf{in}(x_i, x_j) \wedge \mathbf{rotten}(x_i))]]$

This paves the way for our analysis of telescoping.

5 Telescoping with RCs

We are now ready for an analysis of the worst case, namely telescoping out of a RC. The example we mentioned above is repeated in (53):

(53) The picture of HIS$_x$ mother that EVERY$_x$ SOLDIER kept t wrapped in a sock was not much use to HIM$_x$

For simplicity we assume that *his mother* is analyzed with the iota-operator, whereas the definite description is a Russellian quantifier. Moreover, we assume that the restriction's continuation has been plugged. We thus start off with (54):

(54) $[\![$ the$_y$ picture of HIS$_x$ mother $]\!]$ =
$\lambda c \lambda p \exists y \forall u((\textbf{picture}(u, (\iota v)(\textbf{mother}(v, x))) \leftrightarrow y = u) \wedge c(p))$

It is now easy to see that the RC plays the same role as the PP in the inverse linking case. The RC thus translates as:

(55) $[\![$ that$_y$ every soldier$_x$ kept wrapped in a sock $]\!]_y$ =
$\lambda c \lambda p \forall x(\textbf{soldier}(x) \rightarrow \exists z(\textbf{sock}(z) \wedge c(\textbf{kept-wrapped-in}(x, y, z) \wedge p)))$

It is evident that the index y on *that* is the index of an (invisible) RC operator corresponding to a silent relative pronoun that has been moved to SpecC. This index is needed to properly identify variables in a coordination scheme that identifies the y of the RC with the same variable y of the DP it attaches to.

(56) $\lambda c\,(55)((54)(c))$ =
$\lambda c \lambda p \forall x(\textbf{soldier}(x) \rightarrow \exists z(\textbf{sock}(z) \wedge \exists y \forall u((\textbf{picture}(u, (\iota v)(\textbf{mother}(v, x))) \leftrightarrow$
$y = u) \wedge c(\textbf{kept-wrapped-in}(x, y, z) \wedge p))))$

Note that due to unusual beta reduction, *HIS* can be bound by the RC. Likewise, the final step, namely continuing with *was not much use to HIM*, involves binding by beta-reduction, as shown in (57):

(57) $\lambda c\,(56)(\lambda c' \lambda p'.c'(\textbf{not-of-much-use-to}(y, x) \wedge p')(c))$ =
$\lambda c \lambda p \forall x(\textbf{soldier}(x) \rightarrow \exists z(\textbf{sock}(z) \wedge \exists y \forall u((\textbf{picture}(u, (\iota v)(\textbf{mother}(v, x))) \leftrightarrow$
$y = u) \wedge c(\textbf{not-of-much-use-to}(y, x) \wedge \textbf{kept-wrapped-in}(x, y, z) \wedge p))))$

This completes our discussion of example (2)/(15).

Let us finally return to (25), repeated as (58):

(58) der Sohn von keiner Frau$_y$ liebt ihre$_y$ Schwester
the son of no woman$_y$ loves HER$_y$ sister

Compared to previous examples the predicate *son* is relational. As before, if this implies that the structure of the DP is

(59) $[_{DP}$ the $[_{NP}$ son of no woman]]

there is no way to get wide scope for *no woman* in situ. If, on the other hand, the structure is (60) as argued for above,

(60) $[_{DP} [_{DP}$ the$_x$ son$_{x,y}$ $]_x$ [of no$_y$ woman$_y$ $]_y$ $]_x$

we get wide scope for *no woman* with respect to the determiner *the* by the same mechanism already applied above. The index x is the argument index of the sentential predicate, as in *x loves Berta*. The index y, by contrast, gets semantically wide scope (as the index of the quantifier *no*) and may serve as a binder by accidental coindexation with a pronoun, as in *x loves HER$_y$ sister*.

The discussion shows that to some degree telescoping is a consequence of wide scope, and this is in accord with other theories like QR. In contrast to these theories, the actual mechanism of scope taking is local and does not require movement at LF.

The acceptance rate for sentences like (25) is not yet captured in the above system. In theory, it would be possible to separate the ability of taking wide scope from that of delayed binding of variables (i.e. unrestrained beta-reduction), perhaps only for negative quantifiers, but given the 50% acceptance rate of such sentences, we have a 50% chance that such a theory would be too restrictive, hence wrong.

References

Barker, Chris. 2002. Continuations and the nature of quantification. *Natural Language Semantics* 10. 211–242.

Bott, Oliver & Wolfgang Sternefeld. 2017. An event semantics with continuations for incremental interpretation. *Journal of Semantics* 34(2). 201–236. https://doi.org/10.1093/jos/ffw013.

Doron, Edit. 1982. The syntax and semantics of resumptive pronouns. *Texas Linguistics Forum* 19. 1–48.

Gazdar, Gerald, Ewan Klein, Geoffrey Pullum & Ivan Sag. 1985. *Generalized phrase structure grammar*. Oxford: Blackwell.

Groenendijk, Jeroen A. G. & Martin B. J. Stokhof. 1990. Dynamic Montague Grammar. In L. Kálmán et al. (eds.), *Proceedings of the second symposium on logic and language*. Budapest.

Groenendijk, Jeroen A. G. & Martin B. J. Stokhof. 1991. Dynamic Predicate Logic. *Linguistics and Philosophy* 14. 39–100.

Henkin, Leon & Alfred Tarski. 1961. Cylindric algebras. In R. Dilworth (ed.), *Lattice theory, proc. symp. in pure mathematics, vol. 2*, 83–113. Providence, RI: American Mathematical Society.

Hulsey, Sarah & Uli Sauerland. 2006. Sorting out relative clauses. *Natural Language Semantics* 14. 111–137.

Kayne, Richard. 1994. *The antisymmetry of syntax*. Cambridge, MA: The MIT Press.

Klein, Udo & Wolfgang Sternefeld. 2013. Unrestrained beta reduction. In Todd Snider (ed.), *Proceedings of SALT 23*, 257–275. https://journals.linguisticsociety.org/proceedings/index.php/SALT/article/view/2684/2429 (10 October, 2018).

Klein, Udo & Wolfgang Sternefeld. 2017. Same same but different: An alphabetically innocent compositional predicate logic. *Journal of Philosophical Logic* 46(1). 65–95. https://doi.org/10.1007/s10992-016-9394-x.

Link, Godehard. 1984. On the logic of relative clause constructions with multiple heads. In F. Landman & F. Veltman (eds.), *Varieties of formal semantics*, 245–257. Dordrecht: Foris.

Prinzhorn, Martin. 2005. *DP-Struktur und Stellungsbeschränkungen im Deutschen*. Vortrag, Universität Tübingen.

Reinhart, Tanya & Eric Reuland. 1993. Reflexivity. *Linguistic Inquiry* 24. 657–720.

Roberts, Craige. 1989. Modal subordination and pronominal anaphora in discourse. *Linguistics and Philosophy* 12. 683–721.

Ross, John Robert. 1967. On the cyclic nature of English pronominalization. In *To honor Roman Jacobson, vol. 2*, 1669–1682. The Hague/Paris: Mouton.

Safir, Ken. 1999. Vehicle change and reconstruction in A'-chains. *Linguistic Inquiry* 30. 587–620.

Salzmann, Martin. 2006. *Resumptive prolepsis: A study in indirect A'-dependencies*. Leiden University Doctoral dissertation.

Sternefeld, Wolfgang. 2001. Semantic vs. syntactic reconstruction. In Christian Rohrer, Antje Roßdeutscher & Hans Kamp (eds.), *Linguistic form and its computation*, 145–182. Stanford, CA: CSLI Publications.

Sternefeld, Wolfgang. 2006. *Syntax. Eine morphologisch motivierte generative Beschreibung des Deutschen. Band 1*. Tübingen: Stauffenburg Verlag.

Vergnaud, Jean R. 1974. *French relative clauses*. Cambridge, MA: Massachusetts Institute of Technology Doctoral dissertation.

Janina Radó, Andreas Konietzko, and Wolfgang Sternefeld

Telescoping in relative clauses

Experimental evidence

1 Introduction

Sternefeld (this volume) observes that in sentences like (1) a bound reading of the pronoun *his* in (1a) and *him* in (1b) seems possible:

(1) a. The picture of himself$_i$ everybody$_i$ sent in annoyed his$_i$ mother. (Hulsey & Sauerland 2006, ex. 70)

b. [[The picture of his$_i$ mother]$_j$ [that every soldier$_i$ kept t$_j$ wrapped in a sock] was not much use to him]. (Safir 1999: 613)

(2) Der Dozent, der jede Studentin faszinierte, las ihren Text
the lecturer$_{nom}$ that$_{nom}$ every student$_{nom/acc}$ fascinated read her text
nochmal Korrektur.
again proof
The lecturer that fascinated every student proofread her text again.

Hulsey & Sauerland (2006) discuss the possibility of binding of *his* by the quantifier but propose an E-type analysis. In (1b) there is no index on *him* in Safir's paper, but the bound reading is intuitively possible.

In this paper we investigate whether German counterparts to (1) such as (2) allow a bound reading of the pronoun (*ihren* in (2)) and how syntactic and semantic factors influence the availability of the bound reading. This is of theoretical interest as the results bear on the debate concerning the correct analysis of telescoping and relative clauses in general (see Sternefeld this volume). We present two experiments on bound interpretations under telescoping. Experiment 1 establishes that telescoping out of the relative clause in sentences like (2) is possible. Experiment 2 compares various accounts of telescoping by testing the influence of syntactic and semantic factors on the availability of bound readings.

Janina Radó, Goethe University Frankfurt am Main
Andreas Konietzko, University of Tübingen
Wolfgang Sternefeld, University of Tübingen

https://doi.org/10.1515/9783050095158-013

2 Availability of bound variable interpretations

2.1 Experiment 1: Binding out of the relative clause

Experiment 1 was designed to test whether telescoping regularly takes place, that is, whether a quantifier embedded in a relative clause can scope out and bind a pronoun outside the relative clause without much additional effort. To assess that, we compared the preferred interpretations of sentences like (3), where telescoping is necessary for the bound reading with (4), where the quantifier is in the matrix clause and binding the pronoun should be easy.[1]

(3) Der Dozent, der fast jede Studentin faszinierte, las ihren
the lecturer$_{nom}$ that$_{nom}$ almost every student$_{nom/acc}$ fascinated read her
Text nochmal Korrektur.
text again proof
The lecturer that fascinated almost every student proofread her text again.

(4) Fast jede Studentin, die dieser Dozent faszinierte, las
almost every student$_{nom/acc}$ that$_{nom/acc}$ the lecturer$_{nom}$ fascinated read
ihren Text nochmal Korrektur.
her text again proof
Almost every student whom the lecturer fascinated proofread her text again.

The two conditions *telescoping* vs. *binding* (shown in (3) and (4), respectively)[2] were tested in an eye movement study including two further conditions that are not relevant for the present discussion. To check the availability of the bound reading, each sentence was followed by a comprehension question and two answer options, one compatible with the bound reading, the other with a unique referent for the

1 The difference between *der Dozent* in (3) and *dieser Dozent* in (4) had to do with practical considerations: *dieser* is more similar in length to *fast jede* in the parallel condition. This was relevant for the analysis of reading times in region 2 (the relative clause, cf. Figure 1b), which was of crucial interest, but not for region 1, which we did not analyze. Thus in (3) we opted for the intuitively more natural *der*.

2 The corresponding LFs are:

(3-LF) $[_{CP}\ [_{DP}\ [_{DP}\ \text{der}_x\ \text{Dozent}_x\ ]_x\ [_{CP}\ (\text{der})\ [_{DP}\ \text{fast jede}_y\ [_{NP}\ \text{Studentin}_y\ ]]_y\ [_{IP}\ t_x\ t_y\ \text{faszinierte}\ ]]]$
$[_{C'}\ \text{las}\ \lambda z\ [_{IP}\ t_x\ \text{ihren}_y\ \text{Text nochmal Korrektur-}t_z\ ]]]$

(4-LF) $[_{CP}\ [_{DP}\ \text{fast jede}\ [_{NP}\ [_{NP}\ \text{Studentin}\ ][_{CP}\ (\text{die})\ \lambda x\ [_{IP}\ \text{dieser Student}\ t_x\ \text{faszinierte}\ ]]]]$
$\lambda x\ [_{C'}\ \text{las}\ \lambda z\ [_{IP}\ t_x\ \text{ihren}_x\ \text{Text nochmal Korrektur}\ t_z\ ]]]$

pronoun of interest. For (3)/(4) the comprehension question was *How many texts were proofread? (one / several)*.

48 native German speakers from the Tübingen University community read 20 sentences like those in (3) and (4) (plus two additional conditions) together with 138 other sentences (items from unrelated experiments and fillers) while their eye movements were being monitored. The answers to the comprehension questions showed no difference in the availability of bound readings in the two conditions. The bound answer (*several*) was chosen in 84.2% of the cases in the telescoping condition, and in 85% of the cases in the regular binding condition. For the analysis of reading times the sentences were divided into the following regions: first DP, relative clause, matrix verb, pronoun, rest of the sentence. We analyzed the time spent in an analysis region between first entering and first leaving it (first pass times) as well as the total time spent in the region, and regressions. First pass times at the pronoun region and total times across the sentence are displayed in Figure 1. Reading times revealed no additional difficulty in the telescoping condition compared to the binding condition, either on the pronoun itself or on the final region of the sentence (all t's < 1).

These data indicate that telescoping is relatively easy, at least when the interpretation resulting from the quantifier binding the pronoun is plausible. One might even wonder about the high proportion of bound answers in this experiment, especially in light of the fact that the possibility of this interpretation has largely gone unnoticed in the literature. Before we move on to examining factors that influence the availability of bound readings, let us thus briefly compare the present findings to other experimental studies on bound variable interpretations.

2.2 Bound variable interpretations in the experimental literature

Hirschberg & Ward (1991) tested strict and sloppy readings in VP ellipsis with c-commanding and non-c-commanding antecedents. A sample item is given below:

(5) a. Mary said she deserves the scholarship, and so did Cathy.
b. People who study linguistics think it's critical to cognitive science, and so do people who study AI.

The stimuli were presented auditorily. After each item, participants had to choose between two written paraphrases: (a) *Cathy said Mary deserves the scholarship*, (b) *Cathy said Cathy deserves the scholarship*. The sloppy (bound) reading was chosen in 42.9% of the non-c-commanding contexts. In a written control study with the

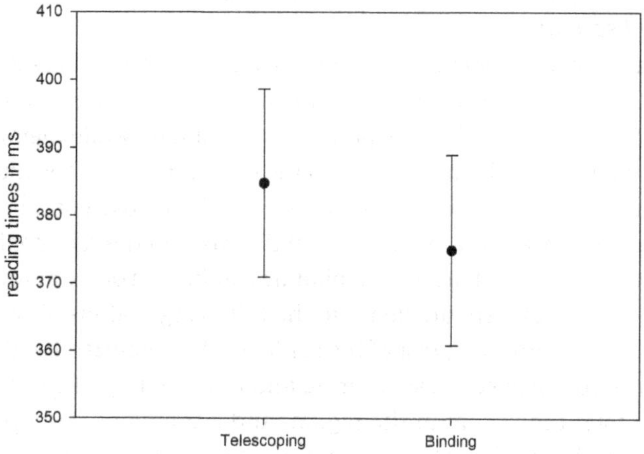

(a) First pass reading times at pronoun

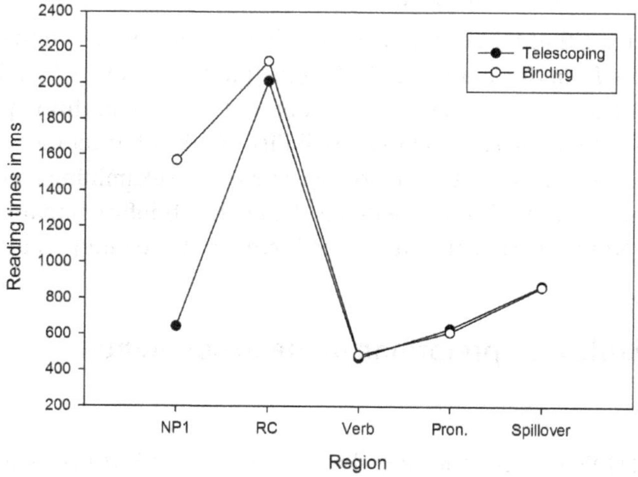

(b) Total reading times across all regions

Fig. 1: Mean reading times in the two conditions. Figure 1a shows the mean first pass times at the pronoun region. Figure 1b shows the mean total reading times across all regions of the sentence.

same items the sloppy reading was reported in 29.7% of the non-c-commanding contexts.

Frazier & Clifton (2000) investigated whether bound or coreferential readings are preferred in sentences such as

(6) Mr. Stevenson helped his wife into the car, and his lawyer did too.

To assess which reading was preferred, participants had to answer a question such as *Who did the lawyer help into the car?*. In sentences like (6) that were not biased either towards a bound or towards a coreferential reading, 48% bound interpretations were reported, and even in the coreferential-biased condition a bound reading was chosen 29% of the time.

Koornneef (2008) used eye-tracking to investigate strict and sloppy readings of the pronoun *her* in Dutch stories given in (7) in their English translation:

(7) a. Lisa and Anouk love the music channel MTV. They were very happy when they were selected for the show "Pimp My Room", in which their rooms were redecorated. Sadly, only Lisa thinks that her pimped room has a touch of class. Oh well, to each their own taste.

b. Lisa and Anouk love the music channel MTV. Lisa was very happy when she was selected for the show "Pimp My Room", in which her room was redecorated. Sadly, only Lisa thinks that her pimped room has a touch of class. Oh well, to each their own taste.

c. Lisa and Anouk love the music channel MTV. They were very happy when they were selected for the show "Pimp My Room", in which their rooms were redecorated. Sadly, Lisa thinks that her pimped room has a touch of class, but Anouk does not. Oh well, to each their own taste.

d. Lisa and Anouk love the music channel MTV. Lisa was very happy when she was selected for the show "Pimp My Room", in which her room was redecorated. Sadly, Lisa thinks that her pimped room has a touch of class, but Anouk does not. Oh well, to each their own taste.

Conditions (7a) and (7c) bias toward a sloppy (bound) reading, whereas in (7b) and (7d) the strict reading is much more plausible. There was a significant main effect (marginal by items) of shorter first fixations on the sloppy conditions at the region *pimped room* immediately after the pronoun. Planned comparisons showed that this effect was limited to the elliptical conditions (7c)–(7d). There was an advantage for sloppy readings in the ellipsis region *but Anouk does not* as well, most strongly in the regression path duration but also in the total fixation duration.

Reading times on the second sentence of the stories provide further support that strict readings are more difficult than sloppy ones. In the strict-biased conditions (7b) and (7d), the biasing sentence (*Lisa was very happy when she …*) was re-read significantly longer than the sloppy *They were very happy when they…*, both in the ellipsis and in the *only*-structures. Thus Koornneef's results, just like Frazier & Clifton's (2000) findings in their self-paced reading experiments provide online evidence that readers prefer sloppy readings in ambiguous elliptical constructions.

Studies using quantifiers, on the other hand, present a mixed picture. Gordon & Hendrick (1998a) collected ratings for bound anaphora on a 5-point scale using the following sentences:

(8) a. Each girl decided what she could do.
  b. Each girl's parents decided what she could do.

Although sentences with a c-commanding quantifier were judged significantly better, sentences where the quantifier did not c-command the pronoun still received average ratings of 4.05.

Carminati, Frazier & Rayner (2002) recorded eye movements in a study using the following materials:

(9) a. Every British soldier aimed and then he killed an enemy soldier.
  b. Every British soldier thought that he killed an enemy soldier.
  c. The British soldier aimed and then he killed an enemy soldier.
  d. The British soldier thought that he killed an enemy soldier.

They report longer reading times in the region after the pronoun for sentences with a quantifier than for those that begin with a definite DP. Moreover, reading times were longer in sentences that contained complement clauses than in sentences with conjoined clauses. However, there was no significant interaction between the two factors, i.e. there was no processing benefit in cases where the pronoun in a complement clause was c-commanded by the quantifier.

In the studies by Carminati, Frazier & Rayner (2002) and Gordon & Hendrick (1998a) it is taken for granted that a bound interpretation was selected but in principle their experimental items were ambiguous between a bound reading and a deictic one where the pronoun picks up a discourse referent. A deictic reading was available in the present experiment as well.[3] However, if that reading was selected then we would expect the answer *one* to the question *How many texts were proofread?*, which was chosen less than 20% of the time. A possible problem may be that there is a pragmatic bias towards answering *several*, since instructors typically read more than one text. While this may be responsible for some of the "bound" answers, it is unlikely that it accounts for all or even the majority of

3 Note that in our materials the definite DP *der Dozent* cannot be interpreted as coreferential with the (feminine) pronoun *ihren* as they do not match in gender.

them. Moreover, it is unlikely that the pragmatic bias had a stronger effect in the telescoping condition than under regular variable binding. The fact that there is no difference between the availability of bound readings in the condition where binding of the pronoun was unproblematic and in the one where telescoping was necessary for the bound interpretation is sufficient to show that telescoping is easily possible in the configuration under consideration here.

3 Experiment 2: Testing theoretical accounts

Having established that telescoping out of a relative clause is possible, we are ready to test some theoretical accounts. As mentioned in Sternefeld (this volume), syntactic approaches predict a subject-object asymmetry in telescoping: Under a syntactic reconstruction analysis, (10a) should not allow a bound reading of *seine Ärztin*, since the object quantifier cannot scope over the subject or its trace. By contrast, the bound reading should be possible in (10b), where the quantifier c-commands the trace in object position. Moreover, *ihm* should never receive a bound interpretation because the quantifier cannot take scope outside the relative clause.

(10) a. Seine Ärztin, die jeden Patienten seit Langem
his doctor$_{nom/acc}$ who$_{nom/acc}$ every$_{acc}$ patient$_{acc}$ since long
gekannt hat, hat ihm ein teures Medikament verschrieben
known has has for-him an expensive medication prescribed
His doctor who has known every patient for a long time prescribed him an expensive medication.

b. Seine Ärztin, die jeder Patient seit Langem gekannt
his doctor$_{nom/acc}$ who$_{nom/acc}$ every$_{nom}$ patient since long known
hat, hat ihm ein teures Medikament verschrieben
has has for-him an expensive medication prescribed
His doctor who every patient has known for a long time prescribed him an expensive medication.

If telescoping results from quantifier raising (QR), then the predictions are reversed: raising the object quantifier in (10a) at LF should be fine, whereas QR of *jeder Patient* into the matrix clause in (10b) should violate the ECP.[4]

4 According to the ECP, all traces must be properly governed and subject traces can only be antecedent governed. The relative pronoun prevents antecedent government in this case as it acts as a barrier (Lasnik & Saito 1984).

On the other hand, a lack of subject/object asymmetry with respect to bound readings may be taken to support semantic theories of telescoping such as Sternefeld (this volume): in such theories both (10a) and (10b) are expected to be equally good.

Another issue briefly mentioned in Sternefeld (this volume) is whether there is a difference between the examples in (10) versus (11).

(11) a. Die Ärztin, die jeden Patienten seit Langem gekannt
the doctor$_{nom/acc}$ who$_{nom/acc}$ every$_{acc}$ patient$_{acc}$ since long known
hat, hat ihm ein teures Medikament verschrieben
has has for-him an expensive medication prescribed
The doctor who has known every patient for a long time prescribed him an expensive medication.

b. Die Ärztin, die jeder Patient seit Langem gekannt
the doctor$_{nom/acc}$ who$_{nom/acc}$ every$_{nom}$ patient since long known
hat, hat ihm ein teures Medikament verschrieben
has has for-him an expensive medication prescribed
The doctor who every patient has known for a long time prescribed him an expensive medication.

We might expect that the processing of forward anaphora is facilitated by cataphoric anaphora, i.e. that telescoping is easier in (10) than in (11).

3.1 Materials and procedures

To test these theoretical issues we conducted a self-paced reading study using the four conditions shown in (10)–(11) and repeated in (12). The sentences were presented phrase-by-phrase using the moving-window technique. The presentation regions are indicated by the slashes in (12).

(12) a. Seine Ärztin,/ die/ jeden Patienten/ seit Langem/ gekannt hat,/ hat/ ihm/ ein teures Medikament/ verschrieben.

b. Seine Ärztin,/ die/ jeder Patient/ seit Langem/ gekannt hat,/ hat/ ihm/ ein teures Medikament/ verschrieben.

c. Die Ärztin,/ die/ jeden Patienten/ seit Langem/ gekannt hat,/ hat/ ihm/ ein teures Medikament/ verschrieben.

d. Die Ärztin,/ die/ jeder Patient/ seit Langem/ gekannt hat,/ hat/ ihm/ ein teures Medikament/ verschrieben.

As the finite verb is in clause-final position in German relative clauses, the subject quantifier and object quantifier cases (12b,d) vs. (12a,c) only differ in the case marking on the QP. To ensure unambiguous case marking and thus correct interpretation of the relative clause, the QP always contained a masculine noun. The matrix subject, by contrast, was feminine so it could not be construed as the antecedent of the masculine pronoun.

As in Experiment 1, the bound readings were assessed using comprehension questions. To avoid the pragmatic bias that may have affected the answers in the previous experiment, the question for the anaphoric reading of *ihm* was made more specific, e.g. for the item in (12) it was *Did each patient get a prescription for an expensive medication?*. The cataphoric reading of *seine* in (12a–b) was tested with the question *Did the sentence say that each patient has known his (own) doctor for a long time?*. Each item was followed by just one comprehension question, thus the anaphoric question appeared with half of the items. The other half of the items received the cataphoric question in conditions (a) and (b) and no question in the remaining two conditions.

24 items like (12) were constructed in four conditions. They were distributed across four presentation lists according to a latin square design. The items were mixed with 48 fillers of superficially similar structure, 16 of which were followed by a comprehension question. 42 native German speakers from the Tübingen University community participated in the experiment for a payment of 5 euros. Participants were tested individually. They were randomly assigned to one of the presentation lists and read the items and fillers in an individually randomized order. An experimental session lasted approximately 30 minutes.

3.2 Predictions

If telescoping is the result of QR into the matrix clause, then it should not be possible in (12b) and (12d) otherwise an ECP-violation will occur. Thus bound readings of *ihm* are only expected in (12a,c), since the object quantifier, but not the subject quantifier can QR out of the relative clause and end up high enough to bind the pronoun. By the same token, *seine* in (12b) should not have a bound reading. Assuming that the pronoun in the subject in (12a–b) acts as a trigger in inducing QR into the matrix clause, we may even expect a reading time difference: if raising of the subject quantifier into the matrix clause is attempted and then rejected because of the ECP, then longer reading times may be observed in the relative clause in (12b) than in (12a). Whether a reading time effect is expected at the pronoun *ihm* is not clear: As the bound interpretation is predicted not to be available in (12b,d) *ihm* will have to be interpreted deicitically, which may or may not take longer than binding.

According to reconstruction theories of relative clause interpretation, the head of the relative clause (*die/seine Ärztin*) is interpreted in its "base" position inside the relative clause. This means that the cataphoric pronoun *seine* in (12b) appears within the scope of the quantifier during some stage of the interpretation, thus it can receive a bound reading. In (12a), however, reconstruction does not make a bound reading possible, since the position the DP is reconstructed into is still higher than the object quantifier. As LF-movement of the quantifier cannot yield new binding relations, *seine* in (12a) should only have a deictic interpretation. Moreover, a bound reading of *ihm* should not be possible in any of the conditions in (12) since the quantifier is presumably clause-bound. Thus the predictions this type of approach makes primarily concern the available readings. Given the discussion above, it is not clear whether any reading time differences are expected.

Semantic approaches such as Sternefeld (this volume) do not require any movement, thus no subject/object asymmetry is expected. The combination of continuation theory (Barker 2002) and delayed binding allows for a bound reading of *seine* both in (12a) and in (12b). Furthermore, Sternefeld conjectures that the bound interpretation of *ihm* may depend on that of *seine* (see Sternefeld this volume for details). If that is the case then we should find more bound readings in (12a–b) than in (12c–d). As with the previous approaches, there are no clear predictions concerning the reading times.

To sum up, the crucial test of the theories is the availability of bound readings of *ihm*: under reconstruction it should not be possible at all, under QR it should only occur with object quantifiers, whereas according to Sternefeld's proposal it should always be allowed. Concerning the bound reading of *seine*, the reconstruction approach predicts it to be available in the subject quantifier condition (12b), the QR approach in (12a), and the semantic approach in both cases.

There is an additional aspect of the materials which may affect reading times. As mentioned above, the DP inside the relative clause is unambiguously case-marked, which clearly indicates whether it is in subject or object position. However, the relative pronoun, which matches the feminine subject DP, is ambiguous: it may be interpreted as nominative or accusative. Its role as subject or object therefore only becomes clear when the full DP has been read. Numerous experiments have shown that readers prefer a subject-before-object order of constituents and take a case-ambiguous initial DP or pronoun to be nominative by default (cf. Bader & Bayer 2006, Bornkessel & Schlesewsky 2006). In case of an object relative clause this will result in a brief temporary misanalysis of the relative clause and reinterpretation when the (nominative-marked) DP has been encountered, which may result in longer reading times.

3.3 Results

The reading times per region, the readings participants reported, and the response times to the comprehension questions were subjected to repeated measures ANOVAs separately by participants and by items with the factors quantifier (subject vs. object quantifier) and determiner in matrix subject (*die* vs. *seine*). Figure 2 shows the proportion of bound readings of the (late) pronoun *ihm* in the four conditions, as well as the time participants took to read the comprehension question and indicate their interpretation of the pronoun, separately for bound and deictic answers.

Across all conditions the bound reading was reported on average on 28.8% of the trials. A repeated measures ANOVA with the factors quantifier (subject vs. object) and determiner in matrix subject (*die* vs. *seine*) revealed no main effects (all F's < 1); the interaction of the factors was marginal ($F_1(1,41) = 3.573$, $p = .066$, $F_2(1,11) = 3.609$, $p = .084$).[5] Planned comparisons showed that bound readings were equally frequent in conditions with a subject or object quantifier following an initial pronoun (*seine*) ($t_1(41) = -1.702$, $p = .096$, $t_2(11) = -1.467$, $p = .170$). There were marginally fewer bound answers when the object quantifier followed *seine* than when it followed an DP with *die* ($t_1(41) = -1.814$, $p = .077$, $t_2(11) = -2.836$, $p = .016$). With subject quantifiers, the numerical difference was reversed but it did not approach statistical significance (t's < 1). In the response times there was a marginally significant main effect of participants providing a bound interpretation faster in the conditions with *seine* than in those with *die* ($F_1(1,41) = 3.772$, $p = .059$, $F_2(1,11) = 4.817$, $p = .051$). There were no other significant effects or interactions (all F's < 1).

Figure 3 shows the proportion of bound readings of the initial pronoun *seine*, as well as the mean reaction times for answering the question that assessed the reading. The initial pronoun received a bound interpretation on average 32.9% of the time. The proportion of bound readings did not differ between the subject-quantifier and the object-quantifier conditions ((12b) and (12a), respectively), both t's < 1. However, with an object quantifier the bound answers were significantly slower than with a subject quantifier ($t_1(22) = 2.265$, $p = .034$, $t_2(11) = 2.146$, $p = .055$). The response times corresponding to the deictic interpretation of the pronoun did not differ from each other ($t_1(37) = 1.432$, $p = .161$, $t_2(11) = 1.928$, $p = .086$).

For the analysis of reading times, residual reading times were calculated for each participant. The mean residual reading times for each presentation region are shown in Figure 4.

---

5 Note that the interpretation of *ihm* was tested after half of the items; the other half received questions about the interpretation of *seine*.

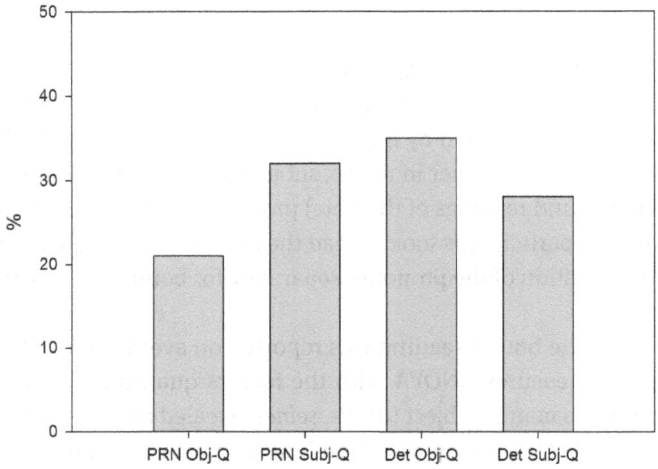

(a) Proportion of bound readings for *ihm*

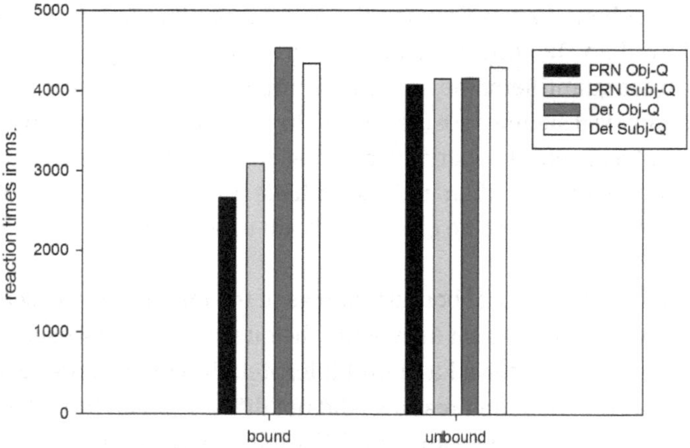

(b) Response times for question about *ihm*

Fig. 2: Reported readings and response times to the question testing the reading of the anaphoric pronoun *ihm*. Figure 2a shows the proportion of bound readings for *ihm*. Figure 2b displays the mean response times per condition, separately for the bound and the deictic answers.

Reading times on the first two regions (subject DP and relative pronoun) are of no theoretical interest. At regions 3 (the quantifier phrase) and 4 (adverb) reading times did not differ from each other: all F's < 1. At region 5 (verb cluster at

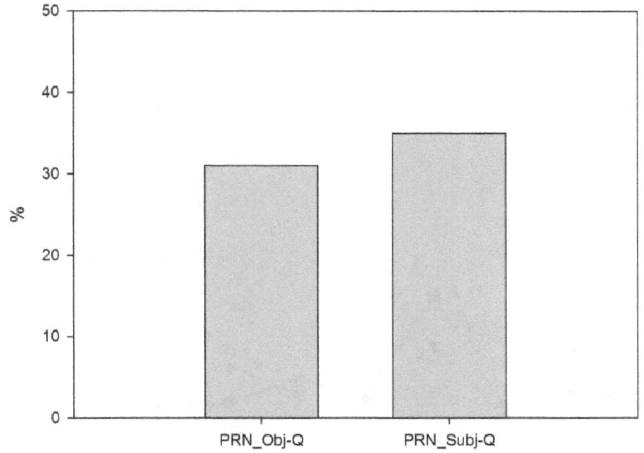

(a) Proportion of bound readings for *seine*

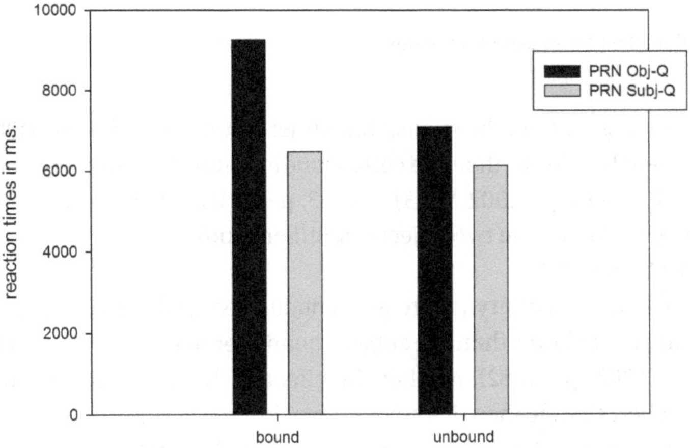

(b) Response times for question about *seine*

Fig. 3: Reported readings and response times to the question testing the reading of the cataphoric pronoun *seine*. Figure 3a shows the proportion of bound readings for *seine*. Figure 3b displays the mean response times per condition, separately for the bound and the deictic answers.

the end of the relative clause) both the main effect of quantifier ($F_1(1,41) = 11.239$, $p = .002$, $F_2(1,23) = 15.097$, $p = .001$), and of *die* vs. *seine* ($F_1(1,41) = 24.108$, $p < .001$, $F_2(1,23) = 16.009$, $p = .001$) were significant. In addition, there was a significant interaction ($F_1(1,41) = 5.275$, $p = .027$, $F_2(1,11) = 8.663$, $p = .007$). This was due to

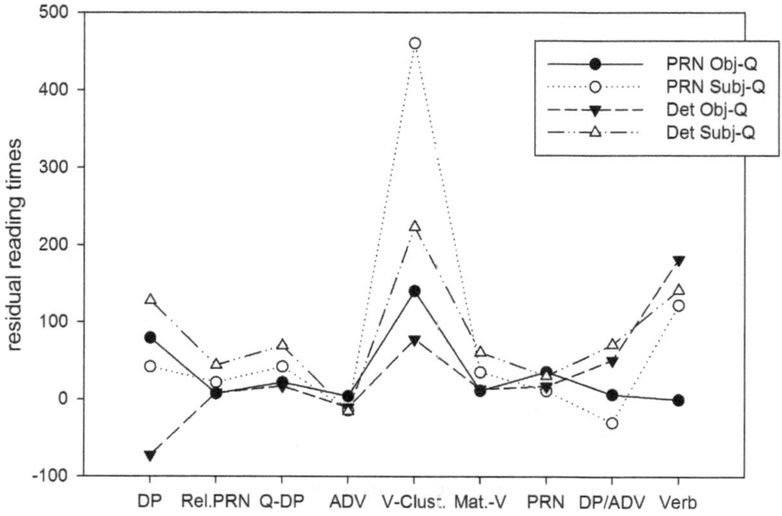

Fig. 4: Mean residual reading times across all regions

particularly long reading times in the subject quantifier condition with *seine* (12b): this condition was reliably slower than the corresponding subject quantifier condition with *die* ($t_1(41) = 3.384$, $p = .002$, $t_2(23) = 6.062$, $p < .001$), whereas there was no reliable difference between the two object-quantifier conditions ($t_1(41) = 1.404$, $p = .168$, $t_2(23) = 1.120$, $p = .274$).

At region 6 (the matrix auxiliary), there was a main effect of the object-quantifier conditions being read slower than the subject-quantifier ones ($F_1(1,41) = 7.932$, $p < .007$, $F_2(1,23) = 3.302$, $p = .082$). Neither the effect of the quantifier nor the interaction approached significance (F's < 1).

At the anaphoric pronoun (region 7, Figure 5 below) neither of the main effects turned out to be reliable (F's < 1) but the interaction was marginally significant ($F_1(1,41) = 3.311$, $p = .076$, $F_2(1,23) = 3.435$, $p = .077$). Pairwise comparisons revealed that reading times were slower when an initial DP with *seine* was followed by an object quantifier as opposed to a subject quantifier ($t_1(41) = 2.355$, $p = .023$, $t_2(23) = 2.132$, $p = .044$). In the corresponding conditions with *die* the numerical data showed the opposite pattern but the difference was not statistically significant ($t_1(41) = -1.866$, $p = .069$, $t_2 < 1$).

At region 8 (adverb), the conditions with *seine* were read significantly faster than those with *die* ($F_1(1,41) = 8.866$, $p = .005$, $F_2(1,23) = 18.306$, $p = .001$). There

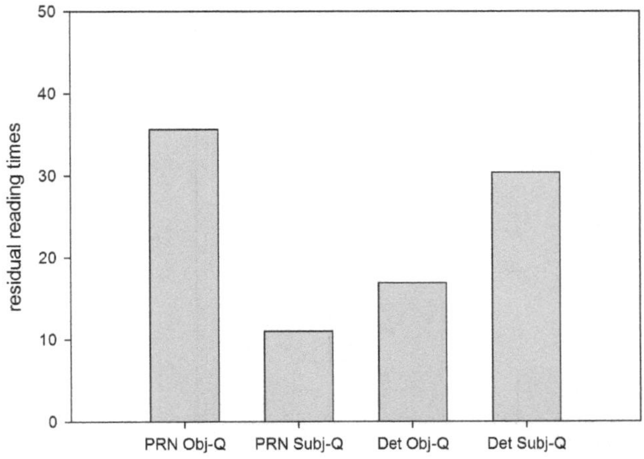

Fig. 5: Mean residual reading times at the pronoun *ihm* (Region 7)

were no other significant effects. The main effect of *seine* vs. *die* persisted on the final region as well ($F_1(1{,}41) = 4.520$, $p = .040$, $F_2(1{,}23) = 6.343$, $p = .019$), whereas the interaction did not reach significance.

The results discussed so far were based on all reading times, irrespective of the reading the participant reported. Recall that only about 33% of the answers provided at the end of the sentence reflected a bound reading of *seine*. Focusing on just those trials, the only region with a considerable reading time difference across conditions was region 5 (the end of the relative clause). As Figure 6 shows, at this region there was a massive slowdown in the subject quantifier condition, just like in the pattern with all observations.

Considering the bound reading of *ihm*, the earliest point in the sentence where we may be able to observe a difference based on the ultimate interpretation is the region of the second pronoun (region 7). At this region there were no significant differences across the four conditions. Crucially, at the next region the pattern is the same as the overall pattern of reading times, showing an advantage of the conditions with *seine* over those with *die*, cf. Figure 7.

Finally, looking at whether the interpretation of *seine* had any effect on the reading ultimately assigned to *ihm*, the only suggestive piece of evidence was relatively longer reading times at the relative pronoun in cases when the bound interpretation was reported, as shown in Figure 8.

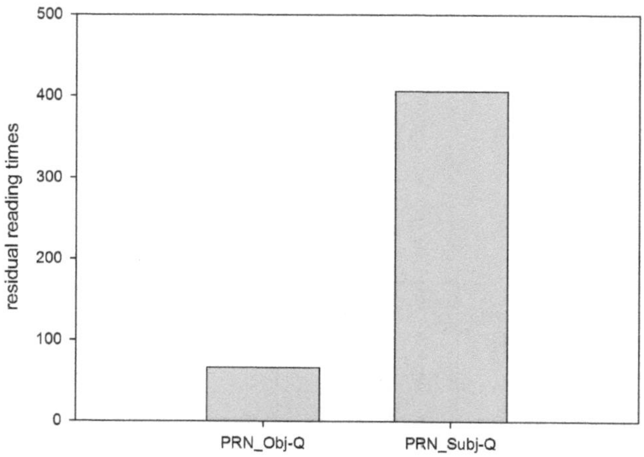

Fig. 6: Mean residual reading times for the bound readings of *seine* at the end of the relative clause (Region 5)

3.4 Discussion

The ca. 30% bound answers for both *seine* and *ihm* provide further evidence that bound readings are easily available. The discrepancy between the proportion of bound answers in Experiment 1 and Experiment 2 probably resulted from different presentation techniques and from the more specific questions used in Experiment 2. As discussed in section 2, in Experiment 1 there was a potential pragmatic bias to answer *several* even when no true bound reading was intended. In the present experiment care was taken to avoid this possibility, which naturally led to fewer bound readings. In addition, the previous experiment used eye-tracking, thus participants were able to go back and re-read earlier portions of the sentence when they encountered the pronoun. In Experiment 2 the moving-window technique made it impossible to reinspect earlier parts of the sentence. Participants thus had to rely on the representation they had constructed up to the point of encountering the pronoun, and that may have discouraged bound interpretations on some of the trials. Note that the proportion of bound readings in the present experiment is much more similar to the findings by other researchers reviewed in Section 2.

Participants' answers to the comprehension questions did not show any subject/object asymmetry with respect to the availability of bound readings. This fact constitutes evidence against both types of syntactic theories. Recall that the QR approach only allows telescoping with an object quantifier, since raising a subject

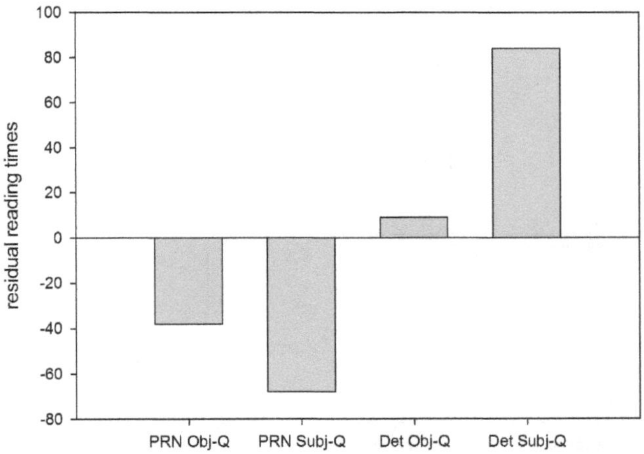

(a) Reading times for the bound interpretation of *ihm*

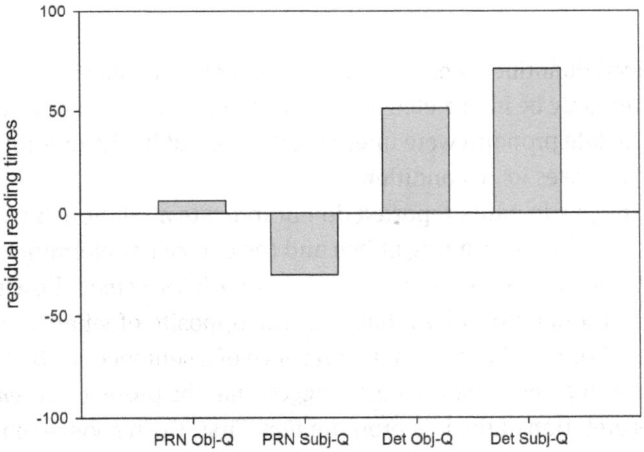

(b) Reading times across all trials

Fig. 7: Mean residual reading times at Region 8. Figure 7a shows the reading times on those trials where a bound reading of *ihm* was reported. Figure 7b displays the mean residual reading times on all trials.

quantifier high enough would result in an ECP-violaton. Under a reconstruction account, on the other hand, the pronoun in the matrix subject should only be able to receive a bound reading in an object relative clause, where it is reconstructed into

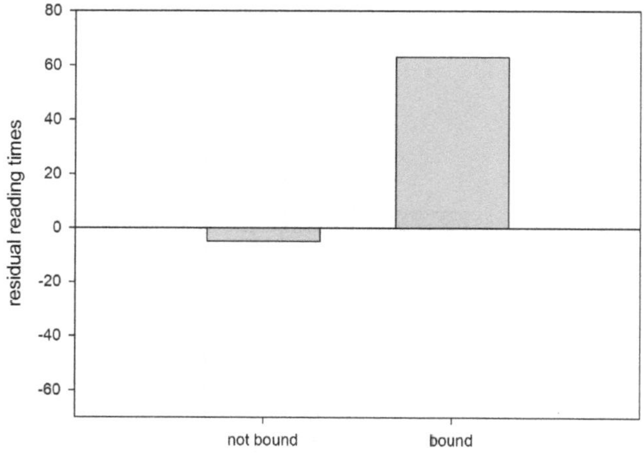

Fig. 8: Mean residual reading times for the bound and deictic readings of *seine* at the relative pronoun (Region 2)

the scope of the (subject) quantifier. Moreover, as the (late) pronoun *ihm* never has to reconstruct, it should only be interpreted deictically. In Experiment 2, however, both the initial and the late pronoun were interpreted as bound by the quantifier in more than 20% of the cases in all conditions.

The interpretations participants reported do not indicate a relationship between the availability of a bound reading of *ihm* and the choice of determiner in the initial DP. In fact, the pattern of bound answers with *die* vs. *seine* following an object quantifier, although not fully reliable, is the opposite of what would be expected if the anaphor benefitted from the presence of a sentence-initial cataphor. However, the reading and response times suggest that the presence of *seine* did facilitate the interpretation of the late pronoun *ihm*. First, the response times corresponding to a bound reading of *ihm* were faster in the conditions with *seine* than with *die*, whereas the choice of determiner in the initial DP did not affect the response times for a deictic interpretation. Furthermore, the significantly faster reading times in the conditions with *seine* at regions 8 and 9 also indicate that the initial pronoun makes the interpretation of the following anaphor easier.

Thus starting with region 8, the two conditions with *seine* are processed in a similar fashion and differently from *die*. However, the reading times on earlier parts of the sentence do not show a clear *seine* vs. *die* difference. Participants seem to encounter processing difficulty at region 5 in the case of *seine* and a subject quantifier, and at region 7 when *seine* is followed by an object quantifier. To explain this difference it may be useful to consider what processing steps are likely to take place at each presentation region.

The interpretation of the initial DP in the conditions with *die* does not require any additional steps beyond lexical-semantic processing and setting up a discourse referent. *Seine*, however, cannot be fully interpreted since an appropriate antecedent is missing. At this point full interpretation may be delayed or an unidentified discourse antecedent may be postulated, resulting in a deictic reading. Gordon & Hendrick's (1998b) findings indicate that readers typically do not associate a later potential antecedent with a possessive pronoun in a sentence-initial subject DP. Instead they tend to assume the existence of an appropriate referent in context. This is consistent with the difference in the contingent reading times at region 2 (Figure 8): no bound reading resulted on those trials where participants quickly moved on to later parts of the sentence.

In line with the general subject-before-object preference documented for German (Bader & Bayer 2006, Bornkessel & Schlesewsky 2006), the case-ambiguous relative pronoun in region 2 is initially interpreted as nominative. This interpretation is disconfirmed in the subject-quantifier conditions (12b,d). The resulting reanalysis is presumably responsible for the significantly longer reading times in the subject-quantifier conditions at the end of the relative clause. Although this effect would be expected to appear right after the quantifier (at region 3 or 4), given the relatively short presentation regions in the present experiment it may have been delayed until region 5. The second main effect observed at this region, namely longer reading times for the conditions with *seine*, was due to the extreme slowdown in the condition with *seine* and a subject quantifier. A possible explanation, consistent with the pattern at later parts of the sentence, is that the extra processing that was needed to recover from the garden-path in the subject quantifier conditions also made the quantifier more salient, and as a consequence, at least on a proportion of the trials it was considered as a potential antecedent for the initial pronoun. This did not necessarily lead to actual binding, but it was sufficient to slow down processing in order to check the viability of a representation where binding could be established. When the second pronoun was encountered two short regions later, the relevant representation was already available, resulting in particularly fast reading in the subject quantifier condition with *seine*. By contrast, the object quantifier could be integrated into the unfolding representation of the sentence without any difficulty. As no additional processing effort was needed, object quantifiers remained less salient during the interpretation of the relative clause and presumably no binding was attempted between the quantifier and the initial pronoun. The kind of representation that would allow a bound interpretation (of both pronouns) was thus only considered when *ihm* was encountered in region 7, leading to considerably slower reading times at this region.

4 Conclusions

Our results indicate that binding out of a relative clause is not particularly difficult. In addition, the observed lack of a subject/object asymmetry with respect to the availability of bound readings constitutes evidence against syntactic theories of telescoping. Moreover, the data suggest that the presence of an initial pronoun may facilitate the binding of a later one within the same sentence. The present evidence is only indirect, based on reading and response times. Follow-up experiments should assess the reading of both pronouns within a sentence to establish a clear connection between the two. If our results are confirmed, they will be difficult to account for in syntactic terms; however, they are compatible with Sternefeld's (this volume) semantic approach to telescoping.

The work reported here focused on the universal quantifier *jede(r)* "every". In order to fully understand telescoping it is necessary to examine other quantifiers as well; we are currently conducting an experiment investigating the availability of bound readings with the negative quantifier *keine* "no". Another possible extension would be to consider the effect of clausal relations on bound interpretations: Intuitively, in the sentence *The poison that every dog ate killed him.* the deictic reading is not available at all. Testing this intuition is left to future research.

References

Bader, Markus & Joseph Bayer. 2006. *Case and linking in language comprehension: Evidence from German.* Heidelberg: Springer.

Barker, Chris. 2002. Continuations and the nature of quantification. *Natural Language Semantics* 10. 211–242.

Bornkessel, Ina & Matthias Schlesewsky. 2006. The extended argument dependency model: A neurocognitive approach to sentence comprehension across languages. *Psychological Review* 113(4). 787–821.

Carminati, Maria Nella, Lyn Frazier & Keith Rayner. 2002. Bound variables and c-command. *Journal of Semantics* 19. 1–34.

Frazier, Lyn & Charles Clifton Jr. 2000. On bound variable interpretations: The LF-only hypothesis. *Journal of Psycholinguistic Research* 29(2). 125–139.

Gordon, Peter C. & Randall Hendrick. 1998a. Dimensions of grammatical coreference. In Morton Ann Gernsbacher & Sharon J. Derry (eds.), *Proceedings of the Twentieth Annual Conference of the Cognitive Science Society*, 424–429. Mahwah, NJ: Lawrence Erlbaum Associates.

Gordon, Peter C. & Randall Hendrick. 1998b. The representation and processing of coreference in discourse. *Cognitive Science* 22. 389–424.

Hirschberg, Julia & Gregory Ward. 1991. Accent and bound anaphora. *Cognitive Linguistics* 2(2). 101–121.

Hulsey, Sarah & Uli Sauerland. 2006. Sorting out relative clauses. *Natural Language Semantics* 14. 111–137.

Koornneef, Arnout Willem. 2008. *Eye-catching anaphora*. Utrecht University Doctoral dissertation.

Lasnik, Howard & Mamoru Saito. 1984. On the nature of proper government. *Linguistic Inquiry* 15. 235–289.

Safir, Ken. 1999. Vehicle change and reconstruction in A'-chains. *Linguistic Inquiry* 30. 587–620.

Friederike Moltmann

Intensional relative clauses and the semantics of variable objects

NPs with intensional relative clauses such as *the book John needs to write* pose a significant challenge for semantic theory. Such NPs act like referential terms, yet they do not stand for a particular actual object. This paper will develop a semantic analysis of such NPs on the basis of the notion of a variable object. The analysis avoids a range of difficulties that a more standard analysis based on the notion of an individual concept would face. Most importantly, unlike the latter, the proposed analysis can be carried over NPs such as *the number of people that fit into the bus*, which describe tropes (particularized properties).

1 Introduction

Individual concepts, functions from possible worlds and times to entities, have become a standard tool in linguistic semantics since Montague (1973), in particular as semantic values of functional NPs such as *the president of the US* in the context below:

(1) The president of the US is elected every four years.

If making use of individual concepts, *the president of the US* will stand for a function mapping a world w and time t to the individual that is the president of the US in w at t.

This paper focuses on NPs with relative clauses containing an intensional verb, as in (2), for which an analysis in terms of individual concepts is equally tempting:

(2) The book John needs to write must have more impact than the one he has already written.

I will call NPs of this sort, that is, definite NPs modified by a relative clause with an intensional verb as predicate 'IR-NPs'. On an analysis using individual concepts, *the book John needs to write* would stand for a function mapping a circumstance in which John fulfills his need to a book written by John in that circumstance.

Friederike Moltmann, Institute for the History and Philosophy of Science and Technology (IHPST) (Paris1/ENS/CNRS)

https://doi.org/10.1515/9783050095158-014

In fact, there is a construction closely related to the one in (2) for which an analysis in terms of individual concepts has been proposed. This is the construction below, analysed by Grosu & Krifka (2007), which involves an intensional verb and the copula verb *be*:

(3) The gifted mathematician John claims to be could solve this problem in no time.

On Grosu & Krifka's (2007) analysis, roughly, the subject of (3) stands for an individual concept mapping any circumstance in which what John claims is true onto a gifted mathematician identical with John in that circumstance.

I will argue that an analysis based on individual concepts raises a range of problems, ontologically, conceptually, and empirically. Focusing on the construction in (2), I will make use of an alternative to the notion of an individual concept, namely the notion of a *variable object*. A variable object is an entity that may have different manifestations as different individuals in different actual or counterfactual circumstances. The notion of a variable object derives from the notion of a variable embodiment, which plays a central role in Kit Fine's metaphysics (Fine 1999). Unlike individual concepts, variable objects are entities, which means, given standard type theory, they are of type *e*. Individual concepts are not so much entities of a particular type, but rather they make up the contribution of certain sorts of occurrences of expressions to the compositional meaning of the sentence. Their type-theoretic type $\langle s, t \rangle$, the type of functions from indices to individuals, captures the fact that NPs of that type can occur only in syntactic contexts in which such a function can compose suitably with the semantic value of a sister constituent. Variable objects, by contrast, are objects and as such able to act as semantic values of referential NPs, which will include functional and IR-NPs.

The main motivation for positing variable objects as the semantic values of functional and IR-NPs comes from constructions in which those NPs appear to describe the bearers of tropes. Tropes are particularized properties, concrete manifestations of properties in objects. Typical examples of tropes are 'the softness of the pillow' and 'the redness of the apple', which are qualitative tropes. 'The length of the paper' and 'the number of planets' can also be considered tropes, namely quantitative tropes. 'The number of planets' will be a number trope, the instantiation of the property of being eight in the plurality of planets (Moltmann 2013a,c). In the sentences below, IR-NPs appear to describe the bearers of tropes: number tropes in (4a) and tropes of causal effect in (4b):

(4) a. The number of people that fit into the bus exceeds the number of people that fit into the car.

b. The impact of the book John needs to write must be greater than the impact of the book he has already written.

There is a crucial difference between (4a) and (4b), though. (4b) requires a modal in the main clause, which (4a) does not. (4b), without the modal, would be unacceptable. As will be discussed, this means that only the NPs in (4a) refer to tropes with variable objects as their bearer. The NPs in (4b), by contrast, refer to 'variable tropes', variable objects whose manifestations are tropes rather than individuals.

The variable-objects account of IR-NPs goes along with a particular compositional analysis of the construction, according to which the head of the relative clause is interpreted in the lower position inside the relative clause. Thus, the account presupposes a syntactic view according which the head noun of an IR-NP originates from inside the relative clause, within a copying theory of movement or a view according to which it can be reconstructed into the lower position.

The paper starts with a few clarifying remarks about tropes and reference to tropes in natural language. It then discusses in greater detail the individual-concept approach to the constructions in (1), (2), and (3). The main part of the paper consists in the introduction of the notion of a variable object, which will first be applied to the semantics of (1) and (2) and then to the semantics of (3) as well. The ontology of variable objects will also be used to explain when IR-NPs require a modal in the main clause and when they don't.

2 Reference to tropes in natural language

It is a common view, at least since Aristotle's 'Categories', that terms of the sort in (5) refer to tropes or particularized properties, that is, particular, non-sharable features of individuals (Williams 1953, Strawson 1959, Wolterstorff 1970, Campbell 1990, Lowe 2006, Mertz 1996):

(5) a. the wisdom of Socrates
b. the softness of the pillow
c. the simplicity of the dress

According to that view, (5a) refers to the particular manifestation of wisdom in Socrates, that is, a wisdom trope that has Socrates as its bearer, (5b) to the manifestation of softness in the pillow, and (5c) to the manifestation of simplicity in the dress.

There are equally good reasons to take the terms below to refer to tropes, namely quantitative tropes, manifestations of being so and so tall or so and so long in an individual (Campbell 1990, Moltmann 2009, 2013a):

(6) a. the height of the building
b. the length of the paper

Quantitative tropes also include number tropes, such as the manifestation of the property of being eight in the plurality of the planets, as below (Moltmann 2013a,c):

(6) c. the number of planets

The number trope that is the manifestation of the property of being eight in the plurality of the planets is a particularized property not shared by any equally numbered plurality.

Qualitative and quantitative tropes, as we refer to them in natural language, exhibit the very same properties characteristic of tropes, which I will turn to now.

2.1 The relation of a trope to its bearer

An important feature of tropes is their dependence on a bearer. Socrates is the bearer of the trope 'Socrates' wisdom' and the planets are the bearers of the trope 'the number of planets'. A trope exists in a world *w* at a time *t* only if its bearer exists in *w* at *t*. Moreover, two tropes are identical only if their bearers are identical.

2.2 Similarity relations

Another important feature of tropes consists in the way they enter similarity relations. Tropes instantiating the same property are similar, and tropes instantiating the same 'natural' property are exactly similar. For example, two redness tropes are similar, and two tropes exhibiting the very same shade of red are exactly similar. In natural language, exact similarity is expressed by *is the same as* (which does not imply numerical distinctness), as below:

(7) a. The quality of this fabric is the same as the quality of that fabric.
b. The impact of John's book was the same as the impact of Bill's book.
c. The height of the desk is the same as the height of the lamp.
d. The length of John's vacation is the same as the length of Mary's vacation.
e. The number of women is the same as the number of men.

Only the *is* of identity expresses numerical identity, rendering the sentences below intuitively false:

(8) a. ?? The quality of this fabric is the quality of that fabric.
b. ?? The impact of John's book was the impact of Bill's book.
c. ?? The number of women is the number of men.
d. ?? The height of the desk is the height of the lamp.

The way *is the same as* and the *is* of identity are understood with the terms in question is a particularly good indication that those terms refer to tropes and not abstract objects such as properties, degrees, or numbers.

2.3 Properties of concreteness

Tropes are as concrete as their bearers. If they have a concrete bearer, they may exhibit properties of concreteness such as the ability of acting as objects of perception – in fact as the immediate objects of perception (Williams 1953, Campbell 1990, Lowe 2006):

(9) a. John noticed the simplicity of the dress.
b. John observed Mary's politeness.
c. John noticed the small number of women that were present.

Tropes may also act as relata of causal relations (Williams 1953), as in the sentences below:

(10) a. The heaviness of the bag made Mary exhausted.
b. The number of passengers caused the boat to sink.
c. The weight of the lamp caused the table to break.

Tropes furthermore may have a temporal duration:[1]

(11) John's happiness lasted only a year.

There are other properties of concreteness that tropes may exhibit. One such property is what one may call 'description independence'. Description independence

1 More problematic is the spatial location of tropes. Even though the philosophical literature considers tropes to be located in space just where the bearer is located at the relevant time, in fact trope-referring terms in general resist predicates of spatial location:

(i) a. ?? John's happiness was in Munich.
b. ?? John's heaviness on the table

consists in that tropes generally have an internal structure 'below' the description used to refer to them. A manifestation of that property is the applicability of predicates of description and qualitative comparison to tropes:

(12) a. John described Mary's beauty.
b. John compared Mary's beauty to Sue's beauty.

Tropes differ in that respect from states and facts which strictly match the content of a canonical description and thus do not accept predicates of description and comparison (on a natural reading):

(13) a. ?? John described (the state of) Mary's being beautiful.
b. ?? John compared (the state of) Mary's being beautiful to (the state of) Sue's being beautiful.

Related to description independence is the ability of tropes to have a measureable extent, allowing, for example, for the application of the predicate *exceed*, which, again, is not applicable, on a natural reading, to states and facts:

(14) a. Mary's happiness exceeds Bill's.
b. ??? The fact that Mary likes Bill exceeds the fact that Mary is tall.
c. ??? The state of Mary's liking Bill exceeds the state of Mary's being tall.

Tropes referred to with the help of predicates, however determinable, unspecific, or quantificational the predicates may be, are always maximally specific – in contrast to states and facts, entities whose nature is 'exhausted' by the content of a canonical description (Moltmann 2013b).

Another characteristic of tropes is that they share with their bearers properties of quantitative comparison. These are properties expressed by predicates like *exceed*, *equal* or *high*. Such predicates apply to tropes as well as their bearers, though in the latter case they require qualification of respect:

(15) a. The eagerness of John exceeds the eagerness of Mary.
b. The sloppiness of John equals the sloppiness of Mary.

(16) a. John exceeds Mary in eagerness.
b. John equals Mary in sloppiness.

(17) a. The height of John exceeds / equals the height of Mary.
b. John exceeds / equals Mary in height.

(18) a. The number of men exceeds the number of women.
b. The men exceed the women in number.

(19) a. The number of participants is high.
b. The participants are high in number.

Those predicates do not apply to abstract objects such as properties or numbers:

(20) a. ?? The property of being very eager exceeds the property of being not so eager.
b. ?? The property of being extremely sloppy exceeds the property of being somewhat sloppy.
c. ?? The number 13 does not equal the number 8.
d. ?? 100 is high.

Thus, predicates of quantitative comparison provide another good indication for trope reference as opposed to reference to abstract objects (Moltmann 2013a,b,c).

3 Trope-reference with intensional relative clauses

We can now try to apply the same types of predicates to NPs as in (4a, b), that is, NPs that appear to refer to tropes, but tropes whose bearers are described by IR-NPs. In general, the various types of predicates can apply, which means that those NPs must indeed refer to tropes.

First, predicates of perception and causation may apply to such NPs:

(21) a. John noticed the number of screws that are missing.
b. The number of screws that are missing caused the table to fall apart.
c. Mary was astonished by the length of the paper John needs to write.
d. Mary noticed the amount of repair that is required to make the machine work again.

Even in the absence of an actual bearer, tropes, under particular circumstances as in (21a, d), may act as objects of perception.

Also predicates of similarity and identity apply to the NPs in question in the same way they did to ordinary trope-referring NPs.

(22) a. The number of women in the room is the same as the number of men in the room.
b. ??? The number of women in the room is the number of men in the room.

(23) a. The number of books Mary wants to write is the same as the number of books Sue wants to write.

b. ??? The number of books Mary wants to write is the number of books Sue wants to write.

Furthermore, predicates of quantitative comparison and evaluation are applicable just as they were to ordinary trope-referring terms. Moreover, such predicates can alternatively apply to the description of the bearer of the tropes in the presence of a qualification of respect:

(24) a. The originality of the book John wants to write needs to exceed the originality of the book John has already written.

b. The book John wants to write needs to exceed the book John has already written in quality.

(25) a. The elegance of the dress that the bridesmaid will wear should not exceed the elegance of the dress that the bride will wear.

b. The dress that the bridesmaid will wear should not exceed the dress that the bride will wear in elegance.

(26) a. The height of the desk John needs exceeds the height of the desk John is using right now.

b. The desk John needs exceeds the desk John is using right now in height.

(27) a. John compared the number of books Mary wants to write to the number of books Sue wants to write.

b. John compared the books Mary wants to write to the number of books Sue wants to write in number.

(28) a. The number of people that fit into the bus is high.

b. The people that fit into the bus are high in number.

Given the behavior of predicates, the parallel between ordinary trope-referring terms and corresponding terms with intensional relative clauses is rather striking and supports the view that the latter are trope-referring terms as well.

4 Individual-concepts

Before turning to trope-referring NPs with IR-NPs, let us first discuss in more detail the individual-concepts approach to functional and IR-NPs.

(29) a. The president of the US is elected every four years.
b. John changed his trainer.
c. The temperature is rising.
d. The number of students has increased.

It is wellknown that functional NPs act referentially in that they can be antecedents of anaphoric pronouns in subsequent sentences, as can IR-NPs:

(30) a. The president of the US is elected every four years. He occupies the most powerful office.
b. The book John needs to write must be at least 200 pages long. It needs to be finished by next year.

According to the standard Montagovian account, functional NPs stand for individual concepts (Montague 1973). This means they are of a different type than that of referential NPs, namely of type $\langle s, e\rangle$, rather than of type e, the type of referential NPs. When predicates like *change, rise, increase* apply to individual concepts, they will also be of a different type than when they apply to individuals. Thus, *increase* when applying to an individual concept is of type $\langle\langle s, e\rangle, t\rangle$, rather than of type $\langle e, t\rangle$.

Predicates according to the Montagovian view can in general be lifted to predicates of individual concepts. A predicate P that unlike *increase, rise,* and *change* does not have a meaning that specifically takes into account the individual concept can be lifted to a predicate P' of individual concepts in virtue of a general meaning postulate, as below:

(31) For a predicate P of individuals and an individual concept f,
$P'_{w,t}(f) = 1$ iff $P_{w,t}(f(w,t)) = 1$ for any world w and time t.

There is an apparent problem for the individual-concept account of functional NPs, and that is the impossibility of replacing a functional NP as in (29b) by an explicit function-referring NP, as in the intuitively invalid inference below:

(32) John changed his trainer.
———
John changed a function.

However, the inference does not follow given that the use of individual-concepts needs to be understood within the context of type theory. In the premise of (32), *change* is of type $\langle e, \langle\langle s, e\rangle, t\rangle\rangle$, whereas in the conclusion it is type $\langle e, \langle e, t\rangle\rangle$, invalidating the inference.

A more serious problem for the individual-concept approach is the possibility of reference to tropes whose bearers are described by functional NPs. Below functional NPs clearly specify the bearers of tropes:

(33) a. The decrease of the number of students caused concern.
b. The increase in the amount of corruption triggered a revolt.
c. The impact of the increasing number of students is noticeable.
d. The rise of the temperature caused the drought.

In these examples, functional NPs describe the bearers of single tropes playing causal roles or acting as objects of perception.

When describing the bearers of tropes, functional NPs can hardly be considered standing for individual concepts (being of type $\langle s, t\rangle$). Moreover, they could not be considered referential NPs referring to functions (in which case they would be of type e), since they could not be substituted by an explicit function-referring NP:

(34) a. ? the change of the function
b. ? the impact of the function
c. ? the rise of the function
d. ? the responsibility of the function

Functions can be bearers of tropes, but they are generally bearers of very different sorts of tropes. As mentioned in the introduction, individual concepts are not meant to be the particular entities that referential NPs refer to, but rather they make up the contribution of the syntactic type of functional NPs to the compositional meaning of the sentence. Functional NPs are not of type e, the type of referential NPs, but of type $\langle s, t\rangle$, the type of individual concepts. But that means that the individual concepts they stand for are not entities of a particular sort at all. Tropes, however, are entities, entities that essentially depend on other entities as their bearers. Such entities must be semantic values of NPs of type e and cannot be semantic values of functional NPs, being of type $\langle s, \langle e, t\rangle\rangle$.

IR-NPs present similar problems. First of all, there are object-related predicates that can apply to IR-NPs, such as *count*, *describe* and *enumerate*:

(35) a. John counted the screws that were missing.
b. John described the personnel that the company needed to hire.
c. John enumerated the things that he needed to buy.

Such predicates apply in (35) with the very same meaning they have when applying to ordinary objects. They do not obtain a derivative meaning according to which they keep track of the values of a function when applied to different circumstances.[2]

2 Note that *count* applies with the very same meaning to ordinary NPs and IR-NPs:
(i) a. What did John count?
b. John counted the legs of the chair and the screws that were missing.
Thus, ordinary NPs and IR-NPs should better not be distinguished in type.

IR-NPs moreover describe the bearers of quantitative tropes in examples such as (4a), repeated below as (36a), and (36b):

(36) a. The number of people that can fit into the bus exceeds the number of people that can fit into the car.
b. The length of the vacation John is allowed to take exceeds the length of the vacation Mary is allowed to take.

In (36a) and (36b) the predicate *exceed* applies to two quantitative tropes whose bearers are described by IR-NPs.

Object-related predicates and trope reference thus indicate that IR-NPs are of type *e*, referring to entities of a suitable sort, just like functional NPs. These entities, on the present view, will be variable objects.

The apparent trope-referring NPs below present a different case:

(37) a. The beauty of the landscape has changed.
b. The amount of corruption in this administration has become more noticeable.
c. The impact of this book has diminished.

(38) a. The number of students has increased.
b. the increasing number of students

(39) a. The number of teachers sometimes exceeds the number of students.
b. The increasing number of students causes problems for the availability of sufficient class rooms.

The NPs in such sentences do not refer to single tropes. Rather (37), (38), and (39) involve typical predicates applying to 'individual concepts'. On the individual-concepts approach, this means that the subject NPs would stand for functions from circumstances to tropes. On the present approach, it means that they refer to variable tropes.

5 Semantic problems with individual-concepts

There are also problems regarding the compositional semantics of IR-NPs for an analysis using individual concepts. There are two options of analyzing (40) as standing for an individual concept:

(40) a. the book John needs to write

I will only outline the two options, focusing on the general idea and their problems and leaving out any formal details.

The first option would be an extension of Grosu & Krifka's (2007) analysis of (41):

(41) the gifted mathematician that John claims to be

Their analysis involves several assumptions. First, it involves type-lifting of all predicates to predicates of individual concepts and all singular terms (including proper names) to terms for individual concepts. Second, it requires treating all intensional verbs as operators quantifying over circumstances (possible worlds and times). Finally, it interprets the head noun *book* in (40a) in the upper position, rather than reconstructing it into the lower position inside the relative clause. Greatly simplifying, this analysis would yield the following as the denotation of (40a):

(40) b. $\min(\{f \mid \text{book}(f)\} \cap \{f \mid [\textit{John needs to write}](f)\})$

The second set mentioned in (40b) would be the set of partial functions mapping a world *w* compatible with the satisfaction of John's needs to an object John writes in *w*.

This analysis raises a range of problems. First of all, it involves an excessive use of individual concepts, involving a lifting of all predicates and singular terms to the type of individual concepts. While raising singular terms and argument positions of predicates to the type of individual concepts is not as such problematic technically, the move seems too far-reaching given the motivation of just getting the semantics of the construction in (40a) right. The construction in (40a) should not really be grounds for abandoning the view that names stand for individuals and that predicates in natural language are generally predicates of individuals.

Second, the analysis makes a rather problematic philosophical assumption by considering all intensional verbs, including attitude verbs, operators quantifying over circumstances. Certainly a great number of philosophers will find such an assumption problematic. The most common view about attitude verbs is that they are not to be analysed as operators quantifying over circumstances, but rather express two-place relations between agents and propositions. Furthermore there are philosophical views according to which modal verbs do not represent operators quantifying over circumstances but correspond to primitive operators ('modalism').[3] The semantic analysis of the construction in (40a) should better not involve a highly controversial philosophical assumption. Rather it should be

3 See, for example, Forbes (1985).

independent of particular views of attitude verbs, modal verbs, or other intensional verbs.

A third problem for the analysis in (40b) concerns a problem of uniqueness, a problem which specifically arises when carrying over Grosu & Krifka's (2007) analysis of (41) to the construction in (40a). The problem of uniqueness does not arise for the construction in (41) because Grosu & Krifka (2007) consider the copula *be* in that construction be the *be* of identity, which means it takes two individual concepts as arguments.

The uniqueness problems arises for *the book John needs to write* because in a given world in which John's need is satisfied, John may have written more than one book meeting his need. In order to guarantee uniqueness, a move is required from the notion of a context of evaluation to that of a truthmaking situation, or rather a satisfaction situation, a situation satisfying John's need.

A satisfaction situation may also impose various constraints on the book John writes in it (constraints the speaker in fact need not know about): not all the books John writes in a world in which his need is satisfied qualify as 'the book John's needs to write'. The complement of *need* may give only a partial characterization of the exact need. Thus, the individual concept denoted by *the book John needs to write* should not take into account entire worlds in which John's need is satisfied, but rather situations satisfying John's need. More precisely, these situations should not just be situations in which John's needs are satisfied, but situations wholly relevant for the satisfaction of John's needs. That is, they should be *exact satisfiers* of John's needs, or *exact truth makers* of the conditions making up John's needs.[4] A given world in which John's needs are satisfied may contain several situations satisfying his need, each containing a different book.[5]

The analysis in (40b) crucially relies on the notion of a circumstance of evaluation, but what is needed is the notion of an exact satisfier or an exact truth maker of the condition in question, John's need. A circumstance of evaluation would not be able to fulfil the latter role because the purpose of the context of evaluation is not only to relativize the truth value of a sentence, but also to fix at the same time the extensions of singular terms and predicates.

In (40a), the truth-making circumstances appear to be determined by a particular condition constitutive of John's need at a time. However, the truth-making circumstances may also depend on a particular event described by the verb, as in the examples below:

4 For the notion of exact truthmaking see Rodriguez-Pereyra (2005), Moltmann (2007, 2013a), and Fine (2012, 2017).

5 For further motivations for the use of situations in NPs with intensional relative clauses, see Moltmann (to appear).

(42) a. the book John promised to write

b. the report John asked Bill to write

In (42a), the circumstances are not determined by a general condition, such as the one constitutive of John's needs, but rather they are determined by a particular event of promising (note that John may have promised different books on different occasions). Similarly in (42b), they depend on a particular event of asking. In (42a), the circumstances are those that satisfy a particular promise, and in (42b) the circumstances are those that satisfy a particular demand. A promise is not the same as an act or promising, though, and a demand is not an act of demanding; rather they are the (non-enduring) 'products' of acts or promising or demanding in the sense of Twardowski (1999). Products, not acts or states, have satisfaction conditions (Moltmann 2013a, 2014, 2017). This means that the individual concepts denoted by IR-NPs depend on the product of an event argument of the intensional verb in question. They will be functions mapping situations exactly satisfying the product of the event in question to individuals of the relevant sort. For example in (42a), the individual concept would be the function mapping a circumstance exactly satisfying a particular promise to a book John writes in that circumstance. Such truth-making situations cannot be viewed as circumstances of evaluation, though, as standardly conceived.

A general problem for the analysis in (40b) was that it makes excessive use of individual concepts. There is a second option of analysing *the book John needs to write*, which appears to avoid that problem. On that analysis, *the book John needs to write* would involve reconstructing the head noun into the lower position inside the relative clause, as in (40c), yielding the analysis in (40d):

(40) c. the book [John needs to write [e $[\text{book}]_N$]]

d. the function f [for any world w compatible with the satisfaction of John's needs, $\text{write}_w(\text{John}, f(w))$ & $\text{book}_w(f(w))$]

In (40c), the first trace would be a trace of individual concepts. This analysis obviously would allow the noun *book* to remain a predicate of individuals.

This analysis raises the very same problem of uniqueness as the first analysis, however. Moreover, just like the first analysis, it is forced to treat all intensional verbs as modal operators quantifying over worlds.

In addition, in its attempt of avoiding type-shifting the analysis cannot go very far. Even though it is plausible that the head noun reconstructs into the lower position, reconstruction of the functional trope noun into a position inside the relative clause is in general impossible: there is no place inside the relative clause for a noun like *impact* in (3a), repeated below:

(43) the impact of the book John needs to write

Impact will have to be interpreted in the upper position. But this means that it will have to denote a function applying to individual concepts.

6 Variable objects

I will propose an account of functional and IR-NPs based on the notion of a variable object and the notion of a variable trope in particular. The notion of a variable object is due to Kit Fine, though the way I will make use of it is not entirely based on Fine's published work.

Variable objects are entities that fall under Fine's (1999) more general notion of a variable embodiment (see also Koslicki 2008). The notion of a variable embodiment for Fine is a central notion in metaphysics and accounts for a great variety of 'ordinary' objects. Fine himself (p.c.) also meant to apply the notion of a variable embodiment to the semantic values of functional NPs as in (13) as well as NPs with intensional relative clauses such as *the book John needs to write*. The notion of a variable embodiment allows an account of functional NPs and IR-NPs that treats them as being of type *e*, while avoiding treating their referents as abstract functions. It hence avoids type-shifting of predicates.

A variable embodiment, according to Fine, is an entity that allows for the replacement of constituting matter or of parts, and more generally that may have different material manifestations in different circumstances. Organisms and artifacts are variable embodiments, but also entities like 'the water in the river'. Trees and houses allow for a replacement of constituting matter and thus may have different material realizations at different times. They should not be identified with their constituting matter, but rather are entities associated with a function mapping a time to their material realization, that is, they are variable embodiments. 'The water in the river' conceived as a variable embodiment will have different realizations as different water quantities at different times (Fine 1999). Variable embodiments differ from 'rigid embodiments', entities which do not allow for a replacement of their immediate parts. An example is a token of the word *be*, which has as its immediate parts a token of *b* and a token of *e*, neither of which can be replaced.

Fine's theory of variable embodiments as formulated in Fine (1999) applies to variable embodiments that may have different manifestations at different times. But the theory is also meant to apply to entities that have different manifestations in different worlds and in fact may lack a manifestation in the actual world (Fine, p.c.). 'The book John needs to write' will be such an entity. It is an entity that has manifestations as different objects in various counterfactual circumstances. The term 'variable object', as used in this paper, is meant to apply to entities that have different manifestations as different objects at different times or in different worlds.

Variable objects generally have properties in a derivative way, on the basis of their manifestations. In particular, a variable object exists at a time or in a world just in case it has a manifestation at that time or in that world. Moreover, a variable object shares its location at a time in a world with that of its manifestation at the time in that world provided it has a manifestation at that time in that world. Finally, a variable object 'inherits' time- and world-relative properties from its manifestations in the relevant circumstances. Thus, variable objects are subject to the following conditions, which generalize the conditions on variable embodiments of Fine (1999) from times to circumstances (pairs of times and worlds or situations):

(44) a. *Existence*
A variable object *e* exists in a circumstance *i* iff *e* has a manifestation in *i*.

b. *Location*
If a variable object *e* exists in a circumstance *i*, then *e*'s location in *i* is that of its manifestation in *i*.

c. *Property Inheritance 1*
A variable object *e* has a (world- or time-relative) property *P* in a circumstance *i* in which *e* exists if *e*'s manifestation in *i* has *P* in *i*.

(44c) accounts for the obligatory presence of a modal with certain IR-NPs, a condition that I will call, following Grosu & Krifka (2007), the *Modal Compatibility Requirement* (MCR). IR-NPs are subject to the MCR if they stand for a variable object that lacks a manifestation in the actual circumstances, for example *the book John needs to write* as in (2), as can be seen below:

(45) ??? The book John needs to write has a greater impact than the book he has already written.

The modal in (2) permits predicating the predicate of a manifestation in a circumstance other than the actual one.

(44c) does not yet capture all the properties a variable object may have. It only accounts for what I will call its 'local properties'. In addition to local properties, which are obtained in the way of (44c), variable objects may have 'global properties', that is, properties that they may have on the basis of several of their manifestations at different times (for example properties of change, rise, or increase). Variable objects moreover may have properties that are not time- or world-relative. A variable object may have a property in a time- and world-independent way in virtue of all manifestations having that property. This requires a second condition of property inheritance:

(44) d. *Property Inheritance 2*

A variable object has a property P (circumstance-independently) if all its manifestations have P in the circumstances in which they exist.

Such a property can nonetheless be attributed to a variable object relative to a time and a world, assuming that having a property circumstance-independently implies having it at all circumstances. Note that there are certain properties, formal properties such a being an object, that by their own nature can borne only circumstance-independently.

The two conditions on property-inheritance in (44c, d) tell when a variable object inherits properties from its manifestations. Given trope theory, this requires corresponding conditions on when a variable object is the bearer of a particular trope in virtue of its manifestations being bearers of corresponding tropes. On a trope-theoretical view, two objects o_1 and o_2 sharing a (fully specific) property translates as o_1 and o_2 being bearers of two tropes t_1 and t_2 that are exactly similar. Within trope theory, Property Inheritance 1 and Property Inheritance 2 can thus be reformulated follows:

(46) a. *Trope 'Inheritance' 1*

A variable object o that exists in a circumstance i bears a trope t in i if o's manifestation in i bears a trope t' in i such that t' is exactly similar to t.[6]

b. *Trope 'Inheritance' 2*

A variable object o bears a trope t (circumstance-independently) if for any circumstance i in which o has a manifestation, o's manifestation in i bears a trope t' such that t' is exactly similar to t in i.

Variable objects are associated with a (partial) function from circumstances to manifestations, but they are not identical to it. That is why variable objects can bear properties of concrete objects, rather than qualifying as abstract. 'Ordinary' objects that are variable embodiments do not generally stand in a 1-1 relation to functions from circumstances to manifestations: not any function from circumstances to manifestations corresponds to a variable objects, but rather variable embodiments are driven by conditions such as those on shape and continuity. It is conceivable that two variable embodiments share the same function from circumstances to manifestations. But this is hardly so for variable objects of the sort 'the book John needs to write'. There is not much more to variable objects of this sort than what

6 In Moltmann (2013d), I argue that in such cases the very same trope is inherited. This result is a trope with multiple bearers. This is of course a nonstandard view about tropes.

is given by the partial function from circumstances to objects. It is reasonable to assume that there is a unique variable object corresponding to the partial function from circumstances to objects. Variable objects are then ordered according to the ordering among their associated functions: a variable object o_1 is part of a variable object o_2 iff the function associated with o_2 is an extension of the function associated with o_2. This relation is important when formulating the semantics of IR-NPs: as definite NPs they generally refer to a minimal variable object satisfying the relative clause.

The variable objects that IR-NPs stand for depend on entities like a 'need'. A need is not a state of needing and thus not a Davidsonian event argument. Crucially, unlike a Davidsonian event or state, an entity like a need has satisfaction conditions. Thus, in the interpretation of an IR-NP, a function *product* needs to be applied to the Davidsonian event, mapping it onto a related entity that has satisfaction conditions. This will allow the embedded sentence to act as a predicate of the product of the event argument. If controlled clauses involve the self-ascription of a property, as on a standard Lewisian account, then the semantics of attitude verbs with an infinitival clausal complement will be as below:[7]

(47) a. For an attitude verb V and a (subject-)controlled clause S
$[\text{V S}] = \lambda ex[\text{V}(e, x) \,\&\, \text{S}(\text{product}(e), x)]$

The infinitival clause will have the syntactic structure in (47b) and will denote the relation in (47b), making use of the standard treatment of controlled clauses as expressing properties of agents:

(47) b. $[\text{PRO to write } [[\text{e}]_{\text{D}}\ [\text{book}]_{\text{NP}}]_{\text{DP}}]_{\text{CP}}$
c. $\lambda xe\, [\forall s\, (s \vDash e \rightarrow (\text{write}_s(x, d) \,\&\, \text{book}_s(d)))]$

For the interpretation of IR-NPs, again the assumption needs to be made that the head noun is interpreted in the lower position inside the relative clause; the lower variable will then stand for a variable object, an object to which the relative clause attributes certain properties in particular circumstances. It will refer to the minimal variable object that is a book and something John writes in any situation satisfying John's need, as in (47e), which is equivalent to (47f):

7 For independent motivations of conceiving of *that*-clause-complements of attitude verbs as predicates of the product of the described event see Moltmann (2014).

(47) d. [the [e] [John needs [to write $[[e]_D$ $[book]_{NP}]_{DP}]]_{CP}]_{DP}$ =

e. min d [$\exists e$ (need(e, John) &
$\forall s$ ($s \models$ prod(e) $\rightarrow$ (write$_s$(John, d) & book$_s$(d))))] =

f. min d [$\exists e$ (need(e, John) &
$\forall s$ ($s \models$ prod(e) $\rightarrow$ (write$_s$(John, $F(d, s)$) & books($F(d, s)$)))))]

There are constructions that make the product of which a clausal complement is predicated linguistically explicit. Thus, the verb *need* alternates with the light-verb construction *have a need*. In fact, Harves & Kayne (2012) argue that the verb *need* is the result of incorporating the copula *have* and the noun *need*. In any case, given the light-verb construction, the product will be available as part of the compositional semantics of the complex predicate *have+a need*. The construction will thus have the following compositional semantics:

(48) the e [John has a need [to write [e book]]] =
min x [$\exists e$ (have(John, e) & need(e) &
$\forall s$ ($s \models e \rightarrow$ (write$_s$(John, d) & book$_s$(d))))]

Using variable objects has a significant advantage over the individual-concept approach to the compositional semantics of functional NPs and IR-NPs. It allows avoiding a type ambiguity among predicates, definite NPs, and pronouns, and it avoids lifting all those expressions to a higher type.

Let us then turn to trope-referring or apparent trope-referring NPs with IR-NPs, as in (49a) and (49b):

(49) a. the impact of the number of students

b. the increase of the number of students

The functional trope nouns *impact* and *increase* in the upper position apply to a variable object and map it onto a trope that is a local trope based on a single circumstance, as in (49a), or a global trope based on a series of circumstances, as in (49b). The two functional trope nouns denote different functions from variable objects to tropes, as indicated below, where F is the function mapping a variable object o and a circumstance i to the manifestation of o in i:

(50) a. For a variable object o and a circumstance i, impact$_i$(o) = the trope that has o as its bearer and is exactly similar to impact$_i$($F(e, i)$).

b. For a variable object o and a circumstance $\langle w, t\rangle$, increase$_i$(o) = the trope that has o as its bearer and is the instantiation of the property $\lambda e'$ [$F(e', w, t_1)$ less than $F(e', w, t_2)$ less than ... for subintervals t_1, t_2, and t_3 of t and $t_1 < t_2 < t_3$ ...]

Impact can also serve to describe a variable trope, though, in a sentence such as (4b), repeated below:

(51) The impact of the book John needs to write must exceed the impact of the book he has already written.

The impact of the book John needs to write stands for a variable trope that has as its manifestation in a relevant circumstance i the impact of the manifestation of the variable object that is 'the book that John needs to write', that is, the impact of a particular book John has written in a non-actual circumstance satisfying John's needs. *The impact of the book John needs to write* in (51) stands for a variable trope, rather than a single trope because of the obligatory presence of the modal. Here the head noun *impact* applies to a variable object and maps it onto a variable trope. The variability of the trope thus is 'driven by' the variability of the bearer. A variable trope driven by the variability of its bearer o has as its manifestation in a circumstance i the trope t that has as its bearer the manifestation of o in i. The noun *impact* in (51) thus denotes the function mapping a variable object onto a variable trope below:

(52) For a variable object e and a circumstance i',
impact$_{i'}(e)$ = the variable trope o such that for any circumstance i in which o has a manifestation $F(e, i)$, impact$_i(F(e, i))$ = the manifestation of o in i.

A variable trope that has manifestations only in counterfactual circumstances requires a modal in the main clause in order to be attributed local properties in the first place. As a variable trope, 'the impact of the book John needs to write' has manifestations only in non-actual circumstances. Ordinary properties can be true of the variable trope in a circumstance i only in virtue of being true of a manifestation of the variable trope in i provided the variable trope has a manifestation in i. If the circumstance i is nonfactual, this means that a modal is required in order to shift the context of evaluation of the predicate to a non-actual context, a context in which the variable trope has a manifestation. Again, the Modal Compatibility Requirement follows straightforwardly from Property Inheritance 1.

7 Exemptions from the Modal Compatibility Requirement

Let us turn to the cases in which a modal is not required in the main clause of a sentence with an IR-NP. The Modal Compatibility Requirement does not hold in (53a) and (53b), in contrast to (54a) and (54b):

(53) a. The number of people that can fit into the bus exceeds the number of people that can fit into the car.
b. The length of the vacation John is allowed to take exceeds the length of the vacation Mary is allowed to take.

(54) a. The impact of the book John needs to write ?? exceeds / ok must exceed / ok might exceed the impact of the book he has already written.
b. The elegance of the dress the bridesmaid should wear ?? does not exceed / ok should not exceed the elegance of the dress that the bride will wear.

The question, of course, is why are (53a, b) are not subject to the MCR? At first sight, the generalization seems to be that IR-NPs referring to quantitative tropes are not subject to the MCR. But this is not right. The MCR is in place below:

(55) ?? The number of people John might invite exceeds the number of people Mary might invite.

Yet the distinction between quantitative and qualitative tropes does matter. This is illustrated by the difference between (56a) and (56b) with a one-place evaluative predicate:

(56) a. The number of papers a student has to write during this program is too high.
b. The quality of the paper John must write ?? is very high / must be very high.

I propose an explanation of the exemptions from the MCR based on general conditions on when a variable object is the bearer of a particular sort of trope on the basis of its instances bearing particular tropes. The reason why quantitative tropes allow for an exemption from the MCR will be ontological. Quantitative tropes enter relations of exact similarity more easily than qualitative tropes, This is what permits a variable object to act as the bearer of a quantitative trope. Let us take (53a). It is quite plausible that the same number of people fit into the bus / the car in the various relevant circumstances, or at least that this is how agents generally perceive things. This means that the number tropes in the relevant circumstances are exactly similar. Given the condition of Trope Inheritance 2, the variable object itself will bear an exactly similar number trope. Trope Inheritance 2 allows a variable object to be the bearer of a single trope. Generally such a trope has to be a quantitative trope and cannot be a qualitative trope. That is because exact similarity among qualitative tropes is unlikely to obtain, given that natural language predicates in general do not express natural qualitative properties, but unspecific, determinable ones. Thus, in (54a), for example, it can hardly be the case that the impact of the book John writes in a situation satisfying John's needs is the very same as the impact of the book he writes in any other situation satisfying his needs. Similarly, in (54b) it will hardly be the case that the elegance of the bridesmaid's dress in one situation satisfying the relevant conditions is the very same as the elegance of her dress in any other situation satisfying the relevant condition.

This account made use of general ontological conditions on variable objects, Trope Inheritance 2, to explain the exemption from the MCR. This in itself can be considered further support for the ontological account of IR-NPs as such.

8 The Grosu/Krifka construction

Let us finally turn to the construction discussed by Grosu & Krifka (2007) in (3) repeated again below:

(57) The gifted mathematician John claims to be could solve this problem in no time.

Let me call NPs of the type in (57) 'G/K-NPs'. Characteristically, G/K-NPs involve a copula such as *be*, *become* or *remain*:[8]

(58) a. The mathematician John wants to become should be able to solve the problem in no time.
b. The honest person that John should remain would pay back his debts in time.

The construction also involves an intensional verb such a *claim* or a modal verb of necessity or possibility, as also in the examples below:[9]

(59) a. The student John has to become in order to satisfy his parents will have to be very disciplined.
b. The painter John could have become might have initiated a new art movement.

8 This means that *be* in G/K-NPs is not the *be* of identity. Further evidence for that is that *is identical to* is rather unacceptable in that construction:

(i) ??? The mathematician John claims to be identical to would be able to solve the problem in no time.

This constitutes a difficulty for Grosu/Krifka's analysis for whom *be* in G/K-NPs expresses the identification of individual concepts (at the relevant circumstances).

9 According to Grosu & Krifka (2007), the construction allows only for modal verbs of necessity. I could not agree with that judgment.

There are significant similarities between the Grosu-Krifka construction and other IR-NPs. Both must involve an intensional verb in the relative clause, both must be definite, and both are subject to the MCR, as illustrated for G/K-NPs below:

(60) a. ??? The student John is in order to satisfy his parents will have to be very disciplined.
b. ??? A famous painter John could have become might have initiated a new art movement.
c. ??? The gifted mathematician John claims to be has solved the problem in no time.

Moreover, as Grosu & Krifka (2007) note, their construction allows for anaphora support, just like IR-NPs. Thus, (57) can be continued by (61):

(61) He would have no difficulty with it at all.

As discussed earlier, Grosu & Krifka (2007) analyse G/K-NPs in terms of individual concepts. Roughly, on their analysis, *the gifted mathematician John claims to be* refers to the smallest partial function that maps a world satisfying John's claim to an entity that is John and a gifted mathematician in that world.

There are the same arguments in favor of conceiving of the referents of G/K-NPs as variable objects rather than individual concepts. In particular, G/K-NPs can also act as the bearers of tropes, in examples such as the following:

(62) a. The talent of the mathematician John claims to be would exceed the talent of the mathematician Mary hopes to become.
b. The influence of the poet John could have become would by far exceed the influence of the painter John did become.
c. The honesty of the person John should remain would consist in him paying back his debts.

Cast in terms of variable objects, the subject of (57) refers to the variable object that has a manifestation in any circumstance exactly satisfying John's claim, namely as an entity that is John and a gifted mathematician.

Thus it is reasonable to carry over the analysis in terms of variable objects to the Grosu/Krifka-construction. There is one particular challenge the construction poses, though, and that concerns the interpretation of the copula. The head noun of the construction should be interpreted in the predicate position of the copula verb. The copula verb then must expresses the identity of the subject referent with the manifestation of the variable object at the relevant circumstance. Of course, this is not compatible with the standard view according to which the predicative complement of the copula verb expresses a property predicated of the subject referent.

There is a recent view, however, concerning copula constructions with indefinite NP complements according to which indefinite complements of the copula do not express an ordinary property to be predicated of the subject referent, but rather define a set so that the subject referent will be identified with its members (Beyssade & Dobrovie-Sorin 2005). This view was meant to explain semantic differences between full indefinite copula complements as in (63a) and bare noun complements as in (63b):

(63) a. John is a mayor.
b. John is mayor.

This view of the copula with an indefinite NP helps solve the present puzzle, namely if the representation of the full indefinite complement D N′ of a copula verb will not be the simple property $\lambda x\,[\mathrm{N}'(x)]$, but rather the property $\lambda y\,[\exists x\,(\mathrm{N}'(x)\ \&\ y = x)]$, as below:

(64) For a copula verb V,
$[\mathrm{V}\ a\ \mathrm{N}'] = \lambda z\,[\mathrm{V}(z, \lambda y\,[\exists x\,(\mathrm{N}'(x)\ \&\ y = x)])]$

The interpretation of the head noun in the lower predicative position can then be considered that of contributing the restriction of the variable that is bound by the relative clause operator. This will give the interpretation of (65a) as in (65b), which is equivalent to (65c), to (65d), and in turn to (65e):

(65) a. the [mathematician [John claims [PRO to be [e mathematician]]]]
b. $\min x\,[\exists e\,(\mathrm{claim}(e, \mathrm{John})\ \&$
$[\textit{PRO to be}\ [\mathrm{e}\ \textit{mathematician}]](\mathrm{product}(e), \mathrm{John}))]$
c. $\min x\,[\exists e\,(\mathrm{claim}(e, \mathrm{John})\ \&$
$\forall s\,(s \vDash \mathrm{product}(e) \rightarrow \mathrm{be}_s(\mathrm{John}, \lambda y\,[\mathrm{M}(x)\ \&\ x = y])))]$
d. $\min x\,[\exists e\,(\mathrm{claim}(e, \mathrm{John})\ \&$
$\forall s\,(s \vDash \mathrm{product}(e) \rightarrow \lambda y\,[\mathrm{M}(x)\ \&\ x = y]_s(\mathrm{John})))]$
e. $\min x\,[\exists e\,(\mathrm{claim}(e, \mathrm{John})\ \&$
$\forall s\,(s \vDash \mathrm{product}(e) \rightarrow \mathrm{M}_s(x)\ \&\ x =_s \mathrm{John}))]$

In (65e) the identity symbol is relativized to a circumstance, allowing for the identity of the manifestation of the variable object with John at the circumstance in question.

9 Intentional verbs

There is a different case of an exemption from the MCR, illustrated below:

(66) The originality of the paper John wants to write exceeds the originality of the papers he has so far written.

Here the relative clause contains a verb that has an interpretation not as an intensional verb, but as an intentional verb. This case is an entirely different one from (4a). In (66), the trope 'the originality of the paper John wants to write' has as its bearer an intentional object, a nonexistent 'object of thought', rather than a variable object (Moltmann 2015). An intentional object is fully present in the world in which the act occurs on which the intentional object depends. It is not an object that has different manifestations in worlds that may exclude the actual one. Only psychological verbs allow for reference to intentional objects, modal verbs of absence like *need* do not. The latter can involve only variable objects and hence are subject to MCR:

(67) a. The house John needs to live in must be / ??? is huge.
b. The house John imagines to be living in is huge.

We can also note that transitive intentional and intensional verbs display the very same contrast:

(68) a. The house John is thinking of is huge.
b. The house John needs must be / ??? is huge.

Obviously, IR-NP transitive intensional verbs involve a similar semantics to that of clausal complement-taking verbs.[10]

10 Conclusion

The aim of this paper was to show that the notion of a variable object allows for an account of an otherwise very puzzling construction of apparent trope-referring terms. The notion of a variable object as such is not a peculiar notion, though, invoked only for the analysis of that construction. Rather, it falls under the more general and ontologically central notion of a variable embodiment (in Fine's metaphysics). As such, it is subject to the very same ontological conditions as drive variable embodiments in general.

10 See also Moltmann (1997, 2013a) for the semantics of intensional transitive verbs involving variable objects and Moltmann (2015) for the semantics of intentional transitive verbs.

References

Beyssade, Claire & Carmen Dobrovie-Sorin. 2005. A syntax-based analysis of predication. In Efthymia Georgala & Jonathan Howell (eds.), *Proceedings of SALT 15*, 44–61. Ithaca, NY: Cornell University. https://doi.org/10.3765/salt.v15i0.2936.

Campbell, Keith. 1990. *Abstract particulars*. Oxford: Blackwell.

Fine, Kit. 1999. Things and their parts. *Midwest Studies of Philosophy* 23. 61–74.

Fine, Kit. 2012. Counterfactuals without possible worlds. *Journal of Philosophy* 109.

Fine, Kit. 2017. Truthmaker semantics. In Bob Hale, Crispin Wright & Alexander Miller (eds.), *A companion to the philosophy of language*, 556–577. New York: Blackwell. https://doi.org/10.1002/9781118972090.ch22.

Forbes, Graeme. 1985. *The metaphysics of modality*. Oxford: Clarendon Press.

Grosu, Alexander & Manfred Krifka. 2007. *The gifted mathematician that you claim to be*: Equational intensional 'reconstruction' relatives. *Linguistics and Philosophy* 30. 445–485. https://doi.org/10.1007/s10988-008-9022-5.

Harves, Stephanie & Richard Kayne. 2012. Having 'need' and needing 'have'. *Linguistic Inquiry* 43(1). 120–132. https://doi.org/10.1162/LING_a_00076.

Koslicki, Kathrin. 2008. *The structure of objects*. Oxford: Oxford University Press.

Lowe, Edward Jonathan. 2006. *The four-category ontology. A metaphysics foundation for natural science*. Oxford: Oxford University Press.

Mertz, Donald W. 1996. *Moderate realism and its logic*. New Haven: Yale University Press.

Moltmann, Friederike. 1997. Intensional verbs and quantifiers. *Natural Language Semantics* 5(1). 1–52.

Moltmann, Friederike. 2007. Events, tropes and truthmaking. *Philosophical Studies* 134. 363–403.

Moltmann, Friederike. 2009. Degree structure as trope structure: A trope-based analysis of comparative and positive adjectives. *Linguistics and Philosophy* 32. 51–94.

Moltmann, Friederike. 2013a. *Abstract objects and the semantics of natural language*. Oxford: Oxford University Press.

Moltmann, Friederike. 2013b. On the distinction between abstract states, concrete states, and tropes. In Alda Mari, Claire Beyssade & Fabio Del Prete (eds.), *Genericity*, 292–311. Oxford: Oxford University Press.

Moltmann, Friederike. 2013c. Reference to numbers in natural language. *Philosophical Studies* 162(3). 499–534. https://doi.org/10.1007/s11098-011-9779-1.

Moltmann, Friederike. 2013d. Tropes, bare demonstratives, and apparent statements of identity. *Nous* 47(2). 346–370. https://doi.org/10.1111/j.1468-0068.2011.00844.x.

Moltmann, Friederike. 2014. Propositions, attitudinal objects, and the distinction between actions and products. *Canadian Journal of Philosophy* 43(5-6). 679–701. https://doi.org/10.1080/00455091.2014.892770.

Moltmann, Friederike. 2015. Quantification with intentional verbs and with intensional verbs. In Alessandro Torza (ed.), *Quantifiers, quantifiers, and quantifiers: Themes in logic, metaphysics, and language* (Synthese Library), 141–168. Dordrecht: Springer.

Moltmann, Friederike. 2017. Cognitive products and the semantics of attitude verbs and deontic modals. In Friederike Moltmann & Mark Textor (eds.), *Act-based conceptions of propositional content*, 254–290. New York: Oxford University Press.

Moltmann, Friederike. to appear. Variable objects and truthmaking. In Mircea Dumitru (ed.), *Metaphysics, meaning, and modality: Themes from Kit Fine*. New York: Oxford University Press.

Montague, Richard. 1973. The proper treatment of quantification in ordinary english. In Jaakko Hintikka, Julius Moravcsik & Patrick Suppes (eds.), *Approaches to natural language*, 221–242. Dordrecht: Reidel.

Rodriguez-Pereyra, Gonzalo. 2005. Why truthmakers? In Helen Beebee & Julian Dodd (eds.), *Truthmakers: The contemporary debate*, 17–31. Oxford: Oxford University Press.

Strawson, Peter Frederick. 1959. *Individuals: An essay in descriptive metaphysics*. London: Methuen.

Twardowski, Kazimierz. 1999. Actions and products (1912). In Johannes Brandl & Jan Woleński (eds.). Trans. by Arthur Szylewicz, *Kazimierz Twardowski: On actions, products and other topics in philosophy*, 103–132. Amsterdam & Atlanta: Rodopi.

Williams, Donald Cary. 1953. On the elements of being. *Review of Metaphysics* 7. 3–18.

Wolterstorff, Nicholas. 1970. *On universals: An essay in ontology*. Chicago: University of Chicago Press.